MW01015027

CCNA Wireless 200-355 Official Cert Guide

DAVID HUCABY, CCIE NO. 4594

Cisco Press
800 East 96th Street
Indianapolis, IN 46240

CCNA Wireless 200-355 Official Cert Guide

David Hucaby

Published by:
Cisco Press
800 East 96th Street
Indianapolis, IN 46240 USA

Printed in the United States of America

2 16

Library of Congress Control Number: 2015955570

ISBN-13: 978-1-58714-457-8

ISBN-10: 1-58714-457-3

Warning and Disclaimer

This book is designed to provide information about preparing for the CCNA Wireless 200-355 exam. Every effort has been made to make this book as complete and as accurate as possible, but no warranty or fitness is implied.

The information is provided on an "as is" basis. The authors, Cisco Press, and Cisco Systems, Inc. shall have neither liability nor responsibility to any person or entity with respect to any loss or damages arising from the information contained in this book or from the use of the discs or programs that may accompany it.

The opinions expressed in this book belong to the author and are not necessarily those of Cisco Systems, Inc.

Trademark Acknowledgments

All terms mentioned in this book that are known to be trademarks or service marks have been appropriately capitalized. Cisco Press or Cisco Systems, Inc., cannot attest to the accuracy of this information. Use of a term in this book should not be regarded as affecting the validity of any trademark or service mark.

Special Sales

For information about buying this title in bulk quantities, or for special sales opportunities (which may include electronic versions; custom cover designs; and content particular to your business, training goals, marketing focus, or branding interests), please contact our corporate sales department at corpsales@pearsoned.com or (800) 382-3419.

For government sales inquiries, please contact governmentsales@pearsoned.com.

For questions about sales outside the U.S., please contact international@pearsoned.com.

Feedback Information

At Cisco Press, our goal is to create in-depth technical books of the highest quality and value. Each book is crafted with care and precision, undergoing rigorous development that involves the unique expertise of members from the professional technical community.

Readers' feedback is a natural continuation of this process. If you have any comments regarding how we could improve the quality of this book, or otherwise alter it to better suit your needs, you can contact us through email at feedback@ciscopress.com. Please make sure to include the book title and ISBN in your message.

We greatly appreciate your assistance.

Publisher: Paul Boger

Associate Publisher: Dave Dusthimer

Business Operation Manager, Cisco Press: Jan Cornelssen

Executive Editor: Mary Beth Ray

Managing Editor: Sandra Schroeder

Senior Development Editor: Christopher Cleveland

Senior Project Editor: Tonya Simpson

Copy Editor: Bill McManus

Technical Editor: Jerome Henry

Editorial Assistant: Vanessa Evans

Cover Designer: Mark Shirar

Composition: Studio Galou

Indexer: Publishing Works

Proofreader: Laura Hernandez

About the Author

David Hucaby, CCIE No. 4594, is a network engineer for a large university healthcare network based on Cisco wireless products. David has bachelor's and master's degrees in electrical engineering from the University of Kentucky. He is the author of several Cisco Press titles, including *CCNP SWITCH Exam Certification Guide*; *Cisco LAN Switching Video Mentor*; *CCNP Security FIREWALL Exam Certification Guide*; *Cisco ASA, PIX, and FWSM Firewall Handbook*, Second Edition; and *Cisco Firewall Video Mentor*.

David lives in Kentucky with his wife, Marci, and two daughters.

About the Technical Reviewer

Jerome Henry, CCIE Wireless No. 24750, is a technical marketing engineer in the Wireless Enterprise Networking Group at Cisco systems. Jerome has close to 17 years of experience teaching technical Cisco courses in more than 15 different countries and 4 different languages, to audiences ranging from bachelor degree students to networking professionals and Cisco internal system engineers.

Focusing on his wireless experience, Jerome joined Cisco in 2012. Before that time, he was consulting and teaching Heterogeneous Networks and Wireless Integration with the European Airespace team, which Cisco later acquired to become its main wireless solution. He then spent several years with a Cisco Learning Partner developing wireless courses and working on training material for new wireless technologies. In addition to his CCIE Wireless certification, Jerome is a Certified Wireless Networking Expert (CWNE No. 45) and has developed several Cisco courses focusing on wireless topics (IUWNE, IUWMS, IUWVN, CUWSS, IAUWS, LBS, CWMN lab guide, and so on) and authored several Wireless books (*CCNP Wireless IUWMS Quick Reference*, *CCNP Wireless CUWSS Quick Reference*, and so on). Jerome also is an IEEE 802.11 group member and participant of Wi-Fi Alliance working groups. With more than 10,000 hours in the classroom, Jerome was awarded the IT Training Award Best Instructor silver medal in 2009. He is based in the Research Triangle Park in North Carolina.

Dedications

As always, this book is dedicated to the most important people in my life: my wife, Marci, my two daughters, Lauren and Kara, and my parents, Reid and Doris Hucaby. Their love, encouragement, and support carry me along. I'm so grateful to God, who gives endurance and encouragement (Romans 15:5), who has allowed me to enjoy networking and working on projects like this, and who invented wireless communication. With a higher purpose.

As the sign in front of a church near my home says: "Prayer: The world's greatest wireless connection."

Acknowledgments

It has been my great pleasure to work on another Cisco Press project. I've now been writing Cisco Press titles continuously for more than 15 years. I have physically worn out several laptop keyboards and probably several Cisco Press editors in the process. I am most thankful that Chris Cleveland has never worn out—he has been the development editor for almost every project I have ever worked on. I can't say enough good things about working with him. I am grateful to Mary Beth Ray for inviting me back to revise this book, Tonya Simpson as the project editor, Bill McManus for raising the copy editing bar to an amazing height, and many other Cisco Press folks who have worked hard to make this book happen.

I am very grateful for the insight, knowledge, and helpful comments that Jerome Henry has provided. He is a tremendous resource for wireless networking expertise and training. Jerome's input has made this a more well-rounded book and me a more educated author.

As always, I have enjoyed the good discussions with my dad, Reid Hucaby, a fellow EE and a seasoned RF engineer, that this book has prompted about all things wireless.

Finally, I am indebted to my co-worker and good friend, Rick Herring, who has been saying for years that I should write a wireless book one day. I always thought he was joking until now.

Contents at a Glance

On the DVD

Contents

On the DVD

Icons Used in This Book

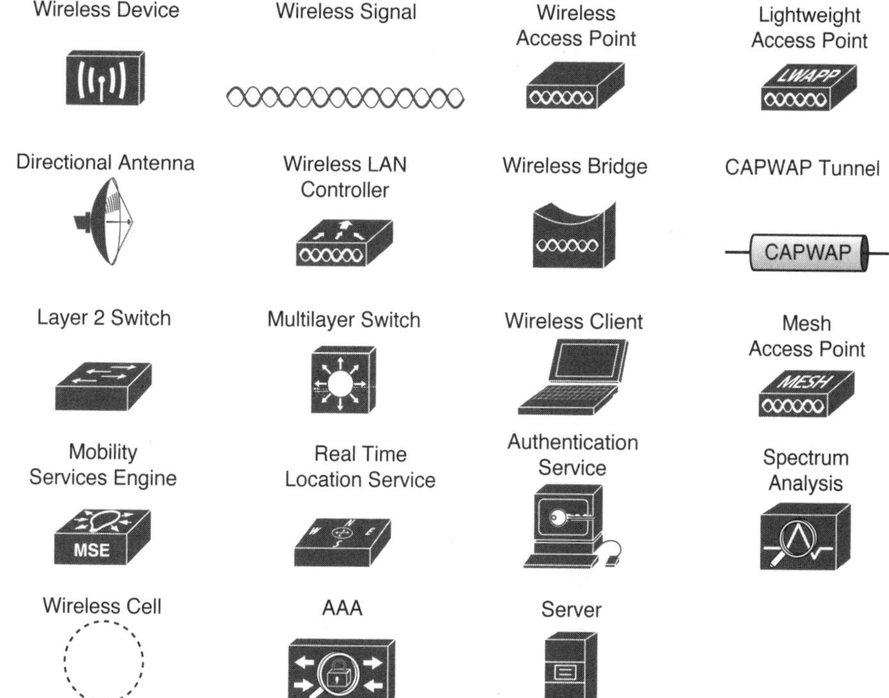

Command Syntax Conventions

The conventions used to present command syntax in this book are the same conventions used in the IOS Command Reference. The Command Reference describes these conventions as follows:

- **Boldface** indicates commands and keywords that are entered literally as shown. In actual configuration examples and output (not general command syntax), boldface indicates commands that are manually input by the user (such as a show command).
- *Italic* indicates arguments for which you supply actual values.
- Vertical bars (|) separate alternative, mutually exclusive elements.
- Square brackets ([ ]) indicate an optional element.
- Braces ({ }) indicate a required choice.
- Braces within brackets ([{ }]) indicate a required choice within an optional element.

Introduction

Welcome to the world of Cisco Certified Network Associate (CCNA) Wireless! As technology continues to evolve, wireless technologies are finding their way to the forefront. This clearly indicates the progression from a fixed wired type of connectivity to a more fluid, mobile workforce that can work when, where, and how they want. Regardless of your background, one of the primary goals of the CCNA Wireless certification is to introduce you to the Cisco Unified Wireless Network (CUWN).

This book is designed to help you prepare for the Cisco CCNA Wireless 200-355 WIFUND (Implementing Cisco Wireless Networking Fundamentals) certification exam. To achieve the CCNA Wireless specialization, you must first pass the CCENT, CCNA Routing and Switching, or any CCIE certification.

Who Should Read This Book

Wireless networking is a complex business. The CCNA Wireless specialization was developed to introduce wireless LANs, the CUWN, and Cisco's wireless product line. The certification tests for proficiency in designing, installing, configuring, monitoring, and troubleshooting wireless networks in an enterprise setting.

How to Use This Book

The book consists of 21 chapters. Each chapter tends to build upon the chapter that precedes it. The chapters of the book cover the following topics:

- **Chapter 1, "RF Signals and Modulation":** This chapter covers the basic theory behind radio frequency (RF) signals and the methods used to carry data wirelessly.
- **Chapter 2, "RF Standards":** This chapter covers the agencies that regulate, standardize, and validate the correct use of wireless LAN devices.
- **Chapter 3, "RF Signals in the Real World":** This chapter explores many of the conditions that can affect wireless signal propagation.
- **Chapter 4, "Understanding Antennas":** This chapter explains some basic antenna theory, in addition to various types of antennas and their application.
- **Chapter 5, "Wireless LAN Topologies":** This chapter explains the topologies that can be used to control access to the wireless medium and provide data exchange between devices.
- **Chapter 6, "Understanding 802.11 Frame Types":** This chapter covers the frame format and frame types that APs and clients must use to communicate successfully. It also discusses the choreography that occurs between an AP and its clients.
- **Chapter 7, "Planning Coverage with Wireless APs":** This chapter explains how wireless coverage can be adjusted to meet a need and how it can be grown to scale over a greater area and a greater number of clients. It also explains how coverage can be measured, surveyed, and validated.

- **Chapter 8, "Understanding Cisco Wireless Architectures":** This chapter describes the autonomous, cloud-based, centralized, and converged wireless architectures and how you can leverage their respective strengths to solve some fundamental problems.
- **Chapter 9, "Implementing Autonomous and Cloud Deployments":** This chapter discusses basic operation of an autonomous AP and how you can connect to it and convert it to lightweight mode, to become a part of a larger, more integrated wireless network. It also provides an introduction of Cisco Meraki cloud-based APs.
- **Chapter 10, "Implementing Controller-based Deployments":** This chapter covers the wireless controller's role in linking wired and wireless networks. It also covers the minimal initial configuration needed to get a controller up on the network where you can manage it more fully.
- **Chapter 11, "Understanding Controller Discovery":** This chapter explains the process that each lightweight AP must go through to discover and bind itself with a controller before wireless clients can be supported.
- **Chapter 12, "Understanding Roaming":** This chapter discusses client mobility from the AP and controller perspectives so that you can design and configure your wireless network properly as it grows over time.
- **Chapter 13, "Understanding RRM":** This chapter covers Radio Resource Management (RRM), a flexible and automatic mechanism that Cisco wireless LAN controllers can use to make wireless network operation more efficient.
- **Chapter 14, "Wireless Security Fundamentals":** This chapter covers many of the methods you can use to secure a wireless network.
- **Chapter 15, "Configuring a WLAN":** This chapter explains how to define and tune a wireless LAN to support wireless clients and connectivity with a wired infrastructure.
- **Chapter 16, "Implementing a Wireless Guest Network":** This chapter discusses the steps you can take to configure a guest network as an extension to your wireless infrastructure.
- **Chapter 17, "Configuring Client Connectivity":** This chapter introduces some of the most common types of wireless clients and how to configure them to join a wireless LAN.
- **Chapter 18, "Managing Cisco Wireless Networks":** This chapter provides an overview of Prime Infrastructure, how you can configure controllers and APs with it, and how you can use it to monitor a variety of things in your network.
- **Chapter 19, "Dealing with Wireless Interference":** This chapter covers some common types of devices that can cause interference and the Cisco CleanAir features that can detect and react to the interference sources.

- **Chapter 20, "Troubleshooting WLAN Connectivity":** This chapter helps you get some perspective about wireless problems, develop a troubleshooting strategy, and become comfortable using the tools at your disposal.
- **Chapter 21, "Final Review":** This short chapter lists the exam preparation tools useful at this point in the study process. It also provides a suggested study plan now that you have completed all of the earlier chapters in this book.
- **Appendix A, "Answers to the 'Do I Know This Already?' Quizzes":** This appendix provides the correct answers to the "Do I Know This Already?" quizzes that you will find at the beginning of each chapter. Brief explanations for the correct answers will also help you complete your understanding of topics covered.
- **Appendix B, "Modulation and Coding Schemes":** This appendix outlines the direct-sequence spread spectrum (DSSS) and orthogonal frequency-division multiplexing (OFDM) data rates used for 802.11b/g and 802.11a; the modulation and coding schemes and data rates used for 802.11n; and the modulation, coding schemes, and data rates used for 802.11ac.
- **Appendix C, "CCNA Wireless 200-355 Exam Updates":** This appendix is a living document that provides you with updated information if Cisco makes minor modifications to the exam upon which this book is based. Be sure to check the online version of this appendix at http://www.ciscopress.com/title/9781587144578 for any updates.
- **Appendix D, "Study Planner":** This spreadsheet is designed as a tool to help you plan and track major study milestones as you prepare for the CCNA Wireless exam.
- **Key Terms Glossary:** The glossary defines all WLAN-related terms that you were asked to define at the end of each chapter.

Each chapter follows the same format and incorporates the following tools to assist you by assessing your current knowledge and emphasizing specific areas of interest within the chapter:

- **Do I Already Know This Quiz?:** Each chapter begins with a quiz to help you assess your current knowledge of the subject. The quiz is divided into specific areas of emphasis that enable you to best determine where to focus your efforts when working through the chapter.
- **Foundation Topics:** The foundation topics are the core sections of each chapter. They focus on the specific protocols, concepts, or skills that you must master to successfully prepare for the examination.
- **Exam Preparation:** Near the end of each chapter, this section highlights the key topics from the chapter and the pages where you can find them for quick review. This section also provides a list of key terms that you should be able to define in preparation for the exam. It is unlikely that you will be able to successfully complete the certification exam by just studying the key topics and key terms, although they are a good tool for last-minute preparation just before taking the exam.

- **DVD-based practice exam:** This book includes a DVD containing several interactive practice exams. It is recommended that you continue to test your knowledge and test-taking skills by using these exams. You will find that your test-taking skills will improve by continued exposure to the test format. Remember that the potential range of exam questions is limitless. Therefore, your goal should not be to "know" every possible answer but to have a sufficient understanding of the subject matter so that you can figure out the correct answer with the information provided.

Certification Exam Topics and This Book

The questions for each certification exam are a closely guarded secret. However, we do know which topics you must know to *successfully* complete this exam. Cisco publishes them as an exam blueprint for Implementing Cisco Wireless Networking Fundamentals (WIFUND), exam 200-355. Table I-1 lists each exam topic listed in the blueprint along with a reference to the book chapter that covers the topic. These are the same topics you should be proficient in when working with Cisco wireless LANs in the real world.

> **Tip** At the time this book is being published, the WIFUND exam is based on Cisco Wireless LAN Controller software release 8.0 and Cisco Prime Infrastructure release 2.2.

Table I-1 WIFUND Exam 200-355 Topics and Chapter References

WIFUND 200-355 Exam Topic	Chapter(s) in Which Topic Is Covered
1.0 RF Fundamentals	
1.1 Describe the propagation of radio waves	
1.1.a Frequency, amplitude, phase, wavelength (characteristics)	1
1.1.b Absorption, reflection, diffraction, scattering, refraction, fading, free space path loss, multipath	3
1.2 Interpret RF signal measurements	
1.2.a Signal strength (RSSI, Transmit power, receive sensitivity)	1
1.2.b Differentiate interference vs. noise	1, 3, 19
1.2.c Device capabilities (smartphones, laptops, tablets)	17
1.2.d Define SNR	1
1.3 Explain the principles of RF mathematics	
1.3.a Compute dBm, mW, Law of 3s and 10s,	1
1.4 Describe Wi-Fi antenna characteristics	
1.4.a Ability to read a radiation pattern chart	4
1.4.b Antenna types and uses	4

WIFUND 200-355 Exam Topic	Chapter(s) in Which Topic Is Covered
1.4.c dBi, dBd, EIRP	1, 4
2.0 802.11 Technology Fundamentals	
2.1 Describe basic Wi-Fi governance	
2.1.a Describe regional regulatory bodies (such as, FCC / ETSI/ NTT)	2
2.1.b IEEE 802.11	2
2.1.c Wi-Fi Alliance	2
2.2 Describe usable channel and power combination	
2.2.a Regional EIRP limitation examples	2
2.2.b ISM, UNII frequency bands	2
2.2.c Describe RRM fundamental	13
2.3 Describe 802.11 fundamentals	
2.3.a Modulation techniques	1, 2
2.3.b Channel width	2
2.3.c MIMO / MU-MIMO	2
2.3.c (i) MRC	2
2.3.c (ii) Beam forming	2
2.3.c (iii) Spatial streams	2
2.3.d Wireless topologies	5
2.3.d (i) IBSS	5
2.3.d (ii) BSS	5
2.3.d (iii) ESS	5
2.3.e Frame types	6
2.3.e (i) Management	6
2.3.e (ii) Control	6
2.3.e (iii) Data	6
3.0 Implementing a Wireless Network	
3.1 Describe the various Cisco wireless architectures	
3.1.a Cloud	8
3.1.b Autonomous	8
3.1.c Split MAC	8

WIFUND 200-355 Exam Topic	Chapter(s) in Which Topic Is Covered
3.1.c (i) FlexConnect	8
3.1.c (ii) Centralized	8
3.1.c (iii) Converged	8
3.2 Describe physical infrastructure connections	
3.2.a Wired infrastructure (AP, WLC, access/trunk ports, LAG)	10
3.3 Describe AP and WLC management access connections	
3.3.a Management connections (Telnet, SSH, HTTP, HTTPS, console)	9, 10
3.3.b IP addressing: IPv4 / IPv6	9, 10
3.3.c Management via wireless	15
4.0 Operating a Wireless Network	
4.1 Execute initial setup procedures Cisco wireless infrastructures	
4.1.a Cloud	9
4.1.b Converged	10
4.1.c Centralized	10
4.1.d Autonomous	9
4.2 Describe the Cisco implementation of the CAPWAP discovery and join process	
4.2.a DHCP	11
4.2.b DNS	11
4.2.c Master-controller	11
4.2.d Primary-secondary-tertiary	11
4.3 Distinguish different lightweight AP modes	8
4.4 Describe and configure the components of a wireless LAN access for client connectivity using GUI only	15
4.5 Identify wireless network and client management and configuration platform options	
4.5.a Controller GUI and CLI	10
4.5.b Prime infrastructure	18
4.5.c Dashboard	9
4.5.d ISE	18
4.6 Maintain wireless network	

WIFUND 200-355 Exam Topic	Chapter(s) in Which Topic Is Covered
4.6.a Perform controller configuration backups	10
4.6.b Perform code updates on controller, APs, and converged access switches	10
4.6.b (i) AireOS: boot loader (FUS), image	10
4.6.b (ii) IOS-XE: bundle, unbundle	10
4.6.b (iii) Autonomous	9
5.0 Configuration of Client Connectivity	
5.1 Identify authentication mechanisms	
5.1.a LDAP, RADIUS, local authentication, WebAuth, 802.1X, PSK	14, 16
5.2 Configuring WLAN authentication mechanisms on the controller	
5.2.a WebAuth, 802.1X, PSK	14, 16
5.2.b TKIP deprecation	14
5.3 Configure client connectivity in different operating systems	
5.3.a Android, MacOS, iOS, Windows	17
5.4 Describe roaming	
5.4.a Layer 2 and Layer 3	12
5.4.b Intracontroller and intercontroller	12
5.4.c Centralized mobility	12
5.4.d Converged mobility	12
5.5 Describe wireless guest networking	
5.5.a Anchor controller	16
5.5.b Foreign controller	16
6.0 Performing Client Connectivity Troubleshooting	
6.1 Validating WLAN configuration settings at the infrastructure side	
6.1.a Security settings	20
6.1.b SSID settings	20
6.2 Validating AP infrastructure settings	
6.2.a Port level configuration	20
6.2.b Power source	20
6.2.c AP and antenna orientation and position	20

WIFUND 200-355 Exam Topic	Chapter(s) in Which Topic Is Covered
6.3 Validate client settings	
6.3.a SSID	17, 20
6.3.b Security	17, 20
6.3.c Device driver version	17
6.4 Employ appropriate controller tools to assist troubleshooting	
6.4.a GUI logs	20
6.4.b CLI show commands	20
6.4.c Monitor pages	
6.4.c (i) CleanAir (controller GUI)	19
6.5 Identify appropriate third-party tools to assist troubleshooting	
6.5.a OS-based Client utilities	20
6.5.b Wi-Fi scanners	20
6.5.c RF mapping tool	20
7.0 Site Survey Process	
7.1 Describe site survey methodologies and their purpose	
7.1.a Offsite (predictive / plan)	7
7.1.b Onsite	7
7.1.b (i) Predeployment (AP on a stick)	7
7.1.b (ii) Post deployment (validation)	7
7.2 Describe passive and active site surveys	7
7.3 Identify proper application of site survey tools	
7.3.a Spectrum analyzer	19
7.3.b Site surveying software	7
7.4 Describe the requirements of client real-time and non-real-time applications	17

Each version of the exam can have topics that emphasize different functions or features, and some topics can be rather broad and generalized. The goal of this book is to provide the most comprehensive coverage to ensure that you are well prepared for the exam. Although some chapters might not address specific exam topics, they provide a foundation that is necessary for a clear understanding of important topics. Your short-term goal might be to pass this exam, but your long-term goal should be to become a qualified wireless networking professional.

It is also important to understand that this book is a "static" reference, whereas the exam topics are dynamic. Cisco can and does change the topics covered on certification exams often.

This exam guide should not be your only reference when preparing for the certification exam. You can find a wealth of information available at Cisco.com that covers each topic in great detail. If you think that you need more detailed information on a specific topic, read the Cisco documentation that focuses on that topic.

Note that as wireless technologies continue to develop, Cisco reserves the right to change the exam topics without notice. Although you can refer to the list of exam topics in Table I-1, always check Cisco.com to verify the actual list of topics to ensure that you are prepared before taking the exam. You can view the current exam topics on any current Cisco certification exam by visiting the Cisco.com website, hovering over Training & Events, and selecting from the Certifications list. Note also that, if needed, Cisco Press might post additional preparatory content on the web page associated with this book at http://www.ciscopress.com/title/9781587144578. It's a good idea to check the website a couple of weeks before taking your exam to be sure that you have up-to-date content.

Taking the CCNA Wireless Certification Exam

As with any Cisco certification exam, you should strive to be thoroughly prepared before taking the exam. There is no way to determine exactly what questions are on the exam, so the best way to prepare is to have a good working knowledge of all subjects covered on the exam. Schedule yourself for the exam and be sure to be rested and ready to focus when taking the exam.

The best place to find out the latest available Cisco training and certifications is under the Training & Events section at Cisco.com.

Tracking Your Status

You can track your certification progress by checking http://www.cisco.com/go/certifications/login. You must create an account the first time you log in to the site.

How to Prepare for an Exam

The best way to prepare for any certification exam is to use a combination of the preparation resources, labs, and practice tests. This guide has integrated some practice questions and example scenarios to help you better prepare. If possible, get some hands-on experience with CUWN equipment. There is no substitute for real-world experience; it is much easier to understand the designs, configurations, and concepts when you can actually work with a live wireless network.

Cisco.com provides a wealth of information about wireless LAN controllers, access points (APs), and wireless management products, and wireless LAN technologies and features.

Assessing Exam Readiness

Exam candidates never really know whether they are adequately prepared for the exam until they have completed about 30 percent of the questions. At that point, if you are not prepared, it is too late. The best way to determine your readiness is to work through the "Do I Know This Already?" quizzes at the beginning of each chapter and review the foundation and key topics presented in each chapter. It is best to work your way through the entire book unless you can complete each subject without having to do any research or look up any answers.

Cisco Wireless Certifications in the Real World

Cisco has one of the most recognized names on the Internet. Cisco Certified wireless specialists can bring quite a bit of knowledge to the table because of their deep understanding of wireless technologies, standards, and networking devices. This is why the Cisco certification carries such high respect in the marketplace. Cisco certifications demonstrate to potential employers and contract holders a certain professionalism, expertise, and dedication required to complete a difficult goal. If Cisco certifications were easy to obtain, everyone would have them.

Exam Registration

The CCNA Wireless WIFUND 200-355 exam is a computer-based exam, with around 60 to 70 multiple-choice, fill-in-the-blank, list-in-order, and simulation-based questions. You can take the exam at any Pearson VUE (http://www.pearsonvue.com) testing center. According to Cisco, the exam should last about 90 minutes. Be aware that when you register for the exam, you might be told to allow a certain amount of time to take the exam that is longer than the testing time indicated by the testing software when you begin. This discrepancy is because the testing center will want you to allow for some time to get settled and take the tutorial about the test engine.

Book Content Updates

Because Cisco occasionally updates exam topics without notice, Cisco Press might post additional preparatory content on the web page associated with this book at http://www.ciscopress.com/title/9781587144578. It is a good idea to check the website a couple of weeks before taking your exam, to review any updated content that might be posted online. We also recommend that you periodically check back to this page on the Cisco Press website to view any errata or supporting book files that may be available.

This chapter covers the following topics:

- **Comparing Wired and Wireless Networks**—This section provides a brief overview of how a wireless network differs from a wired network.
- **Understanding Basic Wireless Theory**—This section discusses radio frequency signals and their properties, such as frequency, bandwidth, phase, wavelength, and power level.
- **Carrying Data over an RF Signal**—This section covers the encoding and modulation methods that are used in wireless LANs.

This chapter covers the following exam topics:

- 1.1—Describe the propagation of radio waves
  - 1.1a—Frequency, amplitude, phase, wavelength (characteristics)
- 1.2—Interpret RF signal measurements
  - 1.2a—Signal strength (RSSI, transmit power, receive sensitivity)
  - 1.2b—Differentiate interference vs. noise
  - 1.2d—Define SNR
- 1.3—Explain the principles of RF mathematics
  - 1.3a—Compute dBm, mW, Law of 3s and 10s
- 1.4—Describe Wi-Fi antenna characteristics
  - 1.4c—dBi, dBd, EIRP
- 2.3—Describe 802.11 fundamentals
  - 2.3a—Modulation techniques

CHAPTER 1

RF Signals and Modulation

Wireless LANs must transmit a signal over radio frequencies (RF) to move data from one device to another. Transmitters and receivers can be fixed in consistent locations or they can be free to move around. This chapter covers the basic theory behind RF signals and the methods used to carry data wirelessly.

"Do I Know This Already?" Quiz

The "Do I Know This Already?" quiz allows you to assess whether you should read this entire chapter thoroughly or jump to the "Exam Preparation Tasks" section. If you are in doubt about your answers to these questions or your own assessment of your knowledge of the topics, read the entire chapter. Table 1-1 lists the major headings in this chapter and their corresponding "Do I Know This Already?" quiz questions. You can find the answers in Appendix A, "Answers to the 'Do I Know This Already?' Quizzes."

Table 1-1 "Do I Know This Already?" Section-to-Question Mapping

Foundation Topics Section	Questions
Comparing Wired and Wireless Networks	1
Understanding Basic Wireless Theory	2–8
Carrying Data Over an RF Signal	9–12

Caution The goal of self-assessment is to gauge your mastery of the topics in this chapter. If you do not know the answer to a question or are only partially sure of the answer, you should mark that question as wrong for purposes of the self-assessment. Giving yourself credit for an answer you correctly guess skews your self-assessment results and might provide you with a false sense of security.

1. Which one of the following is the common standard that defines wireless LAN operation?
   a. IEEE 802.1
   b. IEEE 802.1x
   c. IEEE 802.11
   d. IEEE 802.3
2. Which of the following represent the frequency bands commonly used for wireless LANs? (Choose two.)
   a. 2.4 MHz
   b. 2.4 GHz
   c. 5.5 MHz
   d. 11 GHz
   e. 5 GHz
3. Two transmitters are each operating with a transmit power level of 100 mW. When you compare the two absolute power levels, what is the difference in dB?
   a. 0 dB
   b. 20 dB
   c. 100 dB
   d. You can't compare power levels in dB.
4. A transmitter is configured to use a power level of 17 mW. One day it is reconfigured to transmit at a new power level of 34 mW. How much has the power level increased in dB?
   a. 0 dB
   b. 2 dB
   c. 3 dB
   d. 17 dB
   e. None of these answers are correct; you need a calculator to figure this out.
5. Transmitter A has a power level of 1 mW, and transmitter B is 100 mW. Compare transmitter B to A using dB, and then identify the correct answer from the following choices.
   a. 0 dB
   b. 1 dB
   c. 10 dB
   d. 20 dB
   e. 100 dB

6. A transmitter normally uses an absolute power level of 100 mW. Through the course of needed changes, its power level is reduced to 40 mW. What is the power-level change in dB?
   a. 2.5 dB
   b. 4 dB
   c. −4 dB
   d. −40 dB
   e. None of these answers are correct; where is that calculator?

7. Consider a scenario with a transmitter and a receiver that are separated by some distance. The transmitter uses an absolute power level of 20 dBm. A cable connects the transmitter to its antenna. The receiver also has a cable connecting it to its antenna. Each cable has a loss of 2 dB. The transmitting and receiving antennas each have a gain of 5 dBi. What is the resulting EIRP?
   a. +20 dBm
   b. +23 dBm
   c. +26 dBm
   d. +34 dBm
   e. None of these answers are correct.

8. A receiver picks up an RF signal from a distant transmitter. Which one of the following represents the best signal quality received? Example values are given in parentheses.
   a. Low SNR (10 dB), Low RSSI (−75)
   b. High SNR (30 dB), Low RSSI (−75)
   c. Low SNR (10 dB), High RSSI (−30)
   d. High SNR (30 dB), High RSSI (−30)

9. The typical data rates of 1, 2, 5.5, and 11 Mbps can be supported by which one of the following modulation types?
   a. OFDM
   b. FHSS
   c. DSSS
   d. QAM

10. Put the following modulation schemes in order of the number of possible changes that can be made to the carrier signal, from lowest to highest.
   a. 16-QAM
   b. DQPSK
   c. DBPSK
   d. 64-QAM

11. 64-QAM modulation alters which two of the following aspects of an RF signal?
    a. Frequency
    b. Amplitude
    c. Phase
    d. Quadrature

12. OFDM offers data rates up to 54 Mbps, but DSSS supports much lower limits. Compared with DSSS, which one of the following does OFDM leverage to achieve its superior data rates?
    a. Higher-frequency band
    b. Wider 20-MHz channel width
    c. 48 subcarriers in a channel
    d. Faster chipping rates
    e. Greater number of channels in a band

Foundation Topics

Comparing Wired and Wireless Networks

In a wired network, any two devices that need to communicate with each other must be connected by a wire. (That was obvious!) The "wire" might contain strands of metal or fiber-optic material that run continuously from one end to the other. Data that passes over the wire is bounded by the physical properties of the wire. In fact, the IEEE 802.3 set of standards defines strict guidelines for the Ethernet wire itself, in addition to how devices may connect, send, and receive data over the wire.

Wired connections have been engineered with tight constraints and have few variables that might prevent successful communication. Even the type and size of the wire strands, the number of twists the strands must make around each other over a distance, and the maximum length of the wire must adhere to the standard.

Therefore, a wired network is essentially a bounded medium; data must travel over whatever path the wire or cable takes between two devices. If the cable goes around a corner or lies in a coil, the electrical signals used to carry the data must also go around a corner or around a coil. Because only two devices may connect to a wire, only those two devices may send or transmit data. Even better: The two devices may transmit data to each other simultaneously because they each have a private, direct path to each other.

Wired networks also have some shortcomings. When a device is connected by a wire, it cannot move around very easily or very far. Before a device can connect to a wired network, it must have a connector that is compatible with the one on the end of the wire. As devices get smaller and more mobile, it just is not practical to connect them to a wire.

As its name implies, a wireless network removes the need to be tethered to a wire or cable. Convenience and mobility become paramount, enabling users to move around at will while staying connected to the network. A user can (and often does) bring along many different wireless devices that can all connect to the network easily and seamlessly.

Wireless data must travel through free space, without the constraints and protection of a wire. In the free space environment, many variables can affect the data and its delivery. To minimize the variables, wireless engineering efforts must focus on two things:

- Wireless devices must adhere to a common standard.
- Wireless coverage must exist in the area where devices are expected.

Wireless LANs are based on the IEEE 802.11 standard, which is covered in more detail in Chapter 2, "RF Standards."

Understanding Basic Wireless Theory

To send data across a wired link, an electrical signal is applied at one end and is carried to the other end. The wire itself is continuous and conductive, so the signal can propagate rather easily. A wireless link has no physical strands of anything to carry the signal along.

How then can an electrical signal be sent across the air, or free space? Consider a simple analogy of two people standing far apart, and one person wants to signal something to other. They are connected by a long and somewhat-loose rope; the rope represents free space. The sender at one end decides to lift his end of the rope high and hold it there so that the other end of the rope will also raise and notify the partner. After all, if the rope were a wire, he knows that he could apply a steady voltage at one end of the wire and it would appear at the other end. Figure 1-1 shows the end result; the rope falls back down after a tiny distance, and the receiver never notices a change.

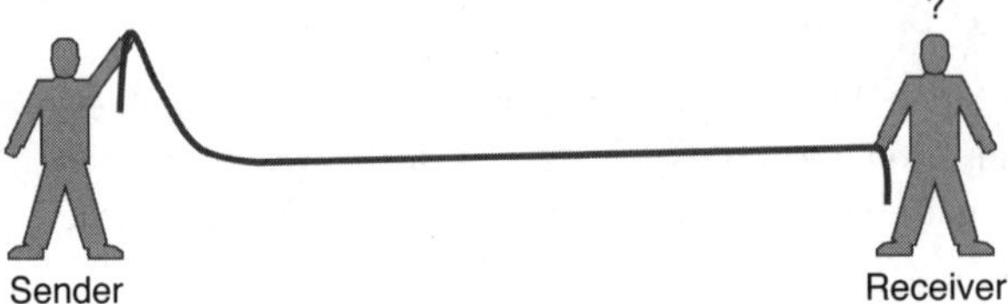

Figure 1-1 *Failed Attempt to Pass a Message Down a Rope*

The sender tries a different strategy. He cannot push the rope, but when he begins to wave it up and down in a steady, regular motion, a curious thing happens. A continuous wave pattern appears along the entire length of the rope, as shown in Figure 1-2. In fact, the waves (each representing one up and down cycle of the sender's arm) actually travel from the sender to the receiver.

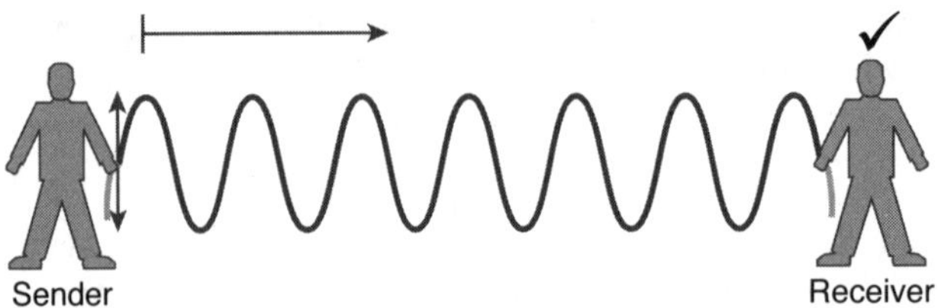

Figure 1-2 *Sending a Continuous Wave Down a Rope*

In free space, a similar principle occurs. The sender (a transmitter) can send an alternating current into a section of wire (an antenna), which sets up moving electric and magnetic fields that propagate out and away as traveling waves. The electric and magnetic fields travel along together and are always at right angles to each other, as shown in Figure 1-3. The signal must keep changing, or alternating, by cycling up and down, to keep the electric and magnetic fields cycling and pushing ever outward.

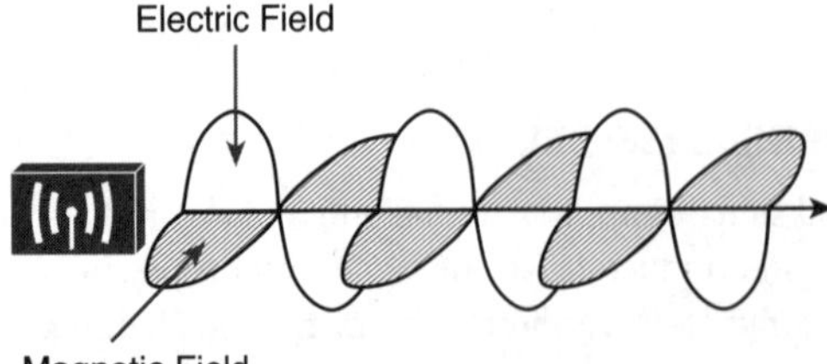

Figure 1-3 *Traveling Electric and Magnetic Waves*

Electromagnetic waves do not travel in a straight line. Instead, they travel by expanding in *all* directions away from the antenna. To get a visual image, think of dropping a pebble into a pond when the surface is still. Where it drops in, the pebble sets the water's surface into a cyclic motion. The waves that result begin small and expand outward, only to be replaced by new waves. In free space, the electromagnetic waves expand outward in all three dimensions.

Figure 1-4 shows a simple idealistic antenna that is a single point at the end of a wire. The waves produced expand outward in a spherical shape. The waves will eventually reach the receiver, in addition to many other locations in other directions.

Tip The idealistic antenna does not really exist, but serves as a reference point to understand wave propagation. In the real world, antennas can be made in various shapes and forms that can limit the direction that the waves are sent. Chapter 4, "Understanding Antennas," covers antennas in more detail.

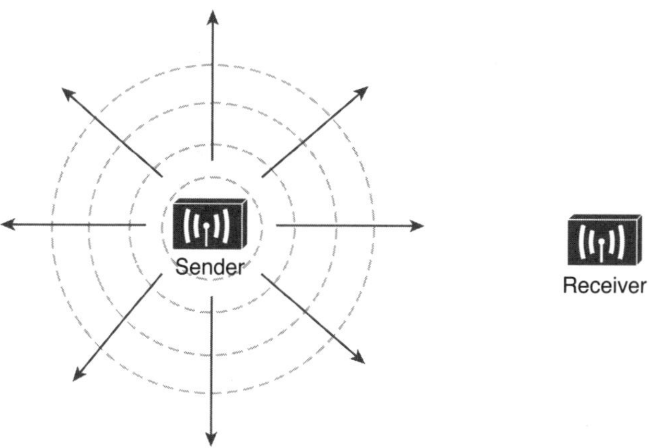

Figure 1-4 *Wave Propagation with an Idealistic Antenna*

At the receiving end of a wireless link, the process is reversed. As the electromagnetic waves reach the receiver's antenna, they induce an electrical signal. If everything works right, the received signal will be a reasonable copy of the original transmitted signal.

Understanding Frequency

The waves involved in a wireless link can be measured and described in several ways. One fundamental property is the *frequency* of the wave, or the number of times the signal makes one complete up and down *cycle* in 1 second. Figure 1-5 shows how a cycle of a wave can be identified. A cycle can begin as the signal rises from the center line, falls through the center line, and rises again to meet the center line. A cycle can also be measured from the center of one peak to the center of the next peak. No matter where you start measuring a cycle, the signal must make a complete sequence back to its starting position where it is ready to repeat the same cyclic pattern again.

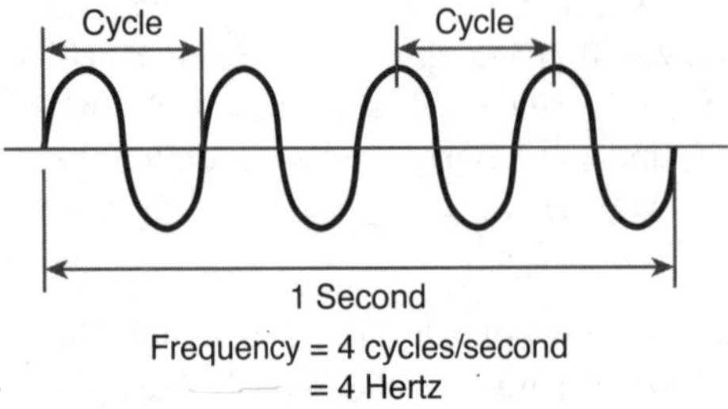

Figure 1-5 *Cycles Within a Wave*

In Figure 1-5, suppose that 1 second has elapsed, as shown. During that 1 second, the signal progressed through four complete cycles. Therefore, its frequency is 4 cycles/second or 4 hertz. A *hertz* (Hz) is the most commonly used frequency unit and is nothing other than one cycle per second.

Frequency can vary over a very wide range. As frequency increases by orders of magnitude, the numbers can become quite large. To keep things simple, the frequency unit name can be modified to denote an increasing number of zeros, as listed in Table 1-2.

Table 1-2 Frequency Unit Names

Unit	Abbreviation	Meaning
Hertz	Hz	Cycles per second
Kilohertz	kHz	1000 Hz
Megahertz	MHz	1,000,000 Hz
Gigahertz	GHz	1,000,000,000 Hz

Figure 1-6 shows a simple representation of the continuous frequency spectrum ranging from 0 Hz to 10^{22} (or 1 followed by 22 zeros) Hz. At the low end of the spectrum are frequencies that are too low to be heard by the human ear, followed by audible sounds. The highest range of frequencies contains light, followed by X, gamma, and cosmic rays.

The frequency range from around 3 kHz to 300 GHz is commonly called *radio frequency* (RF). It includes many different types of radio communication, including low-frequency radio, AM radio, shortwave radio, television, FM radio, microwave, and radar. The microwave category also contains the two main frequency ranges that are used for wireless LAN communication: 2.4 and 5 GHz.

Because a range of frequencies might be used for the same purpose, it is customary to refer to the range as a *band* of frequencies. For example, the range from 530 kHz to around 1710 kHz is used by AM radio stations; therefore it is commonly called the AM band or the AM broadcast band.

One of the two main frequency ranges used for wireless LAN communication lies between 2.400 and 2.4835 GHz. This is usually called the *2.4-GHz band*, even though it does not encompass the entire range between 2.4 and 2.5 GHz. It is much more convenient to refer to the band name instead of the specific range of frequencies included.

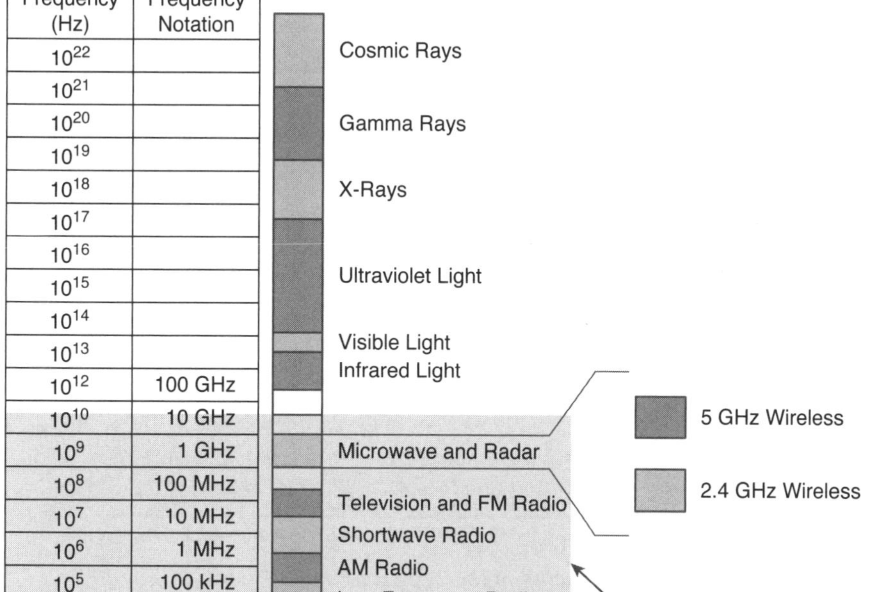

Figure 1-6 *Continuous Frequency Spectrum*

The other wireless LAN range is usually called the *5-GHz band* because it lies between 5.150 and 5.825 GHz. The 5-GHz band actually contains the following four separate and distinct bands:

5.150 to 5.250 GHz

5.250 to 5.350 GHz

5.470 to 5.725 GHz

5.725 to 5.825 GHz

Tip You might have noticed that most of the 5-GHz bands are contiguous except for a gap between 5.350 and 5.470. At the time of this writing, this gap exists and cannot be used for wireless LANs. However, some governmental agencies have moved to reclaim the frequencies and repurpose them for wireless LANs. Efforts are also underway to add 5.825 through 5.925 GHz.

It is interesting that the 5-GHz band can contain several smaller bands. Remember that the term *band* is simply a relative term that is used for convenience. At this point, do not worry about memorizing the band names or exact frequency ranges; Chapter 2 covers this in more detail.

A frequency band contains a continuous range of frequencies. If two devices require a single frequency for a wireless link between them, which frequency can they use? Beyond that, how many unique frequencies can be used within a band?

To keep everything orderly and compatible, bands are usually divided up into a number of distinct *channels*. Each channel is known by a channel number and is assigned to a specific frequency. As long as the channels are defined by a national or international standards body, they can be used consistently in all locations.

For example, Figure 1-7 shows the channel assignment for the 2.4-GHz band that is used for wireless LAN communication. The band contains 14 channels numbered 1 through 14, each assigned a specific frequency. First, notice how much easier it is to refer to channel numbers than the frequencies. Second, notice that the channels are spaced at regular intervals that are 0.005 GHz (or 5 MHz) apart, except for channel 14. The channel spacing is known as the channel separation or channel width.

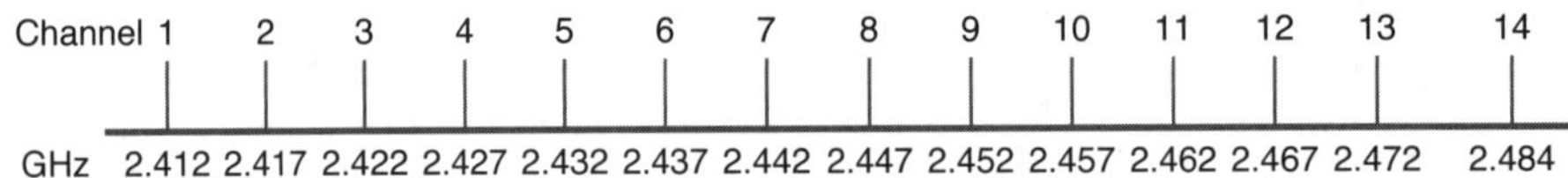

Figure 1-7 *Example of Channel Spacing in the 2.4-GHz Band*

If devices use a specific frequency for a wireless link, why do the channels need to be spaced apart at all? The reason lies with the practical limitations of RF signals, the electronics involved in transmitting and receiving the signals, and the overhead needed to add data to the signal effectively.

In practice, an RF signal is not infinitely narrow; instead, it spills above and below a center frequency to some extent, occupying neighboring frequencies, too. It is the center frequency that defines the channel location within the band. The actual frequency range needed for the transmitted signal is known as the signal *bandwidth*, as shown in Figure 1-8. As its name implies, bandwidth refers to the width of frequency space required within the band. For example, a signal with a 22-MHz bandwidth is bounded at 11 MHz above and below the center frequency. In wireless LANs, the signal bandwidth is defined as part of a standard. Even though the signal might extend farther above and below the center frequency than the bandwidth allows, wireless devices will use something called a spectral mask to ignore parts of the signal that fall outside the bandwidth boundaries.

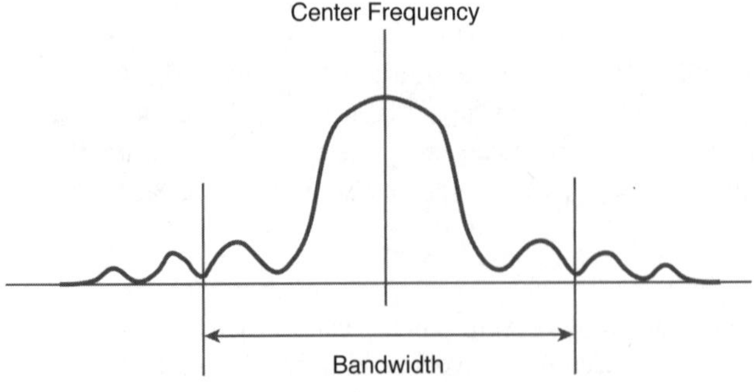

Figure 1-8 *Signal Bandwidth*

Ideally, the signal bandwidth should be less than the channel width so that a different signal could be transmitted on every possible channel with no chance that two signals could overlap and interfere with each other. Figure 1-9 shows such a channel spacing, where the signals on adjacent channels do not overlap. A signal can exist on every possible channel without overlapping with others.

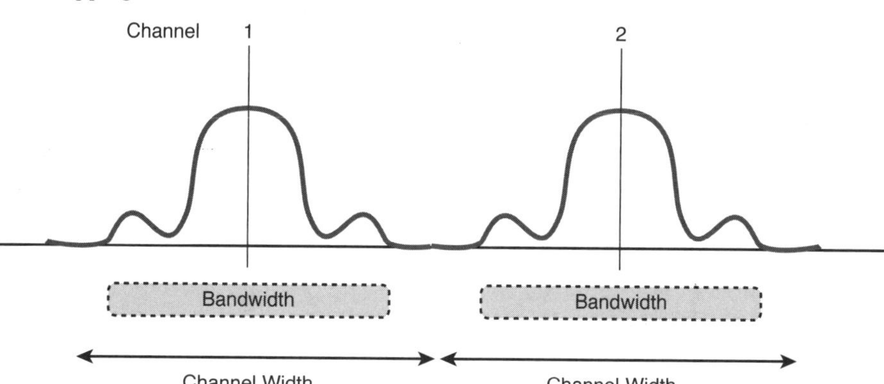

Figure 1-9 *Non-overlapping Channel Spacing*

However, you should not assume that signals centered on the standardized channel assignments will not overlap with each other. It is entirely possible that the channels in a band are narrower than the signal bandwidth, as shown in Figure 1-10. Notice how two signals have been centered on adjacent channel numbers 1 and 2, but they almost entirely overlap each other! The problem is that the signal bandwidth is slightly wider than four channels. In this case, signals centered on adjacent channels cannot possibly coexist without overlapping and interfering. Instead, the signals must be placed on more distant channels to prevent overlapping, thus limiting the number of channels that can be used in the band.

Tip How can channels be numbered such that signals overlap? Sometimes the channels in a band are defined and numbered for a specific use. Later on, another technology might be developed to use the same band and channels, only the newer signals might require more bandwidth than the original channel numbering supported. Such is the case with the 2.4-GHz Wi-Fi band.

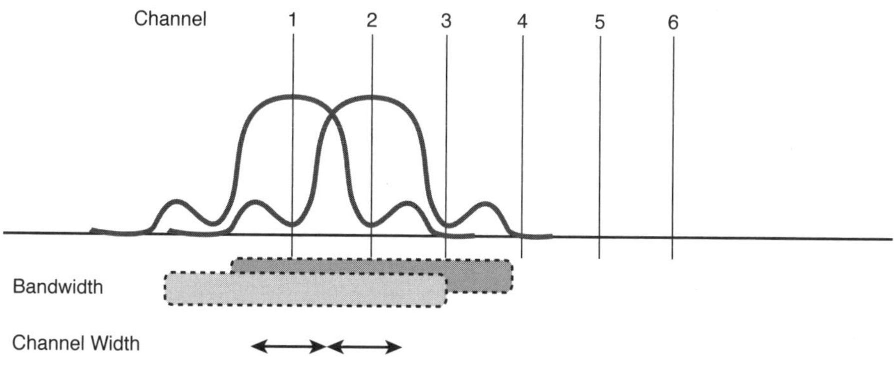

Figure 1-10 *Overlapping Channel Spacing*

Understanding Phase

RF signals are very dependent upon timing because they are always in motion. By their very nature, the signals are made up of electrical and magnetic forces that vary over time. The *phase* of a signal is a measure of shift in time relative to the start of a cycle. Phase is normally measured in degrees, where 0 degrees is at the start of a cycle, and one complete cycle equals 360 degrees. A point that is halfway along the cycle is at the 180-degree mark. Because an oscillating signal is cyclic, you can think of the phase traveling around a circle again and again.

When two identical signals are produced at exactly the same time, their cycles match up and they are said to be *in phase* with each other. If one signal is delayed from the other, the two signals are said to be *out of phase*. Figure 1-11 shows examples of both scenarios.

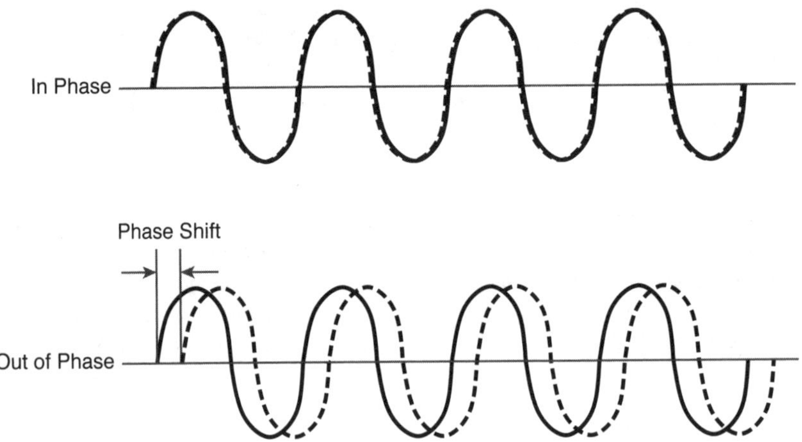

Figure 1-11 *Signals In and Out of Phase*

Phase becomes important as RF signals are received. Signals that are in phase tend to add together, whereas signals that are 180 degrees out of phase tend to cancel each other out. Chapter 3, "RF Signals in the Real World," explores signal phase in greater detail.

Measuring Wavelength

RF signals are usually described by their frequency; however, it is difficult to get a feel for their physical size as they move through free space. The *wavelength* is a measure of the physical distance that a wave travels over one complete cycle. Wavelength is usually designated by the Greek symbol lambda (λ). To get a feel for the dimensions of a wireless LAN signal, assuming you could see it as it travels in front of you, a 2.4-GHz signal would have a wavelength of 4.92 inches, while a 5-GHz signal would be 2.36 inches.

Figure 1-12 shows the wavelength of three different waves. The waves are arranged in order of increasing frequency, from top to bottom. Regardless of the frequency, RF waves travel at a constant speed. In a vacuum, radio waves travel at exactly the speed of light; in air, the velocity is slightly less than the speed of light. Notice that the wavelength decreases as the frequency increases. As the wave cycles get smaller, they cover less distance. Wavelength becomes useful in the design and placement of antennas.

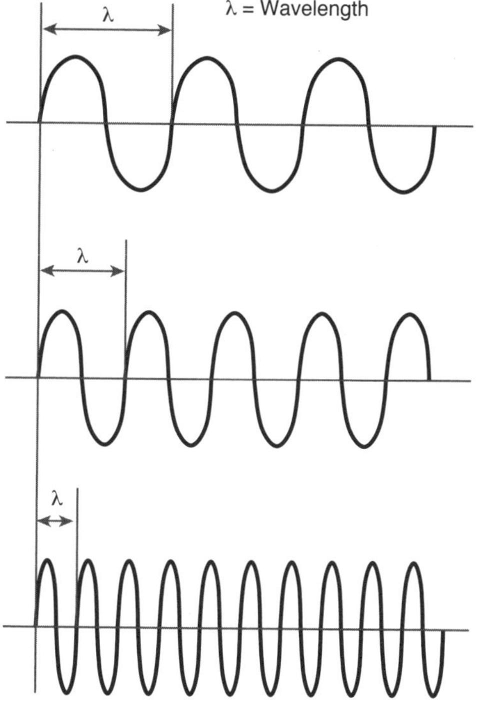

Figure 1-12 *Examples of Increasing Frequency and Decreasing Wavelength*

Understanding RF Power and dB

For an RF signal to be transmitted, propagated through free space, received, and understood with any certainty, it must be sent with enough strength or energy to make the journey. Think about Figure 1-1 again, where the two people are trying to signal each other with a rope. If the sender continuously moves his arm up and down a small distance, he will produce a wave in the rope. However, the wave will dampen out only a short distance away because of factors such as the weight of the rope, gravity, and so on. To move the wave all the way down the rope to reach the receiver, the sender must move his arm up and down with a much greater range of motion and with greater force or strength.

This strength can be measured as the *amplitude*, or the height from the top peak to the bottom peak of the signal's waveform, as shown in Figure 1-13.

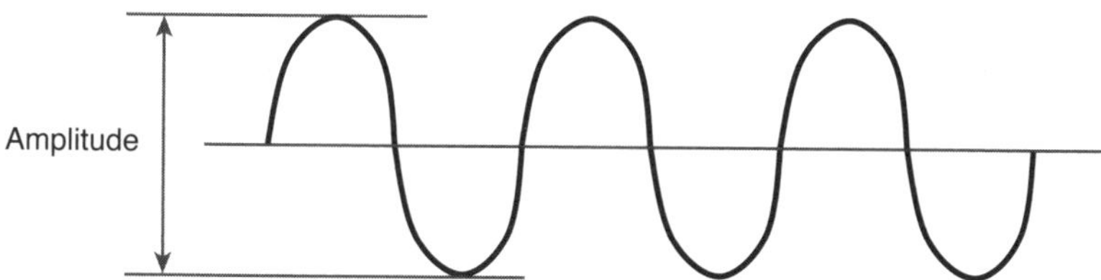

Figure 1-13 *Signal Amplitude*

The strength of an RF signal is usually measured by its power, in watts (W). For example, a typical AM radio station broadcasts at a power of 50,000 W; an FM radio station might use 16,000 W. In comparison, a wireless LAN transmitter usually has a signal strength between 0.1 W (100 mW) and 0.001 W (1 mW).

When power is measured in watts or milliwatts, it is considered to be an absolute power measurement. In other words, something has to measure exactly how much energy is present in the RF signal. This is fairly straightforward when the measurement is taken at the output of a transmitter because the transmit power level is usually known ahead of time.

Sometimes you might need to compare the power level between two different transmitters. For example, suppose that device T1 is transmitting at 1 mW, while T2 is transmitting at 10 mW, as shown in Figure 1-14. Simple subtraction tells you that T2 is 9 mW stronger than T1. You might also notice that T2 is 10 times stronger than T1.

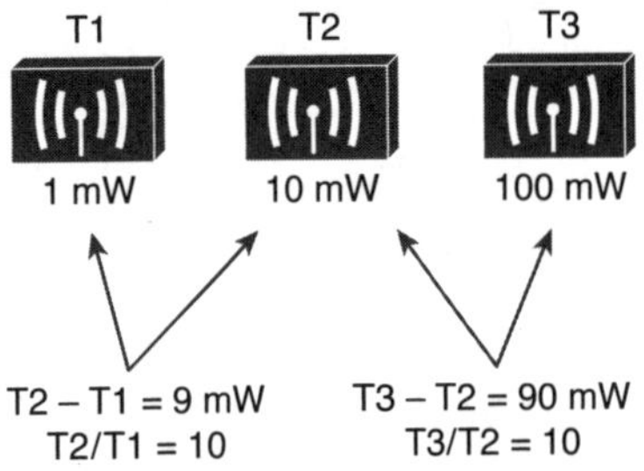

Figure 1-14 *Comparing Power Levels Between Transmitters*

Now compare transmitters T2 and T3, which use 10 mW and 100 mW, respectively. Using subtraction, T2 and T3 differ by 90 mW, but T3 is again 10 times stronger than T2. In each instance, subtraction yields a different result than division. Which method should you use?

Quantities like absolute power values can differ by orders of magnitude. A more surprising example is shown in Figure 1-15, where T4 is 0.00001 mW and T5 is 10 mW. Subtracting the two values gives their difference as 9.99999 mW. However, T5 is 1,000,000 times stronger than T4!

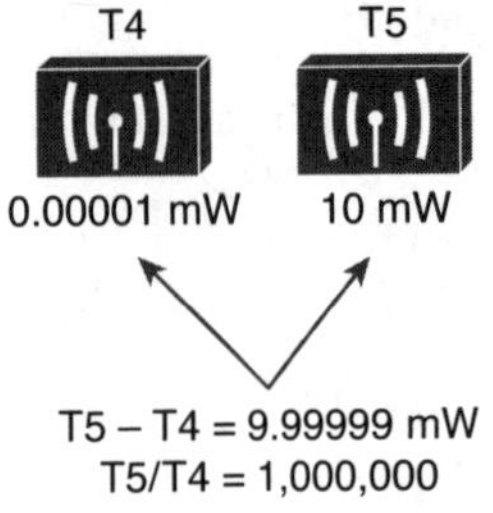

Figure 1-15 *Comparing Power Levels That Differ By Orders of Magnitude*

Because absolute power values can fall anywhere within a huge range, from a tiny decimal number to hundreds, thousands, or greater values, we need a way to transform the exponential range into a linear one. The logarithm function can be leveraged to do just that. In a nutshell, a logarithm takes values that are orders of magnitude apart (0.001, 0.01, 0.1, 1, 10, 100, and 1000, for example) and spaces them evenly within a reasonable range.

> **Tip** The base-10 logarithm function, denoted by $\log_{10}$, computes how many times 10 can be multiplied by itself to equal a number. For example, $\log_{10}(10)$ equals 1 because 10 is used only once to get the result of 10. The $\log_{10}(100)$ equals 2 because 10 is multiplied twice (10 × 10), to reach the result of 100. Computing other $\log_{10}$ values is difficult, requiring the use of a calculator. The good news is that you will not need a calculator or a logarithm on the CCNA Wireless exam. Even so, try to suffer through the few equations in this chapter so that you get a better understanding of power comparisons and measurements.

The *decibel* (dB) is a handy function that uses logarithms to compare one absolute measurement to another. It was originally developed to compare sound intensity levels, but it applies directly to power levels, too. After each power value has been converted to the same logarithmic scale, the two values can be subtracted to find the difference. The following equation is used to calculate a dB value, where P1 and P2 are the absolute power levels of two sources:

$$dB = 10(log_{10}P2 - log_{10}P1)$$

P2 represents the source of interest, and P1 is usually called the *reference* value or the source of comparison.

The difference between the two logarithmic functions can be rewritten as a single logarithm of P2 divided by P1, as follows:

$$dB = 10log_{10}\left(\frac{P2}{P1}\right)$$

Here, the *ratio* of the two absolute power values is computed first; then the result is converted onto a logarithmic scale.

Oddly enough, we end up with the same two methods to compare power levels with dB: a subtraction and a division. Thanks to the logarithm, both methods arrive at identical dB values. Be aware that the ratio or division form of the equation is the most commonly used in the wireless engineering world.

Important dB Laws to Remember

There are three cases where you can use mental math to make power-level comparisons using dB. By adding or subtracting fixed dB amounts, you can compare two power levels through multiplication or division. You should memorize the following three laws, with are based on dB changes of 0, 3, and 10, respectively, and are known as the Law of Zero, Law of 3s, and Law of 10s. You will be tested on them in the CCNA Wireless exam. All other dB cases require a calculator, so you will not be tested on those.

- **Law of Zero**—A value of 0 dB means that the two absolute power values are equal.

  If the two power values are equal, the ratio inside the logarithm is 1, and the $\log_{10}(1)$ is 0. This law is intuitive; if two power levels are the same, one is 0 dB more than the other.

- **Law of 3s**—A value of 3 dB means that the power value of interest is double the reference value; a value of –3 dB means the power value of interest is half the reference.

  When P2 is twice P1, the ratio is always 2. Therefore, $10\log_{10}(2) = 3$ dB.

  When the ratio is 1/2, $10\log_{10}(1/2) = -3$ dB.

  The Law of 3s is not very intuitive, but is still easy to learn. Whenever a power level doubles, it increases by 3 dB. Whenever it is cut in half, it decreases by –3 dB.

- **Law of 10s**—A value of 10 dB means that the power value of interest is 10 times the reference value; a value of –10 dB means the power value of interest is 1/10 of the reference.

  When P2 is 10 times P1, the ratio is always 10. Therefore, $10\log_{10}(10) = 10$ dB.

  When P2 is one tenth of P1, then the ratio is 1/10 and $10\log_{10}(1/10) = -10$ dB.

  The Law of 10s is intuitive because multiplying or dividing by 10 adds or subtracts 10 dB, respectively.

Notice another handy rule of thumb: When absolute power values multiply, the dB value is positive and can be added. When the power values divide, the dB value is negative and can be subtracted. Table 1-3 summarizes the useful dB comparisons.

Table 1-3 Power Changes and Their Corresponding dB Values

Power Change	dB Value
=	0 dB
× 2	+3 dB
/ 2	-3 dB
× 10	+10 dB
/ 10	–10 dB

Try a few example problems to see whether you understand how to compare two power values using dB. In Figure 1-16, sources A, B, and C transmit at 4, 8, and 16 mW, respectively. Source B is double the value of A, so it must be 3 dB greater than A. Likewise, source C is double the value of B, so it must be 3 dB greater than B.

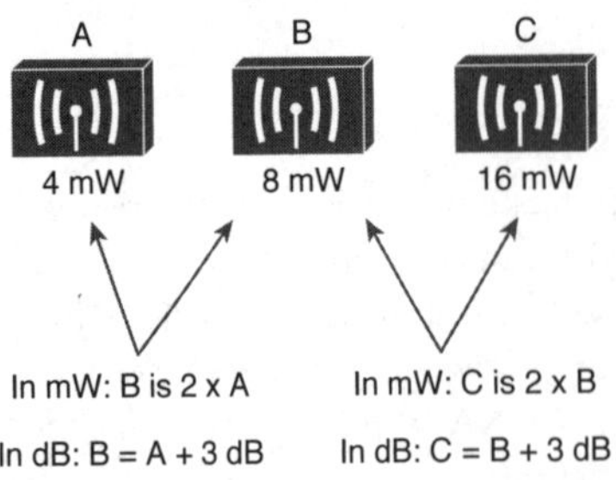

Figure 1-16 *Comparing Power Levels Using dB*

You can also compare sources A and C. To get from A to C, you have to double A, and then double it again. Each time you double a value, just add 3 dB. Therefore, C is 3 dB + 3 dB = 6 dB greater than A.

Next, try the more complicated example shown in Figure 1-17. Keep in mind that dB values can be added and subtracted in succession (in case several multiplication and division operations involving 2 and 10 are needed).

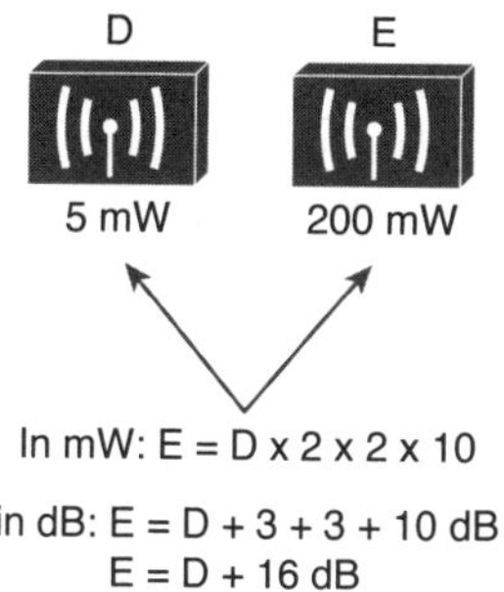

Figure 1-17 *Example of Computing dB with Simple Rules*

Sources D and E have power levels 5 and 200 mW. Try to figure out a way to go from 5 to 200 using only ×2 or ×10 operations. You can double 5 to get 10, then double 10 to get 20, and then multiply by 10 to reach 200 mW. Next, use the dB laws to replace the doubling and ×10 with the dB equivalents. The result is E = D + 3 + 3 + 10 or E = D + 16 dB.

You might also find other ways to reach the same result. For example, you can start with 5 mW, then multiply by 10 to get 50, then double 50 to get 100, then double 100 to reach 200 mW. This time the result is E = D + 10 + 3 + 3 or E = D + 16 dB.

Comparing Power Against a Reference: dBm

Beyond comparing two transmitting sources, a wireless LAN engineer must be concerned about the RF signal propagating from a transmitter to a receiver. After all, transmitting a signal is meaningless unless someone is there to receive it and make use of it.

Figure 1-18 shows a simple scenario with a transmitter and a receiver. Nothing in the real world is ideal, so assume that something along the path of the signal will induce a net loss. At the receiver, the signal strength will be degraded by some amount. Suppose that you are able to measure the power level leaving the transmitter, which is 100 mW. At the receiver, you measure the power level of the arriving signal. It is an incredibly low 0.000031623 mW.

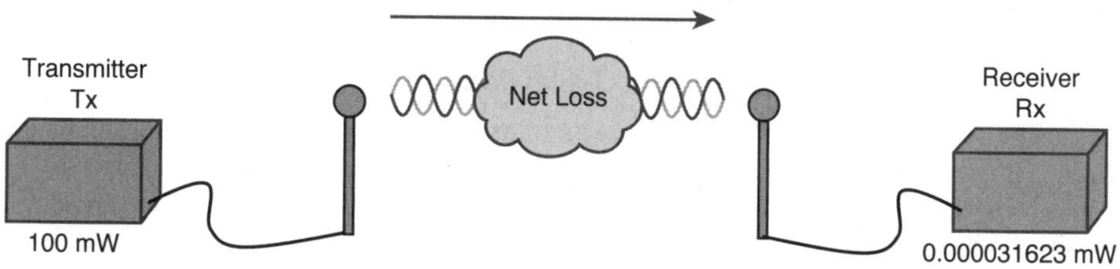

Figure 1-18 *Example of RF Signal Power Loss*

Wouldn't it be nice to quantify the net loss over the signal's path? After all, you might want to try several other transmit power levels or change something about the path between the transmitter and receiver. To design the signal path properly, you would like to make sure that the signal strength arriving at the receiver is at an optimum level.

You could leverage the handy dB formula to compare the received signal strength to the transmitted signal strength, as long as you can remember the formula and have a calculator nearby:

$$dB = 10 log_{10}\left(\frac{0.000031623\,mW}{100\,mW}\right) = -65\,dB$$

The net loss over the signal path turns out to be a decrease of 65 dB. Knowing that, you decide to try a different transmit power level to see what would happen at the receiver. It does not seem very straightforward to use the new transmit power to find the new signal strength at the receiver. That might require more formulas and more time at the calculator.

A better approach is to compare each absolute power along the signal path to one common reference value. Then, regardless of the absolute power values, you could just focus on the changes to the power values that are occurring at various stages along the signal path. In other words, convert every power level to a dB value and simply add them up along the path.

Recall that the dB formula puts the power level of interest on the top of the ratio, with a reference power level on the bottom. In wireless networks, the reference power level is usually 1 mW, so the units are designated by *dBm* (dB-milliwatt).

Returning to the scenario from Figure 1-18, the absolute power values at the transmitter and receiver can be converted to dBm, the results from which are shown in Figure 1-19. Notice that the dBm values can be added along the path: The transmitter dBm plus the net loss in dB equals the received signal in dBm.

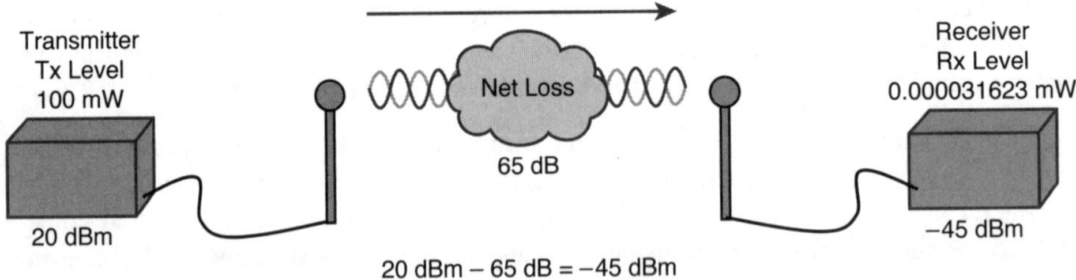

Figure 1-19 *Subtracting dB to Represent a Loss in Signal Strength*

Measuring Power Changes Along the Signal Path

Up to this point, this chapter has considered a transmitter and its antenna to be a single unit. That might seem like a logical assumption because many wireless access points have built-in antennas. In reality, a transmitter, its antenna, and the cable that connects them are all discrete components that not only propagate an RF signal but also affect its absolute power level.

When an antenna is connected to a transmitter, it provides some amount of gain to the resulting RF signal. This effectively increases the dB value of the signal above that of the transmitter alone. Chapter 4 explains this in greater detail; for now, just be aware that antennas provide positive gain.

By itself, an antenna does not generate any amount of absolute power. In other words, when an antenna is disconnected, no milliwatts of power are being pushed out of it. That makes it impossible to measure the antenna's gain in dBm. Instead, an antenna's gain is measured by comparing its performance with that of a reference antenna, then computing a value in dB.

Usually, the reference antenna is an *isotropic antenna*, so the gain is measured in *dBi* (dB-isotropic). An isotropic antenna does not actually exist, because it is ideal in every way. Its size is a tiny point, and it radiates RF equally in every direction. No physical antenna can do that. The isotropic antenna's performance can be calculated according to RF formulas, making it a universal reference for any antenna.

Because of the physical qualities of the cable that connects an antenna to a transmitter, some signal loss always occurs. Cable vendors supply the loss in dB per foot or meter of cable length for each type of cable manufactured.

Once you know the complete combination of transmitter power level, the length of cable, and the antenna gain, you can figure out the actual power level that will be radiated from the antenna. This is known as the *effective isotropic radiated power* (EIRP), measured in dBm.

EIRP is a very important parameter because it is regulated by governmental agencies in most countries. In those cases, a system cannot radiate signals higher than a maximum allowable EIRP. To find the EIRP of a system, simply add the transmitter power level to the antenna gain and subtract the cable loss, as illustrated in Figure 1-20.

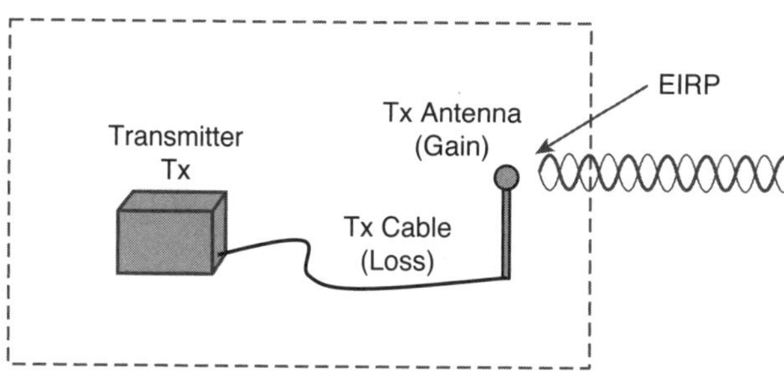

Figure 1-20 *Calculating EIRP*

Suppose a transmitter is configured for a power level of 10 dBm (10 mW). A cable with 5-dB loss connects the transmitter to an antenna with an 8-dBi gain. The resulting EIRP of the system is 10 dBm – 5 dB + 8 dBi, or 13 dBm.

You might notice that the EIRP is made up of decibel-milliwatt (dBm), dB relative to an isotropic antenna (dBi), and decibel (dB) values. Even though the units appear to be different, you can safely combine them for the purposes of calculating the EIRP. The only exception to this is when an antenna's gain is measured in *dBd* (dB-dipole). In that case, a dipole antenna has been used as the reference antenna, rather than an isotropic antenna. A dipole is a simple actual antenna, which has a gain of 2.14 dBi. If an antenna has its gain shown as dBi, you can add 2.14 dBi to that value to get its gain in dBi units instead.

Power-level considerations do not have to stop with the EIRP. You should also be concerned with the complete path of a signal, to make sure that the transmitted signal has sufficient power so that it can effectively reach and be understood by a receiver. This is known as the *link budget.*

The dB values of gains and losses can be combined over any number of stages along a signal's path. Consider Figure 1-21, which shows every component of signal gain or loss along the path from transmitter to receiver.

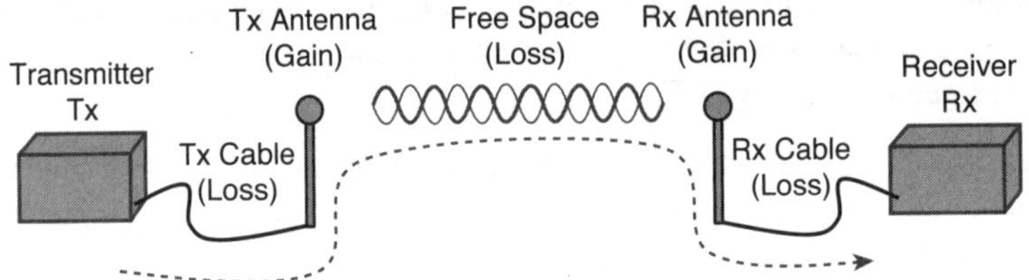

Figure 1-21 *Calculating Received Signal Strength Over the Path of an RF Signal*

At the receiving end, an antenna provides gain to increase the received signal power level. A cable connecting the antenna to the receiver also introduces some loss.

Figure 1-22 shows some example dB values, as well as the resulting sum of the component parts across the entire signal path. The signal begins at 20 dBm at the transmitter, has an EIRP value of 22 dBm at the transmitting antenna (20 dBm – 2 dB + 4 dBi), and arrives at the receiver with a level of –45 dBm.

> **Tip** Notice that every signal gain or loss used in Figure 1-22 is given except for the 69-dB loss between the two antennas. In this case, the loss can be quantified based on the other values given. In reality, it can be calculated as a function of distance and frequency. For perspective, you might see a 69-dB Wi-Fi loss over a distance of about 13 to 28 meters. Free space path loss is covered in greater detail in Chapter 3, "RF Signals in the Real World."

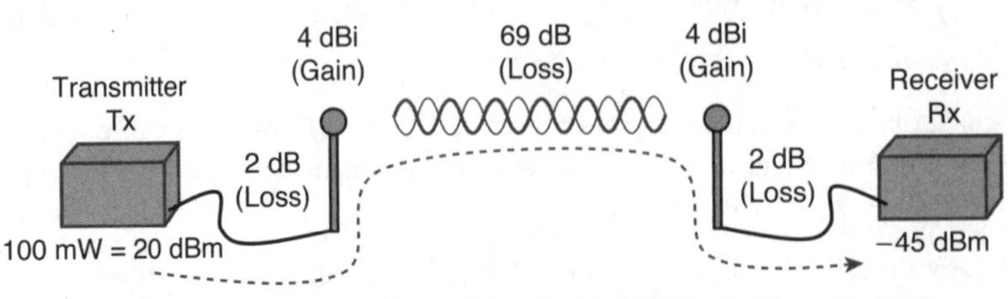

Figure 1-22 *Example of Calculating Received Signal Strength*

If you always begin with the transmitter power expressed in dBm, it is a simple matter to add or subtract the dB components along the signal path to find the signal strength that arrives at the receiver.

Understanding Power Levels at the Receiver

At the receiving end of the signal path, a receiver expects to find a signal on a predetermined frequency, with enough power to contain useful data. Receivers measure a signal's power in dBm according to the *received signal strength indicator* (RSSI) scale.

When you work with wireless LAN devices, the EIRP levels leaving the transmitter's antenna normally range from 100 mW down to 1 mW. This corresponds to the range +20 dBm down to 0 dBm. At the receiver, the power levels are much, much less, ranging from 1 mW all the way down to tiny fractions of a milliwatt, approaching 0 mW. The corresponding range of received signal levels is from 0 dBm down to about –100 dBm.

Therefore, the RSSI of a received signal can range from 0 to –100, where 0 is the strongest and –100 is the weakest. The range of RSSI values can vary between one hardware manufacturer and another. RSSI values are supposed to represent dBm values, but the results are not standardized across all receiver manufacturers. An RSSI value can vary from one receiver hardware to another.

Assuming a transmitter is sending an RF signal with enough power to reach a receiver, what RSSI value is good enough? Every receiver has a *sensitivity level* or a threshold that divides intelligible, useful signals from unintelligible ones. As long as a signal is received with a power level that is greater than the sensitivity level, chances are that the data from the signal can be understood correctly. Figure 1-23 shows an example of how the signal strength at a receiver might change over time. The receiver's sensitivity level is –82 dBm.

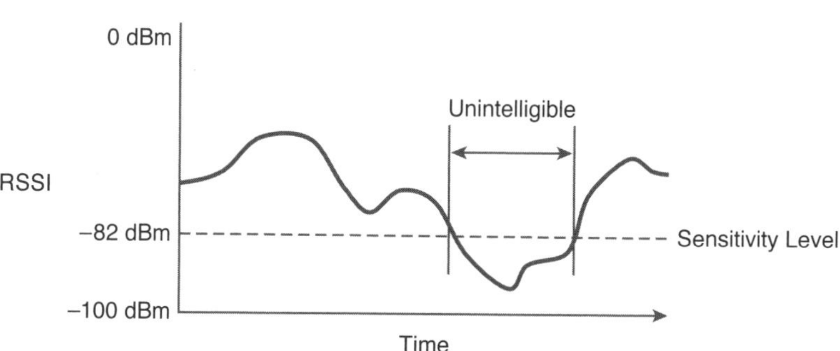

Figure 1-23 *Example of Receiver Sensitivity Level*

The RSSI value focuses on the expected signal alone, without regard to any other signals that may be received, too. All other signals that are received on the same frequency as the one you are trying to receive are simply viewed as *noise*. The noise level, or the average signal strength of the noise, is called the *noise floor*.

It is easy to ignore noise as long as the noise floor is well below what you are trying to hear. For example, two people can whisper in a library effectively because there is very little competing noise. Those same two people would become very frustrated if they tried to whisper to each other in a crowded sports arena.

Receiving an RF signal is no different; its signal strength must be greater than the noise floor by a decent amount so that it can be received and understood correctly. The difference between the signal and the noise is called the *signal-to-noise ratio* (SNR), measured in dB. A higher SNR value is preferred.

Figure 1-24 shows the RSSI of a signal compared with the noise floor that is received. The RSSI averages around –54 dBm. On the left side of the graph, the noise floor is –90 dBm. The resulting SNR is –54 dBm – (–90) dBm or 36 dB. Toward the right side of the graph, the noise floor gradually increases to –65 dBm, reducing the SNR to 11 dB. The signal is so close to the noise that it might not be usable.

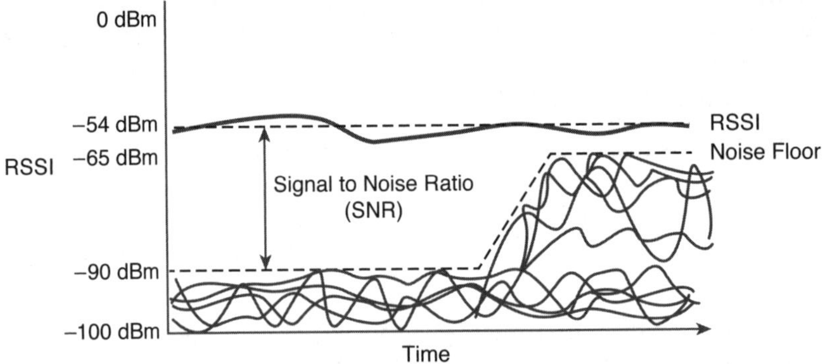

Figure 1-24 *Example of a Changing Noise Floor and SNR*

Carrying Data Over an RF Signal

Up to this point in the chapter, only the RF characteristics of wireless signals have been discussed. The RF signals presented have existed only as simple oscillations in the form of a sine wave. The frequency, amplitude, and phase have all been constant. The steady, predictable frequency is important because a receiver needs to tune to a known frequency to find the signal in the first place.

This basic RF signal is called a *carrier signal* because it is used to carry other useful information. With AM and FM radio signals, the carrier signal also transports audio signals. TV carrier signals have to carry both audio and video. Wireless LAN carrier signals must carry data.

To add data onto the RF signal, the frequency of the original carrier signal must be preserved. Therefore, there must be some scheme of altering some characteristic of the carrier signal to distinguish a 0 bit from a 1 bit. Whatever scheme is used by the transmitter must also be used by the receiver so that the data bits can be correctly interpreted.

Figure 1-25 shows a carrier signal with a constant frequency. The data bits 1001 are to be sent over the carrier signal, but how? One idea might be to simply use the value of each data bit to turn the carrier signal off or on. The Bad Idea 1 plot shows the resulting RF signal. A receiver might be able to notice when the signal is present and has an amplitude and correctly interpret 1 bits, but there is no signal to receive during 0 bits. If the signal becomes weak or is not available for some reason, the receiver will incorrectly think that a long string of 0 bits has been transmitted. A different twist might be to transmit only the upper half of the carrier signal during a 1 bit and the lower half during a 0 bit, as shown in the Bad Idea 2 plot. This time, a portion of the signal is always available for the receiver, but the signal becomes impractical to receive because important pieces of each cycle are missing. In addition, it is very difficult to transmit RF with disjointed alternating cycles.

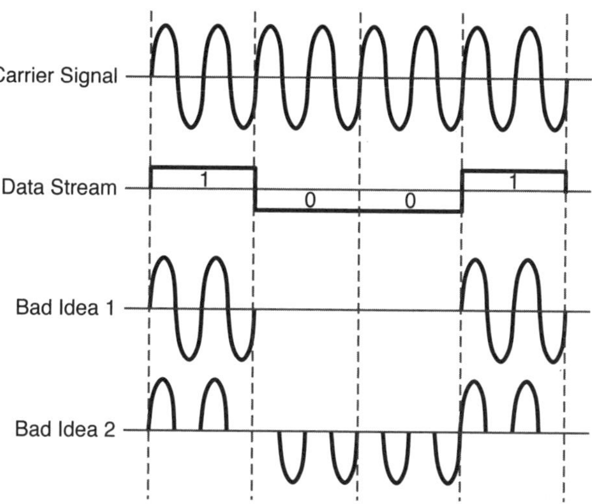

Figure 1-25 *Poor Attempts at Sending Data Over an RF Signal*

Such naive approaches might not be successful, but they do have the right idea: to alter the carrier signal in a way that indicates the information to be carried. This is known as *modulation*, where the carrier signal is modulated or changed according to some other source. At the receiver, the process is reversed; *demodulation* interprets the added information based on changes in the carrier signal.

RF modulation schemes generally have the following goals:

- Carry data at a predefined rate
- Be reasonably immune to interference and noise
- Be practical to transmit and receive

Due to the physical properties of an RF signal, a modulation scheme can alter only the following attributes:

- Frequency, but only by varying slightly above or below the carrier frequency
- Phase
- Amplitude

The modulation techniques require some amount of bandwidth centered on the carrier frequency. This additional bandwidth is partly due to the rate of the data being carried and partly due to the overhead from encoding the data and manipulating the carrier signal. If the data has a relatively low bit rate, such as an audio signal carried over AM or FM radio, the modulation can be straightforward and requires little extra bandwidth. Such signals are called *narrowband* transmissions.

In contrast, wireless LANs must carry data at high bit rates, requiring more bandwidth for modulation. The end result is that the data being sent is spread out across a range of frequencies. This is known as *spread spectrum*. At the physical layer, wireless LANs can be broken down into the following three spread-spectrum categories, which are discussed in subsequent sections:

- Frequency-hopping spread spectrum (FHSS)
- Direct-sequence spread spectrum (DSSS)
- Orthogonal frequency-division multiplexing (OFDM)

FHSS

Early wireless LAN technology took a novel approach as a compromise between avoiding RF interference and needing complex modulation. The wireless band was divided into 79 channels or fewer, with each channel being 1 MHz wide. To avoid narrowband interference, where an interfering signal would affect only a few channels at a time, transmissions would need to continuously "hop" between frequencies all across the band. This is known as *frequency-hopping spread spectrum*.

Figure 1-26 shows an example of how the FHSS technique works, where the sequence begins on channel 2, then moves to channels 25, 64, 10, 45, and so on, through an entire predetermined sequence before repeating again. Hopping between channels has to occur at regular intervals so that the transmitter and receiver can stay synchronized. In addition, the hopping order must be worked out in advance so that the receiver can always tune to the correct frequency in use at any given time.

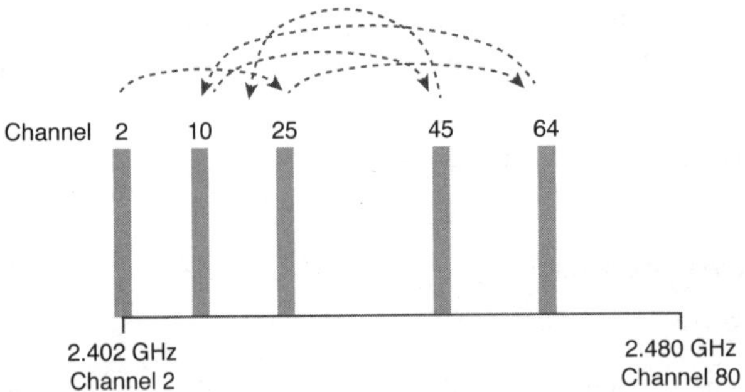

Figure 1-26 *Example FHSS Channel-Hopping Sequence*

Whatever advantage FHSS gained avoiding interference was lost because of the following limitations:

- Narrow 1-MHz channel bandwidth, limiting the data rate to 1 or 2 Mbps.
- Multiple transmitters in an area could eventually collide and interfere with each other on the same channels.

As a result, FHSS fell out of favor and was replaced by another, more robust and scalable spread-spectrum approach: DSSS. Even though FHSS is rarely used now, you should be familiar with it and its place in the evolution of wireless LAN technologies.

DSSS

Direct-sequence spread spectrum uses a small number of fixed, wide channels that can support complex modulation schemes and somewhat scalable data rates. Each channel is 22 MHz wide—a much wider bandwidth compared with the maximum supported 11-Mbps data rate, but wide enough to augment the data by spreading it out and making it more resilient to disruption. In the 2.4-GHz band where DSSS is used, there are 14 possible channels, but only 3 of them that do not overlap. Figure 1-27 shows how channels 1, 6, and 11 are normally used.

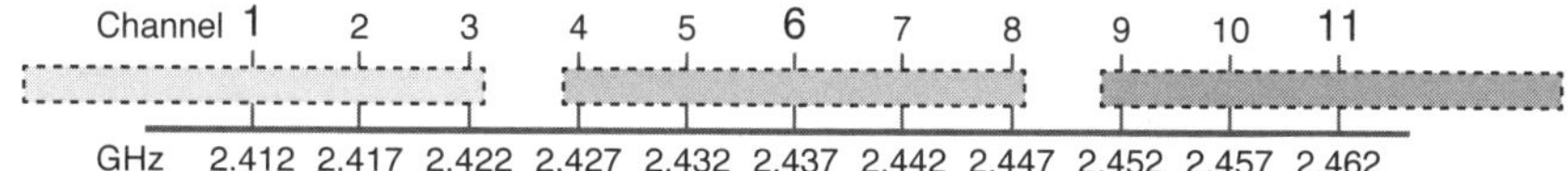

Figure 1-27 *Example Non-overlapping Channels Used for DSSS*

DSSS transmits data in a serial stream, where each data bit is prepared for transmission one at a time. It might seem like a simple matter to transmit the data bits in the order that they are stored or presented to the wireless transmitter; however, RF signals are often affected by external factors like noise or interference that can garble the data at the receiver. For that reason, a wireless transmitter performs several functions to make the data stream less susceptible to being degraded along the transmission path:

- **Scrambler**—The data waiting to be sent is first scrambled in a predetermined manner so that it becomes a randomized string of 0 and 1 bits rather than long sequences of 0 or 1 bits.
- **Coder**—Each data bit is converted into multiple bits of information that contain carefully crafted patterns that can be used to protect against errors due to noise or interference. Each of the new coded bits is called a *chip*. The complete group of chips representing a data bit is called a *symbol*. DSSS uses two encoding techniques: Barker codes and Complementary Code Keying (CCK).
- **Interleaver**—The coded data stream of symbols is spread out into separate blocks so that bursts of interference might affect one block, but not many.
- **Modulator**—The bits contained in each symbol are used to alter or modulate the phase of the carrier signal. This enables the RF signal to carry the binary data bit values.

Figure 1-28 shows the entire data preparation process. At the receiver, the entire process is reversed. The DSSS techniques discussed in this chapter focus only on the coder and modulator functions.

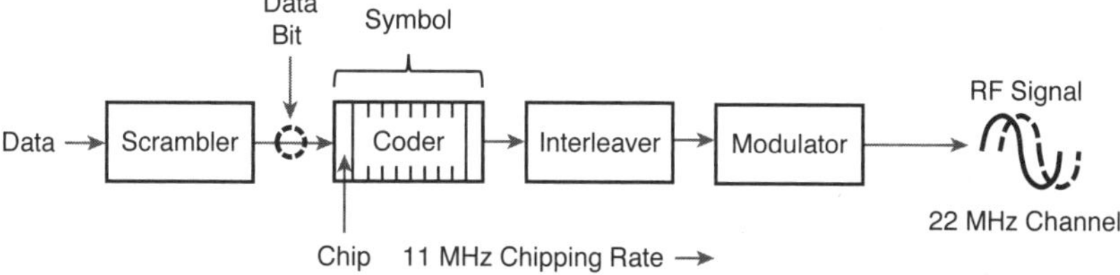

Figure 1-28 *Functional Blocks Used in a DSSS Transmitter*

DSSS has evolved over time to increase the data rate that is modulated onto the RF signal. The following sections describe each DSSS method and data rate, in progression. Regardless of the data rate, DSSS always uses a chipping rate of 11 million chips per second.

1-Mbps Data Rate

To minimize the effect of a low SNR and data loss in cases of narrowband interference, each bit of data is encoded as a sequence of 11 bits called a *Barker 11 code*. The goal is to add enough additional information to each bit of data that its integrity will be preserved when it is sent in a noisy environment.

It might seem ridiculous to turn 1 bit into 11 bits. As an analogy, voice transmissions over an RF signal can be subject to noise and interference, too. Spelling words letter by letter can help, but even single letters can become garbled and ambiguous. For example, the letters *B*, *C*, *D*, *E*, *G*, *P*, *T*, *V*, and *Z* can all sound similar when noise is present. Phonetic alphabets have been developed to remove the ambiguity. Instead of saying the letter *B*, the word *Bravo* is spoken; *C* becomes *Charlie*, *D* becomes *Delta*, and so on. Replacing single letters with longer, unique words makes the listener's job much easier and more accurate.

There are only two possible values for the Barker chips—one corresponding to a 0 data bit (10110111000) and one for a 1 data bit (01001000111). The receiver must also expect the Barker chips and convert them back into single bits of data. The number and sequence of the Barker chip bits have been defined to allow data bits to be recovered if some of the chip bits are lost. In fact, up to 9 of the 11 bits in a single chip can be lost before the original data bit cannot be restored.

Each bit in a Barker chip can be transmitted by using the *differential binary phase shift keying* (DBPSK) modulation scheme. The phase of the carrier signal is shifted or rotated according to the data bit being transmitted, as follows:

0: The phase is not changed.

1: The phase is "rotated" or shifted 180 degrees, such that the signal is suddenly inverted.

DBPSK can modulate 1 bit of data at a time onto the RF signal. With a steady chipping rate of 11 million chips per second, where each symbol (1 original bit) contains 11 chips, the transmitted data rate is 1 Mbps.

2-Mbps Data Rate

It is possible to couple the 1-Mbps strategy with a different modulation scheme to double the data rate. As before, each data bit is coded into an 11-bit Barker code with an 11-MHz chipping rate. This time, chips are taken two at a time and modulated onto the carrier signal by using *differential quadrature phase shift keying* (DQPSK). The two chips are used to affect the carrier signal's phase in four possible ways, each one 90 degrees apart (hence, the name quadrature). The bit patterns produce the following phase shifts:

- **00**—The phase is not changed.
- **01**—Rotate the phase 90 degrees.
- **11**—Rotate the phase 180 degrees.
- **10**—Rotate the phase 270 degrees.

Because DQPSK can modulate data bits in pairs, it is able to transmit twice the data rate of DBPSK, or 2 Mbps.

Figure 1-29 shows examples of DBPSK and DQPSK modulation. Each input data bit combination is shown along with the carrier signal phase rotation that occurs. Phase rotations can occur at several points along a cycle; for simplicity, only rotations at the beginning of the cycle (0 degrees) are shown. Notice how abrupt the phase can change, according to the bits being modulated. The receiver must detect these phase changes when it demodulates the signal so that the original data bits can be recovered.

Tip As you read about wireless modulation techniques, you will often see terms like DBPSK and BPSK mentioned. The two forms reference the same type of modulation (BPSK, in this case), but differ in the reference signal that the receiver uses to detect the phase changes. The nondifferential form (without the initial *D*) means the receiver must compare with the original premodulated signal to find phase changes. The differential form (with the *D*) means the receiver must figure out phase changes by comparing with previous phases already seen in the received signal.

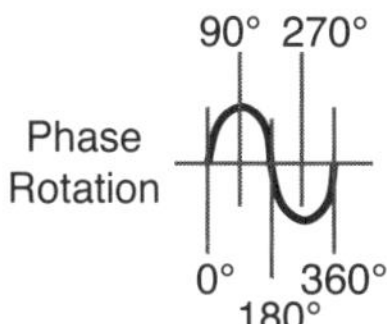

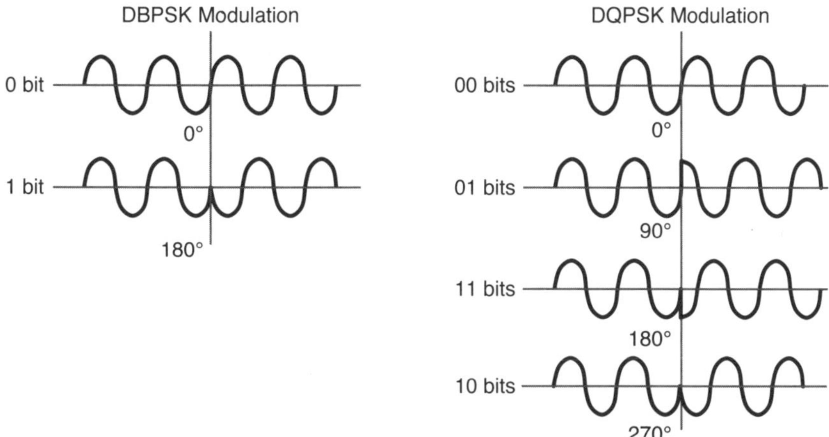

Figure 1-29 *Example Phase Changes During DBPSK and DQPSK Modulation*

5.5-Mbps Data Rate

To gain more efficiency, *Complementary Code Keying* (CCK) can replace the Barker code. CCK can take 4 bits of data at a time and build out redundant information to create a unique 6-chip symbol. Two more bits are added to indicate the modulated phase orientation for the symbol, resulting in 8 chips total. CCK is naturally coupled with DQPSK modulation; the two-phase orientation bits determine four possible carrier signal phase rotation values.

The chipping rate remains steady at 11 MHz, but each symbol contains 8 chips. This results in a symbol rate of 1.375 MHz. Each symbol is based on 4 original data bits, so the effective data rate is 5.5 Mbps.

11-Mbps Data Rate

The 5.5-Mbps CCK data rate can be doubled by making an adjustment to the coder. Instead of taking 4 data bits at a time to make each coder symbol, data can be taken 8 bits at a time to create a unique 8-chip symbol. The CCK symbol rate is still 1.375 MHz, so 8 data bits per symbol results in a data rate of 11 Mbps.

The smaller 8-chip CCK symbol is more efficient than the 11-bit Barker code because more data bits can be sent with each new symbol. At the same time, CCK loses some of the extra bits used by the Barker code to recover information received in a noisy or low SNR environment. In other words, CCK achieves faster data rates at the expense of requiring a stronger, less-noisy signal.

OFDM

DSSS spreads the chips of a single data stream into one wide, 22-MHz channel. It is inherently limited to an 11-Mbps data rate because of the consistent 11-MHz chipping rate that feeds into the RF modulation. To scale beyond that limit, a vastly different approach is needed.

In contrast, orthogonal frequency-division multiplexing (OFDM) sends data bits in *parallel* over multiple frequencies, all contained in a single 20-MHz channel. Each channel is divided into 64 subcarriers (also called subchannels or tones) that are spaced 312.5 kHz apart. The subcarriers are broken down into the following types:

- **Guard**—12 subcarriers are used to help set one channel apart from another and to help receivers lock onto the channel.
- **Pilot**—4 subcarriers are equally spaced and always transmitted to help receivers evaluate the noise state of the channel.
- **Data**—48 subcarriers are devoted to carrying data.

Tip Sometimes you might see OFDM described as having 52 subcarriers (48 for data and 4 for pilot). This is because the 12 guard frequencies are not actually transmitted, but stay silent as channel spacing.

Figure 1-30 shows an example of OFDM, where channel 6 in the 2.4-GHz band is 20 MHz wide with 48 data subcarriers. OFDM is named for the way it takes one channel and divides it into a set of distinct frequencies for its subcarriers. Notice that the subcarriers appear to be spaced too close together, causing them to overlap. In fact, that is the case, but instead of interfering with each other, the overlapped portions are aligned so that they cancel most of the potential interference.

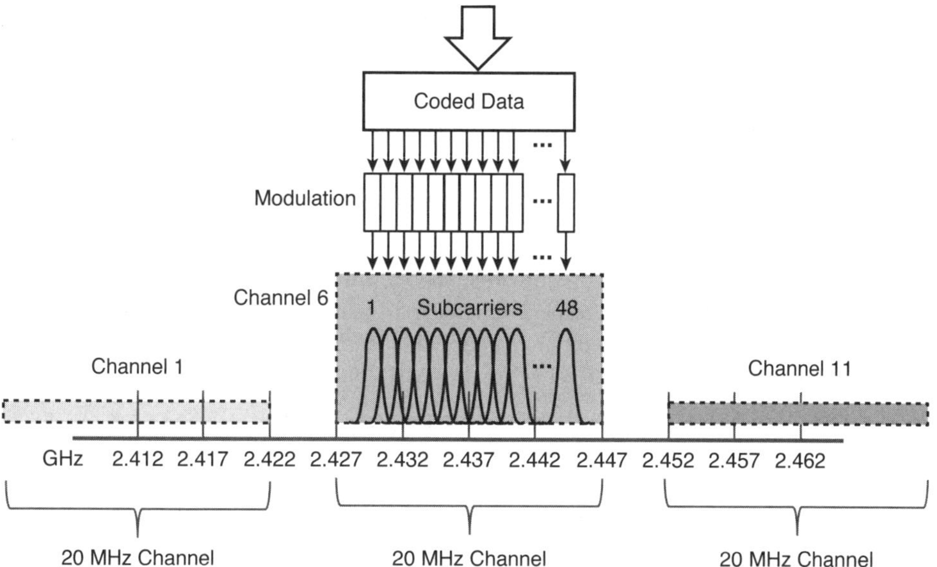

Figure 1-30 *OFDM Operation with 48 Parallel Subcarriers*

OFDM has the usual scrambling, coding, interleaving, and modulating functions, but it gains its scalability by leveraging so many data subcarriers in parallel. Even though the data rates through each subcarrier are relatively low, the sum of all subcarriers results in a high aggregate data rate.

OFDM offers many different data rates through several different modulation schemes. Because OFDM is concerned with moving data in parallel at higher rates, the amount of information that is repeated for resilience can be varied. The coders used with OFDM are named according to the fraction of symbols that are new or unique, and not repeated. For example, BPSK 1/2 designates that one half of the bits are new and one half are repeated. BPSK 3/4 uses a coder that presents three-fourths new data and repeats only one fourth. As a rule of thumb, a greater fraction means a greater data rate, but a lower tolerance for errors.

At the low end of the range, the familiar BPSK modulation can be used along with two different coder ratios. In this case, OFDM still uses 48 subchannels or tones, with a reduced tone rate of 250 Kbps. OFDM with BPSK 1/2 results in a 6-Mbps data rate, whereas BPSK 3/4 gives 9 Mbps. QPSK 1/2 and 3/4 can be used to increase the data rate to 12 and 18 Mbps, respectively.

Recall that QPSK uses 2 data bits to modulate the RF signal, resulting in four possible phase shifts. To achieve data rates greater than 18 Mbps, more bits must be used to modulate the signal. Quadrature amplitude modulation (QAM) combines QPSK phase shifting (*quadrature*) with multiple amplitude levels to get a greater number of unique alterations to the signal. For example, 16-QAM uses 2 bits to select the QPSK phase rotation and 2 bits to select the amplitude level, giving 4 bits or 16 unique modulation changes. Figure 1-31 illustrates a 16-QAM operation.

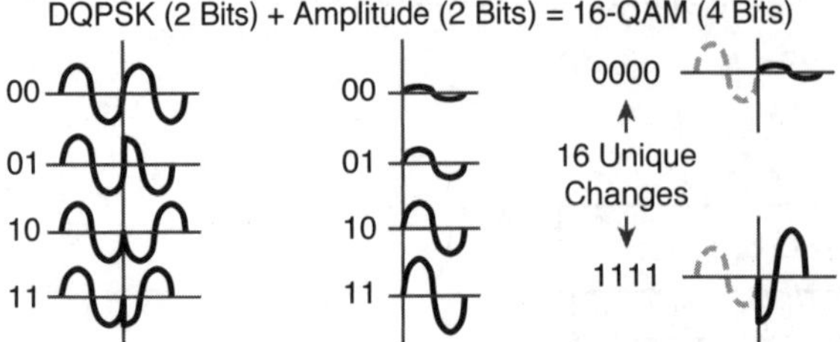

Figure 1-31 *Examples of Phase and Amplitude Changes with 16-QAM*

The number of possible outcomes is always given as a prefix to the QAM name, followed by the coder ratio of new data. In other words, 16-QAM is available in 1/2 and 3/4, providing data rates of 24 and 36 Mbps, respectively. Beyond that, 64-QAM uses 8 phase shifts and 8 amplitude levels to produce 64 unique modulation changes. The 64-QAM 2/3 and 64-QAM 3/4 methods offer 48 and 54 Mbps, respectively.

The same scheme is extended even further with 256-QAM 3/4 and 256-QAM 5/6. As the 256 prefix denotes, 16 different phase shifts and 16 different amplitude levels are combined to produce 256 unique modulation changes, effectively encoding 8 bits of data at a time. With so many shifts and levels in use, receivers can have a difficult job determining the original transmitted values accurately—especially when noise is present. As the modulation schemes get more complex (the QAM prefix gets higher), the signal-to-noise ratio must become greater.

Modulation Summary

Table 1-4 lists all the modulation techniques used in wireless LANs. There are quite a few, and you will have to know them all for the CCNA Wireless exam. The modulation types are broken down by DSSS and OFDM. This will become important as wireless standards are introduced in Chapter 2.

Try to get a feel for the relative data rates, working from the lowest to the highest. Remember that

- *B* in DBPSK stands for binary (two outcomes).
- Q in DQPSK stands for quadrature (four outcomes).
- CCK is coupled with QPSK and replaces Barker 11 to go a bit faster.
- OFDM generally wins out, except at the two slowest BPSK methods, which sit between the two CCK methods.
- QAM leverages both phase and amplitude changes to move the greatest amount of data.
- Higher fractions mean higher data rates.

Table 1-4 Wireless LAN Modulation Techniques

Modulation	DSSS Data Rate (Mbps)	OFDM Data Rate (Mbps)
DBPSK	1	
DQPSK	2	
CCK 4	5.5	
OFDM BPSK 1/2		6
OFDM BPSK 3/4		9
CCK 8	11	
OFDM QPSK 1/2		12
OFDM QPSK 3/4		18
OFDM 16-QAM 1/2		24
OFDM 16-QAM 3/4		36
OFDM 64-QAM 2/3		48
OFDM 64-QAM 3/4		54
OFDM 256-QAM 3/4		78
OFDM 256-QAM 5/6		86[1]

[1] The OFDM 256-QAM 5/6 data rate is approximate but is not supported with a single spatial stream.

To pass data over an RF signal successfully, both a transmitter and receiver have to use the same modulation method. In addition, the pair should use the best data rate possible, given their current environment. If they are located in a noisy environment, where a low SNR or a low RSSI might result, a lower data rate might be preferable. If not, a higher data rate is better.

With so many possible modulation methods available, how do the transmitter and receiver select a common method to use? To complicate things, the transmitter, the receiver, or both might be mobile. As they move around, the SNR and RSSI conditions will likely change from one moment to the next. The most effective approach is to have the transmitter and receiver negotiate a modulation method (and the resulting data rate) dynamically, based on current RF conditions.

Chapter 2 explains the industry standards that are used in wireless LANs and how they influence the modulation techniques that are used.

Exam Preparation Tasks

As mentioned in the section "How to Use This Book" in the Introduction, you have a couple of choices for exam preparation: the exercises here, Chapter 21, "Final Review," and the exam simulation questions on the DVD.

Review All Key Topics

Review the most important topics in this chapter, noted with the Key Topic icon in the outer margin of the page. Table 1-5 lists a reference of these key topics and the page numbers on which each is found.

Table 1-5 Key Topics for Chapter 1

Key Topic Element	Description	Page Number
Paragraph	dB definition	17
List	Important dB laws to remember	17
Table 1-3	Power changes and corresponding dB values	18
Paragraph	EIRP calculation	21
Figure 1-23	Receiver sensitivity and noise floor	23
Table 1-4	Modulation technique summary	33

Key Terms

Define the following key terms from this chapter and check your answers in the glossary:

amplitude, band, bandwidth, Barker code, carrier signal, channel, chip, coder, Complementary Code Keying (CCK), decibel (dB), dBd, dBi, dBm, demodulation, differential binary phase shift keying (DBPSK), differential quadrature phase shift keying (DQPSK), direct-sequence spread spectrum (DSSS), effective isotropic radiated power (EIRP), frequency, frequency-hopping spread spectrum (FHSS), hertz (Hz), in phase, isotropic antenna, link budget, modulation, narrowband, noise floor, orthogonal frequency-division multiplexing (OFDM), out of phase, phase, quadrature amplitude modulation (QAM), radio frequency (RF), received signal strength indicator (RSSI), sensitivity level, signal-to-noise ratio (SNR), spread spectrum, symbol, wavelength

This chapter covers the following topics:

- **Regulatory Bodies**—This section describes the organizations that regulate radio frequency spectrum and its uses.
- **IEEE Standards Body**—This section discusses the IEEE and the 802.11 standards that define wireless LAN operation.
- **802.11 Channel Use**—This section covers each of the frequency bands used for 802.11 wireless LANs and the encoding and modulation methods that are used in wireless LANs.
- **IEEE 802.11 Standards**—This section describes the standards that define the progressive generations of 802.11 wireless LANs.
- **Wi-Fi Alliance**—This section introduces the global industry association that promotes and certifies wireless LAN products to ensure interoperability.

This chapter covers the following exam topics:

- 2.1—Describe basic Wi-Fi governance
  - 2.1a—Describe regional regulatory bodies
  - 2.1b—IEEE 802.11
  - 2.1c—Wi-Fi Alliance
- 2.2—Describe usable channel and power combination
  - 2.2a—Regional EIRP limitation examples
  - 2.2b—ISM, UNII frequency bands
- 2.3—Describe 802.11 fundamentals
  - 2.3a—Modulation techniques
  - 2.3b—Channel width
  - 2.3c—MIMO/MU-MIMO
    - 2.3c(i)—MRC
    - 2.3c(ii)—Beam forming
    - 2.3c(iii)—Spatial streams

CHAPTER 2

RF Standards

To communicate successfully, wireless devices must first find each other in the radio frequency (RF) spectrum and then use compatible methods to generate RF signals, modulate and encode data, negotiate communication parameters and features, and so on—all without interfering with the operation of other wireless devices. This chapter covers the agencies that regulate, standardize, and validate the correct use of wireless LAN devices.

"Do I Know This Already?" Quiz

The "Do I Know This Already?" quiz allows you to assess whether you should read this entire chapter thoroughly or jump to the "Exam Preparation Tasks" section. If you are in doubt about your answers to these questions or your own assessment of your knowledge of the topics, read the entire chapter. Table 2-1 lists the major headings in this chapter and their corresponding "Do I Know This Already?" quiz questions. You can find the answers in Appendix A, "Answers to the 'Do I Know This Already?' Quizzes."

Table 2-1 "Do I Know This Already?" Section-to-Question Mapping

Foundation Topics Section	Questions
Regulatory Bodies	1–3
IEEE Standards Body	4
802.11 Channel Use	5–6
IEEE 802.11 Standards	7–14
Wi-Fi Alliance	15

Caution The goal of self-assessment is to gauge your mastery of the topics in this chapter. If you do not know the answer to a question or are only partially sure of the answer, you should mark that question as wrong for purposes of the self-assessment. Giving yourself credit for an answer you correctly guess skews your self-assessment results and might provide you with a false sense of security.

1. Which regulatory body allocated the 2.4–2.5-GHz band for industrial, scientific, and medical use?
   a. IEEE
   b. ETSI
   c. ITU-R
   d. FCC
2. The U-NII-1 band is used for which one of the following purposes?
   a. 2.4-GHz wireless LANs
   b. 5-GHz wireless LANs
   c. Medical applications
   d. Point-to-point links
3. In the 2.4-GHz band, the FCC limits the EIRP of a point-to-multipoint link to which one of the following maximum values?
   a. 100 mW
   b. 20 dBm
   c. 50 mW
   d. 36 dBm
4. Wireless LAN operation is defined in which one of the following standards?
   a. 802.1
   b. 802.2
   c. 802.3
   d. 802.11
   e. 802.15
5. Which one of the following specifies the correct list of non-overlapping channels for DSSS use in the 2.4-GHz band?
   a. 1, 2, 3
   b. 1, 5, 10
   c. 1, 6, 11
   d. 1, 8, 13
   e. All of channels 1–14
6. The U-NII-1 band begins at which one of the following channel numbers?
   a. 0
   b. 1
   c. 24
   d. 36

7. Which of the following standards apply to wireless LAN operation in the 5-GHz band? (Choose all that apply.)
   a. IEEE 802.1
   b. IEEE 802.11g
   c. IEEE 802.11a
   d. IEEE 802.11n
   e. IEEE 802.11ac
   f. IEEE 802.11b
   g. IEEE 802.11-2012

8. Which of the following wireless LAN standards use OFDM for transmissions? (Choose all that apply.)
   a. 802.11-1997
   b. 802.11b
   c. 802.11g
   d. 802.11a

9. Which one of the following correctly specifies the maximum theoretical data rate of the 802.11b, 802.11a, and 802.11n standards, respectively?
   a. 11 Mbps, 54 Mbps, 600 Mbps
   b. 54 Mbps, 54 Mbps, 150 Mbps
   c. 1 Mbps, 11 Mbps, 54 Mbps
   d. 11 Mbps, 20 Mbps, 40 Mbps

10. A 2×3 MIMO device correctly describes which one of the following?
    a. A device with two radios and three antennas
    b. A device with two transmitters and three receivers
    c. A device with two bonded channels and three spatial streams
    d. A device with two receivers and three transmitters

11. An 802.11n device can aggregate channels to which one of the following maximum widths?
    a. 5 MHz
    b. 20 MHz
    c. 40 MHz
    d. 80 MHz

12. Which one of the following standards can make use of multiple spatial streams on a transmitter and a receiver? (Choose all that apply.)

    a. 802.11n

    b. 802.11b

    c. 802.11g

    d. 802.11a

    e. 802.11ac

    f. All of these answers are correct.

13. Which one of the following is the highest or best modulation scheme that can be used with 802.11ac devices?

    a. QPSK 3/4

    b. 256-QAM

    c. 128-QAM

    d. 64-QAM

    e. 16-QAM

14. What is the maximum number of spatial streams supported by 802.11ac?

    a. 1

    b. 2

    c. 4

    d. 8

    e. 16

15. Which one of the following organizations certifies 802.11 interoperability?

    a. ITU-R

    b. FCC

    c. IEEE

    d. Wi-Fi Alliance

    e. Cisco

Foundation Topics

Regulatory Bodies

The entire frequency spectrum is composed of all possible frequencies, from very low up to cosmic rays. The part of the spectrum that is usable for radio communication, the radio frequency (RF) portion, ranges from about 3 kHz to 300 GHz. Frequencies within the RF spectrum are available because they exist everywhere, but it would not be wise to use any frequency at will. For example, suppose someone decides to set up a radio transmitter to broadcast a signal on 123.45 MHz. Unless other people know about the transmitter's frequency and have radio receivers that can tune to that frequency, no one will be able to receive the signal. Even further, a frequency might be used by one entity for a specific purpose, while another entity might try to use the same frequency for a different purpose. To keep the RF spectrum organized and open for fair use, regulatory bodies were formed.

ITU-R

A telecommunications regulatory body regulates or decides which part of the RF spectrum can be used for a particular purpose, in addition to how it can be used. A country might have its own regulatory body that controls RF spectrum use within its borders, but RF signals can be more far-reaching than that. For example, one purpose for shortwave radio stations is to broadcast from one country around the earth to reach other countries. In a similar manner, one radio manufacturer might sell its equipment internationally, where a transmitter or receiver might be used in any global location.

To provide a hierarchy to manage the RF spectrum globally, the United Nations set up the International Telecommunication Union Radiocommunication Sector (ITU-R; http://www.itu.int). The ITU-R maintains spectrum and frequency assignments in three distinct regions:

- **Region 1:** Europe, Africa, and Northern Asia
- **Region 2:** North and South America
- **Region 3:** Southern Asia and Australasia

While the ITU-R strives to make the RF spectrum usable by all countries, it also tries to make sure that the RF signals from one country do not interfere with the signals of another country. It also attempts to determine the expected usages of each segment of the spectrum. The ITU-R even keeps track of geostationary satellite orbits and frequencies so that signals for one country's satellites do not harmfully interfere with those of another country.

Most bands in the RF spectrum are tightly regulated, requiring you to apply for a license from a regulatory body before using a specific frequency. The regulatory bodies typically determine the allowed type of emission and set limits on things like the emission source and power. Licensed bands might seem restrictive, for a good reason: "Harmful" or disruptive interference is kept to a minimum because frequencies are reserved for approved transmitters, purposes, and locations. To use a frequency in a licensed band, someone has to submit an application to a regulatory body that governs frequency use in a given country, wait for approval, and then abide by any restrictions that are imposed.

In contrast, the ITU-R allocated the following two frequency ranges specifically for industrial, scientific, and medical (ISM) applications. Although there are other ISM bands, too, there are mainly two that apply to wireless LANs:

2.400 to 2.500 GHz

5.725 to 5.825 GHz

The purposes for these bands are broad and access is open to anyone who wants to use them. In other words, the ISM bands are unlicensed and no registration or approval is needed to transmit on one of the frequencies.

While unlicensed bands are more accessible and convenient to use, they are much more vulnerable to interference and misuse. For example, suppose that you decide to set up a transmitter in your office to use one frequency. The next day, someone in a neighboring office sets up his own transmitter to broadcast on the same or an overlapping frequency. Because the band is unlicensed, you can do little to relieve the interference other than move your transmitter to a different frequency or use diplomacy to convince your neighbor to move his transmitter instead.

Fortunately, all the frequency bands used for wireless LANs are unlicensed. You can purchase a wireless LAN device and begin to use it immediately—provided you abide by the rules set up by the regulatory agency that governs RF use in your country. Usually, unlicensed transmitters must stay within an approved frequency range and transmit within an approved maximum power level. Several national regulatory agencies are discussed in the following sections.

FCC

In the United States, the Federal Communications Commission (FCC; http://www.fcc.gov) regulates RF frequencies, channels, and transmission power. Some other countries choose to follow the FCC rules, too. In addition to the 2.4–2.5-GHz ISM band allocated by the ITU-R, the FCC has allocated the Unlicensed National Information Infrastructure (U-NII) frequency space in the 5-GHz band for wireless LAN use. U-NII is actually four separate sub-bands, as follows:

U-NII-1 (Band 1): 5.15 to 5.25 GHz

U-NII-2 (Band 2): 5.25 to 5.35 GHz

U-NII-2 Extended (Band 3): 5.47 to 5.725 GHz

U-NII-3 (Band 4): 5.725 to 5.825 GHz (also allocated as ISM)

> **Tip** As you read and work with the 5-GHz bands, be aware that you may see various forms of the band names. For example, the 5.15–5.25-GHz band is often referenced by names like U-NII-1, UNII-1, U-NII Low, and so on.

All transmitting equipment must be approved by the FCC before it can be sold to users. For the 2.4- and 5-GHz unlicensed bands, the FCC requires strict limits on the effective isotropic radiated power (EIRP). Recall from Chapter 1, "RF Signals and Modulation," that the

EIRP is the net power level that is being transmitted from an antenna that is connected to a transmitter.

You must be aware of the EIRP limits and make sure that your wireless LAN equipment does not exceed the limits. If the FCC has to approve wireless transmitters, it might seem logical that the maximum EIRP of the equipment would have to be approved, too. Why would you, as a wireless user, have to worry about staying within the limits? Some transmitters are sold without antennas, so you are free to buy and install your own. Without considering the EIRP limit, you might choose an antenna that has too much gain, which would raise the EIRP too high.

In an effort to prevent users from exceeding the EIRP limits, the FCC requires all removable antennas to have a unique, nonstandard connector, based on the transmitter manufacturer. The original idea was to require both transmitter and antenna to be purchased from the same manufacturer, preventing the end user from mixing and matching parts from different vendors.

Cisco uses a variant of the threaded Neill-Concelman (TNC) connector on its equipment. The reverse polarity TNC (RP-TNC) connector is identical to the TNC, but has key male and female parts reversed so that antennas with TNC connectors cannot be connected. Figure 2-1 shows the male version of the regular TNC and RP-TNC connector side by side.

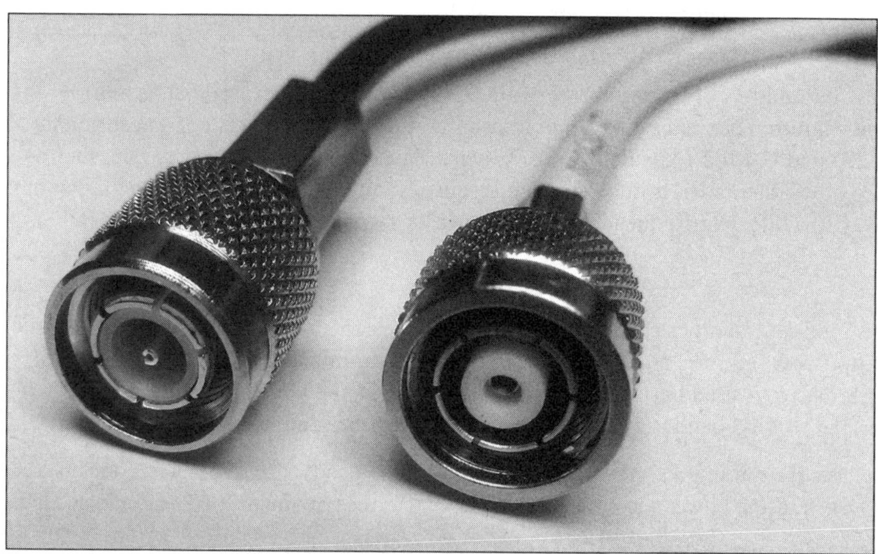

Figure 2-1 *Comparison Between TNC (left) and Cisco RP-TNC Connector (right)*

In practice, you can find all sorts of antennas from a wide variety of manufacturers that all have RP-TNC connectors. In other words, you cannot depend on the FCC and the RP-TNC connector to limit the EIRP of your wireless equipment; you have to do that yourself.

Transmitters in the 2.4-GHz band can be used indoors or outdoors. The power emitted at the transmitter must be limited to 30 dBm and the EIRP limited to 36 dBm. An antenna gain of +6 dBi is assumed. However, there is some flexibility according to the following two rules, based on the intended spread of the signal:

- **Point-to-multipoint links**—Where the transmitted signal propagates in all directions, you can make adjustments according to a *1:1* rule. For each dBm you remove from the transmitter, one dBi can be added to the antenna gain, as long as the EIRP is no greater than 36 dBm.
- **Point-to-point links**—Where the transmitted signal propagates in one general direction, you can make adjustments according to a *3:1* rule. For each dBm you remove from the transmitter, 3 dBi can be added to the antenna gain. The resulting EIRP can exceed 36 dBm but cannot be greater than 56 dBm.

Transmitters in the 5-GHz bands must follow the FCC limits listed in Table 2-2. In each of the U-NII bands, you can make power adjustments according to the 1:1 rule. Notice that the U-NII-1 band is the only one restricted to indoor use.

Table 2-2 FCC Requirements in the 5-GHz U-NII Bands

Band	Allowed Use	Transmitter Max	EIRP Max
U-NII-1	Indoor only	17 dBm (50 mW)	23 dBm
U-NII-2	Indoor or outdoor	24 dBm (250 mW)	30 dBm
U-NII-2 Extended	Indoor or outdoor	24 dBm (250 mW)	30 dBm
U-NII-3	Indoor or outdoor	30 dBm (1 W)	36 dBm

Normally, transmitters operating in any of the 2.4- and 5-GHz unlicensed bands must endure any interference caused by other transmitters. The FCC requires one exception in the U-NII-2 and U-NII-2 Extended bands: When a signal from an approved device, such as a military or weather radar, is detected on a frequency, all other transmitters must move out of the way to a different frequency. This is known as *dynamic frequency selection* (DFS).

ETSI

In Europe and several other countries, the European Telecommunication Standards Institute (ETSI; http://www.etsi.org) regulates radio transmitter use. Like the FCC, the ETSI allows wireless LANs to be used in the 2.4-GHz ISM and most of the same 5-GHz U-NII bands; however, the U-NII-3 band is a licensed band and cannot be used.

Table 2-3 lists the transmitter requirements for each of the bands. The ETSI allows adjustments to the transmit power and antenna gain, as long as the maximum EIRP is not exceeded.

Table 2-3 ETSI Requirements in the 2.4- and 5-GHz Bands

Band	Allowed Use	EIRP Max
2.4 GHz ISM	Indoor or outdoor	20 dBm
U-NII-1	Indoor only	23 dBm
U-NII-2	Indoor only	23 dBm
U-NII-2 Extended	Indoor or outdoor	30 dBm
U-NII-3	Licensed	N/A

The ETSI regulations also include DFS, which requires wireless LAN transmitters to move to a random frequency after a radar signal is detected.

Other Regulatory Bodies

Wireless LAN equipment use is regulated outside the Americas and Europe, too. Does each country have its own set of regulations? Not necessarily; a country might have its own or it can adhere to all or parts of the regulations of a larger, more established regulatory body. Countries that use a common set of RF regulations are known as a regulatory domain.

For example, a Cisco wireless device that is compatible with the American regulatory domain can also be used in Canada, many Latin and South American countries, and in the Philippines.

Cisco manufactures wireless devices for use in at least 13 different regulatory domains. The basic wireless LAN operation is identical in all domains, but the frequency ranges, channels, and maximum transmit powers can differ.

IEEE Standards Body

To pass data over a wireless link, many parameters have to be defined and standardized. Wireless LANs rarely involve just one transmitter and receiver; normally, many devices must contend for use of airtime on a frequency. The Institute of Electric and Electronic Engineers (IEEE; http://ieee.org) maintains the industry standards that are used for wireless LANs, among many others.

The IEEE is a professional organization made up of engineers from around the world. It is organized as a collection of "societies" that are focused on particular engineering areas. For example, the IEEE Computer Society develops and maintains standards on a variety of topics related to computing, including Ethernet and wireless LANs.

The IEEE 802 standards all deal with local-area networks and metropolitan-area networks (LANs and MANs, respectively). The standards mainly deal with the physical and data link layers of the OSI model, and with transporting variable-size data packets across a network media. As you explore the portion of the 802 standards that are dedicated to wireless LANs, you will find that they focus on accessing the shared RF media (physical layer or Layer 1) and on sending and receiving data frames (data link layer or Layer 2).

> **Tip** What is the significance of the number 802? The Local Network Standards Committee of the IEEE Computer Society first met in February 1980, to begin work on "Project 802," the first LAN standard. The number 802 was the next sequential project number, but also fit the odd coincidence of the date—year 80, second month.

To develop networking standards, the IEEE is organized into working groups, which have an open membership. Each working group is assigned an index number that is appended to the 802 standards family number. For example, 802.1 refers to the first working group, which developed standards for network bridging. Table 2-4 lists a few familiar 802 working groups. Notice that the eleventh working group, 802.11, is responsible for the wireless LAN standards that are used by Cisco, many other wireless vendors, and users like yourself. For the remainder of this chapter, the focus will be on 802.11.

Table 2-4 Example IEEE 802 Working Groups

Name	Description
802.1	Network bridging (includes Spanning Tree Protocol)
802.2	Link-layer control
802.3	Ethernet
802.4	Token Bus
802.5	Token Ring MAC layer
...	
802.11	Wireless LANs
...	
802.15	Wireless PANs (personal-area networks such as Bluetooth, ZigBee, and so on)

As a new improvement is needed or the technology advances, a study group (SG) researches the topic to see whether an amendment to the 802.11 standard is needed. Each time a new amendment is necessary, a new task group (TG) is formed to collaborate and develop it. Task groups are assigned a suffix letter in alphabetic order. For example, as amendments are introduced, their names become 802.11a, 802.11b, 802.11c, and so on. If there are enough amendments to reach letter *z*, any subsequent amendments are given a two-letter suffix, beginning with the letter *a* followed by letters *a* through *z*. At the time of this writing, the 802.11 working group had assigned amendments 802.11aa through 802.11ay.

Once a draft amendment is completed, it must be voted on and ratified. At that point, manufacturers can then begin to build products that operate according to all or a part of the standard. For example, when the 802.11n amendment was finalized and published, the new features of 802.11n were then added to many wireless LAN devices.

Sometimes an amendment takes a very long time to get through the development, voting, and final approval processes, so many manufacturers will decide to move ahead and implement the draft amendment into their products early. Usually a manufacturer has to decide whether the draft amendment is stable enough to implement into device hardware or is likely to receive drastic changes before it is ratified. This scenario occurred with the 802.11n amendment. Many manufacturers offered early implementations as "Draft N-compliant" products, which may or may not have been compatible with similar products from other manufacturers.

The 802.11 standards usually have the year they were ratified added to their names. For example, the original 802.11 standard was issued in 1997, so it is now known as 802.11-1997. Likewise, the name 802.11a-1999 means that the 802.11a amendment was ratified in 1999.

Periodically, the IEEE 802 working group chooses to revise the 802.11 standard as a whole. When this occurs, every amendment that has been ratified since the last 802.11 revision is "rolled up" and absorbed into the new updated standard. The idea is to maintain one document that defines the entire standard, as of a certain date, so that wireless developers can find all of the technical details in one place.

Even though the amendments become part of the larger standard, their names are still commonly used to reference the specific functions they introduced. Since its introduction in 1997, the 802.11 standard has been revised in 1999, 2007, and 2012. The current 802.11-2012 standard is more than 2700 pages long, and the 2016 revision is projected to be at least 3700 pages!

802.11 Channel Use

Chapter 1 introduced RF frequency, bands, and channels in a generic fashion. Wireless devices built around the 802.11 standard must also have a standardized concept of the same RF parameters. As wireless devices move around, they should be able to detect and participate in wireless LANs as they become available, regardless of geographic location.

The following sections describe the 802.11 channel definitions in the 2.4- and 5-GHz bands.

Channels in the 2.4-GHz ISM Band

In the 2.4-GHz ISM band, the frequency space is divided up into 14 channels, numbered 1 through 14. With the exception of channel 14, the channels are spaced 5 MHz apart, as listed in Table 2-5.

Table 2-5 IEEE 802.11 Channel Layout in the 2.4-GHz Band

Channel	Frequency (GHz)
1	2.412
2	2.417
3	2.422
4	2.427
5	2.432
6	2.437
7	2.442
8	2.447
9	2.452
10	2.457
11	2.462
12	2.467
13	2.472
14	2.484

The 802.11 standard allows either direct-sequence spread spectrum (DSSS) or orthogonal frequency-division multiplexing (OFDM) modulation and coding schemes to be used in the 2.4-GHz band. DSSS radios require each channel to be 22 MHz wide, and OFDM requires 20 MHz. Either way, with only 5 MHz between channels, transmissions on neighboring channels are bound to overlap and interfere with each other. (This condition is covered in Chapter 3, "RF Signals in the Real World.")

Even though the band is made up of 14 channels, not all of them may be used in all countries. For example, the FCC limits the band to channels 1 through 11 only. The ETSI permits channels 1 through 13. Japan permits all 14 channels to be used, but channel 14 has some restrictions.

Figure 2-2 shows how 802.11 signals can overlap on neighboring 2.4-GHz channels. The only way to prevent transmitters on nearby channels from interfering with each other is to keep them on channels that are spaced farther apart. The most common arrangement is to use only channels 1, 6, and 11, which do not overlap with each other at all.

> **Tip** One scheme uses channels 1, 5, 9, and 13 to gain an extra channel, but it is not commonly used. With DSSS, the channels end up overlapping, which violates the 802.11 definition for adjacent channels and also raises the noise floor. Only the OFDM 20-MHz-wide channels can avoid overlapping each other. Channel 13 presents an interesting case because it is not supported on all wireless clients in all areas of the world.

Key Topic

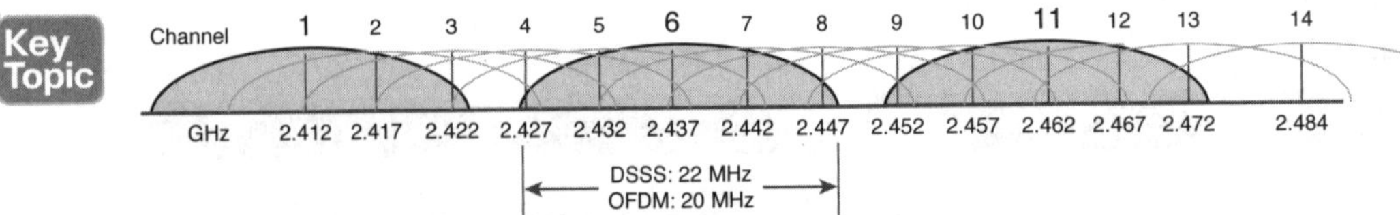

Figure 2-2 *Channel Layout in the 2.4-GHz Band*

Why should you be concerned about non-overlapping channels? After all, having three non-overlapping channels might seem like plenty. Problems can arise when you need to set up several wireless LAN transmitters in the same general area. You could set the first three transmitters to each use a different channel, but the fourth or fifth ones would have to reuse one of the three non-overlapping channels.

Reusing channels becomes a puzzle that you have to solve when you administer a growing wireless LAN. Chapter 7, "Planning Coverage with Wireless APs," covers channel reuse in greater detail. Be aware that the three-channel limitation also applies to every transmitter located in an area—regardless of whether you administer them. Because the 2.4-GHz band is unlicensed, anyone is free to bring up a transmitter on any of the three non-overlapping channels without consulting you or anybody else. In fact, they might decide to set their transmitter to use any of the 14 available channels, thinking that none of them overlap.

Channels in the 5-GHz U-NII Bands

Recall that the 5-GHz band is organized as four separate, smaller bands: U-NII-1, U-NII-2, U-NII-2 Extended, and U-NII-3. The bands are all divided into channels that are 20 MHz apart, as listed in Table 2-6.

Table 2-6 IEEE 802.11 Channel Layout in the 5-GHz Bands

Band	Channel	Frequency (GHz)
U-NII-1	36	5.180
	40	5.200
	44	5.220
	48	5.240
U-NII-2	52	5.260
	56	5.280
	60	5.300
	64	5.320
U-NII-2 Extended	100	5.500
	104	5.520
	108	5.540
	112	5.560
	116	5.580
	120	5.600
	124	5.620
	128	5.640
	132	5.660
	136	5.680
	140	5.700
U-NII-3	149	5.745
	153	5.765
	157	5.785
	161	5.805

The fact that the 5-GHz space is divided into four different bands might seem confusing. Even worse is the channel numbering. For instance, why is the first channel in the U-NII-1 band called channel 36 instead of channel 1? And why are neighboring channels actually four channel numbers apart?

The answers lie in the 802.11 standard itself: The entire 5-GHz frequency space is defined as a sequence of channels spaced 5 MHz apart, beginning with channel 0 at 5.000 GHz. Therefore, the first U-NII-1 channel is located at 5.180 GHz, which corresponds to channel number 36. Each U-NII channel is 20 MHz wide, so an adjacent channel is located four 5-MHz channel widths, or four channel numbers, away.

The FCC originally allocated three separate bands as U-NII-1, U-NII-2, and U-NII-3, each having four 20-MHz channels. In 2004, the FCC added the U-NII-2 Extended band, which offered 11 additional 20-MHz channels. Figure 2-3 shows the complete frequency layout of the four bands. Notice that the U-NII-1 and U-NII-2 bands are contiguous, but that the U-NII-2 Extended and U-NII-3 bands are separated by a range of frequencies that are unusable at the time of this writing but that might become available in the future.

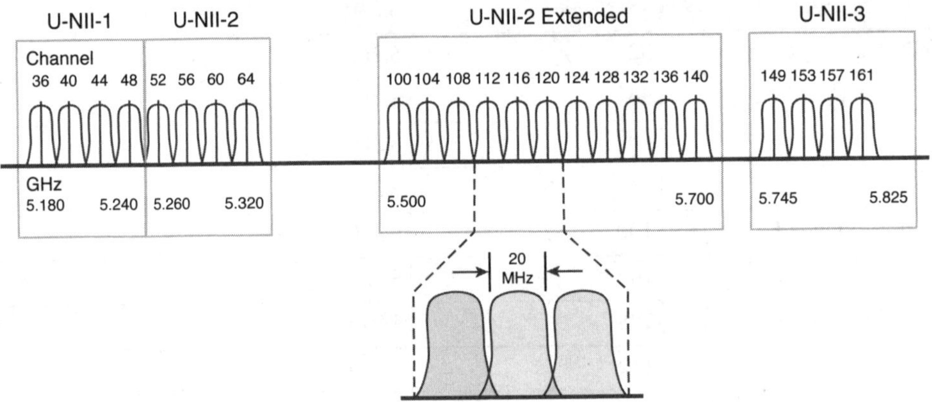

Figure 2-3 *Channel Layout in the 5-GHz U-NII Bands*

> **Tip** The U-NII-1, -2, and -3 bands each have four channels. Sometimes you may find 802.11 devices that support a fifth channel in the U-NII-3 band as channel 165.

The 802.11 standard allows only OFDM modulation and coding schemes to be used in the U-NII bands. OFDM requires a 20-MHz channel width, which fits perfectly with the 20-MHz spacing in the U-NII bands. In other words, neighboring channels can be used in the same area without overlap or interference.

With all four U-NII bands set aside for wireless LANs, a total of 23 non-overlapping channels are available. This is quite a contrast to the three non-overlapping channels in the 2.4-GHz band. Having 23 channels at your disposal gives you much more flexibility in a crowded environment. The additional channels can also be leveraged to scale wireless LAN performance, as explained in the 802.11n and 802.11ac sections later in this chapter.

IEEE 802.11 Standards

The 802.11 standard defines the mechanisms that devices can use to communicate wirelessly with each other. Through 802.11, RF signals, modulation, coding, bands, channels, and data rates all come together to provide a robust communication medium.

Since the original IEEE 802.11 standard was published in 1997, there have been many amendments added to it. The amendments cover almost every conceivable aspect of wireless LAN communication, including things like quality of service (QoS), security, RF measurements, wireless management, more efficient mobility, and ever-increasing throughput.

By now, most of the amendments have been rolled up into the overall 802.11 standard and no longer stand alone. Even so, the amendments may live on and be recognized in the industry by their original task group names. For example, the 802.11b amendment was approved in 1999, was rolled up into 802.11 in 2007, but is still recognized by its name today. When you shop for wireless LAN devices, you will often find the 802.11a, b, g, and n amendments listed in the specifications.

The following sections discuss the progression of 802.11 amendments that have allowed wireless LANs to steadily increase in performance over time. The original amendment names are used to distinguish each one. At the CCNA level, you should become familiar with these amendments. As you read through the remainder of this chapter, notice how the transmission types, modulation types, and data rates presented in Chapter 1 fit into the 802.11 standard.

802.11-1997

The original 802.11 standard was ratified in 1997. It included two main transmission types that were available at the time: FHSS and DSSS, for use only in the 2.4-GHz band. The theoretical data rates included 1 and 2 Mbps, as listed in Table 2-7.

Table 2-7 IEEE 802.11-1997 Data Rates

Band	Transmission Type	Modulation	Data Rate
2.4 GHz	FHSS	—	1, 2 Mbps
	DSSS	DBPSK	1 Mbps
		DQPSK	2 Mbps

802.11b

To increase throughput over the original 802.11-1997 standard, 802.11b was introduced in 1999. It offered data rates of 5.5 and 11 Mbps through the use of Complementary Code Keying (CCK). Because 802.11b was based on DSSS and was used in the 2.4-GHz band, it was backward compatible with the original standard. Devices could select either 1, 2, 5.5, or 11 Mbps by simply changing the modulation and coding schemes. Table 2-8 lists the new data rates introduced in 802.11b.

Table 2-8 IEEE 802.11b Data Rates

Band	Transmission Type	Modulation	Data Rate
2.4 GHz	DSSS	DQPSK with CCK	5.5 Mbps
			11 Mbps

802.11g

With 802.11b, the DSSS maximum data rate was limited to 11 Mbps. To increase data rates further, a different transmission type was needed. The 802.11g amendment was based on OFDM and was introduced in 2003. It is commonly called Extended Rate PHY (ERP) or ERP-OFDM. Whenever you see *ERP*, think of 802.11g in the 2.4-GHz band. Table 2-9 lists the data rates available with 802.11g.

Table 2-9 IEEE 802.11g Data Rates

Band	Transmission Type	Modulation	Data Rate
2.4 GHz	ERP-OFDM	BPSK 1/2	6 Mbps
		BPSK 3/4	9 Mbps
		QPSK 1/2	12 Mbps
		QPSK 3/4	18 Mbps
		16-QAM 1/2	24 Mbps
		16-QAM 3/4	36 Mbps
		64-QAM 2/3	48 Mbps
		64-QAM 3/4	54 Mbps

By selecting one of eight different modulation schemes, wireless devices can choose data rates of 6, 9, 12, 18, 24, 36, 48, or 54 Mbps. The higher data rates can be used when the signal strength and signal-to-noise ratio (SNR) are optimal.

Clearly, 802.11g offers far superior throughput than 802.11b. It might seem logical to simply use 802.11g and its higher data rates everywhere. Sometimes that is not possible because 802.11b-only devices are still being used on a wireless LAN. Notice that 802.11g and 802.11b use completely different transmission types—OFDM versus DSSS. This means that 802.11g and 802.11b devices cannot communicate directly because they cannot understand each other's RF signals.

Oddly enough, 802.11g was designed to be backward compatible with legacy 802.11b devices. Devices using 802.11g and OFDM are able to downgrade and understand 802.11b DSSS messages. However, the reverse is not true; 802.11b devices are limited to DSSS, so they are not able to understand any OFDM data. When two 802.11g devices are communicating with OFDM, 802.11b devices cannot understand any of the transmissions, so they might interrupt with transmissions of their own.

To allow both OFDM and DSSS devices to coexist on a wireless LAN, 802.11g offers a *protection mechanism*. The idea is to precede each 802.11g OFDM transmission with DSSS flags that 802.11b devices can understand. Figure 2-4 compares the basic sequence of events as data is transmitted in a native 802.11g OFDM network and when the 802.11g protection mechanism is enabled. When an 802.11g device is ready to transmit data in protection mode, it first sends a Request to Send (RTS) and a Clear to Send (CTS) message using

DSSS (and a low data rate) that informs all 802.11b devices that an OFDM transmission will follow. Any 802.11b devices that are listening must wait a predefined time until the transmission is complete because the OFDM transmission is unintelligible.

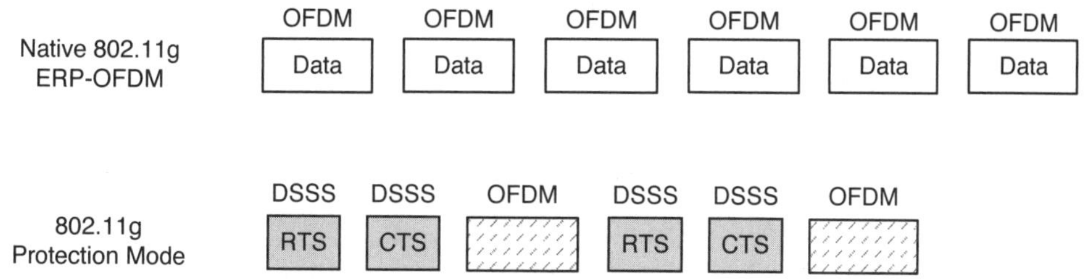

Figure 2-4 *Comparison of 802.11g Native and Protected Mode Transmissions*

Protection mode is enforced if an 802.11b device is detected on a wireless LAN. If the 802.11b device leaves the local network, protection mode is lifted. While the protection mechanism enables 802.11b and 802.11g devices to share the wireless medium, it also reduces throughput significantly—often by one half or more. To get the most performance out of an 802.11g network, you should make sure that there are no 802.11b-only devices in use.

Be aware that 802.11g has the following limitations:

- It is used in the 2.4-GHz band, which offers only three non-overlapping channels.
- OFDM devices are limited to a maximum transmit power of 15 dBm, rather than the 20 dBm limit for DSSS. This is due to the way the RF energy is spread across the channel width.

802.11a

Both 802.11b and 802.11g share one problem: They live in the 2.4-GHz ISM band. Having only three non-overlapping channels can limit wireless LAN growth in an area—assuming that all 802.11 devices stay within those three channels and do not cause unnecessary interference. Even worse, the ISM band is not limited to 802.11 devices. A wide variety of transmitters—even microwave ovens—can use the 2.4-GHz band without any regard for channels at all.

With too few channels and the potential for interference, the 802.11a amendment was introduced to utilize the 5-GHz U-NII bands for wireless LANs. Only one of the four U-NII bands is designated as ISM, so the chance for non-802.11 interference is very low. In addition, many more channels are available for use.

The 802.11a amendment restricts devices to use OFDM only. The end result is a set of modulation schemes and data rates that are identical to those used for 802.11g, but with less chance for interference and more room for growth. Table 2-10 lists the data rates available with 802.11a.

Table 2-10 IEEE 802.11a Data Rates

Band	Transmission Type	Modulation	Data Rate
5 GHz	OFDM	BPSK 1/2	6 Mbps
		BPSK 3/4	9 Mbps
		QPSK 1/2	12 Mbps
		QPSK 3/4	18 Mbps
		16-QAM 1/2	24 Mbps
		16-QAM 3/4	36 Mbps
		64-QAM 2/3	48 Mbps
		64-QAM 3/4	54 Mbps

802.11a was not designed to be backward compatible with anything else, so there is no need to support data rates below 6 Mbps or to support DSSS at all. Wireless devices can select one of the eight modulation schemes to support data rates of 6, 9, 12, 18, 24, 36, 48, or 54 Mbps.

802.11a is based on OFDM channels that are 20 MHz wide. Even though the U-NII bands have channels that are spaced 20 MHz apart (a perfect fit), signals on adjacent channels might still have a small amount of overlap. Therefore, 802.11a recommends that transmitters in the same geographic space stay separated by one channel. In other words, one transmitter might use channel 36, but another should use channel 44 rather than the adjacent channel 40.

Tip If the 802.11 amendment letters come in chronological order, how could the higher-performance 802.11a come before the lower-performance 802.11b? Actually, interference on the 2.4-GHz ISM band was so prevalent that a move to the 5-GHz bands was proposed right away. The 802.11a amendment was introduced in 1999—earlier in the same year as 802.11b. OFDM did come to the 2.4-GHz band, too, with 802.11g in 2003, mainly because migrating to 802.11a and 5 GHz required an investment in new hardware.

802.11n

Under the best conditions, both 802.11g and 802.11a are capable of offering a 54-Mbps data rate. Each amendment was introduced in the days when wired Ethernet devices used 10- or 100-Mbps connections. As the speed of Ethernet connections has progressed, 802.11 amendments have been introduced to keep in step.

The 802.11n amendment was published in 2009 in an effort to scale wireless LAN performance to a theoretical maximum of 600 Mbps. The amendment defines a number of techniques known as *high throughput* (HT) that can be applied to either the 2.4- or 5-GHz band. 802.11n was designed to be backward compatible with OFDM used in 802.11g and 802.11a.

Before 802.11n, wireless devices used a single transmitter and a single receiver. In other words, the components formed one radio, resulting in a single *radio chain*. This is also known as a single-in, single-out (SISO) system. The secret to 802.11n's better performance is its use of multiple radio components, forming multiple radio chains. For example, an 802.11n device can have multiple antennas, multiple transmitters, and multiple receivers at its disposal. This is known as a multiple-input, multiple-output (MIMO) system.

802.11n devices are characterized according to the number of radio chains available. This is described in the form T×R, where *T* is the number of transmitters and *R* is the number of receivers. A 2×2 MIMO device has two transmitters and two receivers, and a 2×3 device has two transmitters and three receivers. The 802.11n amendment requires at least two radio chains (2×2), up to a maximum of four (4×4). Figure 2-5 compares the traditional 1×1 SISO device with 2×2 and 2×3 MIMO devices.

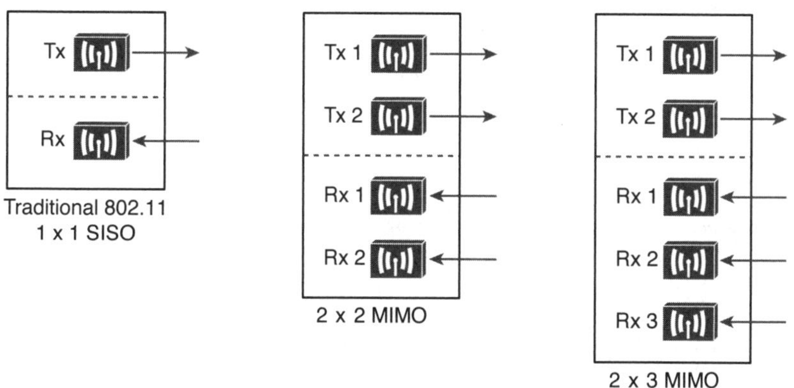

Figure 2-5 *Example SISO and MIMO Devices*

The multiple radio chains can be leveraged in a variety of ways. In fact, 802.11n has a rich set of features that can make many aspects of wireless communication more efficient. You should be familiar with the following features that improve throughput:

- Channel aggregation
- Spatial multiplexing (SM)
- MAC layer efficiency

You should also become familiar with the following features that improve the reliability of the 802.11n RF signals:

- Transmit beamforming (T×BF)
- Maximal-ratio combining (MRC)

Each of these features is described in the sections that follow.

Channel Aggregation

Normally, an 802.11a or 802.11g wireless LAN device has one transmitter and one receiver that operate on one 20-MHz channel only. The transmitter and receiver can be configured or tuned to operate on different channels in a band, but only one channel at a time. Each 20-MHz OFDM channel has 48 subcarriers to carry data in parallel.

The 802.11n amendment increased the 20-MHz channel throughput by increasing the number of data subcarriers to 52. In addition, it introduced radios that could operate on either a single 20-MHz channel or a single 40-MHz channel. By doubling the channel width to 40 MHz, the throughput is also doubled.

Aggregated channels must always bond two adjacent 20-MHz channels. Figure 2-6 shows a comparison between two 20-MHz channels and one 40-MHz channel, formed from channels 36 and 40 in the 5-GHz band. Notice that the 20-MHz channels have a quiet space below and above, providing some separation between channels. When two 20-MHz channels are aggregated or bonded, the quiet space below and above remain, separating 40-MHz channels from each other. However, the quiet space that used to sit between the two 20-MHz channels can be used for additional subcarriers in the 40-MHz channel, for a total of 108. As more subcarriers are utilized, more data can be carried over time.

Key Topic

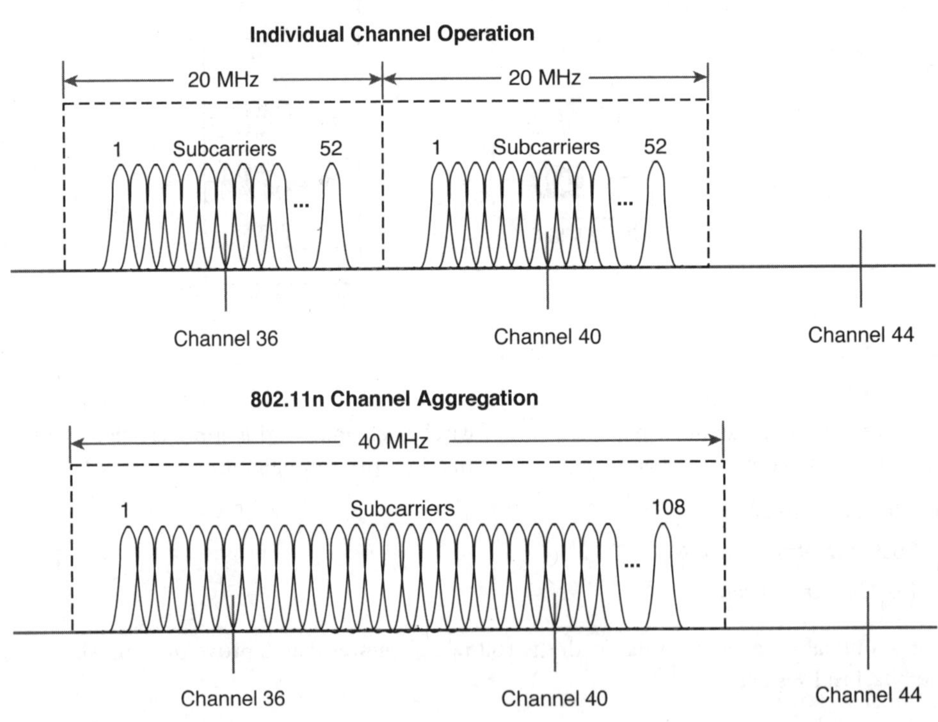

Figure 2-6 *Comparing 20-MHz Channels to an 802.11n 4-MHz Channel*

When channels are aggregated, the total number of available channels in a band decreases. For example, the 5-GHz band is made up of 23 non-overlapping 20-MHz channels. If aggregated 40-MHz channels are used instead, only 11 non-overlapping channels would be possible. That still gives plenty of channels to work with.

Now consider the 2.4-GHz band, which has only three non-overlapping channels. It just is not practical to try to aggregate any of them into 40-MHz channels. Therefore, channel aggregation is not recommended and not normally attempted on any 2.4-GHz channels.

Spatial Multiplexing

Channel aggregation can double the throughput by doubling the channel width—all with a single radio chain. An 802.11n device can have multiple radio chains waiting to be used. To increase data throughput even more, data can be multiplexed or distributed across two or more radio chains—all operating on the same channel, but separated through spatial diversity. This is known as *spatial multiplexing*.

How can several radios transmit on the same channel without interfering with each other? The key is to try to keep each signal isolated or easily distinguished from the others. Each radio chain has its own antenna; if each antenna is spaced some distance apart, the signals arriving at the receiver's antennas (also appropriately spaced) will likely be out of phase with each other or at different amplitudes. This is especially true if the signals bounce off some objects along the way, making each antenna's signal travel over a slightly different path to reach the receiver.

In addition, data can be distributed across the transmitter's radio chains in a known fashion. In fact, several independent streams of data can be processed as *spatial streams* that are multiplexed over the radio chains. The receiver must be able to interpret the arriving signals and rebuild the original data streams by reversing the transmitter's multiplexing function.

Spatial multiplexing requires a good deal of digital signal processing on both the transmitting and receiving end. This pays off by increasing the throughput over the channel—the more spatial streams that are available, the more data that can be sent over the channel.

The number of spatial streams that a device can support is usually designated by adding a colon and a number to the MIMO radio specification. For example, a 3×3:2 MIMO device would have three transmitters, three receivers, and would support two unique spatial streams. Figure 2-7 shows spatial multiplexing between two 3×3:2 MIMO devices. A 3×3:3 device would be similar, but would support three spatial streams.

Tip Notice that a MIMO device can support a different number of unique spatial streams than it has transmitters or receivers. It might seem logical that each spatial stream is assigned to a transmitter/receiver, but that is not true. Spatial streams are processed so that they are distributed across multiple radio chains. The number of possible spatial streams depends on the processing capacity and the transmitter feature set of the 802.11n device—not on the number of its radios.

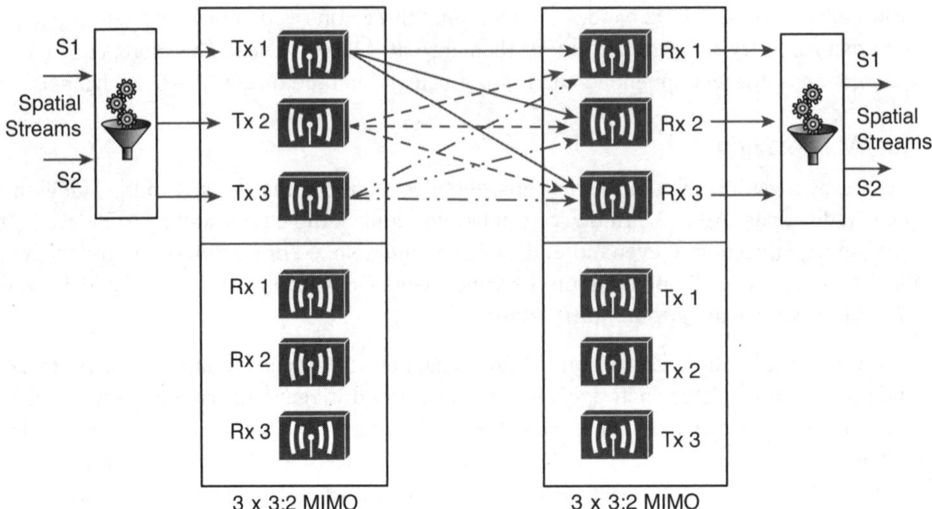

Figure 2-7 *Spatial Multiplexing Between Two 3×3:2 MIMO Devices*

802.11n devices come with a variety of MIMO capabilities. Ideally, two devices should support an identical number of spatial streams to multiplex and demultiplex the data streams correctly. That is not always possible or even likely because more spatial streams usually translates to a greater cost. What happens when two devices have mismatched spatial stream support? They negotiate the wireless connection by informing each other of their capabilities. Then they can use the lowest number of spatial streams that they have in common, but a transmitting device can leverage an additional spatial stream to repeat some information for increased redundancy.

MAC Layer Efficiency

Even without multiple radio chains, 802.11n offers some important methods to make data communication more efficient. Two of the methods are as follows:

- **Block acknowledgment**—Normally, 802.11 requires that each frame of data transmitted must be acknowledged by the recipient. If a frame goes unacknowledged, the transmitter can assume that the frame was lost and needs to be resent. The overhead of having acknowledgment messages interleaved with every transmitted frame is inefficient; it uses up airtime on the shared media.

  With 802.11n, data frames can be transmitted in one burst. Only one acknowledgment is expected from the recipient after the burst is complete. More airtime can be spent sending data, increasing the overall throughput.

- **Guard interval**—As OFDM symbols are transmitted, they can take different paths to reach the receiver. If two symbols somehow arrive too close together, they can interfere with each other and corrupt the received data. This is known as *intersymbol interference* (ISI). The 802.11 standard requires a *guard interval* (GI), a period of 800 nanoseconds, between each OFDM symbol that is transmitted to protect against ISI.

  As an option, you can configure 802.11n devices to use a much shorter 400-nanosecond guard interval. This allows OFDM symbols to be transmitted more often, increasing throughput by about 10 percent, at the expense of making data corruption more likely.

Transmit Beamforming

When a transmitter with a single radio chain sends an RF signal, any receivers that are present have an equal opportunity to receive and interpret the signal. In other words, the transmitter does nothing to prefer one receiver over another; each is at the mercy of its environment and surrounding conditions to receive at a decent SNR.

The 802.11n amendment offers a method to customize the transmitted signal to prefer one receiver over others. By leveraging MIMO, the same signal can be transmitted over multiple antennas to reach specific client locations more efficiently.

Usually multiple signals travel over slightly different paths to reach a receiver, so they can arrive delayed and out of phase with each other. This is normally destructive, resulting in a lower SNR and a corrupted signal. With *transmit beamforming* (T×BF), the phase of the signal is altered as it is fed into each transmitting antenna so that the resulting signals will all arrive in phase at a specific receiver. This has a constructive effect, improving the signal quality and SNR.

Figure 2-8 shows an 802.11n device using transmit beamforming to target device B. The phase of each copy of the transmitted signal is adjusted so that all three signals arrive at device B more or less in phase with each other. The same three signal copies also arrive at device A, which is not targeted by T×BF. As a result, the signals arrive as is and are out of phase.

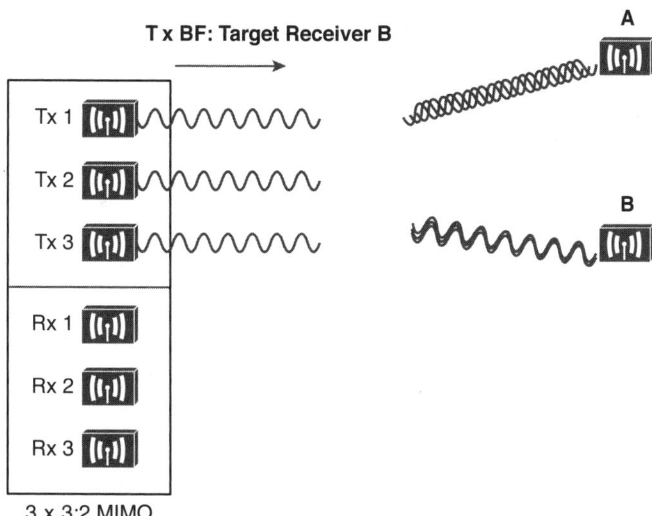

Figure 2-8 *Using Transmit Beamforming to Target a Specific Receiving Device*

The location and RF conditions can be unique for each receiver in an area. Therefore, transmit beamforming can use explicit feedback from an 802.11n device at the far end, enabling the transmitter to make the appropriate adjustments to the transmitted signal phase. As T×BF information is collected about each far end device, a transmitter can keep a table of the devices and phase adjustments so that it can send focused transmissions to each one dynamically. Although the feedback process sounds straightforward, it is complex to implement. The 802.11n amendment allowed four different feedback mechanisms to be used. To date, no practical feedback mechanism has been implemented due to compatibility issues among vendors and mechanisms.

Cisco also offers ClientLink, which performs a similar transmit beamforming function; however, ClientLink does not require explicit feedback from an 802.11n device at all. Based on data that is received from a far end device, the phase values can be calculated and performed on data transmissions that are returned to it. In this case, the far end device can be 802.11n or legacy 802.11a/g.

Maximal-Ratio Combining

When an RF signal is received on a device, it may look very little like the original transmitted signal. The signal may be degraded or distorted due to a variety of conditions. If that same signal can be transmitted over multiple antennas, as in the case of a MIMO device, then 802.11n can attempt to restore it to its original state.

An 802.11n device can use multiple antennas and radio chains to receive the multiple transmitted copies of the signal. One copy might be better than the others, or one copy might be better for a time, and then become worse than the others. In any event, 802.11n offers *maximal-ratio combining* (MRC), a feature that can combine the copies to produce one signal that represents the best version at any given time. The end result is a reconstructed signal with an improved SNR and receiver sensitivity.

802.11n Modulation and Coding Schemes

Recall that 802.11g and 802.11a are both based on OFDM and can use binary phase shift keying (BPSK), quadrature phase shift keying (QPSK), 16-QAM (quadrature amplitude modulation), and 64-QAM modulation schemes. Depending on conditions affecting the RF signal, wireless devices can choose one of the eight possible modulation and coding schemes. The 802.11n amendment is somewhat backward compatible with 802.11a and 802.11g, as it supports the same eight schemes. However, as the schemes are applied to an increasing number of spatial streams, the number of combinations multiplies.

802.11n supports a total of 32 possible schemes (8 per spatial stream)—so many that they are known by a modulation and coding scheme (MCS) index number. Beyond that, channel aggregation and guard interval selection add even more variables to the mix. In all, 802.11n has 128 possible data rates. For your reference, Appendix B, "Modulation and Coding Schemes," lists all of the MCS and data rates.

802.11ac

The many features and high throughput of 802.11n might make it seem like the end-all wireless LAN technology. As with most any aspect of computing, the current state of the art is never good enough. The 802.11ac amendment, finalized in 2013, takes the best of

802.11n and offers a new generation that is much faster and more scalable. The goal is to bring wireless on a par with Gigabit Ethernet through a set of capabilities known as *very high throughput* (VHT). Once 802.11ac is fully implemented, it should support a maximum data rate of 6.93 Gbps! Some of the most notable improvements are outlined in the list that follows and further described in the ensuing sections. As you read through the improvements, you might notice that they sound familiar from the list of 802.11n features, but are greatly enhanced.

- **Better channel aggregation**—40-MHz bonded channels can be bonded again into channels that are 80 or 160 MHz wide. Because of the extensive use of channels, 802.11ac can be used only in the 5-GHz band.
- **More dense modulation**—256-QAM is used to modulate the RF signal in 256 different ways, taking more data at one time and boosting throughput.
- **MAC layer efficiency**—More data can be aggregated with less overhead.
- **Explicit T×BF**—To simplify and scale transmit beamforming, only a single feedback method is supported.
- **Scalable MIMO**—Up to eight spatial streams can be used.
- **Multi-user MIMO (MU-MIMO)**—An 802.11ac access point (AP) can send multiple frames to multiple receiving devices simultaneously.

Robust Channel Aggregation

The 5-GHz band is made up of many channels, each one 20 MHz wide, as illustrated in Figure 2-9, where 802.11a must always use 20-MHz channels. One improvement with 802.11n is that two channels can be aggregated, forming a single 40-MHz channel, to increase throughput. The 802.11ac amendment supports an even better channel aggregation scheme, where the channel width can be 20, 40, 80, or 160 MHz. As always, to support efficient roaming and to minimize neighboring channel interference, the channels should not overlap. With 23 available channels, the number of non-overlapping aggregated channels decreases as the channel width increases. For example, there are only eleven 40-MHz channels, five 80-MHz channels, and two 160-MHz channels available.

To maximize channel use, 802.11ac offers something really clever—the channel width can vary dynamically, on a frame-by-frame basis. This means that wide channels can overlap within the band, but cannot be used at the same time. Every transmission does not normally require a wide channel, so the channel space can be negotiated for each frame. If a wide channel is needed and is currently available, it can be used. If some fraction of it is already in use, then the remainder can be claimed for a transmission.

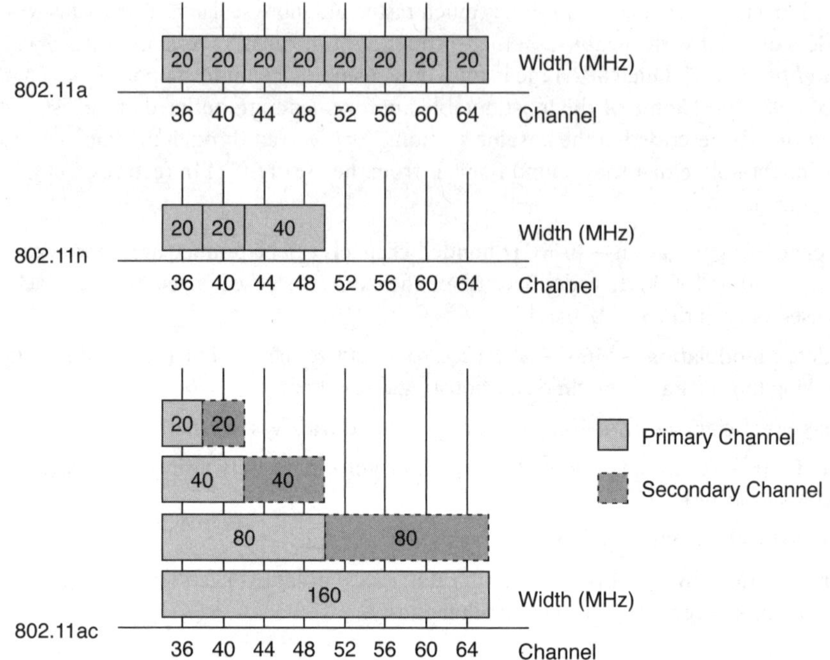

Figure 2-9 *Channel Width Comparison Between 802.11a, 802.11n, and 802.11ac*

Suppose two APs are located in the same general area so that their cells overlap. Ideally, the two APs should operate on separate non-overlapping channels to minimize co-channel and neighboring channel interference. As the channel layout in Figure 2-10 shows, the two APs can use their assigned 20- and 40-MHz channels at any time without interfering with each other. However, notice that their 80- and 160-MHz channels do overlap completely. Either AP can claim the wider channel and transmit as long as the other AP (or some other device) is not currently transmitting there.

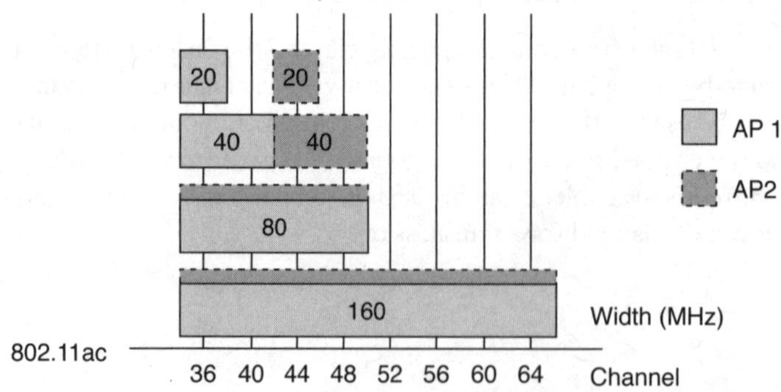

Figure 2-10 *Channel Aggregation and Dynamic Use with 802.11ac*

Contention for a wide channel is handled through the use of the Request-to-Send (RTS) and Clear-to-Send (CTS) frames. If one AP is ready to transmit on an aggregated channel, it first sends an RTS frame on its primary 20-MHz channel and duplicates the RTS frame on all other 20-MHz channels that are components of the wider channel. By doing so, the AP is requesting use of the full channel width for one frame. The intended receiver checks to see if the full channel is free, then replies with CTS frames on each free 20-MHz component channel. The AP can then gauge which parts of the wide channel are free and transmit there.

Dense Modulation

Devices using 802.11ac can take advantage of 256-QAM modulation for higher data throughput. The difference between 256-QAM and 64-QAM (the best 802.11n offering) is about 25 percent higher data rates. However, you cannot simply expect to use 256-QAM in all circumstances, because it also requires a higher SNR, which usually means the client must be located closer to the AP.

The 802.11ac amendment also simplifies the list of modulation and coding scheme (MCS) choices that can be used between an AP and a client. There are 10 possible MCS values, listed in Table 2-11, as opposed to 32 or more choices with 802.11n. Notice that the 802.11ac MCS choices are tied only to the actual modulation and coding schemes used—not to the number of spatial streams or the channel width, as 802.11n uses. All of those parameters still work together to produce a long list of possible maximum data rates, but 802.11ac tends to loosen the restrictions so that each parameter can be selected independently.

Table 2-11 IEEE 802.11ac Modulation and Coding Schemes

MCS Index	Modulation and Coding Scheme
0	BPSK 1/2
1	QPSK 1/2
2	QPSK 3/4
3	16-QAM 1/2
4	16-QAM 3/4
5	64-QAM 2/3
6	64-QAM 3/4
7	64-QAM 5/6
8	256-QAM 3/4
9	256-QAM 5/6

You can find complete MCS and data rate information for both 802.11ac and 802.11n in Appendix B.

MAC Layer Efficiency

To improve the efficiency of frame transmission, 802.11n introduced frame aggregation. In a nutshell, more data can be sent in a single wireless frame, avoiding the 802.11 header overhead that would be required for each smaller frame. To build an aggregated frame, the sender places multiple payloads (known as MAC Service Data Units, or MSDUs) inside one

802.11 frame (a PLCP Service Data Unit, or PSDU, with one header and one trailer) that will be transmitted over the air.

Regardless of the wireless protocol being used, each individual frame (MSDU) inside the aggregated frame is limited to 2304 bytes. How large can the aggregated frame be? In traditional wired networks, the transmitted frame would be limited to the MTU size. With wireless networks, devices contend for air time so the frame size is bounded by a time limit of about 5.5 milliseconds. At 802.11n data speeds, 64 KB can be transmitted in 5.5 ms; at the maximum 802.11ac speed, about 4.5 MB can be sent as a single frame!

Rather than marking each frame as individual or aggregated, 802.11ac expects every frame to be an aggregate. Each MSDU within an 802.11ac frame contains a familiar MAC header and MAC addresses.

Like 802.11n, 802.11ac supports two guard intervals—400 and 800 nanoseconds.

Explicit Transmit Beamforming

Transmit beamforming is an attempt to "focus" or direct a transmission toward a specific client by adjusting the phase of several spatial streams. With 802.11n, transmit beamforming can be either explicit, requiring feedback from the client, or passive, where the AP infers information about the client from received signals. The explicit method must be negotiated between the AP and the client, but no standardized or common methods have been developed—especially ones that are compatible across multiple vendors.

The 802.11ac amendment specifies only one transmit beamforming method, called *Null Data Packet* (NDP). The AP first transmits an NDP Announcement frame to identify itself and any 802.11ac clients that might be present within range. Any interested clients respond, while all other clients simply ignore the announcement. The AP then sends an NDP frame as a way to "sound" a channel. When the clients receive the NDP, they compute a matrix of information about the channel conditions and how the NDP was received and return that matrix to the AP. From that point on, the AP can make beamforming adjustments that are customized for each 802.11ac client each time it transmits a frame.

Scalable MIMO

The 802.11n amendment introduced multiple spatial streams that can be used to multiplex data across several different paths from the transmitter to the receiver. Each path requires a separate radio chain and antenna, as well as physical conditions that create multipath signal propagation. 802.11n supports up to four spatial streams on a device. The 802.11ac amendment takes this concept even further—up to eight spatial streams can be used.

Such a large number of spatial streams brings some challenges though. Each radio chain requires physical space for circuitry and an antenna, as well as additional power. Mobile devices might not easily be able to support many radio chains due to their small size and limited battery power.

Multi-user MIMO

Recall that 802.11n supports MIMO using multiple spatial streams simultaneously—all dedicated to data transfer between an AP and one wireless user. 802.11ac can take that concept even further by sending data in the downstream direction, from an AP across multiple spatial streams to *multiple* users simultaneously. Naturally, the multipath conditions must be conducive for the spatial streams to reach the intended clients, wherever they are located at the time. Explicit transmit beamforming comes in very handy for this purpose, as it enables the AP to tailor transmissions to each specific client. MU-MIMO is not possible from a wireless client toward other devices in the upstream direction.

MU-MIMO also brings a heavy signal processing burden on the transmitter in order to multiplex the wireless frames across the spatial streams.

802.11ac Implementation

After reading through the list of 802.11ac improvements and enhancements, you might think some or all of them would be difficult to implement. In fact, 802.11ac was designed to be a bit too progressive for the wireless technology at the time. Rather than waiting on hardware technologies to catch up before the amendment was ratified, 802.11ac has been broken up into two waves or phases. Wave 1 includes almost every feature, with performance limits that are reasonable for current hardware. Wave 2 begins in 2016, giving hardware developers time to produce more advanced products that will extend the Wave 1 features further. Table 2-12 lists the features and capabilities offered in each of the two waves, as tested by the Wi-Fi Alliance.

Table 2-12 Features and Capabilities Tested in IEEE 802.11ac Waves

Feature	Wave 1	Wave 2
Maximum channel width	80 MHz	160 MHz
Maximum spatial streams	3	4
Maximum modulation	256-QAM (optional)	256-QAM
MU-MIMO	No	Yes
Maximum typical data speed tested	1.3 Gbps	2.6 Gbps

Tip As discussed earlier in this chapter, 802.11ac was expected to support up to eight spatial streams and a maximum data speed of 6.93 Gbps. Why does Table 2-12 list Wave 2 with four spatial streams and a maximum data speed of 2.6 Gbps? Wave 2 is not necessarily the finish line for 802.11ac development; it is the second milestone. Past that, there should be further development to bring about four more spatial streams, which should bring the data speed up to 6.93 Gbps accordingly.

802.11 in Other Frequency Bands

Throughout this book, you will find references to the two main frequency bands, 2.4 and 5 GHz, but few others. That is because the bulk of the 802.11 standard and its amendments have been focused on using those common public bands—not because 802.11 cannot be used elsewhere in the frequency spectrum.

You should be aware of several amendments that apply 802.11 to other bands too, including the following:

- **802.11ad**—A multi-gigabit technology that allows devices to operate in the unlicensed 60-GHz band. At that frequency, signals tend to propagate less through physical objects. The end result is increased data rates but reduced range, making 802.11ad more suitable for very high speed wireless links within a room.
- **802.11af**—Allows unlicensed 802.11 operation in the spectrum known historically as the Television White Space (TVWS), between 54 and 790 MHz. Many of 802.11ac's features are leveraged, such as OFDM, 10 MCS choices, channel aggregation, multiple spatial streams, and MU-MIMO. The lower frequencies used tend to penetrate physical objects better, improving the effective range.
- **802.11ah**—Allows devices to communicate on frequencies below 1 GHz. The emphasis is on a greater range (1 km), lower power consumption, and connectivity to a large number of devices dispersed over the coverage area.

Wi-Fi Alliance

All wireless LAN products must adhere to the IEEE 802.11 set of standards to be compatible with each other. Even though the 802.11 standards are very thorough and lengthy, it is still possible for one manufacturer to build a product based on one interpretation of a standard feature, while another manufacturer works with a different interpretation. This is especially true when products are developed while an 802.11 amendment is still in draft form. In addition, manufacturers are not obligated to implement every function described in a standard; they may pick and choose certain parts or implement the entire standard, and may even add in some proprietary features.

The Wi-Fi Alliance (http://wi-fi.org) is a nonprofit industry association made up of wireless manufacturers around the world, all devoted to promoting wireless use. To address the problem of incompatible wireless products, the Wi-Fi Alliance introduced the Wi-Fi CERTIFIED program in 2000. Wireless products are tested in authorized testing labs against stringent criteria that represent correct implementation of a standard. If a product passes the tests, then it is certified and receives a Wi-Fi CERTIFIED stamp of approval, using the logo shown in Figure 2-11.

Figure 2-11 *Wi-Fi Alliance Certification Logo*

The Wi-Fi Alliance has many certification programs that are based around common sets of features—not just specific 802.11 amendments. The end result is an effort to make Wi-Fi better by assuring a better user experience. The following list describes some example programs:

- **Wi-Fi Certified n**—Products using 802.11n correctly implement features like multiple spatial streams, channel aggregation, block acknowledgement, and dual-band operation.
- **Wi-Fi Certified ac**—Products using 802.11ac correctly implement all of its features, including each of the two 802.11ac waves.
- **Wi-Fi Direct**—Products can interoperate without the use of an AP for printing, display, and content sharing.
- **WPA2**—Products correctly implement premium personal and enterprise wireless security features.
- **Protected Management Frames**—Extends premium security to protect Wi-Fi management frames between an AP and wireless devices.
- **Wi-Fi Protected Setup (WPS)**—Products offer an easy-to-use initial configuration of wireless security features.
- **Wi-Fi Multimedia (WMM)**—Wi-Fi products interoperate to prioritize and handle various types of traffic with quality-of-service (QoS) mechanisms.
- **Voice-Personal**—Tests the performance of Wi-Fi devices to make sure they can deliver good voice quality wirelessly.
- **Voice-Enterprise**—Tests the ability of Wi-Fi devices to deliver good voice quality, efficient roaming, and robust management while voice-capable devices are mobile.

Tip Remember that the IEEE develops and maintains the 802.11 set of standards. The Wi-Fi Alliance tests and certifies product interoperability and the feature set functionality according to the IEEE standards and its own technical specifications.

Exam Preparation Tasks

As mentioned in the section, "How to Use This Book," in the Introduction, you have a couple of choices for exam preparation: the exercises here, Chapter 21, "Final Review," and the exam simulation questions on the DVD.

Review All Key Topics

Review the most important topics in this chapter, noted with the Key Topic icon in the outer margin of the page. Table 2-13 lists a reference of these key topics and the page numbers on which each is found.

Table 2-13 Key Topics for Chapter 2

Key Topic Element	Description	Page Number
List	ISM band allocation	42
List	U-NII band allocation	42
List, Table 2-2	2.4-GHz and 5-GHz EIRP rules	44
Figure 2-2	Channel layout in the 2.4-GHz band	48
Table 2-7	802.11-1997 data rates	51
Table 2-8	802.11b data rates	51
Table 2-9	802.11g data rates	52
Table 2-10	802.11a data rates	54
Figure 2-6	802.11n channel aggregation	56
Paragraph	802.11n spatial stream notation	57
List	802.11ac features	61
Table 2-11	802.11ac modulation and coding schemes	63
Table 2-12	802.11ac waves	65

802.11 Protocol Summary

Table 2-14 lists each of the 802.11 protocols by their amendment nomenclature. You can use this table to review and compare the basic specifications of each. As you review, keep in mind that the maximum data rate is most impacted by a combination of the channel width, the number of spatial streams, and the modulation density.

Table 2-14 802.11 Protocol Summary

	Band (GHz)	Channel Width (MHz)	Modulation	Spatial Streams	Max Data Rate
802.11b	2.4	22	DBPSK or DQPSK	1	11 Mbps
802.11g	2.4	20	BPSK, QPSK, 16-QAM, 64-QAM	1	54 Mbps
802.11a	5	20	BPSK, QPSK, 16-QAM, 64-QAM	1	54 Mbps
802.11n	2.4 5	20 or 40	BPSK, QPSK, 16-QAM, 64-QAM	1–4	600 Mbps
802.11ac	5	20, 40, 80, 160	BPSK, QPSK, 16-QAM, 64-QAM, 256-QAM	1–8	6.933 Gbps

Define Key Terms

Define the following key terms from this chapter and check your answers in the glossary:

block acknowledgment, channel aggregations, guard interval (GI), high throughput (HT), intersymbol interference (ISI), maximal-ratio combining (MRC), Null Data Packet (NDP), protection mechanism, spatial multiplexing, spatial stream, transmit beamforming (T×BF)

This chapter covers the following topics:

- **Interference**—This section describes several types of external interference that can adversely affect a wireless signal.
- **Free Space Path Loss**—This section explains why a radio frequency signal degrades as it travels through free space.
- **Effects of Physical Objects**—This section explores what happens when an RF signal meets various physical objects, resulting in effects such as reflection, absorption, refraction, and diffraction.

This chapter covers the following exam topics:

- 1.1—Describe the propagation of radio waves
  - 1.1b—Absorption, reflection, diffraction, scattering, refraction, fading, free space path loss, multipath
- 1.2—Interpret RF signal measurements
  - 1.2b—Differentiate interference vs. noise

CHAPTER 3

RF Signals in the Real World

Radio frequency (RF) signals travel through the air as electromagnetic waves. In an ideal setting, a signal would arrive at the receiver exactly as the transmitter sent it. In the real world, this is not always the case. Many things affect RF signals as they travel from a transmitter to a receiver. This chapter explores many of the conditions that can affect wireless signal propagation.

"Do I Know This Already?" Quiz

The "Do I Know This Already?" quiz allows you to assess whether you should read this entire chapter thoroughly or jump to the "Exam Preparation Tasks" section. If you are in doubt about your answers to these questions or your own assessment of your knowledge of the topics, read the entire chapter. Table 3-1 lists the major headings in this chapter and their corresponding "Do I Know This Already?" quiz questions. You can find the answers in Appendix A, "Answers to the 'Do I Know This Already?' Quizzes."

Table 3-1 "Do I Know This Already?" Section-to-Question Mapping

Foundation Topics Section	Questions
Interference	1–4
Free Space Path Loss	5–7
Effects of Physical Objects	8–10

Caution The goal of self-assessment is to gauge your mastery of the topics in this chapter. If you do not know the answer to a question or are only partially sure of the answer, you should mark that question as wrong for purposes of the self-assessment. Giving yourself credit for an answer you correctly guess skews your self-assessment results and might provide you with a false sense of security.

1. An 802.11 transmitter is configured to send a signal on channel 11. Someone reports a problem receiving the signal, so you investigate and find a second transmitter broadcasting on channel 11. Which one of the following best describes the problem?
   a. Path interference
   b. Adjacent channel interference
   c. Co-channel interference
   d. Cross-channel interference
2. Suppose that you place a new 802.11n transmitter in a building, but notice that there are other signals already coming from transmitters in the same general area. To avoid interference problems, how much greater should your transmitter's signal be above all of the others to provide the best signal?
   a. 0 dB
   b. +3 dB
   c. +5 dB
   d. +10 dB
   e. +20 dB
3. An existing transmitter in your office sends its signal on 2.4-GHz channel 1. Suppose that someone in a neighboring office sets up a new wireless router. He notices your signal on channel 1, so he chooses channel 2 instead. Which one of the following might adversely affect the wireless operation?
   a. Co-channel interference
   b. Neighboring channel interference
   c. Wideband interference
   d. Excessive SNR
4. Which one of the following is the best strategy for avoiding interference between neighboring channels in the 2.4-GHz band?
   a. Use any channel number that seems to be available
   b. Leverage 802.11n for 40-MHz aggregated channels
   c. Use only channels that are spaced four numbers apart, beginning with channel 1
   d. Use only channels that are spaced five numbers apart, beginning with channel 1
5. Which one of the following is the primary cause of free space path loss?
   a. Spreading
   b. Absorption
   c. Humidity levels
   d. Magnetic field decay

6. Which one of the following has the shortest effective range in free space, assuming that the same transmit power level is used for each?
   a. An 802.11g device
   b. An 802.11a device
   c. An 802.11b device
   d. None of these answers
7. Suppose that an 802.11a device moves away from a transmitter. As the signal strength decreases, which one of the following might the device or the transmitter do to improve the signal quality along the way?
   a. Aggregate more channels
   b. Use more radio chains
   c. Switch to a more complex modulation scheme
   d. Switch to a less-complex modulation scheme
8. When RF signals are reflected by objects in a building, which one of the following best describes the result that might be experienced at a receiver?
   a. Fresnel loss
   b. Multipath
   c. Cross-channel fading
   d. Free space path loss
9. Which one of the following best describes the effect that a building material has as an RF signal passes through a wall?
   a. Reflection
   b. Refraction
   c. Diffraction
   d. Absorption
   e. Multipath
10. Which one of the following best describes the first Fresnel zone?
   a. The area covered by one transmitter on a channel
   b. The area around a signal path that should be kept clear of any obstructions
   c. The area around a signal path that is blocked by the earth's curvature
   d. The area around a transmitter that represents the range of a signal

Foundation Topics

Interference

The idea behind WLAN modulation is to pack as much data as possible into the wireless signal, and to minimize the amount of data that might be lost due to interference or noise. When data is lost, it must be retransmitted, using more of the wireless resources. Therefore, it is always best if a transmitter is configured to use a channel that is open and is clear from any other transmitter.

Co-Channel Interference

Whenever one transmitter's signal overlaps another on a frequency or channel, the signals interfere with each other. Interference can be described by the way the signals overlap. For example, *co-channel interference* occurs when two or more transmitters use the same channel. In Figure 3-1, Transmitters A and B are both transmitting an RF signal on channel 6 in the 2.4-GHz band.

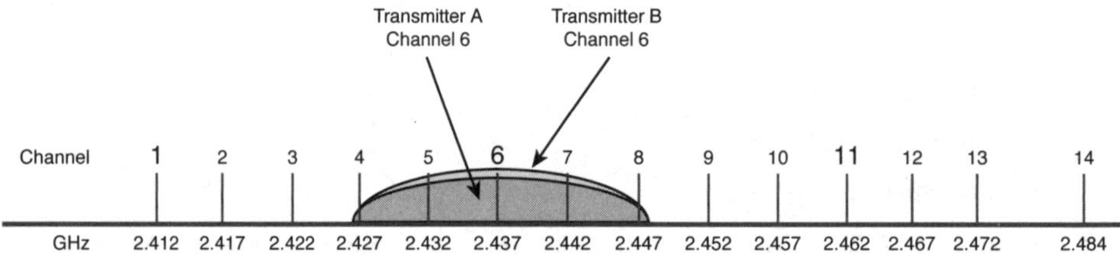

Figure 3-1 *Co-Channel Interference*

Because the two 802.11 transmitters are using the same channel, their signals completely overlap and the whole 22-MHz channel bandwidth is affected. This might not be a problem if the transmitters are not sending data at the same time. After all, wireless LAN devices must contend for use of the airtime; if nobody is transmitting at a given time, someone may use the channel.

When both transmitters are busy sending data, the channel can become very congested. The two signals begin to interfere and cause data corruption, which causes devices to retransmit lost data, which uses more airtime, and so on.

In the real world, co-channel interference is often a necessary evil. The 2.4-GHz band offers only three non-overlapping channels. If you have many transmitters in a building or area, you are bound to have some of them transmitting on the same channel as others. The best solution is to use careful planning when you select the channel for each transmitter. For instance, two nearby transmitters should never be placed on the same channel because their strong signals would be more likely to interfere.

Instead, a transmitter should only share a channel with other distant transmitters whose received signals are much weaker. A best practice is to place a transmitter on a channel only if its signal will be stronger than any other received signal by some margin. A common margin is at least 19 dB, as shown in Figure 3-2.

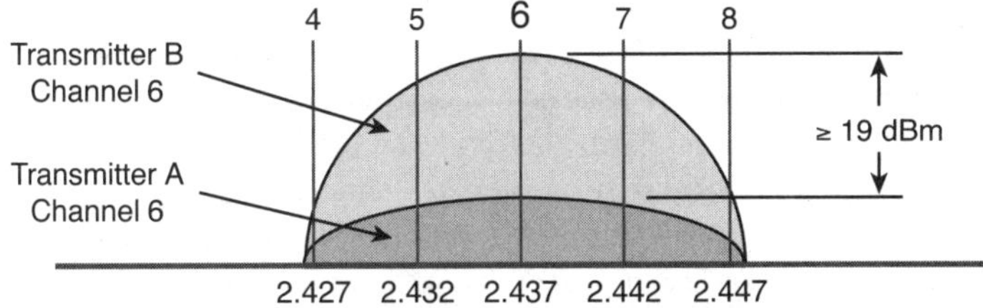

Figure 3-2 *Maintaining Signal Separation to Minimize Co-Channel Interference*

Having at least 19-dB separation helps maintain a healthy signal-to-noise ratio (SNR) in the area surrounding the transmitter. Be aware that this margin differs according to the modulation and coding scheme that is in use. For example, simple BPSK modulation may need less than 10 dB, while 19 dB may be enough to support 64-QAM modulation (54 Mbps) for 802.11g or 802.11a. The 256-QAM modulation used in 802.11ac requires much more—anywhere from 31 to 50 dB!

Note Channel assignment is covered in more detail in Chapter 7, "Planning Coverage with Wireless APs."

Neighboring Channel Interference

Suppose that two transmitters are placed on two different channels. However, the channels are spaced too closely together such that they overlap each other. Perhaps someone decided to use neighboring channels, rather than reuse the same channel, to avoid co-channel interference. More likely, two different people have transmitters located in the same general area and decided to use slightly different channel numbers—not realizing that neighboring channels in the 2.4-GHz band overlap.

The end result is *interference on both channels* because a portion of one signal overlaps a portion of another signal. In Figure 3-3, transmitter A is using channel 6, while transmitter B is using channel 7. The two signals do not completely overlap, but the interference between them is enough to be detrimental to both.

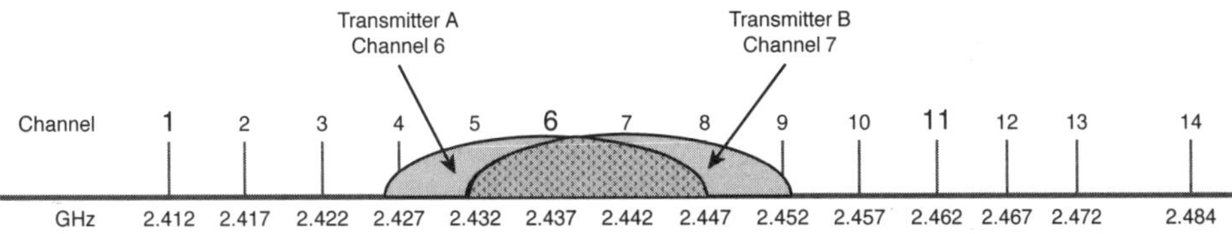

Figure 3-3 *Adjacent Channel Interference*

Tip Do you think of neighboring channels as having adjacent channel numbers? You are not alone; after all, channel numbers 1 and 2 are adjacent. Interference between neighboring channels is commonly called *adjacent channel interference*. Technically, this term is incorrect and is often misused. The 802.11 standard defines adjacent channels as non-overlapping channels. Therefore, by definition, it is impossible for adjacent channels to overlap and interfere. Be aware that the CCNA Wireless exam strictly uses the terminology found in the 802.11 standard. *Adjacent* channels cannot overlap, but *neighboring* channels can.

To remedy the situation, all transmitters in an area should be configured to use the three non-overlapping 2.4-GHz channels: 1, 6, and 11. In the 5-GHz band, adjacent channel interference is not a problem because the channels do not significantly overlap; the channels are 20 MHz wide, whereas the orthogonal frequency-division multiplexing (OFDM) signals have a bandwidth of 20 MHz. As a best practice, you should still avoid placing neighboring access points on neighboring 5-GHz channels, just to avoid the possibility of raising the noise floor.

Non-802.11 Interference

Recall that the 2.4-GHz band is an ISM band. This means that your 802.11 wireless LAN devices might share the same frequency space as non-802.11 devices. That might not sound like a bad situation because the devices could simply be configured to use different, non-overlapping channels.

In practice, such an elegant solution might not be possible. Many non-802.11 devices do not sit on any one channel; they use frequency-hopping spread spectrum (FHSS) to hop around on a variety of channels at any given time. Even worse, some devices do not adhere to any channel scheme at all. Figure 3-4 shows transmitters A, B, and C using channels 1, 6, and 11, which is a perfect world—until someone decides to warm up her lunch. A nearby microwave oven also uses RF energy in the 2.4-GHz ISM band to radiate the food. Because it is poorly shielded, the RF energy escapes and interferes with most of the 802.11b/g channels nearby. The microwave's transmission is also constant, rendering the wireless LAN channels mostly useless.

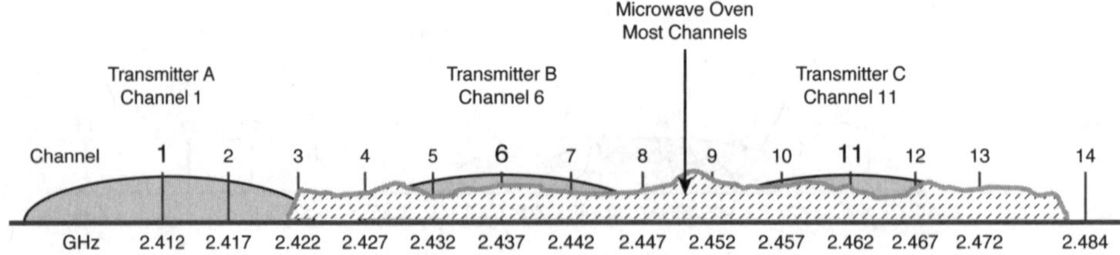

Figure 3-4 *Non-802.11 Interference from a Microwave Oven*

To mitigate interference from non-802.11 devices, you have to eliminate the source. Leaky microwave ovens should be replaced with better models that have proper RF shielding. Devices like 2.4-GHz FHSS cordless phones or wireless video cameras should be replaced with models that operate in a non-802.11 band.

Note Noise and interference are topics that are covered in more detail in Chapter 19, "Dealing with Wireless Interference."

Free Space Path Loss

Whenever an RF signal is transmitted from an antenna, its amplitude decreases as it travels through free space. Even if there are no obstacles in the path between the transmitter and receiver, the signal strength will weaken. This is known as *free space path loss*.

What is it about free space that causes an RF signal to be degraded? Is it the air or maybe the earth's magnetic field? No, even signals sent to and from spacecraft in the vacuum of outer space are degraded.

Recall that an RF signal propagates through free space as a wave, not as a ray or straight line. The wave has a three-dimensional curved shape that expands as it travels. It is this expansion or spreading that causes the signal strength to weaken.

Figure 3-5 shows a cutaway view of the free space loss principle. Suppose the antenna is a tiny point, such that the transmitted RF energy travels in every direction. The wave that is produced would take the form of a sphere; as the wave travels outward, the sphere increases in size. Therefore, the same amount of energy coming out of the tiny point is soon spread over an ever expanding sphere in free space. The concentration of that energy gets weaker as the distance from the antenna increases.

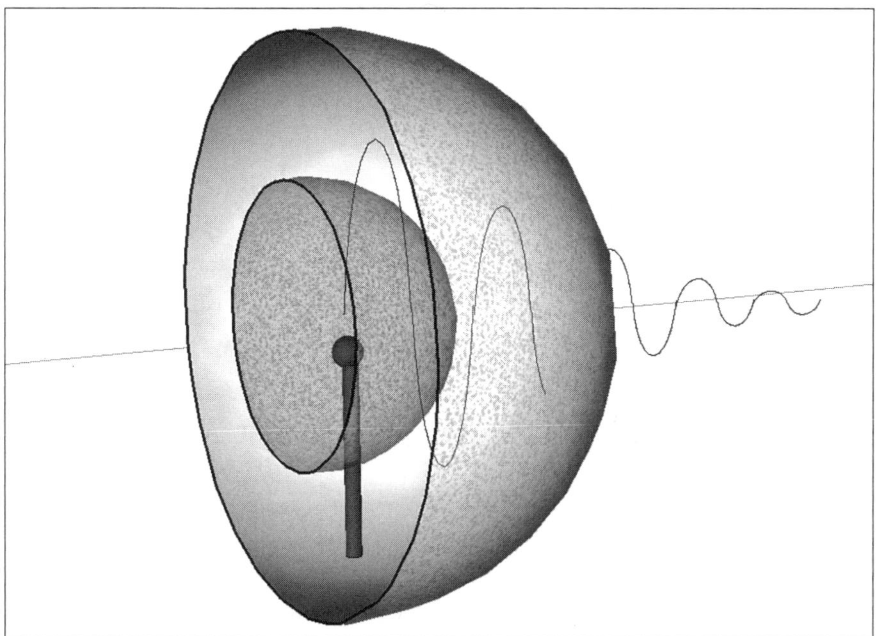

Figure 3-5 *Free Space Loss Due to Wave Spreading*

Even if you could devise an antenna that could focus the transmitted energy into a tight beam, the energy would still travel as a wave and would spread out over a distance. Regardless of the antenna used, the amount of signal strength loss is consistent.

The free space path loss (FSPL) in dB can be calculated according to the following equation:

$$FSPL\ (dB) = 20\log_{10}(d) + 20\log_{10}(f) + 32.44$$

where *d* is the distance from the transmitter in kilometers and *f* is the frequency in megahertz. Do not worry, though: you will not have to know this equation for the CCNA Wireless exam. It is presented here to show two interesting facts:

- Free space path loss is an exponential function; the signal strength falls off quickly near the transmitter, but more slowly farther away.
- The loss is a function of distance and frequency only.

With the formula, you can calculate the free space path loss for any given scenario, but you will not have to for the exam. Just be aware that the free space path loss is always an important component of the link budget, along with antenna gain and cable loss.

You should also be aware that the free space path loss is greater in the 5-GHz band than it is in the 2.4-GHz band. In the equation, as the frequency increases, so does the loss in dB. This means that 802.11b/g/n devices (2.4 GHz) have a greater effective range than 802.11a/n (5 GHz) devices, assuming an equal transmitted signal strength. Figure 3-6 shows the range difference, where both transmitters have an effective isotropic radiated power (EIRP) of 14 dBm and the effective range ends where a receiver's received signal strength indicator (RSSI) equals –67 dBm.

Key Topic

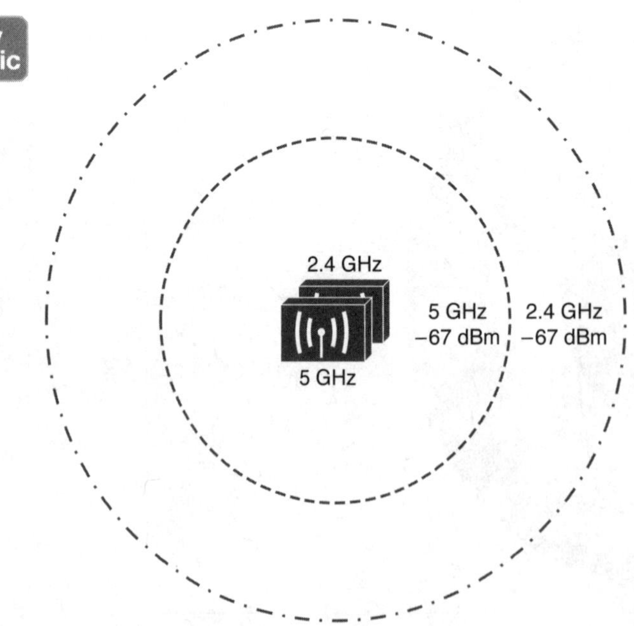

Figure 3-6 *Effective Range of 2.4-GHz and 5-GHz Transmitters*

Tip To get a feel for the actual range difference between 2.4 and 5 GHz, a receiver was carried away from the two transmitters until the RSSI reached –67 dBm. On a 2.4-GHz channel, the range was measured to be 140 feet, whereas at 5 GHz it was reduced to 80 feet. While the free space path loss is the largest contributor to the difference, other factors like antenna size and receiver sensitivity that differ between the 2.4 and 5 GHz radios have some effect, too.

Mitigating the Effects of Free Space Path Loss

One simple solution to overcome free space path loss is to increase the transmitter's output power. Increasing the antenna gain can also boost the EIRP. Having a greater signal strength before the free space path loss occurs translates to a greater RSSI value at a distant receiver after the loss. This approach might work fine for an isolated transmitter, but can cause interference problems when several transmitters are located in an area.

A more robust solution is to just cope with the effects of free space path loss. Wireless devices are usually mobile and can move closer to or farther away from a transmitter at will. As a receiver gets closer to a transmitter, the RSSI increases. This, in turn, translates to an increased SNR. Recall from Chapter 1, "RF Signals and Modulation," that more complex modulation and coding schemes can be used to transport more data when the SNR is high. As a receiver gets farther away from a transmitter, the RSSI (and SNR) decreases. More basic modulation and coding schemes are needed there because of the increase in noise and the need to repeat more data.

802.11 devices have a clever way to adjust their modulation and coding schemes based on the current RSSI and SNR conditions. If the conditions are favorable for good signal quality and higher data rates, a complex modulation and coding scheme is used. As the conditions deteriorate, less-complex schemes can be selected, resulting in a greater range but lower data rates. The scheme selection is commonly known as *dynamic rate shifting* (DRS). As its name implies, it can be performed dynamically with no manual intervention.

Tip Although DRS is inherently used in 802.11 devices, it is not defined in the 802.11 standard. Each manufacturer can have its own approach to DRS; so all devices don't necessarily select the same scheme at the same location. DRS is also known by many alternative names, such as *link adaptation*, *adaptive modulation and coding* (AMC), *rate adaptation*, and so on.

Figure 3-7 illustrates DRS operation on the 2.4-GHz band. Each concentric circle represents the range supported by a particular modulation and coding scheme. The figure is somewhat simplistic because it assumes a consistent power level across all modulation types. Notice that the white circles denote OFDM modulation (802.11g) and that the shaded circles contain DSSS modulation (802.11b). None of the 802.11n modulation types are shown, for simplicity. The data rates are arranged in order of increasing circle size or range from the transmitter.

Key Topic

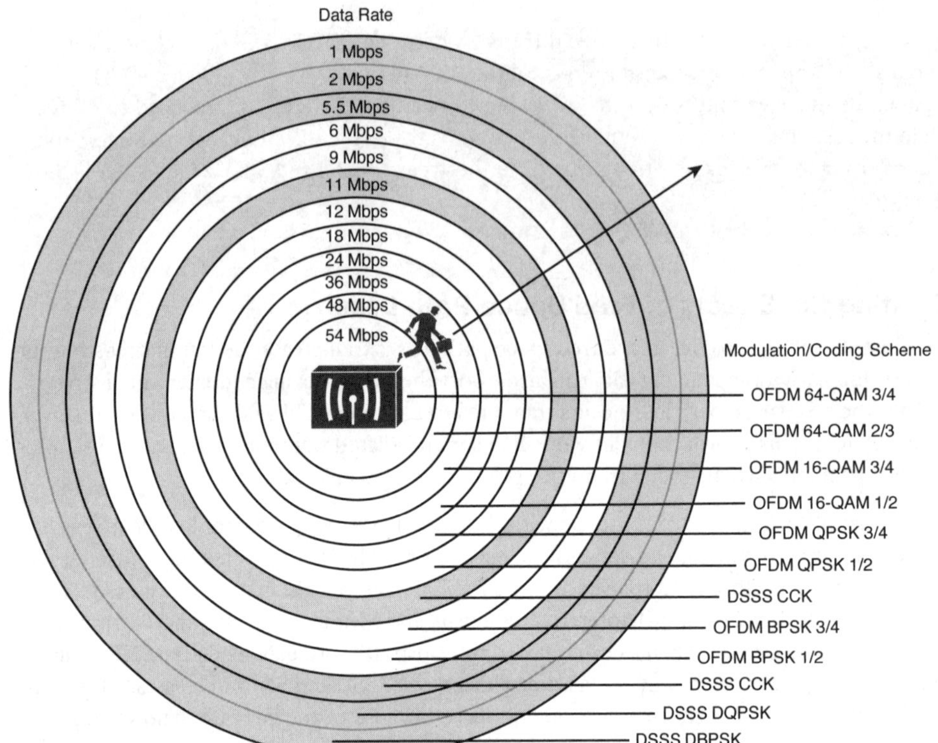

Figure 3-7 *Dynamic Rate Shifting as a Function of Range*

Suppose that a mobile user starts out near the transmitter, within the innermost circle, where the received signal is strong and SNR is high. Most likely, wireless transmissions will use the OFDM 64-QAM 3/4 modulation and coding scheme to achieve a data rate of 54 Mbps. As the user walks away from the transmitter, the RSSI and SNR fall by some amount. The new RF conditions will likely trigger a shift to a different modulation and coding scheme, resulting in a lower data rate.

In a nutshell, each move into a larger concentric circle causes a dynamic shift to a reduced data rate, in an effort to maintain the data integrity to the outer reaches of the transmitter's range.

The 5-GHz band looks very similar to Figure 3-7, except that every circle uses an OFDM modulation scheme corresponding to 802.11a, 802.11n, or 802.11ac.

Effects of Physical Objects

As an RF signal propagates through free space, it might encounter physical objects in its path. Objects and materials can affect an RF signal in a variety of ways, mostly in a degrading or destructive fashion. The following sections cover the most common scenarios.

Reflection

If an RF signal traveling as a wave meets a dense reflective material, the signal can be reflected. Think of the light emitted from a light bulb; while most of the light is traveling in all directions away from the bulb, some might be reflected from objects in a room. The reflected light might travel back toward the bulb or toward another area of the room, making that area even brighter.

Figure 3-8 depicts a reflected RF signal. Indoor objects such as metal furniture, filing cabinets, and metal doors can cause reflection. An outdoor wireless signal can be reflected by objects such as a body of water, reflective glass on a building, or the surface of the earth.

Key Topic

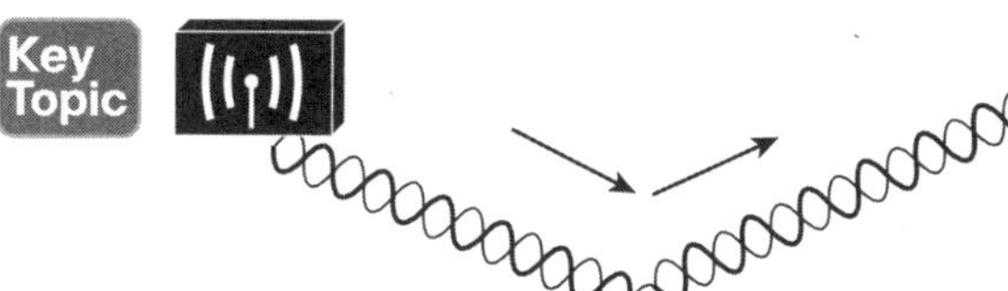

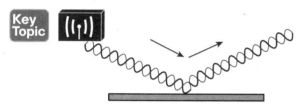

Figure 3-8 *Reflection of an RF Signal*

A reflection is not necessarily bad, because it is just a copy of the original signal. However, if both the copy and the original reach a receiver, they can arrive out of phase with each other. This is because the reflection takes a different path than the original, causing it to arrive slightly later. This is known as *multipath*. When the receiver combines the two signals, the result is a poor representation of the original signal. The combined signal can be weak and distorted, causing the data to be corrupted.

In Figure 3-9, the original signal, along with two different reflections, arrive at the receiver embedded in a laptop computer. The two reflections each take a different path and arrive at different times.

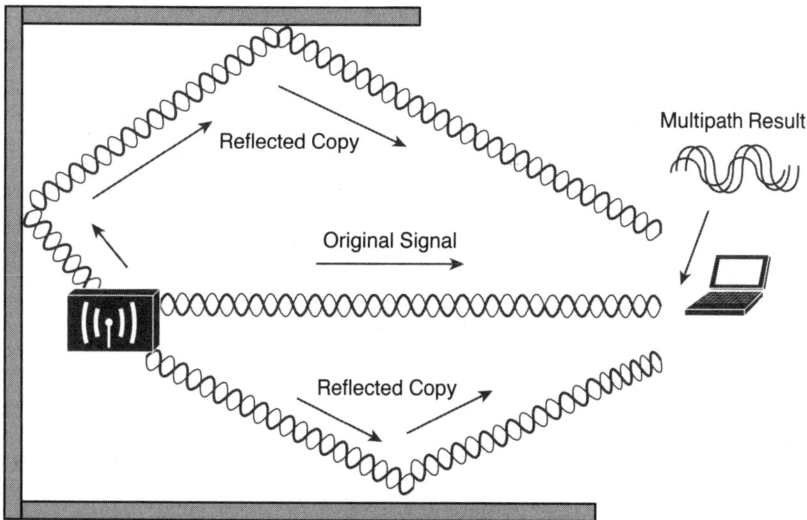

Figure 3-9 *Multipath Transmissions*

When multipath transmissions occur, there can be two outcomes:

- If the receiver has a single radio chain, then all of the arriving signals (original and reflected) are combined into one poor, error prone composite signal.
- If the receiver has multiple radio chains and supports multiple-input, multiple-output (MIMO), each arriving signal will be received on each of the different antennas and radios. Further processing can improve the signal quality to extract the multiple data streams—making something good out of a bad situation.

Absorption

If an RF signal passes into a material that can absorb some of its energy, the signal will be attenuated. The more dense the material, the more the signal will be attenuated. Figure 3-10 shows how a signal is affected by absorption and how a receiver might be affected by the lower signal strength.

Key Topic

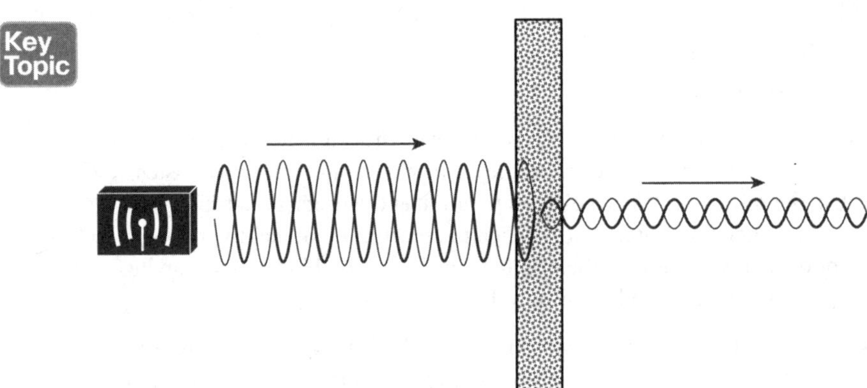

Figure 3-10 *Absorption of an RF Signal*

One common example of absorption is when a wireless signal passes through a wall in a building. Different wall materials absorb different amounts of energy. For example, a wall constructed from gypsum or drywall might attenuate a signal by –4 dBm. A solid concrete wall might attenuate it by –12 dBm. The thicker the wall or the more dense the material, the greater the attenuation will be.

In outdoor wireless scenarios, RF signals frequently have to travel through water. The water might be contained in tree leaves positioned along the wireless path. Even in unobstructed space, the signal might encounter water in the form of rain, snow, hail, or fog. As the air is filled with heavier rain or snow, the signal will be attenuated more. Because weather conditions change over time, an RF signal will be attenuated accordingly—a strong signal on a clear day can fade or become weaker on rainy days.

Another less-obvious example of absorption is the human body, which is made up mostly of water. A person will usually hold a laptop computer, tablet PC, or a smartphone close to his or her body. Depending on how the person is oriented with respect to the transmitter, his body could sit between the transmitter and the receiver, attenuating the signal. For example, a hand covering a phone antenna can decrease a received signal by 6–8 dB; a person's head might attenuate the signal received by a phone antenna by almost 30 dB. Likewise, a classroom or auditorium might be filled with human bodies, each with the potential to attenuate the signal from a transmitter.

> **Tip** To gain perspective, a quick experiment revealed that a human body attenuated a 2.4-GHz signal by –5 dBm.

Scattering

When an RF signal passes into a medium that is rough, uneven, or made up of very small particles, the signal can be scattered into many different directions. This is because the tiny irregular surfaces of the medium can reflect the signal, as shown in Figure 3-11. Scattering can occur when a wireless signal passes through a dusty or sandy environment.

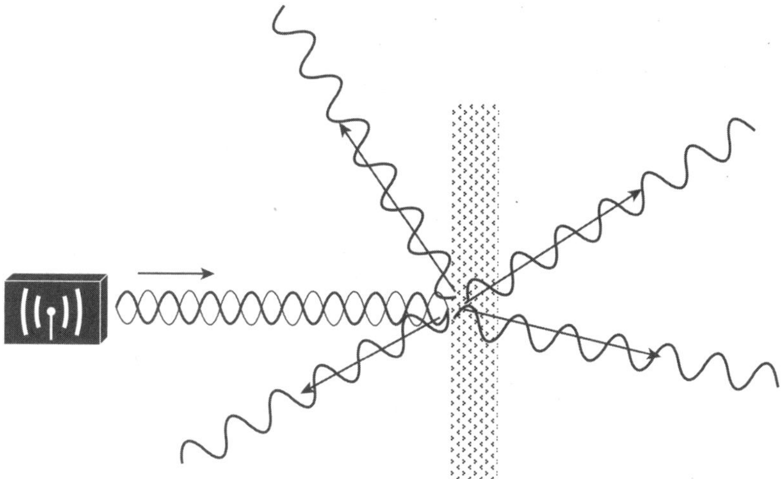

Figure 3-11 *Scattering an RF Signal*

Refraction

When an RF signal meets the boundary between media of two different densities, it can also be refracted. Think of reflection as bouncing off a surface and refraction as being bent while passing through a surface.

A refracted signal will have a different angle from the original, as illustrated in Figure 3-12. The speed of the wave can also be affected as it passes through the different materials. A signal can be refracted when it passes through layers of air having different densities or through building walls with different densities, for example.

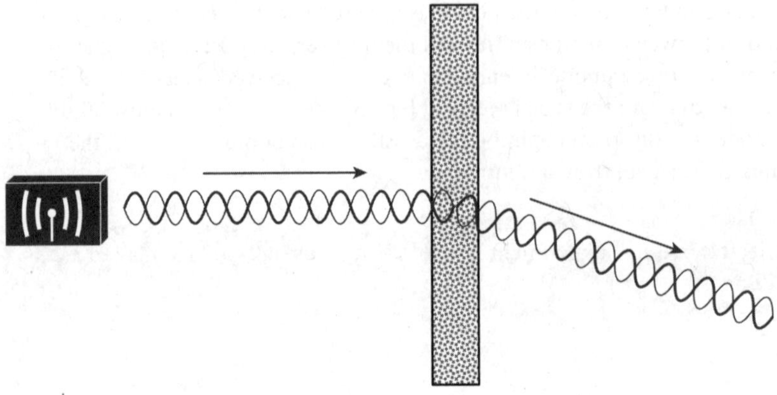

Figure 3-12 *Refraction of an RF Signal*

Diffraction

Suppose an RF signal approaches an opaque object, or one that is able to absorb the energy that strikes it. You might think that the object would produce a shadow in place of the signal that is absorbed, much like an object might make a shadow as light shines on it. If a shadow formed, it might make a dead or silent zone in the RF signal behind the object.

With RF propagation, however, the signal tends to bend around the object and eventually rejoin to complete the wave. Figure 3-13 shows how a radio-opaque object can cause diffraction of an RF signal. Diffraction is best viewed as concentric waves, rather than an oscillating signal, so that its effect on the actual waves can be seen. In the figure, diffraction has caused the signal to "heal" itself around an absorbing object. This makes reception possible even when a building stands between the transmitter and receiver. However, the signal is never quite like the original again, as it has been distorted by the diffraction.

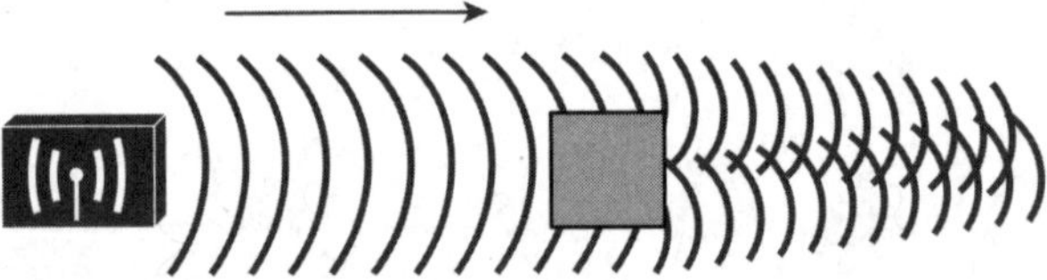

Figure 3-13 *Diffraction of an RF Signal*

Fresnel Zones

If an object is standing free, so that an RF signal traveling parallel with the ground is diffracted around it on both sides, the signal will often fill in the object's "shadow" as it continues to propagate. However, if a standing object such as a building or a mountain obstructs the signal, the signal can be adversely affected in the vertical direction.

In Figure 3-14, a building partially obstructs the path of the signal. Because of diffraction along the front and top of the building, the signal is bent and also attenuated. This causes the signal to be masked behind most of the height of the building.

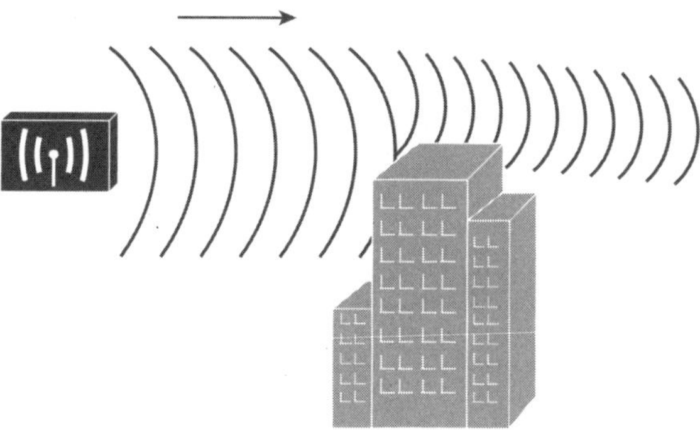

Figure 3-14 *Standing Obstacle Diffracts a Signal*

This is especially important in narrow line-of-sight wireless transmission, which is suited for very long distances. These signals do not propagate in all directions; rather, they are focused into a tight cone-shaped pattern, as shown in Figure 3-15. For a line-of-sight path, the signal must be clear of any obstructions between the transmitter's antenna and the receiver's antenna. Paths between buildings or between cities commonly have other buildings, trees, or other objects that might block the signal. In those cases, the antennas must be raised higher than the obstructions to get a clear path.

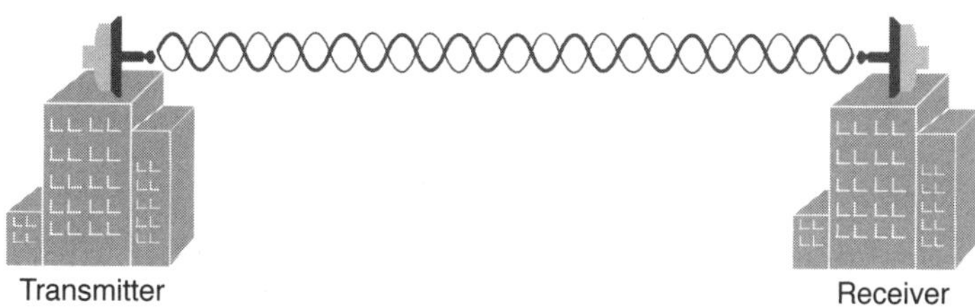

Figure 3-15 *Line-of-Sight Wireless Signal*

Over a very long distance, the curvature of the earth actually becomes an obstacle that can affect the signal. At ground level, beyond a distance of about two miles, the far end cannot be seen because it lies slightly below the horizon. Nevertheless, a wireless signal tends to propagate along the same curve, following the atmosphere around the earth's curvature.

Even narrow line-of-sight signals can be affected by diffraction, even if an object does not directly block the signal. There is an elliptical-shaped volume around the line of sight that must also remain free of obstructions. This is called the *Fresnel zone*, as shown in Figure 3-16. If an object penetrates the Fresnel zone anywhere along the path, some portion of the RF signal can be diffracted by it. That portion of the signal gets bent, causing it to be delayed or altered so that it affects the overall signal arriving at the receiver.

Tip Actually, there are many concentric Fresnel zones surrounding the line-of-sight path. Only the innermost, or first, Fresnel zone is described in this section and taken into account because it affects the transmitted signal the most. Fresnel zones are numbered incrementally as their size increases. Oddly enough, the odd-numbered Fresnel zones have a destructive effect on signals, whereas the even-numbered zones can have a constructive effect and add to the signal's power.

Key Topic

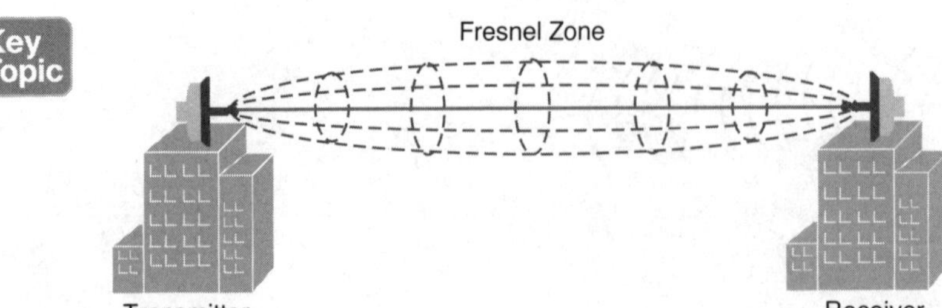

Figure 3-16 *Fresnel Zone*

In Figure 3-17, a building lies along the signal's path, but does not obstruct the beam of the signal; however, it does penetrate the Fresnel zone, so the received signal will be negatively affected.

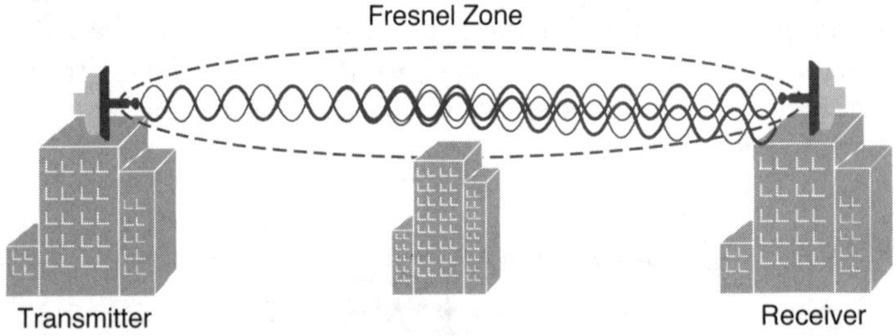

Figure 3-17 *Signal Degradation Due to a Fresnel Zone Obstruction*

As a rule, you should raise the antennas of a line-of-sight system so that even the bottom of the Fresnel zone is higher than any obstruction. Remember that as the path gets very long, even the curvature of the earth can enter the Fresnel zone and cause problems, as Figure 3-18 shows.

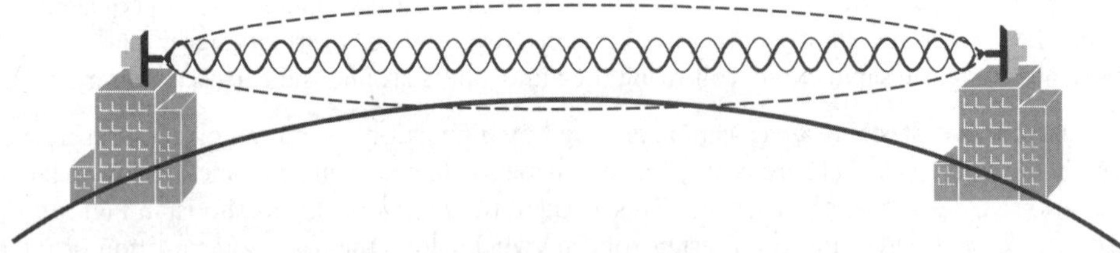

Figure 3-18 *Earth's Curvature Enters the Fresnel Zone*

The radius of the Fresnel zone can be calculated according to a complex formula. However, you should only be concerned with the idea that the Fresnel zone exists and should remain clear. Table 3-2 gives some example values of the Fresnel zone radius at the midpoint of some line-of-sight path lengths for wireless frequencies in the 2.4-GHz band.

Table 3-2 Fresnel Zone Radius Values

Path Length	Fresnel Zone Radius at Path Midpoint
0.5 mile	16 feet
1.0 mile	23 feet
2.0 miles	33 feet
5.0 miles	52 feet
10.0 miles	72 feet

Exam Preparation Tasks

As mentioned in the section, "How to Use This Book," in the Introduction, you have a couple of choices for exam preparation: the exercises here, Chapter 21, "Final Review," and the exam simulation questions on the DVD.

Review All Key Topics

Review the most important topics in this chapter, noted with the Key Topic icon in the outer margin of the page. Table 3-3 lists a reference of these key topics and the page numbers on which each is found.

Table 3-3 Key Topics for Chapter 3

Key Topic Element	Description	Page Number
Figure 3-2	Co-channel interference	75
Figure 3-6	Free space path loss affecting signal range	78
Figure 3-7	Changing modulation and coding schemes with DRS	80
Figure 3-8	Reflection	81
Figure 3-10	Absorption	82
Figure 3-16	Fresnel zone	86

Define Key Terms

Define the following key terms from this chapter and check your answers in the glossary:

absorption, adjacent channel interference, co-channel interference, diffraction, dynamic rate shifting, free space path loss, Fresnel zone, multipath, reflection, refraction, scattering

This chapter covers the following topics:

- **Antenna Characteristics**—This section describes the radiation pattern, gain, beamwidth, and polarization of an antenna.
- **Antenna Types**—This section covers the two basic types of antennas and their applications.
- **Adding Antenna Accessories**—This section explains several devices that can be added to an antenna to increase or reduce signal strength and to protect connected equipment from lightning damage.

This chapter covers the following exam topics:

- 1.4—Describe Wi-Fi antenna characteristics
  - 1.4a—Ability to read a radiation pattern chart
  - 1.4b—Antenna types and uses
  - 1.4c—dBi, dBd, EIRP

CHAPTER 4

Understanding Antennas

Chapters 1 through 3 covered radio frequency (RF) signals, as used by 802.11 devices, and their propagation from the perspective of a transmitter and a receiver. By considering the link budget, or the net signal strength gain between a transmitter and receiver, you can make sure that a signal will arrive in good condition at its destination. The antenna gain is an important piece of the equation, but it does not completely describe an antenna's construction or performance. This chapter explains some basic antenna theory, in addition to various types of antennas and their application.

"Do I Know This Already?" Quiz

The "Do I Know This Already?" quiz allows you to assess whether you should read this entire chapter thoroughly or jump to the "Exam Preparation Tasks" section. If you are in doubt about your answers to these questions or your own assessment of your knowledge of the topics, read the entire chapter. Table 4-1 lists the major headings in this chapter and their corresponding "Do I Know This Already?" quiz questions. You can find the answers in Appendix A, "Answers to the 'Do I Know This Already?' Quizzes."

Table 4-1 "Do I Know This Already?" Section-to-Question Mapping

Foundation Topics Section	Questions
Antenna Characteristics	1–5
Antenna Types	6–9
Adding Antenna Accessories	10

Caution The goal of self-assessment is to gauge your mastery of the topics in this chapter. If you do not know the answer to a question or are only partially sure of the answer, you should mark that question as wrong for purposes of the self-assessment. Giving yourself credit for an answer you correctly guess skews your self-assessment results and might provide you with a false sense of security.

1. Which two of the following plots are used to show the radiation pattern of an antenna?
   a. A plane
   b. E plane
   c. XY plane
   d. H plane
   e. YZ-plane
2. Which one of the following is another name for the H plane radiation pattern?
   a. Horizon plane
   b. Azimuth plane
   c. Heat map
   d. Lateral plane
3. Which one of the following answers correctly identifies the antenna parameter that is measured at 3 dB below the strongest point on a radiation pattern plot?
   a. Half life
   b. Decay point
   c. Cut off point
   d. Beamwidth
   e. Sensitivity
4. The orientation of an electromagnetic wave is best described by which one of the following?
   a. Phase
   b. Amplitude
   c. Modulation
   d. Polarization
   e. Azimuth
5. A Cisco dipole antenna is mounted so that it points straight upward and has a radiation pattern that extends in all directions horizontally. Which one of the following best describes the antenna's likely polarization?
   a. Horizontal polarization
   b. Vertical polarization
   c. Dual polarization
   d. Elliptical polarization

6. Which one of the following antennas would probably have the greatest gain?
   a. Patch
   b. Dish
   c. Yagi
   d. Dipole
   e. Integrated
7. An omnidirectional antenna usually has which of the following characteristics? (Choose two.)
   a. Low gain
   b. Small beamwidth
   c. High gain
   d. Zero gain
   e. Large beamwidth
8. A standard indoor Cisco wireless access point is mounted on the ceiling and has antennas that are hidden inside the case. Which one of the following describes the antennas?
   a. Patch antennas
   b. Monopole antennas
   c. Omnidirectional antennas
   d. Isotropic antennas
9. A dipole antenna is connected to a transmitter. You would like to leverage the directional quality of the antenna. Based on the radiation pattern of the antenna, what would happen if you orient the antenna such that its cylindrical shape points directly at a distant receiver?
   a. The receiver would pick up a stronger signal.
   b. The receiver would pick up a weaker signal.
   c. The antenna is omnidirectional, so the orientation would not matter.
   d. This is pointless unless the receiver's dipole is also aimed directly at the transmitter.
10. Which one of the following is not true about a lightning arrestor?
   a. It is connected inline between a transmitter and an antenna.
   b. It protects against large transient spikes of energy.
   c. It protects against lightning strikes on an antenna.
   d. It directs energy to the ground, rather than the transmitter equipment.
   e. Every outdoor antenna needs one.

Foundation Topics

Antenna Characteristics

The world of wireless LANs would be rather simple if all antennas were created equal—too simple, in fact. To provide good wireless LAN coverage in a building, an outdoor area, or between two locations, you might be faced with a number of variables. For example, an office space might be arranged as a group of open cubicles or as a strip of closed offices down a long hallway. You might have to cover a large open lobby, a large open classroom, a section of a crowded sports arena, an oblong portion of a hospital roof where helicopters land, a large expanse of an outdoor park, city streets where public safety vehicles travel, and so on.

In other words, one type of antenna cannot fit every application. Instead, antennas come in many sizes and shapes, each with its own gain value and intended purpose. The following sections describe antenna characteristics in more detail.

Radiation Patterns

Recall from Chapter 1, "RF Signals and Modulation," that antenna gain is normally a comparison of one antenna against an isotropic antenna, and is measured in dBi (decibel-isotropic). An isotropic antenna does not actually exist because it is ideal, perfect, and impossible to construct. It is also the simplest, most basic antenna possible, which makes it a good starting place for antenna theory.

An isotropic antenna is shaped like a tiny round point. When an alternating current is applied, an RF signal is produced and the electromagnetic waves are radiated equally in all directions. The energy produced by the antenna takes the form of an ever-expanding sphere. If you were to move all around an isotropic antenna at a fixed distance, you would find that the signal strength is the same.

To describe the antenna's performance, you might draw a sphere with a diameter that is proportional to the signal strength, as shown in Figure 4-1. Most likely, you would draw the sphere on a logarithmic scale so that very large and very small numbers could be shown on the same linear plot. A plot that shows the relative signal strength around an antenna is known as the *radiation pattern*.

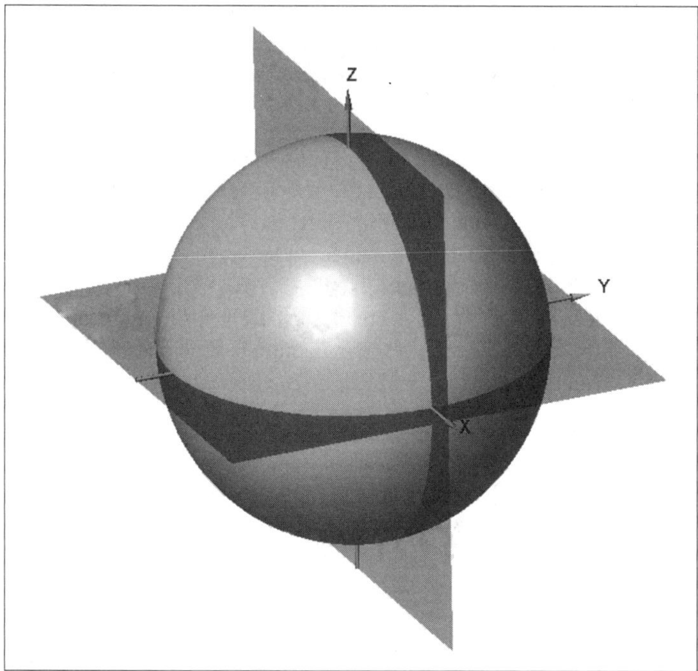

Figure 4-1 *Plotting the Radiation Pattern of an Isotropic Antenna*

It is rather difficult to show a three-dimensional plot or shape on a two-dimensional document—especially if the shape is complex or unusual. After all, most physical antennas are not ideal, so their radiation pattern is not a simple sphere. Instead, you could slice through the three-dimensional plot with two orthogonal planes and show the two outlines that are formed from the plot. In Figure 4-1, the sphere is cut by the XY plane, which lies flat along the horizon, and by the XZ plane, which lies vertically along the elevation of the sphere. Figure 4-2 shows the resulting cuts.

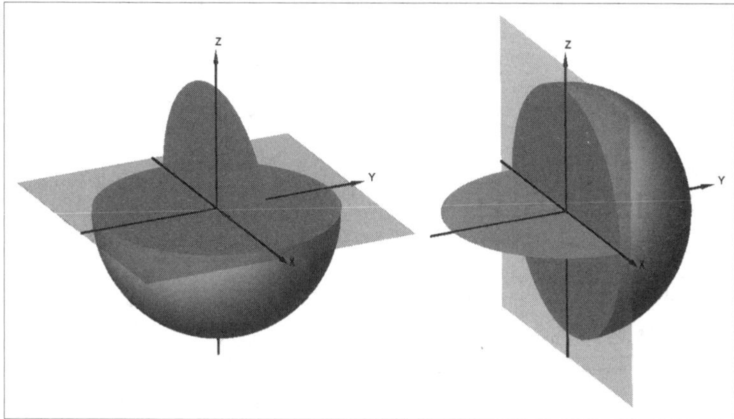

Figure 4-2 *Cutting the Radiation Pattern with Two Planes*

The plane at the left is known as the *H plane* or the *horizontal* (*azimuth*) *plane*, and usually shows a top-down view of the radiation pattern through the center of the antenna. The plane at the right is known as the *E plane* or *elevation plane*, and shows a side view of the same radiation pattern.

The outline of each plot can be recorded on a polar plot, as shown by the heavy dark lines in Figure 4-3. A polar plot contains concentric circles that represent relative changes in the signal strength as measured at a constant distance from the antenna. The outermost circle usually represents the strongest signal strength, and the inner circles represent weaker signal strength. Although the circles are labeled with numbers like 0, –5, –10, –15, and so on, they do not necessarily represent any absolute dB values. Instead, they are measurements that are relative to the maximum value at the outside circle. If the maximum is shown at the outer ring, everything else will be less than the maximum and will lie further inward.

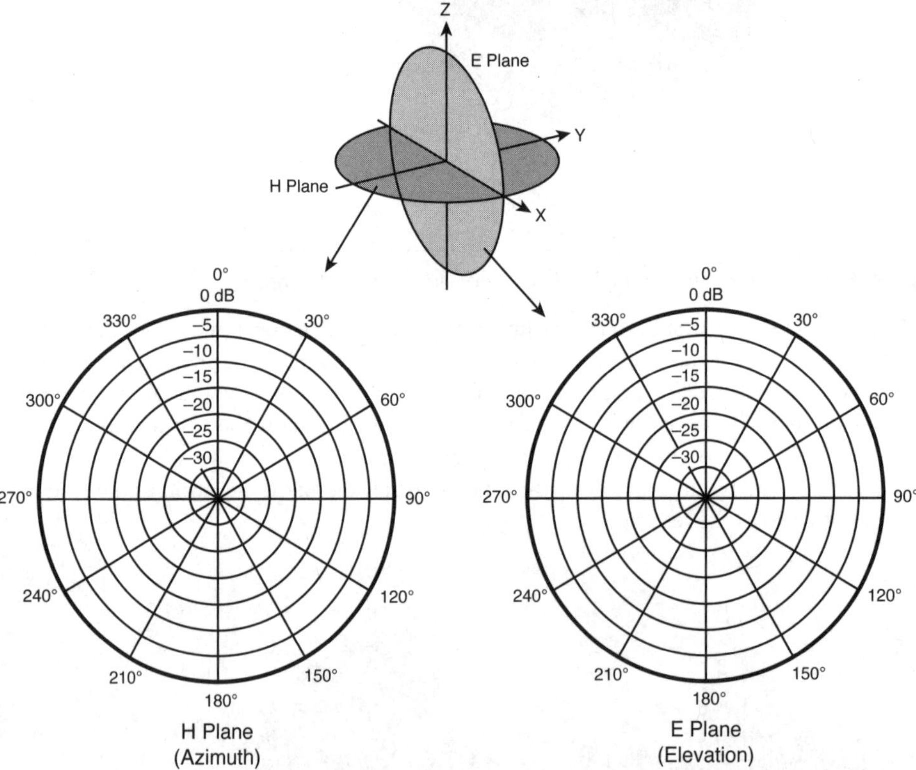

Figure 4-3 *Recording an Isotropic Antenna Pattern on E and H Polar Plots*

The circles are also divided into sectors so that a full sweep of 360 degrees can be plotted. This allows measurements to be taken at every angle around the antenna in the plane shown.

Are you confused? You aren't alone. The E and H polar plots of the radiation pattern are presented here because most antenna manufacturers include them in their product literature. The antenna is always placed at the center of the polar plots, but you will not always be able to figure out how the antenna is oriented with respect to the E and H planes. Cisco usually includes a small picture of the antenna at the center of the plots as a handy reference.

As a wireless engineer, you will have to look at various antenna patterns and try to figure out whether the antenna is a good match for the environment you are trying to cover with an RF signal. You will need a good bit of imagination to merge the two plots into a 3D picture in your mind. As various antennas are described in this chapter, the plots, planes, and a 3D rendering are presented to help you get a feel for the thinking process.

Gain

Antennas are passive devices; they do not amplify a transmitter's signal with any circuitry or external power. Instead, they amplify or add gain to the signal by shaping the RF energy as it is propagated into free space. In other words, the *gain* of an antenna is a measure of how effectively it can focus RF energy in a certain direction.

Because an isotropic antenna radiates RF energy in all directions equally, it cannot focus the energy in any certain direction. Recall from Chapter 1 that the gain of an antenna in dBi is measured relative to an isotropic antenna. When an isotropic antenna is compared with itself, the result is a gain of $10\log_{10}(1)$ or 0 dBi.

Think of a zero gain antenna producing a perfect sphere. If the sphere is made of rubber, you could press on it in various locations and change its shape. As the sphere is deformed, it expands in other directions. Figure 4-4 shows some simple examples, along with some example gain values. As you work through this chapter and examine antennas on your own, notice how the gain is lower for omnidirectional antennas, which are made to cover a widespread area, and higher for directional antennas, which are built to cover more focused areas.

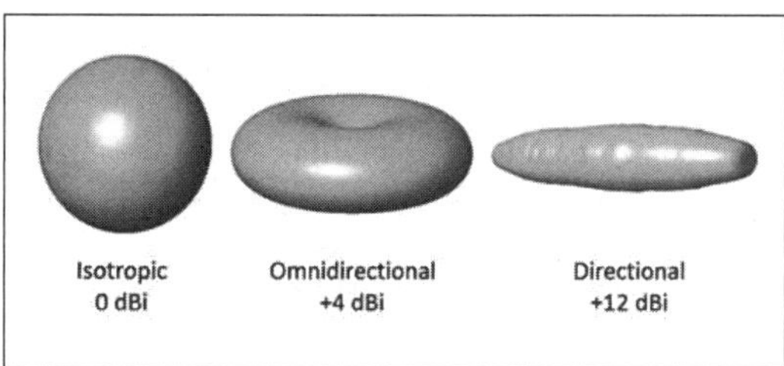

Figure 4-4 *Radiation Patterns for the Three Basic Antenna Types*

> **Tip** The gain itself is typically not indicated on either E or H plane radiation pattern plots. The only way to find an antenna's gain is to look at the manufacturer's specifications.

Beamwidth

The antenna gain can be an indicator of how focused an antenna's pattern might be, but it is really more suited for link budget calculations. Instead, many manufacturers list the *beamwidth* of an antenna as a measure of the antenna's focus. Beamwidth is normally listed in degrees for both the H and E planes.

The beamwidth is determined by finding the strongest point on the plot, which is usually somewhere on the outer circle. Next, the plot is followed in either direction until the value decreases by 3 dB, indicating the point where the signal is one-half the strongest power. A line is drawn from the center of the plot to intersect each 3-dB point, and then the angle between the two lines is measured. Figure 4-5 shows a simple example. The H plane has a beamwidth of 30 degrees, and the E plane has a beamwidth of 55 degrees.

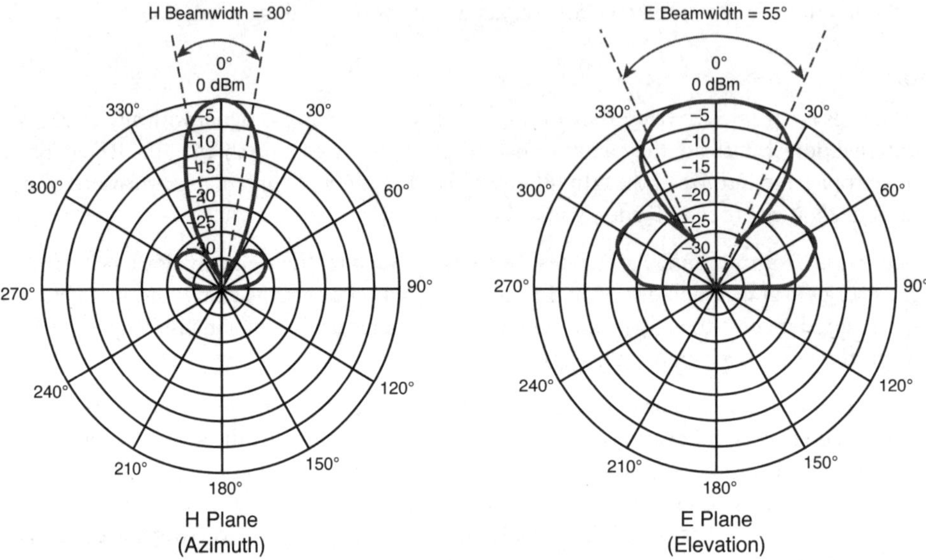

Figure 4-5 *Example of Antenna Beamwidth Measurement*

Polarization

When an alternating current is applied to an antenna, an electromagnetic wave is produced. From Chapter 1, you learned that the wave has two components: an electrical field wave and a magnetic field wave. The electrical portion of the wave will always leave the antenna in a certain orientation. For example, a simple dipole antenna that is mounted pointing vertically will produce a wave that oscillates up and down in a vertical direction as it travels through free space. This is true of most Cisco antennas when they are mounted according to Cisco recommendations. Other types of antennas might be designed to produce waves that oscillate back and forth horizontally. Still others might produce waves that actually twist in a three-dimensional spiral motion through space.

The electrical field wave's orientation, with respect to the horizon, is called the antenna *polarization*. Antennas that produce vertical oscillation are vertically polarized; ones that produce horizontal oscillation are horizontally polarized. (Keep in mind that there is always a magnetic field wave too, which is oriented at 90 degrees from the electrical field wave.) By itself, the antenna polarization is not of critical importance. However, the antenna polarization at the transmitter must be matched to the polarization at the receiver. If the polarization is mismatched, the received signal can be severely degraded.

Figure 4-6 illustrates antenna polarization. The transmitter and receiver along the top both use vertical polarization, so the received signal is optimized. The pair along the bottom is mismatched, causing the signal to be poorly received.

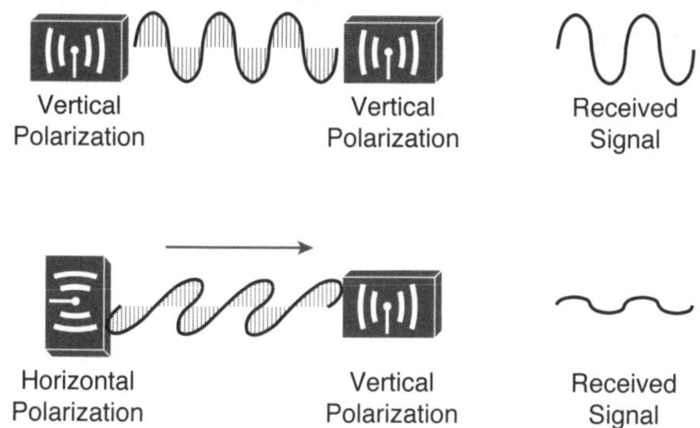

4

Figure 4-6 *Matching the Antenna Polarization Between Transmitter and Receiver*

> **Tip** Even though Cisco antennas are designed to use vertical polarization, someone might mount an antenna in an unexpected orientation. For example, suppose you mount a transmitter with its antennas pointing upward. After you leave, someone knocks the antennas so that they are turned sideways. Not only does that change the radiation pattern you were expecting, it also changes the polarization. If the antenna is located indoors, where multipath conditions exist, MIMO can help mitigate the polarization mismatch by combining several received copies of the signal.

Antenna Types

Wireless LAN antennas are available in a variety of styles, shapes, and radiation patterns. In addition, antennas are normally rated for indoor or outdoor use, depending on weather resistance and mounting options. Antennas are usually designed for a specific frequency range and are approved by the local regulatory body, such as the FCC in the United States. There are two basic types of antennas, omnidirectional and directional, which are discussed in the following sections.

> **Tip** You can learn more about the full line of Cisco antennas in the *Cisco Aironet Antennas and Accessories Reference Guide*, at http://www.cisco.com/en/US/prod/collateral/wireless/ps7183/ps469/at_a_glance_c45-513837.pdf.

Omnidirectional Antennas

An omnidirectional antenna is usually made in the shape of a thin cylinder. It tends to propagate a signal equally in all directions away from the cylinder, but not along the cylinder's length. The result is a donut-shaped pattern that extends further in the H plane than the E plane. This type of antenna is well suited for broad coverage of a large room or floor area where the antenna is located in the center. Because an omnidirectional antenna distributes the RF energy throughout a broad area, it has a relatively low gain.

A common type of omnidirectional antenna is the *dipole*, shown in the left portion of Figure 4-7. Some dipole models are articulated such that they can be folded up or down, depending on the mounting orientation, whereas others are rigid and fixed. As its name implies, the dipole has two separate wires that radiate an RF signal when an alternating current is applied across them, as shown in the right portion of Figure 4-7. Dipoles usually have a gain of around +2 to +5 dBi.

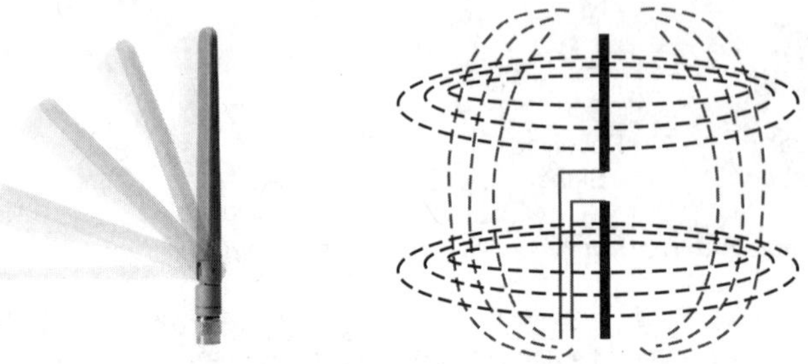

Figure 4-7 *Cisco Dipole Antenna*

The E and H plane radiation patterns for a typical dipole antenna are shown in Figure 4-8. In the E plane, think of the dipole lying on its side in the center of the plot; the H plane is looking down on the top of the dipole. Figure 4-9 takes the patterns a step further, showing how the two planes are superimposed and merged to reveal the three-dimensional radiation pattern.

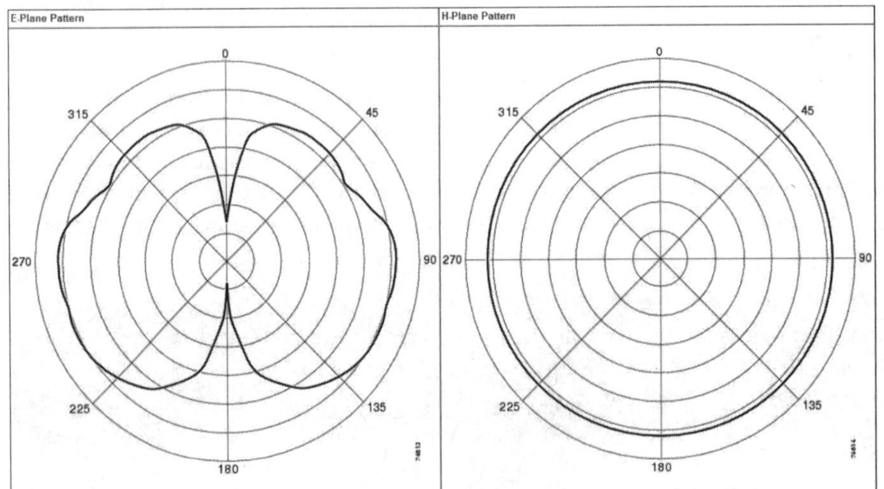

Figure 4-8 *E and H Radiation Patterns for a Typical Dipole Antenna*

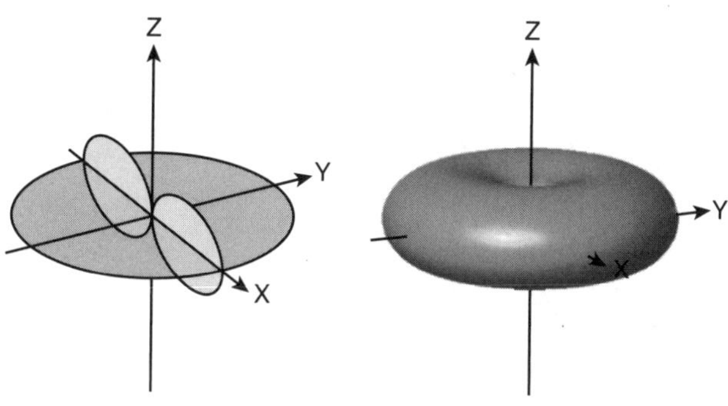

Figure 4-9 *Dipole Radiation Pattern in Three Dimensions*

Dipoles are often connected to wireless LAN devices that mount on the ceilings of rooms and hallways. Most dipole antennas are between 3.5 and 5.5 inches long, so they are not always aesthetically pleasing when they stick down from a ceiling. For this reason, Cisco offers several monopole antennas as an alternative.

Monopole antennas are very short—less than 2 inches in length, as shown in Figure 4-10. To achieve such a small size, they contain only one short length of wire. You can think of this as a compromised dipole antenna, where one of the antenna segments stands out away from the wireless device. The other segment is moved down into the device, in the form of a metal ground plane. Therefore, monopole antennas can be used only on devices that have a large, flat metal casing. The radiation pattern is similar to that of a dipole, but not quite as symmetrical. Monopole antennas have a typical gain of 2.2 dBi in the 2.4- and 5-GHz bands.

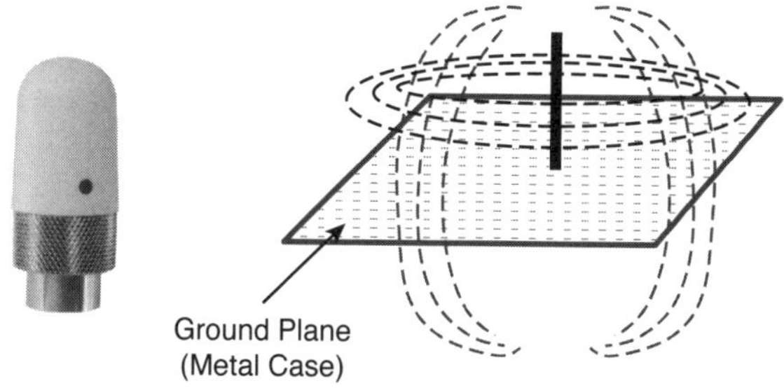

Figure 4-10 *Cisco Monopole Antenna*

To reduce the size of an omnidirectional antenna even further, many Cisco wireless access points (APs) have integrated antennas that are hidden inside the device's smooth case. For example, the AP shown in Figure 4-11 has six tiny antennas hidden inside it.

Figure 4-11 *Cisco Wireless Access Point with Integrated Omnidirectional Antennas*

Integrated omnidirectional antennas typically have a gain of 2 dBi in the 2.4-GHz band and 5 dBi in the 5-GHz band. The E and H plane radiation patterns are shown in Figure 4-12. When the two planes are merged, the three-dimensional pattern shown in Figure 4-13 is revealed.

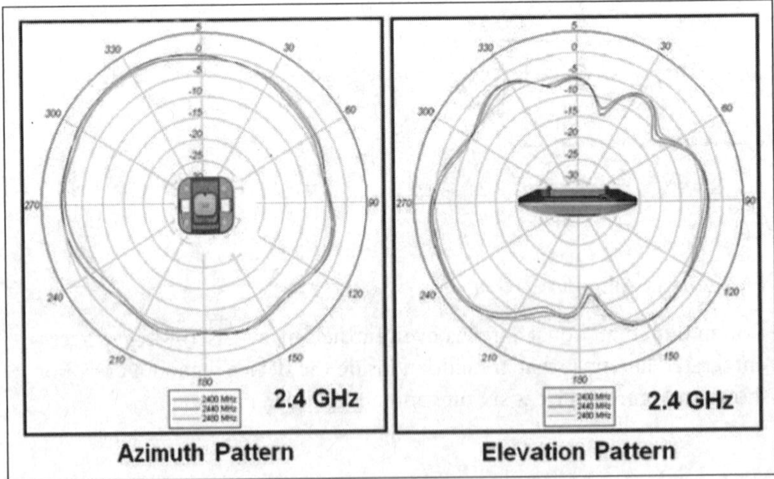

Figure 4-12 *E and H Radiation Patterns for a Typical Integrated Omnidirectional Antenna*

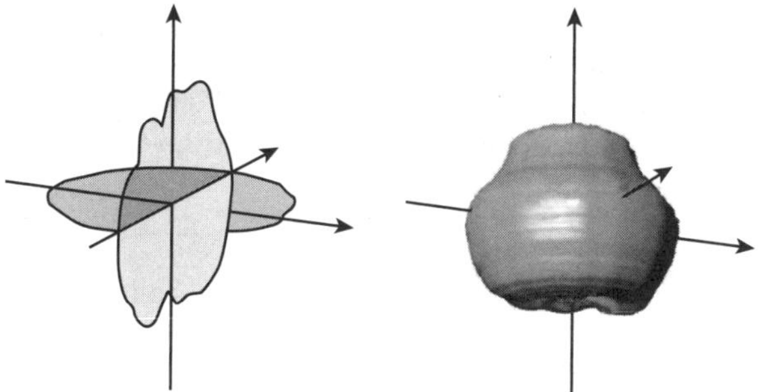

Figure 4-13 *Integrated Omnidirectional Antenna Radiation Pattern in 3D*

> **Tip** What about wireless LAN adapters that are used in mobile devices like laptops and smartphones? Because the adapters are so small, their antennas must also be tiny. As a result, USB wireless adapters often have a gain of 0 dBi, while some smartphones even have a negative gain! This does not mean that the antennas do not radiate or receive signals. Instead, the antennas just have a lower performance compared with other, larger devices.

Directional Antennas

Directional antennas have a higher gain than omnidirectional antennas because they focus the RF energy in one general direction. Typical applications include elongated indoor areas, such as the rooms along a long hallway or the aisles in a warehouse. They can also be used to cover outdoor areas out away from a building or long distances between buildings.

Patch antennas have a flat rectangular shape, as shown in Figure 4-14, so that they can be mounted on a wall.

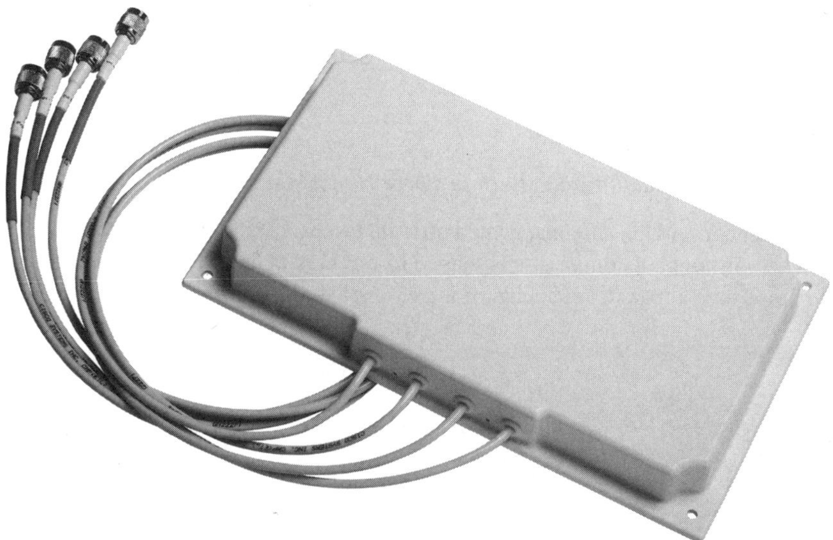

Figure 4-14 *Typical Cisco Patch Antenna*

Patch antennas produce a broad egg-shaped pattern that extends out away from the flat patch surface. The E and H radiation pattern plots are shown in Figure 4-15. When the planes are merged as shown in Figure 4-16, you can see the somewhat broad directional pattern that results. Patch antennas have a typical gain of about 6 to 8 dBi in the 2.4-GHz band and 7 to 10 dBi at 5 GHz.

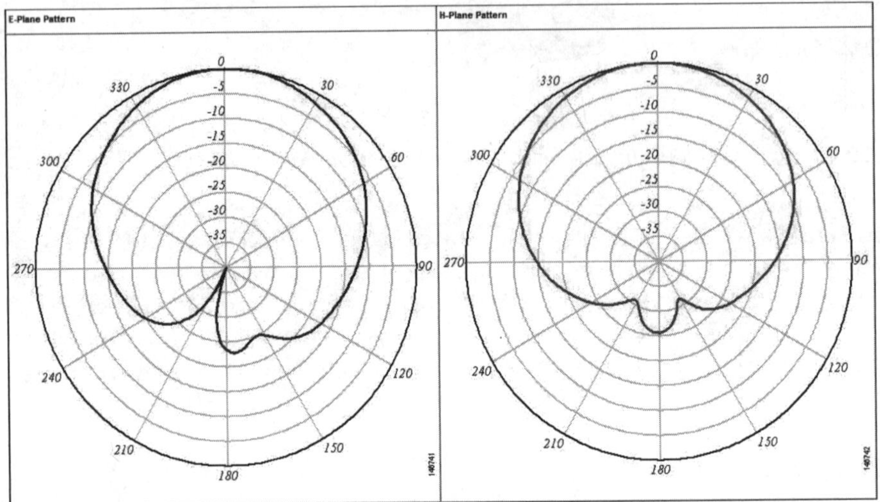

Figure 4-15 *E and H Radiation Patterns for a Typical Patch Antenna*

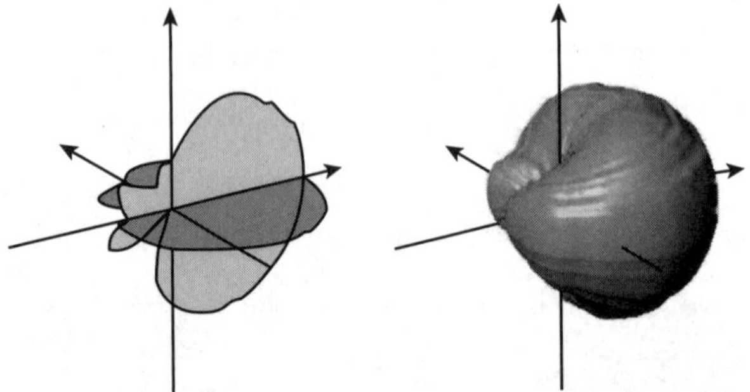

Figure 4-16 *Patch Antenna Radiation Pattern in Three Dimensions*

Figure 4-17 shows the Yagi-Uda antenna, named after its inventors, and more commonly known as the Yagi. Although its outer case is shaped like a thick cylinder, the antenna is actually made up of several parallel elements of increasing length.

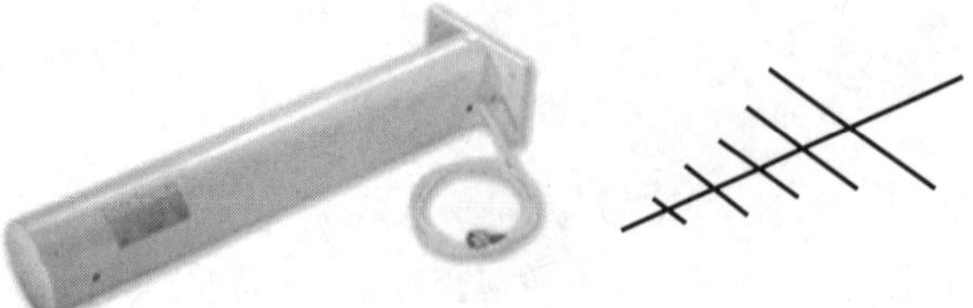

Figure 4-17 *Cisco Yagi Antenna*

Figure 4-18 shows the E and H radiation pattern plots. A Yagi produces a more focused egg-shaped pattern that extends out along the antenna's length, as shown in Figure 4-19. Yagi antennas have a gain of about 10-14 dBi in the 2.4-GHz band. Cisco does not offer a 5-GHz Yagi.

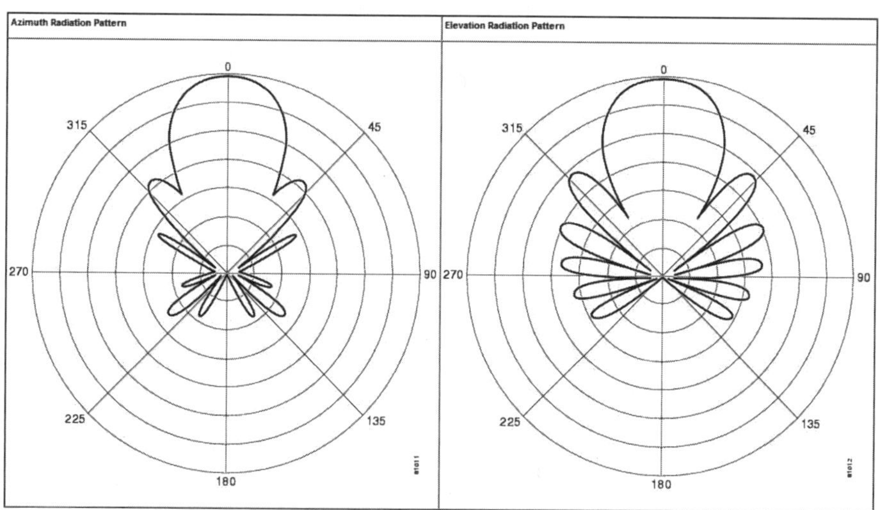

Figure 4-18 *E and H Radiation Patterns for a Typical Yagi Antenna*

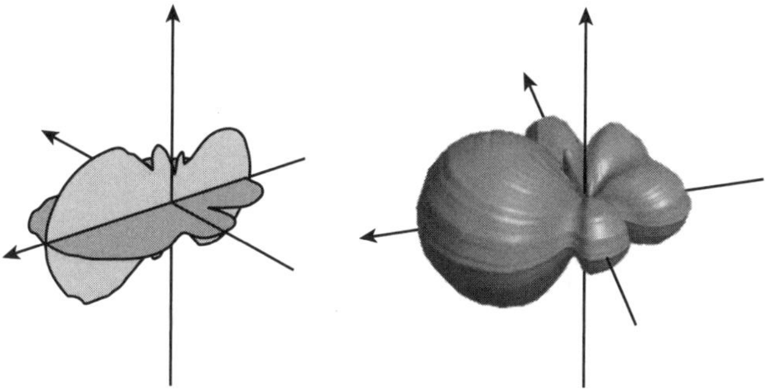

Figure 4-19 *Yagi Antenna Radiation Pattern in Three Dimensions*

In a line-of-sight wireless path, an RF signal must be propagated a long distance using a narrow beam. Highly directional antennas are tailored for that use, but focus the RF energy along one narrow elliptical pattern. Because the target is only one receiver location, the antenna does not have to cover any area outside of the line of sight.

Dish antennas, such as the one shown in Figure 4-20, use a parabolic dish to focus received signals onto an antenna mounted at the center. The parabolic shape is important because any waves arriving from the line of sight will be reflected onto the center antenna element that faces the dish. Transmitted waves are just the reverse; they are aimed at the dish and reflected such that they are propagated away from the dish along the line of sight.

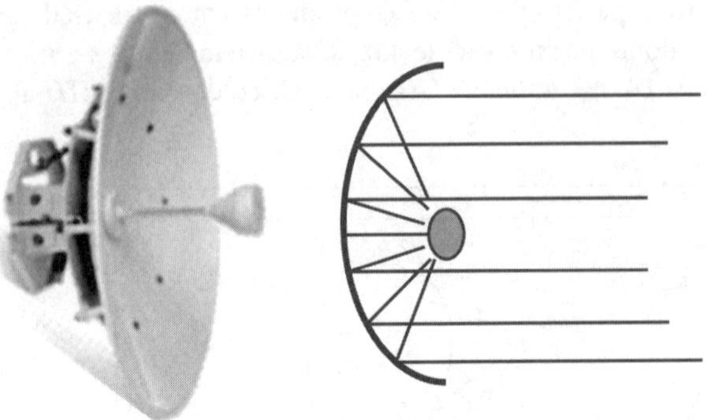

Figure 4-20 *Cisco Parabolic Dish Antenna*

Figure 4-21 shows the radiation patterns in the E and H planes, which are merged into three dimensions in Figure 4-22. Notice how the antenna's coverage pattern is long and narrow, extending out away from the dish. The focused pattern gives the antenna a gain of between 20 and 30 dBi—the highest gain of all the wireless LAN antennas.

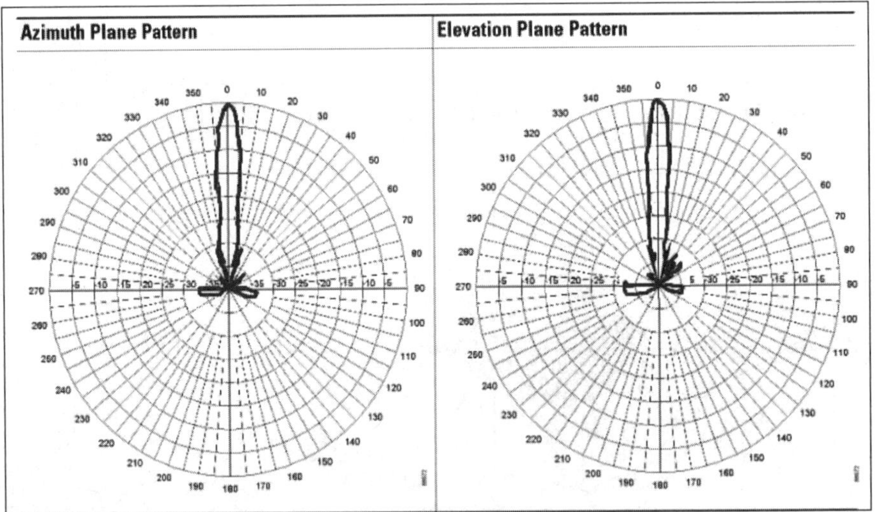

Figure 4-21 *E and H Radiation Patterns for a Parabolic Dish Antenna*

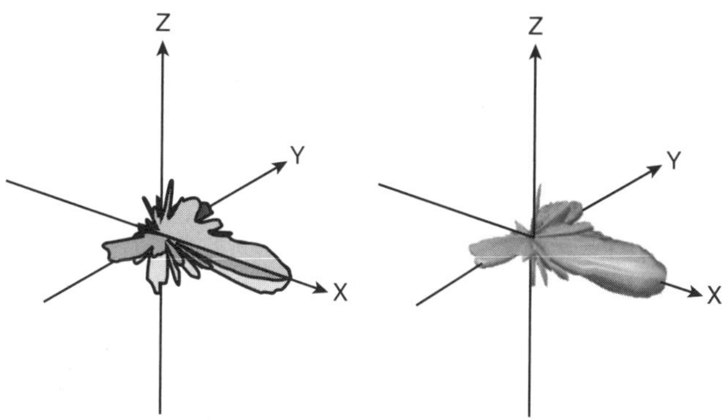

Figure 4-22 *Parabolic Dish Antenna Radiation Pattern in Three Dimensions*

Antenna Summary

Table 4-2 lists each antenna type and style, along with typical beamwidth and gain values. You can use this table as a summary to help compare the antennas side by side. Notice that the beamwidth is the largest for omnidirectional antennas, and then begins to narrow through the progression of directional antennas. The opposite is true of the gain—omnidirectional antennas have the lowest gain, whereas directional antennas increase gain as their beamwidth narrows.

Table 4-2 Summary of Antenna Characteristics

Type	Style	Beamwidth		Gain (dBi)	
		H Plane	E Plane	2.4 GHz	5 GHz
Omnidirectional	Dipole	360°	65°	2.2	3.5
	Monopole	360°	50°	2.2	2.2
	Integrated	360°	150°	2	5
Directional	Patch	50°	50°	6–8	7–10
	Yagi	30°	25°	10–14	—
	Parabolic dish	5°	5°	20–30	20–30

Adding Antenna Accessories

Occasionally, you may find that you are simply not able to meet the path link budget between a transmitter and a receiver. This might be because the distance, and therefore the free space path loss, is too great. Perhaps the transmitter does not offer enough output power, or the cable connecting the transmitter to the antenna is too long or introduces too much loss. You can add an *amplifier* to provide additional gain, provided the EIRP does not exceed the maximum value allowed. An amplifier is an active, powered device that is connected inline between a transmitter and an antenna, as shown in Figure 4-23.

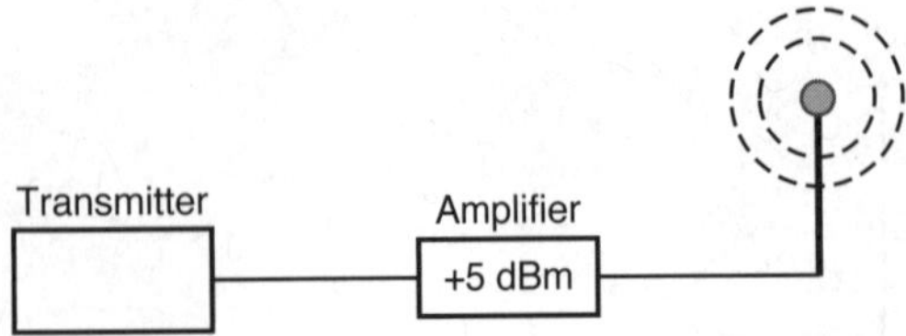

Figure 4-23 *Using an Amplifier to Add 5-dBm Gain*

At other times, you may need to reduce the signal strength of a transmitter beyond what is possible with the transmitter settings. For example, the transmitter may already be configured for its lowest possible transmit power level, but the signal strength is still too great for nearby receivers. You can position an *attenuator*, a passive device that absorbs part of the energy, inline between a transmitter and an antenna, as shown in Figure 4-24.

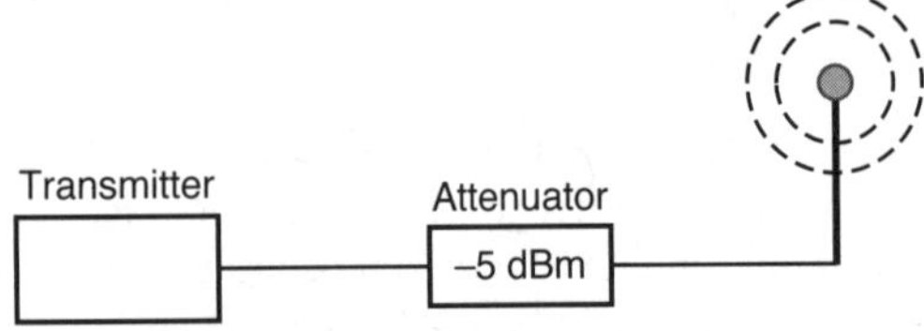

Figure 4-24 *Using an Attenuator to Add 5-dBm Loss*

When a transmitter or receiver is connected to an outdoor antenna, there is always the possibility that lightning will induce a tremendous amount of energy through the antenna—enough to damage the wireless LAN equipment and portions of the network. To protect against such damage, you should always connect a *lightning arrestor* inline between an outdoor antenna and a wireless LAN device, as shown in Figure 4-25.

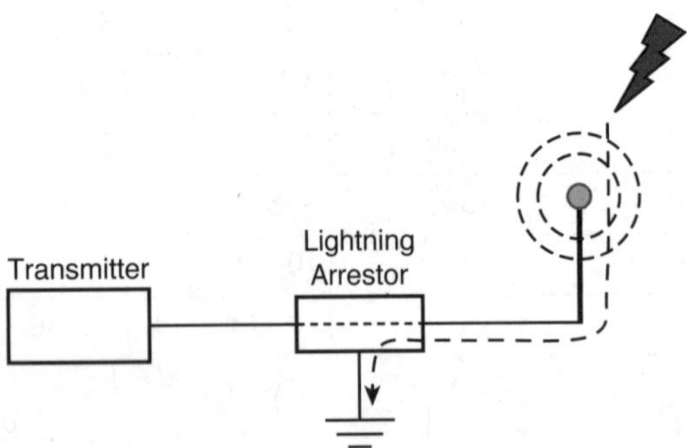

Figure 4-25 *Using a Lightning Arrestor to Protect Sensitive Wireless LAN Equipment*

The lightning arrestor has two connectors that attach to the two ends of coaxial cable, in addition to a grounding lug, which should connect to the nearest building or electrical ground. The RF signal is allowed to pass on through the lightning arrestor, but sudden spikes of electricity will be bypassed to ground. Contrary to its name, a lightning arrestor can never prevent the damage from a direct lightning strike. In can, however, prevent damage that might occur due to static electricity discharges or transient voltage spikes during thunderstorms.

Exam Preparation Tasks

As mentioned in the section, "How to Use This Book," in the Introduction, you have a couple of choices for exam preparation: the exercises here, Chapter 21, "Final Review," and the exam simulation questions on the DVD.

Review All Key Topics

Review the most important topics in this chapter, noted with the Key Topic icon in the outer margin of the page. Table 4-3 lists a reference of these key topics and the page numbers on which each is found.

Table 4-3 Key Topics for Chapter 4

Key Topic Element	Description	Page Number
Figure 4-2	Cutting a radiation pattern into the E and H planes	95
Figure 4-5	Determining the beamwidth of an antenna	98
Figure 4-6	Antenna polarization	99
Table 4-2	A summary of antenna characteristics	107

Define Key Terms

Define the following key terms from this chapter and check your answers in the glossary:

amplifier, attenuator, beamwidth, dipole, directional antenna, E plane, gain, H plane, integrated antenna, lightning arrestor, monopole, omnidirectional antenna, parabolic dish antenna, patch antenna, polar plot, polarization, radiation pattern, Yagi antenna

This chapter covers the following topics:

- **Types of Wireless Networks**—This section gives a brief overview of several major network types and their scales.
- **Wireless LAN Topologies**—This section discusses the basic building blocks of 802.11 wireless LANs and how they work together.
- **Other Wireless Topologies**—This section describes some network topologies that can be used to solve unique problems.

This chapter covers the following exam topics:

- 2.3—Describe 802.11 fundamentals
  - 2.3d—Wireless topologies
    - 2.3d(i)—IBSS
    - 2.3d(ii)—BSS
    - 2.3d(iii)—ESS

CHAPTER 5

Wireless LAN Topologies

Wireless communication usually involves a data exchange between two devices. A wireless LAN goes even further; many devices can participate in sharing the medium for data exchanges. This chapter explains the topologies that can be used to control access to the wireless medium and provide data exchange between devices.

"Do I Know This Already?" Quiz

The "Do I Know This Already?" quiz allows you to assess whether you should read this entire chapter thoroughly or jump to the "Exam Preparation Tasks" section. If you are in doubt about your answers to these questions or your own assessment of your knowledge of the topics, read the entire chapter. Table 5-1 lists the major headings in this chapter and their corresponding "Do I Know This Already?" quiz questions. You can find the answers in Appendix A, "Answers to the 'Do I Know This Already?' Quizzes."

Table 5-1 "Do I Know This Already?" Section-to-Question Mapping

Foundation Topics Section	Questions
Types of Wireless Networks	1
Wireless LAN Topologies	2–8
Other Wireless Topologies	9–10

Caution The goal of self-assessment is to gauge your mastery of the topics in this chapter. If you do not know the answer to a question or are only partially sure of the answer, you should mark that question as wrong for purposes of the self-assessment. Giving yourself credit for an answer you correctly guess skews your self-assessment results and might provide you with a false sense of security.

1. Which two of the following types of wireless networks use the same frequency band?
   a. WPAN
   b. WLAN
   c. WMAN
   d. WWAN
2. Devices using a wireless LAN must operate in which one of the following modes?
   a. Round-robin access
   b. Half duplex
   c. Full duplex
   d. None of these answers
3. An access point is set up to offer wireless coverage in an office. Which one of the following is the correct 802.11 term for the resulting standalone network?
   a. BSA
   b. BSD
   c. BSS
   d. IBSS
4. Which one of the following is used to uniquely identify an AP and the basic service set it maintains with its associated wireless clients?
   a. SSID
   b. BSSID
   c. Ethernet MAC address
   d. Radio MAC address
5. Which one of the following statements is true about a wireless BSS?
   a. A wireless client can send frames directly to any another client at any time.
   b. Once two clients are associated to the BSS, they may communicate directly with each other with no further intervention.
   c. A client must send frames through the AP only when the destination client is associated to a different AP.
   d. A client must send all frames through the AP to reach any other client or coordinate with the AP to reach another client directly.
6. In a Cisco wireless network, which of the following statements full of acronyms are correct? (Choose two.)
   a. The DS connects two BSSs to form an ESS.
   b. The BSA of a BSS looks like a MAC address.
   c. The SSID of a STA must be unique within the ESS.
   d. The BSSID is unique for each SSID in a BSS.

7. A wireless client is configured to associate with the wireless network called BeMyGuest. For the client to roam successfully everywhere within a building, which one of the following correctly identifies the WLAN topology that must be in place?
   a. A basic service set
   b. A distribution system
   c. An extended service set
   d. The SSID BeMyGuest defined on every AP
   e. All of these answers are correct.
8. Which one of the following is also known as an ad hoc wireless network?
   a. DS
   b. ESS
   c. BSA
   d. IBSS
   e. BSS
9. Which one of the following can be used to provide wireless connectivity to a non-wireless device?
   a. Wireless repeater
   b. Workgroup bridge
   c. Transparent bridge
   d. Adaptive bridge
10. Which one of the following is not needed in a Cisco outdoor mesh network?
   a. A BSS function
   b. Ethernet cabling to each AP
   c. A wireless LAN controller
   d. A backhaul network

Foundation Topics

Types of Wireless Networks

The term *wireless LAN* is used quite freely in this book. After all, it is the central theme of the CCNA Wireless exam, but it is only one type of wireless network that you might encounter. Wireless networks can be classified into four main types according to the geographic scope where a signal and service is available. Figure 5-1 gives a general idea of the network types and their scopes.

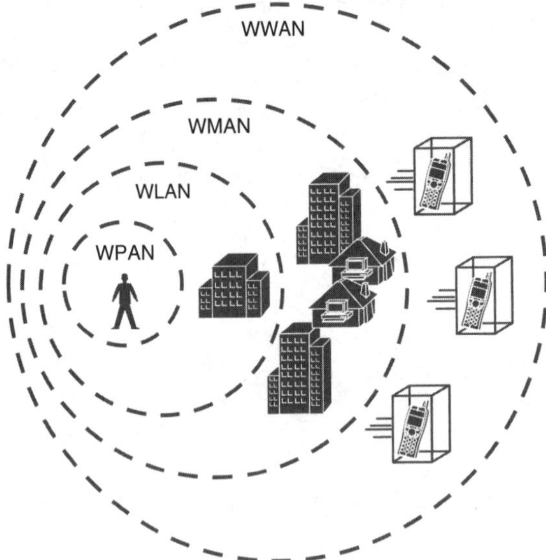

Figure 5-1 *Wireless Network Types and Scopes*

- **Wireless personal-area network (WPAN)**—As its name implies, a WPAN uses low-powered transmitters to create a network with a very short range, usually 20 to 30 feet (7 to 10 meters). WPANs are based on the IEEE 802.15 standard and include technologies like Bluetooth and ZigBee, although ZigBee can have a greater range. Unlicensed ISM frequencies are used, including the 2.4-GHz band.
- **Wireless local-area network (WLAN)**—A wireless service that connects multiple devices using the IEEE 802.11 standard over a medium-sized range, usually up to 300 feet (100 meters). Unlicensed frequencies in the 2.4- and 5-GHz band are used.
- **Wireless metropolitan-area network (WMAN)**—A wireless service over a large geographic area, such as all or a portion of a city. One common example, WiMAX, is based on the IEEE 802.16 standard. Licensed frequencies are commonly used.
- **Wireless wide-area network (WWAN)**—A wireless data service for mobile phones that is offered over a very large geographic area (regional, national, and even global) by telecommunications carriers. Licensed frequencies are used.

The remainder of this chapter focuses on WLANs and how they are constructed.

Wireless LAN Topologies

Up to this point, this book has discussed radio frequency (RF) signals as they travel from a transmitter to a receiver. As Figure 5-2 shows, the transmitter can contact the receiver at any and all times, as long as both devices are tuned to the same frequency (or channel) and use the same modulation and coding scheme. That all sounds simple, except that it is not really practical.

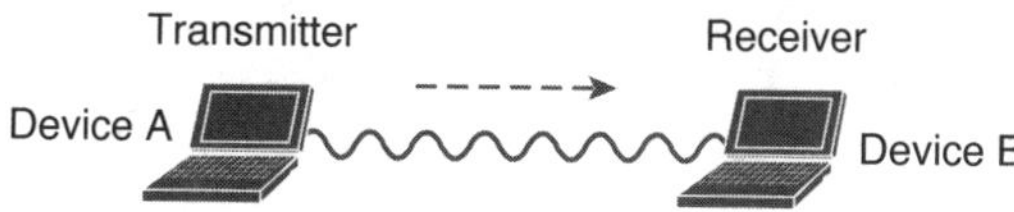

Figure 5-2 *Unidirectional Communication*

To fully leverage wireless communication, data should travel in both directions, as shown in Figure 5-3. Sometimes Device A needs to send data to Device B, while Device B would like to take a turn to send at other times.

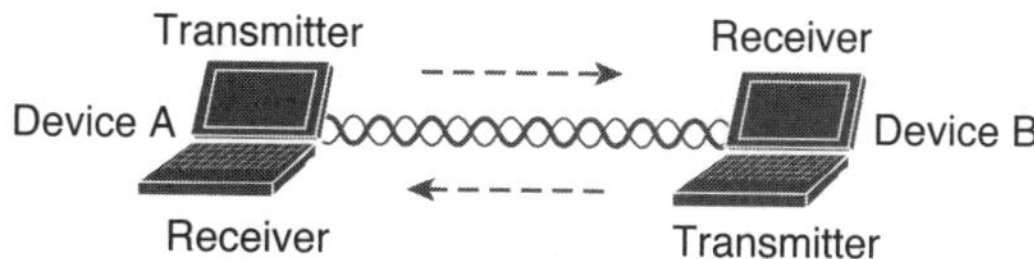

Figure 5-3 *Bidirectional Communication*

Because the two devices are using the same channel, two phrases in the preceding sentence become vitally important: *take a turn* and *send at other times*. As you learned in previous chapters, if multiple signals are received at the same time, they interfere with each other. The likelihood of interference increases as the number of wireless devices grows. For example, Figure 5-4 shows four devices tuned to the same channel and what might happen if some or all of them transmit at the same time.

Figure 5-4 *Interference from Simultaneous Transmissions*

All this talk about waiting turns and avoiding interference should remind you of an Ethernet LAN, where multiple hosts can share common bandwidth and a collision domain. To use the media effectively, all the hosts must operate in half-duplex mode so that they avoid colliding with other transmissions. The side effect is that no host can transmit and receive at the same time on a given frequency.

Tip IEEE 802.11 WLANs are always half duplex because transmissions between stations use the same frequency. Only one station can transmit at any time; otherwise, collisions occur. To achieve full-duplex mode, one station's transmission would have to occur on one frequency while it receives over a different frequency—much like full-duplex Ethernet links work. Although this is certainly possible and practical, the 802.11-2012 standard does not permit full-duplex operation. The 802.11ac amendment will somewhat ease that restriction in its "Wave 2" implementation, through the use of downstream multi-user MIMO (MU-MIMO).

A wireless LAN is similar. Because multiple hosts can share the same channel, they also share the "airtime" or access to that channel at any given time. Therefore, to keep everything clean, only one device should transmit at any given time. To contend for use of the channel, devices based on the 802.11 standard have to determine whether the channel is clear and available before transmitting anything. This process is described in more detail in Chapter 6, "Understanding 802.11 Frame Types."

At the most basic level, there is no inherent organization to a wireless medium or any inherent control over the number of devices that can transmit and receive frames. Any device that has a wireless network adapter can power up at any time and try to communicate. At a minimum, a wireless network should have a way to make sure that every device using a channel can support a common set of parameters, including data rates, 802.11 modulation types, channel width, and so on. Beyond that, there should be a way to control which devices (and users) are allowed to use the wireless medium, and the methods that are used to secure the wireless transmissions.

Basic Service Set

The solution is to make every wireless service area a closed group of mobile devices that forms around a fixed device—before a device can participate, it must advertise its capabilities and then be granted permission to join. The 802.11 standard calls this a *basic service set* (BSS). At the heart of every BSS is a wireless *access point* (AP), as shown in Figure 5-5. The AP operates in *infrastructure mode*, which means it offers the services that are necessary to form the infrastructure of a wireless network.

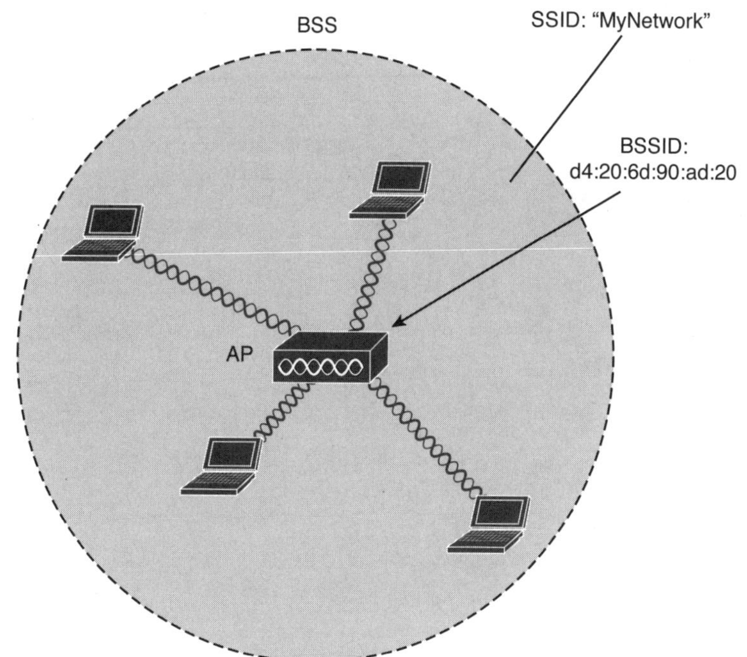

5

Figure 5-5 *802.11 Basic Service Set*

Because the operation of a BSS hinges on the AP, the BSS is bounded by the area where the AP's signal is usable. This is known as the *basic service area* (BSA) or *cell*. In Figure 5-5, the cell is shown as a simple circular area that might result from the radiation pattern of an omnidirectional antenna. Cells can have other shapes too, depending on the antenna that is connected to the AP and on the physical surroundings.

The AP serves as a single point of contact for every device that wants to use the BSS. It advertises the existence of the BSS so that devices can find it and try to join. To do that, the AP uses a unique BSS identifier (BSSID) that is based on the AP's own radio MAC address.

In addition, the AP advertises the wireless network with a service set identifier (SSID), which is a text string containing a logical name. Think of the BSSID as a machine-readable name tag that uniquely identifies the BSS ambassador (the AP), and the SSID as a non-unique, human-readable name tag that identifies the wireless service.

Membership with the BSS is called an *association*. A device must send an association request and the AP must either grant or deny the request. Once associated, a device becomes a client, or an 802.11 *station* (STA), of the BSS. What then? As long as a wireless client remains associated with a BSS, most communications to and from the client must pass *through* the AP, as indicated in Figure 5-6. By using the BSSID as a source or destination address, data frames can be relayed to or from the AP.

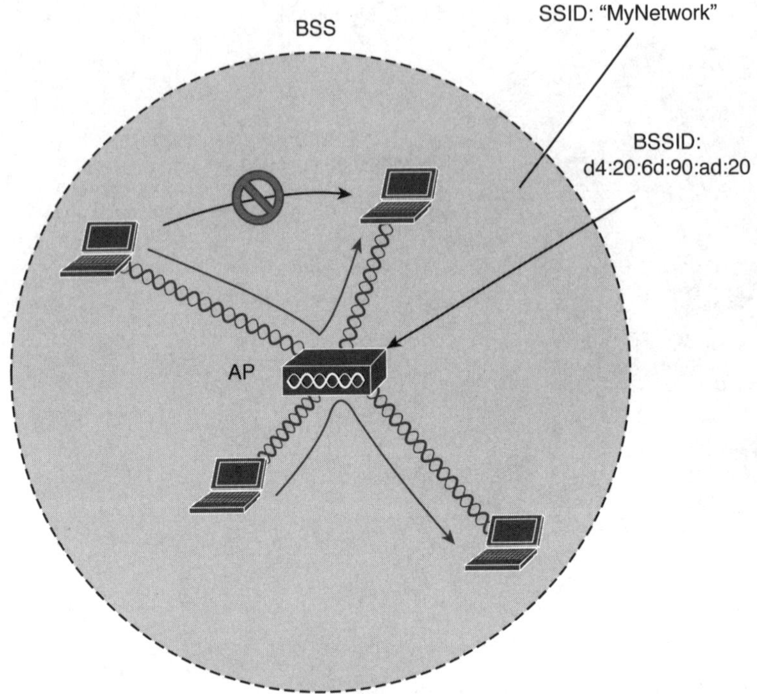

Figure 5-6 *Traffic Flows Within a BSS*

You might be wondering why all client traffic has to traverse the AP at all. Why cannot two clients simply transmit data frames directly to each other and bypass the middleman? If clients are allowed to communicate directly, then the whole idea of organizing and managing a BSS is moot. By sending data through the AP first, the BSS remains stable and under control. The 802.11z amendment, along with a few other Wi-Fi Alliance peer-to-peer mechanisms like Wi-Fi Direct and Near-me Area Network (NAN), provide an exception to the rule, which permits two clients to communicate directly without having to pass through an AP.

Tip Even though data frames are meant to pass through an AP, keep in mind that other devices in the same general area that are listening on the same channel can overhear the transmissions. After all, frames are freely available over the air to anyone that is within range to receive them. If the frames are unencrypted, then anyone may inspect their contents. Only the BSSID value contained within the frames indicates that the intended sender or recipient is the AP.

Distribution System

Notice that a BSS involves a single AP and no explicit connection into a regular Ethernet network. In that setting, the AP and its associated clients make up a standalone network. But the AP's role at the center of the BSS does not just stop with managing the BSS—sooner or later, wireless clients will need to communicate with other devices that are not members of the BSS. Fortunately, an AP can also uplink into an Ethernet network because it has both wireless and wired capabilities. The 802.11 standard refers to the upstream wired Ethernet as the *distribution system* (DS) for the wireless BSS, as shown in Figure 5-7.

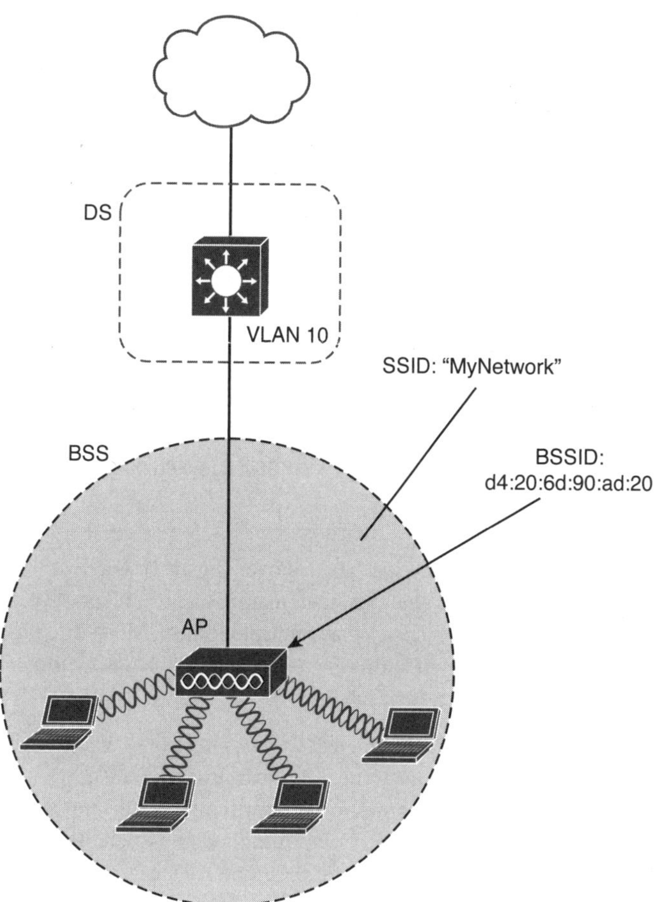

Figure 5-7 *Distribution System Supporting a BSS*

You can think of an AP as a translational bridge, where frames from two dissimilar media (wireless and wired) are translated and then bridged at Layer 2. In simple terms, the AP is in charge of mapping a virtual local-area network (VLAN) to an SSID. In Figure 5-7, the AP maps VLAN 10 to the wireless LAN using SSID "MyNetwork." Clients associated with the "MyNetwork" SSID will appear to be connected to VLAN 10.

This concept can be extended so that multiple VLANs are mapped to multiple SSIDs. To do this, the AP must be connected to the switch by a trunk link that carries the VLANs. In Figure 5-8, VLANs 10, 20, and 30 are trunked to the AP over the DS. The AP uses the 802.1Q tag to map the VLAN numbers to the appropriate SSIDs. For example, VLAN 10 is mapped to SSID "MyNetwork," VLAN 20 is mapped to SSID "YourNetwork," and VLAN 30 to SSID "Guest."

Key Topic

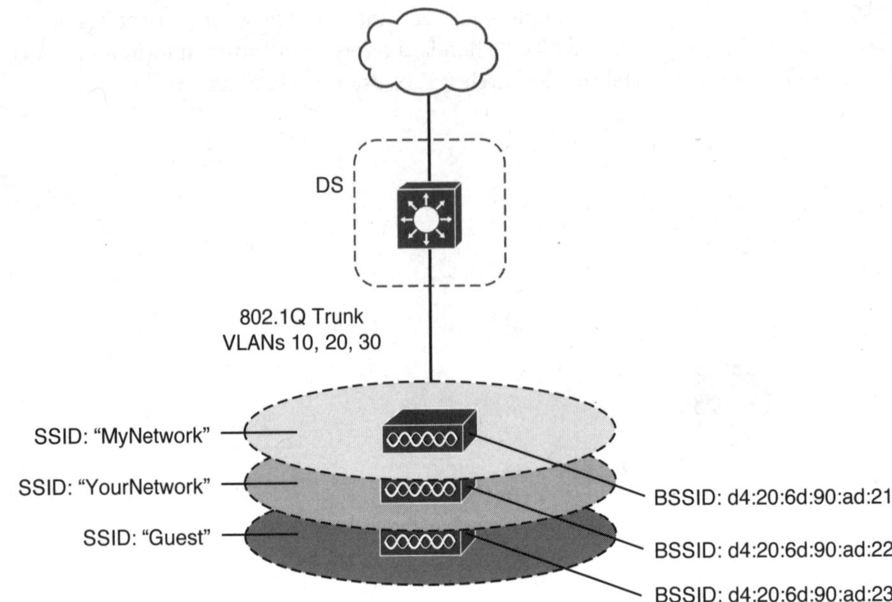

Figure 5-8 *Supporting Multiple SSIDs on One AP*

In effect, when an AP uses multiple SSIDs, it is trunking VLANs over the air to wireless clients. The clients must use the appropriate SSID that has been mapped to the respective VLAN when the AP was configured. The AP then appears as multiple logical APs—one per BSS—with a unique BSSID for each. With Cisco APs, this is usually accomplished by incrementing the last digit of the radio's MAC address for each SSID.

Even though an AP can advertise and support multiple logical wireless networks, each of the SSIDs covers the same geographic area. That is because the AP uses the same transmitter, receiver, antennas, and channel for every SSID that it supports. Beware of one misconception though: Multiple SSIDs can give an illusion of scale. Even though wireless clients can be distributed across many SSIDs, all of those clients must share the same AP's hardware and must contend for airtime on the same channel.

Extended Service Set

Normally, one AP cannot cover the entire area where clients might be located. For example, you might need wireless coverage throughout an entire floor of a business, hotel, hospital, or other large building. To cover more area than a single AP's cell, you simply need to add more APs and spread them out geographically.

When APs are placed at different geographic locations, they can all be interconnected by a switched infrastructure. The 802.11 standard calls this an extended service set (ESS), as shown in Figure 5-9.

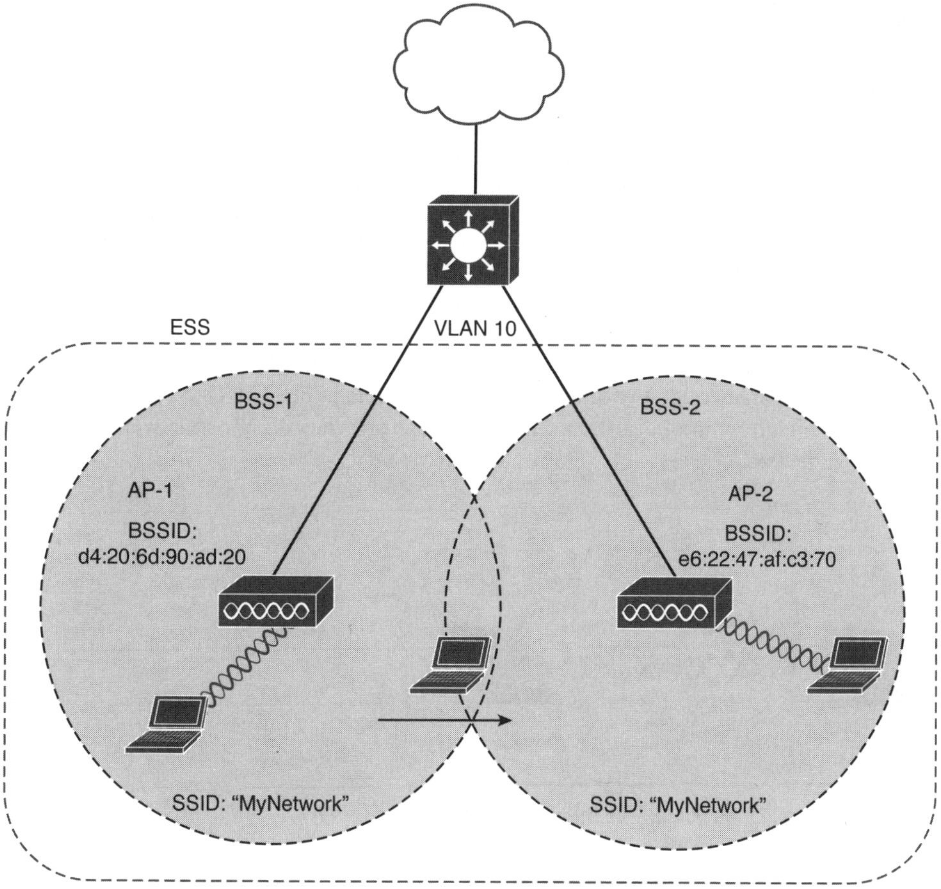

Figure 5-9 *Scaling Wireless Coverage with an 802.11 Extended Service Set*

> **Tip** Chapter 7, "Planning Coverage with Wireless APs," discusses AP and cell placement in greater detail.

The idea is to make multiple APs cooperate so that the wireless service is consistent and seamless from the client's perspective. Ideally, any SSIDs that are defined on one AP should be defined on all the APs in an ESS; otherwise, it would be very cumbersome and inconvenient for a client to be reconfigured each time it moves into a different AP's cell.

Notice that each cell in Figure 5-9 has a unique BSSID, but both cells share one common SSID. Regardless of a client's location within the ESS, the SSID will remain the same but the client can always distinguish one AP from another.

In an ESS, a wireless client can associate with one AP while it is physically located near that AP. If the client later moves to a different location, it can associate with a different nearby AP automatically. Passing from one AP to another is called *roaming* and is covered in Chapter 6.

5

Independent Basic Service Set

Usually a wireless network leverages APs for organization, control, and scalability. Sometimes that is not possible or convenient in an impromptu situation. For example, two people who want to exchange electronic documents at a meeting, might not be able to find a BSS available or might want to avoid having to authenticate to a production network. In addition, many personal printers have the capability to print documents wirelessly, without relying on a regular BSS or AP.

The 802.11 standard allows two or more wireless clients to communicate directly with each other, with no other means of network connectivity. This is known as an *ad hoc* wireless network, or an *independent basic service set* (IBSS), as shown in Figure 5-10. For this to work, one of the devices must take the lead and begin advertising a network name and the necessary radio parameters. Any other device can then join as needed. IBSSs are meant to be organized in an impromptu, distributed fashion; therefore, they do not scale well beyond eight to ten devices.

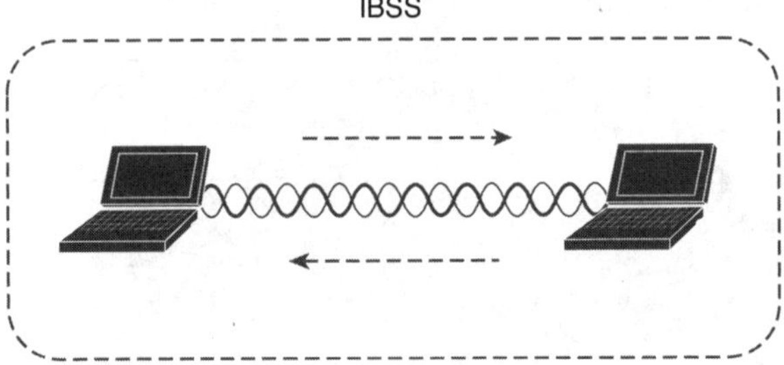

Figure 5-10 *802.11 Independent Basic Service Set*

Other Wireless Topologies

Wireless APs can be configured to operate in noninfrastructure modes when a normal BSS cannot provide the functionality that is needed. The following sections cover the most common modes.

Repeater

Normally, each AP in a wireless network has a wired connection back to the DS or switched infrastructure. To extend wireless coverage, additional APs and their wired connections are added. In some scenarios, it is not possible to run a wired connection to a new AP because the cable distance is too great to support Ethernet communication.

In that case, you can add an additional AP that is configured for *repeater mode*. A wireless repeater takes the signal it receives and repeats or retransmits it. The idea is to move the repeater out away from the AP so that it is still within range of both the AP and the distant client, as shown in Figure 5-11.

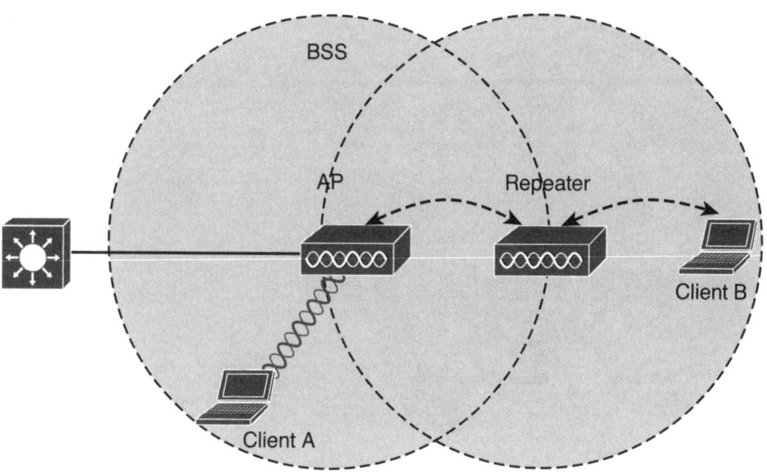

Figure 5-11 *Extending the Range of an AP with a Wireless Repeater*

5

If the repeater has a single radio, there is a possibility that the AP's signal will be received and retransmitted by the repeater, only to be received again by the AP—halving the effective throughput. As a remedy, some repeaters can use two radios to keep the original and repeated signals isolated. One radio is dedicated to signals in the AP's cell, while the other radio is dedicated to signals in the repeater's own cell.

Workgroup Bridge

Suppose you have a device that supports a wired Ethernet link but is not capable of having a wireless connection. You can use a workgroup bridge (WGB) to connect the device's wired network adapter to a wireless network.

Rather than providing a BSS for wireless service, a WGB becomes a wireless client of a BSS. In effect, the WGB acts as an external wireless network adapter for a device that has none. In Figure 5-12, an AP provides a BSS; Client A is a regular wireless client, while Client B is associated with the AP through a WGB.

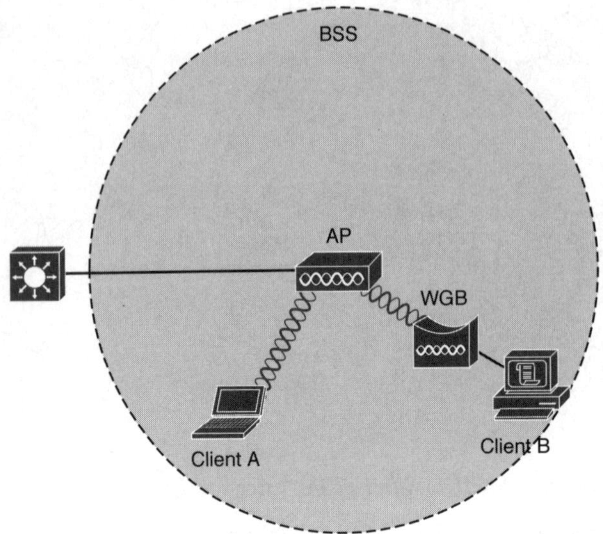

Figure 5-12 *Nonwireless Device Connecting Through a Workgroup Bridge*

You might encounter two types of workgroup bridges:

- **Universal workgroup bridge (uWGB)**—A single wired device can be bridged to a wireless network.
- **Workgroup bridge (WGB)**—A Cisco-proprietary implementation that allows multiple wired devices to be bridged to a wireless network.

Outdoor Bridge

An AP can be configured to act as a bridge to form a single wireless link from one LAN to another over a long distance. Outdoor bridged links are commonly used for connectivity between buildings or between cities.

If the LANs at two locations need to be bridged, a point-to-point bridged link can be used. One bridge mode AP is needed on each end of the wireless link. Directional antennas are normally used with the bridges to maximize the link distance, as shown in Figure 5-13.

Figure 5-13 *Point-to-Point Outdoor Bridge*

Sometimes the LANs at multiple sites need to be bridged. A point-to-multipoint bridged link allows a central site to be bridged to several other sites. The central site bridge is connected to an omnidirectional antenna so that its signal can reach the other sites simultaneously. The bridges at each of the other sites can be connected to a directional antenna aimed at the central site. Figure 5-14 shows the point-to-multipoint scenario.

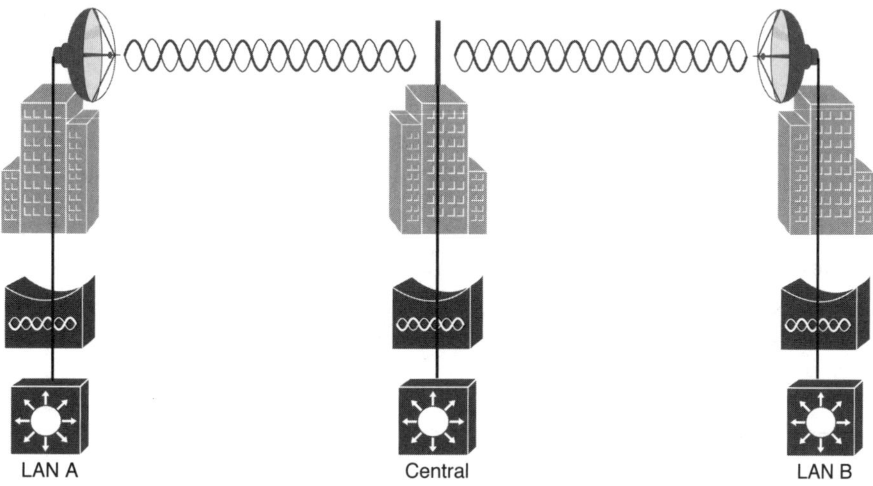

Figure 5-14 *Point-to-Multipoint Outdoor Bridge*

Mesh Network

To provide wireless coverage over a large area, it is not always practical to run Ethernet cabling to every AP that is needed. Instead, you could use multiple APs configured in mesh mode. In a mesh topology, traffic is bridged from AP to AP, in a daisy-chain fashion.

Mesh APs can leverage dual radios—one in the 2.4-GHz band and one in the 5-GHz band. Each mesh AP usually maintains a BSS on a 2.4-GHz channel, with which wireless clients can associate. Client traffic is then usually bridged from AP to AP over 5-GHz channels as a backhaul network. At the edge of the mesh network, the backhaul traffic is bridged to the wired LAN infrastructure. Figure 5-15 shows a typical mesh network. With Cisco APs, you can build a mesh network indoors or outdoors. The mesh network runs its own dynamic routing protocol to work out the best path for backhaul traffic to take across the mesh APs.

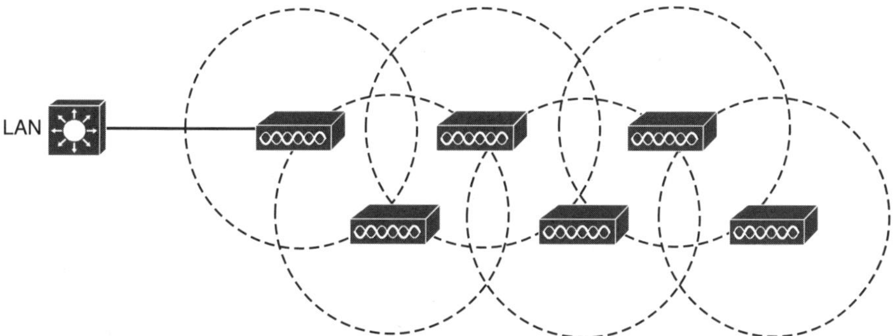

Figure 5-15 *Typical Wireless Mesh Network*

Exam Preparation Tasks

As mentioned in the section, "How to Use This Book," in the Introduction, you have a couple of choices for exam preparation: the exercises here, Chapter 21, "Final Review," and the exam simulation questions on the DVD.

Review All Key Topics

Review the most important topics in this chapter, noted with the Key Topic icon in the outer margin of the page. Table 5-2 lists a reference of these key topics and the page numbers on which each is found.

Table 5-2 Key Topics for Chapter 5

Key Topic Element	Description	Page Number
Figure 5-5	Basic service set	117
Figure 5-8	Multiple SSIDs	120
Figure 5-9	Extended service set	121
Figure 5-12	Workgroup bridge	124
Figure 5-13	Point-to-point bridge	124
Figure 5-15	Mesh network	125

Define Key Terms

Define the following key terms from this chapter and check your answers in the glossary:

access point (AP), ad hoc network, basic service set (BSS), basic service set identifier (BSSID), cell, distribution system (DS), extended service set (ESS), independent basic service set (IBSS), infrastructure mode, mesh network, point-to-point bridge, repeater, roaming, service set identifier (SSID), station (STA), workgroup bridge (WGB)

This chapter covers the following topics:

- **802.11 Frame Format**—This section describes the basic format of wireless LAN frames and the addressing fields they contain.
- **Accessing the Wireless Medium**—This section explains the mechanisms that wireless devices must use to contend for use of a channel when transmitting.
- **802.11 Frame Types**—This section discusses the three basic types of 802.11 frames and their use.
- **Client Housekeeping**—This section discusses many common operations between a wireless client and an access point, based on 802.11 management frames.

This chapter covers the following exam topics:

- 2.3—Describe 802.11 fundamentals
  - 2.3e—Frame types
    - 2.3e(i)—Management
    - 2.3e(ii)—Control
    - 2.3e(iii)—Data

CHAPTER 6

Understanding 802.11 Frame Types

Wireless networks based on the 802.11 standard operate in a very organized and controlled fashion. The standard defines the frame format and frame types that access points (APs) and clients must use to communicate successfully. Before a device transmits on a channel, it must cooperate with all other devices and contend for use of the channel. This chapter covers these topics and the choreography that occurs between an AP and its clients.

"Do I Know This Already?" Quiz

The "Do I Know This Already?" quiz allows you to assess whether you should read this entire chapter thoroughly or jump to the "Exam Preparation Tasks" section. If you are in doubt about your answers to these questions or your own assessment of your knowledge of the topics, read the entire chapter. Table 6-1 lists the major headings in this chapter and their corresponding "Do I Know This Already?" quiz questions. You can find the answers in Appendix A, "Answers to the 'Do I Know This Already?' Quizzes."

Table 6-1 "Do I Know This Already?" Section-to-Question Mapping

Foundation Topics Section	Questions
802.11 Frame Format	1–3
Accessing the Wireless Medium	4–6
802.11 Frame Types	7–8
Client Housekeeping	9–12

Caution The goal of self-assessment is to gauge your mastery of the topics in this chapter. If you do not know the answer to a question or are only partially sure of the answer, you should mark that question as wrong for purposes of the self-assessment. Giving yourself credit for an answer you correctly guess skews your self-assessment results and might provide you with a false sense of security.

1. Which one of the following is the maximum number of address fields defined in an 802.11 frame header?
   a. 1
   b. 2
   c. 3
   d. 4
2. Every 802.11 frame contains 2 flag bits that designate whether the frame is headed to or from which one of the following?
   a. The AP
   b. The DS
   c. The BSS
   d. The ESS
3. The Address1 field in an 802.11 frame always contains which one of the following?
   a. The transmitter address (TA)
   b. The BSSID
   c. The AP's base radio MAC address
   d. The receiver address (RA)
4. To access a wireless channel, 802.11 devices participate in which one of the following?
   a. DCF
   b. GCF
   c. LCM
   d. BSD
5. A wireless client maintains a NAV value that is used for which one of the following purposes?
   a. To navigate the frame through the ESS
   b. To identify the MAC address of the next client to transmit
   c. To predict when the channel might become free
   d. To set the priority of the client's ability to transmit
6. Which one of the following specifies the default amount of time between successive 802.11 data frames?
   a. CCA
   b. IBSS
   c. SIFS
   d. DIFS

7. Which one of the following is the frame type sent to discover APs within the signal range of a wireless client?
   a. Scan
   b. Probe
   c. Beacon
   d. Discovery

8. An ACK frame is an example of which one of the following 802.11 frame types?
   a. Management
   b. Control
   c. Administration
   d. Data

9. A wireless AP advertises mandatory data rates of 1, 2, 5.5, and 11 Mbps. Which of the following represent client data rates that can successfully join the BSS? (Choose all that apply.)
   a. Mandatory: 1 Mbps, Supported: 2, 5.5, 11 Mbps
   b. Mandatory: 2 Mbps, Supported: 1, 5.5, 11 Mbps
   c. Mandatory: 1 Mbps, Supported: None
   d. Mandatory: 5, 11 Mbps; Supported: None

10. In a passive scan, a wireless client uses which one of the following methods to discover nearby APs?
    a. Beacons
    b. Probe requests
    c. ACKs
    d. Discovers

11. When a client attempts to join a BSS, which one of the following frame types is sent first?
    a. Beacon
    b. Rate request
    c. Association request
    d. Authentication request

12. Which one of the following frame types does a client use to roam seamlessly from one BSS to another, within the same ESS and the same SSID?
    a. Association request
    b. Disassociation
    c. Reassociation
    d. Roam request

Foundation Topics

802.11 Frame Format

To understand more about 802.11 frames and how they are transported, it might be useful to compare them with the familiar 802.3 frames.

Ethernet devices based on IEEE 802.3 send and receive frames in the format shown in Figure 6-1. The sender and the intended recipient of a frame are identified by two MAC addresses—a source and a destination. The source address is not used to deliver the frame; rather, it is used for any return traffic that is sent back to the source. When the recipient receives a frame that has its own MAC address as the destination, the frame is then accepted and processed.

Preamble	Destination Address	Source Address	Type	Data	FCS
8 Bytes	6 Bytes	6 Bytes	2 Bytes	46–1500 Bytes	4 Bytes

Figure 6-1 *IEEE 802.3 Ethernet Frame Format*

Suppose that the source and destination hosts are connected by a switched network, as shown in Figure 6-2. The switch that connects the two hosts forwards frames between them as needed, but it does not intervene or actively participate in the exchange. In other words, neither host has to be aware of the switch's existence at all. Frames enter and exit a switch simply because hosts are connected to it through wires or cables. The switch silently forwards the frames based on the destination MAC addresses and the device locations it has learned from the source MAC addresses.

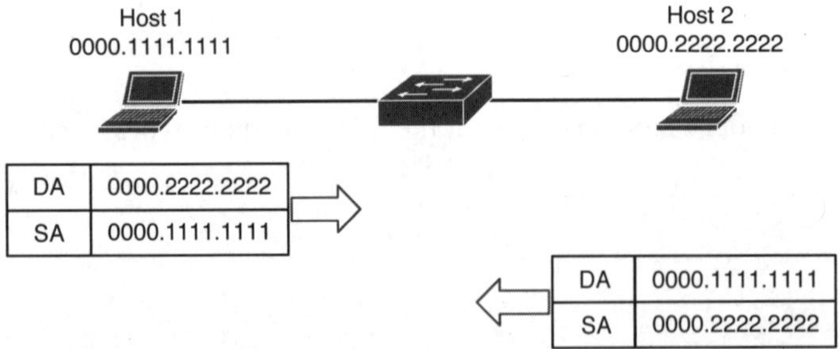

Figure 6-2 *Forwarding 802.3 Frames in a Switched Network*

In contrast, the APs in an 802.11 network are active participants. Recall from Chapter 5, "Wireless LAN Topologies," that an AP acts as the central "hub" or manager of a basic service set (BSS). With the absence of wired connections, a client must join or associate with a specific wireless network by first getting permission from the AP. Then the client must send and receive every frame through the AP or coordinate with the AP for direct client-to-client communication to use 802.11z, Extensions to Direct Link Setup (DLS).

IEEE 802.11 networks are based on traditional MAC addresses. Each client's radio interface must have a unique MAC address so that frames can be sent from and received to that address. To direct frames through an AP, the AP must also have a MAC address of its own. Wireless clients know the AP's address as the BSS identifier (BSSID), which must be included in each frame sent to the AP.

Figure 6-3 shows the basic format of 802.11 frames at the MAC layer, which can carry a maximum payload of 2304 bytes in length. The frame begins with a 2-byte Frame Control field, which identifies such things as the frame type and the direction in which the frame is traveling as it moves from one wireless device to another.

Tip The 802.11n and 802.11ac amendments allow frames to be aggregated and sent as a single unit, to reduce overhead and increase throughput.

Frame Control	Duration /ID	Address1	Address2	Address3	Sequence Control	Address4	Data	FCS
2 Bytes	2 Bytes	6 Bytes	6 Bytes	6 Bytes	2 Bytes	6 Bytes	0–2304 Bytes	4 Bytes

Protocol Version	Type	Subtype	To DS	From DS	More Frag	Retry	Pwr Mgmt	More Data	WEP	Order
Bits: 2	2	4	1	1	1	1	1	1	1	1

Figure 6-3 *IEEE 802.11 Frame Format*

Consider a common scenario where several wireless clients are associated with an AP. This is not a standalone BSS—the AP also connects to an upstream distribution system (DS). Most of the time, wireless frames pass through the AP, either coming from clients toward the DS or coming from the DS toward the clients. Frame motion is indicated by 2 bits, *To DS* and *From DS*, contained in the 802.11 frame header. On the surface, it seems that frames travel in only one of two directions, relative to the DS, as shown in the simple examples of Figure 6-4.

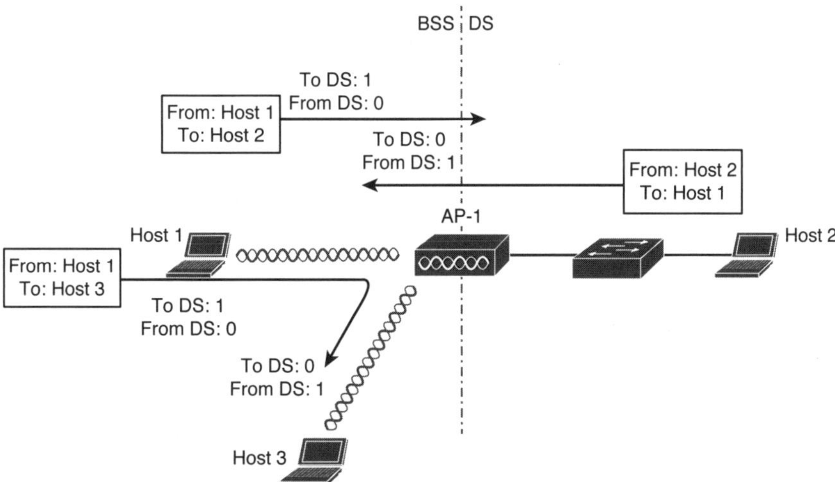

Figure 6-4 *Some Example 802.11 Frames Moving to and from the DS*

With just two frame directions to indicate, a single bit would suffice. Why are there two different direction bits in the frame header? There are two other special cases where frames are destined for something other than a specific wireless client or somewhere in the DS, as shown in Figure 6-5. This gives a total of four possible destinations, or 2 bits' worth of direction values.

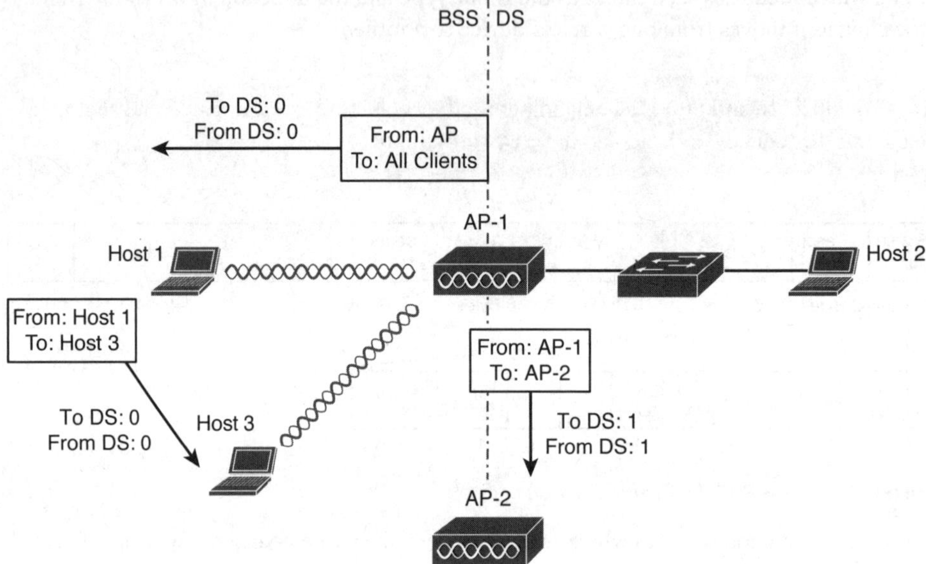

Figure 6-5 *Examples of 802.1.1 Frames That Are Not Moving to and from the DS*

One special case commonly occurs when a frame is sourced or destined from a location that cannot be clearly defined in relation to the DS. In the following examples, both the To DS and From DS bits are set to 0:

- An AP sends a management or control frame, which is broadcast to all wireless clients in the BSS. The AP, and not the DS, is the source of the frame.
- A client sends a management frame to an AP, such that the AP itself is the destination.
- One client sends a frame directly to another client via DLS. The frame is not destined for the AP or the DS.

The other special case is related to mesh AP networks, where frames are relayed from AP to AP over wireless backhaul links. A backhaul link is neither in the BSS nor in the DS, so both direction bits are set to 1.

802.11 Frame Addressing

From an addressing viewpoint, an 802.11 frame header can contain up to four different address fields. In Figure 6-3, you can see them listed with the rather generic names Address1 through Address4. Wireless frames are always sent from a transmitting device to a receiving device. Therefore, each frame header must contain a transmitter address (TA) and a receiver address (RA). The Address1 field always contains the RA, though its exact contents may vary depending on where the frame is headed. Likewise, Address2 always contains the TA.

Address3 contains the final destination address (DA) when the RA is not the final recipient. For example, when a wireless client sends a frame to a destination on the DS, the frame is transmitted from the client's wireless adapter, is received by the AP, but still needs to be forwarded on to the final destination on the DS. Likewise, Address3 can contain the original source address (SA) when the TA is not the originator. Consider a frame sent from a device on the DS to a wireless client. When the frame is sent over the wireless medium, the AP's radio is the transmitter address, but the AP did not originate the frame—a device on the DS did.

Address4 is not present in the frame unless the frame is being transported from one AP to another AP across a wireless link. In that case, the frame has to carry the original SA and DA, in addition to the MAC addresses of a receiver (RA) and transmitter (TA)—the APs relaying the frame over the air.

Table 6-2 lists the possible combinations of frame direction bits, along with the four address field contents. You should become familiar with frame addressing, as the CCNA Wireless exam may cover it. Try to break the table down into parts. First, get comfortable with the To/From DS bits and the reasons behind the frame directions. Next, think about what happens to a frame each step along the way as it travels from its source to its destination. Does it stop at the AP? Does the AP relay it to or from a more distant location? Remember that Address1 and Address2 are always the receiver and transmitter MAC addresses, respectively. Address3 will contain the address of an additional hop, if one is needed.

6

Table 6-2 802.11 Frame Header Direction and Addressing

	To DS	From DS	Address1	Address2	Address3	Address4
Management, control, or DLS	0	0	RA	TA	BSSID	
DS to client	0	1	RA	BSSID	SA or BSSID	
Client to DS	1	0	BSSID	TA	DA or BSSID	
Wireless bridge or mesh	1	1	RA	TA	DA or BSSID	SA or BSSID

Figure 6-6 shows two example frames and their address fields. Frame1 at the top is being sent from Host1 to Host2, while Frame2 at the bottom is coming from Host2 to Host1. Fictitious MAC addresses are used for clarity.

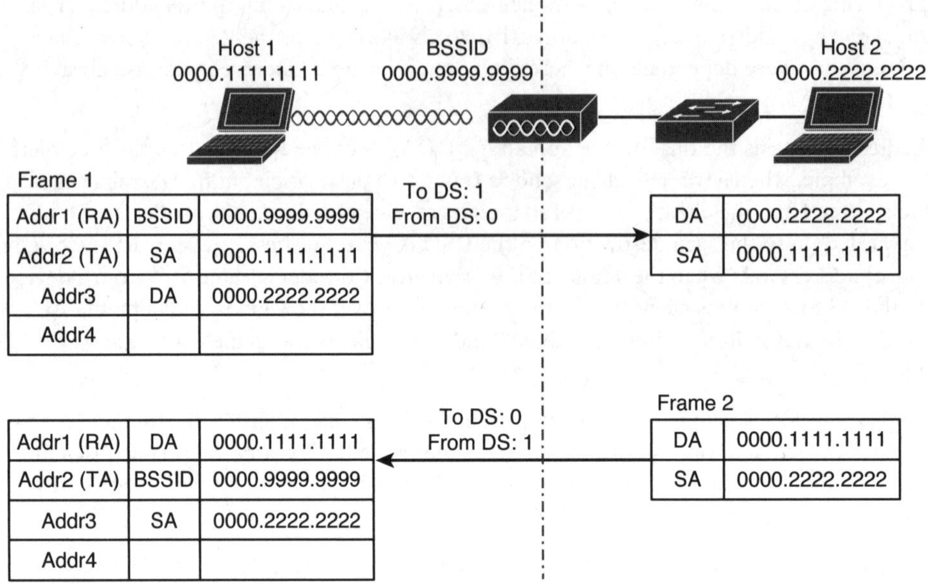

Figure 6-6 *Examples of 802.11 Frame Addressing*

Host1 is sending the frame through the AP to the DS, so the Address1 (RA) contains the BSSID 0000.9999.9999. Frame1 is sourced or transmitted by Host1, so the Address2 (TA) field contains Host1's MAC address, 0000.1111.1111. The frame must pass through the AP, so Host1 populates Address3 with the destination address of Host2, 0000.2222.2222. Once the AP receives Frame1, it finds that Host2 is located on the DS, so the wireless frame is converted into an 802.3 wired frame. The original source and destination addresses are copied into the new frame so that it can be forwarded on to Host2.

On the return trip, Host2 fills in the source and destination addresses of Frame2 in 802.3 format. The switch forwards the frame to the AP, which knows that the destination (Host1) is located within the wireless BSS. The AP populates Address1 (RA) with the destination address of Host1. The AP is transmitting the frame, so Address2 (TA) contains the BSSID. The address of the original source, Host2, is copied into the Address3 field.

Accessing the Wireless Medium

Once a wireless device has data to send, it must access the network medium and try to send it. Remember that a wireless channel is a shared medium and that every device trying to use it must share the airtime and contend for its use. There is no centralized function that coordinates the use of a wireless channel. Instead, this effort is distributed to each device that uses a channel. This is known as a *distributed coordination function* (DCF).

With a shared medium, such as wired Ethernet or wireless, two or more stations transmitting at the same time can cause collisions. A collision ruins the transmitted data, wastes time on the medium, and causes the data to be retransmitted—wasting even more time. When full-duplex operation isn't possible, some collisions are inevitable; therefore, every device should make its best attempt to mitigate and/or hopefully prevent collisions in the first place.

Carrier Sense

Devices based on the 802.3 and 802.11 standards must use the carrier sense multiple access (CSMA) technique to determine if the media is available before transmitting. Wired devices are able to sense an electrical signal on the wire to detect a transmission already in progress. Wireless devices can use a two-fold process to detect a channel in use:

- **Physical carrier sense**—When a wireless client is not transmitting, it can listen to the channel to overhear any other transmissions that might be occurring. In the case of an 802.11n or 802.11ac device, a high-bandwidth frame may involve multiple channels simultaneously, so any secondary channels must also be checked. If it overhears a frame that is destined for its own MAC address, then it receives the frame for processing. Otherwise, if a transmission is detected but the client cannot read the transmitter's MAC address in the header, the client decides that the channel is busy. This process is also known as *clear channel assessment* (CCA). While CCA is effective, it isn't a proactive approach and must be used in conjunction with other methods.
- **Virtual carrier sense**—When a wireless client transmits a frame, it must include a duration field in the Duration/ID frame header field. The duration indicates how much time is required for the whole frame, plus an interframe gap, plus a return ACK frame, to be sent over the channel. This effectively reserves the channel for that length of time. As long as other wireless clients can overhear a frame and its header, they can predict how long they should wait for the frame to complete. Figure 6-7 depicts the frame duration field and its relationship to the frame length in time.

Key Topic

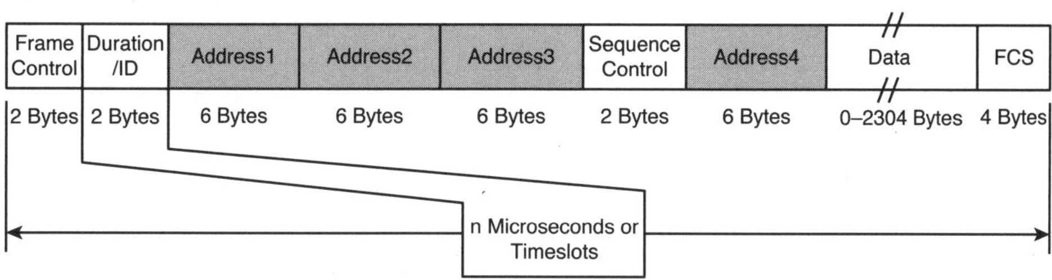

Figure 6-7 *802.11 Frame Duration Field*

Each wireless client must maintain a *network allocation vector* (NAV) timer that is used to predict when the channel will become free. Each time a frame is overheard on the channel, its Duration value is loaded into the NAV. The NAV timer then counts down while the client waits to transmit.

The NAV timer must be at zero before a client can contend for use of the channel. That sounds simple, but the contention process is still a bit more complex. Sensing the carrier alone can alert a client when the medium is quiet and available—except that every client on the channel will come to the same conclusion at the same time! If multiple clients have frames to transmit and all decide that the channel is free at the same time, collisions are still likely.

Collision Avoidance

The 802.3 and 802.11 standards differ when it comes to dealing with collisions. Wired devices can *detect* collisions in real time so that they can back off and wait a random time to try again. This is known as CSMA/CD (collision detection).

Wireless devices always operate in half-duplex mode, which prevents a client from receiving signals on a channel while it is transmitting. This means that a transmitting wireless client can't detect when a collision occurs at all. Therefore, 802.11 devices must try to *avoid* collisions in the first place, resulting in the CSMA/CA (collision avoidance) scheme.

Wireless clients avoid collisions by backing off and waiting a random time *before* transmitting. Here, time is measured in two ways: by *timeslot*, a counting tempo at regular intervals, and by a unit called the SIFS, which is defined later in this section. If a client has a frame to transmit, it must wait until the channel is quiet, then it chooses a random number (0 to 31) of timeslots to use as a *backoff timer*. If there are multiple clients with frames ready to transmit, their random backoff timer values will lessen the likelihood that they will contend to use a channel at the same time. In fact, the range of random timer values is called the *contention window*.

If the channel becomes busy before the backoff timer reaches zero, the timer is paused and the overheard frame duration value is added to the NAV. The waiting client can transmit only when every timer mechanism has expired and the channel is available.

Believe it or not, there is one more timing scheme that controls frame transmission. The 802.11 standard defines a few different *interframe space* periods that provide a safety cushion between frames. These periods of silence give the channel enough time for signals to dampen out—especially when multipath is involved and some reflected copies take longer to propagate than others.

Several different interframe space periods are used, according to the type and priority of the frame being transmitted:

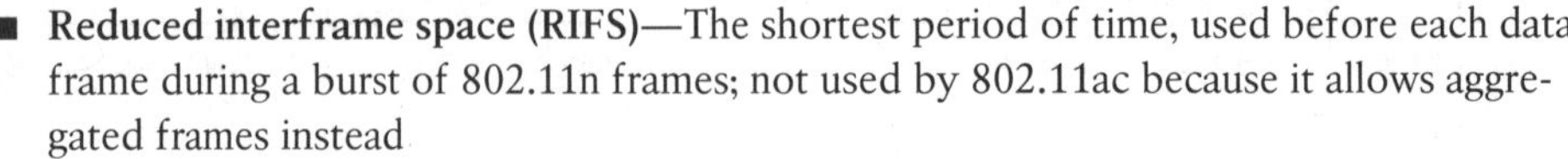

- **Reduced interframe space (RIFS)**—The shortest period of time, used before each data frame during a burst of 802.11n frames; not used by 802.11ac because it allows aggregated frames instead
- **Short interframe space (SIFS)**—Used between data frames and frame acknowledgements or CTS 802.11g protection mode control frames
- **Distributed interframe space (DIFS)**—The default period used after most standard priority frame types
- **Extended interframe space (EIFS)**—The longest period of time, used after collisions and before retransmitted frames

Tip If you feel confused about all the timer mechanisms, try to remember this simple rule. Before a device can transmit on a channel, it must do the following:

1. Wait until the channel is quiet for a DIFS period.
2. Choose a random number and count down the backoff timer.
3. Listen during the countdown; stop counting if another station's transmission is heard; resume counting after the channel has been quiet for a DIFS period.
4. Once the countdown reaches zero and the channel is clear, the client may transmit.

Assuming all of the carrier sense and collision avoidance methods have worked, how does a transmitting client know that the frame it just sent arrived in good condition? During transmission, the receiver must be off, so there is no way to listen to the channel. Instead, every client must rely on a very rudimentary feedback mechanism. Each time a client receives a unicast frame, it must send a unicast acknowledgement frame back to the sender. The 802.11 standard requires this one-to-one response for every frame received, except in the case of 802.11n, 802.11ac, and 802.11e (WMM) blocks of frames, which require one acknowledgement for a whole block of frames.

If a transmitted frame fails and is not acknowledged, the sending client must try again by retransmitting the frame. The client chooses a new backoff timer value from a contention window that is double the previous range. In effect, this relaxes the conditions on the channel to give the retransmitted frame a better chance of surviving. With every failed attempt, the contention window is doubled, up to a maximum of 1023 timeslots.

Figure 6-8 shows an example of the DCF operation within a wireless cell.

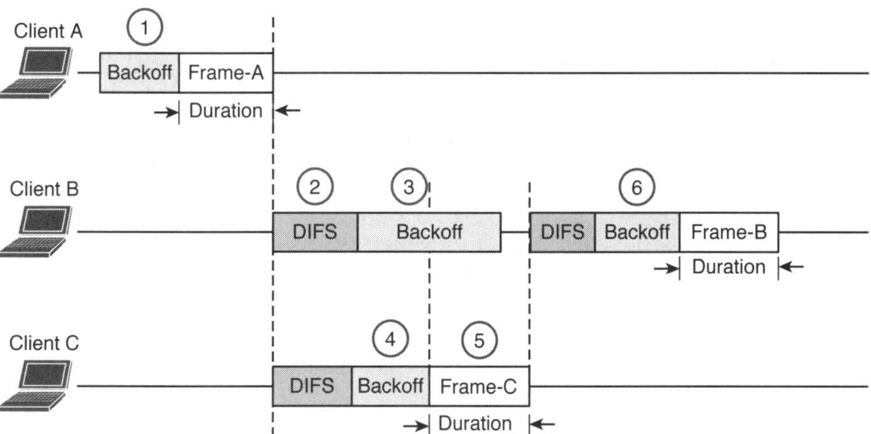

Figure 6-8 *Avoiding Collisions with the DCF Process*

The following sequence of events occurs:

1. Client A has been waiting at least a DIFS period and determines that no other devices are transmitting. Client A waits a random backoff timer period before transmitting Frame-A. The frame's duration is advertised in the header's duration field.
2. Client B has a frame to transmit. It must wait until Client A's frame is completed and then wait until a DIFS period has expired.
3. Client B waits a random backoff time before attempting to transmit.
4. While Client B is waiting, Client C has a frame to transmit. Like Client B, Client C must wait until the DIFS period after Client A's transmission has elapsed. Client C then listens and detects that no one else is transmitting. It then waits a random backoff time that is shorter than Client B's backoff timer.
5. Client C transmits a frame and advertises the frame duration in the duration field.
6. Client B must now wait the duration of Client C's frame plus a DIFS period plus the remainder of its own backoff timer before attempting to transmit.

802.11 Frame Types

The 802.11 standard defines three different frame types that can be used:

- Management frames
- Control frames
- Data frames

The frame type is identified by a 2-bit Type field and a 4-bit SubType field in the Frame Control portion of the header. This implies that each of the three frame types can have several different subtypes that perform various functions. The frame types and their most common subtypes are discussed in the following sections.

Management Frames

Management frames are used to advertise a BSS and its capabilities and to manage clients as they join or leave the BSS. For example, 802.11ac management frames include very high throughput (VHT) capabilities such as channel width, guard interval, beamforming, and MCS support. Management frames are also used to manage clients as they join or leave the BSS. A client must first locate a candidate BSS to join, authenticate itself to an AP, and associate itself with the BSS.

Although there are 14 different management frame subtypes available, you should become familiar with just the following for the CCNA Wireless exam:

- **Beacon**—The AP broadcasts this frame to advertise the BSS, the data rates necessary and allowed in the BSS, an optional security set identifier (SSID) string, and vendor-specific information when necessary. Beacons are sent to any and all devices in the BSA about ten times per second (100-ms intervals). If the AP supports multiple SSIDs, a different beacon is broadcast for each SSID.

  A wireless device can learn about BSSs within range by listening to the beacons that are received. This is known as *passive scanning*.
- **Probe**—A wireless device can send probe request frames to ask any APs within range or a specific AP to provide information about their BSSs. An AP answers by sending a probe response that contains most of the beacon information. Probing for BSS information is known as *active scanning*.
- **Authentication and deauthentication**—To join a BSS, a wireless device must first send an authentication request frame to an AP. The AP can support either *Open System authentication*, where any valid 802.11 device is authenticated without any other sort of verification, or *shared key authentication*, where a valid 802.11 device must exchange a Wired Equivalent Privacy (WEP) key that matches the key used by the AP. The AP sends the result of the authentication in an authentication response frame.

  If a device wants to leave the authenticated state, it can send a deauthentication frame to the AP. However, the AP can force a device out of the authenticated state by sending it a deauthentication frame.

Tip It might seem odd that Open System and WEP are the only two authentication methods offered in authentication request frames. The intent is to simply screen devices to make sure they are 802.11 compliant. Beyond that, wireless networks can offer robust authentication methods through a different method of frame exchanges. Those methods are covered in Chapter 14, "Wireless Security Fundamentals."

- **Association, disassociation, and reassociation**—Once a device is authenticated, it can send an association request frame to the AP to ask permission to join the BSS. If the device supports compatible parameters and is allowed to join, then the AP will reply with an association response frame, along with a unique association identifier (AID) for that client.

  If a device wants to gracefully leave a BSS, it can send a disassociation frame to the AP. An AP can also decide to drop a client by sending it a disassociation frame.

  When a client wants to leave one BSS for another, while staying within the same SSID, it can send a reassociation request frame to the new AP. In effect, the client is attempting to reassociate with the SSID, not an AP. The new AP responds with a reassociation response frame. (Moving from one BSS to another is covered in greater detail in Chapter 12, "Understanding Roaming.")
- **Action**—An action frame provides a way to communicate an extended management action to be taken. For example, in the 802.11k amendment, a wireless station can use action frames to request radio measurement information from other devices, as well as a report of neighboring APs to make its roaming decisions more efficient. The 802.11v amendment uses action frames to allow network-assisted client power savings. The 802.11y amendment leverages action frames to allow an AP to announce an impending channel change or channel width change to its associated clients.

Control Frames

Control frames are used to gain control of and to help deliver data over a channel. Control frames contain only frame header information and no data payload. There are nine different control frames possible. Be familiar with the following four:

- **ACK**—A short frame that is sent as an acknowledgment of a unicast frame that has been received.
- **Block ACK**—A short frame that is sent as an acknowledgment of a burst of frames sent as a single block of data.
- **PS-Poll (Power Save Poll)**—A frame sent from a client to an AP to request the next frame that was buffered while the client's radio was powered down.
- **RTS/CTS**—Frames that are used to reserve a channel. RTS/CTS frames carry a Duration value that reserves the channel airtime for the frame they are protecting. RTS/CTS frames may also be used to help avoid collisions between clients that cannot hear each other because of the distance between them. When clients cannot hear each other, they also cannot hear the Duration values or detect a carrier to know when to cease transmitting. As long as the clients can hear the AP when it sends RTS/CTS frames, they can remain silent while others are transmitting.

In contrast, RTS and CTS frames are not needed for hidden nodes or backward compatibility with 802.11ac. This is because all devices on the 5-GHz band use OFDM, so 802.11a, 802.11n, and 802.11ac stations can all understand the same frame header information. Instead, RTS and CTS frames are used with 802.11ac to reserve channel space. Recall that the bandwidth can change on a frame-by-frame basis—one frame may require a 20-MHz channel, while the next frame may require 80 MHz or 160 MHz. The RTS and CTS frames are duplicated and sent on each secondary channel that makes up the appropriate bandwidth to signal that those channels are needed and are free to be used for a frame.

Data Frames

Data is sent to and from clients in data frames. A data frame contains up to four address fields that identify the sender and recipient and identify the BSSID and any wireless link involved with forwarding the frame. The 802.11 standard defines 15 different data frame subtypes, but you should just be aware of a generic data frame and its addressing mechanism.

Client Housekeeping

Recall from Chapter 1, "RF Signals and Modulation," that a client and an AP have to use the same modulation and coding scheme (MCS) to successfully communicate. The scheme can be changed dynamically, if needed, as long as both ends agree on the choice. The MCS directly affects the data rate between the client and the AP.

An AP is configured with a set of data rates that it can use. Each data rate can be set to one of the following states:

- **Disabled**—The AP will not use the data rate for any client communication.
- **Supported**—The AP can use the data rate if a client also supports its use, but the client is not required to support it.
- **Mandatory**—The AP can use the data rate and expects every client to support it. This is also known as an 802.11 *BSS basic rate*.

At least one data rate must be mandatory to provide a common rate that can be used for management and control frames. In fact, the AP will always send broadcast management frames using the lowest mandatory rate. The idea is to leverage a lower data rate to get better signal-to-noise ratio (SNR) and greater signal range to reliably manage client devices within the BSS.

Other data rates can be configured as supported. Normal data frames and unicast management frames will be sent at whatever supported rate is most optimal between the client and the AP. Acknowledgment frames are sent at the first mandatory rate that is below the current optimal data rate.

APs advertise their mandatory and supported data rates in each beacon frame so that potential clients can know what is available. By default, 802.11b/g/n radios are configured with 1-, 2-, 5.5-, and 11-Mbps data rates as mandatory; 802.11a/n/ac radios consider 6, 12, and 24 Mbps to be mandatory.

Before a wireless device can join a BSS, it must be satisfied that it can support the AP's list of advertised data rates. The device can then announce its own set of mandatory and supported data rates in an association request frame. The AP compares the client's list of data rates with its own. If the client can support all of the AP's mandatory rates, the client can take the next step to be associated with the BSS.

Wireless clients can be mobile and transient. The following sections describe how a wireless client and a BSS interact using management frames in a variety of common scenarios.

A Client Scans for APs

To join a BSS, a wireless device first has to scan its surroundings to look for any live APs that might offer network service. Beyond that, the device might need to build a list of SSIDs that are available. A device can scan the wireless horizon in two ways:

- **Passive scan**—The device simply listens for any beacon frames broadcast from nearby APs. Passive scanning has a couple of drawbacks: a device must wait until beacons are broadcast at the next interval, which might not be soon enough in a time critical situation; and beacons don't always contain specific SSID names, so a device cannot always depend on learning that a desired SSID exists on an AP.

  In Figure 6-9, Host-1 is able to receive beacons from AP-1 and AP-2. The beacon frames specify the BSSIDs and SSIDs that are offered, as well as supported data rates and other information about their BSSs.

6

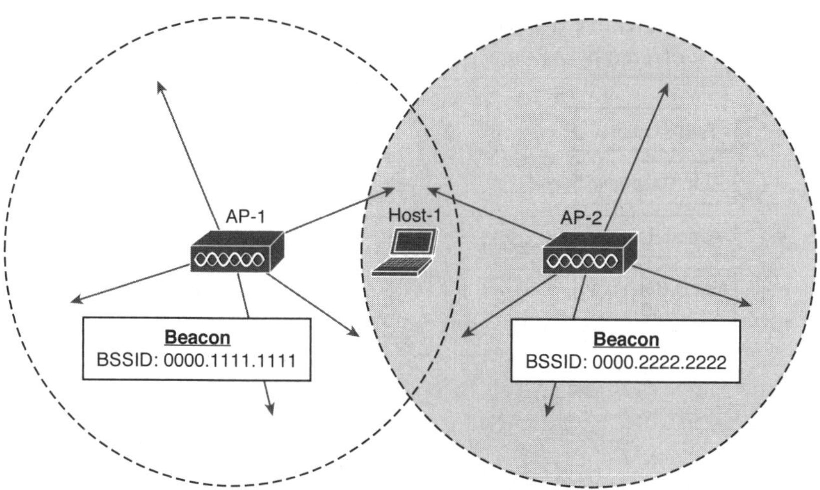

Figure 6-9 *Using a Passive Scan to Discover BSSs*

- **Active scan**—The device must take an active role and broadcast a probe request frame to ask any APs within range to identify themselves. The device can include a specific SSID name in the request. Any APs that receive the probe request must send a unicast probe response frame back to the device.

  In Figure 6-10, a device broadcasts a probe request to look for any APs that can offer the "guest" SSID. Both AP-1 and AP-2 receive the request and send probe responses containing their BSSIDs and other information about the BSS and SSID.

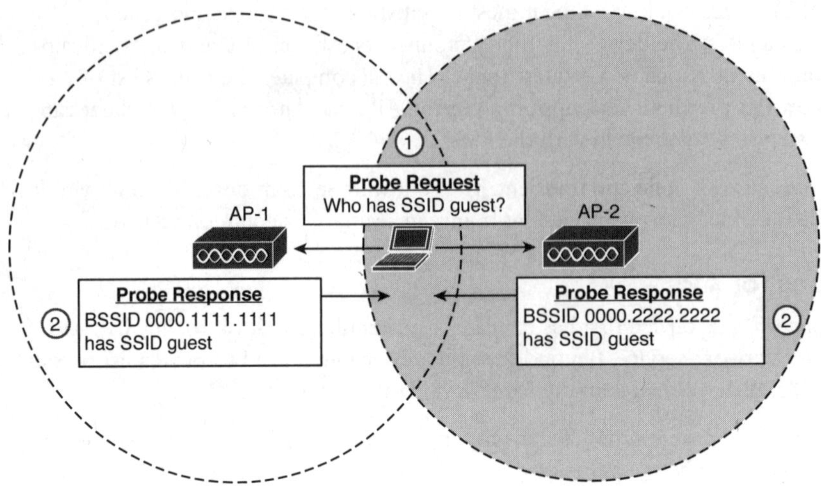

Figure 6-10 *Using an Active Scan to Discover BSSs*

A Client Joins a BSS

Suppose a wireless device is not currently joined to a wireless network. The device comes within range of two different APs that form a single ESS and offer a common SSID. The device performs an active scan and discovers the two APs. Through some algorithm, it decides that AP-1 is more preferable than AP-2. Figure 6-11 shows the steps that the device takes to join the network offered by AP-1.

Key Topic

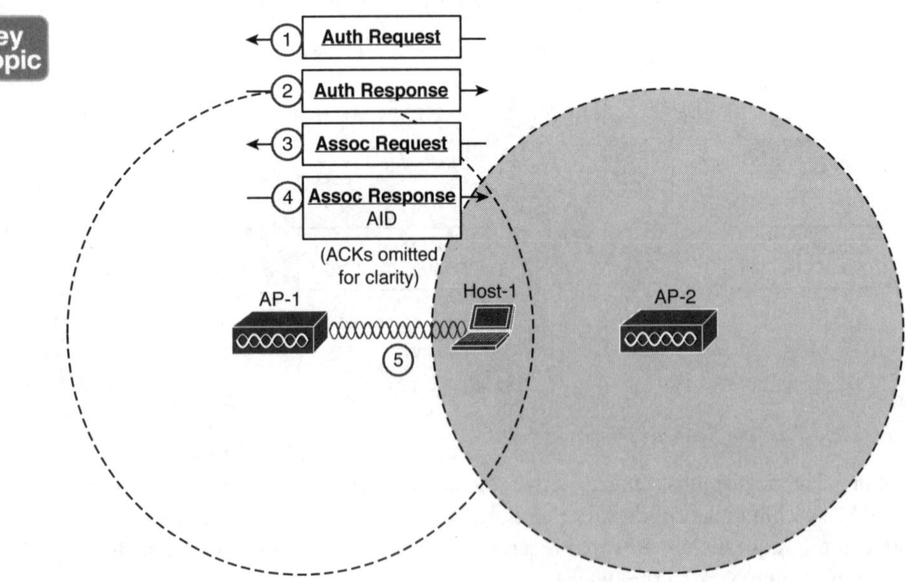

Figure 6-11 *Wireless Client Joining a BSS*

Step 1. Host-1 sends an authentication request frame to AP-1's BSSID address.

Step 2. If AP-1 is satisfied with the host's identity, it sends an authentication response frame back to Host-1.

Step 3. Now that Host-1 is known to the AP, it must ask for BSS membership by sending an association request frame to AP-1. Host-1 includes a list of its 802.11 capabilities, the SSID it wants to join, a list of data rates and channels it supports, and any parameters that are needed to secure the wireless link to the AP.

Step 4. If the AP is satisfied with the request, it sends an association response frame back to Host-1.

Step 5. The response also contains the AID that uniquely identifies Host-1 as an associated client. In effect, the AID is Host-1's membership card while it remains a part of the BSS.

A Client Leaves a BSS

Once a wireless device successfully becomes a client of a BSS, it keeps that relationship with the AP until something happens to remove it. For example, a wireless client might be removed if it violates a security policy, is recognized as a rogue device, has a session that stays idle for too long, and so on.

A client can be removed from a BSS if the AP sends it a disassociation or a deauthentication frame. If a client is disassociated, it loses only its associated status but is still authenticated. To rejoin the BSS, the client can simply reassociate. Deauthentication is a bit more drastic. Once that happens, the device must start the whole authentication and association process over again. In Figure 6-12, Client-A has been forced to leave the BSS through either disassociation or deauthentication.

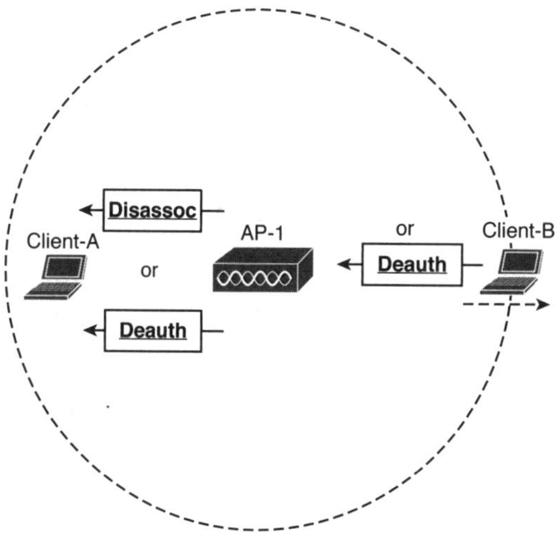

Figure 6-12 *Disassociating and Deauthenticating—Two Ways to Leave a BSS*

A client can gracefully remove itself from a BSS, when needed. To do this, the client simply notifies the AP by sending it a deauthentication frame. In Figure 6-12, Client-B has sent a deauthentication frame for itself to AP-1.

What happens if a client physically leaves a BSS without informing the AP? For example, suppose Client-B in Figure 6-12 reaches the edge of AP-1's cell, but does not send a deauthentication frame? Once it goes outside the cell range, the AP might not even notice. Even before it leaves the cell, the client might just go into sleep mode and stop communicating with the AP altogether. In this case, the AP maintains the AID entry for the device, in case it returns to the cell or wakes up, but only for a certain amount of time. Cisco APs age out unresponsive clients after 5 minutes. In case the client is still listening, the AP also sends a deauthentication frame to it.

A Client Moves Between BSSs

When a wireless client is within range of several APs, it must choose to associate with only one of them. A client can join only one BSS at any given time. If the client changes its location, it might stay within its original BSS or it might move out of range and into the cell of an adjacent BSS. Moving seamlessly from one BSS to another is called *roaming*.

The basic roaming process is not much different than finding and associating with a BSS, except that the client does this while it is actively associated with another BSS. To switch BSSs seamlessly, the client must recognize that it is nearing the cell boundary and that it needs to find other potential cells to move into before losing the signal completely.

Figure 6-13 illustrates the basic steps of the roaming process.

The wireless client begins with an active association with AP-1 using SSID "guest":

Step 1. Client-1 notices that the signal from AP-1 is degrading. Based on various conditions like the received signal strength indicator (RSSI) and SNR, the client will decide that it needs to roam.

Step 2. Client-1 begins to search for a successor BSS to move into. It broadcasts a probe request frame to look for nearby APs that can offer the same "guest" SSID.

Step 3. AP-2 receives the probe request and returns a probe response, advertising its BSSID and the "guest" SSID. Other APs may also hear the request and send probe responses of their own.

Step 4. Client-1 must decide which AP is the best candidate out of all probe responses that are received. It then sends a reassociation request frame to the new AP, asking to transfer its ESS membership from AP-1's BSS to AP-2.

Step 5. AP-2 communicates with AP-1 over the wired DS network to begin the client handoff. Client-1's association will be moved from AP-1 to AP-2. Any frames that are destined for the client during the handoff will be buffered on AP-1, then relayed to AP-2 and transmitted to the client.

Step 6. If the reassociation is accepted, AP-2 will inform the client with a reassociation response frame.

Key Topic

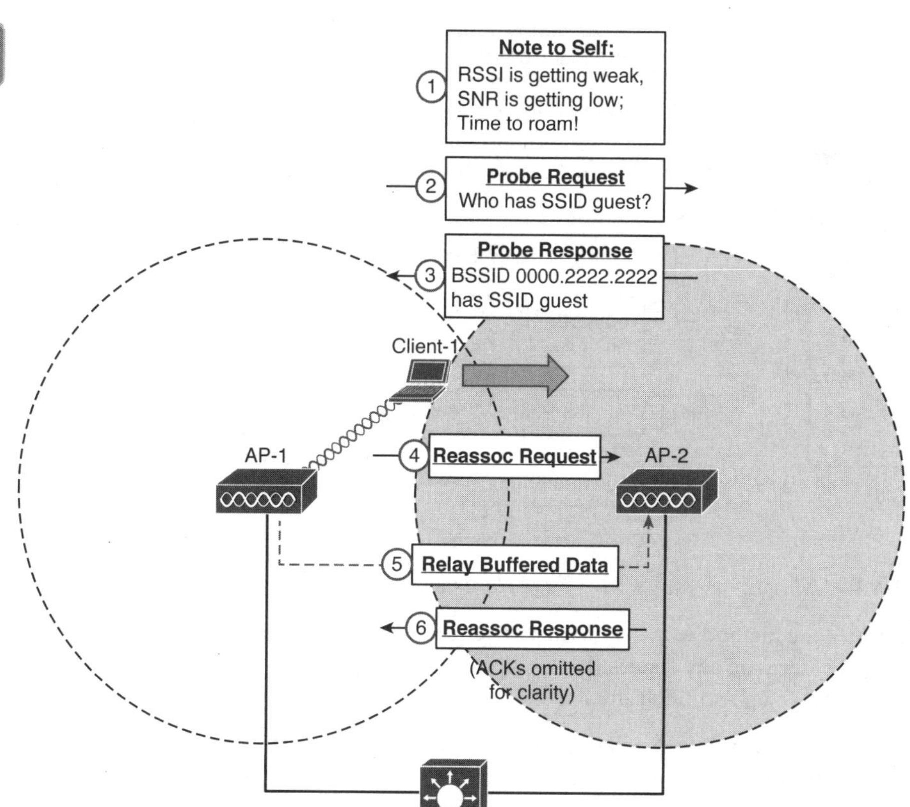

Figure 6-13 *Roaming Between Two BSSs*

A Client Saves Power

Wireless devices are commonly small in size and powered by batteries. Because the devices are mobile and carried around, it is not very practical to stop and charge the batteries. To maximize the battery life, the device should conserve as much power as possible.

By default, the radio (both transmitter and receiver) is powered on all the time, so that the device is always ready to send and receive data. That might be good for performance, but applies a constant drain on the battery. Fortunately, the 802.11 standard defines some methods to save power by putting the radio to sleep when it is not needed.

Tip Be aware that a device's radio sleeping is different than the whole device sleeping, as when you close the lid on a laptop. While a radio is sleeping, its transmitter and receiver are powered down for a short amount of time and cannot send or receive wireless frames. In contrast, when a laptop is sleeping, most of its functions are paused for a long period of time. While asleep, a laptop can become disassociated from the AP; when it wakes, it must probe and associate again. The "legacy" method was defined in the original 802.11 standard and is described by Figure 6-14 and the following sequence of steps. (For simplicity, the ACK frames that acknowledge each frame have been omitted.)

6

Key Topic

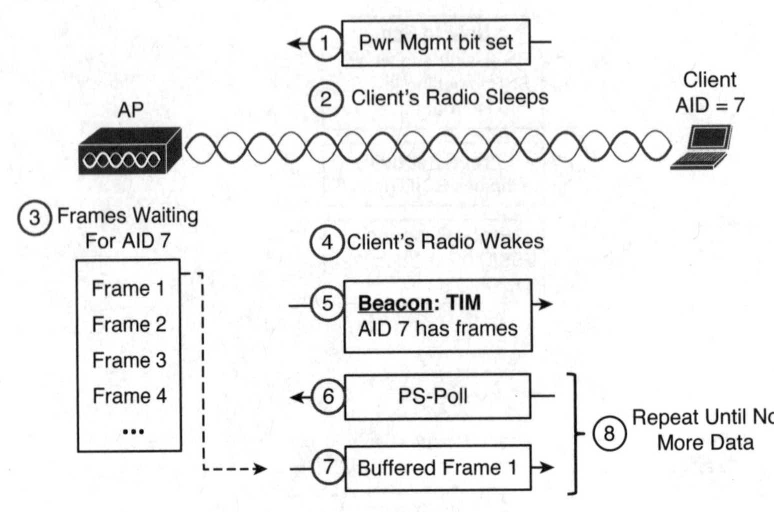

Figure 6-14 *Using the Legacy Power Save Delivery Method*

In a nutshell, the method works by letting the client's radio power down and go to sleep while the AP stores up any frames that are destined for the client. The client's radio must periodically wake up and fetch any buffered frames from the AP:

Step 1. The client informs the AP that it is entering power save mode by setting the Power Management bit in the Frame Control field of the frame header (refer to Figure 6-3).

Step 2. The client shifts its wireless radio into a very low power or "sleep" mode.

Step 3. The AP begins to buffer any unicast frames that are destined for the client while it is in power save mode.

Step 4. To check for any potentially buffered frames, the client's radio must wake up in time to receive a beacon frame.

Step 5. The beacon can contain a *traffic indication map* (TIM), or a list of AID entries for clients that have buffered frames. The client, known as AID 7, has frames available and is listed in the TIM.

Step 6. The client can begin to retrieve its buffered frames one by one. To do so, it must send a PS-Poll management frame to the AP.

Step 7. The AP sends the next buffered frame to the client, along with a flag that indicates more buffered frames are available.

Step 8. The client and AP continue the exchange in Steps 6 and 7 until no more frames are available in the buffer.

Broadcast and multicast frames become special cases for clients that have radios in power save mode. Such frames are not destined for any specific client; rather, they are destined for mass delivery. Sleeping radios will miss the frames unless the AP somehow intervenes.

An AP can also buffer broadcast and multicast frames and deliver them at regular intervals. The *delivery traffic indication message* (DTIM) is a beacon that is sent at some multiple of regular beacon periods. The DTIM period is advertised in every beacon so that all clients know to wake up their radios in time to receive the next DTIM. At that time, the DTIM is sent, followed by any buffered broadcast and multicast frames.

The legacy TIM and DTIM schemes have one drawback—they are AP-centric. Even though a client needs to conserve its battery power, it is the AP that dictates when and how often the client's radio should wake up and consume more power.

Ideally, a client should have more control over its own power consumption. The 802.11e amendment, certified by the Wi-Fi Alliance and known as *Wi-Fi Multimedia* (WMM), introduced a new quality-of-service (QoS) mechanism along with a new and improved power save mode that is more client-centric.

Traffic to and from a wireless client can be handled according to four different categories, in order of decreasing time-critical delivery: voice, video, best effort, and background. While a client is in a power save mode, the AP buffers its frames in four queues that correspond to the QoS categories. When the client is ready to wake its radio up, it sends a frame marked for one of the queues. The AP responds by sending the buffered frames in that queue to the client in a burst.

This method is known as *unscheduled automatic power save delivery* (U-APSD), and must be supported on both the client and the AP. The client does not have to request each frame, and the client does not have to wake its radio up until it is ready to do so. Figure 6-15 illustrates the sequence of steps involved in U-APSD, which are detailed in the list that follows.

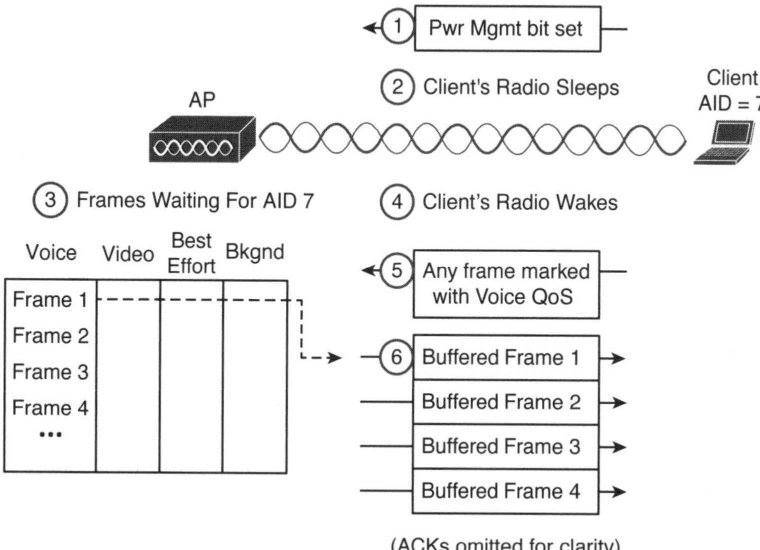

Figure 6-15 *Using the U-APSD Power Save Delivery Method*

Step 1. The client informs the AP that it is entering power save mode by setting the Power Management bit in a frame.

Step 2. The client puts its radio into power down or sleep mode.

Step 3. The AP buffers any frames destined for the client in the appropriate QoS queues.

Step 4. The client decides to wake its radio.

Step 5. The client is ready to receive any buffered frames from the "voice" queue, so it marks a frame as voice and signals the AP that it is awake.

Step 6. The AP sends the frames it has buffered in the voice queue in a burst.

Exam Preparation Tasks

As mentioned in the section, "How to Use This Book," in the Introduction, you have a couple of choices for exam preparation: the exercises here, Chapter 21, "Final Review," and the exam simulation questions on the DVD.

Review All Key Topics

Review the most important topics in this chapter, noted with the Key Topic icon in the outer margin of the page. Table 6-3 lists a reference of these key topics and the page numbers on which each is found.

Table 6-3 Key Topics for Chapter 6

Key Topic Element	Description	Page Number
Figure 6-3	802.11 frame format	133
Figure 6-7	802.11 Frame Duration (NAV) field	137
Figure 6-8	Avoiding collisions with DCF	139
List	802.11 frame types	140
List	Client scanning methods	143
Figure 6-11	Joining a BSS	144
Figure 6-13	Roaming between BSSs	147
Figure 6-14	Legacy power save mode	148

Define Key Terms

Define the following key terms from this chapter and check your answers in the glossary:

active scanning, association, backoff timer, BSS basic rate, clear channel assessment (CCA), collision avoidance, contention window, delivery traffic indication message (DTIM), distributed coordination function (DCF), interframe space, network allocation vector (NAV), open system authentication, passive scanning, physical carrier sense, reassociation, shared key authentication, traffic indication map (TIM), unscheduled automatic power save delivery (U-APSD), virtual carrier sense, Wireless Multimedia (WMM)

This chapter covers the following topics:

- **AP Cell Size**—This section discusses how the size of a wireless cell affects things like coverage area, performance, and efficiency.
- **Adding APs to an ESS**—This section covers the process of growing an extended service set, with an emphasis on client roaming and proper layout of wireless channels over an area.
- **Designing and Validating Coverage with Site Surveys**—This section discusses methods you can use to predict and measure RF coverage within an area so that you can know how the wireless LAN will work in an actual physical environment.

This chapter covers the following exam topics:

- 7.0—Site Survey Process
- 7.1—Describe site survey methodologies and their purpose
  - 7.1.a—Offsite (predictive / plan)
  - 7.1.b—Onsite
    - 7.1.b(i)—Predeployment (AP on a stick)
    - 7.1.b(ii)—Post deployment (validation)
- 7.2—Describe passive and active site surveys
- 7.3—Identify proper application of site survey tools
  - 7.3.a—Spectrum analyzer
  - 7.3.b—Site surveying software

CHAPTER 7

Planning Coverage with Wireless APs

Chapters 1 through 6 covered wireless communication with a focus on a single access point (AP) exchanging data with one or more clients. A single AP may be sufficient for home or small office use, but most wireless LANs involve a greater geographic area and require more APs. This chapter explains how wireless coverage can be adjusted to meet a need and how it can be grown to scale over a greater area and a greater number of clients. You will also learn about various types of site survey that you can use to verify RF coverage over an area. As you work through this chapter, remember that two things are important: the size of the BSA or AP cell and the location of cells in relation to each other.

"Do I Know This Already?" Quiz

The "Do I Know This Already?" quiz allows you to assess whether you should read this entire chapter thoroughly or jump to the "Exam Preparation Tasks" section. If you are in doubt about your answers to these questions or your own assessment of your knowledge of the topics, read the entire chapter. Table 7-1 lists the major headings in this chapter and their corresponding "Do I Know This Already?" quiz questions. You can find the answers in Appendix A, "Answers to the 'Do I Know This Already?' Quizzes."

Table 7-1 "Do I Know This Already?" Section-to-Question Mapping

Foundation Topics Section	Questions
AP Cell Size	1–4
Adding APs to an ESS	5–10
Designing and Validating Coverage with Site Surveys	11–15

Caution The goal of self-assessment is to gauge your mastery of the topics in this chapter. If you do not know the answer to a question or are only partially sure of the answer, you should mark that question as wrong for purposes of the self-assessment. Giving yourself credit for an answer you correctly guess skews your self-assessment results and might provide you with a false sense of security.

1. Which of the following parameters can be adjusted on an AP to change the size of its cell or BSA? (Choose all that apply.)
   a. Channel number within a band
   b. Transmit power
   c. Supported modulation and coding schemes
   d. Supported data rates
2. An AP has been configured to use channel 1 with a transmit power of 20 dBm. With the AP located in the center of the lobby, you have determined that its signal will reach all locations in the lobby area. However, some users with small battery-operated devices report connectivity problems when they move toward the outer walls of the lobby. Which of the following approaches will probably fix the problem? (Choose two.)
   a. Increase the AP's transmit power to increase its range
   b. Increase the client device's transmit power
   c. Adjust the client device's roaming algorithm
   d. Enable some lower data rates on the AP
3. Suppose that an AP is configured to offer the following data rates to its clients: 2, 5.5, 6, 9, 11, 12, 18, 24, 36, and 48 Mbps. Which one of the following strategies should be used to reduce the AP's cell size?
   a. Enable the 1-Mbps data rate
   b. Enable the 54-Mbps data rate
   c. Disable the 36- and 48-Mbps data rates
   d. Disable the 2-Mbps data rate
4. All the APs on the second floor of a building are part of a single ESS. Each AP has been configured with a transmit power level of 14 dBm. In addition, each AP has been configured to use a non-overlapping channel that is different from its adjacent neighbors. All APs have been configured to offer only the 24-, 36-, 48-, and 54-Mbps data rates; all other rates are disabled. One day, one of the APs fails and someone replaces it. Afterward, users begin to call and complain about poor performance and roaming. You discover that the problems are not occurring in the area covered by the replacement AP; instead, they are occurring about two APs away from it. Which one of the following could be causing the problem?
   a. The replacement AP has its radios disabled.
   b. The replacement AP is using a transmit level of 1 dBm.
   c. The replacement AP is using the 1- and 2-Mbps data rates.
   d. The replacement AP is new and cannot be causing the problem.

5. Which one of the following determines when a wireless client will roam from one AP to another?
   a. The current AP detects a weak signal coming from the client and forces the client to roam.
   b. The next AP overhears the client's signal and asks it to roam.
   c. The client's roaming algorithm reaches a threshold in signal quality.
   d. The client loses its IP address.
6. Which one of the following 802.11 frames is used to trigger a roam from one AP to another within an ESS?
   a. Association request
   b. Disassociation request
   c. Probe
   d. Reassociation request
7. Which one of the following statements is true about roaming?
   a. All wireless clients use the same algorithms to trigger a roaming condition.
   b. Wireless clients can scan available channels to look for a new AP when roaming.
   c. Wireless clients must roam from one AP to another on the same channel.
   d. The 802.11 standard defines a set of roaming algorithms for clients.
8. Which one of the following statements is true about a good wireless LAN design?
   a. Neighboring APs should use the same channel to promote good roaming.
   b. APs should be positioned so that their cells overlap.
   c. APs should be positioned so that their cells do not overlap at all.
   d. APs should use channels that overlap each other.
9. When you are designing the AP channel layout for an area, which one of the following is the most important consideration?
   a. The number of channels is conserved.
   b. APs in different areas use different channels.
   c. Adjacent APs use non-overlapping channels.
   d. Clients are grouped into common channels.
10. An AP is located in the main office on the third floor of a building. The AP is configured to use channel 6 in the 2.4-GHz band. Which of the following conditions might hinder clients as they move around on the third floor and need to roam? (Choose all that apply.)
    a. Two other APs in the third-floor main office area use channel 6.
    b. None of the fourth-floor APs directly above the main office use channel 6.
    c. One of the second-floor APs directly below the main office uses channel 6.
    d. All of these answers are correct.

11. Which one of the following is the best type of wireless LAN survey to perform for a new building that is under construction, where APs have not yet been deployed?
    a. Predictive survey
    b. Passive survey
    c. Active survey
    d. Performance survey

12. Suppose you would like to survey the coverage area in a new building to make sure that mobile client devices can associate with APs and roam between them. Which one of the following surveys should you perform?
    a. Predictive survey
    b. Passive survey
    c. Active survey
    d. Performance survey

13. To troubleshoot some possible RF coverage issues in a large auditorium, you would like to see a heatmap of every AP (both legitimate and rogue) that can be received at every location. You would also like to see the signal strength of each AP, SNR, and evidence of any co-channel interference. Which one of the following survey types would be best for this purpose?
    a. Predictive survey
    b. Passive survey
    c. Active survey
    d. Performance survey

14. The term "AP-on-a-stick" correctly refers to which one of the following?
    a. An AP that has a single cable connecting it to the wired network
    b. An AP with a single antenna, with MIMO disabled
    c. An AP that is mounted on a tall object to determine its cell size
    d. An AP that bridges traffic from one SSID to another

15. In an active site survey, how many APs can the survey device associate with and measure at any given time?
    a. 1
    b. 2
    c. 16
    d. As many as can be overheard

Foundation Topics

AP Cell Size

The basic service area (BSA) or cell that is provided by an AP can vary, depending on several factors. Obviously, the cell size determines the geographic area where wireless service will be offered. AP cell size can also affect the performance of the APs as clients move around or gather in one place.

Remember that a wireless LAN is a shared medium. Within a single AP cell, all of the clients associated with that AP must share the bandwidth and contend for access. If the cell is large, a large number of clients could potentially gather and use that AP. If the cell size is reduced, the number of simultaneous clients can also be reduced.

The signal from an AP does not simply stop at the boundary of its cell. Instead, the signal continues to expand ad infinitum, growing exponentially weaker. Devices inside the cell boundary can communicate with the AP. Devices outside the boundary cannot because the signal strength of either the client or the AP is too weak for the pair to find any usable modulation that can be used to exchange information. You can control the size of a cell by changing the parameters that are described in the following sections.

Tuning Cell Size with Transmit Power

7

To use a wireless LAN, devices must be located within the range of an AP's signal and have an active association with the AP. This area is known as the BSA or cell. Consider the scenario shown in Figure 7-1. PC-1 through PC-4 are within the cell's perimeter and are associated with the AP. PC-5, however, is outside the cell and cannot form an association or participate in the basic service set (BSS).

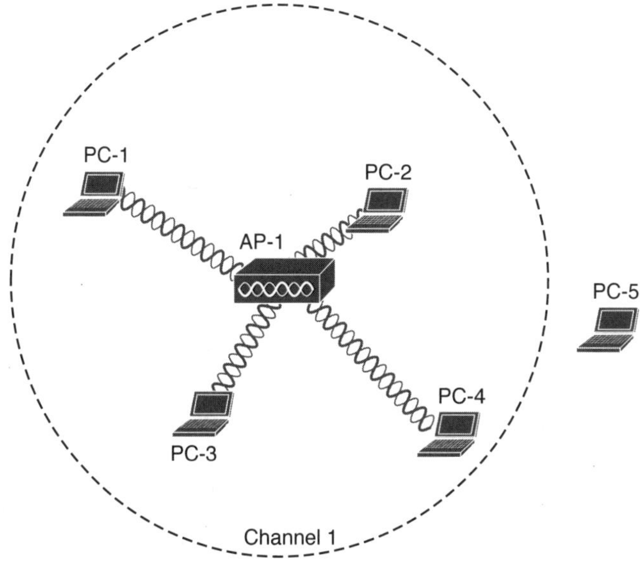

Figure 7-1 *Example Cell That Includes All but One Client*

If the area outside a cell is a legitimate location where wireless devices might be present, the coverage area should probably be extended there. How can that be accomplished? The most straightforward approach is to increase the transmit power or signal strength leaving the AP's antenna. A greater signal strength will overcome some of the free space path loss so that the usable signal reaches farther away from the AP.

Figure 7-2 shows the effect of changing the AP's transmit power level. The original cell from Figure 7-1 is shown as the second concentric circle, where the transmit power level was set to 17 dBm. If the level is increased to 20 dBm, the cell grows into the area shown by the outermost circle. Notice that PC-5 now falls within the cell boundary. If the transmit power level is decreased to 10 dBm, the cell shrinks and includes only clients PC-2 and PC-3. Why would you ever want to decrease a cell's size? That question will be answered later in this section.

Key Topic

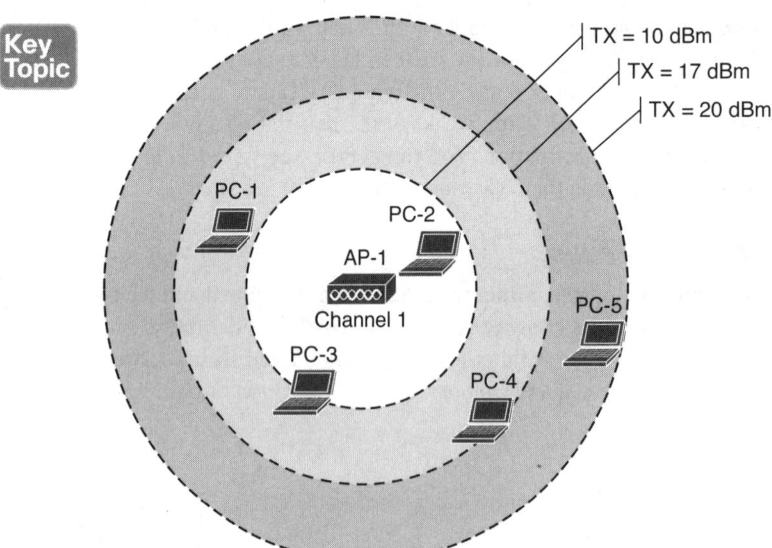

Figure 7-2 *Effects of the Transmit Power Level on Cell Size*

How should you decide on a transmit power level value? Cisco APs offer a fixed number of settings on each radio—in the United States, for example, there are eight different values for 2.4-GHz radios and seven values for 5-GHz radios. Most 802.11 scenarios fall within government regulations that limit the effective isotropic radiated power (EIRP) to a maximum transmit power level of 20 dBm (100 mW). You could just configure an AP to run wide open at maximum power, but that is not always appropriate or beneficial.

One thing to consider is the two-way nature of wireless communications. By increasing the AP's transmit power, the AP might reach a distant client, but can the client's own signal reach the AP? Notice client PC-5 in Figure 7-3. If the AP transmit power level is increased to 20 dBm (the outermost circle), PC-5 is included in the cell. However, PC-5's wireless transmitter has a lesser transmit power level; in its current location, PC-5 has a coverage area that falls short of including the AP. This scenario is known as the *asymmetric power* problem, where the two communicating devices have differing transmit power levels that might prevent them from reaching each other.

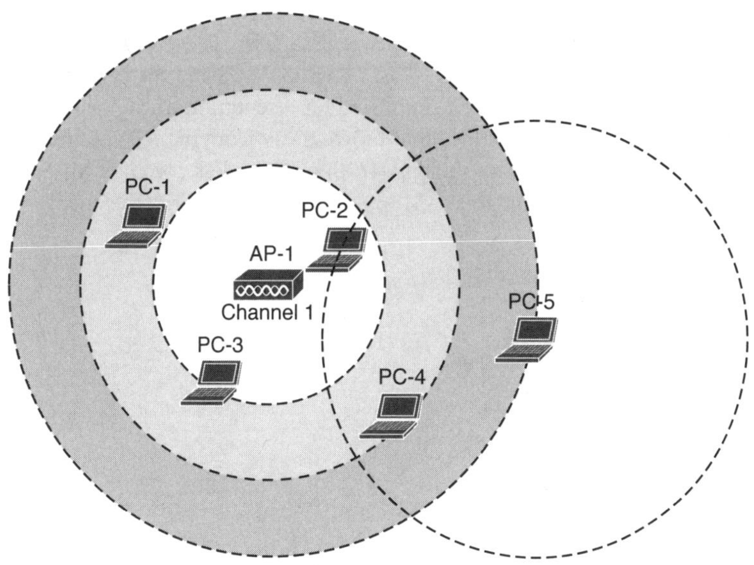

Figure 7-3 *Asymmetric Power Problem*

> **Tip** The discussion in this section is focused on setting the transmit power of the AP to an appropriate level. Keep in mind that by doing so, you are ultimately affecting the received signal strength indicator (RSSI) that the client will experience. As you work with wireless LANs, you will always need to tune things to meet requirements at the client location, to provide a quality user experience.

Tuning Cell Size with Data Rates

Setting the transmit power level is a simplistic approach to defining the cell size, but that is not the only variable involved. The cell size of an AP is actually a compromise between its transmit power and the data rates that it offers.

Recall from Chapters 1 and 3 that higher data rates must use more complex modulation and coding schemes (MCSs), which offer the greatest throughput but require the best signal conditions. The signal must be greater than the receiver sensitivity and the signal-to-noise ratio (SNR) must be high enough to support the MCS that is needed for a certain data rate. As the data rates go higher, so must the SNR.

> **Tip** The data rate can also be raised by increasing the number of spatial streams and the channel width. However, spatial streams can be leveraged only if the physical environment between an AP and a client creates multipath conditions. Each additional spatial stream also requires a higher SNR. Wider channels bring more throughput, but require an even higher SNR.

Usually, a higher SNR translates to having the client located closer to the AP. Less complex MCSs can work further away from an AP, but offer slower data rates. Therefore, at the perimeter of a cell, a client is likely to be using the least complex MCS and the lowest data rate. Figure 7-4 uses concentric circles to show a simplified representation of the range of each data rate used in the 2.4-GHz band. As the client moves away from the AP and the current MCS becomes less reliable, dynamic rate shifting (DRS) selects a less complex MCS. In the figure, the client will probably resort to a 1-Mbps data rate by the time the client reaches the outer edge of the cell.

Key Topic

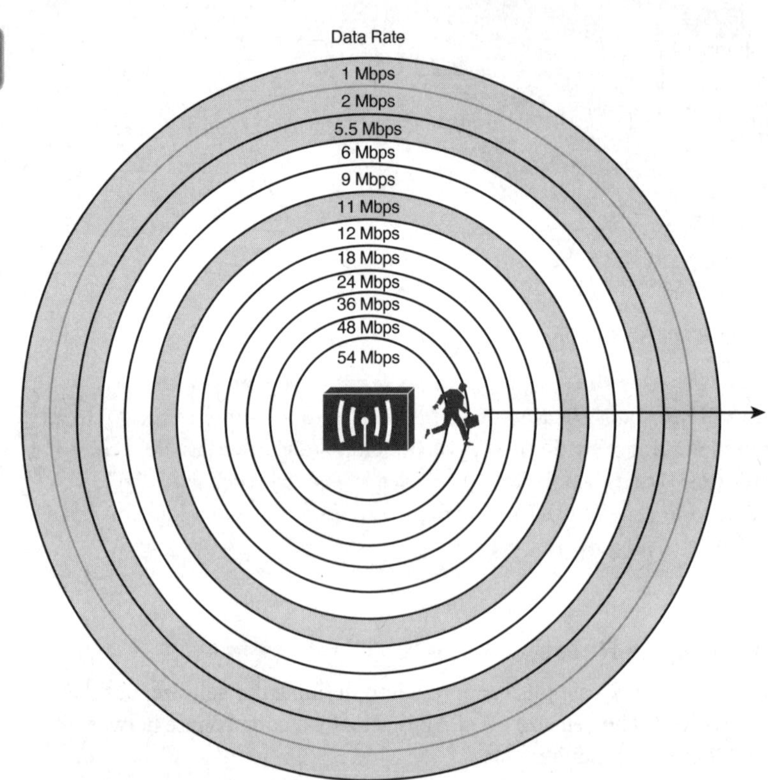

Figure 7-4 *Relationship of Data Rates and Cell Range*

To design a wireless LAN for best performance, you would most likely need to disable some of the lower data rates. For example, you could disable the 1-, 2-, and 5.5-Mbps rates in the 2.4-GHz band to force clients to use higher rates and better modulation and coding schemes. That would improve throughput for individual clients and would also benefit the BSS as a whole by eliminating the slower rates that use more time on a channel.

As you disable lower data rates, the corresponding outer concentric circles in Figure 7-4 become irrelevant. This effectively *reduces* the usable size of the AP's cell, even though the radio frequency (RF) footprint remains the same. After all, you haven't reduced the transmit power level, which would reduce the extent of the RF energy.

Tip As smaller usable cells are placed closer together, their available data rates are indeed higher. Be aware that at the same time, their RF footprints can remain large and overlap each other, resulting in a higher noise floor.

Even though Figure 7-4 depicts the 2.4-GHz band, the same principles apply to the 5-GHz band. As a client moves away from an AP, the MCS is stepped down according to the RF conditions at the client's location. Clients and APs using 802.11n have eight MCS options per spatial stream, while 802.11ac has ten. Figure 7-5 depicts an 802.11ac client as it moves away from an AP. The client might start out using MCS 9 very near the AP, shifting down incrementally through the remaining MCS numbers each time the SNR falls below a corresponding threshold. On the client, you might be able to see this reported as a data rate or an MCS number, both shown in the figure.

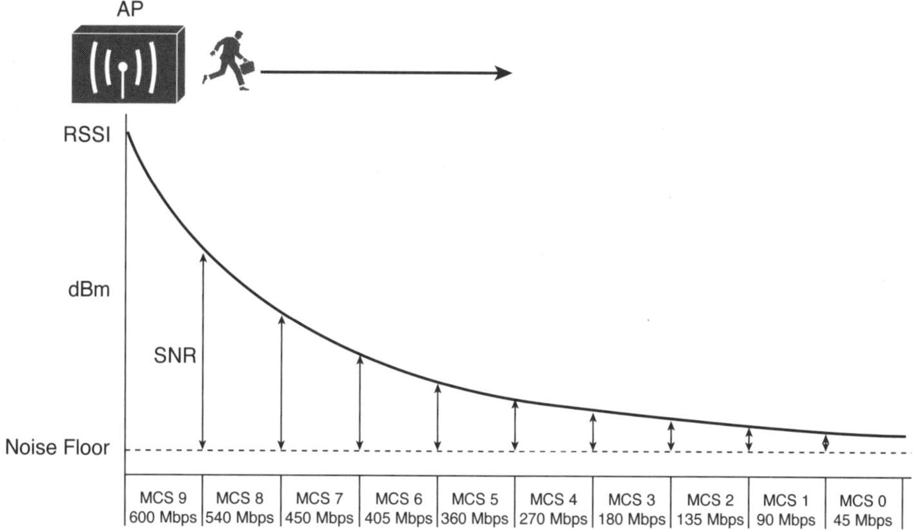

Figure 7-5 *Relationship of MCS, Data Rates, and Cell Range for 802.11ac*

So far, this section has discussed factors that affect the size of a single AP cell. If you need to cover a large area, such as the entire floor of a building, one cell will not suffice. To provide robust wireless coverage to an ever-increasing area, you should use the following two-pronged approach:

- Tune the cell size based on data rates and performance.
- Add additional APs to build an ESS that covers more area.

Adding APs requires careful consideration for client mobility and the use of wireless channels. These topics are covered in the next section.

Adding APs to an ESS

If a client is associated with an AP, it can maintain the association as long as it stays within range of the AP. Consider the cell shown in Figure 7-6. As long as the client stays within points A and B, three conditions are met:

- The client is able to receive the AP's signal at an acceptable level.
- The AP is able to receive the client's signal.
- One of the acceptable modulations can be successfully used between the client and the AP.

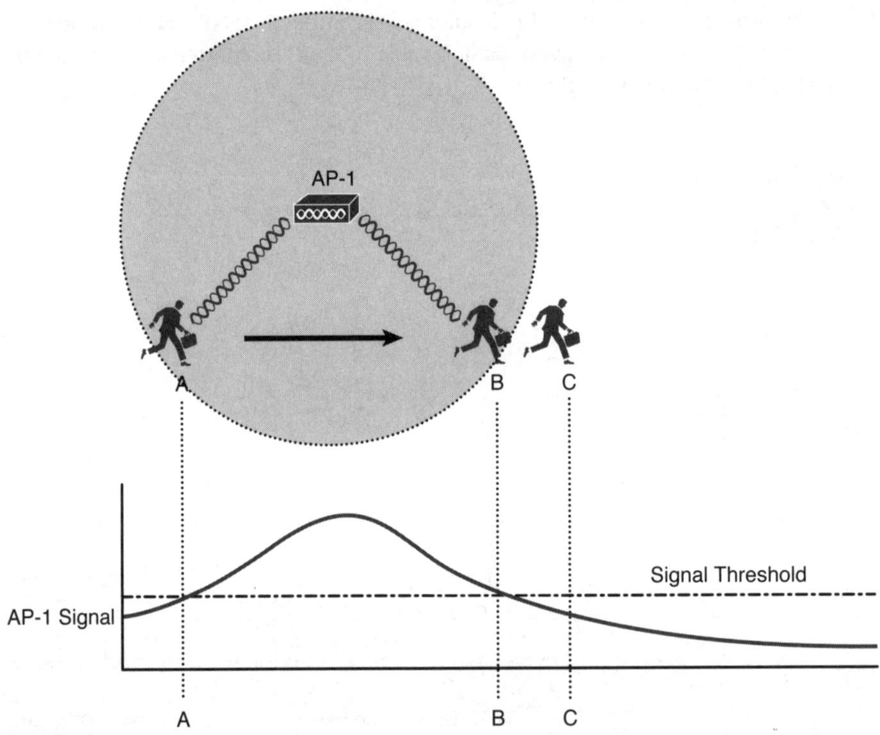

Figure 7-6 *Mobile Client Moving Within an AP Cell*

As soon as the client goes outside the cell range at point C, one or more of the conditions fail and the client loses the association. In the figure, the AP's signal has fallen below an acceptable threshold.

Other APs can be added so that the client can move within a larger area; however, the APs must be carefully deployed to allow the client to roam from AP to AP. *Roaming* is the process of moving an association from one AP to the next, so that the wireless connection is maintained as the client moves.

In Figure 7-7, a new AP has been added alongside AP-1, each using the same channel. It might seem intuitive to build a larger coverage area by using a single channel. Usually this turns out to be a bad idea because the client may experience an excessive amount of frame collisions in the area between the two cells.

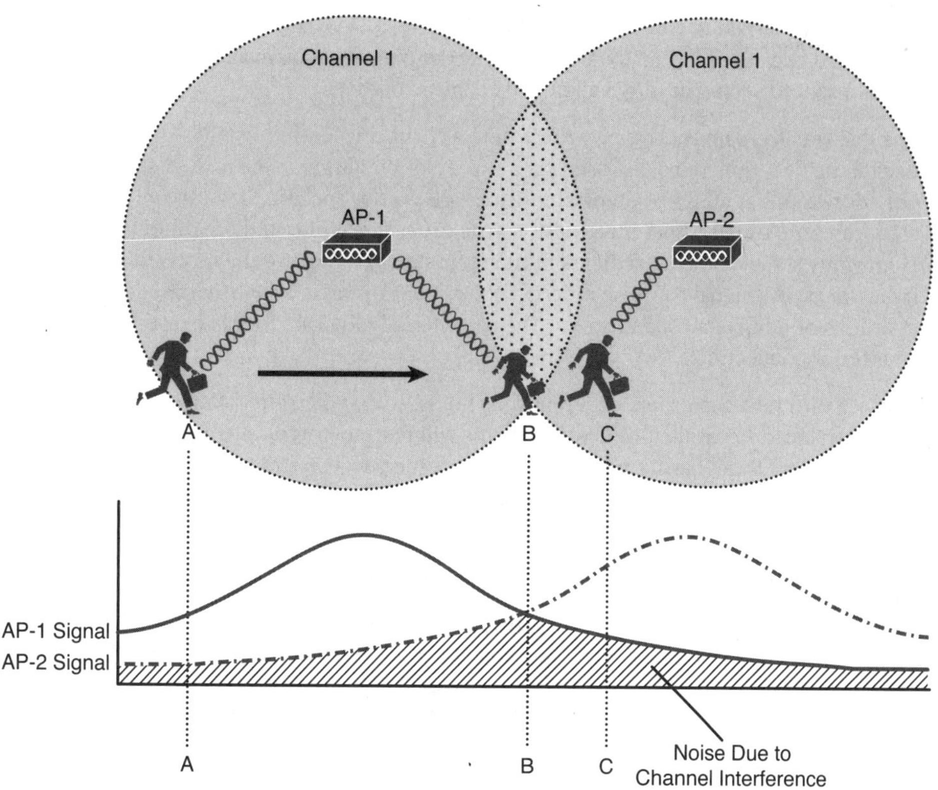

Figure 7-7 *Pitfalls of Reusing Channels in Adjacent APs*

7

Remember that the signal from an AP does not actually stop at the edge of the cell; rather, it continues to propagate as it eventually dies off. This is shown by the signal strength graph of each AP. The client is able to form an association with AP-1 at point A. Even at that location, some portion of AP-2's signal can be received, albeit at a lower level. Because AP-2 is using the same channel as AP-1, the two APs (and any clients within range) can essentially interfere with each other through co-channel interference.

Ideally, when the client in Figure 7-7 moves to location B, it should begin to anticipate the need to roam or transfer its association from AP-1 to AP-2. Notice that AP-1 and AP-2 are spaced appropriately for roaming, where their cells have some overlap. The two APs are out of range of each other, so they are not aware of each other's transmissions on the same channel. Each AP will coordinate the use of the channel with devices that are inside its own cell, but not with the other AP and devices in the other cell. As a result, the client around location B will probably experience so many collisions that it may never be able to roam cleanly.

The Roaming Process

What enables a client to roam in the first place? First, adjacent APs *should* be configured to use different non-overlapping channels. For example, an AP using channel 1 must not be adjacent to other APs also using channel 1. Instead, a neighboring AP should use channel 6 or higher to avoid any frequency overlap with channel 1 in the 2.4-GHz band. This ensures that clients will be able to receive signals from a nearby AP without interference from other APs. As you learned in Chapter 2, "RF Standards," the 5-GHz band is much more flexible in this regard because it has many more non-overlapping channels available. In fact, all channels are spaced such that they will not overlap each other.

The decision to roam is driven by the wireless client driver—not by the AP. Wireless clients decide that it is time to roam based on a variety of conditions. The 802.11 standard does not address this at all, so roaming algorithms are vendor specific. In addition, the roaming algorithms are usually "secret recipes," so the exact thresholds and conditions are hidden from view. Some of the ingredients in the roaming algorithm are the received signal strength indicator (RSSI), signal-to-noise ratio (SNR), a count of missed AP beacons, errors due to collisions or interference, and so on. These are usually logical choices because they indicate an inferior connection.

Because different clients use different thresholds, some will try to roam earlier than others at a given location within a cell. Some clients will tend to "latch on" to an existing association until the AP can hardly be heard, whereas others will attempt to roam whenever a better AP is discovered. You might find that some client drivers have advanced options that let you select the roaming "aggressiveness," affecting how quickly the client will try to roam away from an AP association. Figure 7-8 depicts a clean roam between two APs that have been correctly configured with non-overlapping channels 1 and 6. The two AP signal strengths are also shown as a graph corresponding to the client's location. At location A, the client has a clear signal from AP-1, so it maintains an association with that AP.

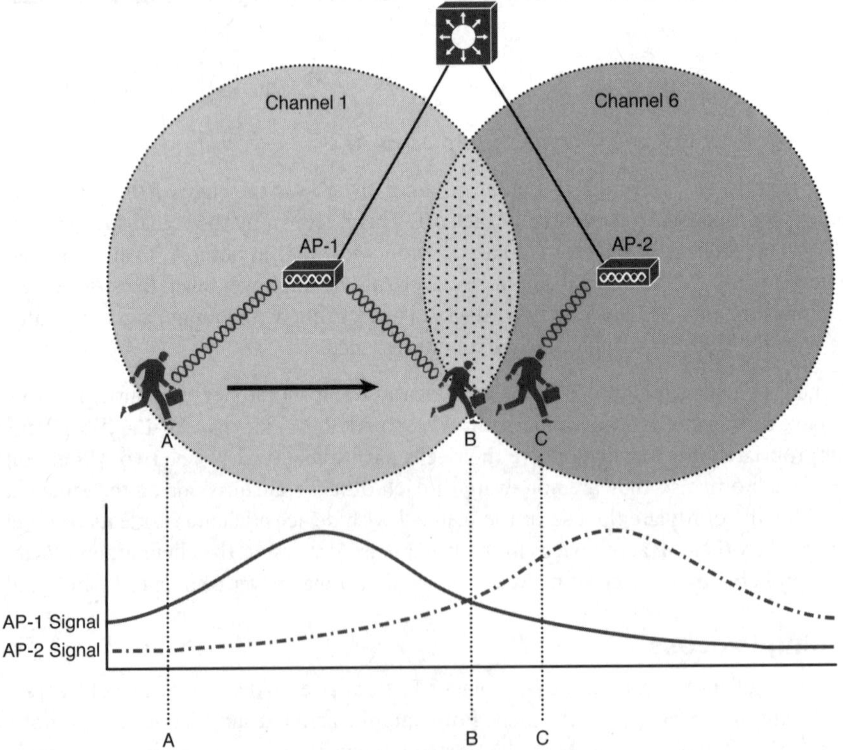

Figure 7-8 *Client Roaming Correctly Between Two APs*

As the client moves toward location B, it decides that AP-1's signal is no longer optimal. Somewhere along the way, the client begins to gather more information about any neighboring AP cells. The client can passively scan by tuning its radio to other channels and listening for beacons transmitted from other APs. During the time that the radio is tuned away from the associated channel, the client might lose packets that have been sent to it. A client might use active scanning instead, where it sends probe requests to seek out a better AP where it can move its association. The client does not know what channel is used on the next AP it encounters, so it must send the probes over every possible channel. Again, the client must take time to tune its radio away from the current AP's channel so it can scan other channels and send probes.

You might think of this as someone watching television. As the current program gets boring or nears its end, the viewer begins to "channel surf" and scans other channels for a better program. One thing to keep in mind: While the viewer is scanning channels, he cannot keep watching the original program. Some of that program will be missed. This is also true of wireless clients. While a radio is scanning other channels, packets arriving on the original channel will be dropped because they cannot be received. Therefore, there is a trade-off between staying available on a single channel and attempting to roam to other APs.

Tip The 802.11k-2008 amendment, now incorporated into the 802.11-2012 standard, defines a more efficient roaming scheme where a client can ask an AP for a list of other nearby APs. By requesting a list of potential candidate APs in bulk, the client does not have to spend time scanning channels and sending probe requests. This technique is commonly called AP assisted roaming.

After the client is satisfied with all of the beacons or probe responses it receives, it evaluates them to see which AP offers the most potential for a new association. Returning to Figure 7-8, when the client nears location B, it receives a probe response from AP-2 on channel 6. At location C, the client sends a reassociation frame to AP-2 and moves its association to that BSS.

How much should cells overlap each other to promote good roaming? Cisco recommends 10–15 percent overlap for most data applications and 15–20 percent overlap for voice. The idea is to give a client device some continued coverage even after the RSSI of its associated AP falls below a threshold and a roam might be triggered. The client can probe and reassociate with the next AP before it completely loses contact with the previous AP. Seamless roaming is especially important for time-critical applications like voice traffic.

WLAN Channel Layout

The previous section laid the foundation for roaming by describing movement between two AP cells. Most scenarios require more than two APs to cover the appropriate area within a building. Therefore, you need to consider the layout and configuration of more and more APs to scale the design to fit your wireless environment.

For example, to cover the entire area of a warehouse or one floor of a building, APs must be placed at regular intervals throughout that space. A site survey is a vital step toward deciding on AP placement, as actual live measurements are taken with an AP staged at various points in the actual space. This method also takes any factors like free space loss and absorption into account, as the signal strength is measured within the actual environment where clients are located. Site surveys are covered later in this chapter.

To minimize channel overlap and interference, APs cells should be designed so that adjacent APs use different channels. For simplicity and a convenient design constraint, the examples in this section use the three non-overlapping 2.4-GHz channels. The cells could be laid out in a regular, alternating pattern, as shown in Figure 7-9.

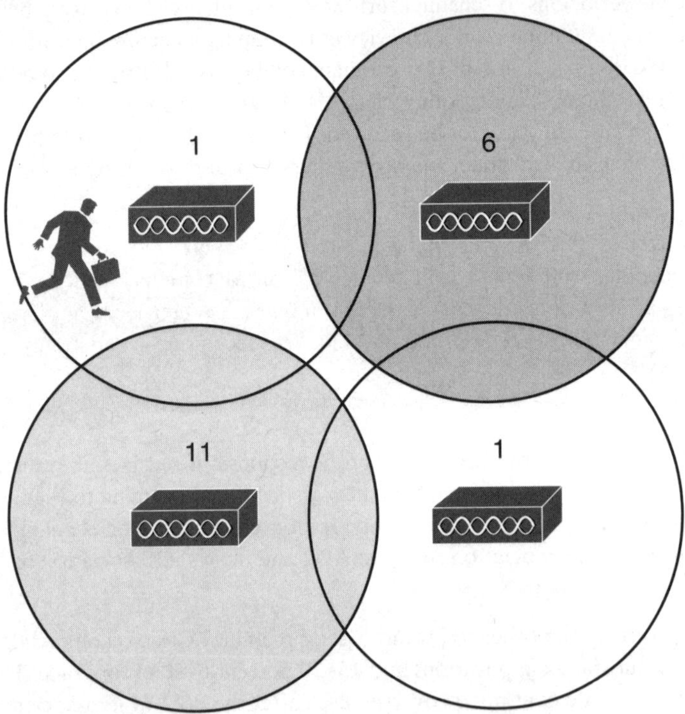

Figure 7-9 *Holes in an Alternating Channel Pattern*

However, notice what is happening in the center where the cells meet; there is a small hole in RF coverage. If a client roams through that hole, his wireless signal could drop completely. In addition, if the cells were brought closer together to close this hole, the two cells using channel 1 would overlap and begin interfering with each other.

Instead, you should lay the cells out in a "honeycomb" fashion, as shown in Figure 7-10. This pattern is seamless, leaving no holes in coverage. In addition, notice how the two cells using channel 1 are well separated, providing isolation from interference. As far as ordering channels in the pattern, there are several different variations using combinations of the three channels, but the result is basically the same.

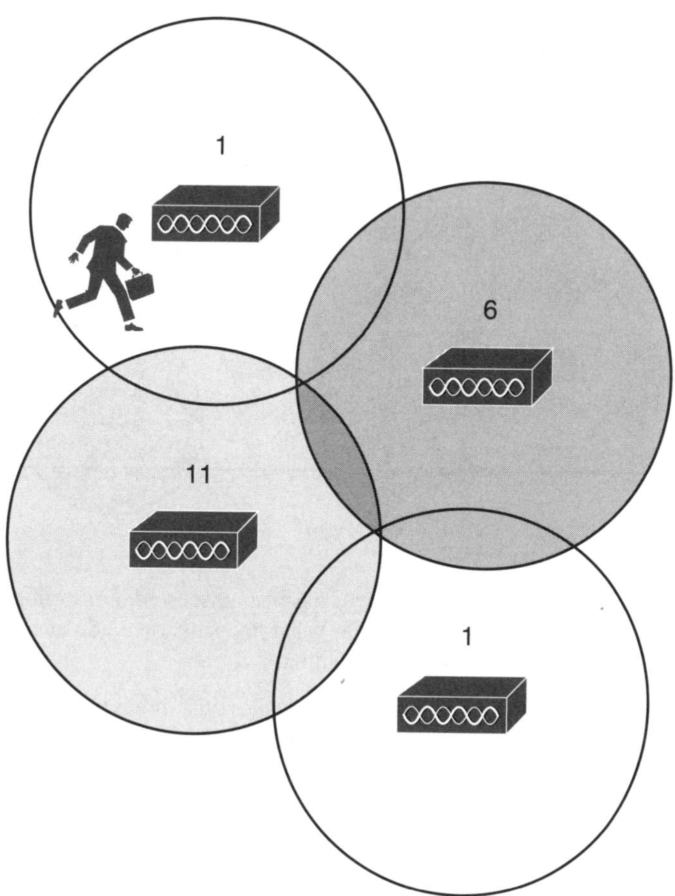

Figure 7-10 *Better Alternating Channel Pattern*

Notice that as the client shown in the channel 1 cell moves around, it will roam into adjacent cells on different channels. For roaming to work properly, a client must be able to move from one channel into a completely different channel.

Alternating channels to avoid overlap is commonly called *channel reuse*. The basic pattern shown in Figure 7-10 can be repeated to expand over a larger area, as shown in Figure 7-11. Naturally, this ideal layout uses perfect circles that are positioned regularly across the building. In practice, cells can take on different shapes and the AP locations may end up being irregularly spaced.

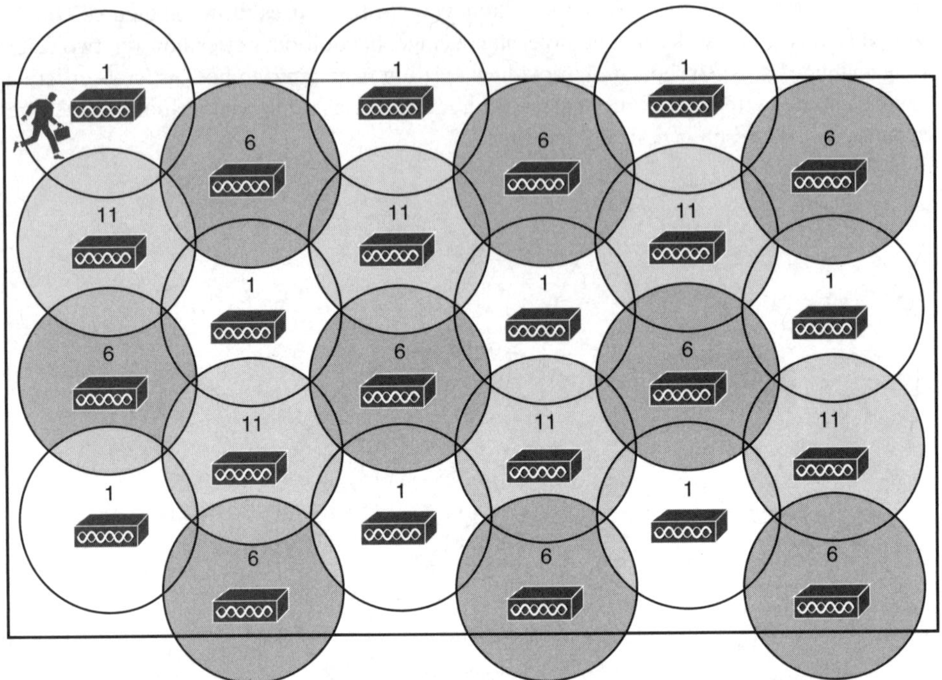

Figure 7-11 *Channel Reuse Over a Large Area*

So far, only the channel layout of a two-dimensional area has been discussed. For example, Figure 7-11 might represent only one floor of a building. What happens when you need to design a wireless LAN for multiple floors in the same building?

Recall that an RF signal propagating from an antenna actually takes on a three-dimensional shape. With an omnidirectional antenna, the pattern is somewhat like a donut shape with the antenna at the center. The signal extends outward, giving the cell a circular shape along the floor. The signal also extends upward and downward to a lesser extent—affecting AP cells on adjacent floors as well.

Consider the building with three floors shown in Figure 7-12. The same two-dimensional channel layout from Figure 7-11 is being used on the first floor. The floors in the figure are shown greatly separated, so that you can see the channel patterns and numbers. In reality, the cells on adjacent floors would touch or overlap, just as adjacent cells on the same floor do.

The pattern of alternating channels exists within the plane of a floor and between floors. It is easy to think of RF signals traveling in two dimensions over the area of one floor, when they actually travel in three dimensions. This means that signals may pass through the floor and ceiling materials into adjacent floors, after being somewhat absorbed or attenuated by the materials. In theory, channel 1 on the first floor should not overlap with channel 1 directly above it on the second floor or below it in the basement.

When you consider each of the tasks involved in designing and maintaining a wireless LAN, it can really become a puzzle to solve. The cell size, transmit power, and channel assignment all have to be coordinated for each and every AP. Roaming also becomes an issue on a large scale, if mobile clients are able to move throughout an entire campus wireless network.

The good news is that Chapter 13, "Understanding RRM," explains how to solve many of these puzzles automatically.

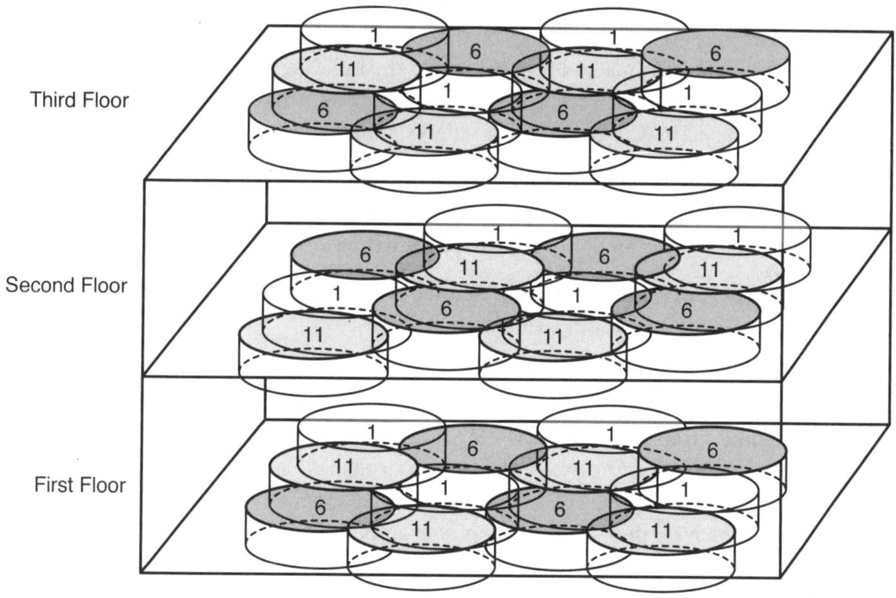

Figure 7-12 *Channel Layout in Three Dimensions*

Designing and Validating Coverage with Site Surveys

In the previous sections, you learned about the parameters you can adjust to affect the size of a BSS or AP cell. Those parameters are all configured at the AP to determine how far its signal will reach toward client devices and what potential data rates will be available. If you simply adjust the AP parameters with no other input, how can you know that clients within an area surrounding an AP will actually be able to use a certain data rate? Or will clients be able to associate with the AP at all? You also learned about selecting and reusing channels when multiple APs are located in the same geographic area. How can you know that the APs do not overlap on the same channel or that clients can use the APs in every possible location?

To verify wireless LAN coverage and performance, you have to shift your perspective toward that of a wireless client. Site surveys offer a way to either predict or actually take measurements of the RF conditions that a client experiences at various locations within the wireless coverage area. Site surveys usually produce colored heatmaps that depict things like signal strength, SNR, data rates, and so on, that are superimposed on actual floor plans or maps. In the following sections, you will learn more about the different types of site surveys and the tools you can use to produce them.

Applications and Their Requirements

To verify wireless coverage and performance, it is important to have an idea about what you want to measure and what target you are trying to hit. For example, suppose you want to verify that a wireless user sitting in a classroom will have an acceptable wireless experience.

What signal strength should you expect to find at that user's seat? What SNR is acceptable there? What typical data rates are needed for that user?

Beyond that, suppose the entire classroom fills with other wireless users. How many users can associate with one AP without dragging down the performance? Now suppose that the wireless client becomes mobile and moves around the building. Will the client be able to roam and maintain a connection regardless of his location? What if the client is a wireless phone or a video device? Will the voice or video stream be acceptable as the client roams?

To answer these questions, you should begin by becoming familiar with the devices and applications that will be used in the wireless environment. Make a list of requirements for each type of device, including the following information:

- **Type of device**—Smartphones, laptops, tablets, wireless phones, RFID tags, and so on, including manufacturer and operating system
- **Wi-Fi capabilities**—Supported protocols (802.11b/g/n/a/ac), number of spatial streams, maximum transmit power, and roaming aggressiveness (if known).
- **Throughput and jitter requirements**—Most devices will make use of "normal" data that has no special requirements or expectations other than what the users consider to be decent responsive throughput. Wireless devices that support voice or video communication will usually have a limit on the acceptable amount of jitter. As well, these devices will need seamless roaming so that the voice or video calls are not dropped or interrupted as the clients move around.

Tip Client throughput will likely leverage the MIMO capabilities of 802.11n and 802.11ac. Remember that multiple spatial streams require multiple paths to reach their destination. Indoor environments with offices, hallways, and large furniture are usually good places to support multipath. You won't necessarily be able to measure or survey multipath conditions though; MIMO is usually difficult to predict or measure with most site survey tools.

Sometimes real-time location services (RTLS) are needed to automatically determine the location of wireless devices. RTLS can be used to track assets like healthcare equipment, to track rogue devices that might be causing problems on the network, to locate sources of wireless interference, and to track the locations of wireless clients within a building or campus. A device is located by triangulating the RSSI from several APs that can receive its signal.

When location-based services are required, it is usually best to change the AP layout within a floor of a building. The outermost APs should be placed near the perimeter of the building to improve the triangulation results.

You should also use a critical eye as you walk through a building before you begin a design or site survey. It is one thing to select AP locations on a two-dimensional floor plan; it is quite another to find suitable locations for every AP in the actual building. For example, your proposed location for an AP might coincide with an obstruction such as a large air duct, concrete pillar, lighting fixture, and so on. The location might also end up in an area that has a vaulted ceiling or is open to the floors above it. Even worse, the building owner might not want any of the APs to be visible, preferring that you hide them from view.

The CCNA Wireless exam requires you to have a good working knowledge of wireless site surveys. The exam may not require you to know how to perform a site survey, but you should be able to gather information about an environment and know what to expect from a survey.

Site Survey Types and Tools

To perform a site survey, you will need a way to gather data about RF parameters at each location within an area of interest. You could use a brute-force approach and collect the data manually, moving from one location to another while recording volumes of data about the RSSI, SNR, channel, modulation, data rates, and so on—for each AP that can be received. Instead, your site survey work will be much more efficient if you use a software tool that is designed for site surveys.

Site survey tools can be grouped into three basic categories based on their installation base:

- **Standalone**—Survey applications that are typically installed on a laptop and used offsite or carried onsite
- **Server-based**—Survey applications that are installed on a stationary server and are usually part of a larger integrated package that includes WLAN management tools
- **Cloud-based**—Survey applications that can be used for designing or predicting actual survey results without collecting RF data

The following are the three basic types of site survey that you can perform as you plan and deploy a wireless network:

- **Predictive survey**—Analyze the environment to select AP locations when no APs have been deployed yet; also called planning survey.
- **Passive survey**—Analyze information that is overheard by listening to existing APs as you move throughout an area.
- **Active survey**—Analyze the survey device itself as it interacts with the APs as you move throughout an area, in order to gauge the correct cell size. An active survey is also used to associate with APs that are already in production to measure cell size and gauge how the survey client interacts with the APs during live associations and roaming.

Table 7-2 lists the survey types along with examples of the different types of survey tools.

Table 7-2 Wireless Survey Types and Tools

Survey Type	Common Survey Tools
Predictive	Fluke Networks AirMagnet Planner (standalone) Ekahau Site Survey + Wi-Fi Planner (standalone)
	Cisco Prime Infrastructure (server-based)
	Cisco Predictive RF Planner (cloud-based; for Cisco Partners only)
	Aerohive Wi-Fi Planner (cloud-based; for Aerohive APs only)
Passive	Fluke Networks AirMagnet Survey Pro (standalone) Ekahau Site Survey (standalone)
Active	Fluke Networks AirMagnet Survey Pro (standalone) Ekahau Site Survey (standalone)

You can also use a spectrum analyzer to detect and identify any sources of interference you might encounter in the wireless coverage area. You can use tools like AirMagnet Spectrum XT (airmagnet.com) or MetaGeek Chanalyzer (http://metageek.com) to gather data and analyze RF spectrum activity. Cisco APs can be configured as remote spectrum sensors that software like Chanalyzer and Cisco Spectrum Expert can leverage to import RF spectrum data.

To prepare for the CCNA Wireless exam, you should understand the purpose of each survey type, when it should be used, and the basic process of carrying it out. Each survey type is described in the sections that follow.

Tip Performing a site survey can be an involved process that requires a thorough knowledge of the survey tools. If that sounds like it could be a course and exam all to itself, you're right—Conducting Cisco Unified Wireless Site Surveys (CUWSS, exam 642-732) or Wi-Fi Design (WIDESIGN, exam 300-360) is one component of the CCNP Wireless certification track.

Predictive or Planning Surveys

Suppose you would like to offer Wi-Fi in a building or an outdoor area where no APs currently exist. How could you figure out how many APs to purchase and where to mount each one? You might have gained some prior knowledge or rules of thumb about AP signal strength by noticing how many bars are shown on a smartphone or laptop as you move past an AP. For example, maybe you realized that a device maintained connectivity in a setting where the APs were spaced some distance apart. You could then hope that your new area would have good coverage by mounting APs in a matrix, spaced 40 feet apart. That approach sounds simple, but is not very scientific. At the least, it does not take into account any effects that the building construction materials or large objects might have on the RF signals.

A better approach would be to conduct a *planning* or *pre-deployment survey*. In a nutshell, the survey tool uses a diagram of the coverage area and knowledge of any materials such as walls, doors, and other large objects to calculate the signal strength that a client might experience at any location within the area. The end result is a heatmap where colors are superimposed over the area diagram to represent quantities like signal strength, data rates, and so on. Because all of this information is computed based on the RF propagation from every AP, you end up with a useful representation of the actual RF coverage that a real user might experience. The survey also computes the number of APs needed to cover the area.

As an example, the ESS tool is used to perform a planning survey on a large area of a building floor. A floor plan is imported and calibrated, then walls are drawn over the wall lines in the plan. The survey tool offers a wide selection of wall materials, each having a specific attenuation in dBm, as shown in Figure 7-13. The RF coverage area is marked on the plan, then the coverage parameters (minimum usable RSSI, 802.11 band, client density, and so on) are set. The tool computes the number of APs that are needed, then computes a heatmap of the resulting signal strength over the entire coverage area. In Figure 7-14, the tool has chosen and placed eight APs in default locations. You can manually drag the APs to different locations if needed.

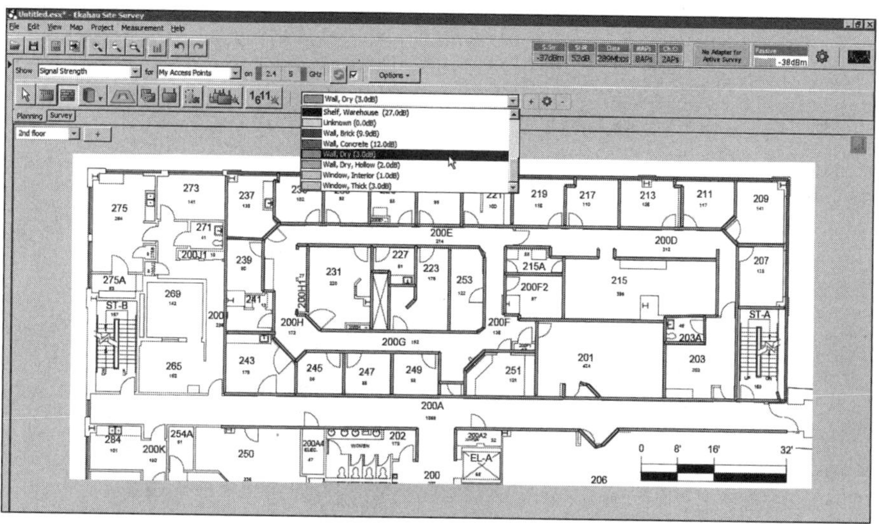

Figure 7-13 *Beginning Predictive Survey with Wall Material Identification*

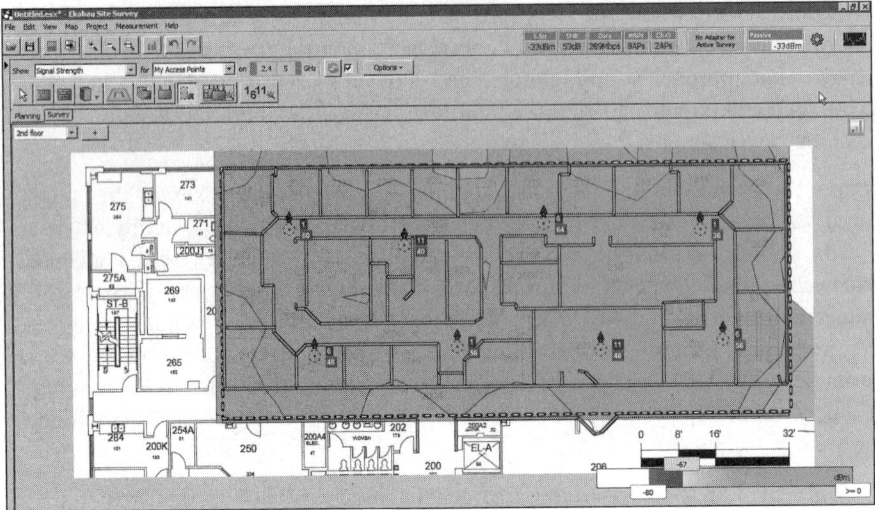

Figure 7-14 *Predictive Survey Results with Eight APs*

Passive Site Surveys

To measure the effects of any existing APs in an area, you can use a site survey tool to perform a *passive site survey*. As its name implies, the survey tool passively scans through the wireless bands and channels to listen for any AP that sends a beacon or a probe response frame. The tool records the APs overheard, including their BSSIDs, RSSI, SNR, channels, and many other parameters, for each location in the survey area. That information is presented as a heatmap superimposed on the building floor plan or outdoor map, as shown in Figure 7-15.

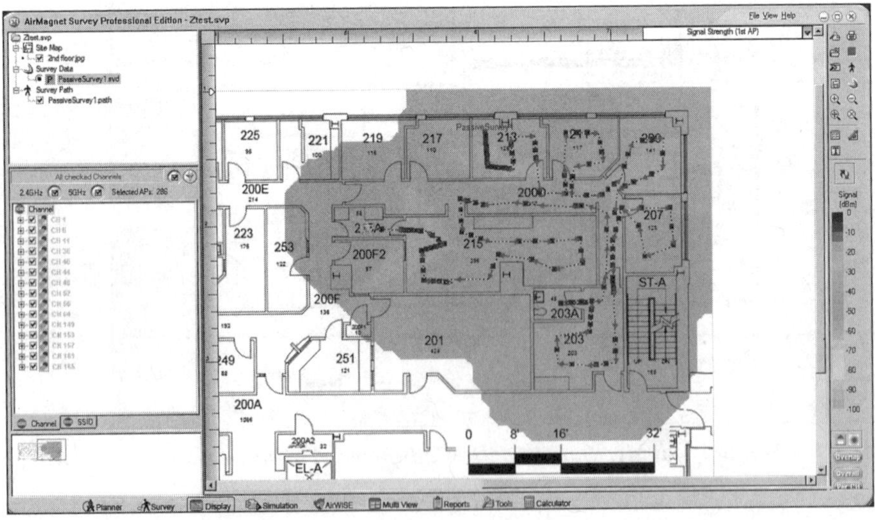

Figure 7-15 *Performing a Passive Site Survey*

To perform the survey, the user must load a map showing the area to be surveyed and define the map's scale. Once the survey is initiated, the user clicks her current location, then walks methodically through the area as the survey tool collects signal and RF data at each location. The tool can operate in one of two modes: *click-and-go* or *continuous scan*. In click-and-go mode, the user clicks each location where a sample should be taken, walks to the next position, clicks for another sample, and so on. In continuous scan mode, the user clicks once to start data collection, then clicks again at the end of a straight walking path. Between clicks, the tool automatically samples at regular intervals, simplifying the user's interaction.

The end result is a heatmap like the one displayed in Figure 7-15, which also shows the path that the user walked during the survey. Notice how the user walked into and around each room and hallway within the area surveyed. Each dash or dot along the path represents a data sample. The survey tool (AirMagnet Survey in this case) calculates the RF parameters that might be received at every other location on the heatmap. The overall signal strength is shown in the figure, although you can display many other views, too.

Remember that a passive site survey is useful for gauging the apparent RF coverage over an area and for identifying APs (both legitimate and rogue). All measurements are taken by listening only; the survey tool never actually associates with any of the APs. Therefore, a passive survey will not reveal any information about actual data rates, throughput, or roaming activity from a client perspective.

7

Tip Passive surveys base everything on listening to beacon frames sent by APs. Remember that beacons are management frames and are sent at the lowest mandatory data rate that the AP supports. As a result, the beacons might be received at a greater distance from the AP than regular data frames used by associated clients. In other words, passive site surveys are useful as initial or cursory surveys or in troubleshooting scenarios.

Active Site Surveys

Predictive surveys are usually based around theoretical calculations and not actual measurements. You can add a level of accuracy by taking some coarse measurements with an actual AP. The AP is mounted on a tripod, ladder, or pole, at the same height it would be mounted when deployed. Power is applied to the AP and signal strength measurements are taken by walking toward and away from the AP until the desired cell edge is determined. Then the AP is moved where the center of an adjacent cell is expected to be and more cell edge measurements are taken. Because the AP is mounted on a pole or stick, this survey method is commonly called *AP-on-a-stick*. Because the survey is done by associating to a live AP, the survey process is called an *active survey*.

The idea behind an AP-on-a-stick survey is to choose a starting point in the coverage area, determine the first cell boundary, then move the AP and measure other cells until the entire area has been covered. More specifically, you would determine the edge of the cell boundary to be when the AP's signal falls to –67 dBm. Then you would move the AP to a new location where its cell overlaps the previous cell by 20 percent, then move the AP again, and so on. Some people choose the initial starting location to be in one corner of the coverage area, while others will choose a place that is next to a hard obstacle, such as a stairwell, bathroom, or elevator shaft, or where an AP is certain to be located.

Figure 7-16 illustrates this process, beginning with location 1. Once the survey is complete, you will have a good idea of the overlapping cells, as well as the number and location of the APs that are needed.

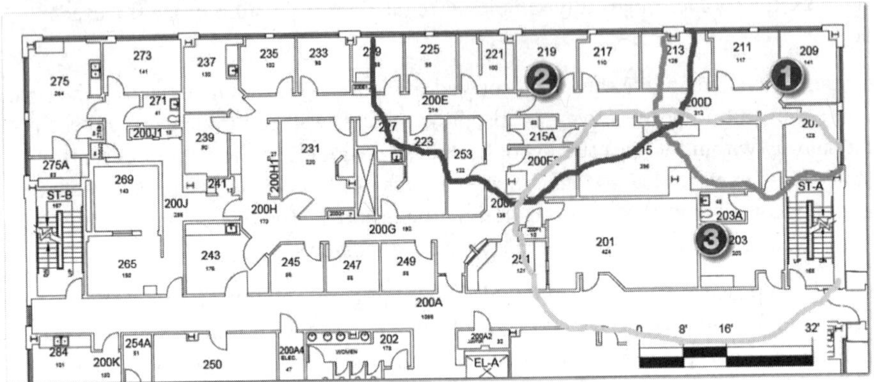

Figure 7-16 *Sequence of AP Locations in an AP-on-a-Stick Survey*

AP-on-a-stick surveys can produce realistic results taken in the actual physical environment of the coverage area. As you might imagine, it is also a time-consuming and tedious process.

A passive site survey offers a wealth of information about RF conditions and the availability of APs throughout an area, but it does not reveal how an actual client device would behave or perform with the APs. To add a client's perspective, you can perform a full *active site survey*.

In an active site survey, the survey device acts as a regular wireless client by associating to an AP. As the survey device is carried throughout the survey area, it is free to associate and roam. Measurements of the client's associations, data transmissions, and roaming activity are recorded as they occur.

An active site survey begins much like a passive survey. A plan of the survey area is imported into the survey tool and calibrated, and then the survey user begins walking on a path through the area. The survey client can be configured for one of two active survey methods:

- **BSSID method**—The survey is locked to a specific BSSID so that the client stays associated to a single AP, to measure a single cell.
- **SSID method**—The client can associate and roam to any AP as needed—all over a consistent SSID.

Figure 7-17 shows an example of an active site survey. A heatmap depicting the RSSI of the associated AP is shown along with the survey path.

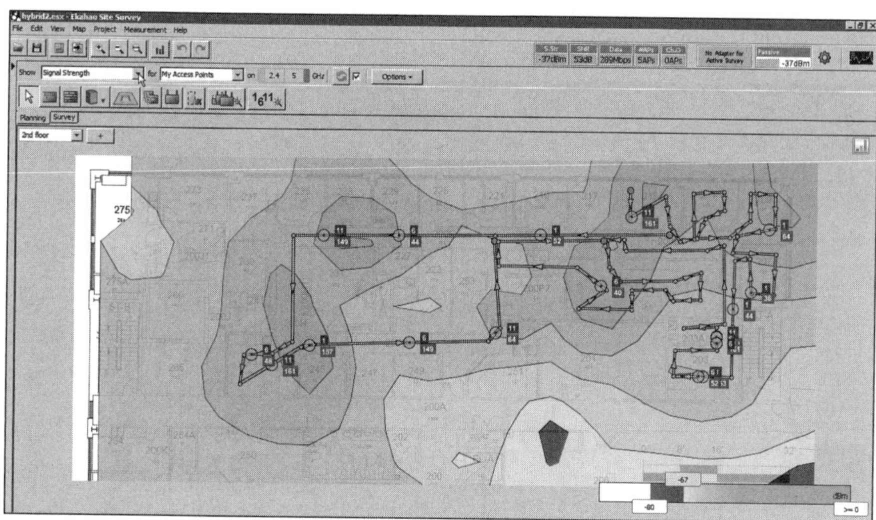

Figure 7-17 *Displaying AP Signal Strength in an Active Site Survey*

An active survey might also ping a target IP address at regular intervals to measure the round-trip time as the survey progresses. Figure 7-18 shows an active survey heatmap that displays ping round-trip times that were measured and extrapolated over the surveyed area. As well, the survey tool can leverage the iperf tool to send data streams between the survey device and an iperf server to gauge the actual throughput over the wireless network.

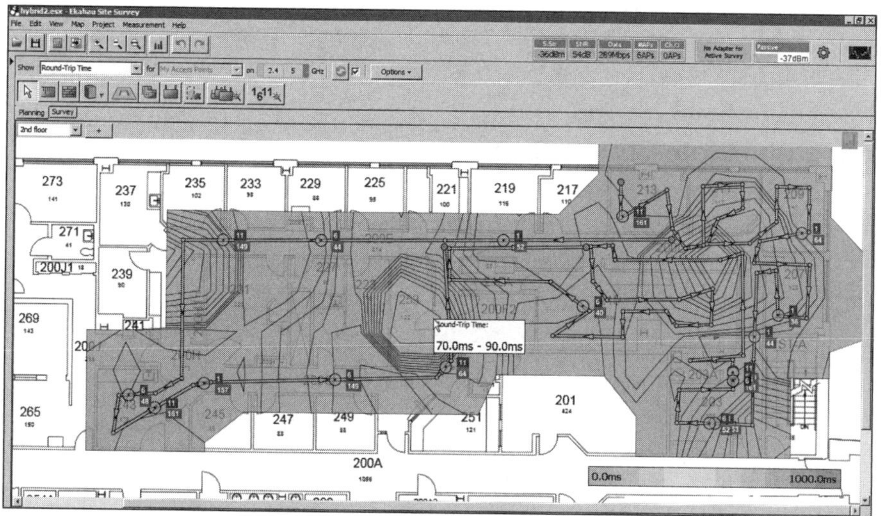

Figure 7-18 *Displaying Ping Round-Trip Times Measured in an Active Site Survey*

An active site survey also records each AP that the survey device associates with. The associated AP data can be presented in a heatmap, as shown in Figure 7-19. Each color represents a unique AP, so you can easily see where the survey client roamed by noticing where the color changes along the survey path.

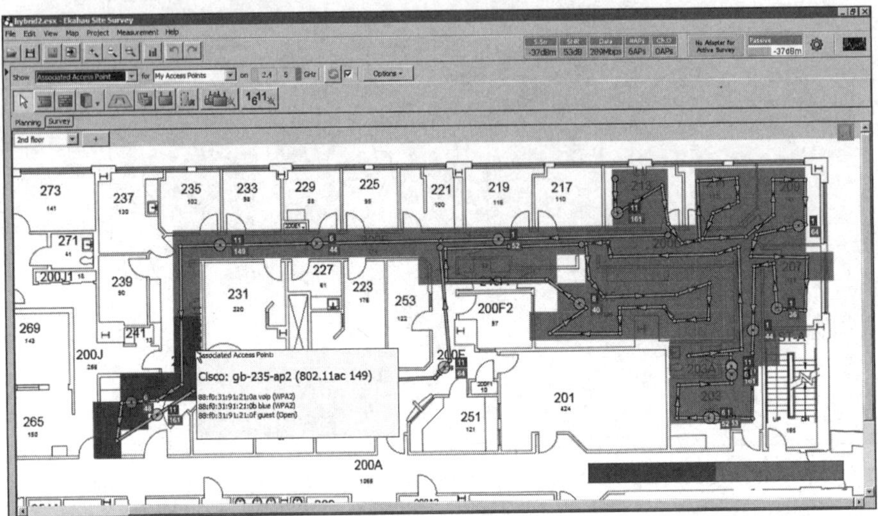

Figure 7-19 *Displaying Client Roaming Behavior in an Active Site Survey*

> **Tip** An active site survey uses the survey device as an actual wireless client, so the measurements taken from it represent the behavior of the device's wireless adapter, antenna, driver, and operating system. The survey results may not necessarily match the behavior of a different client device and software.

Developing a Complete Survey Strategy

Now that you have gotten a taste of the predictive, passive, and active surveys, what is the best practice for using them? A new network deployment has three distinct phases, as listed in Table 7-3: pre-deployment, deployment, and post-deployment, all named for their relation to APs being installed or deployed.

Table 7-3 AP Deployment Phases and Relevant Survey Types

Deployment Phase	Type of Site Survey to Perform	Goals
Pre-deployment	1. Predictive or planning survey	Determine how many APs will be needed to cover the area, as well as their projected locations.
	2. Passive survey	Gauge any existing APs, their channels, and signal strength.
	3. Spectrum analysis sweep	Make a sweep of the area by walking with a spectrum analyzer, such as AirMagnet Spectrum XT or MetaGeek Chanalyzer. Look for any sources of interference and try to pin down their locations. Chapter 19, "Dealing with Wireless Interference," covers spectrum analysis in more detail.
	4. "AP-on-a-stick" active survey	Gauge AP cell sizes and confirm proposed AP locations.
Deploy the APs	None	
Post-deployment	1. Passive survey	Verify every aspect of the operational wireless network.
	2. Active survey	Verify client operation, roaming, and performance across the entire area, over all APs.

The pre-deployment phase can be the most extensive because you need to plan for your AP layout, gauge any existing APs or interferers, then validate your design. Notice how many different survey types are involved—predictive, passive, spectrum analysis, and active. Each of these could require a complete walking pass through the entire coverage area, as well as a significant investment in time and effort. You can reduce the amount of work if a survey begins to produce acceptable results. For example, if the active AP-on-a-stick survey verifies your predictive design and AP layout after a few initial AP locations, then you might decide that no further results are needed.

Post-deployment is focused on verifying that the new AP deployment meets all of the requirements for acceptable service and performance. The post-deployment phase involves a passive survey and an active survey over the entire coverage area. The goals are to verify RF coverage, cell and channel overlap, SNR, noise floor, and bleed-through between floors and to check for rogue APs and interference sources. At this phase, it is very important to make sure the wireless network works properly before it is put into production.

Tip Passive and active surveys normally require two separate passes through an area to collect their data. Some standalone survey tools support a hybrid survey model and can perform both passive and active surveys in a single pass. This requires multiple wireless adapters that can be dedicated to each type of survey.

Exam Preparation Tasks

As mentioned in the section, "How to Use This Book," in the Introduction, you have a couple of choices for exam preparation: the exercises here, Chapter 21, "Final Review," and the exam simulation questions on the DVD.

Review All Key Topics

Review the most important topics in this chapter, noted with the Key Topic icon in the outer margin of the page. Table 7-4 lists a reference of these key topics and the page numbers on which each is found.

Table 7-4 Key Topics for Chapter 7

Key Topic Element	Description	Page Number
Figure 7-2	The effects of transmit power on cell size	158
Figure 7-4	The effects of data rate on cell size	160
Figure 7-8	Roaming between BSSs	164
Figure 7-10	Optimizing channel layout for roaming	167
List	Site survey types	171

Define Key Terms

Define the following key terms from this chapter and check your answers in the glossary:

active site survey, AP-on-a-stick, asymmetric power problem, BSSID method, channel reuse, passive site survey, post-deployment site survey, pre-deployment site survey, predictive survey, SSID method

Site Survey Type and Application Highlights

You can use Table 7-5 to review the various survey types, their applications, and purposes. The table also lists how relevant survey tools interact with APs during the survey process.

Table 7-5 Review of Site Survey Types and Applications

Site Survey Type	Application	Purpose	Survey Tool Interaction with APs
Planning	Pre-deployment (offsite)	Plan AP locations for deployment	None; all measurements are calculated
Passive	Pre- and post-deployment (onsite)	Verify existing AP layout and operation; troubleshooting	Listening only
Active	Pre- and post-deployment (onsite)	Verify client-AP interaction, functionality, and performance	Full association and roaming

This chapter covers the following topics:

- **Distributed Architectures**—This section discusses a wireless network formed by autonomous access points and managed either individually or through a cloud-based means.
- **Split-MAC Architectures**—This section describes wireless networks that can be built from lightweight access points and wireless LAN controllers.
- **Cisco Wireless Network Building Blocks**—This section covers the Cisco devices that are necessary to build a wireless network with one of the common architectures.

This chapter covers the following exam topics:

- 3.0—Implementing a Wireless Network
- 3.1—Describe the various Cisco wireless architectures
    - 3.1a—Cloud
    - 3.1b—Autonomous
    - 3.1c—Split MAC
        - 3.1c(i)—FlexConnect
        - 3.1c(ii)—Centralized
        - 3.1c(iii)—Converged
- 4.0 Operating a Wireless Network
    - 4.3 Distinguish different lightweight AP modes

CHAPTER 8

Understanding Cisco Wireless Architectures

In previous chapters, you learned about how a single access point (AP) can provide a basic service set (BSS) for a cell area and how multiple APs can be connected to form an extended service set (ESS) for a larger network. In this chapter, you will learn more about different approaches or architectures that allow APs to be networked together for an enterprise. You will also learn how some architectures are more scalable than others, and how to manage each type of wireless network architecture.

"Do I Know This Already?" Quiz

The "Do I Know This Already?" quiz allows you to assess whether you should read this entire chapter thoroughly or jump to the "Exam Preparation Tasks" section. If you are in doubt about your answers to these questions or your own assessment of your knowledge of the topics, read the entire chapter. Table 8-1 lists the major headings in this chapter and their corresponding "Do I Know This Already?" quiz questions. You can find the answers in Appendix A, "Answers to the 'Do I Know This Already?' Quizzes."

Table 8-1 "Do I Know This Already?" Section-to-Question Mapping

Foundation Topics Section	Questions
Distributed Architectures	1–3
Split-MAC Architectures	4–12
Cisco Wireless Network Building Blocks	13–15

Caution The goal of self-assessment is to gauge your mastery of the topics in this chapter. If you do not know the answer to a question or are only partially sure of the answer, you should mark that question as wrong for purposes of the self-assessment. Giving yourself credit for an answer you correctly guess skews your self-assessment results and might provide you with a false sense of security.

1. Which one of the following terms best describes a Cisco wireless access point that operates in a standalone, independent manner?
   a. Autonomous AP
   b. Independent AP
   c. Lightweight AP
   d. Embedded AP
2. Suppose that an autonomous AP is used to support wireless clients. Which one of the following paths would traffic usually take when passing from one wireless client to another?
   a. Through the AP only
   b. Through the AP and its controller
   c. Through the controller only
   d. None of these answers (because traffic can go directly over the air)
3. The Cisco Meraki cloud-based APs are most accurately described by which one of the following statements?
   a. Autonomous APs joined to a WLC
   b. Autonomous APs centrally managed
   c. Lightweight APs joined to a WLC
   d. Lightweight APs centrally managed
4. Suppose that a lightweight AP in default local mode is used to support wireless clients. Which one of the following paths would traffic usually take when passing from one wireless client to another?
   a. Through the AP only
   b. Through the AP and its controller
   c. Through the controller only
   d. None of these answers (because traffic must go directly over the air)
5. A lightweight access point is said to participate in which one of the following architectures?
   a. Light-MAC
   b. Tunnel-MAC
   c. Split-MAC
   d. Big-MAC
6. How does a lightweight access point communicate with a wireless LAN controller?
   a. Through an IPsec tunnel
   b. Through a CAPWAP tunnel
   c. Through a GRE tunnel
   d. Directly over Layer 2

7. Which one of the following types of traffic is sent securely over a CAPWAP tunnel by default?
   a. Control messages
   b. Client data
   c. DHCP requests
   d. 802.11 beacons

8. Which one of the following is not needed for a lightweight AP in default local mode to be able to support three SSIDs that are bound to three VLANs?
   a. A trunk link carrying three VLANs
   b. An access link bound to a single VLAN
   c. A WLC connected to three VLANs
   d. A CAPWAP tunnel to a WLC

9. A centralized wireless network is built with one WLC and 32 lightweight APs. Which one of the following best describes the resulting architecture?
   a. A direct Layer 2 path from the WLC to each of the 32 LAPs, all using the same IP subnet
   b. A direct Layer 3 path from the WLC to each of the 32 LAPs, all using the same IP subnet
   c. 32 CAPWAP tunnels daisy-chained between the LAPs, one CAPWAP tunnel to the WLC
   d. 32 CAPWAP tunnels—one tunnel from the WLC to each LAP, with no IP subnet restrictions

10. A converged wireless network architecture has which one of the following unique features?
   a. An access layer switch can also function as an AP.
   b. All WLCs are converged into one device.
   c. Large groups of APs connect to a single access layer switch.
   d. An access layer switch can also function as a WLC.

11. Which one of the following wireless architectures usually requires the most controllers to support the same number of lightweight APs?
   a. Autonomous
   b. Cloud-based
   c. Converged
   d. Centralized

12. The FlexConnect architecture is normally used in which of the following scenarios?

a. APs located in a main campus

b. APs located in remote branch sites

c. APs located in the cloud

d. None of the above, because FlexConnect is a Catalyst switch feature

13. A Cisco centralized wireless network is built with 1000 lightweight APs and a Cisco 5520 WLC. Suppose wireless coverage needs to be offered in several additional buildings, which will double the number of APs in use. Which of the following strategies would work? (Choose all that apply.)

a. Add another 5520 WLC.

b. Replace the 5520 with a WLC that offers a greater AP capacity.

c. The 5520 will become full, so replace the APs with models that can cover twice the area.

d. Do nothing; you can have only one WLC in a network and no other model offers more APs than the 5520.

14. Which of the following Cisco Aironet AP models should you choose if you expect to see 802.11ac Wave 2 clients in the near future? (Choose all that apply.)

a. 1700

b. 1850

c. 2700

d. 3700

15. Five Cisco Catalyst 3850 switches are configured as a single switch stack. The switches are also configured as a controller to support a converged wireless network. What is the maximum number of lightweight APs that can be joined to the switch stack?

a. 10

b. 50

c. 500

d. 1000

Foundation Topics

You can build a Cisco wireless network according to several different architectures that are described in the sections that follow. As you work through this chapter, think about how each architecture can be applied to specific environments—how easy it would be to manage, deploy, and troubleshoot the network, how the APs can be controlled, and how data would move through the network.

Distributed Architectures

An AP's primary function is to bridge wireless data from the air to a normal wired network. An AP can accept "connections" from a number of wireless clients so that they become members of the LAN, as if the same clients were using wired connections.

APs act as the central point of access (hence the AP name), controlling client access to the wireless LAN. An *autonomous AP* is self-contained; it is equipped with both wired and wireless hardware so that the wireless client associations can be terminated onto a wired connection locally at the AP. The APs and their data connections must be distributed across the coverage area and across the network. They can be managed in an autonomous fashion or through a cloud-based mechanism.

Autonomous Architecture

Autonomous APs are self-contained, each offering one or more fully functional, standalone basic service sets (BSSs). They are also a natural extension of a switched network, connecting wireless service set identifiers (SSIDs) to wired virtual LANs (VLANs) at the access layer. Figure 8-1 shows the basic architecture; even though only four APs are shown, a typical enterprise network could consist of hundreds or thousands of APs.

8

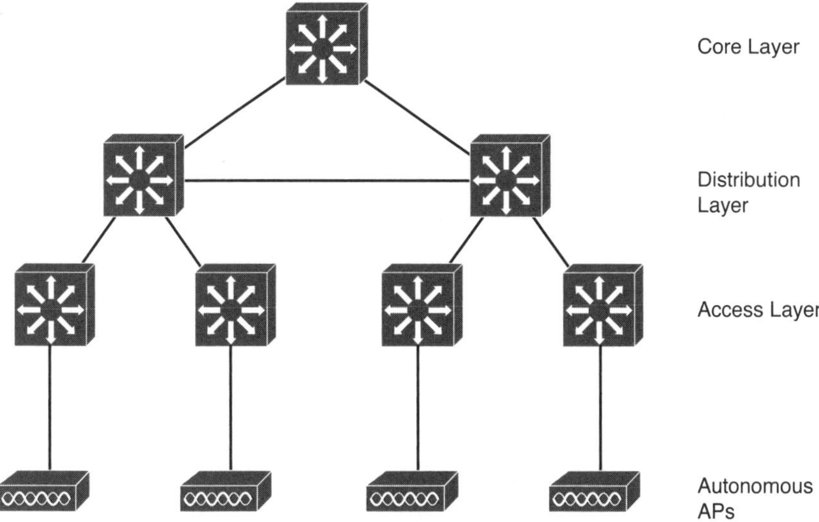

Figure 8-1 *Wireless Network Architecture with Autonomous APs*

What exactly does an autonomous AP need to become a part of the network? Refer to Figure 8-2, which focuses on just one AP and its connections. The wireless network consists of two SSIDs: wlan100 and wlan200. These correspond to wired VLANs 100 and 200, respectively. The VLANs must be trunked from the distribution layer switch (where routing commonly takes place) to the access layer, where they are extended further over a trunk link to the AP.

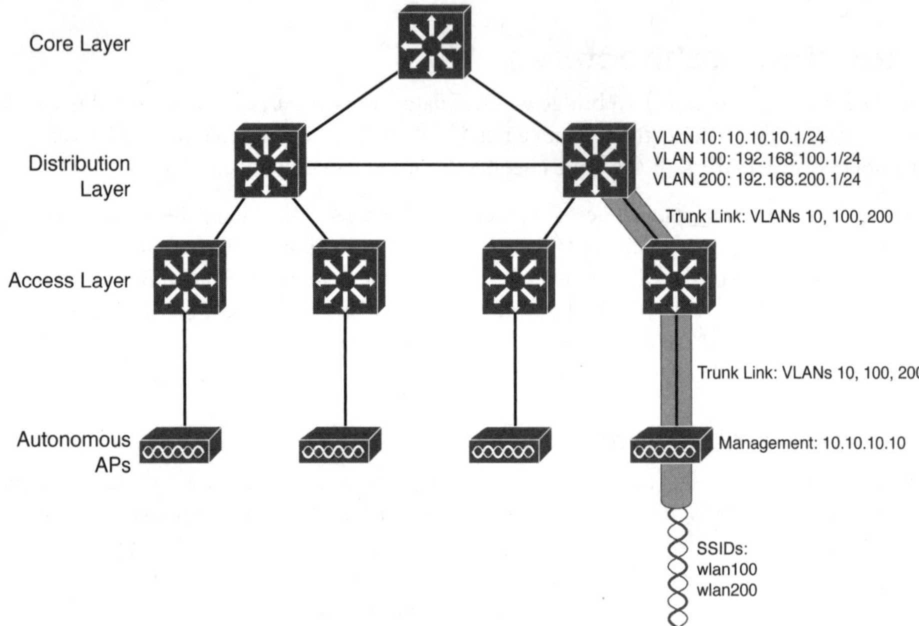

Figure 8-2 *Network Architecture Supporting a Single Autonomous AP*

An autonomous AP offers a short and simple path for data to travel between the wireless and wired networks. As Figure 8-3 shows, data has to travel only through the AP to reach the network on the other side. Two wireless users that are associated to the same autonomous AP can reach each other through the AP, without having to pass up into the wired network. As you work through the wireless architectures discussed in the rest of the chapter, notice the data path that is required for each.

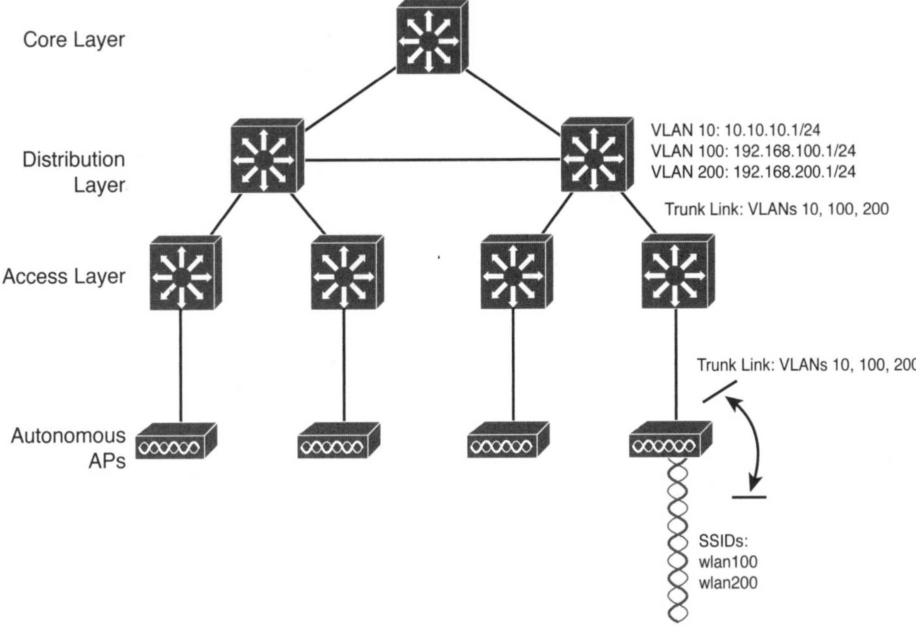

Figure 8-3 *Data Path Between Autonomous Wireless and Wired Networks*

An autonomous AP must also be configured with a management IP address (10.10.10.10) so that you can remotely manage it. After all, you will want to configure SSIDs, VLANs, and many RF parameters like the channel and transmit power to be used. The management address is not normally part of any of the data VLANs, so a dedicated management VLAN (VLAN 10 in the figures) must be added to the trunk links to reach the AP. Each AP must be configured and maintained individually unless you leverage a management platform such as Cisco Prime Infrastructure.

Because the data and management VLANs may need to reach every autonomous AP, the network configuration and efficiency can become cumbersome as the network scales. For example, you will likely want to offer the same SSID on many APs so that wireless clients can associate with that SSID in most any location or while roaming between two APs. You might also want to extend the corresponding VLAN to each and every AP so that clients do not have to request a new IP address for each new association.

Because SSIDs and their VLANs must be extended at Layer 2, you should consider how they are extended throughout the switched network. Figure 8-4 shows an example of a single VLAN's extent in the data plane. Working top to bottom, follow VLAN 100 as it reaches through the network. VLAN 100 is routed within the distribution layer and must be carried over trunk links to the access layer switches and then to each autonomous AP. In effect, VLAN 100 must extend end to end across the whole infrastructure—something that is considered a bad practice.

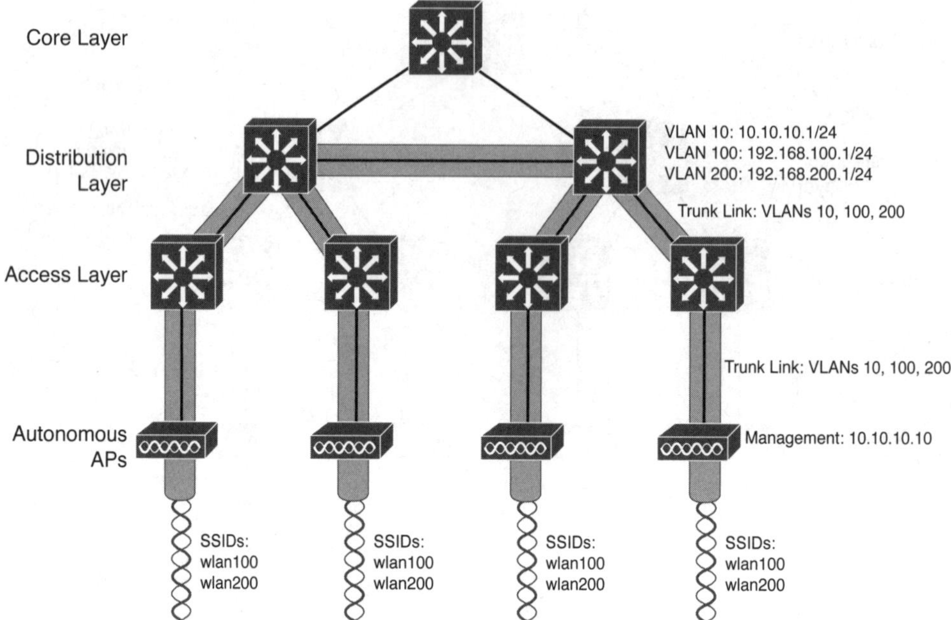

Figure 8-4 *Extent of a Data VLAN in a Network of Autonomous APs*

That might sound straightforward until you have to add a new VLAN and configure every switch and AP in your network. Even worse, suppose your network has redundant links between each layer of switches. The Spanning Tree Protocol (STP) running on each switch becomes a vital ingredient to prevent bridging loops from forming and corrupting the network. For these reasons, client roaming across autonomous APs is typically limited to the Layer 2 domain, or the extent of a single VLAN. As the wireless network expands, the infrastructure becomes more difficult to configure correctly and becomes less efficient.

Cloud-based Architecture

Recall that an autonomous AP needs quite a bit of configuration and management. To help manage more and more autonomous APs as the wireless network grows, you could place an AP management platform such as Cisco Prime Infrastructure in a central location within the enterprise. The management platform would need to be purchased, configured, and maintained too.

A simpler approach is a cloud-based architecture, where the AP management function is pushed out of the enterprise and into the Internet cloud. Cisco Meraki is cloud-based and offers centralized management of wireless, switched, and security network built from Meraki products. For example, through the cloud networking service, you can manage APs, monitor wireless performance and activity, generate reports, and so on.

Cisco Meraki APs can be deployed automatically, once you register with the Meraki cloud. Each AP will contact the cloud when it powers up and will self-configure. From that point on, you can manage the AP through the Meraki cloud dashboard.

Figure 8-5 illustrates the basic cloud-based architecture. Notice that the network is arranged identically to that of the autonomous AP network. That is because the APs in a cloud-based network are all autonomous, too. The most visible difference is that all of the APs are managed, controlled, and monitored centrally from the cloud.

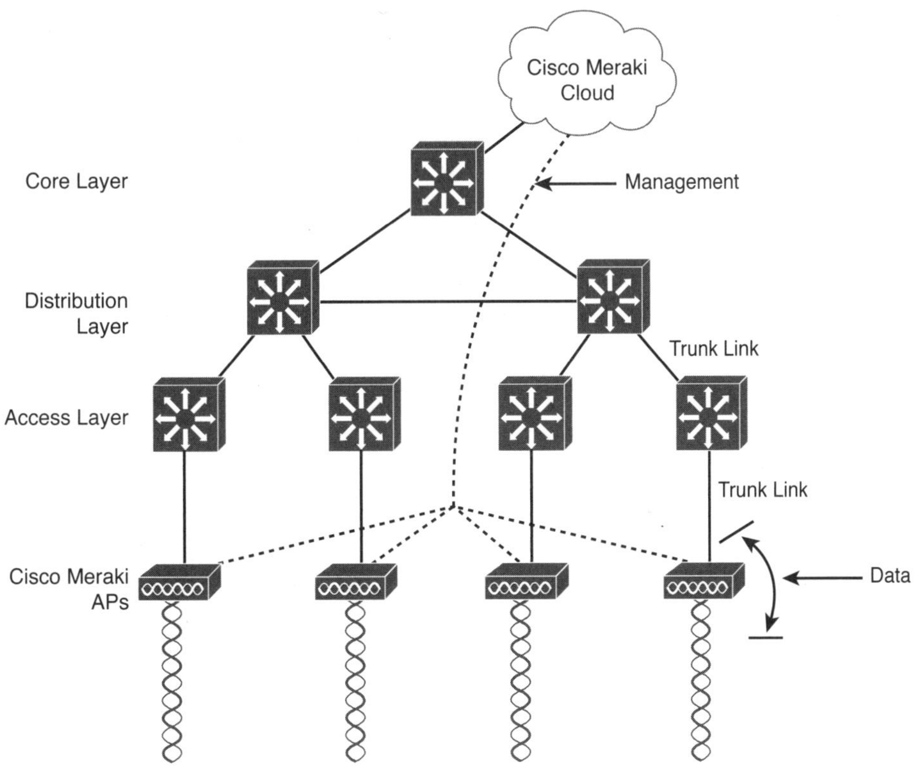

Figure 8-5 *Cisco Meraki Cloud-Based Wireless Network Architecture*

From the cloud, you can push out code upgrades and configuration changes to the APs in the enterprise. The Cisco Meraki cloud also adds the intelligence needed to instruct each AP on which channel and transmit power level to use. It can also collect information from all of the APs about things such as RF interference, rogue or unexpected wireless devices that were overheard, and wireless usage statistics.

Finally, there are a couple of things you should observe about the cloud-based architecture. The data path from the wireless network to the wired network is very short; the autonomous AP links the two networks. Data to and from wireless clients does not have to travel up into the cloud and back; the cloud is used to bring management functions into the data plane.

Also, notice that the network in Figure 8-5 consists of two distinct paths—one for data traffic and another for management traffic, corresponding to the following two functions:

- **A control plane**—Traffic used to control, configure, manage, and monitor the AP itself
- **A data plane**—End-user traffic passing through the AP

8

This division will become important in the following sections as other types of architecture are discussed.

Split-MAC Architectures

Because autonomous APs are...well, autonomous, managing their RF operation can be quite difficult. As a network administrator, you are in charge of selecting and configuring the channel used by each AP and detecting and dealing with any rogue APs that might be interfering. You must also manage things such as the transmit power level to make sure that the wireless coverage is sufficient, does not overlap too much, and there aren't any coverage holes—even when an AP's radio fails.

Managing wireless network security can also be difficult. Each autonomous AP handles its own security policies, with no central point of entry between the wireless and wired networks. That means there is no convenient place to monitor traffic for things such as intrusion detection and prevention, quality of service, bandwidth policing, and so on.

To overcome the limitations of distributed autonomous APs, many of the functions found within autonomous APs have to be shifted toward some central location. In Figure 8-6, most of the activities performed by an autonomous AP on the left are broken up into two groups—real-time processes on the top and management processes on the bottom.

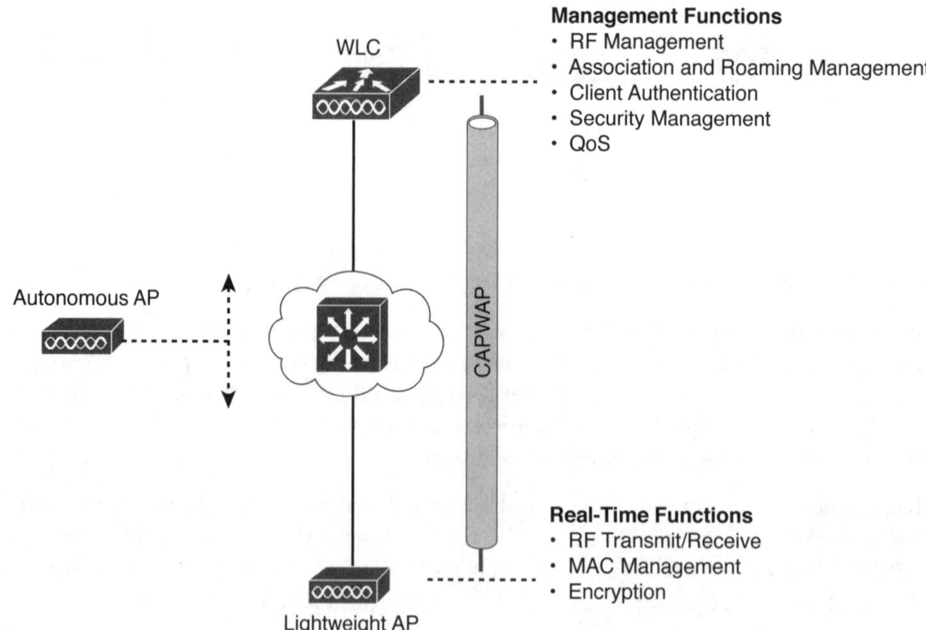

Figure 8-6 *Autonomous Versus Lightweight Access Point*

The real-time processes involve sending and receiving 802.11 frames, beacons, and probe messages. 802.11 data encryption is also handled in real time, on a per-packet basis. The AP must interact with wireless clients on some low level, known as the *media access control* (MAC) layer. These functions must stay with the AP, closest to the clients.

The management functions are not integral to handling frames over the RF channels, but are things that should be centrally administered. Therefore, those functions are moved to a centrally located platform away from the AP.

In the Cisco unified wireless network, a *lightweight access point* (LAP) performs only the real-time 802.11 operation. The LAP gets its name because the code image and the local intelligence are stripped down, or lightweight, compared to the traditional autonomous AP.

The management functions are usually performed on a *wireless LAN controller* (WLC), which controls many LAPs. This is shown in the bottom right portion of Figure 8-6. Notice that the LAP is left with duties in Layers 1 and 2, where frames are moved into and out of the RF domain. The LAP becomes totally dependent on the WLC for every other WLAN function, such as authenticating users, managing security policies, and even selecting RF channels and output power.

Tip Remember that a lightweight AP cannot normally operate on its own—it is very dependent upon a WLC somewhere in the network. The only exception is the FlexConnect architecture, which is discussed later in this chapter.

The LAP-WLC division of labor is known as a *split-MAC architecture*, where the normal MAC operations are pulled apart into two distinct locations. This occurs for every LAP in the network; each one must boot and bind itself to a WLC to support wireless clients. The WLC becomes the central hub that supports a number of LAPs scattered about in the network.

How does an LAP bind with a WLC to form a complete working access point? The two devices must use a tunneling protocol between them, to carry 802.11-related messages and also client data. Remember that the LAP and WLC can be located on the same VLAN or IP subnet, but they do not have to be. Instead, they can be located on two entirely different IP subnets in two entirely different locations.

The Control and Provisioning of Wireless Access Points (CAPWAP) tunneling protocol makes this all possible by encapsulating the data between the LAP and WLC within new IP packets. The tunneled data can then be switched or routed across the campus network. As Figure 8-7 shows, the CAPWAP relationship actually consists of the following two tunnels:

- **CAPWAP control messages**—Used for exchanges that are used to configure the LAP and manage its operation. The control messages are authenticated and encrypted, so that the LAP is securely controlled by only the WLC, then transported using UDP port 5246 at the controller.
- **CAPWAP data**—Used for packets traveling to and from wireless clients that are associated with the LAP. Data packets are transported using UDP port 5247 at the controller, but are not encrypted by default. When data encryption is enabled for an LAP, packets are protected with Datagram Transport Layer Security (DTLS).

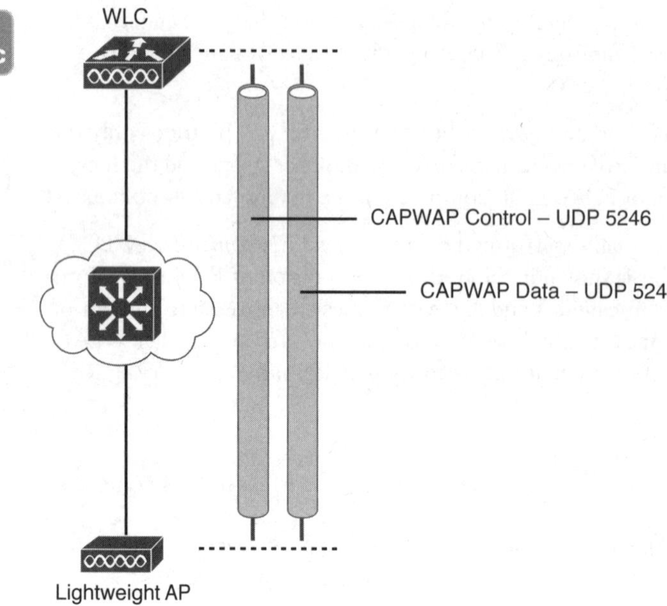

Figure 8-7 *Linking an LAP and WLC with CAPWAP*

> **Tip** CAPWAP is defined in RFCs 5415, 5416, 5417, and 5418. CAPWAP is based on the Lightweight Access Point Protocol (LWAPP), which was a legacy Cisco proprietary solution.

Every LAP and WLC must also authenticate each other with digital certificates. An X.509 certificate is preinstalled in each device when it is purchased. By using certificates behind the scenes, every device is properly authenticated before becoming part of the wireless network. This process helps assure that no rogue non-CAPWAP AP can be introduced into the network. The LAP-WLC association is covered in greater detail in Chapter 11, "Understanding Controller Discovery."

The CAPWAP tunneling allows the LAP and WLC to be separated geographically and logically. It also breaks the dependence on Layer 2 connectivity between them. For example, Figure 8-8 uses shaded areas to show the extent of VLAN 100. Notice how VLAN 100 exists at the WLC and in the air as SSID 100, near the wireless clients—but not in between the LAP and the WLC. Instead, traffic to and from clients associated with SSID 100 is transported across the network infrastructure encapsulated inside the CAPWAP data tunnel. The tunnel exists between the IP address of the WLC and the IP address of the LAP, which allows all of the tunneled packets to be routed at Layer 3.

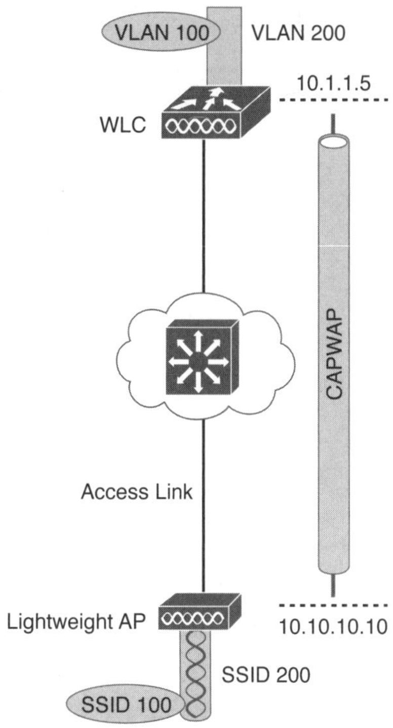

Figure 8-8 *Extent of VLAN 100 in a Cisco Wireless Network*

8

Also, notice how the LAP is known by only a single IP address 10.10.10.10. Because the LAP sits on the access layer where its CAPWAP tunnels terminate, it can use one IP address for both management and tunneling. No trunk link is needed because all of the VLANs it supports are encapsulated and tunneled.

As the wireless network grows, the WLC simply builds more CAPWAP tunnels to reach more APs. Figure 8-9 depicts a network with four LAPs. Each LAP has a control and a data tunnel back to the centralized WLC. SSID 100 can exist on every AP, and VLAN 100 can reach every AP through the network of tunnels.

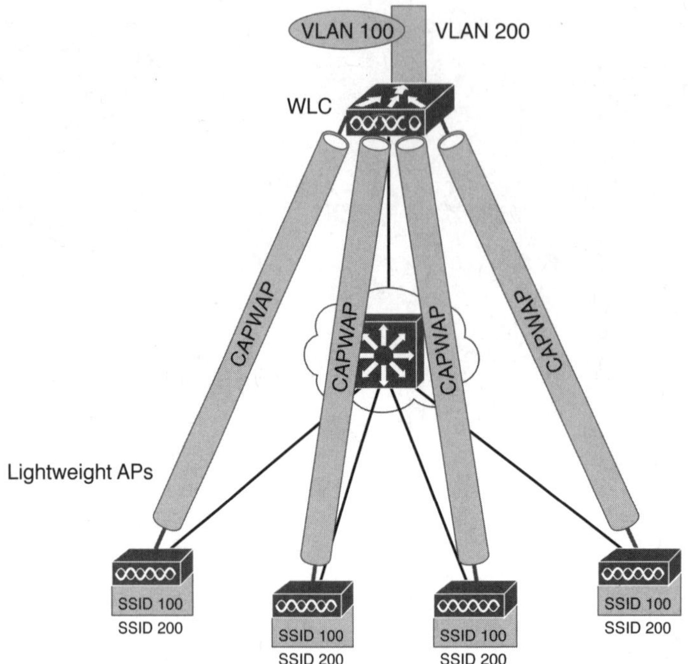

Figure 8-9 *Using CAPWAP Tunnels to Connect LAPs to One Central WLC*

Once CAPWAP tunnels are built from a WLC to one or more lightweight APs, the WLC can begin offering a variety of additional functions. Think of all the puzzles and shortcomings that were discussed for the traditional autonomous WLAN architecture as you read over the following list of WLC activities:

- **Dynamic channel assignment**—The WLC can automatically choose and configure the RF channel used by each LAP, based on other active access points in the area.
- **Transmit power optimization**—The WLC can automatically set the transmit power of each LAP based on the coverage area needed.
- **Self-healing wireless coverage**—If an LAP radio dies, the coverage hole can be "healed" by turning up the transmit power of surrounding LAPs automatically.
- **Flexible client roaming**—Clients can roam between LAPs at either Layer 2 or Layer 3 with very fast roaming times.
- **Dynamic client load balancing**—If two or more LAPs are positioned to cover the same geographic area, the WLC can associate clients with the least used LAP. This distributes the client load across the LAPs.
- **RF monitoring**—The WLC manages each LAP so that it scans channels to monitor the RF usage. By listening to a channel, the WLC can remotely gather information about RF interference, noise, signals from neighboring LAPs, and signals from rogue APs or ad hoc clients.

- **Security management**—The WLC can authenticate clients from a central service and can require wireless clients to obtain an IP address from a trusted DHCP server before allowing them to associate and access the WLAN.
- **Wireless intrusion protection system**—Leveraging its central location, the WLC can monitor client data to detect and prevent malicious activity.

The split-MAC concept can be applied to several different network architectures, as described in the following sections. Each architecture places the WLC in a different location within the network—a choice that also affects how many WLCs are needed.

Centralized Wireless Network Architecture

Suppose you want to deploy a WLC to support multiple lightweight APs in your network. Where should you put the WLC? One approach is to locate the WLC in a central location so that you can maximize the number of APs joined to it. This tends to follow the concept that most of the resources users need to reach are located in a central location such as a data center or the Internet. Traffic to and from wireless users would travel over CAPWAP tunnels that reach into the center of the network, near the core, as shown in Figure 8-10. A centralized WLC also provides a convenient place to enforce security policies that affect all wireless users.

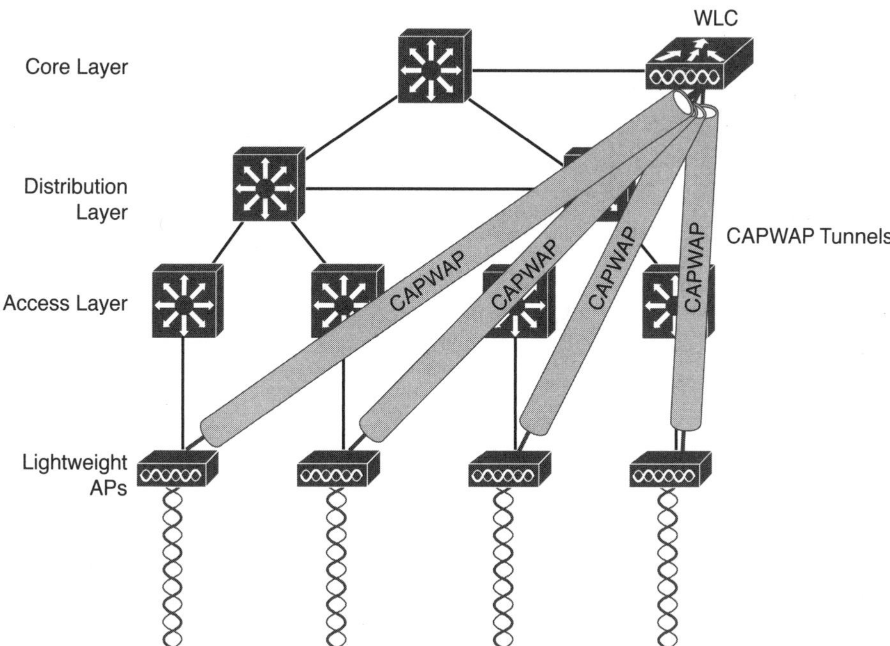

Figure 8-10 *WLC Location in a Centralized Wireless Network*

Figure 8-10 shows four LAPs joined to a single WLC. Your network might have more LAPs—many, many more. A large enterprise network might have thousands of LAPs connected to its access layer. Scalability then becomes an important factor in the centralized

8

design. Each Cisco WLC model has a maximum number of LAPs that it supports. If you have more LAPs than the maximum, you will need to add more WLCs to the design, each located centrally.

Tip Cisco offers WLC models that support a maximum of 75 LAPs up to 6000 LAPs. Each model also has a maximum number of wireless clients. The cost of the WLC is generally proportional to the maximum number of LAPs and clients supported. You can find an overview of specific models later in this chapter.

Notice how the centralized architecture affects wireless user mobility. For example, Figure 8-11 illustrates a wireless user that is moving through the coverage areas of the four APs from Figure 8-10. As the user moves, he might associate with many different LAPs in the access layer. Because all of the LAPs are joined to a single WLC, that WLC can easily maintain the user's connectivity to all other areas of the network.

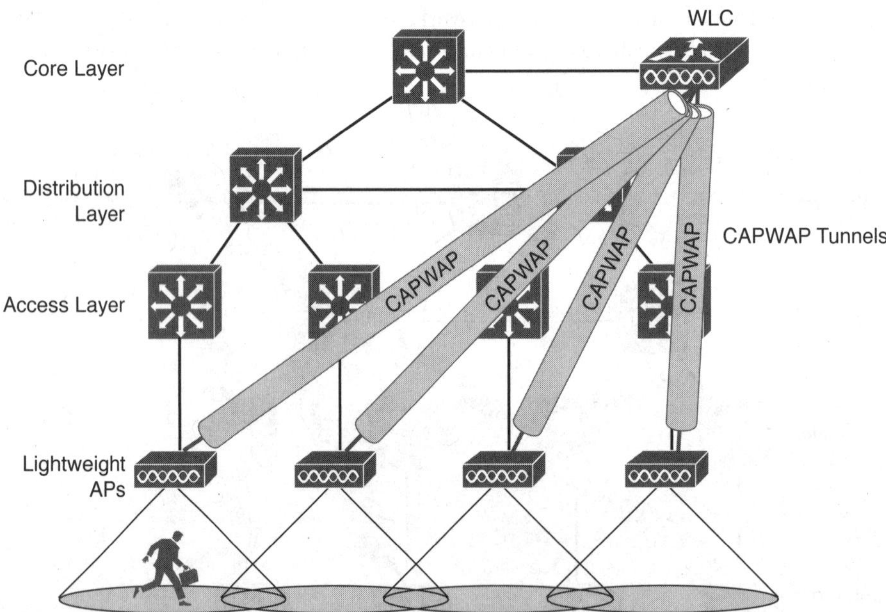

Figure 8-11 *User Mobility in a Centralized Wireless Network*

Locating the WLC centrally also affects the path that wireless data must take. For a wireless user to reach a wired network segment, the traffic is tunneled from the LAP to the WLC as shown in Figure 8-12. Notice that the tunnel extends the full expanse of the network hierarchy from the access layer to the core layer.

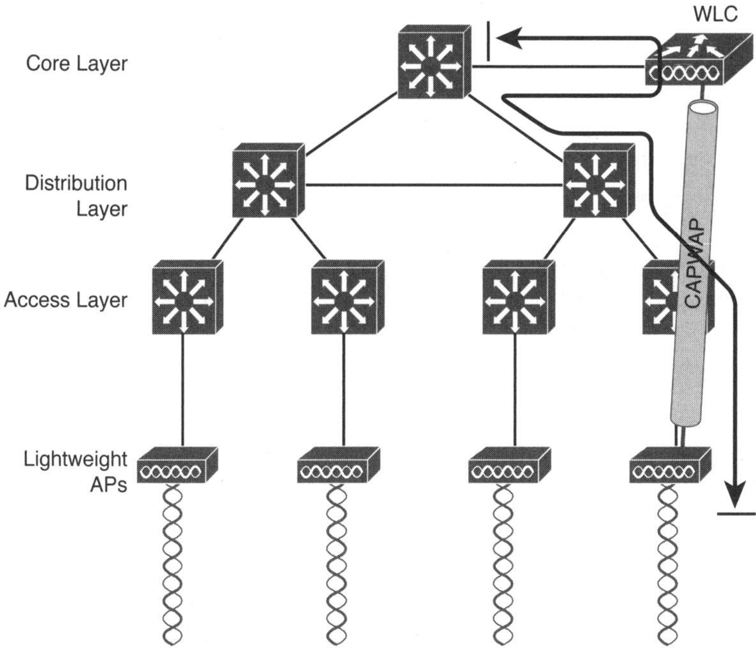

Figure 8-12 *Traffic Path in a Centralized Wireless Network*

The length of the tunnel path is not a great concern for wireless users trying to reach centralized resources. If the wireless users need to reach a local resource in the access layer or other wireless users, then the path becomes much more interesting. Recall that two wireless users associated with an autonomous AP can reach each other through the AP. In contrast, the path between two wireless users in a centralized network is shown in Figure 8-13. From Client A, the traffic must pass through the LAP, where it is encapsulated in the CAPWAP tunnel, then travel up to the core layer to reach the WLC, where it is unencapsulated, To go on to Client B, the process then reverses and the traffic goes back down through the tunnel to reach the AP and back out into the air.

8

Tip The length of the tunnel path can be a great concern for the LAPs, however. The round-trip time (RTT) between an LAP and a controller should be less than 100 ms so that wireless communication can be maintained in near real time. If the path has more latency than that, the LAPs may decide that the controller is not responding fast enough, causing them to disconnect and find another, more responsive controller.

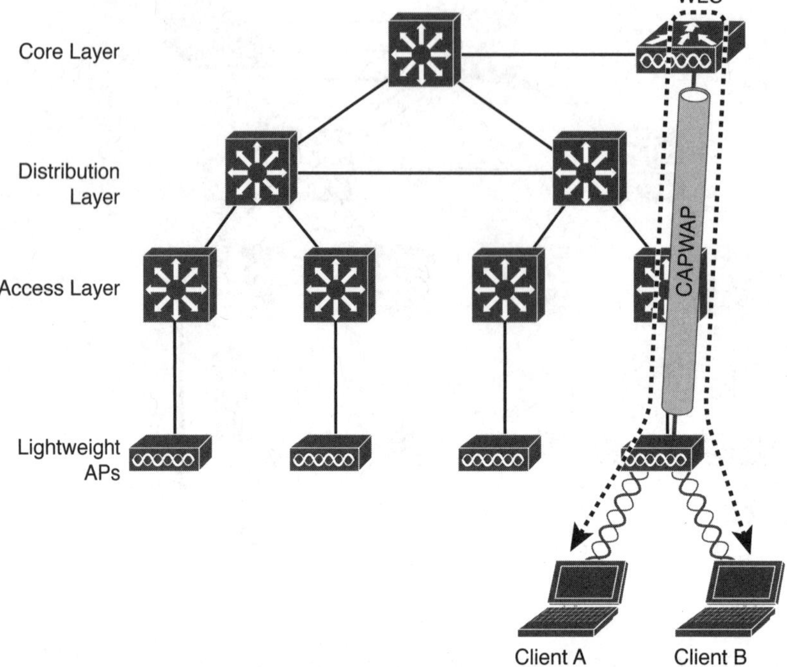

Figure 8-13 *Traffic Path Between Wireless Clients in a Centralized Wireless Network*

Such "hairpin" paths can be rather inefficient because both ends of the split-MAC mechanism must be traversed in both directions. Now consider an enterprise that has some branch sites that are located some distance away from the main campus. LAPs can be deployed at the branch site too, joining to a centralized WLC back at headquarters. Wireless users at the branch site might need to access local file servers or printers, so their traffic paths must hairpin over the WAN link that ultimately connects to the WLC. The branch users become totally dependent on the WAN link—if the link goes down, the CAPWAP tunnel will fail. Once that happens, the users can be cut off from their local resources, too.

Tip Cisco LAPs can remedy this situation by providing local access through the FlexConnect feature. The additional FlexConnect architecture is discussed later in this chapter.

Converged Wireless Network Architecture

As an alternative to the centralized wireless architecture, where WLCs are located near the core layer, the WLC function can be moved further down in the network hierarchy. Relocating the WLCs does two things:

- The WLC function is moved closer to the LAPs (and the wireless users).
- The WLC function becomes distributed, rather than centralized.

The access layer turns out to be a convenient location for the WLCs. After all, wireless users ultimately connect to a WLC, which serves as a virtual access layer. Why not move the wireless access layer to coincide with the wired access layer? With all types of user access merged into one layer, it becomes much easier to do things like apply common access and security policies that affect all users. This is known as a *converged wireless network* architecture. To distinguish the two approaches, centralized controllers are known as WLCs, while converged controllers are known as Wireless Control Modules (WCMs).

Tip As you prepare for the exam, remember the distinction between the centralized and converged architectures, with regard to the WLC and WCM functions. One other difference is that WLCs run the Cisco AireOS software, while WCMs are based on the Cisco IOS-XE software that runs on the Catalyst switches that host the WCMs.

As you might imagine, distributing the controller function into the access layer increases the number of controllers that are needed. One controller is needed per access switch stack or chassis. The idea is to push more controllers down closer to the users, which also reduces the number of APs and clients that connect to each one. How can this be accomplished? The Cisco Catalyst 3650, 3850, and 4500 (Supervisor 8-E only) product families are commonly used as access layer switches, plus they can offer converged-access WCM functions without needing any additional hardware. Table 8-2 lists the AP and client capacity of each switch platform.

Table 8-2 Converged Access Switch Wireless Capacities

Platform	Lightweight APs Supported	Wireless Clients Supported
Catalyst 3650 (per stack)	25	1000
Catalyst 3850 (per stack)	50	2000
Catalyst 4500 (per chassis)	50	2000

It might seem odd that the number of supported APs is rather low, when the physical port density of a switch is rather large. For instance, a Catalyst 3850 switch stack can consist of up to 432 wired ports (nine 48-port switches), but only 50 APs can be connected to the entire stack of switches. If you think of this from a wireless perspective, it makes more sense. Each AP is connected to the switch stack by a twisted-pair cable that is limited to a length of 100 meters. Therefore, all of the APs must be located within a 100 meter radius of the access switch. There are not too many AP cells that can physically fit into that area.

Figure 8-14 shows the basic converged wireless network architecture. Notice that each access switch performs both switching and WLC functions. Each AP connects to an access switch for network connectivity as well as split-MAC functionality, so the CAPWAP tunnel becomes really short—it exists only over the length of the cable connecting the AP! The arrow shows the length of the data path between the wireless and wired networks.

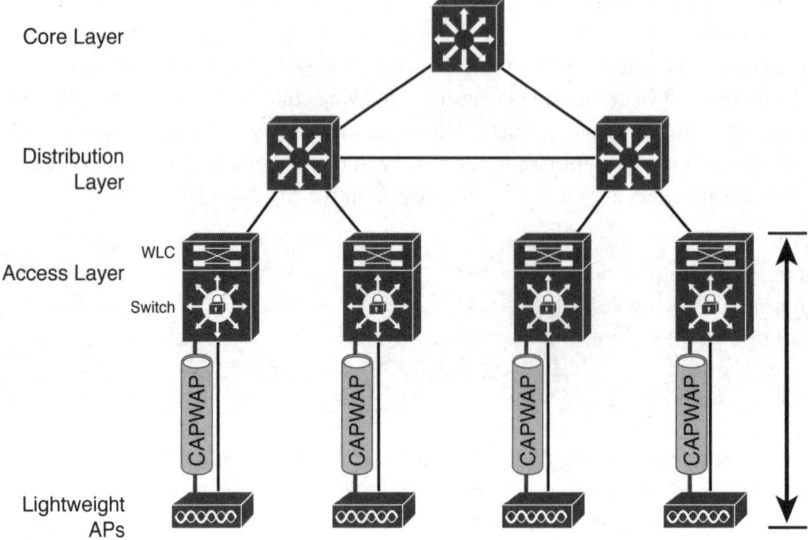

Figure 8-14 *WLC Location in a Converged Wireless Network*

One other advantage of the converged network architecture relates to wireless scalability. APs offering 802.11ac Wave 1 can use common 1-Gbps switch ports without limiting the throughput. Wave 2, however, has the potential to go well beyond 1 Gbps, which requires something more than a single 10/100/1000-Mbps switch port. Cisco offers proprietary Multigigabit Ethernet ports on several models in the Catalyst 3850 and 4500 families, where APs can connect over single cables. Multigigabit Ethernet can operate at speeds of 100 Mbps, 1 Gbps, 2.5 Gbps, and 5 Gbps over Cat5e cabling and up to 10 Gbps over Cat6a cabling speeds.

The converged model also solves some connectivity problems at branch sites by bringing a fully functional WLC onsite, within the access layer switch. With a local WLC, the APs can continue to operate without a dependency upon a WLC at the main site through a WAN connection.

How does the converged architecture affect user mobility? With more WLCs and fewer APs joined to each, you might expect that a mobile user will pass through more WLCs than in a centralized architecture. Figure 8-15 shows the basic network and AP layout. As a wireless user travels along, she could encounter many different WLCs as she roams from AP to AP. Therefore, some greater coordination must be used to support roaming in the converged model. Chapter 12, "Understanding Roaming," discusses this in greater detail.

If the CAPWAP tunnel is relatively short in a converged network, that must mean that wireless devices can reach each other more efficiently. Indeed, as Figure 8-16 shows, the traffic path from one user to another must pass through an LAP, the access switch (and WLC), and back down through the LAP. In contrast, traffic from a wireless user to a central resource such as a data center or the Internet travels through the CAPWAP tunnel, is unencapsulated at the access layer switch (and WLC), then travels normally up through the rest of the network layers.

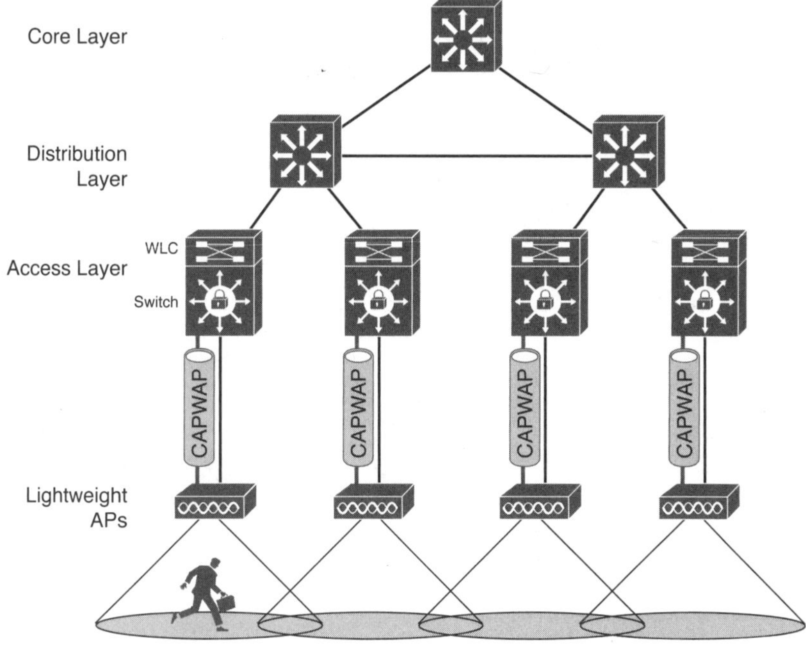

Figure 8-15 *User Mobility in a Converged Wireless Network*

Key Topic

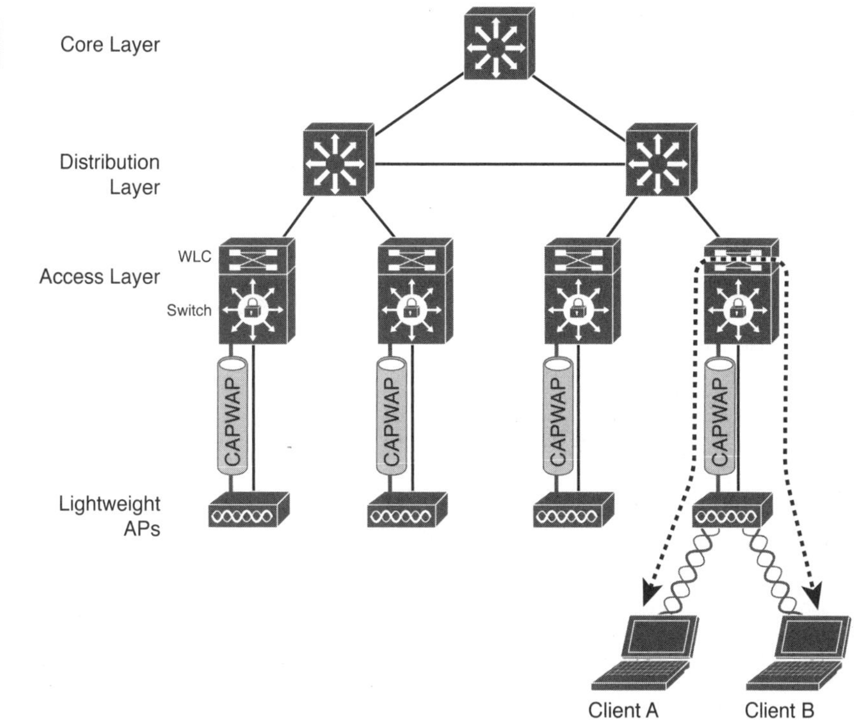

Figure 8-16 *Traffic Path in a Converged Wireless Network*

8

FlexConnect Wireless Network Architecture

In a switched campus infrastructure, the split-MAC traffic pattern is not a big problem because the WLC can be centrally located and bandwidth is plentiful. Suppose that the network grows to include some remote branch sites. LAPs are placed at the branch sites, but the only WLC is located back at the main campus. This scenario forces wireless traffic to traverse the CAPWAP tunnel between branch and main sites to reach centralized resources, as Figure 8-17 shows. Branch-site users might also need to access local nonwireless resources such as a file server and printers. In that case, the traffic path follows the CAPWAP tunnel to the WLC, then back through the tunnel to the branch site again. Such a path, as depicted in Figure 8-18, might not be efficient at all, especially when the bandwidth to the remote site is limited.

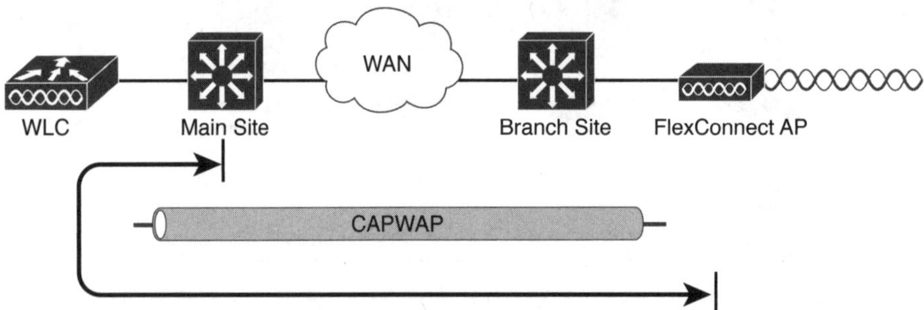

Figure 8-17 *Split-MAC Architecture at a Branch Site*

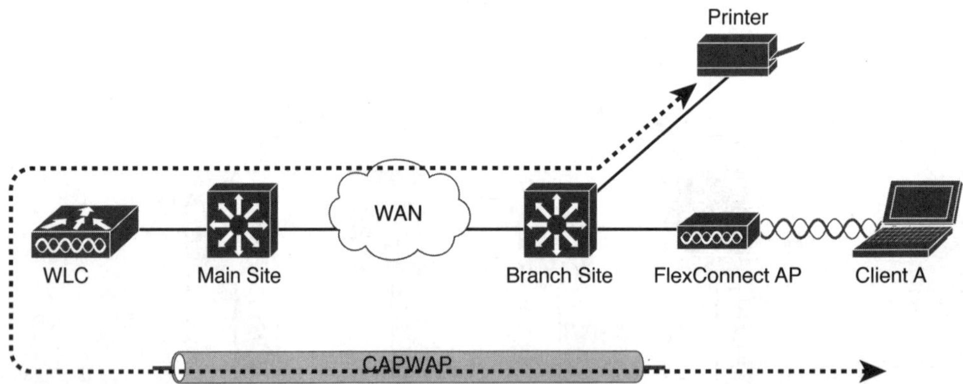

Figure 8-18 *Traffic Path to Reach Nonwireless Resources in a Branch Site*

To address the inefficiency, you can leverage the FlexConnect mode on the remote-site LAPs. Remote-site traffic that needs to traverse the CAPWAP data tunnel to reach the WLC will be transported as usual. However, wireless traffic that is destined for branch-site networks can stay within the branch site; the branch-site LAPs are able to locally switch the traffic without traversing the CAPWAP tunnel. Even if the remote-site link goes down, severing the CAPWAP tunnel completely, FlexConnect allows the LAP to keep switching traffic locally to maintain wireless connectivity inside the remote site, as illustrated in the scenario in Figure 8-19. A FlexConnect AP can operate in two modes: when it can reach the WLC, it operates in *connected mode*; when the path to the WLC is broken, the AP operates in *standalone mode*.

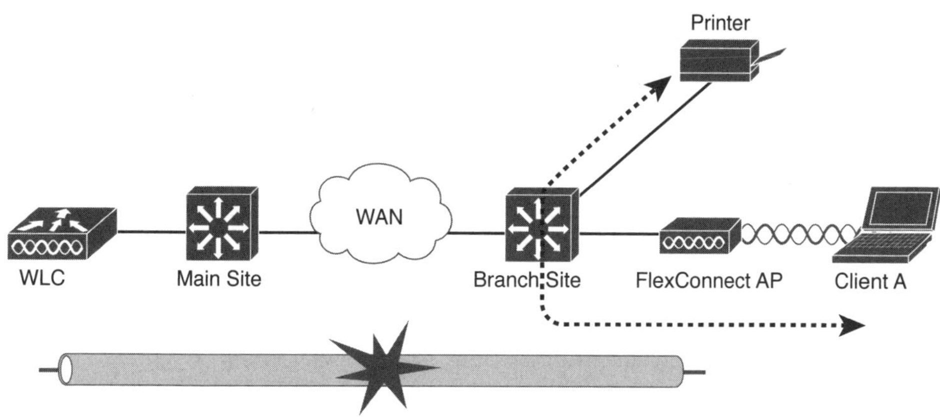

Figure 8-19 *Traffic Path During FlexConnect Local Switching*

> **Tip** FlexConnect was previously known as the Hybrid Remote Edge Access Point (H-REAP) feature. To maintain connectivity between the WLC and the branch-site LAP, the WAN link should have a round-trip latency less than 300 ms for normal data and less than 100 ms for data and voice traffic.

8

Cisco Wireless Network Building Blocks

A successful Cisco wireless network design can involve APs, WLCs, and a platform to manage them all. The following sections describe the Cisco hardware you can use as building blocks.

Cisco Wireless LAN Controllers

Cisco WLCs are available in many platforms, differing mainly in the form factor and the number of managed LAPs. The WLC platforms are listed in Table 8-3, arranged in ascending order by the maximum number of LAPs supported.

Table 8-3 Cisco WLC and WCM Platforms and Capabilities

Model	Architecture	APs Supported	Clients Supported
Catalyst 3650	Converged (WCM)	25 per switch stack	1000
Catalyst 3850	Converged (WCM)	50 per switch stack	2000
Catalyst 4500	Converged (WCM)	50	2000

Model	Architecture	APs Supported	Clients Supported
2504	Centralized (WLC)	75	1000
Virtual WLC	Centralized (WLC)	200	6000
5520	Centralized (WLC)	1500	20,000
5760	Centralized (WLC)	1000	12,000
WiSM2[1]	Centralized (WLC)	1000	15,000
Flex 7510[2]	Centralized (WLC)	6000	64,000
8510	Centralized (WLC)	6000	64,000
8540	Centralized (WLC)	6000	64,000

1. The WiSM2 is a module that must be installed in a Catalyst 6500 chassis.

2. Flex 7510 also supports up to 6000 branch locations with FlexConnect APs.

Use Table 8-3 to become familiar with the entire spectrum of Cisco WLCs—not to memorize their specifications. Be aware of the relative AP capacity and architecture based on the model. Generally, the number of supported LAPs rises as the model number increases. Products that support a low number of LAPs are usually meant for small campus sites, while products that support 1000 or 6000 LAPs are flagship models that are meant for very large enterprises.

Many WLCs are standalone appliances, while others are integrated in Catalyst switch chassis. The Wireless Service Module 2 (WiSM2) is unique because it can be integrated into an existing Catalyst 6500 switch. Up to seven WiSM2 modules can live in a single switch chassis.

The virtual WLC (vWLC) is an interesting product because it consists of software only, running under a VMware Hypervisor. You might use it in a small enterprise or in a lab scenario. Because of its virtual nature, vWLC can coexist with other Cisco wireless management software on a single VMware platform. The vWLC cannot support any APs in local mode; all APs must be configured for FlexConnect instead.

Be aware that you can deploy several WLCs in a network, to handle a growing number of LAPs. In addition, multiple WLCs offer some redundancy so that LAPs can recover from a WLC failure. High availability and redundancy are covered in Chapter 11.

Cisco APs

Cisco Meraki APs are the building blocks for a cloud-based architecture. Table 8-4 lists the AP models with their basic capabilities.

Table 8-4 Cisco Meraki Cloud-based Access Points and Their Capabilities

Model	Spectrum Analysis	Antennas	802.11	Radios
Meraki MR18	Yes	Internal	n	2×2:2
Meraki MR26	Yes	Internal	n	3×3:3

Model	Spectrum Analysis	Antennas	802.11	Radios
Meraki MR32	Yes	Internal	n, ac Wave 1	2×2:2
Meraki MR34	Yes	Internal	n, ac Wave 1	3×3:3
Meraki MR66	Yes	External	n	2×2:2
Meraki MR72	Yes	External	n, ac Wave 1	2×2:2

Cisco also offers a complete line of LAPs that are designed to connect to a WLC to offer fully functional wireless service. Table 8-5 lists many of the LAP models, along with their spectrum analysis capability, antenna location, and 802.11 radio support. All of the models except the 1850 can run an autonomous AP image instead of a lightweight AP image.

Table 8-5 Cisco Lightweight Access Points and Their Capabilities

Model	Spectrum Analysis	Antennas	802.11	Radios
700W[1]	No	Internal	n	2×2:2
1700	Yes	Internal	n, ac Wave 1	3×3:2
1850	Yes	Internal/External	n, ac Wave 2	2.4 GHz: 3×4:3 5 GHz: 4×4:4 SU-MIMO 5 GHz: 4×4:3 MU-MIMO
2700	Yes	Internal/External	n, ac Wave 1	3×4:3
3700	Yes	Internal/External	n, ac Wave 1 + expansion module	4×4:3

1. Includes four 10/100/1000Base-T ports, one with PoE

The 1700, 2700, and 3700 models offer progressively larger feature sets and more robust radio chains. The 3700 is unique because it is modular and can provide "future-proof" upgrades. It can accept one of the following additional modules:

- **Cisco Aironet Wireless Security Module**—Performs channel scanning and intrusion protection with dedicated radios
- **Cisco Universal Small Cell 5310 Module**—Extends 3G cellular service to AP locations within buildings
- **Cisco Aironet 802.11ac Wave 2 Module**—Available in the future; extends 802.11ac capabilities beyond Wave 1

The 1850 model is the first Cisco AP to offer fully integrated 802.11ac Wave 2. Notice how the number of radio chains changes to support 802.11n on 2.4 GHz and 802.11ac on 5 GHz. Wave 2 allows the AP to operate in multiuser multiple-input, multiple-output (MU-MIMO) mode.

With spectrum analysis capabilities, an AP can detect and identify sources of non-802.11 interference. In cooperation with a WLC, APs can also make adjustments to avoid the interference. When the AP and WLC are used in conjunction with Cisco Mobility Services Engine (MSE) and a Cisco wireless management platform, interferers can even be located on a map! This enables the wireless network to be self-healing, able to pinpoint and recover from external problems dynamically. Spectrum analysis through the Cisco CleanAir feature is discussed further in Chapter 19, "Dealing with Wireless Interference."

The main difference between models pertains to 802.11ac support and MIMO operation, with a differing number of radios and spatial streams. Recall from Chapter 2, "RF Standards," that a radio described as 2×3:2 has two transmitters, three receivers, and two spatial streams. As the number of radios and spatial streams increases, the AP is able to provide a greater throughput for its clients. Notice how the number of radios and spatial streams increase with 802.11ac Wave 1 and Wave 2 support.

Note Tables 8-4 and 8-5 list only the APs that are used to provide a straightforward BSS. Cisco also offers the 1500 family of LAPs, which are used to build an outdoor wireless mesh network. Likewise, Cisco Meraki offers the MR66 and MR72 outdoor mesh APs. Mesh networks are outside the scope of this book and the CCNA Wireless exam.

Many Cisco APs can operate in either autonomous or lightweight mode, depending on which code image is loaded and run. From the WLC, you can also configure a lightweight AP to operate in one of the following special-purpose modes:

- **Local**—The default lightweight mode that offers one or more functioning BSSs on a specific channel. During times that it is not transmitting, the LAP will scan the other channels to measure the noise floor, measure interference, discover rogue devices, and match against intrusion detection system (IDS) events.
- **Monitor**—The LAP does not transmit at all, but its receiver is enabled to act as a dedicated sensor. The LAP checks for IDS events, detects rogue access points, and determines the position of stations through location-based services (LBS).
- **FlexConnect**—An LAP at a remote site can locally switch traffic between an SSID and a VLAN if its CAPWAP tunnel to the WLC is down and if it is configured to do so.
- **Sniffer**—An LAP dedicates its radios to receiving 802.11 traffic from other sources, much like a sniffer or packet capture device. The captured traffic is then forwarded to a PC running network analyzer software such as Wildpackets OmniPeek or WireShark, where it can be analyzed further.
- **Rogue detector**—An LAP dedicates itself to detecting rogue devices by correlating MAC addresses heard on the wired network with those heard over the air. Rogue devices are those that appear on both networks.
- **Bridge**—An LAP becomes a dedicated bridge (point to point or point to multipoint) between two networks. Two LAPs in bridge mode can be used to link two locations separated by a distance. Multiple LAPs in bridge mode can form an indoor or outdoor mesh network.
- **Flex+Bridge**—FlexConnect operation is enabled on a mesh AP.
- **SE-Connect**—The LAP dedicates its radios to spectrum analysis on all wireless channels. You can remotely connect a PC running software such as MetaGeek Chanalyzer or Cisco Spectrum Expert to the LAP to collect and analyze the spectrum analysis data to discover sources of interference.

Exam Preparation Tasks

As mentioned in the section, "How to Use This Book," in the Introduction, you have a couple of choices for exam preparation: the exercises here, Chapter 21, "Final Review," and the exam simulation questions on the DVD.

Review All Key Topics

Review the most important topics in this chapter, noted with the Key Topic icon in the outer margin of the page. Table 8-6 lists a reference of these key topics and the page numbers on which each is found.

Table 8-6 Key Topics for Chapter 8

Key Topic Element	Description	Page Number
Figure 8-2	Autonomous AP architecture	188
Figure 8-5	Cloud-based architecture	191
Figure 8-6	Split-MAC architecture	192
Figure 8-7	CAPWAP operation	194
Figure 8-13	Centralized architecture traffic pattern	200
Figure 8-16	Converged architecture traffic pattern	203
Figure 8-19	FlexConnect architecture traffic pattern	205

This chapter covers the following topics:

- **Initially Configuring an Autonomous AP**—This section explains how to connect and configure an access point to form a functional basic service set and how to upgrade the AP's software.
- **Initially Configuring a Cloud-based AP**—This section discusses the initial configuration of a Cisco Meraki access point.

This chapter covers the following exam topics:

- 3.3—Describe AP and WLC management access connections
  - 3.3.a—Management connections (Telnet, SSH, HTTP, HTTPS, console)
  - 3.3.b—IP addressing: IPv4 / IPv6
- 4.0—Operating a Wireless Network
- 4.1—Execute initial setup procedures Cisco wireless infrastructures
  - 4.1a—Cloud
  - 4.1d—Autonomous
- 4.5—Identify wireless network and client management and configuration platform options
  - 4.5.c—Dashboard
- 4.6—Maintain wireless network
  - 4.6b—Perform code updates on controller, APs, and converged access switches
  - 4.6b(iii)—Autonomous

CHAPTER 9

Implementing Autonomous and Cloud Deployments

Autonomous and cloud-based wireless access points (APs) are self-contained and standalone, offering a fully functional BSS. At the CCNA Wireless level, you are expected to be able to install an autonomous or cloud-based AP, find its IP address, connect to it, and configure it. In addition, you should know how to convert an autonomous AP to lightweight mode, to become a part of a larger, more integrated wireless network. This chapter covers the skills you will need to develop.

"Do I Know This Already?" Quiz

The "Do I Know This Already?" quiz allows you to assess whether you should read this entire chapter thoroughly or jump to the "Exam Preparation Tasks" section. If you are in doubt about your answers to these questions or your own assessment of your knowledge of the topics, read the entire chapter. Table 9-1 lists the major headings in this chapter and their corresponding "Do I Know This Already?" quiz questions. You can find the answers in Appendix A, "Answers to the 'Do I Know This Already?' Quizzes."

Table 9-1 "Do I Know This Already?" Section-to-Question Mapping

Foundation Topics Section	Questions
Initially Configuring an Autonomous AP	1–10
Initially Configuring a Cloud-based AP	11–12

Caution The goal of self-assessment is to gauge your mastery of the topics in this chapter. If you do not know the answer to a question or are only partially sure of the answer, you should mark that question as wrong for purposes of the self-assessment. Giving yourself credit for an answer you correctly guess skews your self-assessment results and might provide you with a false sense of security.

1. Suppose that you need to set up an autonomous AP so that it will offer three different SSIDs to clients. The AP will be connected to a wired network infrastructure. Which one of the following is a true statement about the AP?
   a. It can support only one SSID, which must be carried over an access link.
   b. It can support multiple SSIDs over an access link.
   c. It can support multiple SSIDs over an 802.1Q trunk link.
   d. An autonomous AP needs a centralized controller to support SSIDs.
2. Which one of the following is a true statement?
   a. An autonomous AP cannot connect to a DS.
   b. An autonomous AP connects through a centralized controller.
   c. An autonomous AP operates in a standalone fashion.
   d. None of these answers are correct.
3. Which of the following ports are available on an autonomous AP? (Choose all that apply.)
   a. Console port
   b. Service port
   c. Ethernet port
   d. Dynamic interface
4. After looking at a sticker on the back of an autonomous AP, you see MAC C4:7D:4F:12:34:56 listed. Which one of the following is a safe assumption?
   a. The string of numbers is the 2.4-GHz radio base MAC address.
   b. The string of numbers is the 5-GHz radio base MAC address.
   c. The string of numbers is the Ethernet port MAC address.
   d. All of the above are correct.
5. Which methods can be used to assign an IP address to an autonomous AP? (Choose all that apply.)
   a. DHCP
   b. Static through the CLI
   c. TFTP
   d. DNS
6. If the IP address of an autonomous AP is not yet known, which of the following methods could you use to find it? (Choose all that apply.)
   a. DHCP server logs
   b. CDP
   c. AP console CLI
   d. AP management GUI

7. In its default configuration, which of the following is true of an autonomous AP? (Choose all that apply.)
   a. Both radios are enabled.
   b. Both radios are disabled.
   c. No SSIDs are configured.
   d. One SSID ("Cisco") is configured.

8. Which of the following are correct statements about autonomous AP configuration? (Choose all that apply.)
   a. Each AP radio must offer an identical set of SSIDs.
   b. Each AP radio can offer a unique set of SSIDs.
   c. Each AP must be configured with the IP address of its controller.
   d. An IP address must be configured on the Ethernet0 interface.
   e. An IP address must be configured on the BVI1 interface.

9. To convert an autonomous AP into a lightweight AP, which of the following is needed? (Choose all that apply.)
   a. Enter the **convert lightweight** command in the AP CLI
   b. A TFTP or FTP server
   c. An appropriate lightweight code image
   d. An appropriate autonomous upgrade image

10. To upgrade an autonomous AP to lightweight mode, which one of the following initial command keywords should be used from the CLI?
    a. **upgrade download-sw**
    b. **copy flash: tftp:**
    c. **archive download-sw**
    d. **download upgrade-sw**

11. Which one of the following methods can you use to manage a Cisco Meraki AP?
    a. Console port
    b. CLI via Telnet
    c. Web browser opened to the AP's IP address
    d. Web browser opened to the Cisco Meraki cloud

12. When a new Cisco Meraki AP is first powered on, it automatically connects with which one of the following?
    a. A Cisco wireless LAN controller
    b. A TFTP server located at 10.0.0.1
    c. The Cisco Meraki cloud network
    d. Nothing; as an autonomous AP, it waits for you to configure its IP address

Foundation Topics

Autonomous APs are commonly used in small networks, such as a small office or a remote site. Because the APs are self-contained and self-sufficient, they are fairly easy to set up and configure. The end result is a decentralized, distributed architecture, where each wireless AP touches the wired network independently. Each AP is configured and managed independently too, which can lead to a management nightmare as the number of APs grows.

You can think of an AP as a translational bridge, where frames from two dissimilar media are translated and then bridged at Layer 2. In simple terms, the AP is in charge of mapping a service set identifier (SSID) to a VLAN, or in 802.11 terms, mapping a basic service set (BSS) to a distribution system (DS). This is shown in Figure 9-1, where the AP connects a client that is associated to the SSID "Marketing" with the wired network on VLAN 10. On the wired side, the AP's Ethernet port is connected to a switch port configured for access mode and mapped to VLAN 10.

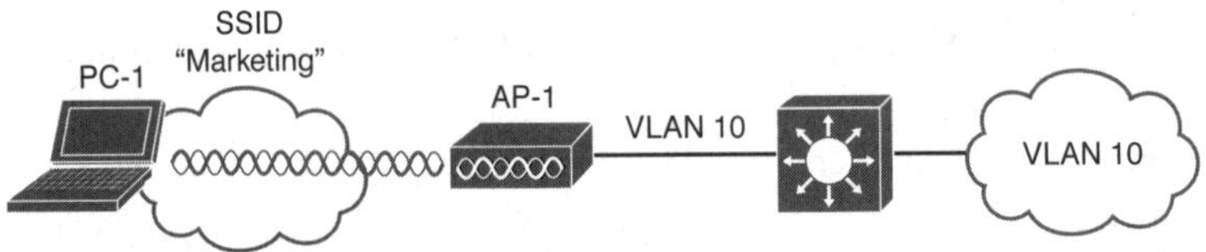

Figure 9-1 *Bridging an SSID to a VLAN*

This concept can be extended so that multiple VLANs are mapped to multiple SSIDs. To do this, the AP must be connected to the switch by a trunk link that carries the VLANs. In Figure 9-2, VLAN 10 and VLAN 20 are both trunked to the AP. The AP uses the 802.1Q tag to map the VLAN numbers to SSIDs. For example, VLAN 10 is mapped to SSID "Marketing," while VLAN 20 is mapped to SSID "Engineering."

Key Topic

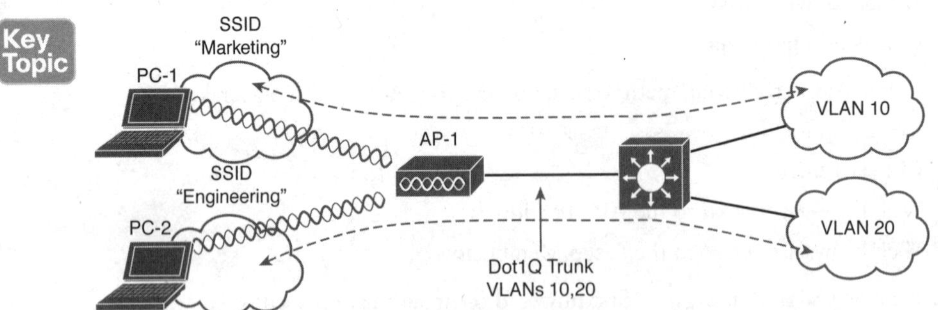

Figure 9-2 *Bridging Multiple SSIDs to VLANs*

In effect, when an AP uses multiple SSIDs, it is trunking VLANs over the air to wireless clients. In the 802.11 space, the VLAN tag is replaced by the SSID. The autonomous AP then becomes an extension of an access layer switch because it bridges SSIDs and VLANs right at the access layer.

Initially Configuring an Autonomous AP

As a wireless engineer, you will likely have to install and configure an autonomous AP. Many Cisco APs can operate in autonomous mode by running an IOS image—much like many other Cisco products. You can configure an AP through any of the following methods:

- A terminal emulator connected to the AP's console port
- Telnet or Secure Shell (SSH) to the AP's IP address
- Use a web browser to access a graphical user interface (GUI) at the AP's IP address

As you read through this chapter, think about the different parameters you might have to configure on an autonomous AP. At a minimum, you would have to configure one or more SSIDs and some wireless security settings. In addition, you would have to set the transmit power level and channel number for each of the AP's radios. Now think about your wireless network as it grows—manually configuring a handful of autonomous APs might not be difficult, but working out the channel reuse layout for 50 or 100 APs in the same building might become a nightmare.

Connecting the AP

Figure 9-3 shows the ports that are available on a typical access point. You should connect the Ethernet port to a switch port on the wired network. The console port can remain disconnected unless you need to use it. A sticker on the AP provides the model and serial numbers, as well as the Ethernet port's MAC address.

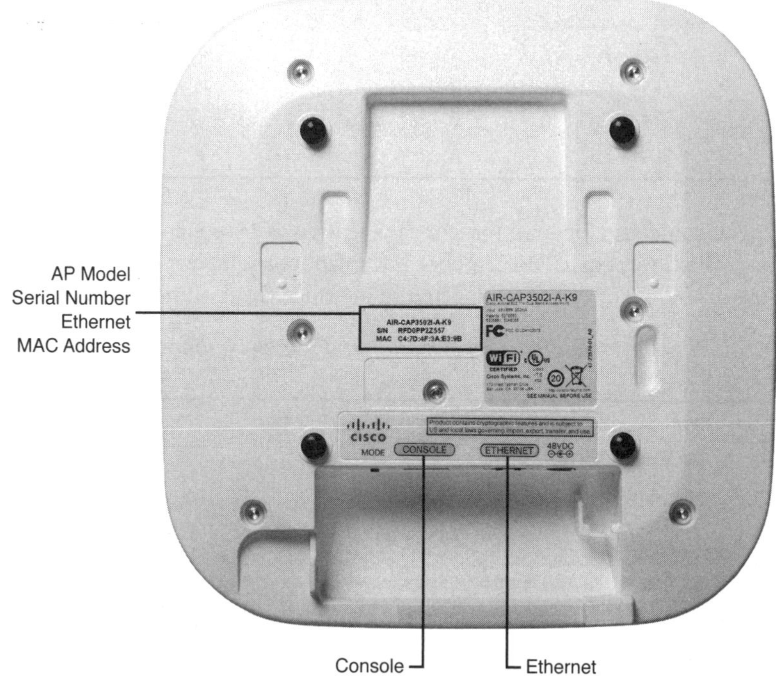

Figure 9-3 *Ports Available on an Autonomous AP*

By default, an AP will try to use Dynamic Host Configuration Protocol (DHCP) to request an IP address for itself. If it is successful, you can connect to it and interact with its GUI or command-line interface (CLI). If not, the AP will use the static IP address 10.0.0.1/26. You can also use the console port to configure a static IP address on the BVI1 interface of the AP, but it is usually more flexible and convenient to let it request an address on its own.

The AP's IP address will not be readily visible because the AP has no way to display it, other than through its user interface and configuration. To find the IP address, you can query the DHCP server that assigned it and look for the AP's MAC address.

Suppose that an AP has MAC address 00:22:bd:19:28:dd. From the output listed in Example 9-1, the MAC address is bound to IP address 192.168.199.44.

Example 9-1 *Finding an Autonomous AP's IP Address*

```
Branch_Office# show ip dhcp binding
Bindings from all pools not associated with VRF:
IP address          Client-ID/              Lease expiration        Type
                    Hardware address/
                    User name
192.168.199.7       0020.6b77.9549          Infinite                Manual
192.168.199.8       000e.3b00.b1a3          Infinite                Manual
192.168.199.9       0004.00d0.378d          Infinite                Manual
192.168.199.14      0100.24f3.da9b.95       May 10 2015 01:09 AM    Automatic
192.168.199.20      0170.f1a1.131c.48       May 09 2015 09:25 PM    Automatic
192.168.199.23      0194.39e5.826c.38       May 09 2015 08:51 PM    Automatic
192.168.199.24      0100.216a.0ac3.a0       May 09 2015 11:21 PM    Automatic
192.168.199.34      0100.166f.6614.6d       May 09 2015 09:33 PM    Automatic
192.168.199.43      01cc.fe3c.4d66.49       May 09 2015 04:59 PM    Automatic
192.168.199.44      0100.22bd.1928.dd       May 10 2015 11:20 AM    Automatic
Branch_Office#
```

As an alternative, you could also log in to the switch where the AP is connected and display detailed Cisco Discovery Protocol (CDP) neighbor information. Example 9-2 shows the output that reveals the IP address of the AP connected to interface GigabitEthernet1/0/1.

Example 9-2 *Displaying CDP Neighbor Information to Find an Autonomous AP's IP Address*

```
Switch# show cdp neighbor gigabitethernet1/0/1 detail
-------------------------
Device ID: ap
Entry address(es):
  IP address: 192.168.199.44
Platform: cisco AIR-CAP3702I-A-K9,  Capabilities: Router Trans-Bridge
Interface: GigabitEthernet1/0/1,  Port ID (outgoing port): GigabitEthernet0.1
Holdtime : 138 sec
```

```
Version :
Cisco IOS Software, C3700 Software (AP3G2-K9W8-M), Version 15.2(4)JB6, RELEASE SOFT-
WARE (fc1)
Technical Support: http://www.cisco.com/techsupport
Copyright (c) 1986-2014 by Cisco Systems, Inc.
Compiled Fri 22-Aug-14 11:52 by prod_rel_team

advertisement version: 2
Duplex: full
Power drawn: 15.400 Watts
Power request id: 52275, Power management id: 7
Power request levels are:16800 15400 13000 0 0
Management address(es):
```

An autonomous AP binds the IP address to its bridged-virtual interface (BVI), which is a logical interface used to bridge the physical wired and wireless interfaces. If you are connected to the AP's console port, you can display the IP address with the **show interface bvi1** command, as shown in Example 9-3.

Example 9-3 *Displaying the BVI IP Address*

```
ap# show interface bvi1
BVI1 is up, line protocol is up
  Hardware is BVI, address is 0022.bd19.28dd (bia 0023.eb81.eb70)
  Internet address is 192.168.199.44/24
  MTU 1500 bytes, BW 54000 Kbit/sec, DLY 5000 usec,
        reliability 255/255, txload 1/255, rxload 1/255
  Encapsulation ARPA, loopback not set
  ARP type: ARPA, ARP Timeout 04:00:00
[output truncated]
```

9

Initially Configuring the AP

By default, an autonomous AP has its radios disabled and does not have any SSIDs configured. This is done to prevent the new AP from interfering with any existing signals before you have a chance to configure it. This also prevents anyone from inadvertently discovering a wireless signal coming from the AP before you can secure it.

Perhaps the easiest method you can use to configure an autonomous AP is to use its web interface. Once you know the AP's IP address, you can open a web browser to it. By default, you can leave the username blank and enter the password as Cisco. The Summary or home page, as shown in Figure 9-4, displays a summary of associated clients, the AP's Ethernet and radio interfaces, and an event log.

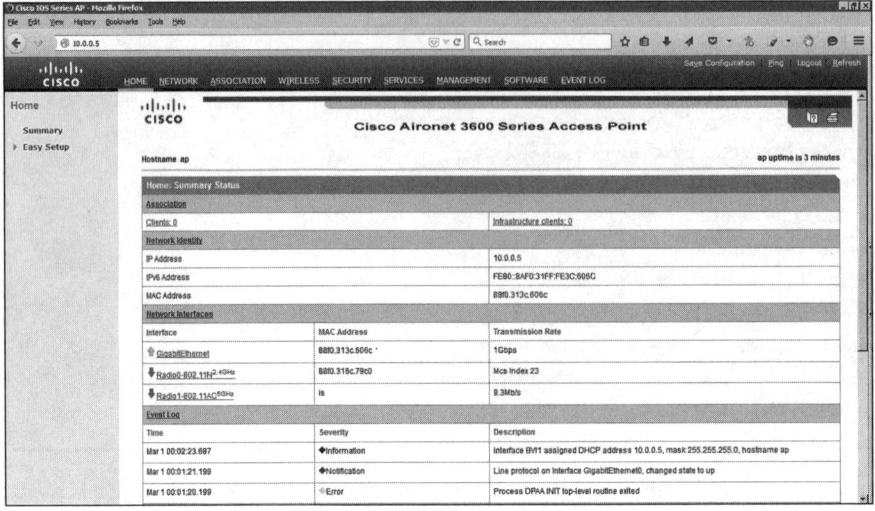

Figure 9-4 *Autonomous AP Web Page*

At the CCNA Wireless level, Cisco expects candidates to be able to perform basic configuration tasks on autonomous APs. Therefore, you should be familiar with only the Summary and Easy Setup menus at the upper-left corner of the web page, as found under the Home tab.

To use the Easy Setup page, as shown in Figure 9-5, you need to enter the following information about the AP:

- Hostname
- Method of IP address assignment
- For a static address: IP address, subnet mask, default gateway
- An administrative username and password
- SNMP community

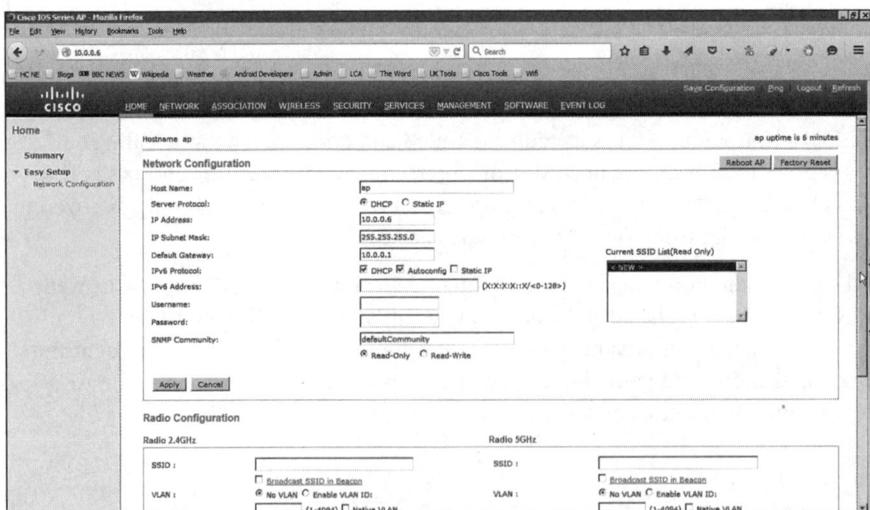

Figure 9-5 *Autonomous AP Easy Setup Page*

You will also need to set some parameters for the 2.4- and 5-GHz radios, which are configured independently in the bottom portion of the Easy Setup page, as shown in Figure 9-6. Enter the name of the first SSID that the AP will provide to wireless users. If the AP will support only a single SSID that is mapped to a single VLAN, select the **No VLAN** radio button. Otherwise, select **Enable VLAN ID** and enter the VLAN number for the SSID.

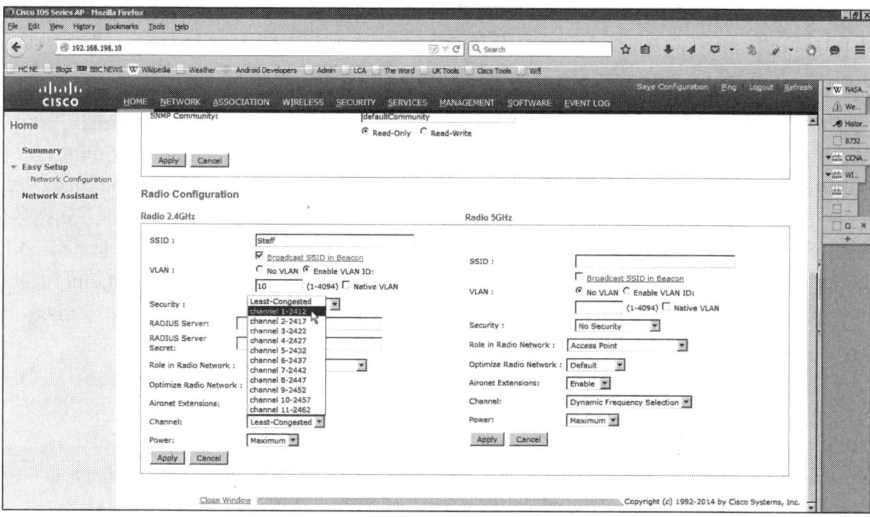

Figure 9-6 *Easy Setup Radio Configuration Page*

Next, select the type of wireless security you want to offer on the SSID. The Security menu options are described in further detail in Chapter 14, "Wireless Security Fundamentals."

By default, each radio is configured to operate in the Access Point role, so that the AP offers an active BSS. You can select one of the following roles instead from the Role in Radio Network drop-down menu:

- **Repeater**—The AP will associate with another nearby AP automatically, to repeat or extend that AP's cell coverage. The Ethernet port will be disabled.
- **Root Bridge**—The AP uses its Ethernet port to connect to bridge the wired network to a remote wireless bridge over a point-to-point or point-to-multipoint link. No wireless clients will be allowed to associate.
- **Non-Root Bridge**—The AP will act as a remote wireless bridge and will connect to a root bridge AP over a wireless link.
- **Workgroup Bridge**—The AP will use one radio to associate with a nearby Cisco access point, as if it is a wireless client. The AP bridges between its radio and its Ethernet port. You can use an AP in workgroup bridge (WGB) mode to provide wireless client capability to wired-only devices.
- **Universal Workgroup Bridge**—The AP will act as a workgroup bridge to associate with Cisco and non-Cisco access points.
- **Scanner**—The AP will use its radio to scan channels and collect data.
- **Spectrum**—The AP will devote its radios to scanning the frequency band and collecting information about RF usage and interference.

The Optimize Radio Network drop-down menu enables you to select how the AP will optimize its cell for wireless clients. By default, the AP will offer data rates that can provide good range and throughput. You can select **Throughput** to leverage higher data rates at the expense of cell range or **Range** to require the lowest data rate for maximum cell range.

Aironet Extensions are Cisco proprietary information elements that Cisco APs can use to interact with Cisco-compatible wireless clients. For example, an AP can provide information about its current client load so that potential clients can choose the least busy AP. Aironet extensions are enabled by default.

At the bottom of the Radio Configuration page, you can select the channel that the AP will use. By default, the channel is set to Least-Congested (2.4 GHz) and Dynamic Frequency Selection (5 GHz) so that the AP will scan and find a channel that it considers to be most viable in its current location. This is not always a best practice because the AP will choose any channel number that it sees fit. That means the 2.4-GHz radio might end up on channel 3 if channels 1 and 11 are already in use. A better practice is to select a specific channel for each radio instead. Each radio has a transmit power setting, too—each defaults to its maximum power rating or a specific dBm level that you select.

Click **Apply** for the settings to take effect.

At this point of the configuration, you do not necessarily have a functional AP because the radios are still disabled. To enable a radio, navigate to the AP's home page and select **Network > Network Interface > Radio0-802.11N2.4GHz** or **Radio1-802.11N5GHz.** Click the **Settings** tab to open it, and then select the **Enable** button next to Enable Radio.

As you are configuring an autonomous AP, keep in mind that the changes you make are applied to the running configuration and will not be saved if the AP loses power or reboots. Click the **Save Configuration** link in the upper-right corner of the screen to save the whole AP configuration into nonvolatile memory.

Tip Although the WIFUND 200-355 exam blueprint topics are limited to the initial "easy" configuration tabs on an autonomous AP, you will need to be proficient with many more complex features on lightweight APs as part of a larger, unified wireless network. Don't worry; lightweight APs (LAPs) and unified networks are covered in detail throughout the remainder of the book.

Once the initial configuration is complete, you may want to configure or monitor other features that the autonomous AP offers. Table 9-2 lists the tabs that are displayed across the top of the GUI, along with common features found in each.

Table 9-2 Cisco Autonomous AP Configuration Tabs and Their Functions

Tab Name	Functions Available
Network	Display a map of neighboring devices Configure AP interfaces and radios
Association	Display a list of associated clients
Wireless	Enable participation in the Cisco Structured Wireless-Aware Network (SWAN) framework
Security	Configure authentication, encryption, and SSIDs Configure a basic wireless intrusion detection system (IDS) Configure MAC address filtering to authenticate clients based on MAC address
Services	Configure AP management protocols such as Telnet, SSH, CDP, DNS, HTTP, SNMP, SNTP Configure QoS policies Define VLANs Configure BandSelect to steer wireless clients toward a specific 802.11 band
Management	Manage guest users Configure web-based authentication (webauth)
Software	Manage AP software Manage AP configuration files
Event Log	Configure and display the AP event logs

Some autonomous AP features are not accessible from the GUI and must be configured or monitored from the CLI instead. For example, the ClientLink feature can be used to enable transmit beamforming (TxBF) to improve communication with each individual client. It must be configured using the CLI through Telnet or SSH by entering the **beamform ofdm** radio interface configuration command.

Upgrading an Autonomous AP

Occasionally you may need to upgrade the IOS software running on an autonomous AP. You can perform software upgrades from a web browser that is opened to the AP's IP address. Download the new autonomous mode image file from Cisco.com onto the machine, then click the **Software** tab and the **Software Upgrade** link, as shown in Figure 9-7. Click the **Browse** button to locate the new software image, then click the **Upgrade** button to begin the upgrade process. Once the upgrade is complete, the AP must be rebooted so that it can begin running the new image.

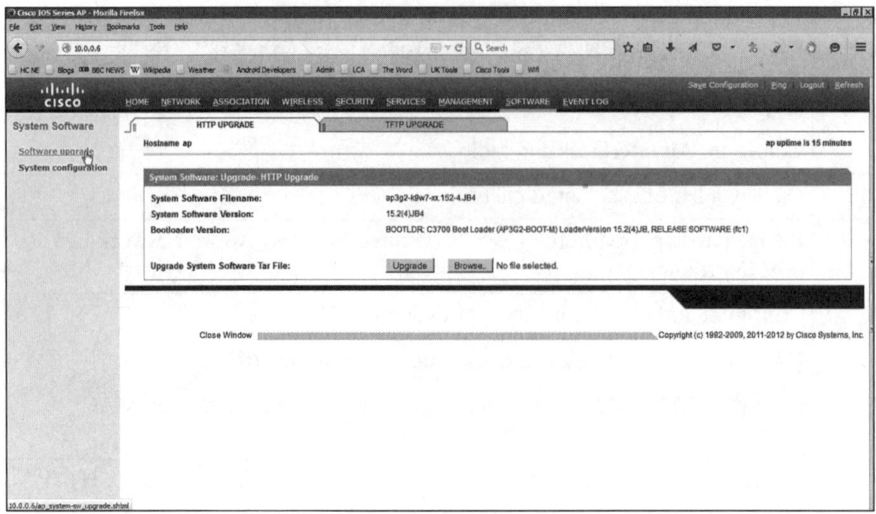

Figure 9-7 *Autonomous AP Software Upgrade Page*

Autonomous APs can be useful in remote sites, small offices, or homes where centralized management is not necessary or practical. In larger environments, a centralized or unified approach is more common. Sometimes you might face a hybrid scenario, where some legacy autonomous APs still exist in a centrally managed network. In that case, you might need to either replace the AP hardware or convert its software image so that it can join the wireless controllers that manage the network. In fact, Cisco expects a CCNA Wireless engineer to know how to convert an autonomous AP to a "lightweight" version that can join a controller.

To convert an AP, you can use one of the following methods, which are described in the subsequent sections:

- Use the Cisco Prime Infrastructure application; all wireless controllers and lightweight APs can be monitored and managed from this one application. The autonomous AP must first be managed, then it can be converted. Cisco Prime Infrastructure is discussed in Chapter 18, "Managing Cisco Wireless Networks," but using it to convert autonomous APs is not covered on the CCNA Wireless exam.
- Use the **archive** command from the autonomous AP's CLI.

You can use the CLI to upgrade the IOS image on an autonomous AP and convert it to lightweight mode. You will also need a TFTP or FTP server along with the appropriate lightweight code image. The process is simple—save the AP's configuration, then use the following command:

```
archive download-sw /overwrite /force-reload {tftp:|ftp:}//location/image-name
```

The lightweight image will be downloaded such that it overwrites the current autonomous IOS image, then the AP will reload and run the new image. Example 9-4 demonstrates the conversion process. The TFTP server is located at 10.0.0.99, and the new lightweight image is named ap3g2-k9w8-tar.153-3.JBB1.tar. If you are using an FTP server, you should specify the FTP username and password that the AP will use with the following commands:

```
ap(config)# ip ftp username username
ap(config)# ip ftp password password
```

Tip Cisco AP image filenames can be difficult to identify. If a filename contains k9w8, as in Example 9-4, it is a lightweight image. If it contains k9w7, it is an autonomous image.

Example 9-4 *Manually Converting an Autonomous AP*

```
ap# archive download-sw /overwrite /reload tftp://10.0.0.99/ap3g2-k9w8-tar.153-3.JBB1.
   tar
examining image...
Loading ap3g2-k9w8-tar.153-3.JBB1.tar from 10.0.0.99 (via BVI1): !
extracting info (282 bytes)
Image info:
    Version Suffix: k9w8-.153-3.JBB1
    Image Name: ap3g2-k9w8-tar.153-3.JBB1
    Version Directory: ap3g2-k9w8-tar.153-3.JBB1
    Ios Image Size: 9421312
    Total Image Size: 9615872
    Image Feature: WIRELESS LAN|LWAPP
    Image Family: C3700
    Wireless Switch Management Version: 8.0.120.0
Extracting files...
ap3g2-k9w8-tar.153-3.JBB1/ (directory) 0 (bytes)0
ap3g2-k9w8-tar.153-3.JBB1/html/ (directory) 0 (bytes)
[output omitted for clarity]
extracting info.ver (282 bytes)
[OK - 9615360 bytes]

Deleting current version: flash:...done.
New software image installed in flash:/ ap3g2-k9w8-tar.153-3.JBB1
Configuring system to use new image...done.
Requested system reload
archive download: takes 107 seconds
```

9

Initially Configuring Cloud-based APs

A cloud-based AP is somewhat similar to an autonomous AP; once configured, it can operate independently to provide fully functional wireless LANs. However, you can configure and manage one or more cloud-based APs from the Cisco Meraki cloud on the Internet.

Meraki APs have only a connector for a power supply and an RJ-45 connector for an Ethernet connection. There is no console port for local administrative access. The initial configuration is fairly straightforward—connect a new AP to the wired network and plug in the AP's power source. As the AP boots up, it will automatically obtain an IP address through DHCP and will contact the Cisco Meraki cloud network for further instructions. From that point on, you perform all configuration and monitoring through a browser that is pointed to the cloud.

> **Tip** If, for some reason, the AP cannot join the Meraki cloud, it will bring up a local WLAN that you can connect to for more information. Once you connect and open a browser to the AP's IP address, you will see an explanation about why the AP is failing to join the cloud.

At this point, you should browse to **https://meraki.cisco.com** and click the **Login** link. The goal is to access the Meraki Dashboard, as shown in Figure 9-8. If you do not already have an account, click the **Create an Account** link. Otherwise, you can enter your username and password to log in.

Key Topic

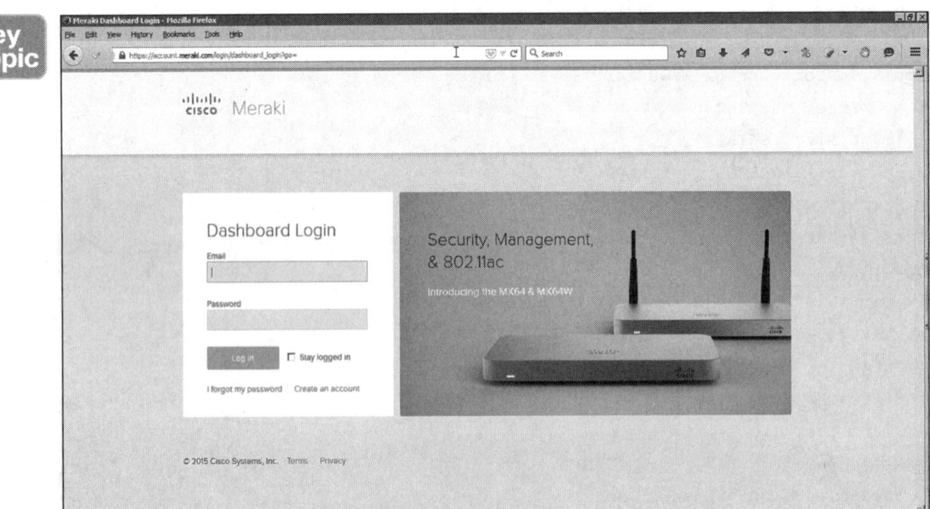

Figure 9-8 *Accessing the Cisco Meraki Dashboard*

Next, you will need to associate APs with your Dashboard account. To do that, select **Network-wide > Configure > Add Devices**, as shown in Figure 9-9, then click the **Claim** button. Then enter each AP serial number in the list that is shown in Figure 9-10 and click the **Claim** button.

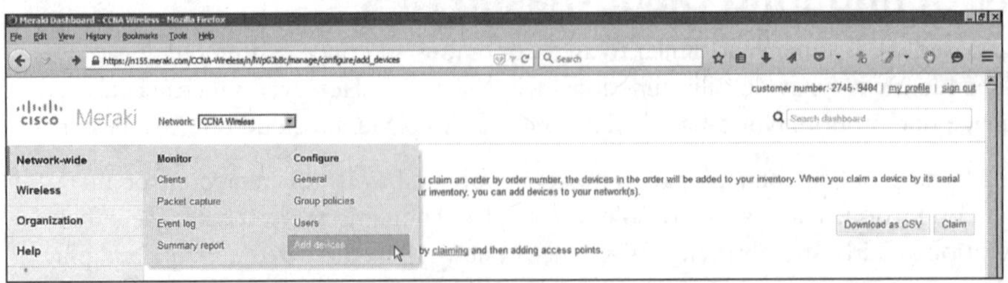

Figure 9-9 *Adding New Cisco Meraki APs*

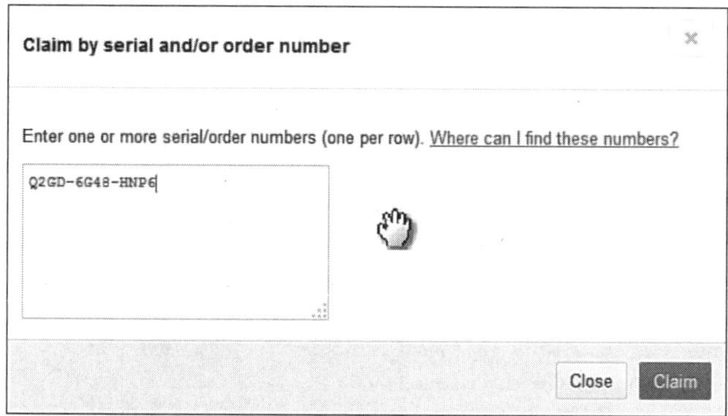

Figure 9-10 *Listing Cisco Meraki APs to Claim*

> **Tip** As you navigate the Cisco Meraki Dashboard, be aware that every function is organized with Monitor and Configuration tasks.

Next, you can configure one or more SSIDs on the AP. Select **Wireless > Configure > SSIDs** as shown in Figure 9-11. The list of SSIDs is displayed in the Configuration Overview: SSIDs page that is shown in Figure 9-12. The first SSID is named "Guest" by default, and only one SSID is enabled by default. You can define up to 15 SSIDs.

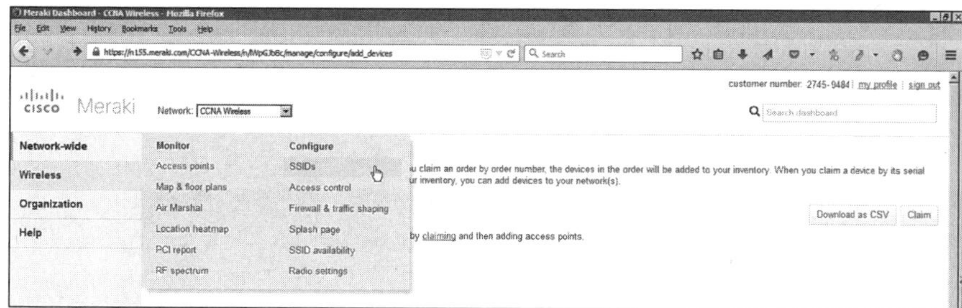

Figure 9-11 *Preparing to Configure SSIDs on a Cisco Meraki AP*

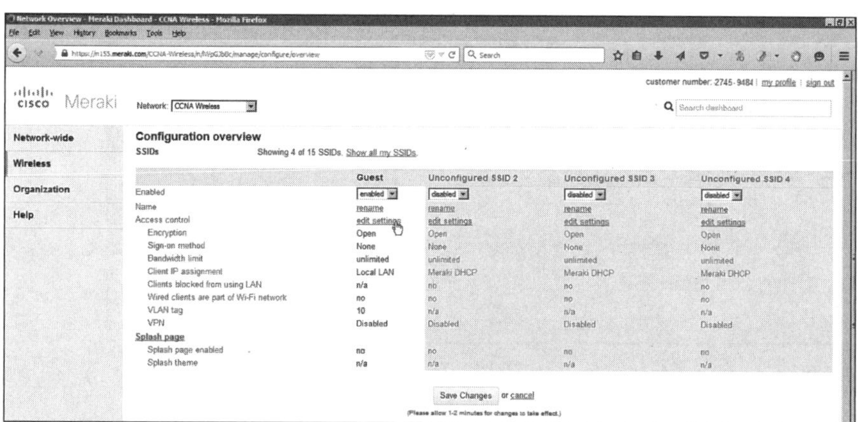

Figure 9-12 *Listing SSIDs to Configure*

You can click the **Rename** link to change the name of an existing SSID or click the **Edit Settings** link to configure the SSID. Figures 9-13 and 9-14 show the top and bottom portions of the page that is displayed when Edit Settings has been clicked under the Guest SSID. In the top portion of the page, you can configure security parameters that control access to the SSID. Further down the page, you can configure IP addressing, VLAN tagging, and wireless parameters. In Figure 9-14, the AP is configured to offer multiple SSIDs that are mapped to VLANs. The AP is configured for Bridge mode, which enables a trunk link and maps SSIDs to VLAN numbers. The Guest SSID is mapped to VLAN 10.

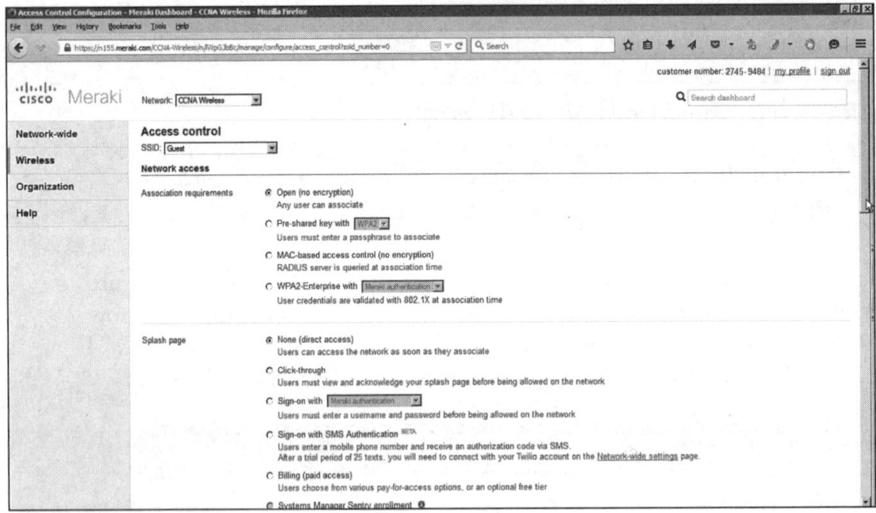

Figure 9-13 *Editing Security Settings for an SSID*

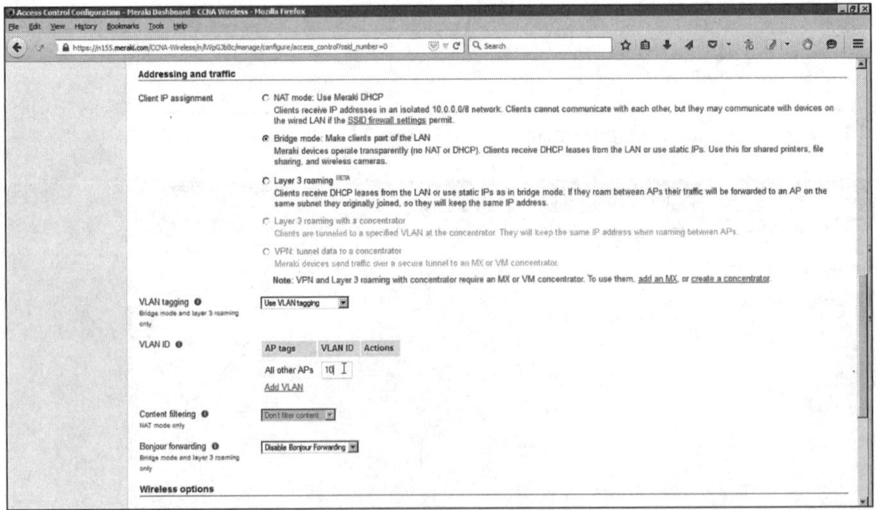

Figure 9-14 *Editing IP Addressing and VLAN Settings for an SSID*

By default, the AP will bridge the wireless and wired LANs, just as an autonomous AP would do. In this case, client roaming is constrained to a single VLAN where all of the cloud-based APs are connected. You can leverage the Layer 3 roaming feature instead, to scale roaming to include APs that are located on different VLANs. As a user roams, traffic will be tunneled from the AP where the user originally associated to another AP where the user currently resides.

Once you are finished configuring the SSID, click the **Save Changes** button. The configuration changes will be pushed out to the AP from the Cisco Meraki cloud network.

You can use the Cisco Meraki cloud-based Dashboard to monitor your APs and to configure some robust features. Table 9-3 lists the tabs that are available along the left side of the Dashboard page.

Table 9-3 Cisco Meraki Dashboard Tabs and Their Functions

Dashboard Tab	Monitor Functions	Configuration Functions
Network-wide	Graph traffic volume and application information Packet capture View logs and reports	AP management functions Bandwidth, firewall, traffic shaping, and splash page policies
Wireless	APs, floor plans, heatmaps RF spectrum analysis	SSIDs Radio settings and automatic adjustments Bandwidth, firewall, traffic shaping, and splash page policies
Organization	Devices in the enterprise Client location analytics Configuration templates	System settings Sync settings across multiple SSIDs Integrate with Mobile Device Management (MDM) Manage device inventory

9

Tip When Cisco Meraki APs boot up and contact the cloud network for the first time, their firmware is automatically upgraded to the most current level. After that, firmware is pushed out from the cloud network to the APs automatically, according to a preset schedule. You can define the schedule by selecting **Network-wide > Configure > General** and scrolling down to the Firmware Upgrades section of the page.

Exam Preparation Tasks

As mentioned in the section, "How to Use This Book," in the Introduction, you have a couple of choices for exam preparation: the exercises here, Chapter 21, "Final Review," and the exam simulation questions on the DVD.

Review All Key Topics

Review the most important topics in this chapter, noted with the Key Topic icon in the outer margin of the page. Table 9-4 lists a reference of these key topics and the page numbers on which each is found.

Table 9-4 Key Topics for Chapter 9

Key Topic Element	Description	Page Number
Figure 9-2	Bridging multiple SSIDs to VLANs	214
Figure 9-4	Autonomous AP web interface	218
Example 9-4	Manually converting an autonomous AP	223
Figure 9-8	Cloud-based AP web interface	224

Define Key Terms

Define the following key term from this chapter and check your answer in the glossary:

autonomous AP

This chapter covers the following topics:

- **Connecting a Centralized Controller**—This section describes the controller ports and interfaces and explains how the controller is connected to the network.
- **Performing an Initial Setup**—This section covers how to provide a bootstrap configuration to a new controller. Both web-based and command-line interface methods of configuration are explored.
- **Maintaining a Wireless Controller**—This section explains how to back up the controller configuration and how to upgrade the software image.

This chapter covers the following exam topics:

- 3.2—Describe physical infrastructure connections
  - 3.2a—Wired infrastructures (AP, WLC, access/trunk ports, LAG)
- 3.3—Describe AP and WLC management access connections
  - 3.3.a—Management connections (Telnet, SSH, HTTP, HTTPS, console)
  - 3.3.b—IP addressing: IPv4/IPv6
- 4.1—Execute initial setup procedures Cisco wireless infrastructures
  - 4.1b—Converged
  - 4.1c—Centralized
- 4.5—Identify wireless network and client management and configuration platform options
  - 4.5.a—Controller GUI and CLI
- 4.6—Maintain wireless network
  - 4.6a—Perform controller configuration backups
  - 4.6b—Perform code updates on controller, APs, and converged access switches
    - 4.6b(i)—AireOS: boot loader (FUS), image
    - 4.6b(ii)—IOS-XE: bundle, unbundle

CHAPTER 10

Implementing Controller-based Deployments

Before you can use a Cisco wireless LAN controller, you must connect it to the switched network. The controller must also link wired networks with wireless ones. You need to understand how to make the necessary connections, both physical and logical, to build a functioning centralized wireless network. The initial deployment of a converged wireless network is simpler because the wireless LAN controller (WLC) is already embedded in the wired network as a part of a Catalyst switch.

This chapter covers the initial deployment concepts needed to connect and initially configure a controller so that you can manage it more fully.

"Do I Know This Already?" Quiz

The "Do I Know This Already?" quiz allows you to assess whether you should read this entire chapter thoroughly or jump to the "Exam Preparation Tasks" section. If you are in doubt about your answers to these questions or your own assessment of your knowledge of the topics, read the entire chapter. Table 10-1 lists the major headings in this chapter and their corresponding "Do I Know This Already?" quiz questions. You can find the answers in Appendix A, "Answers to the 'Do I Know This Already?' Quizzes."

Table 10-1 "Do I Know This Already?" Section-to-Question Mapping

Foundation Topics Section	Questions
Connecting a Centralized Controller	1–7
Performing an Initial Setup	8–10
Maintaining a Wireless Controller	11–16

Caution The goal of self-assessment is to gauge your mastery of the topics in this chapter. If you do not know the answer to a question or are only partially sure of the answer, you should mark that question as wrong for purposes of the self-assessment. Giving yourself credit for an answer you correctly guess skews your self-assessment results and might provide you with a false sense of security.

1. A wireless controller port is used for which one of the following purposes?
   a. Construct CAPWAP tunnel packets
   b. Provide a physical connection to a switch port
   c. Create a logical connection to a WLAN
   d. Provide a physical connection to an AP
2. Which one of the following is used for remote out-of-band management of a controller and the initial controller setup?
   a. Distribution system port
   b. Virtual interface
   c. Service port
   d. AP-manager interface
3. A distribution system port is usually configured in which one of the following modes?
   a. 802.1Q trunk
   b. Access mode
   c. LACP trunk negotiation
   d. Recovery mode
4. Which one of the following correctly describes the single logical link formed by bundling all of a controller's distribution system ports together?
   a. PHY
   b. DSP
   c. LAG
   d. GEC
5. A CAPWAP tunnel terminates on which one of the following controller interfaces?
   a. Virtual interface
   b. Dynamic interface
   c. Service port interface
   d. AP-manager interface
6. Which one of the following is used to relay DHCP requests from wireless clients?
   a. Management interface
   b. Dynamic interface
   c. Virtual interface
   d. Service port interface

7. Which one of the following controller interfaces maps a WLAN to a VLAN?
   a. Bridge interface
   b. Virtual interface
   c. WLAN interface
   d. Dynamic interface
8. Suppose that you have just powered up a new controller. If you connect to the controller's console port, in which one of the following modes will you find the controller?
   a. Initial setup mode
   b. ROMMON mode
   c. Discovery mode
   d. Promiscuous mode
9. Which of the following methods can you use to perform the initial setup of a wireless LAN controller? (Choose all that apply.)
   a. CLI
   b. TFTP
   c. FTP
   d. Web browser
10. To perform an initial configuration of a converged wireless controller, to which one of the following should you connect with your web browser?
    a. Virtual interface
    b. Console port
    c. Dynamic interface
    d. Access switch management address
11. Suppose you use a web browser to access a controller and make a configuration change. You make sure to click on the Apply button. A short time later, the controller loses power and then reboots. Which two of the following answers correctly describes the result?
    a. The Apply button saved the change permanently
    b. The Apply button made the change active, but didn't save it across the reboot
    c. You would need to click the Save Configuration link to save the change permanently
    d. To save the change permanently, you would need to use the **copy run start** command from the CLI

12. To save a copy of a controller's configuration, which of the following methods could you use?
    a. Use **Commands > Upload File**
    b. Use **Commands > Download File**
    c. Use **Commands > Configuration > TFTP**
    d. Use **Commands > Files > Save Configuration**
13. A centralized wireless LAN controller maintains how many code image files?
    a. 1
    b. 2
    c. 3
    d. Unlimited
14. Which two of the following file transfer methods can be used to move a centralized controller code image file onto a controller?
    a. TFTP
    b. RCP
    c. SSH
    d. FTP
    e. XMODEM
    f. HTTP
15. Suppose you need to transfer a code image file from a TFTP server on your PC to a controller. Which of the following file copy directions should you choose?
    a. Download
    b. Upload
    c. None of the above; a controller automatically gets its image from WCS/NCS/PI
    d. None of the above; it isn't possible to transfer an image file via TFTP
16. After copying a new code image file to a controller, how should you copy the same code release to the lightweight APs?
    a. Use **Commands > Download to APs**
    b. Connect to each AP and copy the file there
    c. Put the address of a TFTP server in the DHCP options field
    d. Do nothing; each AP will get the new image as it rejoins the controller

Foundation Topics

Connecting a Centralized Controller

Cisco wireless LAN controllers partner with lightweight access points (LAPs) to provide connectivity between a wired network and mobile wireless clients. The wired network infrastructure also transports the packets that make up the Control and Provisioning of Wireless Access Points (CAPWAP) tunnels between the controllers and the access points (APs). Your first task to begin using a controller is to connect it to the network. From your work with Cisco routers and switches, you probably know that the terms *interface* and *port* are usually interchangeable. For example, switches can come in 24- or 48-port models, and you apply configuration changes to the corresponding interfaces. Cisco wireless controllers differ a bit; ports and interfaces refer to different concepts.

Controller ports are physical connections made to an external wired or switched network, whereas interfaces are logical connections made internally within the controller. The following sections explain each connection type in more detail.

Using Controller Ports

You can connect several different types of controller ports to your network, as shown in Figure 10-1 and discussed in the following list:

- **Service port**—Used for out-of-band management, system recovery, and initial boot functions; always connects to a switch port in access mode
- **Distribution system port**—Used for all normal AP and management traffic; usually connects to a switch port in 802.1Q trunk mode
- **Console port**—Used for out-of-band management, system recovery, and initial boot functions; asynchronous connection to a terminal emulator (9600 baud, 8 data bits, 1 stop bit, by default)
- **Redundancy port**—Used to connect to a peer controller for redundant operation

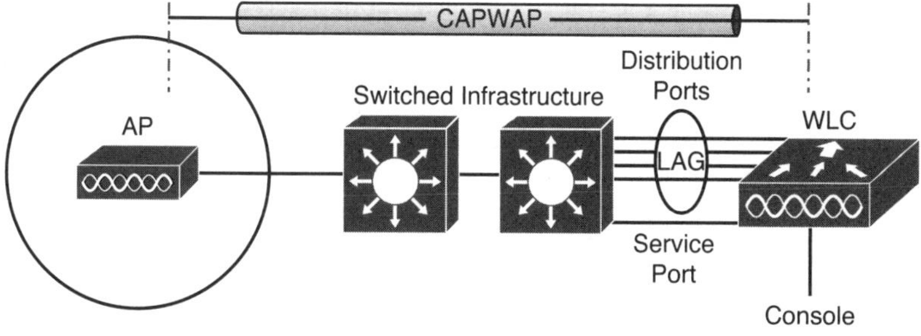

Figure 10-1 *Cisco Wireless LAN Controller Ports*

Controllers can have a single service port that must be connected to a switched network. Usually the service port is assigned to a management VLAN so that you can access the controller with Secure Shell (SSH) or a web browser to perform initial configuration or for maintenance. Notice that the service port supports only a single VLAN, so the corresponding switch port must be configured for access mode only.

Controllers also have multiple distribution system ports that you must connect to the network. These ports carry most of the data coming to and going from the controller. For example, the CAPWAP tunnels (control and data) that connect to each of a controller's APs pass across the distribution system ports. Client data also passes from wireless LANs to wired VLANs over the ports. In addition, any management traffic using a web browser, SSH, Simple Network Management Protocol (SNMP), or Trivial File Transfer Protocol (TFTP) normally reaches the controller through the ports.

Because the distribution system ports must carry data that is associated with many different VLANs, VLAN tags and numbers become very important. For that reason, the distribution system ports always operate in 802.1Q trunking mode. When you connect the ports to a switch, you should also configure the switch ports for unconditional 802.1Q trunk mode.

The distribution system ports can operate independently, each one transporting multiple VLANs to a unique group of internal controller interfaces. For resiliency, you can configure distribution system ports in redundant pairs. One port is primarily used; if it fails, a backup port is used instead.

To get the most use out of each distribution system port, you can configure all of them to operate as a single logical group, much like an EtherChannel on a switch. Controller distribution system ports can be configured as a link aggregation group (LAG) such that they are bundled together to act as one larger link. In Figure 10-1, the four distribution system ports are configured as a LAG. With a LAG configuration, traffic can be load balanced across the individual ports that make up the LAG. In addition, LAG offers resiliency; if one individual port fails, traffic will be redirected to the remaining working ports instead.

Table 10-2 lists common Cisco controller models along with the distribution system and service ports available. As you might expect, the more APs a controller platform supports, the greater distribution system port throughput it needs. In contrast, almost every model uses a 1-Gbps service port because the out-of-band management traffic requirements are fairly small.

Table 10-2 Cisco Controller Models and Supported Distribution and Service Ports

Controller Model	Distribution Ports	Service Port
2504	(4) 1 Gbps	N/A
5508	(8) 1 Gbps	(1) 1 Gbps
5520	(2) 1 or 10 Gbps	(1) 1 Gbps
5760	(6) 1 or 10 Gbps	(1) 1 Gbps
Flex 7510	(2) 10 Gbps	(1) 1 Gbps
8510	(2) 10 Gbps	(1) 1 Gbps
8540	(4) 1 or 10 Gbps	(1) 1 Gbps
WiSM2	(2) 10 Gbps (internal)	(1) 1 Gbps (internal)

Using Controller Interfaces

Through its distribution system ports, a controller connects to multiple VLANs on the switched network. Internally, the controller must somehow map those wired VLANs to equivalent logical wireless networks. For example, suppose that VLAN 10 is set aside for wireless users in the Engineering division of a company. That VLAN must be connected to a unique wireless LAN that exists on a controller and its associated APs. The wireless LAN must then be connected to every client that associates with service set identifier (SSID) "Engineering."

Cisco wireless controllers provide the necessary connectivity through internal interfaces. A controller interface is logical and must be configured with an IP address, subnet mask, default gateway, and a Dynamic Host Configuration Protocol (DHCP) server. Each interface is then assigned to a physical port and a VLAN ID. You can think of an interface as a Layer 3 termination on a VLAN.

Cisco controllers support the following interface types, also shown in Figure 10-2:

- **Management interface**—Used for normal management traffic, such as RADIUS user authentication, WLC-to-WLC communication, web-based and SSH sessions, SNMP, Network Time Protocol (NTP), syslog, and so on.

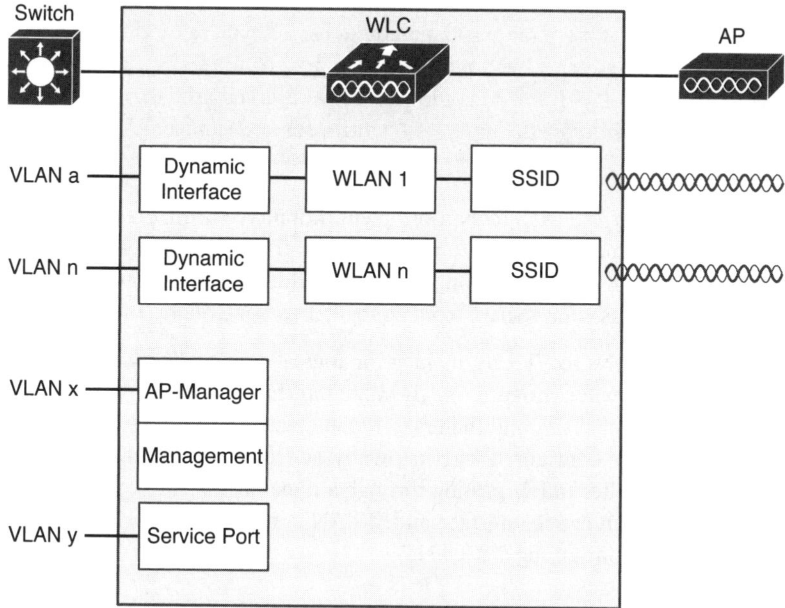

Figure 10-2 *Cisco Wireless LAN Controller Interfaces*

- **AP-manager interface**—A dynamic interface used to terminate CAPWAP tunnels between the controller and its APs. If no AP-manager interface is created, the function is performed by the manager interface instead.
- **Virtual interface**—IP address facing wireless clients when the controller is relaying client DHCP requests, performing client web authentication, and supporting client mobility.

10

- **Service port interface**—Bound to the service port and used for out-of-band management.
- **Dynamic interface**—Used to connect a VLAN to a WLAN.

The management interface faces the switched network, where management users and APs are located. Management traffic will usually consist of protocols like HTTPS, SSH, SNMP, NTP, TFTP, and so on. In addition, management interface traffic consists of CAPWAP packets that carry control and data tunnels to and from the APs.

The virtual interface is used only for certain client-facing operations. For example, when a wireless client issues a DHCP request to obtain an IP address, the controller can relay the request on to a normal DHCP server. From the client's perspective, the DHCP server appears to be the controller's virtual interface address. Clients may see the virtual interface's address, but that address is never used when the controller communicates with other devices on the switched network.

Because the virtual interface is used only for some client management functions, you should configure it with a unique, nonroutable address. For example, you might use 10.1.1.1 because it is within a private address space defined in RFC 1918.

Tip Traditionally, many people have assigned IP address 1.1.1.1 to the virtual interface. Although it is a unique address, it is routable and already in use elsewhere on the Internet. A better practice is to use an IP address from the RFC 1918 private address space that is unused or reserved, such as 192.168.1.1. You could also use a reserved address from RFC 5737 (192.0.2.0/24) that is set aside for documentation purposes and is never used.

The virtual interface address is also used to support client mobility. For that reason, every controller that exists in the same mobility group should be configured with a virtual address that is identical to the others. By using one common virtual address, all the controllers will appear to operate as a cluster as clients roam from controller to controller.

Dynamic interfaces map WLANs to VLANs, making the logical connections between wireless and wired networks. You will configure one dynamic interface for each wireless LAN that is offered by the controller's APs, and then map the interface to the WLAN. Each dynamic interface must also be configured with its own IP address and can act as a DHCP relay for wireless clients. To filter traffic passing through a dynamic interface, you can configure an optional access list. Dynamic interface and WLAN configuration are covered in more detail in Chapter 15, "Configuring a WLAN."

Performing an Initial Setup

When you power up a wireless controller for the first time, it comes up with a minimal default configuration. The distribution system ports are not yet usable, but you can connect to the controller through its console port or through its service port—provided you have connected the service port to a switch or an Ethernet crossover cable. The service port can use a default IP address of 192.168.1.1, or it can request an address through DHCP.

The default configuration has no interfaces or WLANs defined. APs cannot connect to it until you provide some initial setup information and then configure it further after the controller reboots into normal operation.

You can use either a web browser or the command-line interface (CLI) to set up a controller for the first time. Depending on the model and code release running, the WLC could present one of two web-based initial configuration procedures: the initial Configuration Wizard (centralized and converged controllers) or the WLAN Express Setup. All of these methods are covered in the following sections. Through the initial setup, you define the minimum parameters for the controller to become operational—the service port, management interface, virtual interface, WLAN, authentication server, clock, and so on.

Initial Setup of a Centralized Controller with the Configuration Wizard

After you have connected a controller to the network and have powered it up, you can use a web browser to enter a basic configuration. The controller prompts you through the following sequence of steps to configure various parameters as part of the Configuration Wizard:

Step 1. Configure system access.

Connect your PC to the same VLAN and subnet that the controller's service port uses, and then open a web browser to the controller's service port IP address. In Figure 10-3, the service port uses 192.168.1.1 and the Configuration Wizard asks for a system name for the controller, along with an administrative user's ID and password. By default, the username is **admin** and the password is **admin**. The system name is somewhat like a hostname and is used to identify the controller to APs and other controllers. Click the **Next** button to continue.

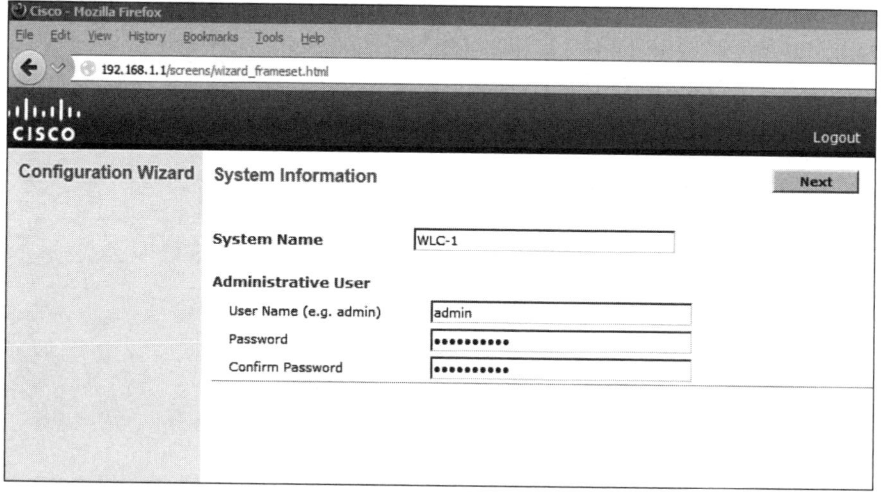

Figure 10-3 *Starting the Configuration Wizard*

10

Step 2. Configure SNMP access.

By default, SNMP Versions 2c and 3 are enabled. Version 3 provides the most secure access and is recommended, whereas Version 2c is not. Version 1 is disabled because it is not considered to be secure. You can enable or disable each version as shown in Figure 10-4. If SNMPv3 is enabled, the controller will remind you to configure an SNMPv3 user once the initial configuration is complete and the controller reboots. Click **Next** to continue.

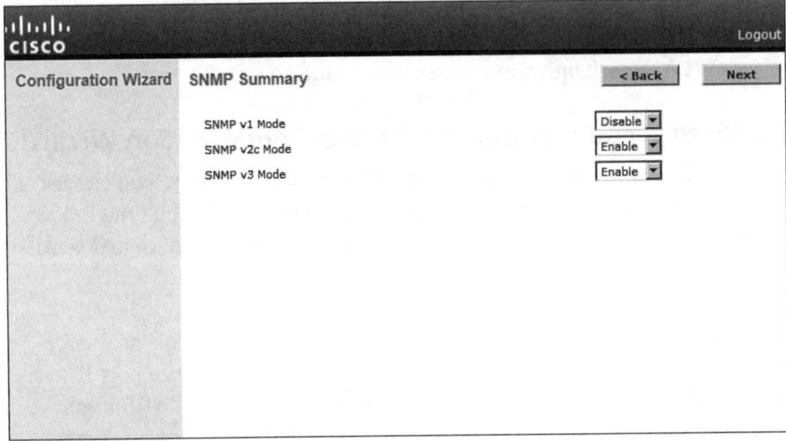

Figure 10-4 *Configuring SNMP Access*

Step 3. Configure the service port.

Although the controller's service port has a default initial IP address (the one you're using to run the initial configuration), you can configure it to use something else in the future. Check the **DHCP Protocol** box to have the controller request an address through DHCP. Otherwise, you can leave the box unchecked and enter a static IP address instead. In Figure 10-5, the service port is configured to use DHCP. The address and netmask shown will be disregarded. Click **Next** to continue.

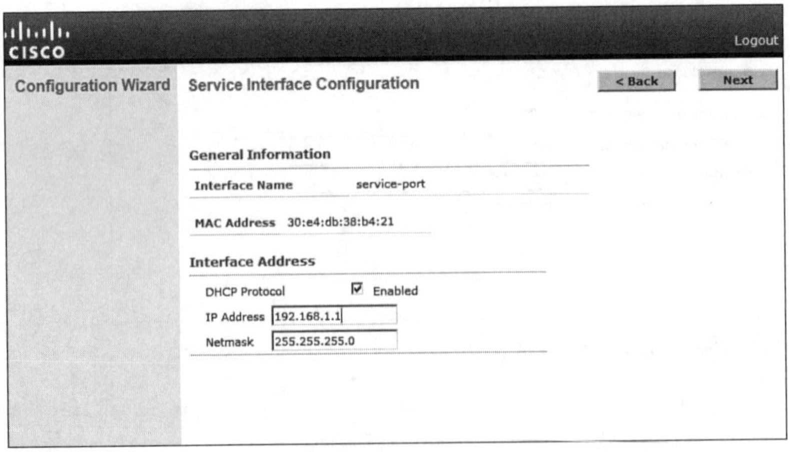

Figure 10-5 *Configuring the Service Port*

Step 4. Configure LAG mode.

By default, all the distribution system ports will be bundled together as a single LAG link, as shown in Figure 10-6. You can disable LAG mode through the drop-down menu. Click **Next** to continue.

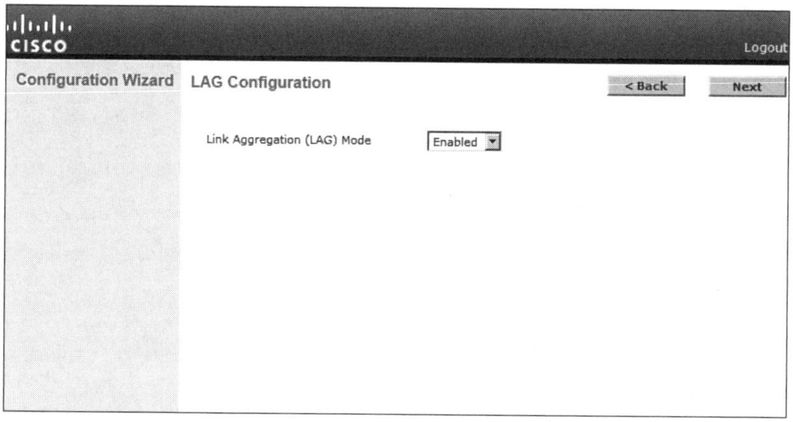

Figure 10-6 *Configuring LAG Mode*

Step 5. Configure the management interface.

By default, a controller can use a single management interface for both management and CAPWAP traffic, if no AP-manager interface is configured. The management interface is configured for VLAN 0 (the 802.1Q trunk native VLAN), with no valid IP address. You can set the VLAN number, IP address, subnet mask, and gateway as shown in Figure 10-7. In this example, the management interface resides on VLAN 50 at 192.168.50.10. You can also configure the primary and secondary DHCP server addresses that the controller will use if it has to relay any DHCP requests from wireless clients. Click **Next** to continue.

> **Tip** You might have noticed that the controller's native VLAN is VLAN 0, whereas Cisco switches use native VLAN 1 as a default. A controller and a switch may communicate over the native VLAN because traffic is *untagged*. Even though the native VLAN numbers differ, it does not matter because no tag is added at all.

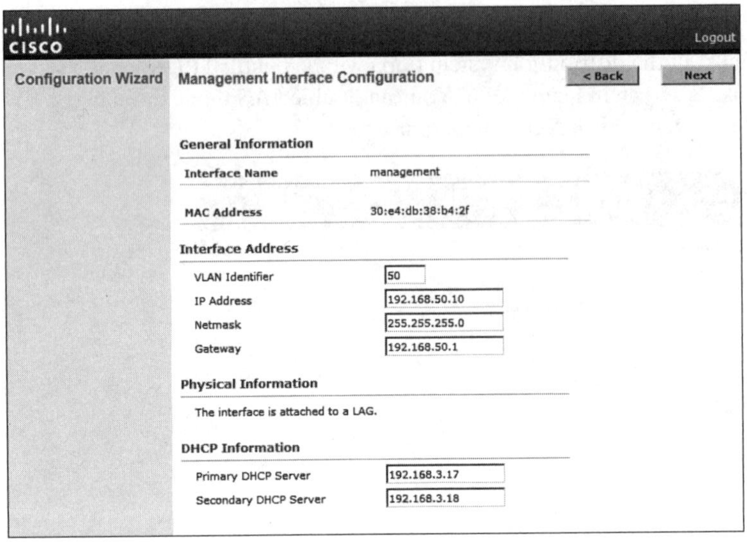

Figure 10-7 *Configuring the Management Interface*

Step 6. Configure the RF mobility domain and country code.

A controller must be configured to use the RF parameters that are defined by the local regulatory body. It also uses an RF mobility domain name to group like controllers together so that things such as AP channel numbers and transmit power can be centrally managed. By default, the RF mobility domain is set to default. You can override that value as shown in Figure 10-8. Although the selected country code is not shown in the figure, it has defaulted to US. Click **Next** to continue.

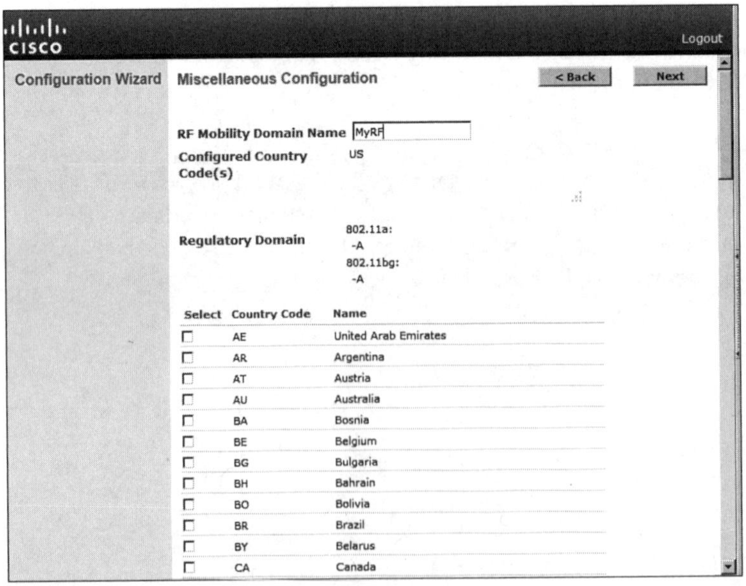

Figure 10-8 *Configuring the RF Regulatory Domain*

Step 7. Configure the virtual interface.

Enter an IP address for the virtual interface, such as the one shown in Figure 10-9. You should have an entry for the virtual interface in your DNS server, to streamline client web authentication. You can also configure a DNS hostname on the controller, but that same name should also exist on the DNS server. Click **Next** to continue.

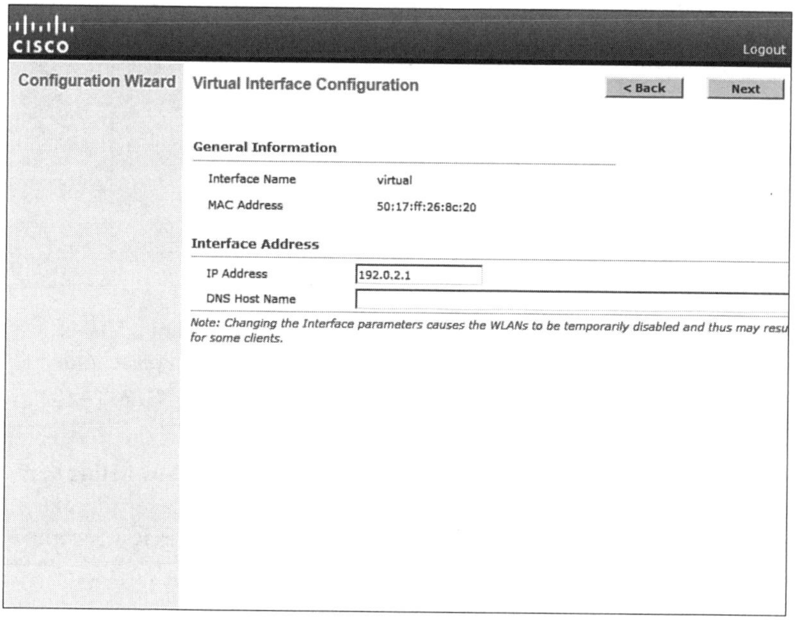

Figure 10-9 *Configuring the Virtual Interface*

Step 8. Configure a WLAN.

During the initial setup, you must define one wireless LAN, as shown in Figure 10-10. The profile name is the name of the WLAN within the controller. The WLAN SSID is the SSID string that will be advertised by any APs that offer the WLAN. You might find it convenient to configure both strings with the same name, as shown in the figure.

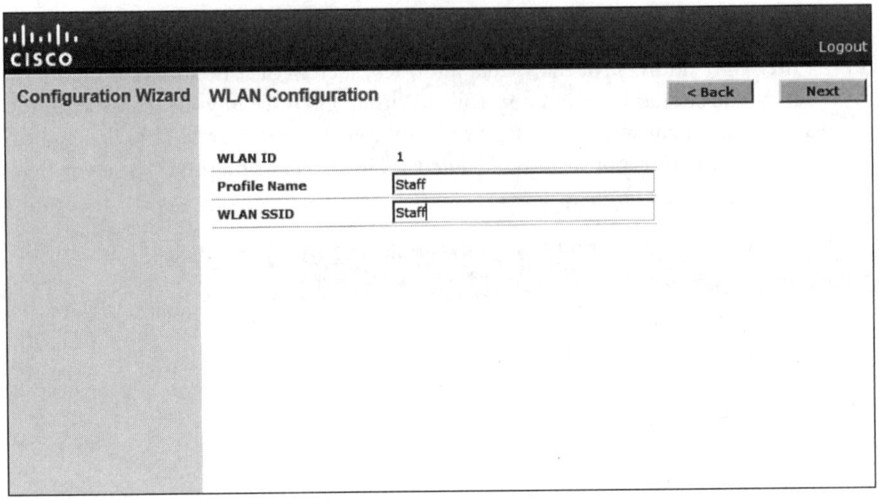

Figure 10-10 *Configuring a WLAN*

Notice that you only need to enter the name of the WLAN—not a VLAN number or an interface name. The initial setup process creates a placeholder for the WLAN. You will complete the WLAN configuration later, when the controller reboots and becomes fully functional.

After you click **Next** to continue, you will see a reminder window noting that the WLAN has been created with the following default wireless security settings: WPA2, AES, and 802.1x authentication. Chapter 14, "Wireless Security Fundamentals," covers these terms in greater detail.

Tip The WLAN Configuration screen also shows a WLAN ID number. As you create new WLANs, the ID number increments. The WLAN ID is an internal index that is used to call the WLAN from other menus, as well as when configuration templates are applied to a controller from a Cisco Prime Infrastructure (PI) management station.

Step 9. Configure a RADIUS server.

As an optional step, you can define a RADIUS server that will be used for client authentication. You can always click the **Skip** button to skip this step and define the server at a later time.

If you choose to define the server now, enter the RADIUS server's IP address, shared secret key, port number, and the server status. Figure 10-11 shows these fields. You use the Server Status field when multiple servers are defined; the controller will send a request to the next server that is in the Enabled state in the list. Click **Apply** to apply the settings and continue to the next step.

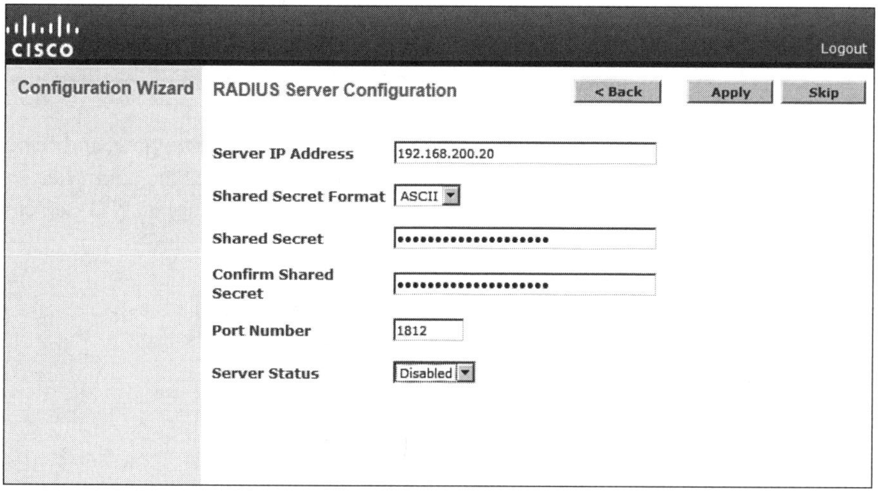

Figure 10-11 *Configuring a RADIUS Server*

Step 10. Configure 802.11 support.

By default, a controller enables 802.11a, 802.11b, and 802.11g support globally for all APs that associate with it. You can override the support settings by changing the check boxes shown in Figure 10-12. When the initial setup is complete and the controller has rebooted into full functionality, you can fine-tune the 802.11 support settings further.

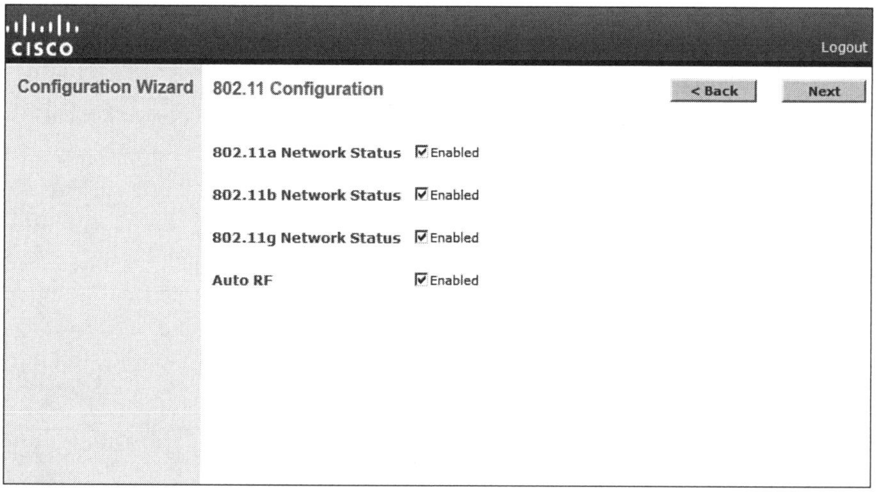

Figure 10-12 *Configuring 802.11 Support*

Also by default, the controller enables Auto-RF, which will automatically determine the channel and transmit power level for each AP's radio. You can always fine-tune the Auto-RF settings globally or on a per-AP basis at a later time. Click **Next** to continue.

The Auto-RF functions are also known as Radio Resource Management (RRM), which is covered in greater detail in Chapter 13, "Understanding RRM."

Step 11. Configure the system clock.

The controller maintains an internal clock. You can set the date, time, and time zone, as shown in Figure 10-13. Click **Next** to continue. After the controller has rebooted and is fully functional, you can configure it to use an NTP server to synchronize its clock.

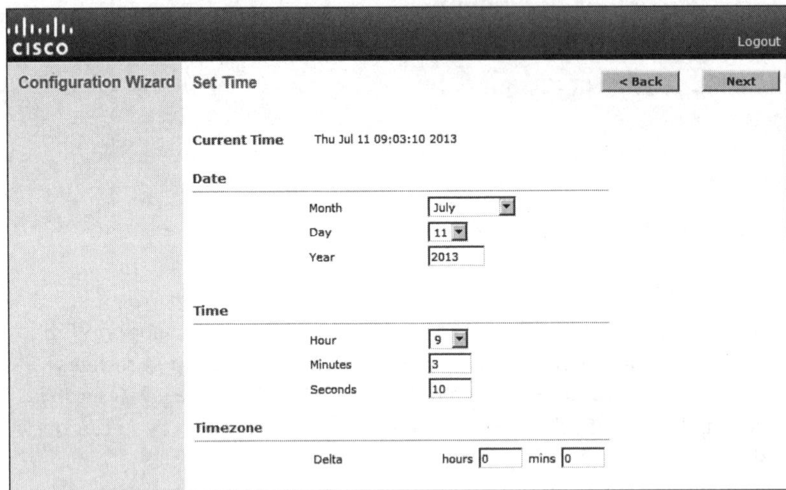

Figure 10-13 *Configuring the System Clock*

Step 12. Reboot the controller.

As a last step, to save the initial configuration and reboot the controller, click the **Save and Reboot** button (see Figure 10-14).

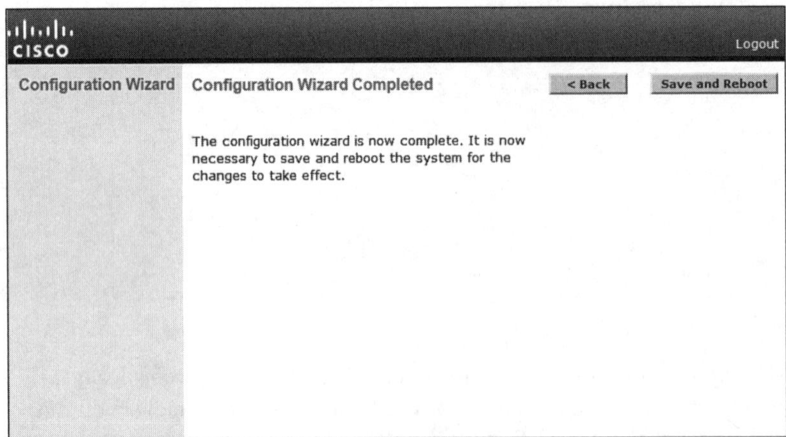

Figure 10-14 *Save and Reboot After Completing the Configuration Wizard*

After the controller has rebooted, it will be fully functional. At that time, you can reposition your PC on the regular wired network and point your web browser toward the controller's management interface IP address. You will have to log in using the administrative user ID and password that you configured in Step 1.

Initial Setup of a Converged Controller with the Configuration Wizard

The initial configuration procedure for a converged Wireless Controller Module (WCM) is very similar to that of a centralized controller. One important difference is that the converged controller shares the same hardware platform and management interface with the access layer switch. That means you must configure all of the WCM features through the switch console port, a Telnet/SSH session, or a web-based GUI, as if you were configuring the switch itself.

To access the Configuration Wizard web page, you must first configure remote web access on the switch and enable the integrated web server. In Example 10-1, VLAN 2 has been created for switch management traffic, including WLC management. The management interface SVI sits on VLAN 2 with IP address 192.168.1.10. Web-based management requires user authentication, so a local username "admin" has been created with privilege level 15 so that configuration changes can be made. Local user authentication is configured for the HTTP server. To increase security, the regular HTTP server is disabled and the HTTPS secure server is enabled.

Example 10-1 *Initial Switch Configuration for Web-based Management*

```
Switch(config)# vlan 2
Switch(config-vlan)# name Switch Management
Switch(config-vlan)# exit
Switch(config)# interface vlan 2
Switch(config-if)# description Management Interface
Switch(config-if)# ip address 192.168.1.10 255.255.255.0
Switch(config-if)# no shutdown
Switch(config-if)# exit
!
Switch(config)# username admin privilege 15 password secretpassword
Switch(config)# ip http authentication local
Switch(config)# no ip http server
Switch(config)# ip http secure-server
```

Next, from your PC, make sure you can reach the management interface address that you just configured. For example, try to ping 192.168.1.10. If the switch is not reachable, verify that you are connected to a switch interface that is assigned to or that can reach the management VLAN. Once you can reach the switch, open a web browser to the switch management address and log in with your credentials. Following Example 10-1, you would open the browser to https://192.168.1.10 to access the switch, as shown in Figure 10-15.

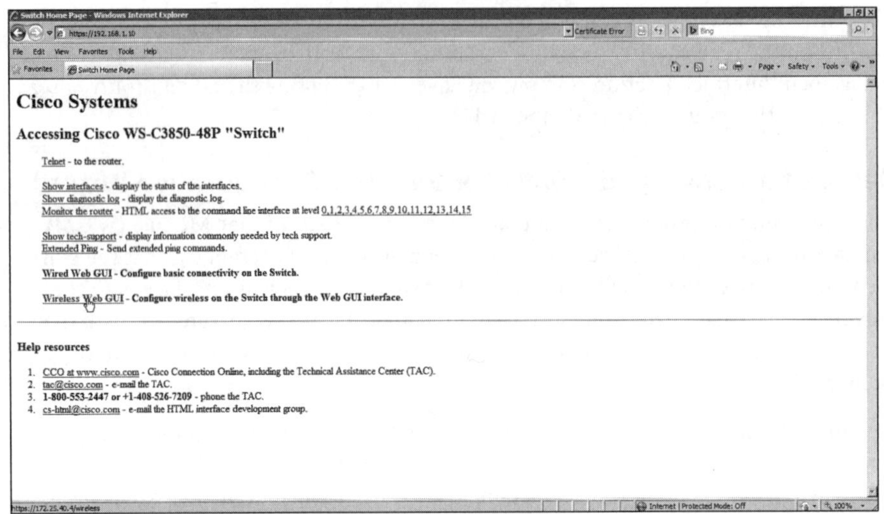

Figure 10-15 *Accessing the Switch Management Web Page*

Click the Wireless Web GUI link to access the WLC management page that is displayed in Figure 10-16. From this page, you can monitor, configure, and administer the converged WLC on the switch. For the initial configuration, select **Configuration > Wizard.**

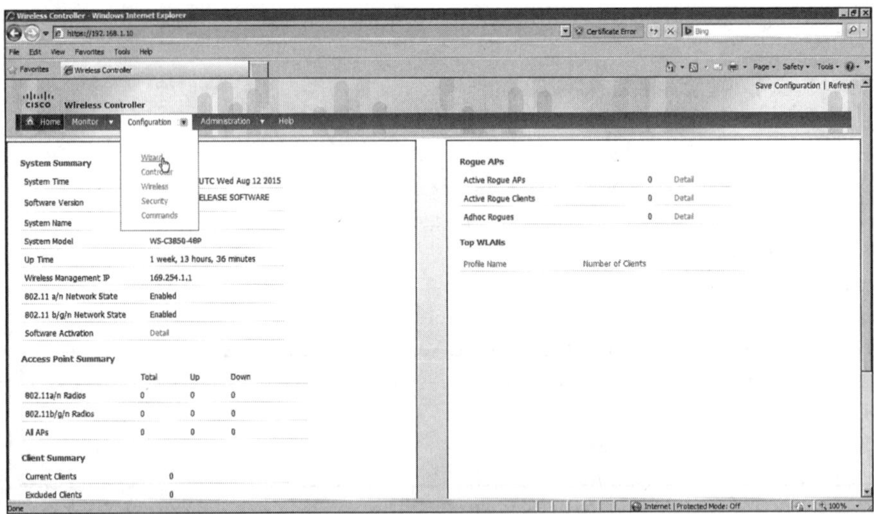

Figure 10-16 *Initiating the WLC Configuration Wizard*

The Configuration Wizard breaks the initial configuration into the following nine steps:

Step 1. **Admin Users**—Configure one username and password for WLC management, as shown in Figure 10-17.

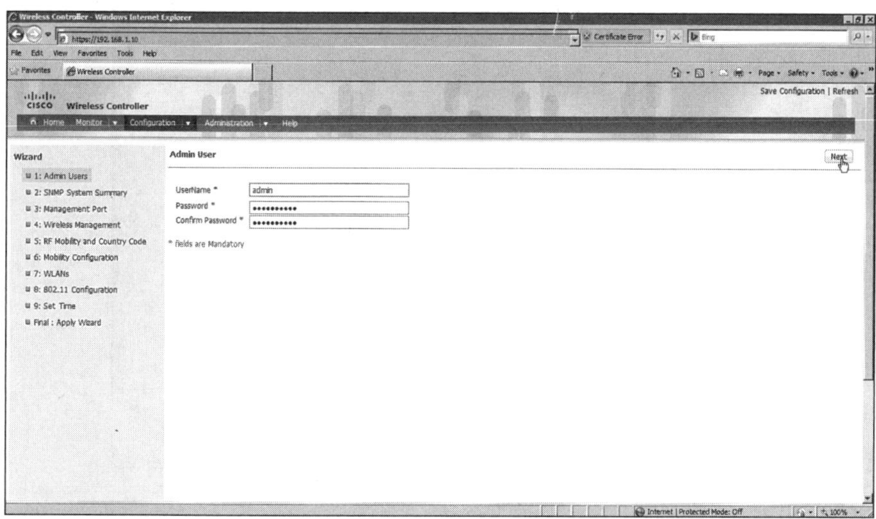

Figure 10-17 *Creating an Administrative User for Converged WLC Management*

Step 2. **SNMP System Summary**—Set basic SNMP parameters as shown in Figure 10-18.

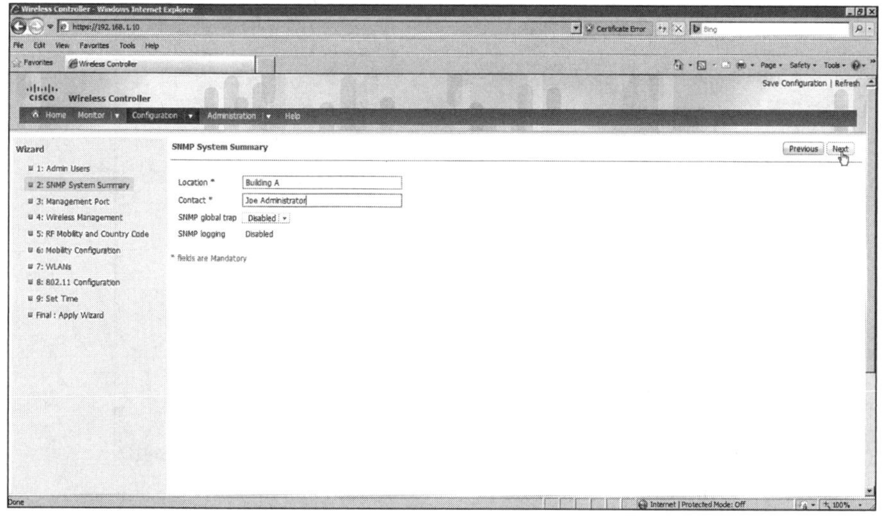

Figure 10-18 *Setting Basic SNMP Parameters on a Converged WLC*

Step 3. **Management Port**—Identify the interface to be used as the WLC service port, along with IP addressing information, as shown in Figure 10-19.

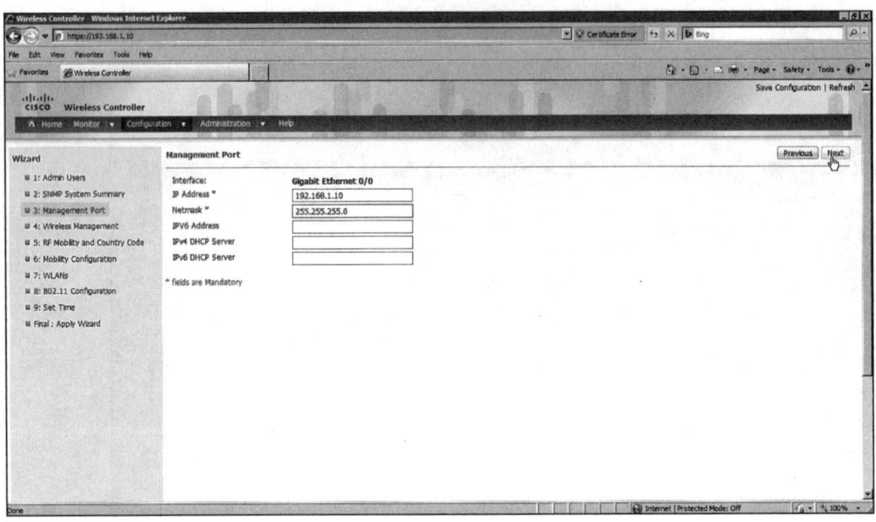

Figure 10-19 *Configuring a Converged WLC Management Port*

Step 4. **Wireless Management**—Configure the management and dynamic interfaces, along with their VLAN numbers and IP addresses, as shown in Figure 10-20.

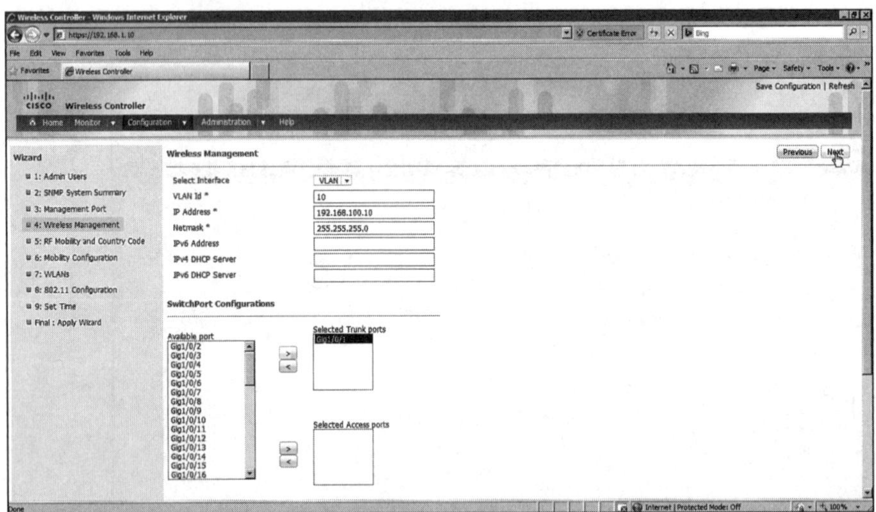

Figure 10-20 *Configuring Converged WLC Wireless Management*

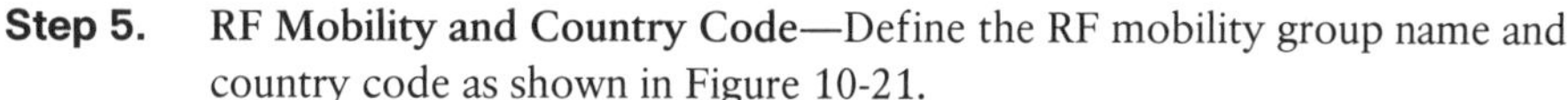

Step 5. **RF Mobility and Country Code**—Define the RF mobility group name and country code as shown in Figure 10-21.

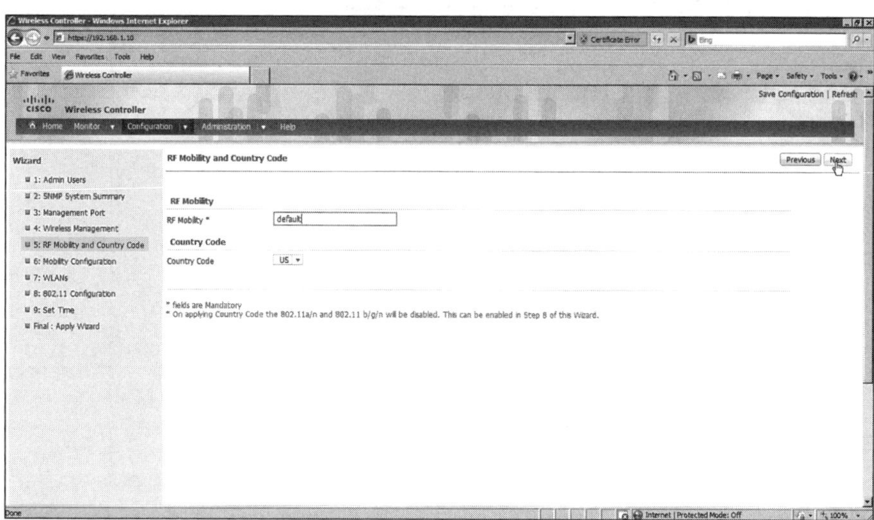

Figure 10-21 *Configuring Converged WLC RF Mobility*

Step 6. **Mobility Configuration**—Set the mobility parameters that will be used to manage roaming clients, as shown in Figure 10-22.

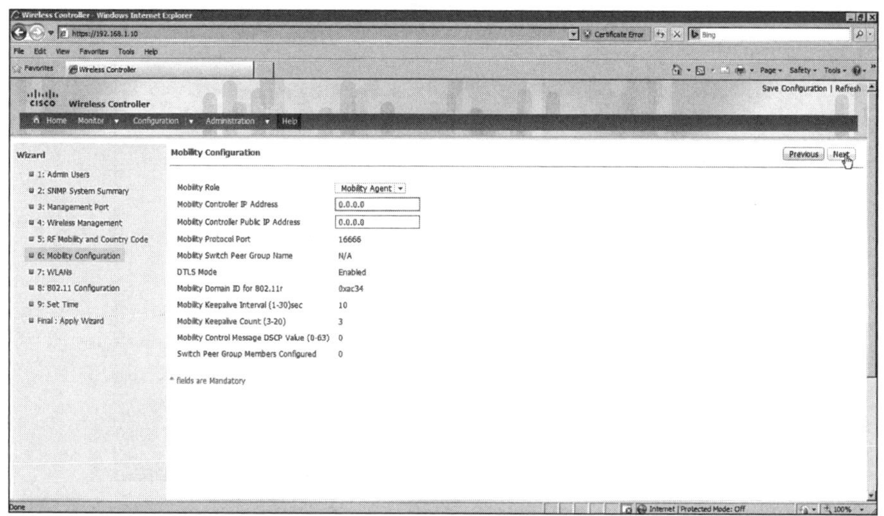

Figure 10-22 *Configuring Converged WLC Mobility*

Step 7. WLANs—Map an SSID to a VLAN using the fields shown in Figure 10-23.

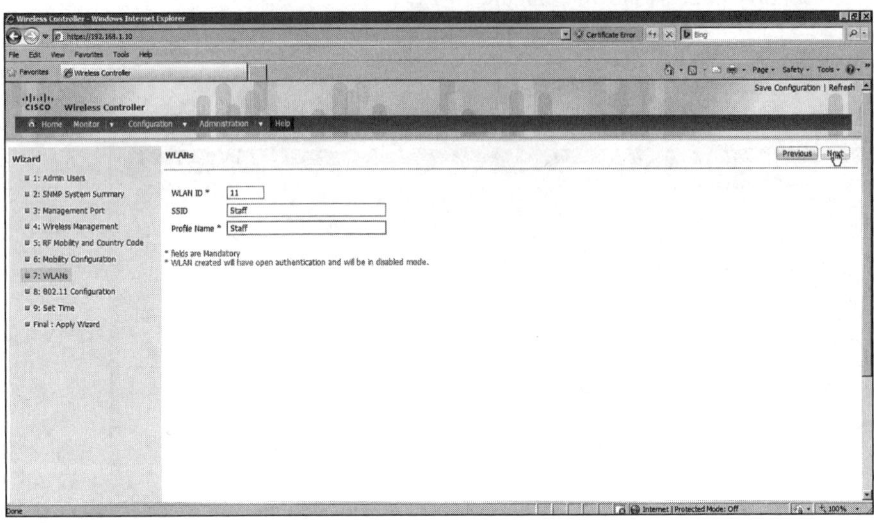

Figure 10-23 *Configuring a WLAN on a Converged WLC*

Step 8. **802.11 Configuration**—Enable the 2.4- and 5-GHz bands as shown in Figure 10-24.

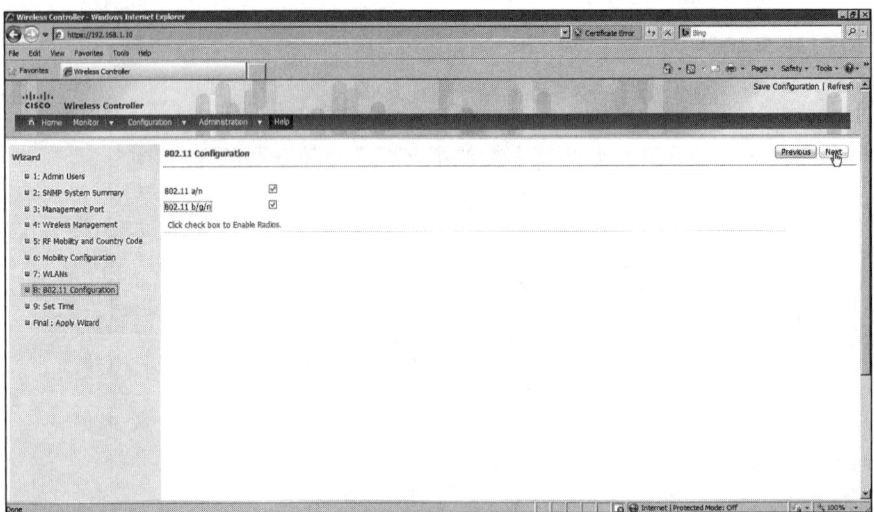

Figure 10-24 *Enabling 802.11 on a Converged WLC*

Step 9. Set Time—Set the WLC clock and calendar using the fields shown in Figure 10-25.

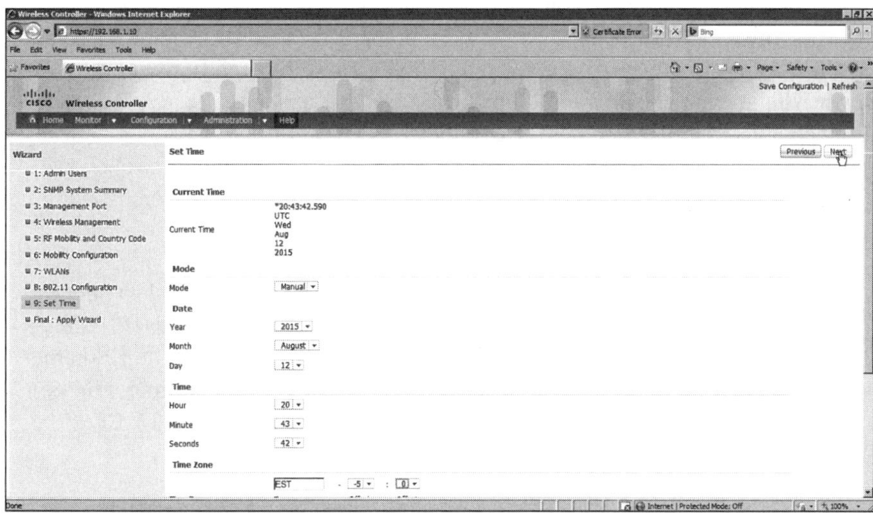

Figure 10-25 *Setting the Clock on a Converged WLC*

At this point, you can view the entire initial configuration on one web page, as shown in Figure 10-26, step Final: Apply Wizard. If everything is correct, click the Apply button in the upper-right corner of the page.

Figure 10-26 *Verifying the Initial Converged WLC Configuration*

The parameters in the converged and centralized WLC configuration wizards are very similar, with one exception. Converged mobility involves a specific role assignment for the access layer switch. The mobility roles and hierarchy are discussed in greater detail in Chapter 12, "Understanding Roaming."

Initial Setup of a Centralized Controller with WLAN Express Setup

Beginning with AireOS 8.1, Cisco WLCs offer an alternate method called WLAN Express Setup (WES) for entering the initial configuration. On the 2504 WLC, WES is available beginning with AireOS 8.0. Through WES, you can prepare a controller by entering parameters into a few web pages. WES differs from the traditional web-based Configuration Wizard by making the initial configuration process more efficient and effective. For example, you can complete the WES process after only two web pages, and WES automatically applies parameters that are considered best practices for you. You can use the following steps to complete WES.

Step 1. Enter an administrative username and password.

Connect your PC to the same VLAN and subnet that the controller's service port uses and then open a web browser to the controller's default IP address 192.168.1.1. On a 2504, you can connect directly to one of the four Ethernet ports instead. Enter a username and password that you will use to configure and maintain the controller in the future, as shown in Figure 10-27. Click the Start button to begin the initial configuration.

Figure 10-27 *Beginning the WLAN Express Setup*

Step 2. Identify the controller.

Next, enter a name for the controller as shown in Figure 10-28. Set the time parameters by selecting the country and timezone, then set the date and time and identify an NTP server. Enter the IP address, subnet mask, and default gateway that the controller will use for management purposes. Select the VLAN number that will be used for management traffic. By default, VLAN 0 is used to signify that management traffic is untagged on the native VLAN of a trunk link. Click the Next button to continue.

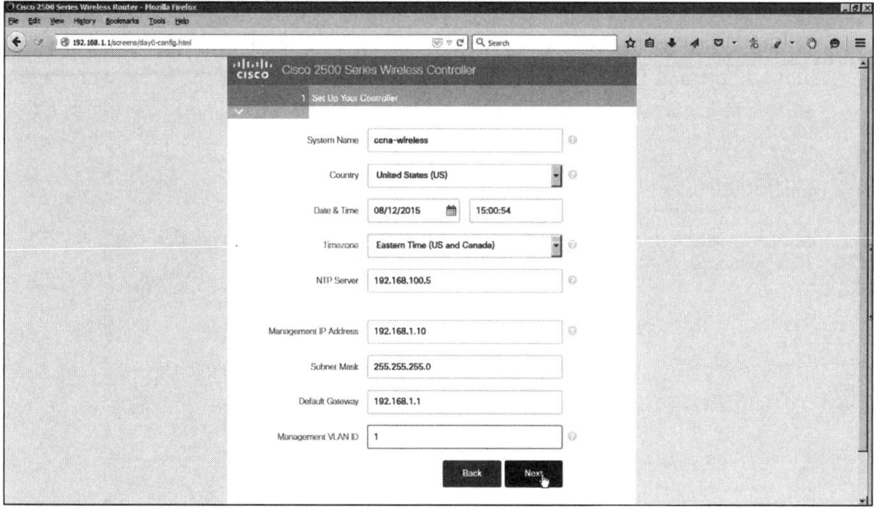

Figure 10-28 *Entering Management Parameters*

Step 3. Configure initial wireless networks.

You can configure up to two WLANs during the express setup: an "Employee" network and a "Guest" network. To enable the WLAN, click the check mark button; to disable the WLAN, click the × button. In Figure 10-29, an Employee network named "staff" is enabled and configured, while the Guest network is disabled. Then for each WLAN that is enabled, enter the network name (SSID), a wireless security method and parameters, and the VLAN number that will be mapped to the WLAN. By default, the management VLAN is selected. You can create a new VLAN by selecting **New VLAN** from the VLAN drop-down menu.

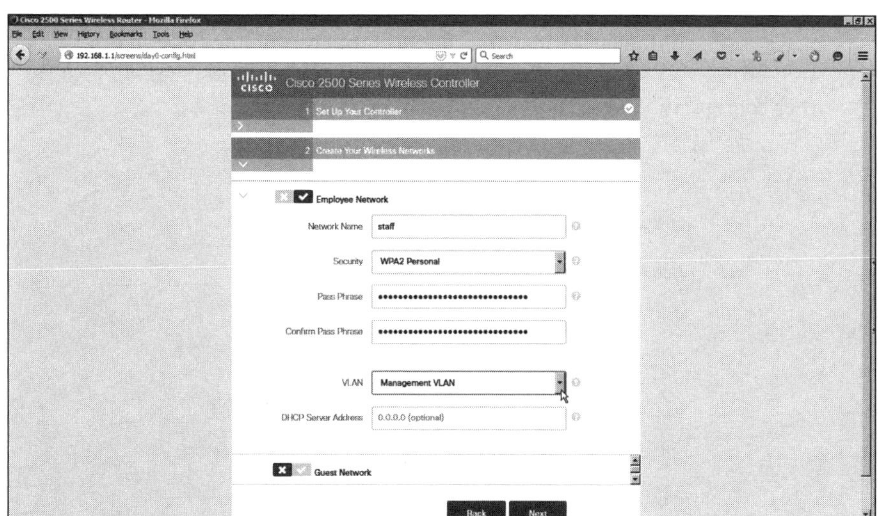

Figure 10-29 *Configuring Initial Wireless Networks*

Enter the IP address that the controller will use on the dynamic interface that is mapped to the VLAN, along with the subnet mask, default gateway address, and an optional DHCP server address. Figure 10-30 shows the same web page shown in Figure 10-29, scrolled down to reveal the VLAN and IP addressing parameters.

Click the **Next** button to continue.

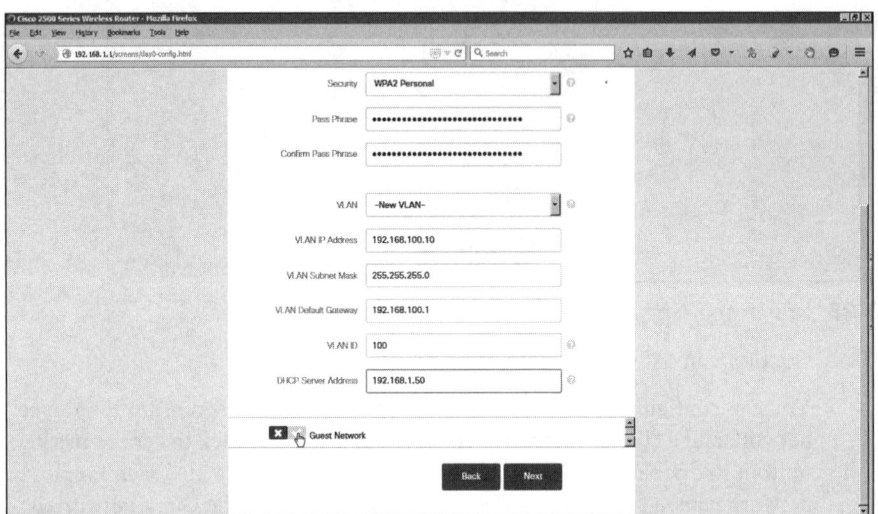

Figure 10-30 *Entering VLAN and IP Address Parameters for a Wireless Network*

Step 4. Verify the initial configuration.

Next, review the parameters you have entered, as shown in Figure 10-31. Click the Back button to return to previous pages to make corrections or click the Apply button to apply the initial configuration. Once applied, the controller will save its configuration and will reboot. From this point, you can open your web browser to the controller's management IP address and continue with further configuration tasks.

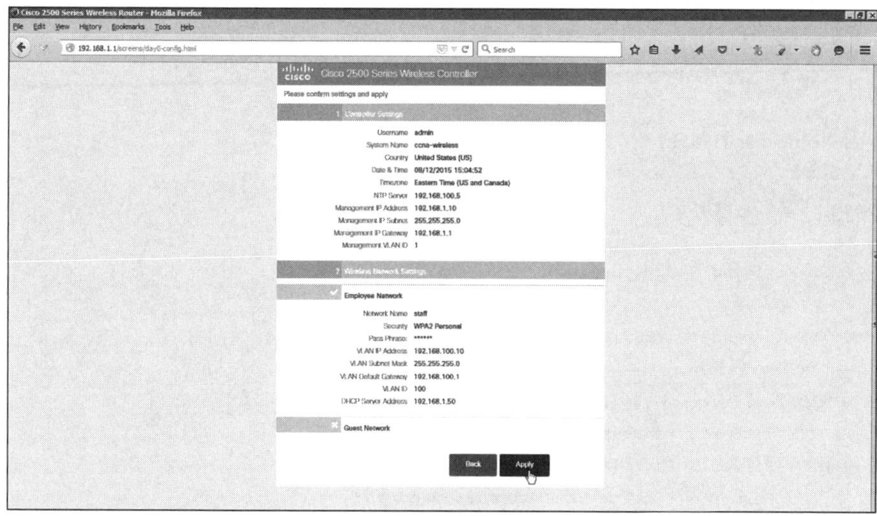

Figure 10-31 *Verifying the Initial Configuration*

Initial Setup of a Centralized Controller with the CLI

As an alternative to using a web browser for the initial setup, you can connect your PC to the controller's asynchronous console port and use the CLI. Your terminal emulator will need to be configured for 9600 baud, 8 data bits, and 1 stop bit—the same settings you use to access the console ports on most Cisco routers and switches.

For comparison, the same parameters used in the web-based initial setup are used to demonstrate the CLI initial setup in Example 10-2. Notice that some CLI prompts end with things like [yes][NO]. You can enter either string option shown (yes or NO) or you can press **Enter** to use the capitalized default value.

Example 10-2 *Using the Controller CLI for Initial Setup*

```
Welcome to the Cisco Wizard Configuration Tool
Use the '-' character to backup
Would you like to terminate autoinstall? [yes]:
AUTO-INSTALL: starting now...

System Name [Cisco_38:b4:2f] (31 characters max): WLC-1
Enter Administrative User Name (24 characters max): admin
Enter Administrative Password (3 to 24 characters): **********
Re-enter Administrative Password                                  : **********

Service Interface IP Address Configuration [static][DHCP]: DHCP

Management Interface IP Address: 192.168.50.10
Management Interface Netmask: 255.255.255.0
Management Interface Default Router: 192.168.50.1
Management Interface VLAN Identifier (0 = untagged): 50
```

10

```
Management Interface DHCP Server IP Address: 192.168.3.17

Virtual Gateway IP Address: 10.1.1.1

Mobility/RF Group Name: MyRF

Network Name (SSID): Staff

Configure DHCP Bridging Mode [yes][NO]:

Allow Static IP Addresses [YES][no]:

Configure a RADIUS Server now? [YES][no]:
Enter the RADIUS Server's Address: 192.168.200.20
Enter the RADIUS Server's Port [1812]:
Enter the RADIUS Server's Secret: thisismysharedsecret

Enter Country Code list (enter 'help' for a list of countries) [US]:

Enable 802.11b Network [YES][no]:
Enable 802.11a Network [YES][no]:
Enable 802.11g Network [YES][no]:
Enable Auto-RF [YES][no]:

Configure a NTP server now? [YES][no]:
Enter the NTP server's IP address: 192.168.200.30
Enter a polling interval between 3600 and 604800 secs: 3600

Configuration correct? If yes, system will save it and reset. [yes][NO]: yes
```

Maintaining a Wireless Controller

Like Cisco routers, switches, and other networking devices, wireless controllers maintain configuration files and run operating system images. As a CCNA Wireless engineer, you will likely be involved in maintaining controllers on a network and dealing with the information and files they use. The following sections explain how you can interface with controllers and APs so that you can upload and download their files.

Backing Up Controller Configurations

As you make configuration changes to a wireless controller, you must click the **Apply** button to make the changes active. This is similar to configuring a router or switch, where changes take effect immediately and are updated in the running configuration but are not saved to the startup configuration. As long as the controller stays up, your changes will stay active. If the controller reboots or loses power, your changes will be lost.

A controller also has nonvolatile storage for its configuration, much like flash memory. You can save the configuration by selecting the **Save Configuration** link at the upper right of any controller web page.

It is important to save the controller configuration to flash memory so that any configuration changes are retained. Beyond that, you should think about saving the configuration to a location away from the controller itself. If the controller hardware ever fails and you receive a replacement, you will need a way to access the configuration so you can import it into the new unit.

From the controller GUI, navigate to **Commands > Upload File; on a WCM, navigate to Configuration > Commands > Upload File.** Select **Configuration** from the file type drop-down menu. Select either TFTP or FTP and enter the IP address, file path, and target filename, as shown in Figure 10-32. The controller configuration will be transferred and saved in cleartext, showing the CLI commands that are used to build the entire configuration. Select the **Configuration File Encryption** checkbox and enter an encryption key string to encrypt the configuration file so that it cannot be read easily. The file contents will be decrypted when they are transferred back onto a WLC.

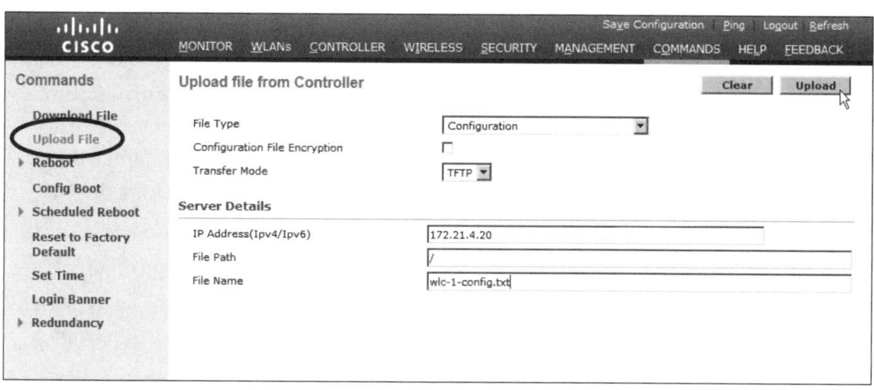

Figure 10-32 *Saving a Wireless Controller Configuration*

When you have an offline copy of the configuration file, you can download the contents to a controller to restore the configuration or to overwrite the configuration that is already in use. This process is just the opposite of uploading the configuration to your PC: Select **Commands > Download File**, select file type **Configuration**, and enter the TFTP or FTP server parameters and filename.

Tip On a WCM, the configuration is contained in the running configuration of the switch platform.

Updating Wireless LAN Controller Code

Like any other network device, a controller requires a code image to operate. Periodically, you might want to upgrade the code image to a new release so that you can take advantage of bug fixes and new features. Less often, you might have to downgrade the code image to return to a more stable version.

A WLC maintains two separate code images: a primary image and a backup image. When a controller boots up, it runs the primary image by default. That means you can download a new image file into the backup position on the controller while it is running, with no interruption of service. To run the new image, you must reboot the controller. You can display the two code image versions by navigating to **Commands > Config Boot**, as shown in Figure 10-33. You can select the image that will be run after the next reboot with the Config Boot Image drop-down menu.

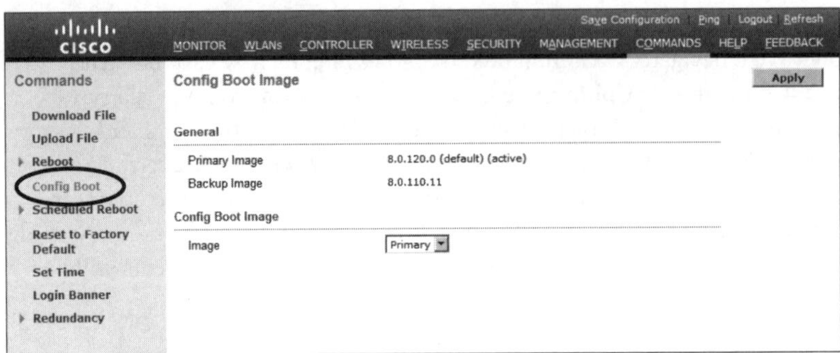

Figure 10-33 *Displaying Controller Code Images*

To download a new code image, go to **Commands > Download File**. The controller can download from a TFTP or an FTP server. Select Code as the file type, then enter the file server's IP address, file path, and code image filename. For an FTP download, enter the credentials required by the FTP server. Next, click the **Download** button to start the file transfer.

Tip The file transfer terminology might be a bit different than you are used to seeing. The terms "download" and "upload" refer to the controller's perspective, as if it acts like a client. You always download to the controller and upload *from* it.

WLC image files are usually named according to the hardware platform and the release number and end with a .aes suffix, as in AIR-WISM2-K9-7-2-115-2.aes. During the download, the WLC will periodically update the web page to display the following sequence of status messages (this process can take several minutes):

1. TFTP Code transfer starting.
2. TFTP receive complete...extracting components.
3. Executing backup script.
4. Writing new RTOS to flash disk.
5. Writing new FP to flash disk.
6. Writing new APIB to flash disk.
7. Executing install_apib script.
8. Executing fini script.
9. TFTP File transfer is successful.

At this point, the new image is ready to be used. You must reboot the controller to run the new image, according to the status message shown in Figure 10-34. Be aware that rebooting the controller will interrupt wireless service. All of the APs joined to the controller will lose contact with it and will rehome to a secondary controller (if one is configured) or begin the controller discovery process to find a new home.

cisco
MONITOR WLANs CONTROLLER WIRELESS SECURITY MANAGEMENT COMMANDS
Commands
Download File
Upload File
Reboot
Config Boot
Scheduled Reboot
Reset to Factory Default
Set Time
Login Banner
Download file to Controller
Clear
Download
File Type: Code
Transfer Mode: TFTP
Server Details
IP Address: 172.21.4.20
Maximum retries: 10
Timeout (seconds): 6
File Path: /
File Name: AIR-WISM2-K9-7-2-115-2.aes
TFTP File transfer is successful. Reboot the controller for update to complete. Optionally, pre-download the image to APs before rebooting to reduce network downtime.
For the new Code to take effect, you need to reboot system. Click Here to get redirected to reboot page.

Figure 10-34 *After an Image Download, the WLC is Ready to Reboot*

You can get ready to reboot the controller by selecting the **Click Here** link at the bottom of the download status or by navigating to **Commands > Reboot**, as shown in Figure 10-35. You can save the current controller configuration and reboot immediately by clicking the **Save and Reboot** button.

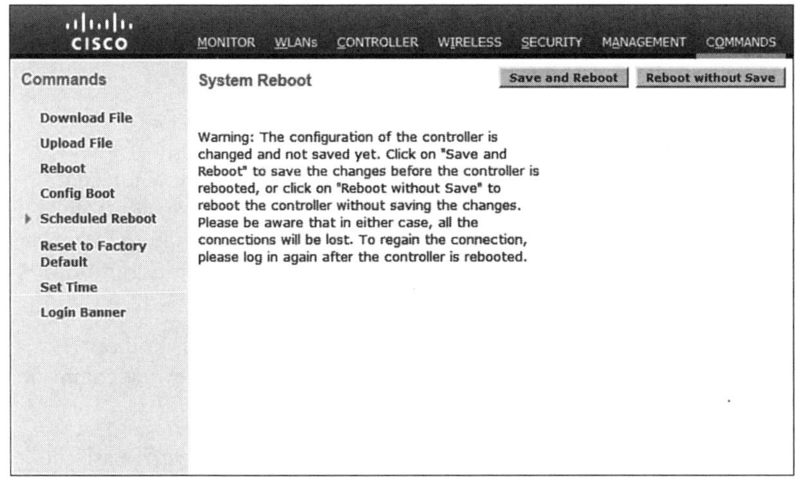

Figure 10-35 *Triggering a WLC Reboot*

After you install a new controller image file, should you install the same code release on the lightweight APs? Recall that the controller manages all aspects of the APs, including their code images. When a lightweight AP joins a controller, it compares its own code release with that of the controller. If the images differ, the AP will download a matching image from the controller automatically. Therefore, after the controller reboots and begins to run a new image, each AP will download the same release as it rejoins the controller.

As you might imagine, the code upgrade process can impose an extensive outage on a wireless network. The controller must be rebooted so that it can begin running the new image. After that, each AP must go offline to download the new image, reboot, and begin running the new image. To lessen the impact to wireless users, controller releases 7.2 and later can "pre-download" or push a new code image to the APs *before* the controller or the APs need to reboot. This prepares the APs ahead of time so that they can reboot in parallel with the controller and begin running the new code image much sooner.

Updating Wireless Control Module Code

A converged wireless network uses Wireless Control Modules (WCMs) rather than WLCs. The functionality is the same from a wireless perspective but differs in the way code images are managed. A WCM is actually a module embedded in a Cisco Catalyst access switch, so the two functions must share the same hardware platform. In addition, the two functions share a common software platform called IOS-XE that provides the traditional Cisco IOS Software for the switch. IOS-XE can also host other software applications, such as WCM and Wireshark.

IOS-XE is actually a bundle of multiple software package files that include things like a base kernel, platform drivers, infrastructure management, a Cisco IOS image, platform-specific functions, and WCM. Devices running IOS-XE can boot in one of two modes: Install Mode or Bundle Mode. The WLC 5760 is an exception because it supports only the Install mode.

Install Mode expands the bundled packages, copies them to flash memory, then boots and runs the appropriate software. Bundle Mode does not expand the packages but boots from the bundle directly. Because Bundle Mode must deal with the bundled packages during boot time, it requires more system resources and sometimes restricts available features. Therefore, Cisco recommends using the default Install Mode instead.

To upgrade the code running on a WCM, you must upgrade the code running on the switch platform. Catalyst 3850 and 3650 switches can be configured as logical switch stacks. A single stack can consist of up to nine individual switches that are connected through their StackWise-480 ports. One switch operates as a master switch, controlling the stack as a whole, while another operates as a standby switch that is ready to take over if the master fails. The master switch maintains the running and startup configurations for all members of the stack.

Also, each switch in the stack should run the same IOS-XE software version. You can upgrade the code image by installing an IOS-XE image bundle with the following command:

```
Switch# software install file source:filename.bin new
```

Over time, you might end up with several software bundles stored on the switch flash filesystem but are no longer used. You can safely remove redundant or extraneous packages with the following command:

```
Switch# software clean file flash: switch switch#
```

Exam Preparation Tasks

As mentioned in the section, "How to Use This Book," in the Introduction, you have a couple of choices for exam preparation: the exercises here, Chapter 21, "Final Review," and the exam simulation questions on the DVD.

Review All Key Topics

Review the most important topics in this chapter, noted with the Key Topic icon in the outer margin of the page. Table 10-3 lists a reference of these key topics and the page numbers on which each is found.

Table 10-3 Key Topics for Chapter 10

Key Topic Element	Description	Page Number
List	Controller ports	235
List	Controller interfaces	237
Figure 10-15	Accessing the WCM interface on a converged access switch	248

Define Key Terms

Define the following key terms from this chapter and check your answers in the glossary:

controller interface, controller port, distribution system port, dynamic interface, link aggregation group (LAG), management interface, service port, virtual interface

This chapter covers the following topics:

- **Discovering a Controller**—This section explains how a lightweight access point discovers and joins a wireless LAN controller.
- **Designing High Availability**—This section discusses what happens when a wireless LAN controller fails and APs need to find a new home. It also covers several common approaches to building networks with redundant controllers.

This chapter covers the following exam topics:

- 4.2—Describe the Cisco implementation of the CAPWAP discovery and join process
    - 4.2a—DHCP
    - 4.2b—DNS
    - 4.2c—Master-controller
    - 4.2d—Primary-secondary-tertiary

CHAPTER 11

Understanding Controller Discovery

Cisco lightweight wireless access points need to be paired with a wireless LAN controller (WLC) to function. Each lightweight access point (LAP) must discover and bind itself with a controller before wireless clients can be supported. This chapter covers the discovery process in detail.

"Do I Know This Already?" Quiz

The "Do I Know This Already?" quiz allows you to assess whether you should read this entire chapter thoroughly or jump to the "Exam Preparation Tasks" section. If you are in doubt about your answers to these questions or your own assessment of your knowledge of the topics, read the entire chapter. Table 11-1 lists the major headings in this chapter and their corresponding "Do I Know This Already?" quiz questions. You can find the answers in Appendix A, "Answers to the 'Do I Know This Already?' Quizzes."

Table 11-1 "Do I Know This Already?" Section-to-Question Mapping

Foundation Topics Section	Questions
Discovering a Controller	1–6
Designing High Availability	7–10

Caution The goal of self-assessment is to gauge your mastery of the topics in this chapter. If you do not know the answer to a question or are only partially sure of the answer, you should mark that question as wrong for purposes of the self-assessment. Giving yourself credit for an answer you correctly guess skews your self-assessment results and might provide you with a false sense of security.

1. Which one of the following comes first in an LAP's state machine, after it boots?
   a. Build a CAPWAP tunnel
   b. Discover WLCs
   c. Download a configuration
   d. Join a WLC
2. If an LAP needs to download a new software image, how does it get the image?
   a. From a TFTP server
   b. From an FTP server
   c. From a WLC
   d. You must preconfigure it.
3. Which of the following are ways that an AP can learn of WLCs that it might join? (Choose all that apply.)
   a. Primed entries
   b. List from a previously joined controller
   c. DHCP
   d. Subnet broadcast
   e. DNS
   f. All of these
4. Which one of the following will an AP try first in order to select a controller to join?
   a. Master controller
   b. Least-loaded controller
   c. Primed address
   d. DHCP option 43
   e. Wait for a controller to send a Join Request
5. If an AP tries every available method to discover a controller, but fails to do so, what happens next?
   a. It broadcasts on every possible subnet.
   b. It tries to contact the default controller at 10.0.0.1.
   c. It reboots and starts discovering again.
   d. It uses IP redirect on the local router.
6. You can configure the priority value on an AP to accomplish which one of the following?
   a. To set the controller it will try to join first
   b. To define which APs will be preferred when joining a controller
   c. To set the SSID that will be advertised first
   d. To identify the least-loaded controller to join

7. Which of the following is the most deterministic strategy you can use to push a specific AP to join a specific controller?
   a. Select the least-loaded controller
   b. Use DHCP option 43
   c. Configure the master controller
   d. Configure the primary controller

8. By default, which one of the following methods and intervals does an AP use to detect a failed controller?
   a. ICMP, 60 seconds
   b. ICMP, 30 seconds
   c. CAPWAP keepalive, 60 seconds
   d. CAPWAP keepalive, 30 seconds
   e. CAPWAP discovery, 30 seconds

9. Suppose that an AP is joined to the WLC that is configured as the primary controller. At a later time, that controller fails and the AP joins its secondary controller. Once the primary controller is restored to service, which feature would allow the AP to rejoin it?
   a. CAPWAP Rejoin
   b. AP Failover
   c. AP Priority
   d. AP Fallback

10. A Cisco unified wireless network architecture consists of two controllers and a number of APs. The APs are distributed equally across the two controllers. Each AP is configured with one controller as primary and the other controller as secondary. Based on this information, which one of the following redundancy models is being used?
   a. No redundancy
   b. N+1 redundancy
   c. N+N redundancy
   d. N+N+1 redundancy

Foundation Topics

Discovering a Controller

Cisco LAPs are designed to be "touch free," so that you can simply unbox a new one and connect it to the wired network, without any need to configure it first. Naturally, you have to configure the switch port, where the AP connects, with the correct access VLAN, access mode, and inline power settings. From that point on, the AP can power up and use a variety of methods to find a viable WLC to join.

AP States

From the time it powers up until it offers a fully functional basic service set (BSS), an LAP operates in a variety of states. Each of the possible states are well defined in the Control and Provisioning of Wireless Access Points (CAPWAP) RFC, but are simplified here for clarity. The AP enters each state in a specific order; the sequence of states is called a *state machine*. You should become familiar with the AP state machine so that you can understand how an AP forms a working relationship with a WLC. If an AP cannot form that relationship for some reason, your knowledge of the state machine can help you troubleshoot the problem.

> **Tip** CAPWAP is defined in RFC 5415, and in a few other RFCs. The terms used in the RFC differ somewhat from the ones used in a Cisco unified wireless network and this book. For example, access controller (AC) refers to a WLC, whereas wireless termination point (WTP) refers to an AP.

The sequence of the most common states, as shown in Figure 11-1, is as follows:

1. **AP boots:** Once an AP receives power, it boots on a small IOS image so that it can work through the remaining states and communicate over its network connection. The AP must also receive an IP address from either a Dynamic Host Configuration Protocol (DHCP) server or a static configuration so that it can communicate over the network.
2. **WLC discovery:** The AP goes through a series of steps to find one or more controllers that it might join. The steps are explained further in the next section.
3. **CAPWAP tunnel:** The AP attempts to build a CAPWAP tunnel with one or more controllers. The tunnel will provide a secure Datagram Transport Layer Security (DTLS) channel for subsequent AP-WLC control messages. The AP and WLC authenticate each other through an exchange of digital certificates.
4. **WLC join:** The AP selects a WLC from a list of candidates, and then sends a CAPWAP Join Request message to it. The WLC replies with a CAPWAP Join Response message. The next section explains how an AP selects a WLC to join.
5. **Download image:** The WLC informs the AP of its software release. If the AP's own software is a different release, the AP will download a matching image from the controller, reboot to apply the new image, and then return to step 1. If the two are running identical releases, no download is needed.

6. **Download config:** The AP pulls configuration parameters down from the WLC and can update existing values with those sent from the controller. Settings include RF, service set identifier (SSID), security, and quality of service (QoS) parameters.
7. **Run state:** Once the AP is fully initialized, the WLC places it in the "run" state. The AP and WLC then begin providing a BSS and begin accepting wireless clients.
8. **Reset:** If an AP is reset by the WLC, it tears down existing client associations and any CAPWAP tunnels to WLCs. The AP then reboots and starts through the entire state machine again.

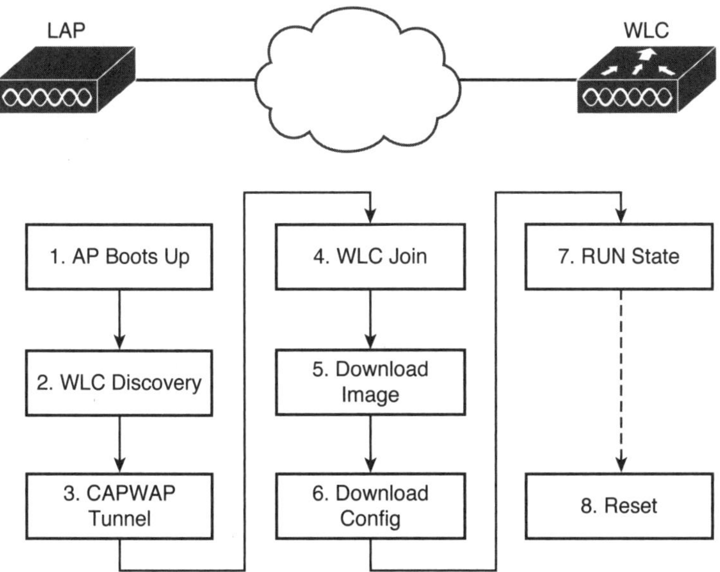

Figure 11-1 *State Machine of an LAP*

Be aware that you cannot control which software image release an LAP runs. Rather, the WLC that the AP joins determines the release, based on its own software version. Downloading a new image can take a considerable amount of time, especially if there are a large number of APs waiting for the same download from one WLC. That might not matter when a newly installed AP is booting and downloading code, because it does not yet have any wireless clients to support.

However, if an existing, live AP happens to reboot or join a different controller, clients can be left hanging with no AP while the image downloads. Some careful planning with your controllers and their software releases will pay off later by minimizing downtime. Consider the following scenarios when an AP might need to download a different release:

- The AP joins a WLC, but has a version mismatch.
- A code upgrade is performed on the WLC itself, requiring all associated APs to upgrade too.
- The WLC fails, causing all associated APs to be dropped and join elsewhere.

If there is a chance that an AP could rehome from one WLC to another, you should make sure that both controllers are running the same code release. Otherwise, the AP move should happen under controlled circumstances, such as during a maintenance window. Fortunately, if you have downloaded a new code release to a controller, but not yet rebooted it to run the new code, you can predownload the new release to the controller's APs. The APs will download the new image, but will keep running the previous release. When it comes time to reboot the controller on the new image, the APs will already have the new image staged without having to take time to download it. The APs can reboot on their new image and join the controller after it has booted and become stable.

Discovering a WLC

An LAP must be very diligent to discover any controllers that it can join—all without any preconfiguration on your part. To accomplish this feat, several methods of discovery are used. The goal of discovery is just to build a list of live candidate controllers that are available, using the following methods:

- Prior knowledge of WLCs
- DHCP and DNS information to suggest some controllers
- Broadcast on the local subnet to solicit controllers

To discover a WLC, an AP sends a unicast CAPWAP Discovery Request to a controller's IP address over UDP port 5246 or a broadcast to the local subnet. If the controller exists and is working, it returns a CAPWAP Discovery Response to the AP. The sequence of discovery steps used is as follows:

Step 1. **Broadcast on the local subnet**—The AP will broadcast a CAPWAP Discovery Request on its local wired subnet. Any WLCs that also exist on the subnet will answer with a CAPWAP Discovery Response.

> **Tip** If the AP and controllers lie on different subnets, you can configure the local router to relay any broadcast requests on UDP port 5246 to specific controller addresses. Use the following configuration commands:

```
router(config)# ip forward-protocol udp 5246
router(config)# interface vlan n
router (config-int)# ip helper-address WLC1-MGMT-ADDR
router(config-int)# ip helper-address WLC2-MGMT-ADDR
```

Step 2. **Use locally stored WLC addresses**—An AP can be "primed" with up to three controllers—a primary, a secondary, and a tertiary. These are stored in non-volatile memory so that the AP can remember them after a reboot or power failure. Otherwise, if an AP has previously joined with a controller, it should have stored up to 8 out of a list of 32 WLC addresses that it received from the last controller it joined. The AP will attempt to contact as many controllers as possible to build a list of candidates.

Step 3. **Use DHCP**—The DHCP server that supplies the AP with an IP address can also send DHCP option 43 to suggest a list of WLC addresses.

Step 4. **Use DNS**—The AP will attempt to resolve the name CISCO-CAPWAP-CONTROLLER.*localdomain* with a DNS request. The *localdomain* string is the domain name learned from DHCP. If the name resolves to an IP address, the controller attempts to contact a WLC at that address.

Step 5. **Reset and try again**—If none of the steps has been successful, the AP resets itself and starts the discovery process all over again.

Selecting a WLC

Once an AP has finished the discovery process, it should have built a list of live candidate controllers. Now it must begin a separate process to select one WLC and attempt to join it. Joining a WLC involves sending it a CAPWAP Join Request and waiting for it to return a CAPWAP Join Response. From that point on, the AP and WLC build a DTLS tunnel to secure their CAPWAP control messages.

The WLC selection process consists of the following three steps:

Step 1. **Try primed addresses**—If the AP has previously joined a controller and has been configured or "primed" with a primary, secondary, and tertiary controller, it will try to join those controllers in succession.

Step 2. **Try the master controller**—If the AP does not know of any candidate controller, it can try to discover one by broadcasting on the local subnet. If a controller has been configured as a master controller, it can respond to the AP's broadcast.

Step 3. **Try the least-loaded controller**—The AP will attempt to join the least-loaded WLC, in an effort to load balance APs across a set of controllers. During the discovery phase, each controller reports its load—the ratio of the number of currently joined APs to the total AP capacity. The least-loaded WLC is the one with the lowest ratio. For example, suppose that a 5508 controller has 20 out of a possible 100 APs joined to it, while a 2504 controller has 20 out of a possible 25 APs. The 5508 would be the least loaded with a ratio of 20/100; the 2504 is more loaded with 20/25.

If an AP discovers a controller, but gets rejected when it tries to join it, what might be the reason? Every controller has a set maximum number of APs that it can support. This is defined by platform or by license. If the controller already has the maximum number of APs joined to it, it will reject any additional APs.

To provide some flexibility in supporting APs on an oversubscribed controller, where more APs are trying to join than a license allows, you can configure the APs with a priority value. All APs begin with a default priority of low. You can change the value to low, medium, high, or critical. A controller will try to accommodate as many higher-priority APs as possible. Once a controller is full of APs, it will reject an AP with the lowest priority to make room for a new one that has a higher priority.

Designing High Availability

Once an AP has discovered, selected, and joined a controller, it must stay joined to that controller to remain functional. Now consider that a single controller might support as many as 1000 or even 6000 APs—enough to cover a very large building or an entire enterprise. If something ever causes the controller to fail, a large number of APs would also fail. In the worst case, where a single controller carries the enterprise, the entire wireless network would become unavailable. That might be catastrophic.

Fortunately, a Cisco AP can discover multiple controllers—not just the one that it chooses to join. Figure 11-2 shows this scenario. If the joined controller becomes unavailable, the AP can simply select the next least-loaded controller and request to join it, as Figure 11-3 depicts. That sounds simple, but it is not very deterministic.

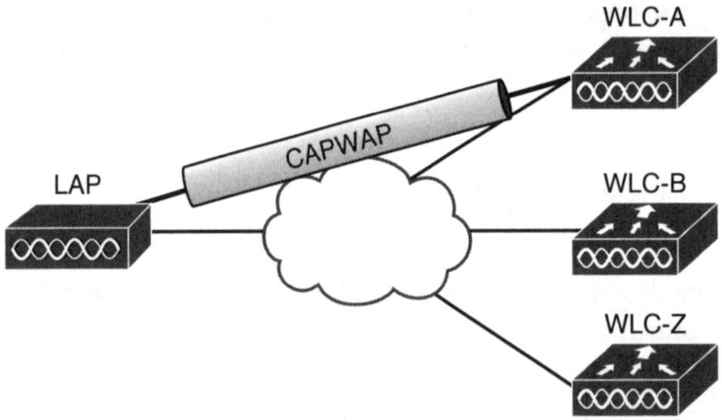

Figure 11-2 *AP Joining One of Several Discovered Controllers*

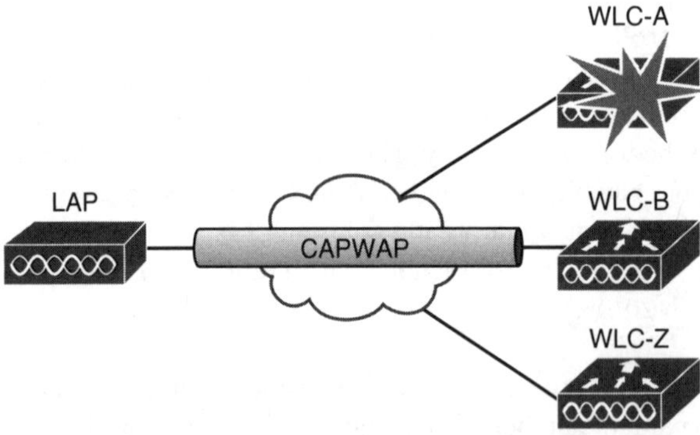

Figure 11-3 *AP Joining a Different Controller After a Failure*

For example, if a controller full of 1000 APs fails, all 1000 APs must detect the failure, discover other candidate controllers, and then select the least-loaded one to join. During that time, wireless clients can be left stranded with no connectivity. You might envision the controller failure as a commercial airline flight that has just been canceled; everyone that purchased a ticket suddenly joins a mad rush to find another flight out.

The most deterministic approach is to leverage the primary, secondary, and tertiary controller fields that every AP stores. If any of these fields are configured with a controller name or address, the AP knows which three controllers to try in sequence before resorting to a more generic search.

Tip When an AP boots and builds a list of potential controllers, it can use CAPWAP to build a tunnel to more than one controller. The AP will join only one controller, which it uses as the primary unit. By building a tunnel with a second controller ahead of time, before the primary controller fails, the AP will not have to spend time building a tunnel to the backup controller before joining it.

As a wireless network grows, you might have several controllers implemented just to support the number of APs that are required. A good network design should also take failures and high availability (HA) into consideration. It is not enough just to have multiple controllers in a network. What if they are all in use and full of APs? There would not be enough room to spare for a large group of additional, displaced APs to join in their time of need. In the commercial flight analogy, there might be other flights departing the airport soon after the cancellation. If those flights are already mostly full of passengers, many people will be left waiting at the gate.

Figure 11-4 illustrates an example network that does not offer enough capacity to fully survive a controller failure. In the "Before" diagram, a group of 400 APs has joined controller WLC-A, and a group of 300 APs has joined WLC-B. Each controller has a maximum capacity of 500 APs. As long as both controllers stay up and functional, the wireless network should work fine. In the "After" diagram, WLC-A has failed. All 400 APs that were previously joined to WLC-A will discover that WLC-B is alive, so they will all try to join it. WLC-B already has 300 APs, so it has room for only 200 more. That means 200 APs will be able to join WLC-B and 200 more will be left out in the cold with no controller to join at all.

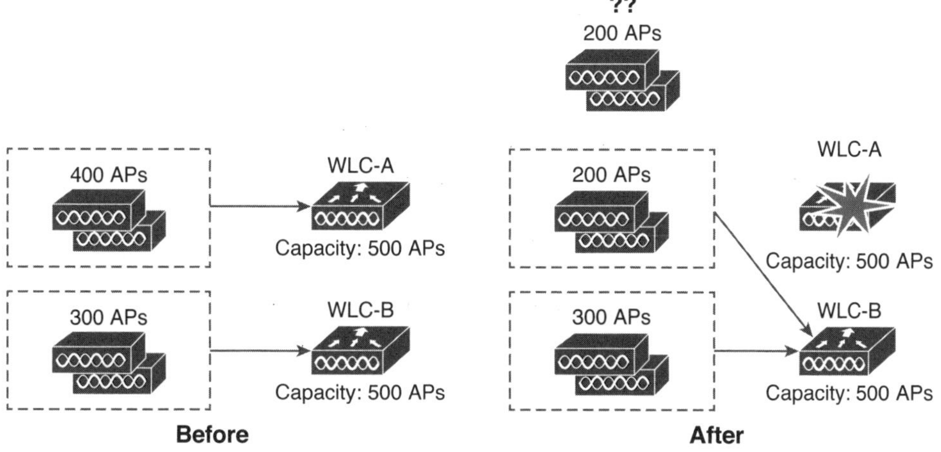

Figure 11-4 *Result of Undersized Controllers During a Failure*

11

Detecting a Controller Failure

When HA is required, make sure that you design your wireless network to support it properly. Fortunately, Cisco APs and controllers are built with HA in mind, so you have several strategies at your disposal. First, it is important to understand how APs detect a controller failure and what action they take to recover from it.

Once an AP joins a controller, it sends keepalive (also called heartbeat) messages to the controller over the wired network at regular intervals. By default, keepalives are sent every 30 seconds. The controller is expected to answer each keepalive as evidence that it is still alive and working. If a keepalive is not answered, an AP will escalate the test by sending four more keepalives at 3-second intervals. If the controller answers, all is well; if it does not answer, the AP presumes that the controller has failed. The AP then moves quickly to find a successor to join.

Using the default values, an AP can detect a controller failure in as little as 35 seconds. You can adjust the regular keepalive timer between 1 and 30 seconds and the escalated or "fast" heartbeat timer between 1 and 10 seconds. By using the minimum values, a failure can be detected after only 6 seconds.

Normally, an AP will stay joined to a controller until it fails. If the AP has been configured with primary and secondary controller information, it will join the primary controller first. If the primary fails, the AP will try to join the secondary until it fails. Even if the primary controller is put back into service, the AP will stay with the secondary. You can change that behavior by enabling the AP Fallback feature—a global controller configuration parameter. If AP Fallback is enabled (the default), an AP can try to rejoin its primary controller at any time, whether its current controller has failed or not.

Building Redundancy

Building a wireless network with one controller and some APs is straightforward, but it does not address what would happen if the controller fails for some reason. Adding another controller or two could provide some redundancy, as long as the APs know how to move from one controller to another when the time comes.

Redundancy is best configured in the most deterministic way possible. The following sections explain how you can configure APs with primary, secondary, and tertiary controller fields to implement various forms of redundancy. As you read through the sections, keep in mind that redundant controllers should be configured similarly so that APs can move from one controller to another without having to undergo any major configuration changes.

N+1 Redundancy

The simplest way to introduce HA into a Cisco unified wireless network is to provide an extra backup controller. This is commonly called N+1 or N:1 redundancy, where *N* represents some number of active controllers and 1 denotes the one backup controller.

By having one backup controller, N+1 redundancy can withstand a failure of only one active controller. As long as the backup controller is sized appropriately, it can accept all of a failed controller's APs. However, once an active controller fails and all its APs rehome to the backup controller, there will be no space to accept any other APs if a second controller fails.

Figure 11-5 illustrates N+1 redundancy with a two-controller network for simplicity. The network could have any number of active controllers, but only one backup controller. WLC-A is the active controller and carries 100 percent of the network's APs. WLC-Z is the backup controller, which normally carries no APs at all. The backup controller sits idle until an active controller fails.

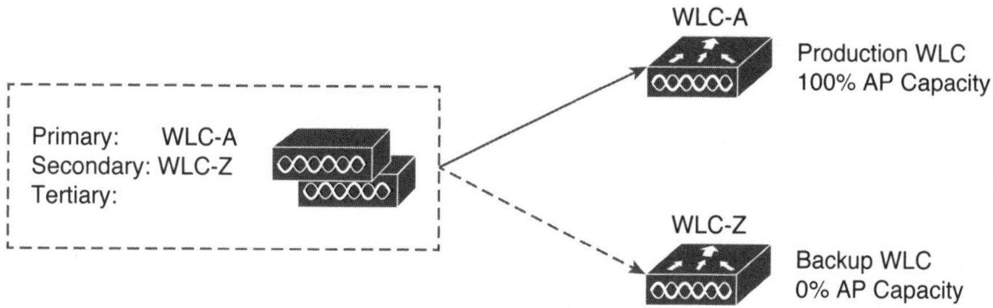

Figure 11-5 *Configuring N+1 Controller Redundancy*

To configure N+1 redundancy, you configure the primary controller field on all APs with the name of an active controller (WLC-A, for example). The secondary controller field is set to the name of the backup controller (WLC-Z).

N+N Redundancy

N+1 design is simple, but it has a couple of shortcomings. First, the backup controller must sit idle and empty of APs until another controller fails. That might not sound like a problem, except that the backup unit must be purchased with the same AP capacity as the active controller it supports. That means the active and backup controllers must be purchased at the same price. Having a full-price device sit empty and idle might seem like a poor use of funds.

Second, the backup controller must be configured identically to every other active controller it has to support. The idea is to make a controller failure as seamless as possible so the APs should not have any noticeable configuration differences when they move from one controller to another.

The N+N redundancy strategy tries to make better use of the available controllers. N+N gets its name from grouping controllers in pairs. If you have one active controller, you would pair it with one other controller; two controllers would be paired with two others, and so on. You might also see the same strategy called N:N or 1+1.

11

By grouping controllers in pairs, you can divide the active role across two separate devices. This makes better use of the AP capacity on each controller. As well, the APs, including their client loads, will be distributed across separate hardware, while still supporting redundancy during a failure. N+N redundancy can support failures of more than one controller, but only if the active controllers are configured in pairs.

Figure 11-6 illustrates the N+N scenario consisting of two controllers, WLC-A and WLC-B. The APs are divided into two groups—one that joins WLC-A as primary controller and another that joins WLC-B as primary. Notice that the primary and secondary controllers are reversed between the two groups of APs. To support the full set of APs during a failure, each controller must not be loaded with more than 50 percent of its AP capacity.

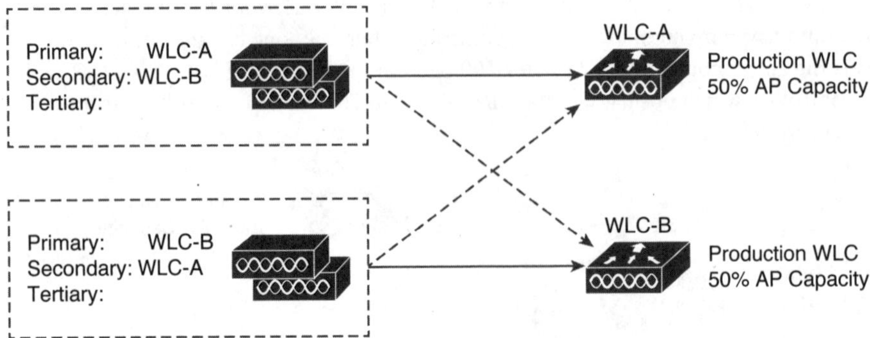

Figure 11-6 *Configuring N+N Controller Redundancy*

Rather than having an extra controller sitting idle waiting for another controller to die, N+N puts all of the controllers to use. However, it also requires more controllers and licenses than you actually need. N+N is an extremely reliable but extremely expensive solution.

N+N+1 Redundancy

What if a scenario calls for more resiliency than the N+N plan can provide? You can simply add one more controller to the mix, as a backup unit. As you might expect, this is commonly called N+N+1 redundancy and combines the advantages of the N+N and N+1 strategies.

Two or more active controllers are configured to share the AP and client load, while reserving some AP capacity for use during a failure. One additional backup controller is set aside as an additional safety net. Figure 11-7 shows a simple example using three controllers—two active (WLC-A and WLC-B) and one backup (WLC-Z). Like N+N redundancy, the two groups of APs are configured with primary and secondary controllers that are the reverse of each other. Each group of APs is also configured with a tertiary controller that points to the backup unit.

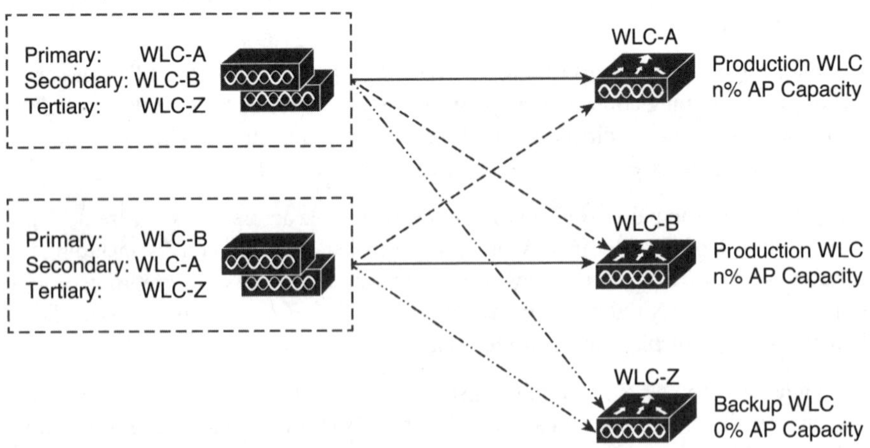

Figure 11-7 *Configuring N+N+1 Controller Redundancy*

If one active controller fails, APs that were joined to it will move to the secondary controller. As long as the two active controllers are not loaded with over 50 percent of their AP capacity, either one may accept the full number of APs. N+N+1 goes one step further; if the other active controller happens to fail, the backup controller is available to carry the load. This means that the active controllers can be loaded to more than 50 percent each because the backup controller will be available to share the load when an active controller fails.

SSO Redundancy

The N+1, N+N, and N+N+1 strategies all address redundancy and fault tolerance, but each still relies on the basic controller discovery and join processes. In other words, APs require a certain amount of time to seek out a new controller when they detect that one has failed.

With Controller Software Release 7.5 or later, Cisco offers AP and client stateful switchover (SSO) redundancy, in addition to the other methods. SSO groups controllers into HA pairs, where one controller takes on the active role while the other is in a hot standby mode. Only the active unit must be purchased with the appropriate license to support the AP count; the standby unit is purchased with an HA license. The standby unit can be paired with an active unit of any license size, as its AP licenses are not really used until it takes on the active role.

Figure 11-8 depicts SSO redundancy. The APs can be configured with only a primary controller name that references the active unit. Because each active controller has its own standby controller, there really is no need to configure a secondary or tertiary controller on the APs unless you need an additional layer of redundancy.

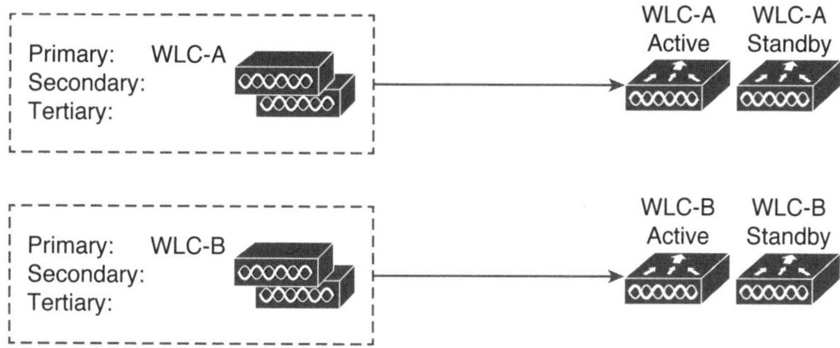

Figure 11-8 *Configuring AP SSO Redundancy*

11

Each AP learns of the HA pair during a CAPWAP discovery phase, then builds a CAPWAP tunnel to the active controller. The active unit keeps CAPWAP tunnels, AP states, client states, configurations, and image files all in sync with the hot standby unit. If the active unit fails, the hot standby unit quickly takes over the active role. The APs do not have to discover another controller to join; the controllers simply swap roles so the APs can stay joined to the active controller in the HA pair.

The APs do not even have to rebuild their CAPWAP tunnels after a failure. The tunnels are synchronized between active and standby, so they are always maintained. The SSO switchover occurs at the controllers—not at the APs.

The active controller also synchronizes the state of each associated client that is in the RUN state with the hot standby controller. If the active fails, the standby will already have the current state information for each client, making the failover process transparent.

Tip The active and standby controllers must always run an identical software image. When one controller is upgraded, its standby peer is also upgraded. That also means when the active unit is rebooted, the standby unit follows suit. At the time of this writing, "hitless" in-service software upgrades are not possible.

The hot standby controller monitors the active unit through keepalives that are sent every 100 ms. If a keepalive is not answered, the standby unit begins to send ICMP echo requests to the active unit to determine what sort of failure has occurred. For example, the active unit could have crashed, lost power, or had its network connectivity severed.

Once the standby unit has declared the active unit as failed, it assumes the active role. The failover may take up to 500 ms, in the case of a crash or power failure, or up to 4 seconds if a network failure has occurred.

SSO is designed to keep the failover process transparent from the AP's perspective, as well as the client's. In fact, the APs know only of the active unit; they are not even aware that the hot standby unit exists. The two controllers share a "mobility" MAC address that initially comes from the first active unit's MAC address. From then on, that address is maintained by whichever unit has the active role at any given time. The controllers also share a common virtual management IP address. Keeping both MAC and IP addresses virtual and consistent allows the APs to stay in contact with the active controller—regardless of which controller currently has that role.

Exam Preparation Tasks

As mentioned in the section, "How to Use This Book," in the Introduction, you have a couple of choices for exam preparation: the exercises here, Chapter 21, "Final Review," and the exam simulation questions on the DVD.

Review All Key Topics

Review the most important topics in this chapter, noted with the Key Topic icon in the outer margin of the page. Table 11-2 lists a reference of these key topics and the page numbers on which each is found.

Table 11-2 Key Topics for Chapter 11

Key Topic Element	Description	Page Number
List	AP states	268
List	Controller discovery methods	270
List	Controller selection process	271
Paragraph	Controller redundancy methods	274

Define Key Terms

Define the following key terms from this chapter and check your answers in the glossary:

CAPWAP Discovery Request, CAPWAP Join Request, N+1 redundancy, N+N redundancy, N+N+1 redundancy, primed controller address, stateful switchover (SSO)

This chapter covers the following topics:

- **Roaming Overview**—This section reviews the fundamentals of wireless client mobility between autonomous access points and between APs that are joined to a common controller.
- **Roaming Between Centralized Controllers**—This section covers wireless client mobility between APs that are bound to different centralized controllers. It also explains how client mobility can be scaled as a network grows.
- **Roaming Between Converged Controllers**—This section explains wireless client mobility when APs are bound to different converged controllers in the access layer. Cisco also calls this New Mobility.

This chapter covers the following exam topics:

- 5.4—Describe roaming
  - 5.4a—Layer 2 and Layer 3
  - 5.4b—Intracontroller and intercontroller
  - 5.4c—Centralized mobility
  - 5.4d—Converged mobility

CHAPTER 12

Understanding Roaming

Wireless client devices are inherently mobile, so you should expect them to move around. This chapter discusses client mobility from the AP and controller perspectives. You should have a good understanding of client roaming so that you can design and configure your wireless network properly as it grows over time.

"Do I Know This Already?" Quiz

The "Do I Know This Already?" quiz allows you to assess whether you should read this entire chapter thoroughly or jump to the "Exam Preparation Tasks" section. If you are in doubt about your answers to these questions or your own assessment of your knowledge of the topics, read the entire chapter. Table 12-1 lists the major headings in this chapter and their corresponding "Do I Know This Already?" quiz questions. You can find the answers in Appendix A, "Answers to the 'Do I Know This Already?' Quizzes."

Table 12-1 "Do I Know This Already?" Section-to-Question Mapping

Foundation Topics Section	Questions
Roaming Overview	1–2
Roaming Between Centralized Controllers	3–11
Roaming Between Converged Controllers	12–15

Caution The goal of self-assessment is to gauge your mastery of the topics in this chapter. If you do not know the answer to a question or are only partially sure of the answer, you should mark that question as wrong for purposes of the self-assessment. Giving yourself credit for an answer you correctly guess skews your self-assessment results and might provide you with a false sense of security.

1. When a client moves its association from one autonomous AP to another, it is actually leaving and joining which one of the following?
   a. SSID
   b. BSS
   c. ESS
   d. DS
2. Which one of the following makes the decision for a device to roam from one AP to another?
   a. The client device
   b. The original AP
   c. The candidate AP
   d. The wireless LAN controller
3. Ten lightweight APs are joined to a wireless LAN controller. If a client roams from one of the APs to another, which one of the following correctly describes the roam?
   a. Autonomous roaming
   b. Intercontroller roaming
   c. Intracontroller roaming
   d. Indirect roaming
4. Which one of the following provides the most efficient means for roaming, as measured by the time to complete the roam?
   a. Layer 2 intercontroller roaming
   b. Layer 3 intercontroller roaming
   c. Intracontroller roaming
   d. All of these answers because each takes an equal amount of time
5. Which one of the following is used to cache authentication key information to make roaming more efficient?
   a. PGP
   b. CCNA
   c. CCKM
   d. EoIP
6. The term *Layer 3 roaming* refers to which one of the following types of client roam in a Cisco unified wireless network?
   a. Autonomous AP roaming
   b. Intracontroller roaming
   c. Intercontroller roaming
   d. RRM roaming

7. In a Layer 2 roam, what mechanism is used to tunnel client data between the two controllers?
    a. GRE tunnel
    b. EoIP tunnel
    c. CAPWAP tunnel
    d. None of these answers
8. When a client roams from one controller to another, it must obtain a new IP address from a DHCP server. True or false?
    a. True
    b. False
9. A client roams from controller A to controller B. If it undergoes a Layer 3 roam, which one of the following best describes the role of controller A?
    a. Foreign controller
    b. Host controller
    c. Master controller
    d. Anchor controller
10. A network consists of four controllers: A, B, C, and D. Mobility group 1 consists of controllers A and B, while mobility group 2 consists of controllers C and D. Which one of the following answers describes what will happen when a client tries to roam between controllers B and C?
    a. Roaming is seamless and efficient.
    b. Roaming is not possible.
    c. Roaming is possible, but CCKM and key caching will not work.
    d. Only Layer 3 roaming is possible.
11. Which one of the following controller functions terminates CAPWAP tunnels from lightweight APs?
    a. MO
    b. MA
    c. MC
    d. MD
12. Before mobility can be successfully implemented in a Cisco converged wireless network, a controller designated as a Mobility Anchor must be linked with which one of the following?
    a. MC
    b. MD
    c. MA
    d. MO

13. Which one of the following roles is used to anchor a wireless client and its IP address to a wired network and IP subnet?
    a. PoP
    b. PoA
    c. PoE
    d. PoC
    e. PoD
14. In a Cisco converged wireless network, multiple controllers can be grouped together into which one of the following entities to make localized roaming more efficient?
    a. High availability group
    b. Mobility Domain
    c. Mobility Subdomain
    d. Mobility Peer Group
    e. Switch Peer Group
15. Each converged controller that is in the access layer must function as which one of the following roles?
    a. MO
    b. MA
    c. MC
    d. ME

Foundation Topics

When a wireless client moves about, the expectations are simple—good, seamless coverage wherever the client goes. Clients know how to roam between access points (APs), but they are ignorant about the wireless network infrastructure. Even in a large network, roaming should be easy, quick, and not disrupt the client's service.

Cisco wireless networks offer several roaming strategies. From your perspective as a wireless engineer, roaming configuration is straightforward. The inner workings can be complex, depending on the size of the wireless network as measured by the number of APs and controllers. As you work through the sections in this chapter, you will review roaming fundamentals, then learn more about how the Cisco wireless controllers handle client roaming and how to configure your controllers to support it properly.

Roaming Overview

To understand how wireless roaming works, you should start simple. The following two sections discuss roaming between access points when no controller is present and when only one controller is present. More complex scenarios are covered later in the chapter.

Roaming Between Autonomous APs

In Chapter 6, "Understanding 802.11 Frame Types," you learned that a wireless client can move from one basic service set (BSS) to another by roaming between APs. A client continuously evaluates the quality of its wireless connection. If the signal quality degrades, the client begins looking for an AP with a better signal. The process is usually quick and simple; active scanning reveals candidate APs, and then the client selects one and tries to reassociate with it.

Figure 12-1 shows a simple scenario with two APs and one client. The client begins with an association to AP-1. Because the APs are running in autonomous mode, each one maintains a table of its associated clients. AP-1 has one client; AP-2 has none.

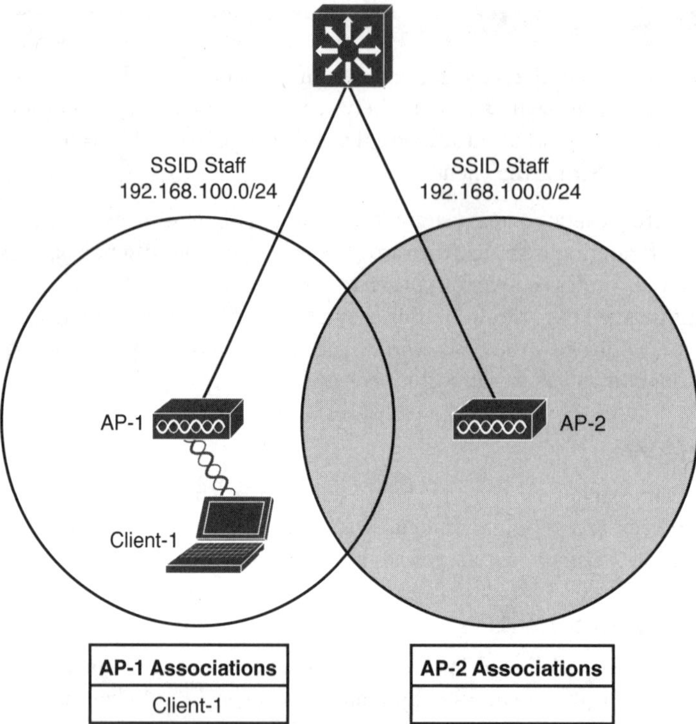

Figure 12-1 *Before Roaming Between Autonomous APs*

Suppose that the client then begins to move into AP-2's cell. Somewhere near the cell boundary, the client decides that the signal from AP-1 has degraded and it should look elsewhere for a stronger signal. The client decides to roam and reassociate with AP-2. Figure 12-2 shows the new scenario after the roam occurs. Notice that both APs have updated their list of associated clients to reflect Client-1's move from AP-1 to AP-2. If AP-1 still has any leftover wireless frames destined for the client after the roam, it forwards them to AP-2 over the wired infrastructure—simply because that is where the client's MAC address now resides.

Naturally, roaming is not limited to only two APs; instead, it occurs between two APs at any given time. To cover a large area, you will probably install many APs in a pattern such that their cells overlap. Figure 12-3 shows a typical pattern. When a wireless client begins to move, it might move along an arbitrary path. Each time the client decides that the signal from one AP has degraded enough, it attempts to roam to a new, better signal from a different AP and cell. The exact location of each roam depends on the client's roaming algorithm. To illustrate typical roaming activity, each roam in Figure 12-3 is marked with a dark ring.

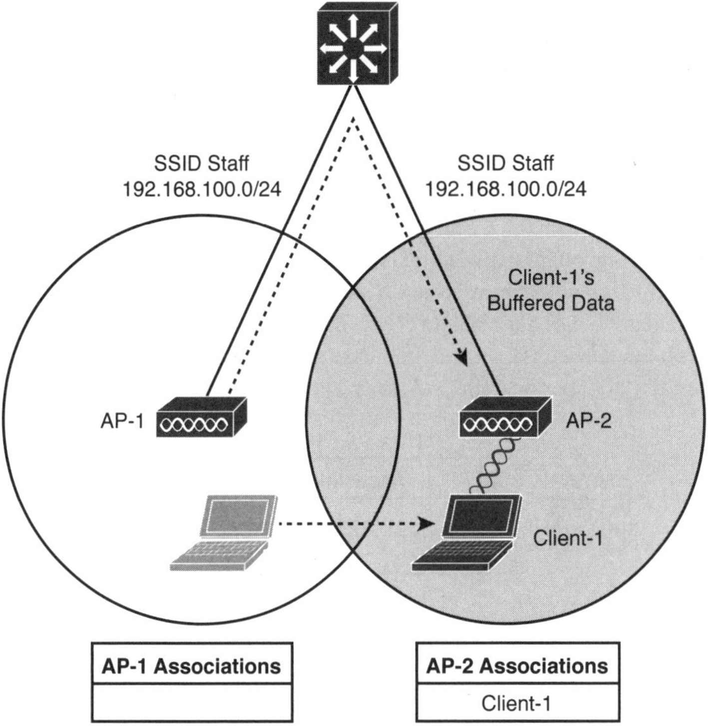

Figure 12-2 *After Roaming Between Autonomous APs*

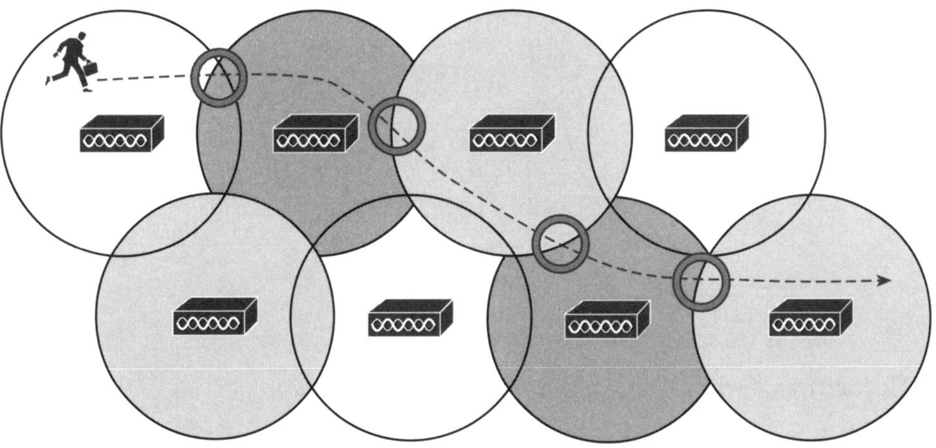

Figure 12-3 *Successive Roams of a Mobile Client*

12

Intracontroller Roaming

In a Cisco wireless network, lightweight APs are bound to a wireless LAN controller through CAPWAP tunnels. The roaming process is similar to that of autonomous APs; clients must still reassociate to new APs as they move about. The only real difference is that the controller handles the roaming process because of the split-MAC architecture.

Figure 12-4 shows a two-AP scenario where both APs connect to a single controller. Client-1 is associated to AP-1, which has a Control and Provisioning of Wireless Access Points (CAPWAP) tunnel to controller WLC-1. The controller maintains a client database that contains detailed information about how to reach and support each client. For simplicity, Figure 12-4 shows the database as a list of the controller's APs, associated clients, and the wireless LAN (WLAN) being used. The actual database also contains client MAC and IP addresses, quality of service (QoS) parameters, and other information.

Key Topic

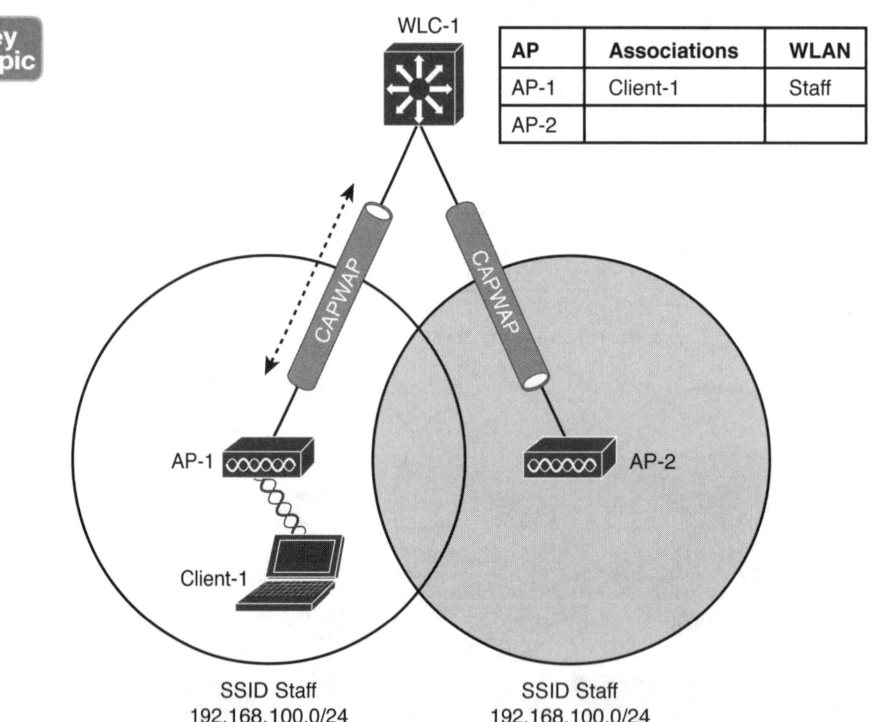

Figure 12-4 *Cisco Wireless Network Before an Intracontroller Roam*

When Client-1 starts moving, it eventually roams to AP-2, as shown in Figure 12-5. Not much has changed except that the controller has updated the client association from AP-1 to AP-2. Because both APs are bound to the same controller, the roam occurs entirely within the controller. This is known as *intra*controller roaming.

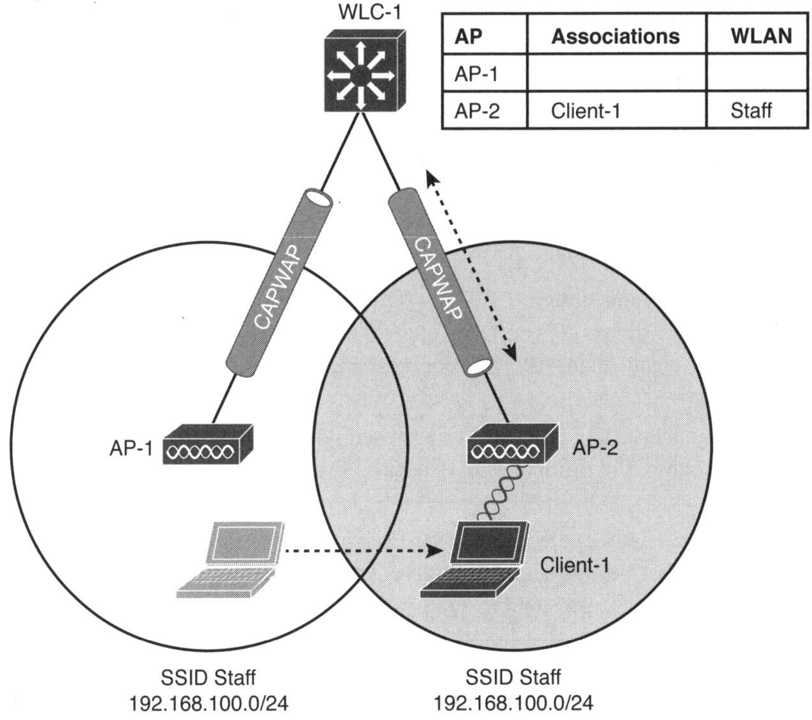

AP	Associations	WLAN
AP-1		
AP-2	Client-1	Staff

Figure 12-5 *Cisco Wireless Network After an Intracontroller Roam*

If both APs involved in a client roam are bound to the same controller, the roaming process is simple and efficient. The controller has to update its client association table so that it knows which CAPWAP tunnel to use to reach the client. Thanks to the simplicity, an intracontroller roam takes less than 10 ms to complete—the amount of processing time needed for the controller to switch the client entry from AP-1 to AP-2. From the client's perspective, an intracontroller roam is no different than any other roam. The client has no knowledge that the two APs are communicating with a controller over CAPWAP tunnels; it simply decides to roam between two APs based on its own signal analysis.

Efficient roaming is especially important when time-critical applications are being used over the wireless network. For example, wireless phones need a consistent connection so that the audio stream is not garbled or interrupted. When a roam occurs, there could be a brief time when the client is not fully associated with either AP. So long as that time is held to a minimum, the end user probably will not even notice that the roam occurred.

Along with the client reassociation, a couple of other processes can occur:

- **DHCP**—The client may be programmed to renew the DHCP lease on its IP address or to request a new address.
- **Client authentication**—The controller might be configured to use an 802.1x method to authenticate each client on a WLAN.

To achieve efficient roaming, both of these processes should be streamlined as much as possible. For instance, if a client roams and tries to renew its IP address, it is essentially cut off from the network until the Dynamic Host Configuration Protocol (DHCP) server responds.

The client authentication process presents the biggest challenge because the dialog between a controller and a RADIUS server, in addition to the cryptographic keys that need to be generated and exchanged between the client and an AP or controller, can take a considerable amount of time to accomplish. Cisco controllers offer three techniques to minimize the time and effort spent on key exchanges during roams:

- **Cisco Centralized Key Management (CCKM)**—One controller maintains a database of clients and keys on behalf of its APs and provides them to other controllers and their APs as needed during client roams. CCKM requires Cisco Compatible Extensions (CCX) support from clients.
- **Key caching**—Each client maintains a list of keys used with prior AP associations and presents them as it roams. The destination AP must be present in this list, which is limited to eight AP-key entries.
- **802.11r**—An 802.11 amendment that addresses fast roaming or fast BSS transition; a client can cache a portion of the authentication server's key and present that to future APs as it roams. The client can also maintain its QoS parameters as it roams.

Each of the fast-roaming strategies requires help on the part of the wireless client. That means the client must have a supplicant or driver software that is compatible with fast roaming and can cache the necessary pieces of the authentication credentials.

Roaming Between Centralized Controllers

As a wireless network grows, one controller might not suffice. When two or more controllers support the APs in an enterprise, the APs can be distributed across them. As always, when clients become mobile, they roam from one AP to another—except they could also be roaming from one controller to another, depending on how neighboring APs are assigned to the controllers. As a network grows, AP roaming can scale too by organizing controllers into mobility groups. The following sections cover intercontroller roaming, mobility groups, and the mechanisms used to coordinate roaming.

Layer 2 Roaming

When a client roams from one AP to another and those APs lie on two different controllers, the client makes an intercontroller roam. Figure 12-6 shows a simple scenario prior to a roam. Controller WLC-1 has one association in its database—that of Client-1 on AP-1. Figure 12-7 shows the result of the client roaming to AP-2.

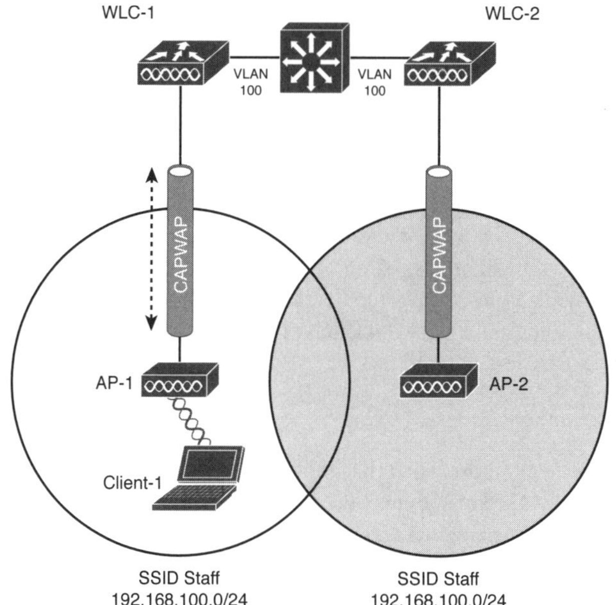

Figure 12-6 *Before an Intercontroller Roam*

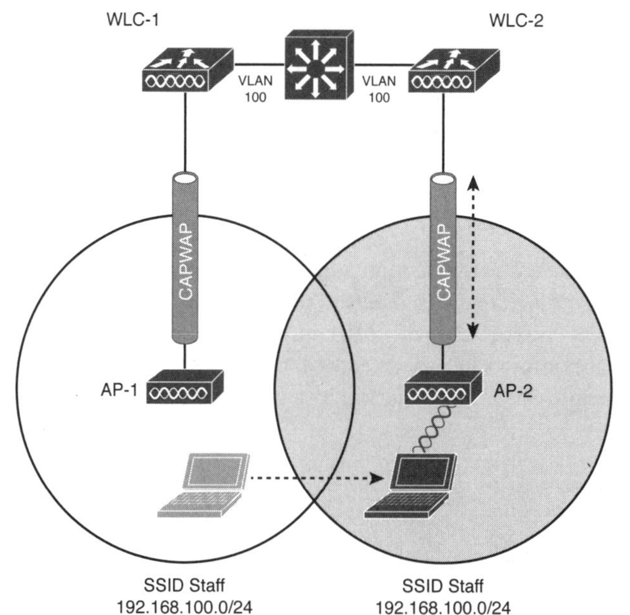

Figure 12-7 *After an Intercontroller Roam*

12

The roam itself is fairly straightforward. When the client decides to roam and reassociate itself with AP-2, it actually moves from one controller to another and the two controllers must coordinate the move. One subtle detail involves the client's IP address. Before the roam, Client-1 is associated with AP-1 and takes an IP address from the VLAN and subnet that are configured on the WLAN supplied by controller WLC-1. In Figure 12-6, WLAN Staff is bound to VLAN 100, so the client uses an address from the 192.168.100.0/24 subnet.

When the client roams to a different AP, it can try to continue using its existing IP address or work with a DHCP server to either renew or request an address. Figure 12-7 shows the client roaming to AP-2, where WLAN Staff is also bound to the same VLAN 100 and 192.168.100.0/24 subnet. Because the client has roamed between APs but stayed on the same VLAN and subnet, it has made a Layer 2 intercontroller roam. Layer 2 roams (commonly called local-to-local roams) are nice for two reasons: The client can keep its same IP address, and the roam is fast (usually less than 20 ms).

Layer 3 Roaming

What if a wireless network grows even more, such that the WLAN interfaces on each controller are assigned to different VLANs and subnets? Breaking a very large WLAN up into individual subnets seems like a good idea from a scalability viewpoint. However, when a wireless client roams from one controller to another, it could easily end up on a different subnet than it started with.

Clients will not usually be able to detect that they have changed subnets. They will be aware of the AP roam but little else. Only clients that aggressively contact a DHCP server after each and every roam will continue to work properly. But to make roaming seamless and efficient, time-consuming processes such as DHCP should be avoided.

No worries—the Cisco wireless network has a clever trick up its sleeve. When a client initiates an intercontroller roam, the two controllers involved can compare the VLAN numbers that are assigned to their respective WLAN interfaces. If the VLAN IDs are the same, nothing special needs to happen; the client undergoes a Layer 2 intercontroller roam and can continue to use its original IP address on the new controller. If the two VLAN IDs differ, the controllers arrange a *Layer 3 roam* (also known as a local-to-foreign roam) that will allow the client to keep using its IP address.

Figure 12-8 illustrates a simple wireless network containing two APs and two controllers. Notice that the two APs offer different IP subnets in their BSSs: 192.168.100.0/24 and 192.168.200.0/24. The client is associated with AP-1 and is using IP address 192.168.100.199. On the surface, it looks like the client will roam into subnet 192.168.200.0/24 if it wanders into AP-2's cell, and will lose connectivity if it tries to keep using its same IP address.

AP	Associations	WLAN	VLAN
AP-1	Client-1	Staff	100

AP	Associations	WLAN	VLAN
AP-2			

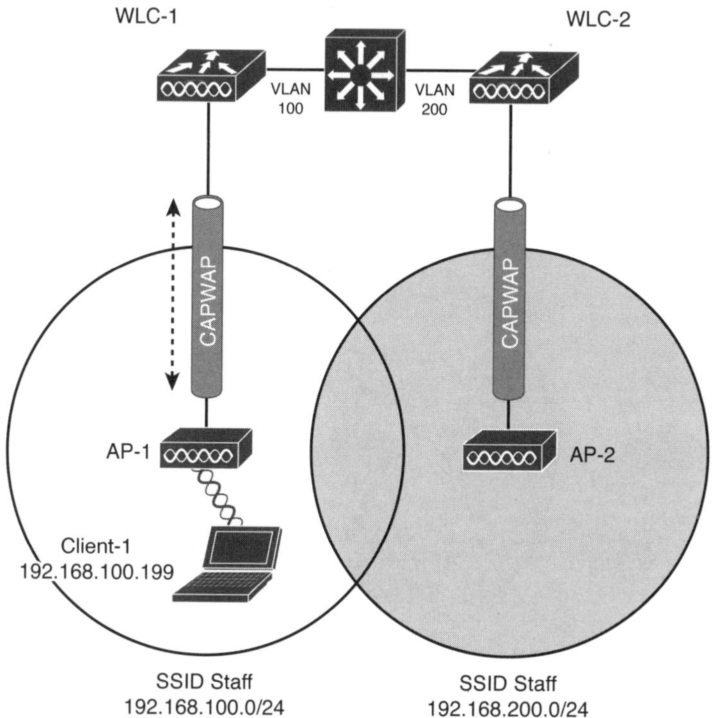

Figure 12-8 *Before a Layer 3 Intercontroller Roam*

A Layer 3 intercontroller roam consists of an extra tunnel that is built between the client's original controller and the controller it has roamed to. The tunnel carries data to and from the client as if it is still associated with the original controller and IP subnet. Figure 12-9 shows the results of a Layer 3 roam. The original controller (WLC-1) is called the *anchor controller*, and the controller with the roamed client is called the *foreign controller*. Think of the client being anchored to the original controller no matter where it roams later. When the client roams away from its anchor, it moves into foreign territory.

AP	Associations	WLAN	VLAN
WLC-2	Client-1 (Mobile)	Staff	100

AP	Associations	WLAN	VLAN
AP-2	Client-1	Staff	

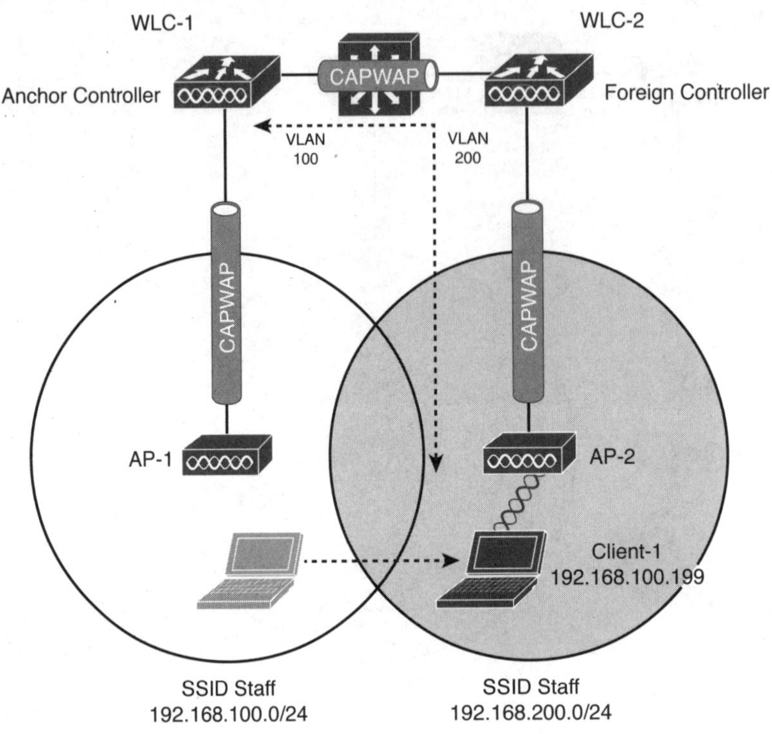

Figure 12-9 *After a Layer 3 Intercontroller Roam*

You can see clients that have undergone a Layer 3 roam by selecting **Monitor > Clients** from the controller graphical user interface (GUI). The client from Figures 12-8 and 12-9 is shown in the WLC-1 client list displayed in Figure 12-10. Notice that the client's protocol is shown as 802.11(Mobile); other clients would be listed as 802.11 only.

Save Configuration

MONITOR WLANs CONTROLLER WIRELESS SECURITY MANAGEMENT COMMANDS HELP FEEDBACK

Clients

Current Filter *None* [Change Filter] [Clear Filter]

Client MAC Addr	AP Name	WLAN Profile	WLAN SSID	Protocol
00:09:ef:06:87:bd	172.22.253.20	Staff	Staff	802.11(Mobile)

Figure 12-10 *Displaying Clients with a Layer 3 Intercontroller Roam*

You can click the client's MAC address to see more details about its state. In Figure 12-11, you can see that the controller has mobility role Anchor and that the Layer 3 mobility peer is 172.22.253.20, or WLC-2.

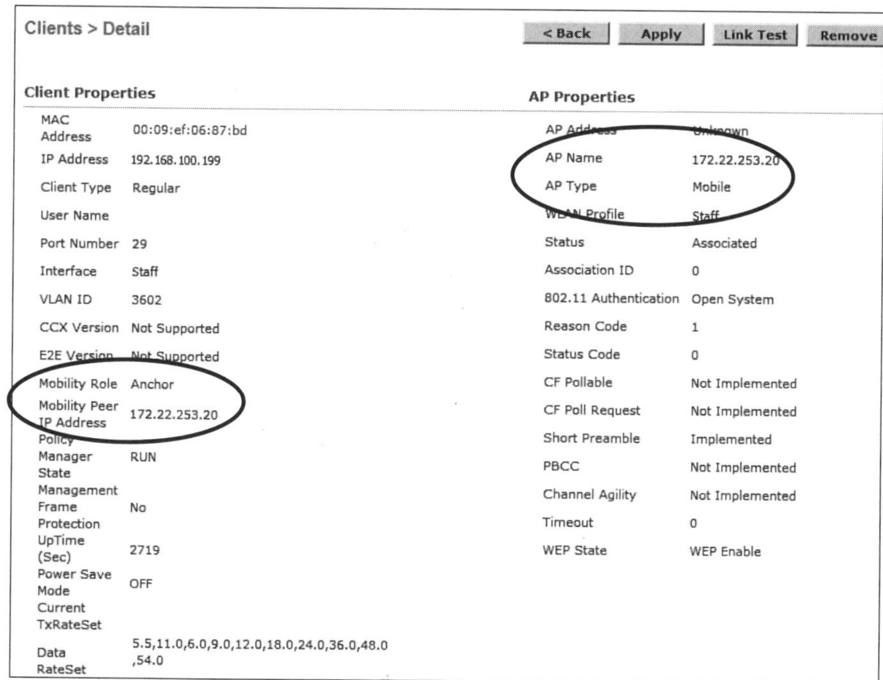

Figure 12-11 *Displaying Client Details on the Anchor Controller*

Due to the Layer 3 roam, the client should have an active association with both the anchor and foreign controllers. On the foreign controller, you can view the client details from a different perspective. In Figure 12-12, the client is shown associated with a foreign controller with IP address 172.22.253.9, or WLC-1. On the foreign controller, the client is associated to an actual AP (AP-2) with a normal AP type.

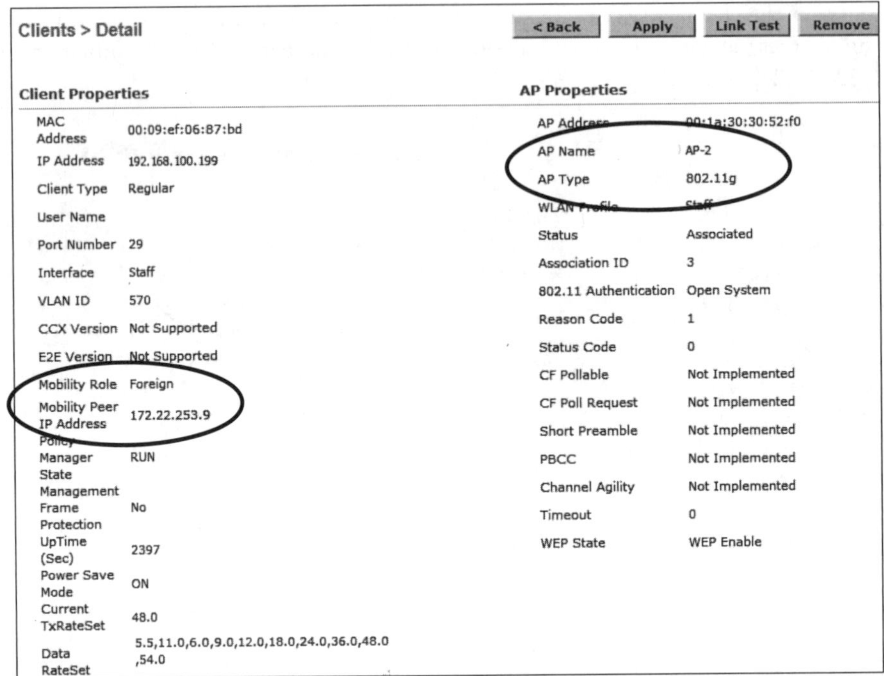

Figure 12-12 *Displaying Client Details on the Foreign Controller*

Recall that Cisco controllers use CAPWAP tunnels to connect with lightweight APs. CAPWAP tunnels are also built between controllers for Layer 3 roaming. The tunnel tethers the client to its original anchor controller (and original IP subnet), regardless of its location or how many controllers it roams through.

Anchor and foreign controllers are normally determined automatically. When a client first associates with an AP and controller, that controller becomes its anchor controller. When the client roams to a different controller, that controller can take on the foreign role. Sometimes you might not want a client's first controller to be its anchor. For example, guest users should not be allowed to associate with just any controller in your network. Instead, you might want guests to be forced onto a specific controller that is situated behind a firewall or contained in a protected environment. You can configure one controller to be a static anchor for a WLAN so that other controllers will direct clients toward it through Layer 3 roaming tunnels. Static anchor controllers are covered in more detail in Chapter 16, "Implementing a Wireless Guest Network."

Scaling Mobility with Mobility Groups

Cisco controllers can be organized into mobility groups to facilitate intercontroller roaming. Mobility groups become important as a wireless network scales and there are more centralized controllers cooperating to provide coverage over a large area.

If two centralized controllers are configured to belong to the same mobility group, clients can roam quickly between them. Layer 2 and Layer 3 roaming are both supported, along with CCKM, key caching, and 802.11r credential caching. If two controllers are assigned to different mobility groups, clients can still roam between them, but the roam is not very efficient. Credentials are not cached and shared, so clients must go through a full authentication during the roam.

Mobility groups have an implied hierarchy as shown in Figure 12-13. Each controller maintains a mobility list that contains its own MAC address and the MAC addresses of other controllers. Each controller in the list is also assigned a mobility group name. In effect, the mobility list gives a controller its view of the outside world; it knows of and trusts only the other controllers configured in the list. If two controllers are not listed in each other's mobility list, they are unknown to each other and clients will not be able to roam between them. Clients will have to associate and authenticate from scratch.

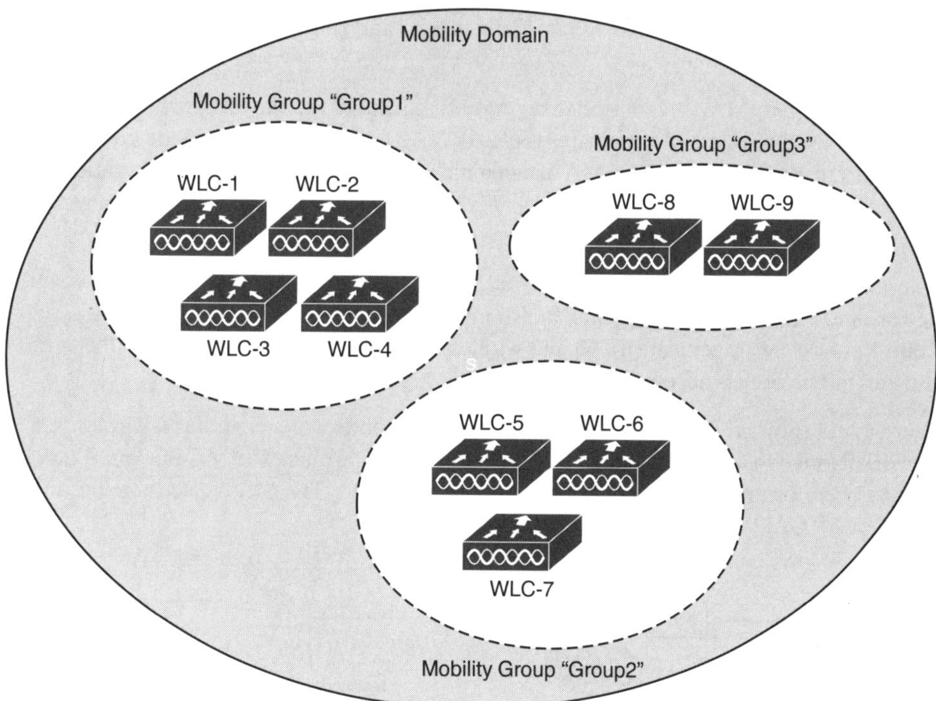

Figure 12-13 *Mobility Group Hierarchy*

You can think of this list as a Mobility Domain. In a centralized controller environment, the list can contain up to 72 controllers, with up to 24 controllers in each mobility group.

To configure a mobility group, use the following steps:

Step 1. Visit each member controller and enter a mobility group name under **Controller > General > Default Mobility Domain Name**.

Step 2. Select **Controller > Mobility Management > Mobility Groups**. Click the **New** button to add one controller MAC address at a time to the group. Otherwise, you can select the **EditAll** button to populate the controller's mobility list with the MAC and IP addresses of other controllers and their mobility group names. The local controller should be the first entry in the list. Click the **Apply** button to make the list entries active.

Step 3. Once you have entered each of the controllers in the mobility group list on each controller, verify that the controllers have joined the group and can communicate with each other. Look on the **Controller > Mobility Management > Mobility Groups** page and make sure each controller is listed with "up" in the **Status** column.

Roaming Coordination with Centralized Controllers

As a mobile client roams between APs, controllers must keep track of its movements, updating tables and building CAPWAP tunnels between controllers if necessary. All of this activity must be coordinated among the controllers that are configured to be part of a mobility group. To do this, controllers have some distinct roles and functions that play important parts in the roaming process.

A *Mobility Agent* (MA) is a controller function that handles mobility tasks facing the clients. For example, an MA terminates the CAPWAP tunnels that connect the controller to the APs that have joined it. An MA also maintains a database of all client associations. Because the MA function faces the clients, it is in a convenient location to handle any security, QoS, and other policies that affect client activity.

In contrast, a *Mobility Controller* (MC) is a function further upstream that manages roaming for one or more Mobility Agents. It also performs higher-level tasks, such as Cisco Radio Resource Management (RRM) and wireless intrusion protection system (wIPS), and manages guest wireless access.

Figure 12-14 shows the MA and MC functions in the context of a centralized wireless network. Notice that both functions are located in the controller. The MC is located there because every centralized controller must operate as an MC. The MA is also there because the client AP CAPWAP tunnels terminate there.

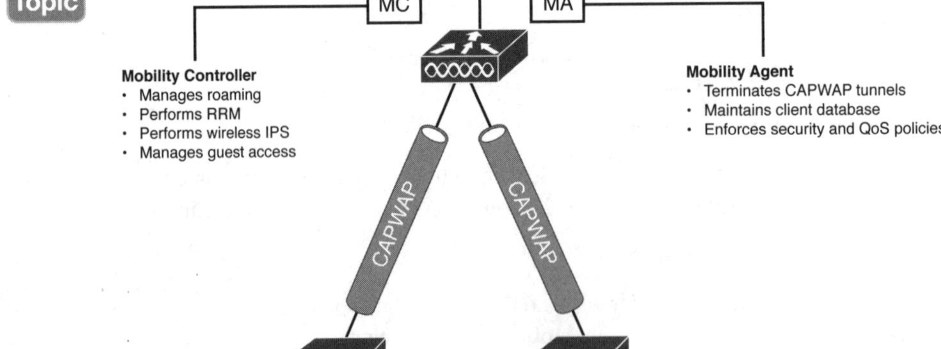

Figure 12-14 *MC and MA Locations in a Centralized Wireless Network*

The MC and MA perform their functions from a controller's perspective. There are also two roaming coordination roles that exist from the client's perspective:

- **Point of Presence (PoP)**—The WLC that anchors a client's IP address, where the client meets the wired network. This is the point where the wireless client's MAC address is seen from the perspective of the wired network. The PoP is also the point at which security policies that affect the client are applied.
- **Point of Attachment (PoA)**—The WLC that terminates the CAPWAP tunnel to the AP where a client is currently located. The PoA is also the point at which QoS and roaming policies can be applied, closest to the client.

Figure 12-15 shows where the PoP and PoA roles are located in a centralized wireless network with a single controller. Regardless of which AP the client is associated with, both PoP and PoA roles are located at the controller.

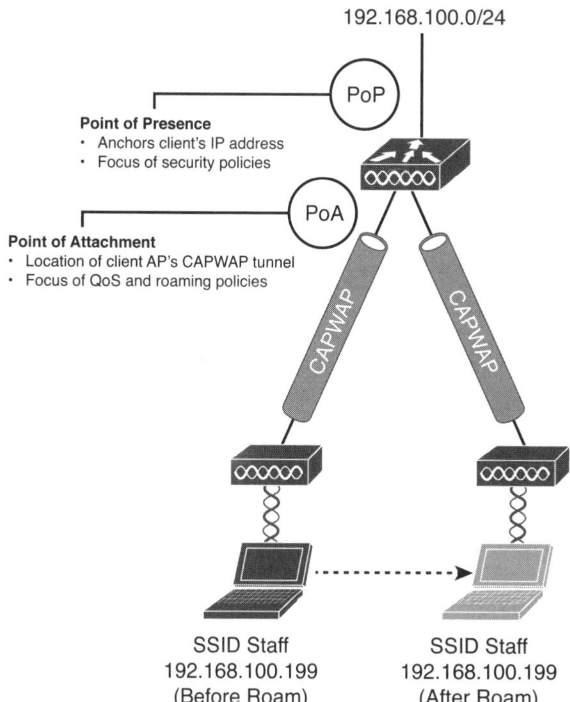

Figure 12-15 *PoP and PoA Locations in a Centralized Wireless Network*

So far, the MC, MA, PoP, and PoA have all been shown to exist on the same controller. What is the point of having all of these distinct functions if they all sit in the same place? The four functions have a somewhat limited use in a centralized wireless network because every controller must act as an MC and an MA. As you will see in the next section, the MC and MA become more distributed in a converged wireless network.

The PoP and PoA are actually dynamic roles that can move around as a client becomes mobile. This becomes more evident with multiple controllers, as shown in Figure 12-16.

Each client has its own PoP and PoA; the PoP always stays with the initial controller that a client joins. You might have realized that the PoP sounds oddly similar to an anchor controller. As a client roams to other APs (and controllers), the PoA follows it.

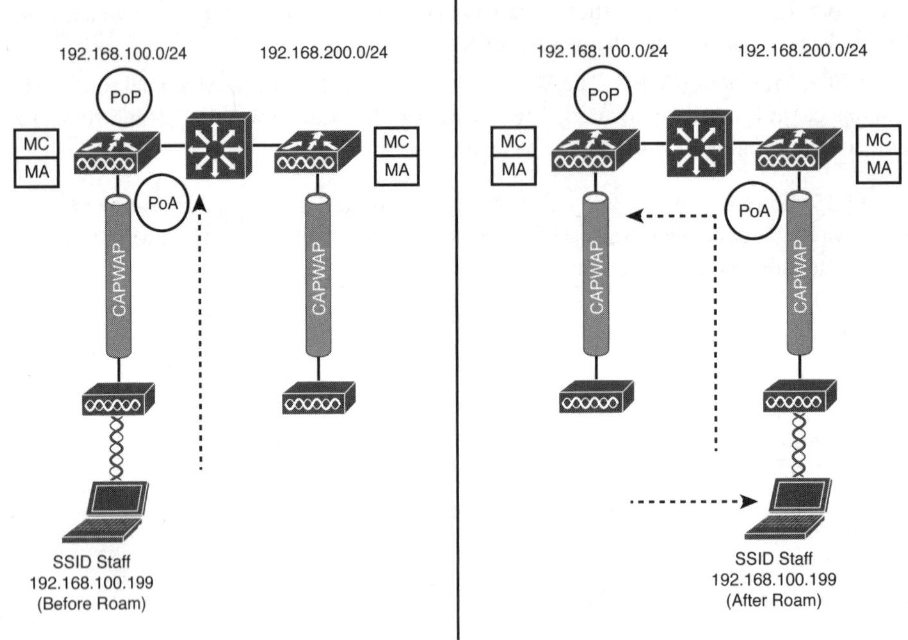

Figure 12-16 *Roaming Functions Before (left) and After (right) a Roam*

Roaming Between Converged Controllers

Now that you are more familiar with the MC and MA functions, you will see how roaming is coordinated in a converged wireless network. Recall from Chapter 8, "Understanding Cisco Wireless Architectures," that a converged network is built by pushing the WLC down into the access layer switches in the form of a Wireless Controller Module (WCM). As a result, the number of APs per WCM is greatly reduced while the number of WCMs may greatly increase. To handle this shift, the converged controllers must be organized into a more scalable hierarchy.

Figure 12-17 illustrates the complete mobility hierarchy, with examples of several common types of controller groupings. There are several distinct layers or group types, which are described in Table 12-2. To get your bearings, first focus on the grouping at the left side of the figure. Notice that there are three controllers labeled "MA." Each of these is a converged controller (WCM) with CAPWAP tunnels connecting to lightweight APs. The MA controllers are all logically connected to an MC, and the MA and MC roles are contained in a single mobility group. That should look familiar from the traditional or centralized roaming structure.

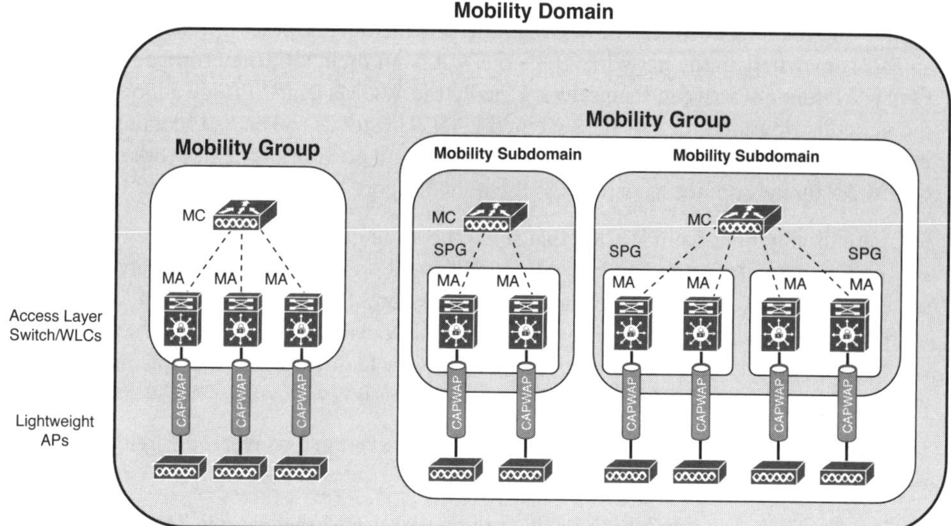

Figure 12-17 *Mobility Hierarchy in a Converged Wireless Network*

Tip Although the MC and MA functions are shown as separate WCMs in Figure 12-17, a WCM can act as both an MA and an MC.

Table 12-2 Converged Controller Roaming Hierarchy

Grouping	Description
Mobility group	A logical grouping of one or more MCs between which efficient roaming is expected
Switch Peer Group (SPG)	A logical grouping of MAs between which frequent and efficient roaming is expected
Mobility subdomain	A logical grouping of one MC along with the MAs relying on the MC for roaming efficiency
Mobility domain	A logical grouping of all member groups within an enterprise

The key to the converged roaming hierarchy is that each WCM functions as an MA and must be joined to an MC. Sometimes the MC function is performed by a separate controller higher up in the network topology. In that case, the MC must be a traditional centralized controller that is configured for converged or "new" mobility. More commonly, the MC is a function that is enabled on one of the MAs. Each set of MAs and their MC form a mobility group.

12

Converged controllers (WCMs) can be configured as a logical Switch Peer Group (SPG), simplifying roaming between the WCMs. The MA members of the SPG must be joined to an MC somewhere in the network. Once the MAs join their MC, they form a full mesh of CAPWAP tunnels between themselves. Usually the WCMs in an SPG are all located within the same distribution block of the switched LAN. This tends to keep all roaming activity that occurs across neighboring APs within the same portion of the network so that the CAPWAP tunnels do not have to cross the network core layer.

SPGs are usually built from WCMs that serve the same geographic area where wireless clients are expected to roam. For example, an SPG might contain WCMs that serve APs in the same building, APs on adjacent floors in a building, or APs in the same general area. One or more SPGs and their MC then form a Mobility Subdomain. Further, multiple subdomains can be grouped into a single mobility group. In a very large network, multiple mobility groups or subdomains can be grouped into a single mobility domain.

Even though there can be an extensive hierarchy involved in a converged wireless network, roaming still occurs according to the same basic rules:

- The client's PoP and PoA both begin at the initial WCM that is used. The PoP anchors the client's IP address there.
- When a client roams, the PoA moves to the WCM where the client is now associated.

The most efficient roam is one that stays within the same WCM. A roam between WCMs in the same SPG is also efficient because the MAs automatically form a full mesh of CAPWAP tunnels to carry roaming traffic.

Roaming between WCMs that are members of different SPGs is not quite as efficient because client traffic must be tunneled through the MC that joins the two SPGs. It is also possible for a client to roam between two mobility subdomains or between two mobility groups. In those cases, the roaming gets less and less efficient, requiring intervention from MCs further and further up the hierarchy.

Exam Preparation Tasks

As mentioned in the section, "How to Use This Book," in the Introduction, you have a couple of choices for exam preparation: the exercises here, Chapter 21, "Final Review," and the exam simulation questions on the DVD.

Review All Key Topics

Review the most important topics in this chapter, noted with the Key Topic icon in the outer margin of the page. Table 12-3 lists a reference of these key topics and the page numbers on which each is found.

Table 12-3 Key Topics for Chapter 12

Key Topic Element	Description	Page Number
Figures 12-4 and 12-5	Intracontroller roaming	288, 289
Figures 12-8 and 12-9	Intercontroller roaming	293, 294
Figure 12-13	Mobility group hierarchy	297
Figure 12-14	Mobility roles	298
Figure 12-15	Client mobility functions	299
Figure 12-17	Mobility hierarchy in a converged wireless network	301

Define Key Terms

Define the following key terms from this chapter and check your answers in the glossary:

anchor controller, foreign controller, intercontroller roaming, intracontroller roaming, Layer 2 roam, Layer 3 roam, Mobility Agent (MA), Mobility Controller (MC), mobility domain, mobility group, mobility subdomain, Point of Attachment (PoA), Point of Presence (PoP), Switch Peer Group (SPG)

This chapter covers the following topics:

- **Configuring 802.11 Support**—This section explains how to configure the data rates in the 2.4- and 5-GHz bands and support for 802.11n high throughput (HT) and 802.11ac very high throughput (VHT) functionality.
- **Understanding RRM**—This section describes the algorithms that can monitor and adjust radio frequency parameters automatically in a wireless network.

This chapter covers the following exam topics:

- 2.2—Describe usable channel and power combination
  - 2.2c—Describe RRM fundamentals

CHAPTER 13

Understanding RRM

In Chapter 7, "Planning Coverage with Wireless APs," you learned how to size access point (AP) cells appropriately by disabling data rates and changing the transmit power levels. You also learned how important a proper channel layout is to promote efficient roaming and minimize co-channel interference. You probably also realized how difficult these tasks are when you have to tune the radio frequency (RF) parameters manually across a large number of APs.

In this chapter, you learn about Cisco Radio Resource Management (RRM), a flexible and automatic mechanism that Cisco Wireless LAN controllers can use to make your life much easier.

"Do I Know This Already?" Quiz

The "Do I Know This Already?" quiz allows you to assess whether you should read this entire chapter thoroughly or jump to the "Exam Preparation Tasks" section. If you are in doubt about your answers to these questions or your own assessment of your knowledge of the topics, read the entire chapter. Table 13-1 lists the major headings in this chapter and their corresponding "Do I Know This Already?" quiz questions. You can find the answers in Appendix A, "Answers to the 'Do I Know This Already?' Quizzes."

Table 13-1 "Do I Know This Already?" Section-to-Question Mapping

Foundation Topics Section	Questions
Configuring 802.11 Support	1–4
Understanding RRM	5–10

Caution The goal of self-assessment is to gauge your mastery of the topics in this chapter. If you do not know the answer to a question or are only partially sure of the answer, you should mark that question as wrong for purposes of the self-assessment. Giving yourself credit for an answer you correctly guess skews your self-assessment results and might provide you with a false sense of security.

1. Which one of the following correctly describes a mandatory data rate?
   a. A data rate that must be used by wireless clients all the time
   b. The highest data rate used by an AP and its clients
   c. A data rate that must be supported by a client before it can associate with an AP
   d. A data rate required by the IEEE 802.11 standards body
2. You can configure only one data rate as mandatory on an AP. True or false?
   a. True
   b. False
3. An AP sends 802.11 broadcast management frames at which one of the following data rates?
   a. The highest mandatory data rate
   b. The lowest mandatory data rate
   c. The lowest supported data rate
   d. All supported data rates
4. Which one of the following is the default state of 802.11n and 802.11ac support and the default channel width on a Cisco wireless LAN controller?
   a. Disabled; 20-MHz channels
   b. Enabled; 20-MHz channels
   c. Enabled; 40-MHz channels
   d. Disabled; 40-MHz channels
   e. Enabled; 80-MHz channels
5. Which one of the following correctly identifies the scope of the RRM algorithms?
   a. All APs joined to one controller
   b. All APs joined to all controllers
   c. All APs joined to controllers in an RF group
   d. All APs of a specific model
6. An RF group is automatically formed by which one of the following?
   a. All APs that share the same channel
   b. All clients that share the same SSID
   c. Any controllers that can overhear neighbor messages with identical RF group names sent between their APs
   d. All controllers that can overhear neighbor messages with identical mobility group names sent between their APs

7. The TPC algorithm is used for which one of the following purposes?
   a. To adjust the transmission control protocol rate
   b. To detect problems in transmission perimeter coverage
   c. To adjust the transmitting primary channel
   d. To adjust the transmit power level
8. If the DCA algorithm detects that an AP is experiencing interference or excessive noise, what might it do to mitigate the problem?
   a. Increase the AP's transmit power level
   b. Decrease the AP's transmit power level
   c. Change the AP's channel number
   d. Direct the client to a different band
9. Which one of the following runs the DCA algorithm?
   a. RF group leader
   b. Master controller
   c. Each controller
   d. NCS or Cisco Prime Infrastructure
10. The 5-GHz radio in one of several APs in a building has failed. Which one of the following algorithms should be able to detect the failure?
    a. CCA
    b. DCA
    c. Dead radio detection
    d. Coverage hole detection

Foundation Topics

Configuring 802.11 Support

Cisco controllers and most APs can support wireless LANs in both the 2.4- and 5-GHz bands. By default, both bands are enabled; however, you can view or change a number of parameters by browsing to the Wireless tab in the controller, shown in Figure 13-1.

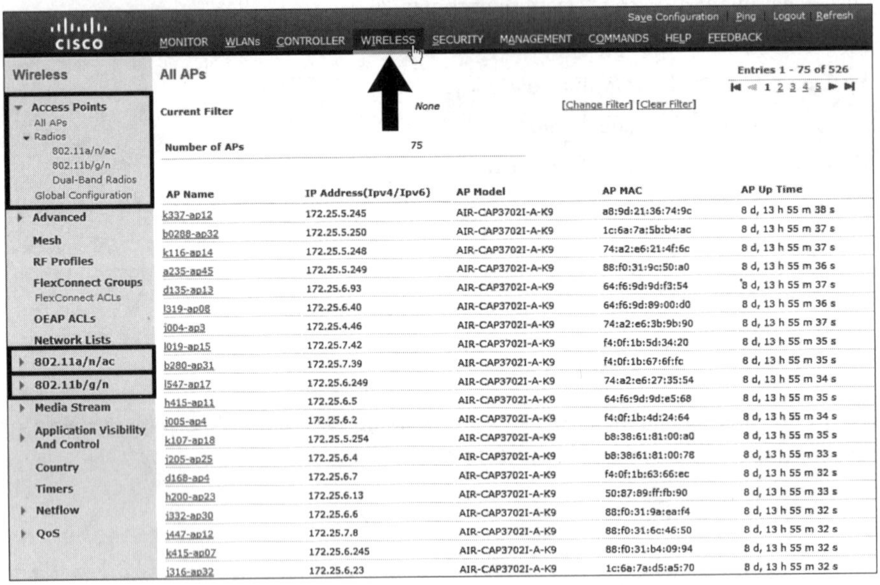

Figure 13-1 *Wireless Tab on a Cisco Controller GUI*

The wireless parameters are organized under a list of links that are found on the left side of the web page. At the CCNA level, you should be familiar with the following links:

- **Access Points**—Used to verify and configure RF things like transmit power level and channel number on individual APs
- **802.11a/n/ac**—Used to configure global parameters for the 5-GHz band
- **802.11b/g/n**—Used to configure global parameters for the 2.4-GHz band

The initial web page displays a list of all APs that are currently joined to the controller, as if you had selected **Wireless > Access Points > All APs**. The remaining configuration is covered in the sections that follow.

Configuring Data Rates

You can enable or disable the 2.4- or 5-GHz bands by selecting **802.11b/g/n** or **802.11a/n/ac**, respectively, and then clicking the **Network** link. Figures 13-2 and 13-3 show the two network configuration pages. Make sure that the **802.11b/g** or **802.11a Network Status** check box is checked to enable the 2.4- or 5-GHz radios on all APs.

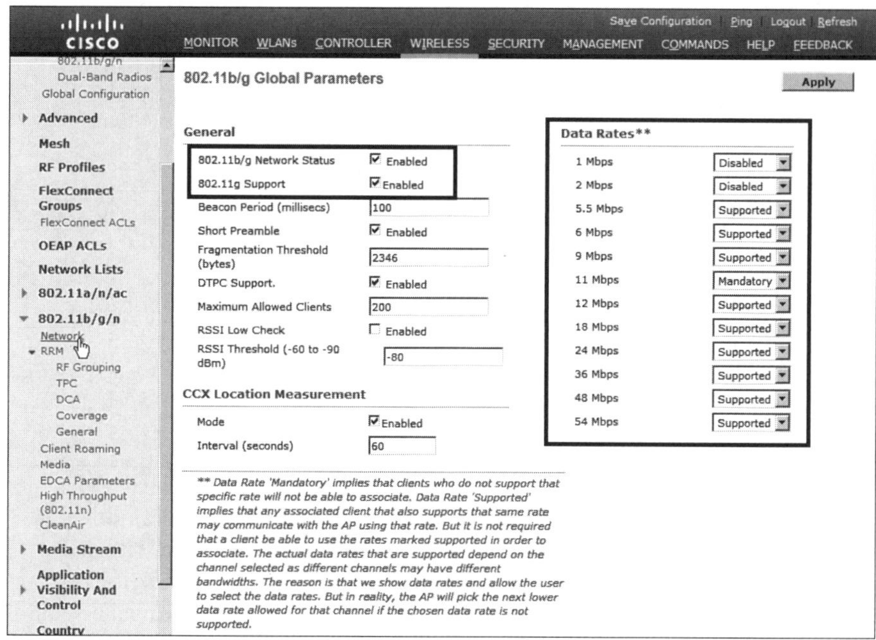

Figure 13-2 *Configuring 2.4-GHz Radios*

On the right side of the network web pages, as shown in Figures 13-2 and 13-3, you can configure the individual data rates (and the corresponding modulation and coding schemes) that are supported on each band. Each data rate can have one of the following states:

- **Mandatory**—A client must be able to use the data rate and Modulation Coding Scheme (MCS) to associate with an AP.
- **Supported**—A client can associate with an AP even if it cannot use the data rate.
- **Disabled**—An AP will not use the data rate with any clients.

By default, all data rates are enabled and supported. In the 2.4-GHz band, the 1-, 2-, 5.5-, and 11-Mbps rates are all marked as mandatory, based on the initial IEEE requirement that all clients be able to support each possible modulation type defined in 802.11b. In the 5-GHz band, the 6-, 12-, and 24-Mbps rates are marked as mandatory.

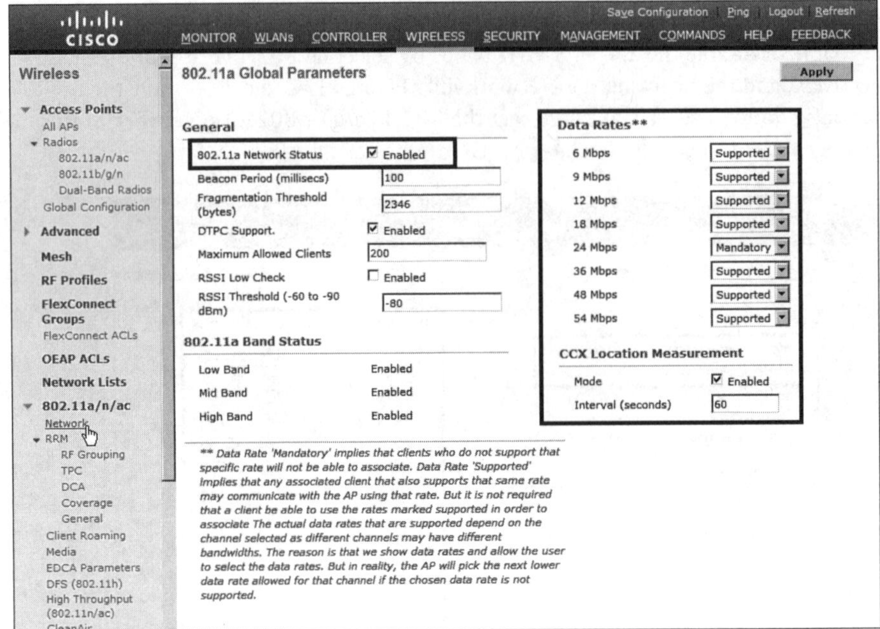

Figure 13-3 *Configuring 5-GHz Radios*

You can change the state of any data rate by selecting a new state from the drop-down menu. Remember that you can disable lower data rates to decrease the AP cell size and make channel use more efficient. Just make sure that your actions do not shrink the cells too much, leaving holes or gaps in the coverage between APs. Also be sure that all of your wireless clients can use the same set of mandatory and supported data rates.

Be sure to click the **Apply** button to make any configuration changes active. Any wireless networks that are already in production on the controller might be disrupted while the new configuration takes effect.

Configuring 802.11n and 802.11ac Support

You might have noticed that you can configure plenty of data rates, but 802.11n and 802.11ac are never mentioned on the wireless network configuration pages. That is because 802.11n and 802.11ac are considered to be rich sets of high-throughput enhancements and must be configured separately.

By default, 802.11n and 802.11ac are enabled. To check or change their state, go to **Wireless > 802.11a/n/ac** or **802.11b/g/n > High Throughput (802.11n/ac)**. Figure 13-4 shows the 5-GHz 802.11n/ac configuration page. Check the **11n Mode** and **11ac Mode** check boxes to enable 802.11n and 802.11ac, respectively. By default, every possible MCS is enabled and supported.

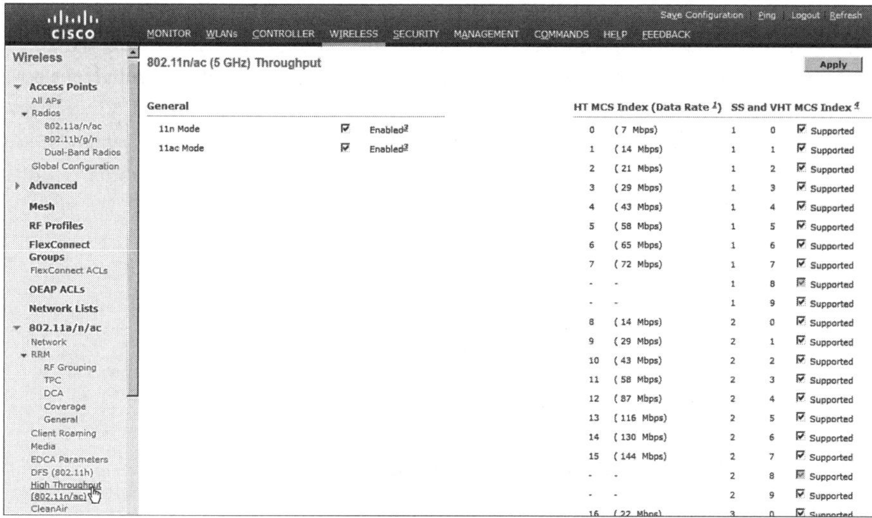

Figure 13-4 *Configuring 802.11n and 802.11ac Support*

Recall that 802.11n can bond one 20-MHz channel to an adjacent 20-MHz channel to effectively double the channel width; 802.11ac can scale even further By default, the controller will use only a single 20-MHz channel on each AP. You can configure channel bonding as a part of the dynamic channel allocation (DCA) configuration for the 5-GHz band only, as covered in the following section.

Understanding RRM

Suppose that you need to provide wireless coverage in a rectangular-shaped building. Using the information you have learned from this book, you decide to use six APs and locate them such that they form a staggered, regular pattern. The pattern shown in Figure 13-5 should create optimum conditions for roaming and channel use. (The building dimensions have not been mentioned, just to keep things simple.)

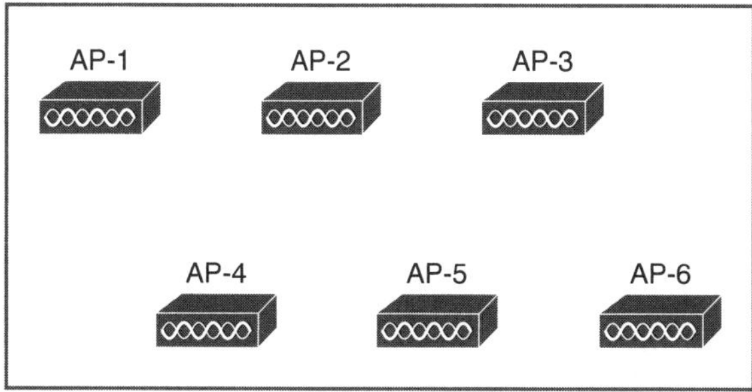

Figure 13-5 *Hypothetical AP Layout*

So far, you have considered the layout pattern and an average cell size, but you still have to tackle the puzzle of selecting the transmit power level and channel number for each AP. The transmit power level will affect the final cell size, and the channel assignment will affect co-channel interference and roaming handoff. At this point, if all the APs are powered up, they might all end up transmitting at maximum power on the same channel. Figure 13-6 shows one possible scenario; each of the AP cells overlaps its neighbors by about 50 percent, and all the APs are fighting to use channel 1!

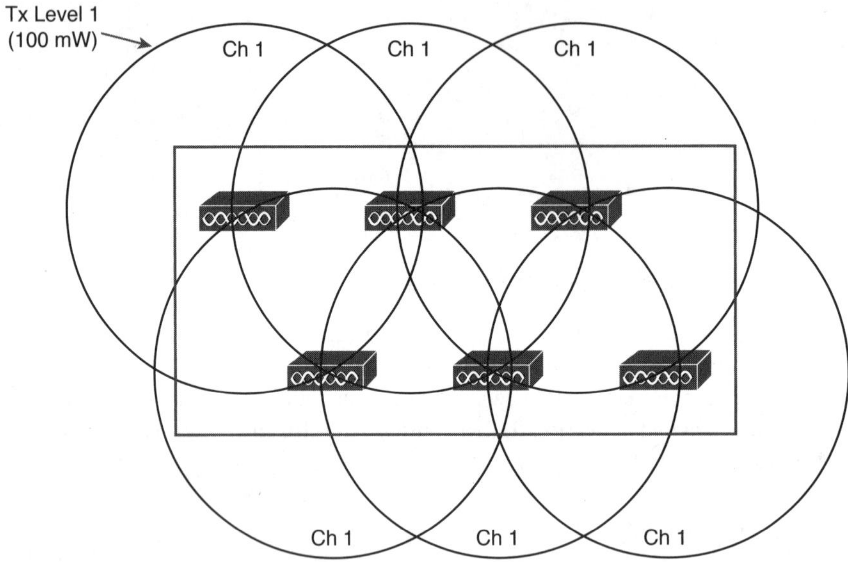

Figure 13-6 *Poorly Configured RF Coverage*

Where do you begin to prevent such mayhem? Because the AP locations are already nailed down, you can figure out the transmit power level that will give the proper cell overlap. Then you can work your way through the AP layout and choose an alternating pattern of channel numbers. With six APs, that might not be a daunting task.

Do not forget to repeat the task for both 2.4- and 5-GHz bands.

Also, if you plan on using 802.11n or 802.11ac with channel widths greater than 20 MHz, do not forget to reserve the extra channels needed for that. Be aware that only the 5-GHz band is capable of supporting wide channels.

If you happen to notice that an AP fails one day, you could always reconfigure its neighboring APs to increase their transmit power level to expand their cells and cover the hole.

If you introduce another AP or two in the future, do not forget to revisit the entire configuration again to make room for cells and channels.

Did your life as the wireless LAN administrator just become depressing and tedious? Cisco Radio Resource Management (RRM) can handle all these tasks regularly and automatically. RRM consists of several algorithms that can look at a large portion of a wireless network and work out an optimum transmit power level and channel number for each AP. If conditions that affect the RF coverage change over time, RRM can detect that and make the appropriate adjustments.

RF Groups

RRM works by monitoring a number of APs and working out optimal RF settings for each one. The APs that are included in the RRM algorithms are contained in a single RF group. An RF group is formed for each band that is supported—one group for 2.4-GHz AP radios and another for 5-GHz AP radios. By default, an RF group contains all the APs that are joined to a single controller.

You can also configure a controller to automatically populate its RF group. In that case, the RF group can expand to include APs from multiple controllers, provided the following two conditions are met:

- The controllers share a common RF group name.
- At least one AP from one controller can be overheard by an AP on another controller.

When an RF group touches more than one controller, the controllers form a type of cluster so that they all participate in any RF adjustments that are needed. Every AP sends a Neighbor Discovery Packet (NDP) at maximum transmit power and at 60-second intervals, by default. If two controllers are close enough in proximity for an AP on one to hear an AP on the other at a received signal strength indicator (RSSI) of –80 dBm or greater, they are close enough to belong to the same RF group. Up to 20 controllers and 1000 APs can join to form a single RF group.

Figure 13-7 shows a simple scenario with four controllers and four APs, resulting in two separate RF groups. AP-1 and AP-2 are both joined to controller WLC-1, so they are members of one RF group by default. AP-3, joined to WLC-2, is located near enough to AP-1 and AP-2 that neighbor advertisements are overheard. As a result, controller WLC-2 joins the RF group with WLC-1. However, AP-4, joined to controller WLC-3, is not close enough to pass the neighbor test. Even though AP-4's cell intersects the cells of AP-2 and AP-3, the APs themselves are not within range. Therefore, controller WLC-3 resides in a different RF group by itself.

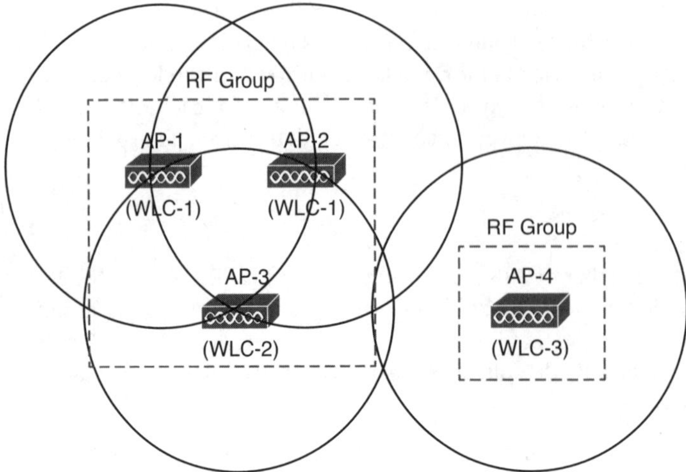

Figure 13-7 *Automatic RF Group Discovery and Formation*

One controller in each group is elected as an RF group leader, although you can override that by configuring one controller as a static leader. The leader collects and analyzes information from all APs in the group about their RF conditions in real time. You can access the RF group leader configuration information by selecting **Wireless > 802.11a/n/ac** or **802.11b/g/n > RRM > RF Grouping.** In Figure 13-8, the controller is in automatic RF group mode and is a member of an RF group along with two other controllers. The RF group leader is controller WLC-1.

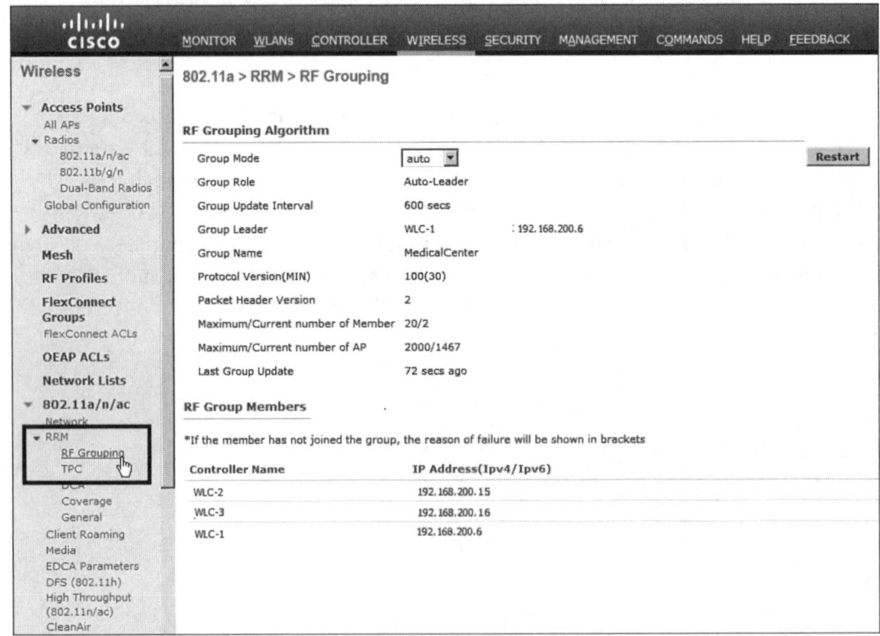

Figure 13-8 *Displaying RF Group Information*

Radio resource monitoring is used to gather and report information from the APs. Each AP is assigned to transmit and receive on a single channel, so it can easily detect noise and interference on that channel, as well as the channel utilization. The AP can also keep a list of clients and other APs that it hears transmitting on that channel.

Each AP can also spend a short bit of time (less than 60 ms) tuning its receiver to all of the other channels that are available. By scanning channels other than the one normally used, an AP can measure noise and interference all across the band from its own vantage point. The AP can also detect unexpected transmissions coming from rogue clients and APs, or devices that are not formally joined to the Cisco wireless network.

Based on the radio resource monitoring data, RRM can make the following decisions about APs in an RF group:

- **Transmit power control (TPC)**—RRM can set the transmit power level of each AP.
- **Dynamic channel allocation (DCA)**—RRM can select the channel number for each AP.
- **Coverage hole detection mitigation (CHDM)**—Based on information gathered from client associations, RRM can detect an area with weak RF coverage and increase an AP's transmit power level to compensate.

The RRM algorithms are designed to keep the entire wireless network as stable and efficient as possible. The TPC and DCA algorithms run independently because they perform very different functions. By default, the algorithms are run every 600 seconds (10 minutes). If conditions in the RF environment change, such as interference or the addition or failure of an AP, RRM can discover and react to the changes at the next interval. The RRM algorithms are discussed in more detail in the following sections.

TPC

The TPC algorithm focuses on one goal: setting each AP's transmit power level to an appropriate value so that it offers good coverage for clients while avoiding interference with neighboring APs that are using the same channel. Figure 13-9 illustrates this process. APs that were once transmitting too strongly and overlapping each other's cells are adjusted for proper coverage, reducing the cell size more appropriately to support clients.

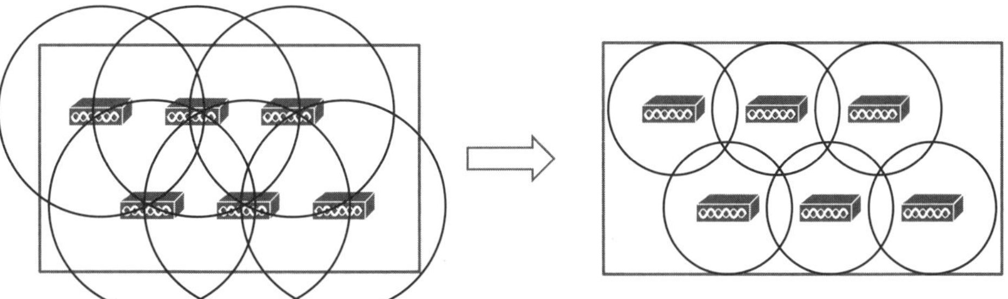

Figure 13-9 *Basic Concept of the TPC Algorithm*

13

Controllers have no knowledge of the physical location of each AP. By looking at Figure 13-9, you can see that the APs are arranged in a nice, evenly spaced pattern, but the controller cannot see that. When an AP joins a controller, only the AP's MAC address, IP address, and some basic information are advertised to the controller. If the locations of neighboring APs cannot be known, each AP must resort to using the RSSI of its neighbors as a measure of how closely their cells touch or overlap its own.

During the time each AP scans the channels to listen for RF conditions and other APs, it forms a list of its neighbors and their RSSI values. Each of those lists is sent to the local controller and on to the RF group leader where they are used by the TPC algorithm.

TPC works on one band at a time, making adjustments to APs as needed. If an AP has been heard with an RSSI above a threshold (–70 dBm by default) by at least three of its neighbors, TPC considers the AP's cell to be overlapping the cells of its three neighbors too much. The AP's transmit power level will be decreased by 3 dB, and then its RSSI will be evaluated again. This process is repeated for all APs at regular intervals until the neighbor that is measuring the third-strongest RSSI value for the AP no longer measures the RSSI greater than the threshold.

Although you probably will not have to make any configuration changes for the TPC algorithm, it is still useful to understand its settings. **TPC** runs on the 2.4- and 5-GHz bands independently. You can see the settings by selecting **Wireless > 802.11a/n/ac** or **802.11b/g/n > RRM > TPC**. Figure 13-10 shows the TPC configuration for the 5-GHz band.

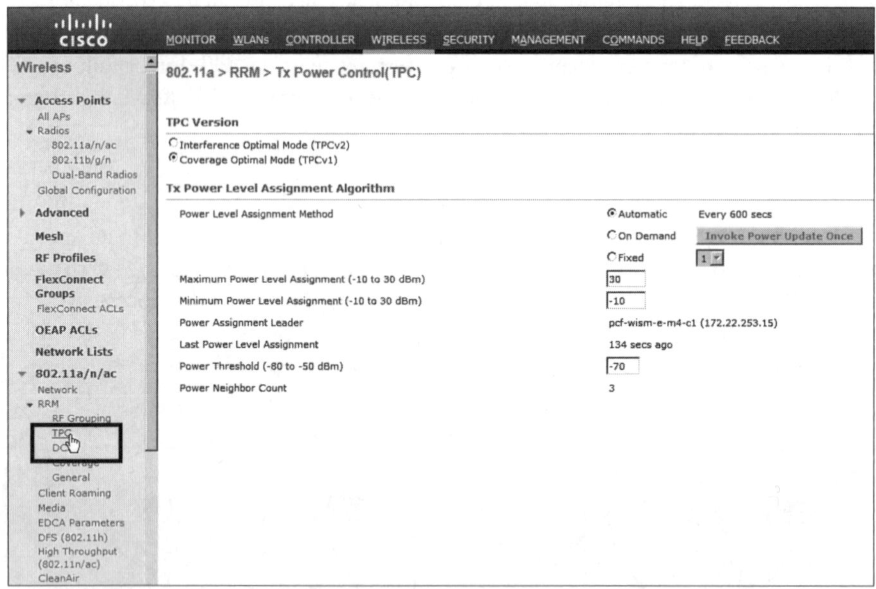

Figure 13-10 *Adjusting the RRM TPC Algorithm Parameters*

Actually, there are two different TPC algorithms as you can see in the figure. TPCv1 (the default), also known as Coverage Optimal Mode, works toward making adjustments that give the best RF coverage, while keeping signals sufficient and stable. TPCv2, also known as Interference Optimal Mode, focuses on avoiding negative impacts that TPCv1 might have had, where the power among AP cells ends up being imbalanced, causing some cells to interfere with others. TPCv2 requires proper tuning of RF parameters in order to work properly. While TPCv2 might sound superior, it should only be enabled in specific cases that are outside the scope of the CCNA Wireless exam or when directed by Cisco TAC.

By default, TPC runs automatically every 10 minutes. This is the recommended mode because any changes in the RF environment can be detected and compensated for without any intervention. As an alternative, you can select **On Demand** to run the algorithm immediately; then the resulting transmit power levels will be frozen until TPC is manually triggered again. If you would rather have the controller set the transmit power level on all APs to one fixed value, you can select **Fixed** and choose the power level from the drop-down menu.

Cisco controllers determine the transmit power level according to an index from 1 to 8, rather than discrete dBm or mW values. A value of 1 corresponds to the maximum power level that is allowed in the AP's regulatory domain. Each increment in the power level number reduces the transmit power by 3 dBm. You might remember from Chapter 1 that reducing by 3 dBm also means that the power in mW is cut in half. As an example, Table 13-2 lists the power levels used in the 2.4-GHz and 5-GHz bands on a Cisco 3700 AP in the Americas or European domains.

Table 13-2 AP Transmit Power Level Numbers, dBm, and mW Values in the 2.4-GHz Band

Power Level	dBm (2.4 GHz)	dBm (5 GHz)	mW
1	23	23	200
2	20	20	100
3	17	17	50
4	14	14	25
5	11	11	12.5
6	8	8	6.25
7	5	Unused	3.125
8	2	Unused	1.56

With every iteration, the TPC algorithm can continue adjusting the transmit power levels until no further changes are needed. As a result, some APs might end up higher or lower than you might want. For example, it is usually best to match the AP transmit power level with that of the clients. Suppose that some of the clients have a fixed power level of 25 mW; if TPC ends up reducing some APs to 10 mW, the AP and client power levels will be mismatched.

To prevent such a condition, you can set minimum and maximum power level boundaries for the TPC algorithm. By default, the minimum level is set to –10 dBm and the maximum to 30 dBm, as shown in Figure 13-10.

Whenever you change the TPC parameters in a controller configuration, remember to make the same changes to all controllers that might be members of the same RF group. No matter which controller might become the RF group leader, the parameters should be identical.

Tip What transmit power level does an AP use when it first powers up? A new AP right out of the box will power up at its maximum power level. After the TPC algorithm has run and adjusted an AP's power level, that level is remembered the next time the AP is power cycled.

DCA

Recall from Chapter 7, "Planning Coverage with Wireless APs," and Chapter 12, "Understanding Roaming," that a proper channel assignment is vital for efficient use of air time and for client mobility. When neighboring APs use the same channel, they can interfere with each other. Ideally, adjacent APs should use different, non-overlapping channels. Working out a channel layout for many APs can be a difficult puzzle, but the DCA algorithm can work out optimum solutions automatically for all APs in an RF group.

When a new AP first powers up, it uses the first non-overlapping channel in each band—channel 1 for 2.4 GHz and channel 36 for 5 GHz. Consider a simplistic scenario where all APs are new and powered up for the first time. You would end up with a building full of overlapping cells competing for the use of 2.4-GHz channel 1, as shown in simplified form in Figure 13-11. The DCA algorithm works to correct this situation by finding a channel that each AP in the RF group can use without overlapping or interfering with other APs. Like TPC, DCA works out one channel layout in the 2.4-GHz band and another layout in the 5-GHz band.

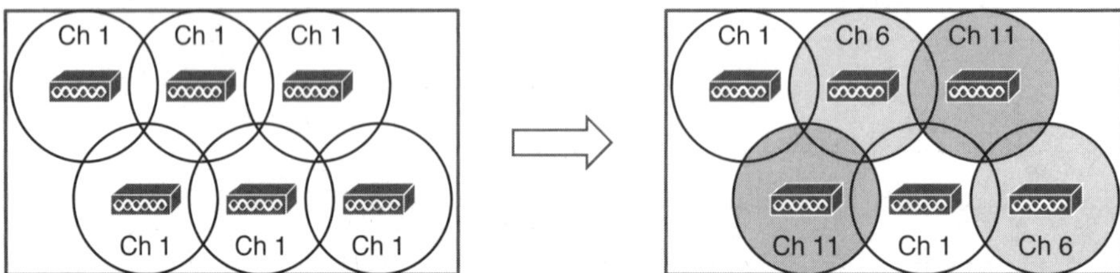

Figure 13-11 *Basic Concept of the DCA Algorithm*

DCA does not just solve the channel layout puzzle once for all APs. The algorithm runs every 10 minutes by default, so that it can detect any conditions that might require an AP's channel to change. APs in the RF group are monitored for the metrics listed in Table 13-3 that can influence the channel reassignment decision.

Table 13-3 Metrics Affecting DCA Decisions

Metric	Default State	Description
RSSI of neighboring APs	Always enabled	If DCA detects co-channel interference, it may move an AP to a different channel.
802.11 interference	Enabled	If transmissions from APs and devices that are not part of the wireless network are detected, DCA may choose to move an AP to a different channel.

Metric	Default State	Description
Non-802.11 noise	Enabled	If excessive noise is present on a channel, DCA may choose to avoid using it.
AP traffic load	Disabled	If an AP is heavily used, DCA may not change its channel to keep client disruption to a minimum.
Persistent interference	Disabled	If an interference source with a high duty cycle is detected on a channel, DCA may choose to avoid using it.

The DCA algorithm tends to look at each AP individually to find the ones with the worst RF conditions. Changing the channel of even one AP can affect many other APs if there are not other alternative channels available. Channel layout is a puzzle that may require several iterations to solve. For this reason, the controller that is the RF group leader will undergo an RRM startup mode after it is elected. The startup mode consists of ten DCA iterations at 10-minute intervals, or a total of 100 minutes before the channel layout reaches a steady state.

The end result of DCA is a channel layout that takes a variety of conditions into account. The channel layout is not just limited to the two dimensions of a single floor space in a building; it also extends to three-dimensional space because the RF signals from one floor can bleed through to another. As long as the APs on different floors belong to the same RF group, co-channel interference between them should be minimized.

You can display and configure the DCA parameters of either the 2.4- or 5-GHz band by selecting **Wireless > 802.11a/n/ac** or **802.11b/g/n > RRM > DCA**. Figure 13-12 shows the 802.11a/n/ac configuration.

By default, the DCA algorithm runs automatically at 10-minute intervals. You can change the interval time, select **Freeze** to run DCA manually on demand, or turn it **Off** completely. You can also select the conditions to avoid, which will trigger a channel change on an AP.

The DCA parameters also include the 802.11n channel width. By default, 20-MHz channels will be used. If you have enabled 802.11n in the 5-GHz band and want to enable 40-MHz channels, be sure to select **40 MHz** as the channel width. If you have 802.11ac enabled, you can choose between 20-, 40-, and 80-MHz channel width. The DCA algorithm will solve the channel assignment puzzle automatically, even with wide channels.

Tip You might be wondering why 802.11ac can support 80- and 160-MHz channel widths, but 160 MHz is not an option on the controller depicted in Figure 13-12. The reason is twofold: (1) Full 160-MHz channel width is not supported until 802.11ac Wave 2; and (2) the CCNA Wireless 200-355 exam uses AireOS 8.0, which supports only Wave 1. In addition, the available spectrum does not currently support more than two 160-MHz channels. Both reasons will be solved over time, as new hardware is developed and as new spectrum is reclaimed and set aside in the 5-GHz band.

The bottom portion of the web page contains a list of channels that DCA can use as it assigns channels to APs in the respective band. This list is populated with channel numbers by default, but you can edit the list as needed. You can also enable or disable individual channel use by using the list of **Select** check boxes.

The DCA algorithm normally runs on an automatic schedule or manually on demand. Event-Driven RRM (ED-RRM) takes this a step further; DCA can be triggered based on RF events that occur in real time. The CleanAir feature, covered in more detail in Chapter 19, "Dealing with Wireless Interference," provides the triggers for ED-RRM. By default, ED-RRM is disabled. You can enable it with the **EDRRM** check box at the very bottom of the web page.

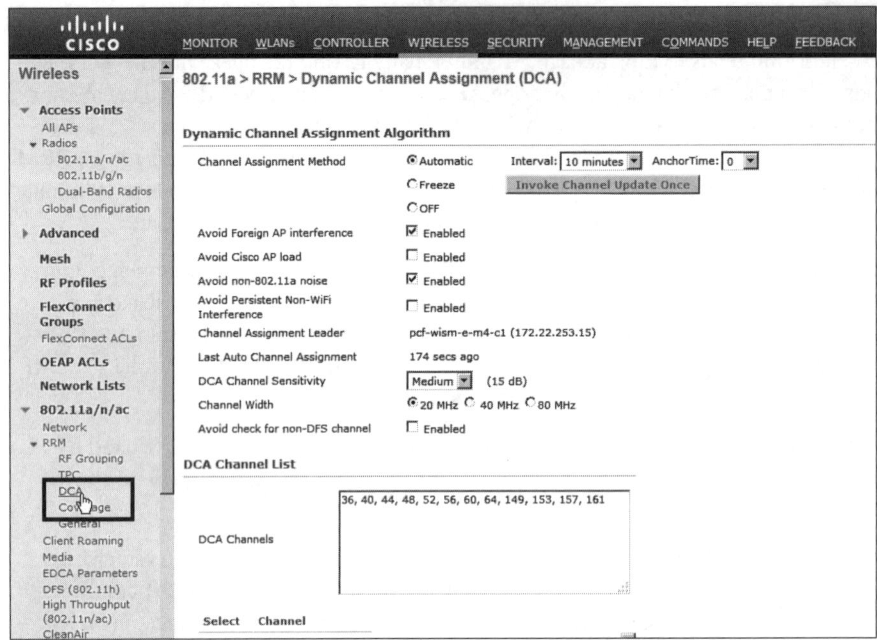

Figure 13-12 *Adjusting the RRM DCA Algorithm Parameters*

Coverage Hole Detection Mitigation

The TPC algorithm normally reduces AP transmit power levels to make cell sizes appropriate. Sometimes you might find that your best intentions at providing RF coverage with a good AP layout still come up short. For example, you might discover that signals are weak in some small area of a building due to the building construction or surrounding obstacles. You might also have an AP radio that happens to fail, causing a larger coverage hole. How would you discover such a condition? You could make a habit of surveying the RF coverage often. More likely, your wireless users will discover a weakness or hole in the coverage and complain to you about it.

A Cisco controller-based wireless network offers an additional RRM algorithm that can detect coverage holes and take action to address them. Coverage hole detection mitigation (CHDM) can alert you to a hole that it has discovered and it can increase an AP's transmit power level to compensate for the hole.

CHDM is useful in two cases:

- Extending coverage in a weak area
- Rapidly healing a coverage hole caused by an AP or radio failure, sooner than the TPC algorithm can detect and correct

The algorithm does not run at regular intervals like TPC and DCA do. Instead, it monitors the RF conditions of wireless clients and decides when to take action. In effect, the algorithm leverages your wireless users who are out in the field and tries to notice a problem before they do.

Every controller maintains a database of associated clients and their RSSI and signal-to-noise ratio (SNR) values. It might seem logical to think that a low RSSI or SNR would mean a client is experiencing a hole in coverage. Assuming the client and its AP are using the same transmit power levels, if the AP is receiving the client at a low level, the client must also be receiving the AP at a low level. This might not be true at all; the client might just be exiting the building and getting too far away from the AP. The client might also have a "sticky" roaming behavior, where it maintains an association with one AP until the RSSI falls to a very low level before reassociating elsewhere.

CHDM tries to rule out conditions that are experienced by small numbers of clients and signal conditions due to client roaming behavior. A valid coverage hole is detected when some number of clients, all associated to the same AP, have RSSI values that fall below a threshold. In addition, the coverage hole condition must exist longer than a threshold of time without the client roaming to a different AP.

By default, the following conditions must all be met for a coverage hole to be detected:

- Client RSSI at the AP is at or below –80 dBm.
- The low RSSI condition must last at least 60 seconds over the past 180 seconds.
- The condition must affect at least three clients or more than 25 percent of the clients on a single AP.

Be aware that CHDM runs on a per-band basis. Unlike TPC and DCA, which operate on the entire RF group of controllers, CHDM runs on each controller independently, on a per-AP radio basis.

You can display and configure the CHDM thresholds by selecting **Wireless > 802.11a/n/ac** or **802.11b/g/n > RRM > Coverage**. Figure 13-13 shows the threshold parameters for the 5-GHz 802.11a band.

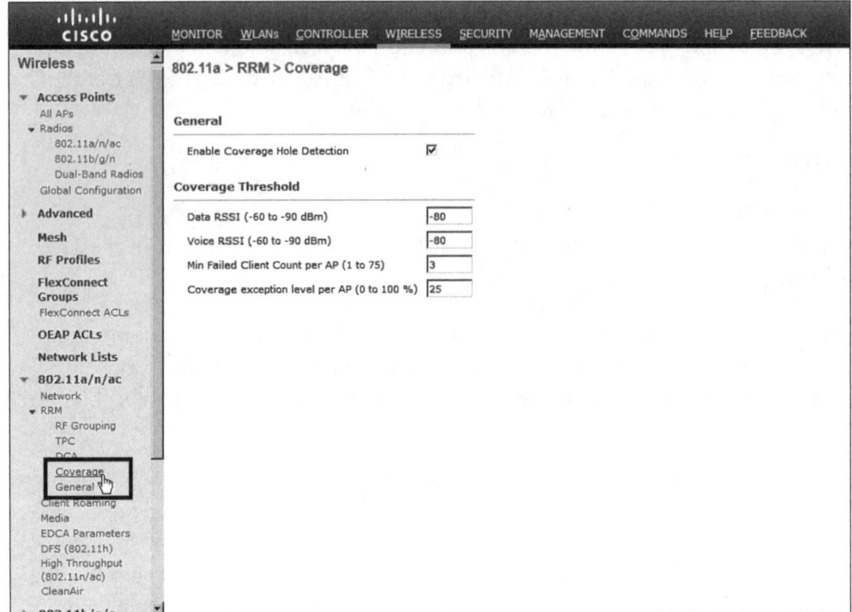

Figure 13-13 *Displaying Coverage Threshold Parameters for the 5-GHz 802.11a Band*

Manual RF Configuration

You might sometimes want to keep RRM from changing the RF conditions in parts of your wireless network. For instance, you might have client devices that operate at a fixed transmit power level. Ideally, the AP and client power levels should be identical or matched. If RRM raises or lowers AP power levels at a later time, then asymmetric power levels would result.

You can override RRM on a per-AP basis by selecting **Wireless > Access Points > Radios > 802.11a/n/ac** or **802.11b/g/n.** From the list of APs displayed, choose a specific AP and select the drop-down menu at the far-right side of the list. From this menu, select **Configure**, as shown in Figure 13-14.

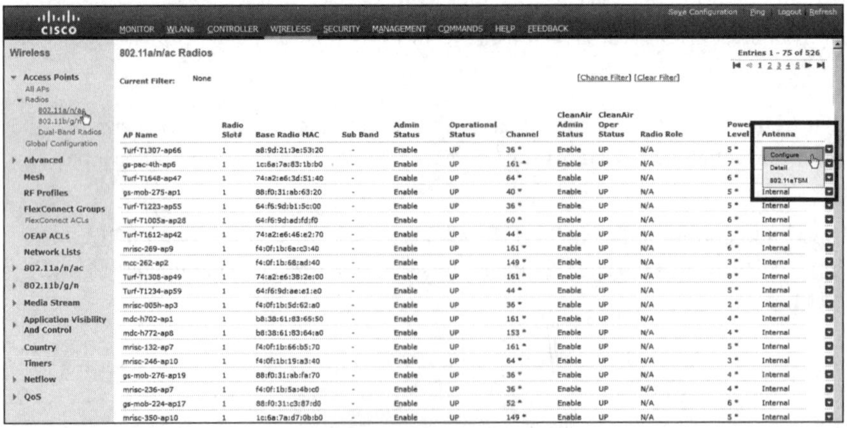

Figure 13-14 *Selecting an AP for Manual Configuration*

On the AP configuration page, as shown in Figure 13-15, you can set the channel under RF Channel Assignment or the transmit power under Tx Power Level Assignment. By default, the **Global** radio button is selected for each, which allows the value to be determined globally within the RF group. You can set a specific channel or power level by selecting the **Custom** radio button and then choosing a value from the drop-down list. In the figure, the AP's transmit power level has been manually set to 3.

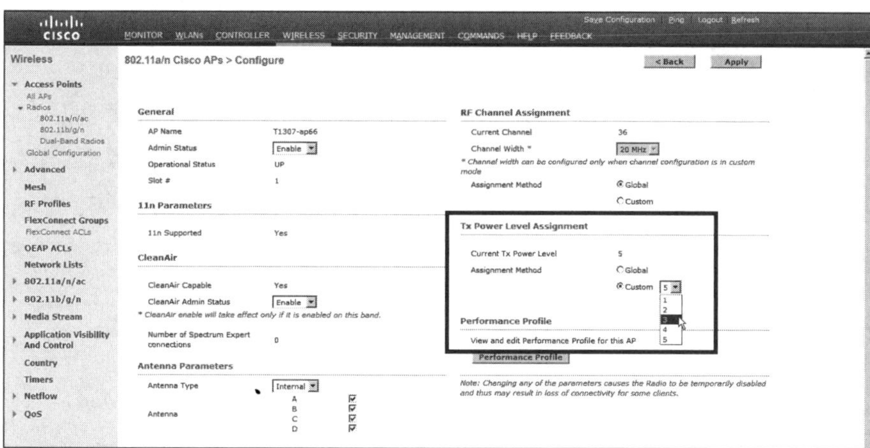

Figure 13-15 *Manually Setting the Transmit Power Level of an AP*

Tip You should let RRM automatically adjust both channels and transmit power levels whenever possible.

Verifying RRM Results

The RRM algorithms can either run at regular intervals or on demand. You can display the channel number and transmit power level that are being used on every AP by selecting **Wireless > Access Points > Radios > 802.11a/n/ac** or **802.11b/g/n**, as shown in Figure 13-15. The controller displays an asterisk next to values that have been set through RRM. Otherwise, if no asterisk appears, the value has been set manually.

To get a much better feel for the RRM results, you can use the Cisco Prime Infrastructure management system (covered in Chapter 18, "Managing Cisco Wireless Networks") to view APs on a graphical representation of an area. The map in Figure 13-16 displays each AP's location on a building floor plan, along with its channel number and transmit power level for the 2.4-GHz band. Figure 13-17 shows the same map for the 5-GHz band. Seeing the physical arrangement of APs and their cells can help you get a much better idea how the channels are assigned and reused.

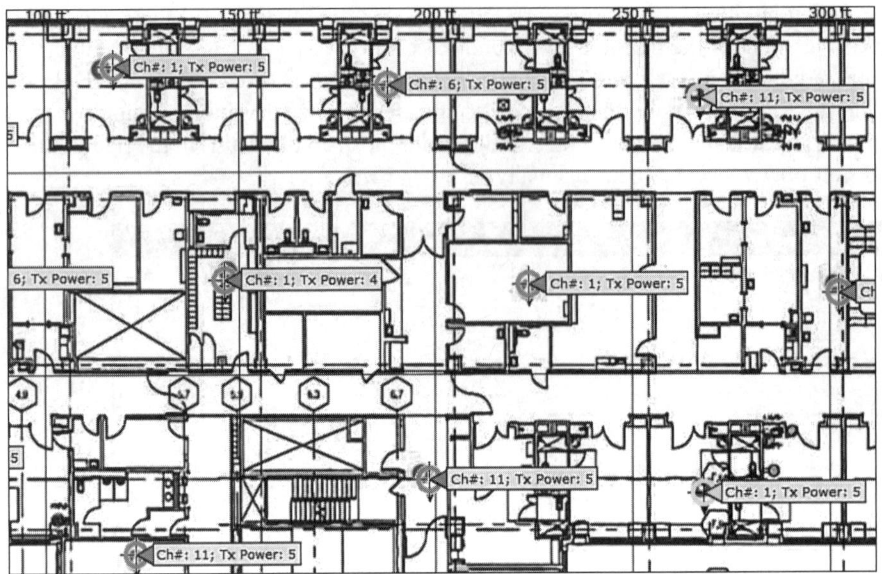

Figure 13-16 *Displaying 2.4-GHz RRM Results in Cisco Prime Infrastructure Maps*

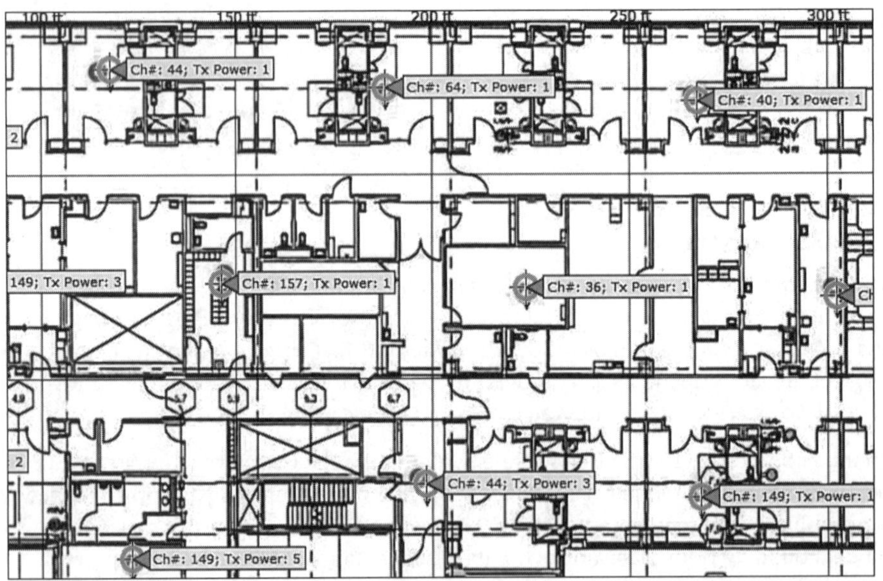

Figure 13-17 *Displaying 5-GHz RRM Results in Cisco Prime Infrastructure Maps*

Exam Preparation Tasks

As mentioned in the section, "How to Use This Book," in the Introduction, you have a couple of choices for exam preparation: the exercises here, Chapter 21, "Final Review," and the exam simulation questions on the DVD.

Review All Key Topics

Review the most important topics in this chapter, noted with the Key Topic icon in the outer margin of the page. Table 13-4 lists a reference of these key topics and the page numbers on which each is found.

Table 13-4 Key Topics for Chapter 13

Key Topic Element	Description	Page Number
List	Data rate states	309
Figure 13-7	RF group formation	314
Figure 13-9	TPC operation	315
Table 13-2	AP transmit power level numbers	317
Figure 13-11	DCA operation	318
List	Coverage hole detection criteria	321

Define Key Terms

Define the following key terms from this chapter and check your answers in the glossary:

coverage hole, dynamic channel allocation (DCA), mandatory data rate, Radio Resource Management (RRM), RF group, RF group leader, supported data rate, transmit power control (TPC)

This chapter covers the following topics:

- **Anatomy of a Secure Connection**—This section provides an overview of the types of information that should be protected over a wireless connection and the functions that you can use to provide protection.
- **Wireless Client Authentication Methods**—This section describes many of the common methods that you can use to authenticate clients on a wireless network.
- **Wireless Privacy and Integrity Methods**—This section discusses two methods that you can leverage to keep data obscured from eavesdroppers and to discover when data has been tampered with over a wireless connection.
- **WPA and WPA2**—This section explains two important industry standards that specify a suite of security methods for wireless security.
- **Securing Management Frames with MFP**—This section discusses a method that you can use to prevent attacks that use management frames to disrupt a wireless network.
- **Configuring Wireless Security**—This section covers the configuration steps needed to implement WPA and WPA2 security on a wireless LAN.

This chapter covers the following exam topics:

- 5.0—Configuration of Client Connectivity
  - 5.1—Identify authentication mechanisms
    - 5.1a—LDAP, RADIUS, local authentication, WebAuth, 802.1X, PSK
  - 5.2—Configuring WLAN authentication mechanisms on the controller
    - 5.2a—WebAuth, 802.1X, PSK
    - 5.2b—TKIP deprecation

CHAPTER 14

Wireless Security Fundamentals

As you know by now, wireless networks are complex. Many technologies and protocols work behind the scenes to give end users a stable, yet mobile, connection to a wired network infrastructure. From the user's perspective, a wireless connection should seem no different than a wired connection. A wired connection can give users a sense of security; data traveling over a wire is probably not going to be overheard by others. A wireless connection is inherently different; data traveling over the air can be overheard by anyone within range.

Therefore, securing a wireless network becomes just as important as any other aspect. A comprehensive approach to wireless security focuses on the following areas:

- Identifying the endpoints of a wireless connection
- Identifying the end user
- Protecting the wireless data from eavesdroppers
- Protecting the wireless data from tampering

The identification process is performed through various authentication schemes. Protecting wireless data involves security functions like encryption and frame authentication.

This chapter covers many of the methods you can use to secure a wireless network. Be warned—wireless security can be a confusing topic because it is filled with many acronyms. Some of the acronyms rhyme like words from a children's book. In fact, this chapter is a story about WEP, PSK, TKIP, MIC, AES, EAP, EAP-FAST, EAP-TLS, LEAP, PEAP, WPA, WPA2, CCMP, and on and on it goes. When you finish with this chapter, though, you will come away with a clear view of what these terms mean and how they all fit together.

As a CCNA Wireless engineer, you will need to have a basic understanding of the wireless security framework and the common methods you can use to build it. You will also need to know how to configure the most robust methods in a wireless network.

"Do I Know This Already?" Quiz

The "Do I Know This Already?" quiz allows you to assess whether you should read this entire chapter thoroughly or jump to the "Exam Preparation Tasks" section. If you are in doubt about your answers to these questions or your own assessment of your knowledge of the topics, read the entire chapter. Table 14-1 lists the major headings in this chapter and their corresponding "Do I Know This Already?" quiz questions. You can find the answers in Appendix A, "Answers to the 'Do I Know This Already?' Quizzes."

Table 14-1 "Do I Know This Already?" Section-to-Question Mapping

Foundation Topics Section	Questions
Anatomy of a Secure Connection	1–2
Wireless Client Authentication Methods	3–7
Wireless Privacy and Integrity Methods	8
WPA and WPA2	9–10
Securing Management Frames with MFP	11
Configuring Wireless Security	12–13

Caution The goal of self-assessment is to gauge your mastery of the topics in this chapter. If you do not know the answer to a question or are only partially sure of the answer, you should mark that question as wrong for purposes of the self-assessment. Giving yourself credit for an answer you correctly guess skews your self-assessment results and might provide you with a false sense of security.

1. Which of the following are necessary components of a secure wireless connection? (Choose all that apply.)
   - **a.** Encryption
   - **b.** MIC
   - **c.** Authentication
   - **d.** All of these answers are correct.
2. Which one of the following is used to protect the integrity of data in a wireless frame?
   - **a.** WIPS
   - **b.** WEP
   - **c.** MIC
   - **d.** EAP
3. Which one of the following is a wireless encryption method that has been found to be vulnerable and is not recommended for use?
   - **a.** AES
   - **b.** WPA
   - **c.** EAP
   - **d.** WEP

4. Which one of the following is used as the 802.11 authentication method when 802.1x is used on a WLAN?
   a. Open authentication
   b. WEP
   c. EAP
   d. WPA
5. A Cisco WLC is configured for 802.1x authentication, using an external RADIUS server. The controller takes on which one of the following roles?
   a. Authentication server
   b. Supplicant
   c. Authenticator
   d. Adjudicator
6. Which one of the following authentication methods uses a certificate to authenticate the AS but not the client?
   a. LEAP
   b. PEAP
   c. EAP-FAST
   d. EAP-TLS
7. Which one of the following authentication methods requires digital certificates on both the AS and the supplicants?
   a. TKIP
   b. PEAP
   c. WEP
   d. EAP-TLS
8. Which one of the following is currently the most secure data encryption and integrity method for wireless data?
   a. WEP
   b. TKIP
   c. CCMP
   d. WPA
9. WPA2 differs from WPA in which one of the following ways?
   a. Allows TKIP
   b. Mandates CCMP
   c. Allows WEP
   d. Allows TLS

10. A pre-shared key is used in which of the following wireless security configurations?
    a. WPA personal mode
    b. WPA enterprise mode
    c. WPA2 personal mode
    d. WPA2 enterprise mode

11. Which of the following is required to implement MFP on a WLAN to protect both the wireless infrastructure and the client? (Select all that apply.)
    a. WPA
    b. WPA2
    c. CCXv4 or v5
    d. CCXv5
    e. WEP

12. Which one of the following options should you select to configure WPA2 personal on a WLAN?
    a. 802.1x
    b. PSK
    c. TKIP
    d. CCMP

13. Which of the following wireless security methods have been deprecated due to their weaknesses? (Choose all that apply.)
    a. AES
    b. TKIP
    c. WEP
    d. CCMP
    e. EAP

Foundation Topics

Anatomy of a Secure Connection

In the previous chapters of this book, you have learned about wireless clients forming associations with wireless access points (APs) and passing data back and forth across the air. The main focus has been on the radio frequency (RF) conditions, the modulation schemes, and the management of airtime that are all necessary to send data from one place to another successfully.

As long as all clients and APs conform to the 802.11 standard, they can all coexist—even on the same channel. Not every 802.11 device is friendly and trustworthy, however. Sometimes it is easy to forget that transmitted frames do not just go directly from the sender to the receiver, as in a wired or switched connection. Instead, they travel according to the transmitter's antenna pattern, potentially reaching any receiver that is within range.

Consider the scenario in Figure 14-1. The wireless client opens a session with some remote entity and shares a confidential password. Because two untrusted users are also located within range of the client's signal, they may also learn the password by capturing frames that have been sent on the channel. The convenience of wireless communication also makes it easy for transmissions to be overheard and exploited by malicious users.

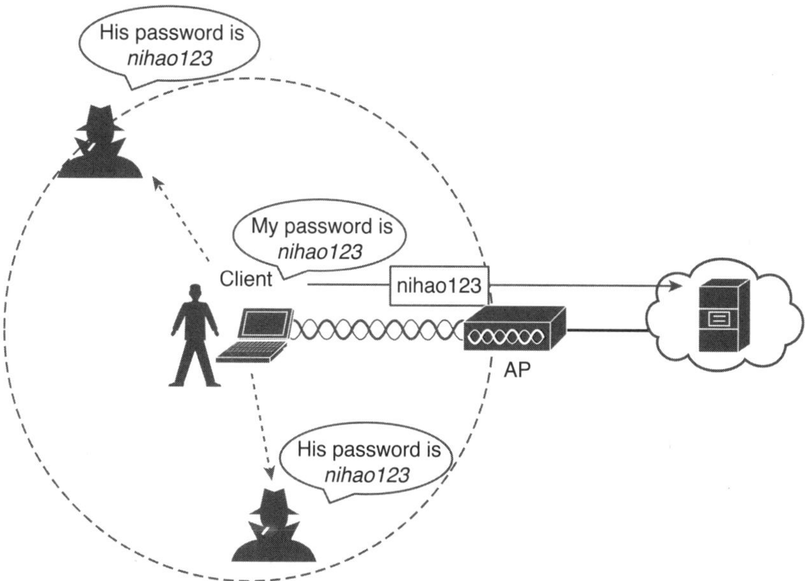

Figure 14-1 *Wireless Transmissions Reaching Unintended Recipients*

If data is sent through open space, how can it be secured so that it stays private and intact? The 802.11 standard offers a framework of wireless security mechanisms that can be used to add trust, privacy, and integrity to a wireless network. A Cisco unified wireless network can go even further by detecting and preventing malicious activity. The following sections give an overview of the wireless security framework. Each element is described in more detail later in the chapter.

Authentication

In Chapter 6, "Understanding 802.11 Frame Types," you learned that wireless clients must discover a basic service set (BSS) and then request permission to associate with it. Clients should be authenticated by some means before they can become functioning members of the wireless LAN. Why?

Suppose that your wireless network connects to corporate resources where confidential information can be accessed. In that case, only devices known to be trusted and expected should be given access. Guest users, if they are permitted at all, should be allowed to join a different guest WLAN where they can access nonconfidential or public resources. Rogue clients, which are not expected or welcomed, should not be permitted to associate at all. After all, they are not affiliated with the corporate network and are likely to be unknown devices that happen to be within range of your network.

To control access, wireless networks can authenticate the client devices before they are allowed to associate. Potential clients must identify themselves by presenting some form of credentials to the APs. Figure 14-2 shows the basic client authentication process.

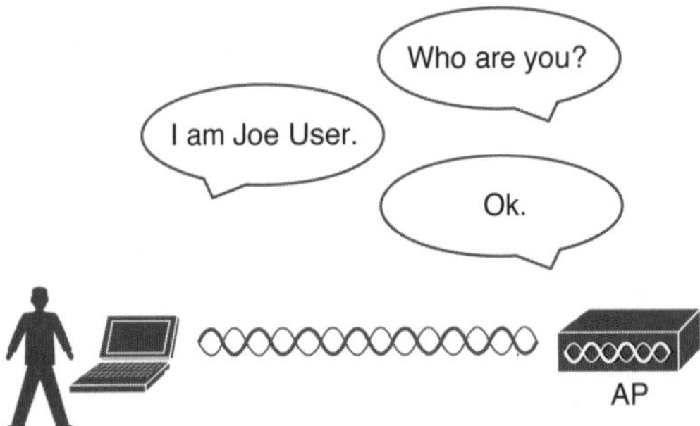

Figure 14-2 *Authenticating a Wireless Client*

Wireless authentication can take many forms. Some methods require only a static text string that is common across all trusted clients and APs. The text string is stored on the client device and presented directly to the AP when needed. What might happen if the device was stolen or lost? Most likely, any user who possessed the device could still authenticate to the network. Other more stringent authentication methods require interaction with a corporate user database. In those cases, the end user must enter a valid username and password—something that would not be known to a thief or an imposter.

If you have ever joined a wireless network, you might have focused on authenticating your device or yourself, while implicitly trusting the nearest AP. For example, if you turn on your wireless device and find a wireless network that is available at your workplace, you probably join it without hesitating. The same is true for wireless networks in an airport, a hotel, a hot spot, or in your home—you expect the AP that is advertising the SSID to be owned and operated by the entity where you are located. But how can you be sure?

Normally, the only piece of information you have is the SSID being broadcast or advertised by an AP. If the SSID looks familiar, you will likely choose to join it. Perhaps your computer is configured to automatically connect to a known SSID so that it associates without your intervention. Either way, you might unwittingly join the same SSID even if it was being advertised by an imposter.

Some common attacks focus on a malicious user pretending to be an AP. The fake AP can send beacons, answer probes, and associate clients just like the real AP it is impersonating. Once a client associates with the fake AP, the attacker can easily intercept all communication to and from the client from its central position. A fake AP could also send spoofed management frames to disassociate or deauthenticate legitimate and active clients, just to disrupt normal network operation.

To prevent this type of man-in-the-middle attack, the client should authenticate the AP before the client itself is authenticated. Figure 14-3 shows a simple scenario. Even further, any management frames received by a client should be authenticated too, as proof that they were sent by a legitimate and expected AP.

Figure 14-3 *Authenticating a Wireless AP*

Message Privacy

Suppose that the client in Figure 14-3 must authenticate before joining the wireless network. It might also authenticate the AP and its management frames after it associates but before it is itself authenticated. The client's relationship with the AP might become much more trusted, but data passing to and from the client is still available to eavesdroppers on the same channel.

To protect data privacy on a wireless network, the data should be encrypted for its journey through free space. This is accomplished by encrypting the data payload in each wireless frame just prior to being transmitted, then decrypting it as it is received. The idea is to use an encryption method that the transmitter and receiver share, so the data can be encrypted and decrypted successfully.

In wireless networks, each WLAN may support only one authentication and encryption scheme, so all clients must use the same encryption method when they associate. You might think that having one encryption method in common would allow every client to eavesdrop on every other client. That is not necessarily the case because the AP should securely negotiate an encryption key to use for each associated client.

Ideally, the AP and a client are the only two devices that have the encryption keys in common so that they can understand each other's data. No other device should know about or be able to use the same keys to eavesdrop and decrypt the data. In Figure 14-4, the client's confidential password information has been encrypted before being transmitted. The AP can decrypt it successfully before forwarding it onto the wired network, but other wireless devices cannot.

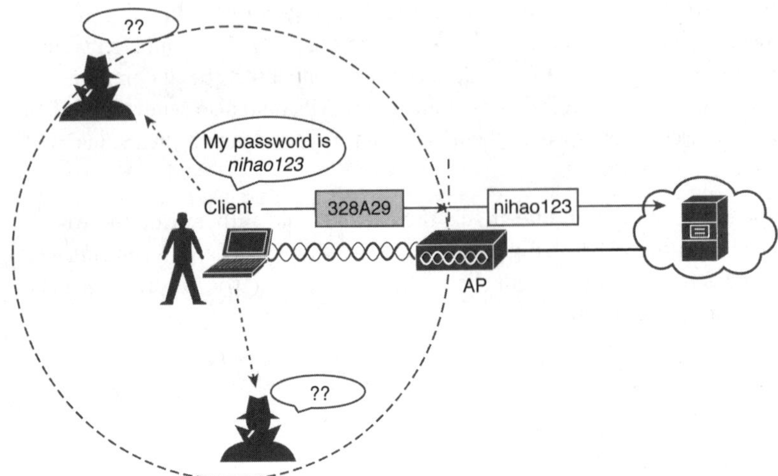

Figure 14-4 *Encrypting Wireless Data to Protect Data Privacy*

The AP also maintains a "group key" that it uses when it needs to send encrypted data to all clients in its cell at one time. Each of the associated clients uses the same group key to decrypt the data.

Message Integrity

Encrypting data obscures it from view while it is traveling over a public or untrusted network. The intended recipient should be able to decrypt the message and recover the original contents, but what if someone managed to alter the contents along the way? The recipient would have a very difficult time discovering that the original data had been modified.

A message integrity check (MIC) is a security tool that can protect against data tampering. You can think of a MIC as a way for the sender to add a secret stamp inside the encrypted data frame. The stamp is based on the contents of the data bits to be transmitted. Once the recipient decrypts the frame, it can compare the secret stamp to its own idea of what the stamp should be, based on the data bits that were received. If the two stamps are identical, the recipient can safely assume that the data has not been tampered with. Figure 14-5 shows the MIC process.

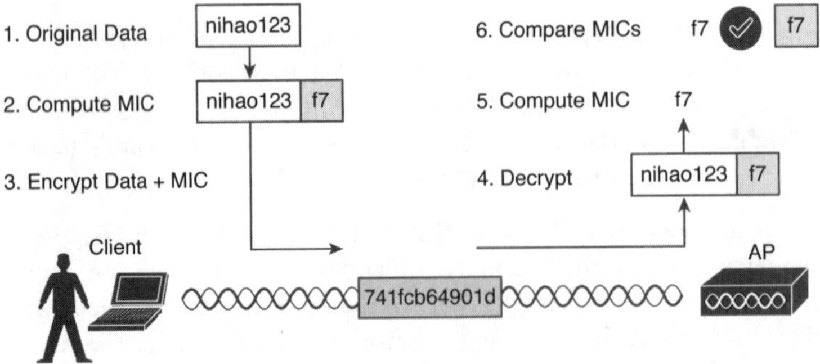

Figure 14-5 *Checking Message Integrity over a Wireless Network*

Intrusion Protection

Many of the tools in the wireless security framework operate as choreographed steps between a client and an AP. Because both the client and the AP are active participants in securing the connection between them, the data they are exchanging can be protected. In other words, much of the security framework focuses on keeping attackers from joining the wireless network and from tampering with existing associations.

Wireless attacks do not stop there; they can involve malicious activity from a variety of angles or vectors. A wireless intrusion detection system (IDS) can monitor wireless activity and compare that against a database of known signatures or patterns. Cisco APs can recognize some signatures and inform their controllers. Controllers have a set of 17 signatures that can match against data coming from many APs. Controller-based IDS can also detect rogue APs and contain them, if needed.

Cisco Prime Infrastructure (PI) is a wireless management system that can go even further by offering a wireless intrusion protection system (wIPS). The wIPS can recognize a rich set of hundreds of signatures, implementing customizable policies to blacklist clients or rogue devices and block SSIDs. It can also integrate with Cisco Mobility Services Engine (MSE) for granular analysis. Chapter 18, "Managing Cisco Wireless Networks," discusses the PI platform in greater detail.

For the CCNA Wireless exam, you should understand the basics of wireless IPS. Know that wireless security threats can be grouped into the following categories:

- Rogue devices
- Ad hoc networks
- Client association issues
- Passive or active attacks

Despite your best efforts to configure and secure every piece of your wireless network, someone could always bring in his own AP or wireless router and connect it to the wired network. A rogue AP is one that is not part of your wireless infrastructure but that is close enough to be overheard or to cause interference. Any clients that associate with a rogue AP are known as *rogue clients*. Cisco controllers can discover both.

Controllers can collect beacon information that is overheard by legitimate APs. Rogue AP detection algorithms running on the controllers and Prime Infrastructure can classify APs as rogue if they do not appear in the database of APs known to your network. As a wireless network administrator, you can override the classification and declare an AP as either friendly or rogue.

When coupled with an MSE, Prime Infrastructure can locate rogue APs so that you can go and find them. Controllers can even transmit special probe frames to determine if a rogue AP is connected to your wired network. This happens if the probe frames are received by the rogue AP over the air and then delivered back to the controller through the wired network.

Controllers can go one step further and attempt to contain the rogue AP so that it does not become a security risk to your own network. Over-the-air rogue containment works by listening for any wireless clients that associate with a rogue AP. The controller then sends spoofed deauthentication frames to those clients so that they think the rogue AP has dropped them.

Based on information gathered by the controllers, a wIPS can detect many types of wireless network attacks. Attacks can range from completely passive, such as an eavesdropper silently capturing wireless frames, to active ones that attempt to disrupt wireless service. For example, an attacker might send a flood of association requests to an AP to overwhelm it with fake potential clients—to the point where the AP can no longer service real clients. Another type of attack is similar to Cisco's rogue containment, where the attacker sends spoofed deauthentication frames to legitimate clients to continually knock them off the network.

Tip In a nutshell, controller-based IDS can detect and contain, while PI-based wIPS can detect, contain, and prevent. Although you should not need to know the specifics about wireless IDS and IPS and their respective attack signatures, you can investigate further on your own by navigating to **Security > Wireless Protection Policies** on a controller and **Services > Mobility Services > wIPS Profiles** in Prime Infrastructure.

Wireless Client Authentication Methods

You can use many different methods to authenticate wireless clients as they try to associate with the network. The methods have been introduced over time, and have evolved as security weaknesses have been exposed and wireless hardware has advanced. This section covers the most common authentication methods you might encounter.

Open Authentication

In Chapter 6, you learned about the frames that are used when a client asks to join a wireless network. The original 802.11 standard offered only two choices to authenticate a client: open authentication and WEP.

Open authentication is true to its name; it offers open access to a WLAN. The only requirement is that a client must use an 802.11 authentication request before it attempts to associate with an AP. No other credentials are needed.

When would you want to use open authentication? After all, it does not sound very secure, because it is not. With no challenge, any 802.11 client may authenticate to access the network. That is, in fact, the whole purpose of open authentication—to validate that a client is a valid 802.11 device by authenticating the wireless hardware and the protocol. Authenticating the user's identity is handled as a true security process through other means.

You have probably seen a WLAN with open authentication when you have visited a public location. If any client screening is used at all, it comes in the form of web authentication (WebAuth). A client can associate right away, but must open a web browser to see and accept the terms for use and enter basic credentials. From that point, network access is opened up for the client. Most client operating systems flag such networks to warn you that your wireless data will not be secured in any way if you join. Figure 14-6 shows an open WLAN discovered on a Windows-based client. Notice the shield-shaped caution icon and the security type Unsecured.

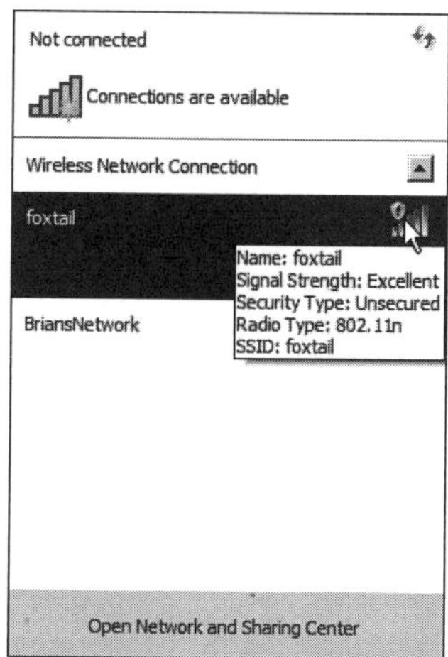

Figure 14-6 *Discovering a WLAN with Open Authentication*

WEP

As you might expect, open authentication offers nothing that can obscure or encrypt the data being sent between a client and an AP. As an alternative, the 802.11 standard has traditionally defined Wired Equivalent Privacy (WEP) as a method to make a wireless link more like or equivalent to a wired connection.

WEP uses the RC4 cipher algorithm to make every wireless data frame private and hidden from eavesdroppers. The same algorithm encrypts data at the sender and decrypts it at the receiver. The algorithm uses a string of bits as a key, commonly called a WEP key, to derive other encryption keys—one per wireless frame. As long as the sender and receiver have an identical key, one can decrypt what the other encrypts.

You can configure up to four WEP keys to be used on a WLAN, although only one of them can be active. The key number is included in the wireless frame so that the sender and receiver can know which one of the four to use.

WEP is known as a shared-key security method. The same key must be shared between the sender and receiver ahead of time, so that each can derive other mutually agreeable encryption keys. In fact, every potential client and AP must share the same key ahead of time so that any client can associate with the AP.

The WEP key can also be used as an optional authentication method as well as an encryption tool. Unless a client can use the correct WEP key, it cannot associate with an AP. The AP tests the client's knowledge of the WEP key by sending it a random challenge phrase. The client encrypts the challenge phrase with WEP and returns the result to the AP. The AP can compare the client's encryption with its own to see whether the two WEP keys yield identical results.

WEP keys can be either 40 or 104 bits long, represented by a string of 10 or 26 hex digits. As a rule of thumb, longer keys offer more unique bits for the algorithm, resulting in more robust encryption. Except in WEP's case, that is. Because WEP was defined in the original

802.11 standard in 1999, every wireless adapter was built with encryption hardware specific to WEP. In 2001, a number of weaknesses were discovered and revealed, so work began to find better wireless security methods. By 2004, the 802.11i amendment was ratified and WEP was officially deprecated. Both WEP encryption and WEP shared-key authentication are widely considered to be weak methods to secure a wireless LAN.

You might think such a clear call to move away from a weak or flawed security method would be easy and quick to achieve. In practice, it has taken many years to move away from WEP. Why?

Because WEP was implemented in wireless adapter hardware, any better security schemes had to leverage variations of WEP without the benefit of new cryptographic hardware. Wireless hardware manufacturers are usually reluctant to commit to build products until the technology is firmly established in the IEEE 802.11 standard. Therefore, WEP was an underlying theme for a very long time. In fact, for backward compatibility, you will still find it supported by clients, APs, and controllers even today. As you work through the rest of this chapter, notice how wireless security schemes have evolved and improved, and notice how many of them leverage WEP to some extent.

802.1x/EAP

With only open authentication and WEP available in the original 802.11 standard, a more secure authentication method was needed. Client authentication generally involves some sort of challenge, a response, and then a decision to grant access. Behind the scenes, it can also involve an exchange of session or encryption keys, in addition to other parameters needed for client access. Each authentication method might have unique requirements as a unique way to pass information between the client and the AP.

Rather than build additional authentication methods into the 802.11 standard, a more flexible and scalable authentication framework, the Extensible Authentication Protocol (EAP), was chosen. As its name implies, EAP is extensible and does not consist of any one authentication method. Instead, EAP defines a set of common functions that actual authentication methods can use to authenticate users. As you read through this section, notice how many authentication methods have *EAP* in their names. Each method is unique and different, but each one follows the EAP framework.

EAP has another interesting quality: It can integrate with the IEEE 802.1x port-based access control standard. When 802.1x is enabled, it limits access to a network media until a client authenticates. This means that a wireless client might be able to associate with an AP, but will not be able to pass data to any other part of the network until it successfully authenticates.

With open and WEP authentication, wireless clients are authenticated locally at the AP without further intervention. The scenario changes with 802.1x; the client uses open authentication to associate with the AP, and then the actual client authentication process occurs at a dedicated authentication server. Figure 14-7 shows the three-party 802.1x arrangement that consists of the following entities:

- **Supplicant**—The client device that is requesting access
- **Authenticator**—The network device that provides access to the network (usually a wireless LAN controller [WLC])
- **Authentication server (AS)**—The device that takes user or client credentials and permits or denies network access based on a user database and policies (usually a RADIUS server)

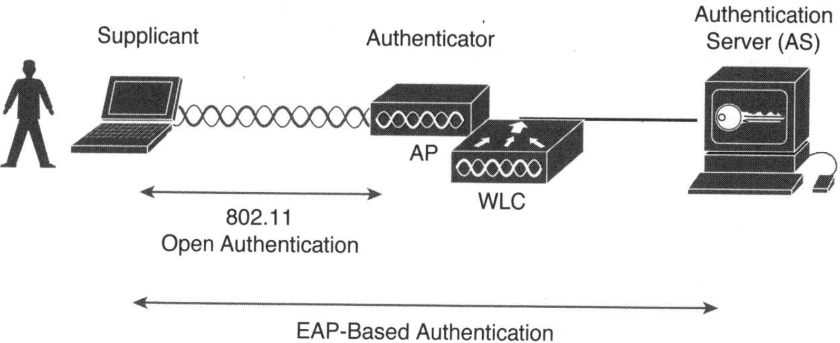

Figure 14-7 *802.1x Client Authentication Roles*

The controller becomes a middleman in the client authentication process, controlling user access with 802.1x and communicating with the authentication server using the EAP framework.

The following sections provide an overview of several common EAP-based authentication methods.

LEAP

As an early attempt to address the weaknesses in WEP, Cisco developed a proprietary wireless authentication method called Lightweight EAP (LEAP). To authenticate, the client must supply username and password credentials. Both the authentication server and the client exchange challenge messages that are then encrypted and returned. This provides mutual authentication; as long as the messages can be decrypted successfully, the client and the AS have essentially authenticated each other.

At the time, WEP-based hardware was still widely used. Therefore, LEAP attempted to overcome WEP weaknesses by using dynamic WEP keys that changed frequently. Nevertheless, the method used to encrypt the challenge messages was found to be vulnerable, so LEAP has since been deprecated. Even though wireless clients and controllers still offer LEAP, you should not use it.

EAP-FAST

Cisco developed a more secure method called EAP Flexible Authentication by Secure Tunneling (EAP-FAST). Authentication credentials are protected by passing a protected access credential (PAC) between the AS and the supplicant. The PAC is a form of shared secret that is generated by the AS and used for mutual authentication. EAP-FAST is a sequence of three phases:

- **Phase 0**—The PAC is generated or provisioned and installed on the client.
- **Phase 1**—After the supplicant and AS have authenticated each other, they negotiate a Transport Layer Security (TLS) tunnel.
- **Phase 2**—The end user can then be authenticated through the TLS tunnel for additional security.

Notice that two separate authentication processes occur in EAP-FAST—one between the AS and the supplicant and another with the end user. These occur in a nested fashion, as an outer authentication (outside the TLS tunnel) and an inner authentication (inside the TLS tunnel).

The PAC is made up of three parts:

- **PAC key**—A 32-octet key used to establish the tunnel
- **PAC-Opaque**—A variable length field that contains the user credentials
- **PAC-Info**—A variable length field used to pass information about the PAC issuer, PAC key lifetime, and so on

Like other EAP-based methods, a RADIUS server is required. However, the RADIUS server must also operate as an EAP-FAST server to be able to generate PACs, one per user.

PEAP

Like EAP-FAST, the Protected EAP (PEAP) method uses an inner and outer authentication; however, the AS presents a digital certificate to authenticate itself with the supplicant in the outer authentication. If the supplicant is satisfied with the identity of the AS, the two will build a TLS tunnel to be used for the inner client authentication and encryption key exchange.

The digital certificate of the AS consists of data in a standard format that identifies the owner and is "signed" or validated by a third party. The third party is known as a certificate authority (CA) and is known and trusted by both the AS and the supplicants. The supplicant must also possess the CA certificate just so that it can validate the one it receives from the AS. The certificate is also used to pass a public key, in plain view, which can be used to help decrypt messages from the AS.

Notice that only the AS has a certificate for PEAP. That means the supplicant can readily authenticate the AS. The client does not have or use a certificate of its own, so it must be authenticated within the TLS tunnel using one of the following two methods:

- **MSCHAPv2**—Microsoft Challenge Authentication Protocol version 2
- **GTC**—Generic Token Card; a hardware device that generates one-time passwords for the user or a manually generated password

EAP-TLS

PEAP leverages a digital certificate on the AS as a robust method to authenticate the RADIUS server. It is easy to obtain and install a certificate on a single server, but the clients are left to identify themselves through other means. EAP Transport Layer Security (EAP-TLS) goes one step further by requiring certificates on the AS and on every client device.

With EAP-TLS, the AS and the supplicant exchange certificates and can authenticate each other. A TLS tunnel is built afterward so that encryption key material can be securely exchanged.

EAP-TLS is considered to be the most secure wireless authentication method available; however, implementing it can sometimes be complex. Along with the AS, each wireless client must obtain and install a certificate. Manually installing certificates on hundreds or thousands of clients can be impractical. Instead, you would need to implement a Public Key Infrastructure (PKI) that could supply certificates securely and efficiently and revoke them when a client or user should no longer have access to the network. This usually involves setting up your own CA or building a trust relationship with a third-party CA that can supply certificates to your clients.

Tip EAP-TLS is practical only if the wireless clients can accept and use digital certificates. Many wireless devices, such as communicators, medical devices, and RFID tags, have an underlying operating system that cannot interface with a CA or use certificates.

Wireless Privacy and Integrity Methods

The original 802.11 standard supported only one method to secure wireless data from eavesdroppers: WEP. As you have learned in this chapter, WEP has been compromised, deprecated, and can no longer be recommended. What other options are available to encrypt data and protect its integrity as it travels through free space?

TKIP

During the time when WEP was embedded in wireless client and AP hardware, yet was known to be vulnerable, the Temporal Key Integrity Protocol (TKIP) was developed. TKIP is the product of the 802.11i working group and the Wi-Fi Alliance.

TKIP adds the following security features using legacy hardware and the underlying WEP encryption:

- MIC—An efficient algorithm to add a hash value to each frame as a message integrity check to prevent tampering; commonly called "Michael" as an informal reference to MIC.
- **Time stamp**—A time stamp is added into the MIC to prevent replay attacks that attempt to reuse or replay frames that have already been sent
- **Sender's MAC address**—The MIC also includes the sender's MAC address as evidence of the frame source.
- **TKIP sequence counter**—Provides a record of frames sent by a unique MAC address, to prevent frames from being replayed as an attack.
- **Key mixing algorithm**—Computes a unique 128-bit WEP key for each frame.
- **Longer initialization vector (IV)**—The IV size is doubled from 24 to 48 bits, making it virtually impossible to exhaust all WEP keys by brute-force calculation.

TKIP became a reasonably secure stopgap security method, buying time until the 802.11i standard could be ratified. Some attacks have been created against TKIP, so it, too, should be avoided if a better method is available. In fact, TKIP was deprecated in the 802.11-2012 standard.

CCMP

The Counter/CBC-MAC Protocol (CCMP) is that better method. CCMP consists of two algorithms:

- AES counter mode encryption
- Cipher Block Chaining Message Authentication Code (CBC-MAC) used as a message integrity check

The Advanced Encryption Standard (AES) is the current encryption algorithm adopted by U.S. National Institutes of Standards and Technology (NIST) and the U.S. government, and widely used around the world. In other words, AES is open, publicly accessible, and represents the most secure encryption method available today.

Before CCMP can be used to secure a wireless network, the client devices and APs must support the AES counter mode and CBC-MAC in hardware. CCMP cannot be used on legacy devices that support only WEP or TKIP. How can you know if a device supports CCMP? Look for the WPA2 designation, which is described in the following section.

WPA and WPA2

This chapter covers a variety of authentication methods and encryption and message integrity algorithms. When it comes time to configure a WLAN with wireless security, should you try to select some combination of schemes based on which one is best or which one is not deprecated? Which authentication methods are compatible with which encryption algorithms?

The Wi-Fi Alliance has worked out a couple of ways to do that. The IEEE 802.11i standard defines best practice wireless security methods. While that standard was still being developed, the Wi-Fi Alliance introduced its Wi-Fi Protected Access (WPA) industry certification. WPA was based on parts of 802.11i and included 802.1x authentication, TKIP, and a method for dynamic encryption key management.

Once 802.11i was ratified and published, the Wi-Fi Alliance included it in full in its WPA Version 2 (WPA2) certification. WPA2 offers the capabilities of WPA, to be backward compatible, while adding the superior CCMP algorithms. Table 14-2 summarizes the simple differences between WPA and WPA2.

Table 14-2 Comparing WPA and WPA2

	WPA	WPA2
Authentication	Pre-shared key or 802.1x	Pre-shared key or 802.1x
Encryption and MIC	TKIP or AES (CCMP)	AES (CCMP)
Key management	Dynamic key management	Dynamic key management

Notice that WPA and WPA2 specify 802.1x, which implies EAP-based authentication, but they do not require any specific EAP method. Instead, the Wi-Fi Alliance certifies interoperability with methods like EAP-TLS, PEAP, EAP-TTLS, and EAP-SIM.

Also notice that WPA can support either TKIP or AES for its data privacy and integrity, while WPA2 supports only AES. This is because TKIP has been deprecated. You should avoid using WPA and leverage WPA2 instead.

The WPA and WPA2 standards also support two authentication modes, based on the scale of the deployment:

- **Personal mode**—A pre-shared key is used to authenticate clients on a WLAN.
- **Enterprise mode**—An 802.1x EAP-based authentication method must be used to authenticate clients.

Tip Personal mode is usually easier to deploy in a small environment or with clients that are embedded in certain devices. Be aware that every device using the WLAN must be configured with an identical pre-shared key. If you ever need to update or change the key, you must touch every device.

Securing Management Frames with MFP

Normally, APs send 802.11 management frames on a BSS with no effort to secure the contents. When clients receive management frames, they assume that the frames were sent by legitimate APs that control their own BSSs. Malicious users can exploit this implicit trust by crafting their own spoofed management frames that appear to come from actual APs.

To mitigate attacks that leverage AP management frames, Cisco developed Management Frame Protection (MFP), which is available in the following two forms:

- **Infrastructure MFP**—To protect the integrity of management frames, APs add a MIC toward the end of each frame; other neighboring APs also participating in infrastructure MFP can determine whether overheard management frames have been tampered with and can alert their controllers.
- **Client MFP**—Protects the integrity of management frames through a MIC and encryption that only associated clients and neighboring APs can understand.

Notice that infrastructure MFP is based on a coordinated effort of APs only. Participating APs compute and tag management frames with a MIC value and then listen to detect any evidence of tampering. Wireless clients cannot participate.

Client MFP, in contrast, uses a MIC to protect management frame integrity and adds end-to-end encryption to protect the privacy of management frame contents. Clients must be capable of participating too, to decrypt the management frames and validate the MIC value. Clients using MFP can safely ignore any disassociation, deauthentication, and WMM quality of service (QoS) action frames that are broadcast and any unicast frames that are not signed.

To use client MFP, client devices must support Cisco Compatible Extensions Version 5 (CCXv5) and must use WPA2 with either TKIP or CCMP. This implies that the clients already have a secure relationship with the AP. This same secure link is used to send trusted management frames. The frames are encrypted in a way that only the MFP-capable client can understand. Infrastructure MFP does not require any special client feature.

The 802.11w amendment also addresses protection for management frames using a service called Protected Management Frames (PMF). Only management frames that are considered to be robust are protected: disassociation, deauthentication, and robust action. 802.11w uses security associations (SAs) to protect management frames to clients and an SA tear-down protection mechanism to keep malicious devices from spoofing information to tear down existing sessions. 802.11w also protects robust management frames that are broadcast or multicast using the Broadcast/Multicast Integrity Protocol (BIP). 802.11w can be used only on WLANs that are configured for WPA2 personal mode (pre-shared key) or WPA2 enterprise mode (802.1X) security.

Configuring Wireless Security

Wireless security is fairly straightforward to configure. Each WLAN has its own security policies. You can configure the security settings when you create a new WLAN or you can edit the parameters of an existing one. Keep in mind that you should use WPA2 and CCMP as a best practice. You can select personal or enterprise mode based on your environment and its security policies.

According to the CCNA Wireless exam blueprint, you should know how to configure WPA2 with pre-shared keys and 802.1x. You should also know how to configure EAP and RADIUS support on Cisco wireless LAN controllers. These topics are covered in the following sections.

Tip Wireless security methods are configured on a per-WLAN basis. The configuration steps you learn in this chapter will be applied in Chapter 15, "Configuring a WLAN."

Configuring WPA2 Personal

You can configure WPA2 personal mode and the pre-shared key in one step. Navigate to **WLANs** and select **Create New** or select the **WLAN ID** of an existing WLAN to edit. Make sure that the parameters on the General tab are set appropriately.

Next, select the **Security > Layer 2** tab. In the Layer 2 Security drop-down menu, select **WPA+WPA2**, as shown in Figure 14-8 for the WLAN named secure. In the WPA+WPA2 Parameters section of the Layer 2 page, you can enable WPA or WPA2 with the **WPA Policy** and **WPA2 Policy-AES** check boxes. In Figure 14-9, WPA2 has been selected.

Tip The controller will allow you to enable both WPA and WPA2 check boxes. You should do that only if you have legacy clients that require WPA support and are mixed in with newer WPA2 clients. Be aware that the WLAN will only be as secure as the weakest security suite you configure on it. Ideally, you should use WPA2 with AES/CCMP and try to avoid any other hybrid mode. Hybrid modes such as WPA with AES and WPA2 with TKIP can cause compatibility issues; in addition, they have been deprecated.

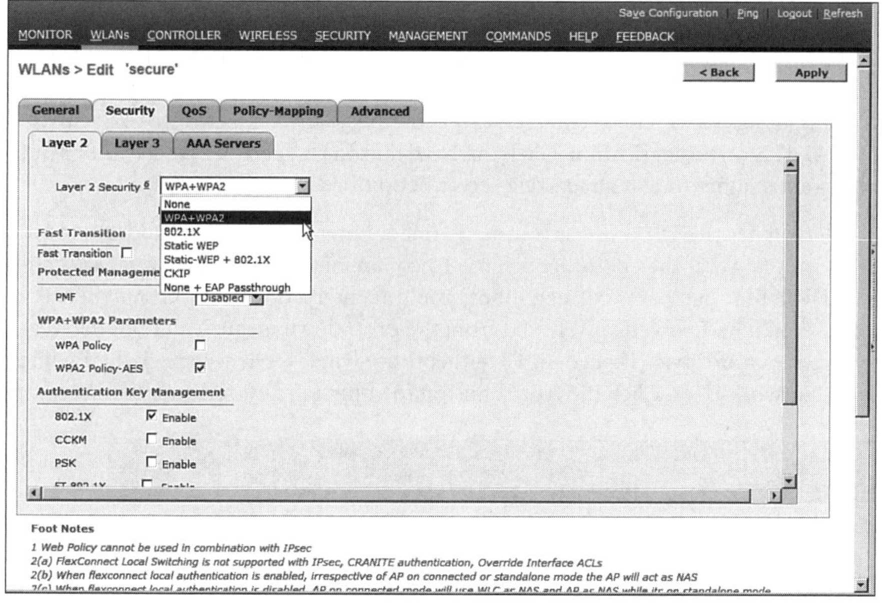

Figure 14-8 *Selecting the WPA+WPA2 Security Suite for a WLAN*

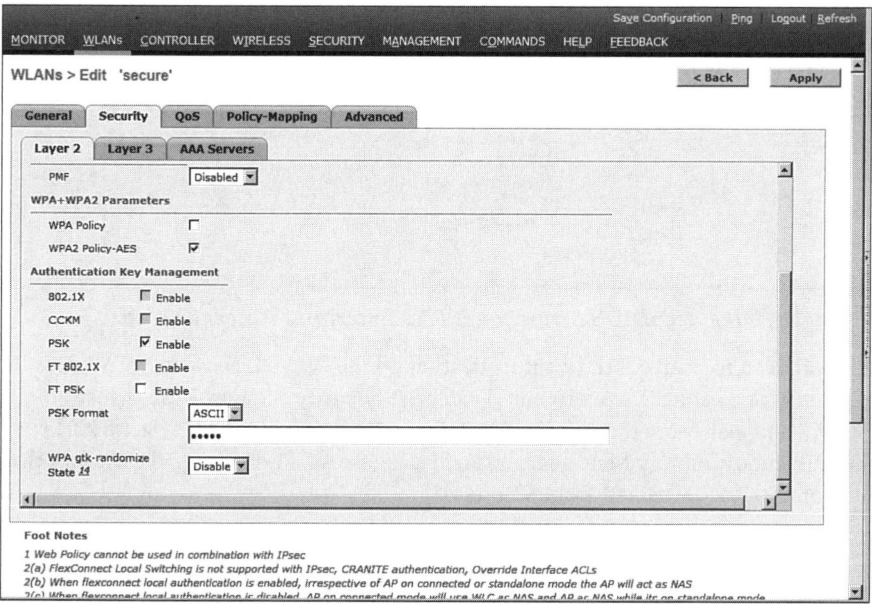

Figure 14-9 *Selecting WPA or WPA2-AES and Authentication Key Management*

For WPA2 personal mode, select to enable PSK under the Authentication Key Management settings section. This will use a pre-shared key to authenticate clients on the WLAN. Be sure to click the **Apply** button to apply the WLAN changes you have made.

Configuring WPA2 Enterprise Mode

You can use WPA2 enterprise mode to authenticate wireless clients with 802.1x and EAP through an external RADIUS server located somewhere on the wired network. You should begin by configuring one or more RADIUS servers on the controller. Navigate to **Security > AAA > RADIUS > Authentication.** Click the **New** button to define a new server or select the Server Index number to edit an existing server definition.

In Figure 14-10, a new RADIUS server is being defined. Enter the server's IP address and the shared secret key that the controller will use to communicate with the server. Make sure that the RADIUS port number is correct; if not, you can enter a different port number. The server status should be **Enabled**, as selected from the drop-down menu. You can disable a server to take it out of service if needed. To authenticate wireless clients, check the **Enable** box next to **Network User.** Click the **Apply** button to apply the new settings.

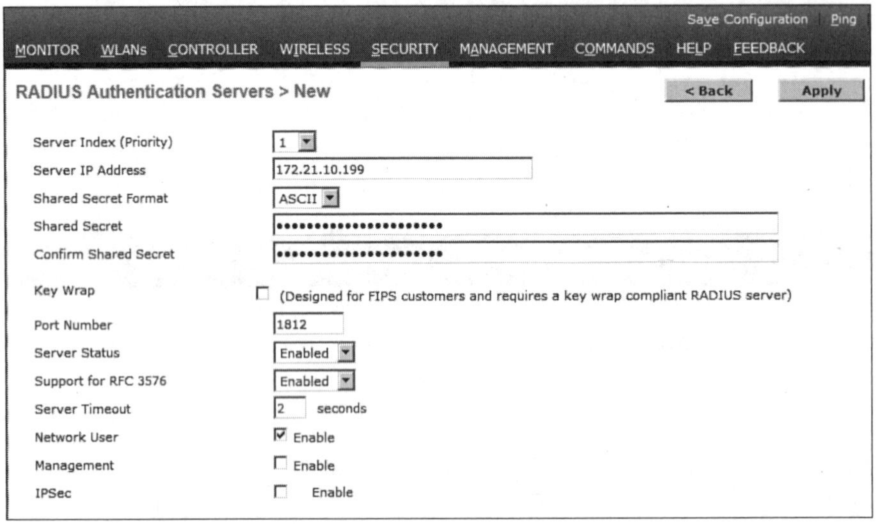

Figure 14-10 *Defining a RADIUS Server for WPA2 Enterprise Authentication*

Next, you will need to enable 802.1x authentication on the WLAN. Navigate to WLANs and select a new or existing WLAN to edit. Under the **Security > Layer 2** tab, select **WPA+WPA2** and make sure that the **WPA2 Policy-AES** box is checked. Select **802.1x** under the Authentication Key Management section. Figure 14-11 illustrates the settings that are needed on the WLAN named MoreSecure.

Tip The default settings for a new WLAN are WPA2 with AES and 802.1x.

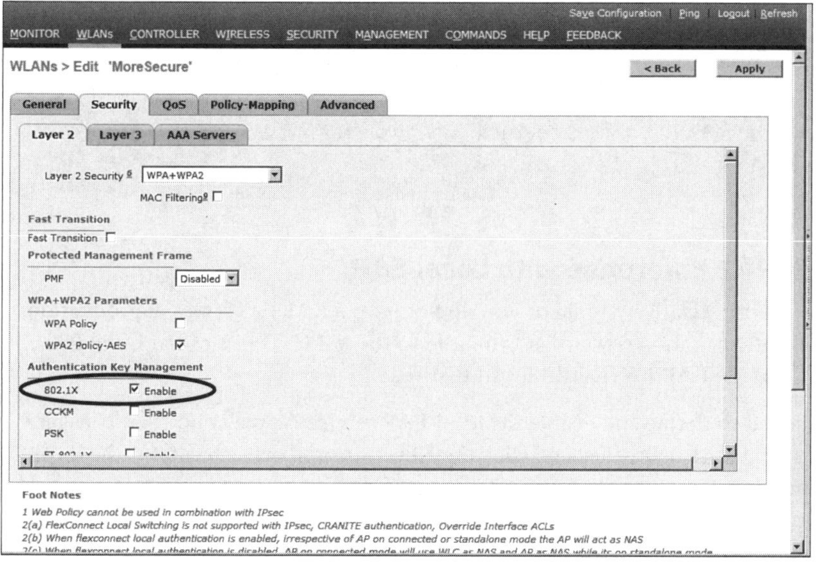

Figure 14-11 *Enabling WPA2 Enterprise Mode with 802.1x Authentication*

By default, a controller will use the global list of RADIUS servers in the order you have defined under **Security > AAA > RADIUS > Authentication.** You can override that list on the AAA Servers tab, where you can define which RADIUS servers will be used for 802.1x authentication. You can define up to three RADIUS servers that will be tried in sequential order, designated as Server 1, Server 2, and Server 3. Choose a predefined server by clicking the drop-down menu next to one of the server entries. In Figure 14-12, the RADIUS server at 172.21.10.176 will be used as Server 1. After you finish selecting servers, you can edit other WLAN parameters or click the **Apply** button to make your configuration changes operational.

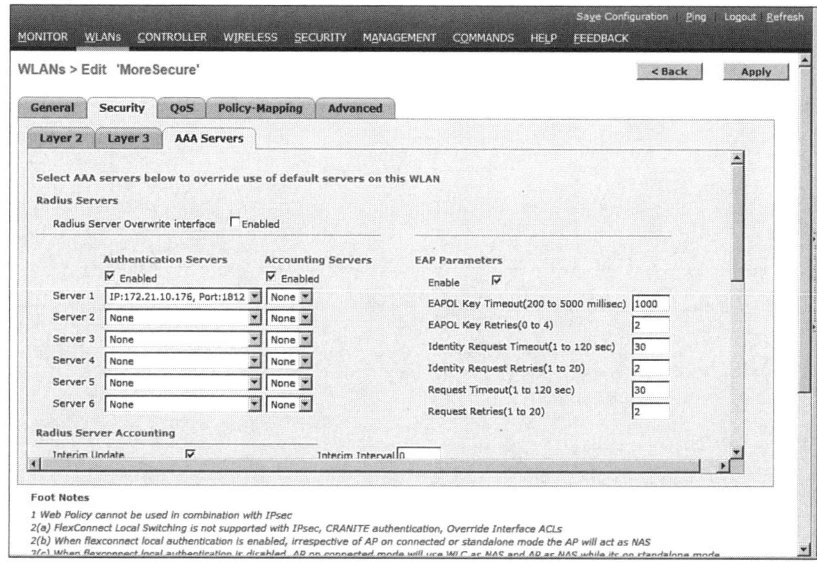

Figure 14-12 *Selecting RADIUS Servers to Authenticate Clients in the WLAN*

Tip As you worked through the WPA2 enterprise configuration, did you notice that you never saw an option to use a specific authentication method like PEAP or EAP-TLS? The controller only has to know that 802.1x will be in use. The actual authentication methods are configured on the RADIUS server. The client's supplicant must also be configured to match what the server is using.

Configuring WPA2 Enterprise with Local EAP

If your environment is relatively small or you do not have a RADIUS server in production, you can use an authentication server that is built in to the WLC. This is called Local EAP, which supports LEAP, EAP-FAST, PEAP, and EAP-TLS.

First, you will need to define and enable the local EAP service on the controller. Navigate to **Security > Local EAP > Profiles** and click the **New** button. Enter a name for the local EAP profile, which will be used to define the authentication server methods. In Figure 14-13, a new profile called MyLocalEAP has been defined. Click the **Apply** button to create the profile. Now you should see the new profile listed, along with the authentication methods it supports, as shown in Figure 14-14. From this list, you can check or uncheck the boxes to enable or disable each method.

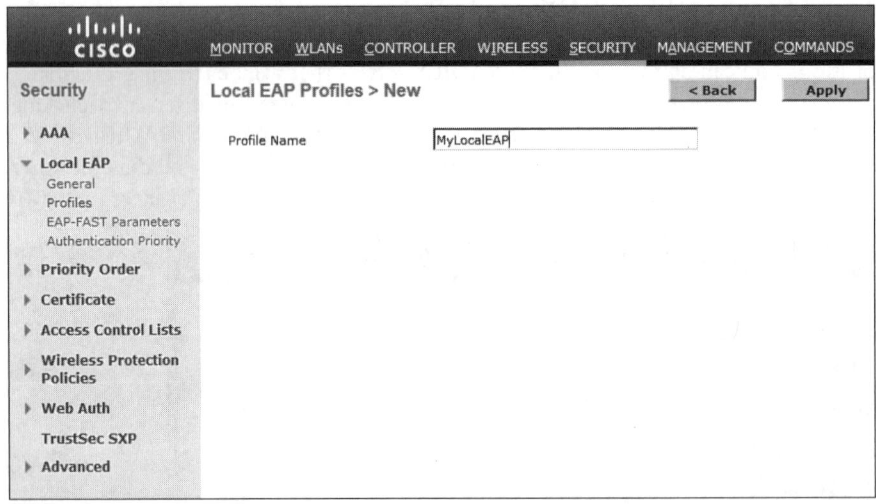

Figure 14-13 *Defining a Local EAP Profile on a Controller*

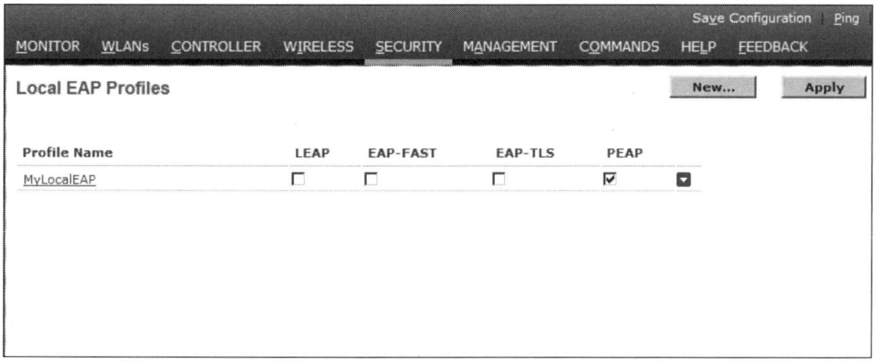

Figure 14-14 *Displaying Configured Local EAP Profiles*

Select the profile name to edit its parameters. In Figure 14-15, the profile named MyLocalEAP has been configured to use PEAP. Click the **Apply** button to activate your changes.

Figure 14-15 *Configuring a Local EAP Profile to Use PEAP*

Next, you need to configure the WLAN to use the Local EAP server rather than a regular external RADIUS server. Navigate to WLANs, select the WLAN ID, and then select the **Security > Layer 2** tab and enable WPA2, AES, and 802.1x as before.

If you have defined any RADIUS servers in the global list under **Security > AAA > RADIUS > Authentication** or any specific RADIUS servers in the WLAN configuration, the controller will use those first. Local EAP will then be used as a backup method.

To make Local EAP the primary authentication method, you must make sure that no RADIUS servers are defined on the controller. Select the **AAA Servers** tab and make sure that all three RADIUS servers use **None** from the drop-down menu. In the Local EAP

Authentication section, check the **Enabled** box to begin using the Local EAP server. Select the EAP profile name that you have previously configured. In Figure 14-16, the Local EAP authentication server is enabled and will use the MyLocalEAP profile, which was configured for PEAP.

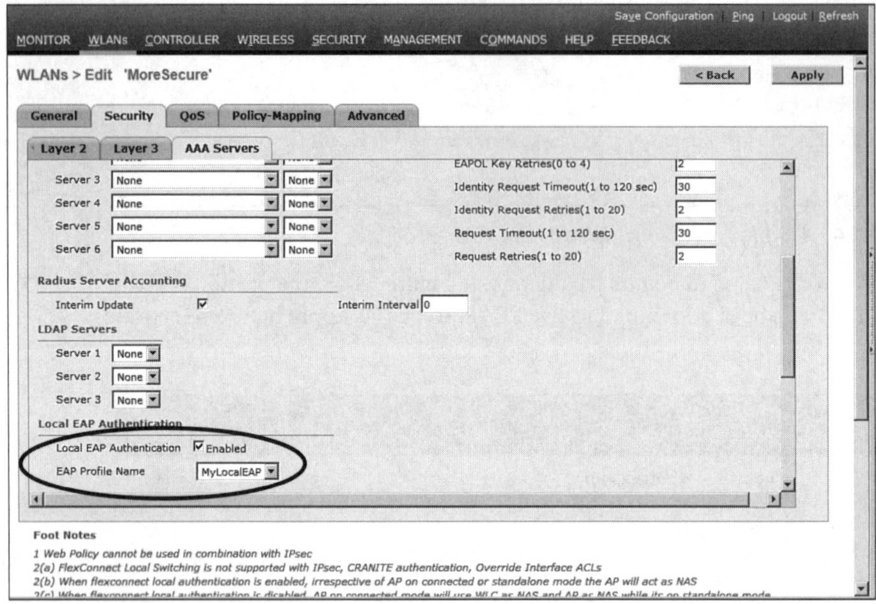

Figure 14-16 *Enabling Local EAP Authentication for a WLAN*

Because the Local EAP server is local to the controller, you will have to maintain a local database of users or define one or more LDAP servers on the controller. You can create users by navigating to **Security > AAA > Local Net Users**.

Exam Preparation Tasks

As mentioned in the section, "How to Use This Book," in the Introduction, you have a couple of choices for exam preparation: the exercises here, Chapter 21, "Final Review," and the exam simulation questions on the DVD.

Review All Key Topics

Review the most important topics in this chapter, noted with the Key Topic icon in the outer margin of the page. Table 14-3 lists a reference of these key topics and the page numbers on which each is found.

Table 14-3 Key Topics for Chapter 14

Key Topic Element	Description	Page Number
List	802.1x entities	339
Table 14-2	WPA and WPA2 comparison	342

Define Key Terms

Define the following key terms from this chapter and check your answers in the glossary:

802.11w, 802.1x, authentication server (AS), authenticator, certificate authority (CA), Counter/CBC-MAC Protocol (CCMP), EAP Flexible Authentication by Secure Tunneling (EAP-FAST), EAP Transport Layer Security (EAP-TLS), enterprise mode, Extensible Authentication Protocol (EAP), Lightweight EAP (LEAP), Management Frame Protection (MFP), message integrity check (MIC), open authentication, personal mode, protected access credential (PAC), Protected EAP (PEAP), Protected Management Frame (PMF), Public Key Infrastructure (PKI), RADIUS server, supplicant, Temporal Key Integrity Protocol (TKIP), Wired Equivalent Privacy (WEP), wireless intrusion protection system (wIPS), Wi-Fi Protected Access (WPA), WPA Version 2 (WPA2)

This chapter covers the following topics:

- **WLAN Overview**—This section provides a review of WLAN concepts and rules of thumb for their use.
- **Configuring a WLAN**—This section covers the steps necessary to create a WLAN on a Cisco wireless LAN controller.

This chapter covers the following exam topics:

- 3.3—Describe AP and WLC management access connections
  - 3.3c—Management via wireless
- 4.4—Describe and configure the components of a wireless LAN access for client connectivity using GUI only

CHAPTER 15

Configuring a WLAN

A wireless LAN controller (WLC) sits somewhere between wireless access points (APs) and a wired network. In this chapter, you learn how to define and tune a wireless LAN (WLAN) to reach devices on each of those networks. In addition, based on the concepts you learned in Chapter 14, "Wireless Security Fundamentals," you will be able to configure basic security parameters for the WLAN.

"Do I Know This Already?" Quiz

The "Do I Know This Already?" quiz allows you to assess whether you should read this entire chapter thoroughly or jump to the "Exam Preparation Tasks" section. If you are in doubt about your answers to these questions or your own assessment of your knowledge of the topics, read the entire chapter. Table 15-1 lists the major headings in this chapter and their corresponding "Do I Know This Already?" quiz questions. You can find the answers in Appendix A, "Answers to the 'Do I Know This Already?' Quizzes."

Table 15-1 "Do I Know This Already?" Section-to-Question Mapping

Foundation Topics Section	Questions
WLAN Overview	1–4
Configuring a WLAN	5–6

Caution The goal of self-assessment is to gauge your mastery of the topics in this chapter. If you do not know the answer to a question or are only partially sure of the answer, you should mark that question as wrong for purposes of the self-assessment. Giving yourself credit for an answer you correctly guess skews your self-assessment results and might provide you with a false sense of security.

1. Which two of the following things are bound together when a new WLAN is created?
   a. VLAN
   b. AP
   c. Controller interface
   d. SSID
2. What is the maximum number of WLANs you can configure on a Cisco wireless controller?
   a. 8
   b. 16
   c. 512
   d. 1024
3. What is the maximum number of WLANs that can be enabled on a Cisco lightweight AP?
   a. 8
   b. 16
   c. 512
   d. 1024
4. Which one of the following is a limiting factor when multiple WLANs are offered on an AP and its radio channel?
   a. The speed of the controller interface
   b. The airtime used for each WLAN's beacons
   c. Co-channel interference between WLANs on the AP
   d. The number of APs joined to the controller
5. Which of the following parameters are necessary when creating a new WLAN with the controller GUI? (Choose all that apply.)
   a. SSID
   b. VLAN number
   c. Interface
   d. BSSID
   e. IP subnet
6. The WLAN ID number is advertised to wireless clients. True or false?
   a. True
   b. False

Foundation Topics

WLAN Overview

Recall from Chapter 8, "Understanding Cisco Wireless Architectures," that a wireless LAN controller and an access point work in concert to provide network connectivity to wireless clients. From a wireless perspective, the AP advertises a service set identifier (SSID) for the client to join. From a wired perspective, the controller connects to a virtual LAN (VLAN) through one of its dynamic interfaces. To complete the path between the SSID and the VLAN, as illustrated in Figure 15-1, you must first define a WLAN on the controller.

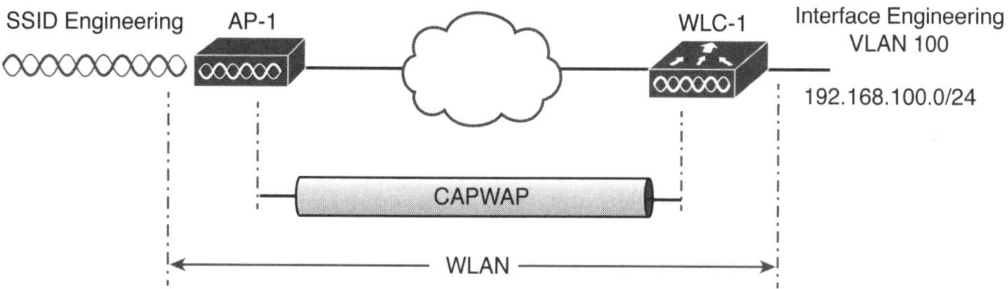

Figure 15-1 *Connecting Wired and Wireless Networks with a WLAN*

The controller will bind the WLAN to one of its interfaces and then push the WLAN configuration out to all of its APs by default. From that point on, wireless clients will be able to learn about the new WLAN and will be able to probe and join the new basic service set (BSS).

Like VLANs, you can use WLANs to segregate wireless users and their traffic into logical networks. Users associated with one WLAN cannot cross over into another one unless their traffic is bridged or routed from one VLAN to another through the wired network infrastructure.

Before you begin to create new WLANs, it is usually wise to plan your wireless network first. In a large enterprise, you might have to support a wide variety of wireless devices, user communities, security policies, and so on. You might be tempted to create a new WLAN for every occasion, just to keep groups of users isolated from each other or to support different types of devices. Although that is an appealing strategy, you should be aware of two limitations:

- Cisco controllers support a maximum of 512 WLANs, but only 16 of them can be actively configured on an AP. The Cisco 2504 Wireless Controller is limited to a maximum of 16 WLANs.
- Advertising each WLAN uses up valuable airtime.

Every AP must broadcast beacon management frames at regular intervals to advertise the existence of a BSS. Because each WLAN is bound to a BSS, each WLAN must be advertised with its own beacons. Beacons are normally sent ten times per second, or once every 100 ms, at the lowest mandatory data rate. The more WLANs you have created, the more beacons you will need to announce them.

Even further, the lower the mandatory date rate, the more time each beacon will take to be transmitted. The end result is this: If you create too many WLANs, a channel can be starved of any usable airtime. Clients will have a hard time transmitting their own data because the channel is overly busy with beacon transmissions. As a rule of thumb, always limit the number of WLANs to five or fewer; a maximum of three WLANs is best.

Configuring a WLAN

By default, a controller has no configuration and therefore no WLANs. Before you create a new WLAN, think about the following parameters it will need to have:

- SSID
- Controller interface and VLAN number
- Type of wireless security needed

As you work through this chapter, you will create the appropriate dynamic controller interface to support the new WLAN, then you will enter the necessary WLAN parameters. Both the centralized and converged wireless architectures are covered, as you can use a similar GUI for each type of WLC.

Configuring a RADIUS Server

If your new WLAN will use a security scheme that requires a RADIUS server, you need to define the server first. On a centralized controller, select **Security > AAA > RADIUS > Authentication** to see a list of servers that have already been configured, as shown in Figure 15-2. If multiple servers are defined, the controller will try them in sequential order. Click **New** to create a new server.

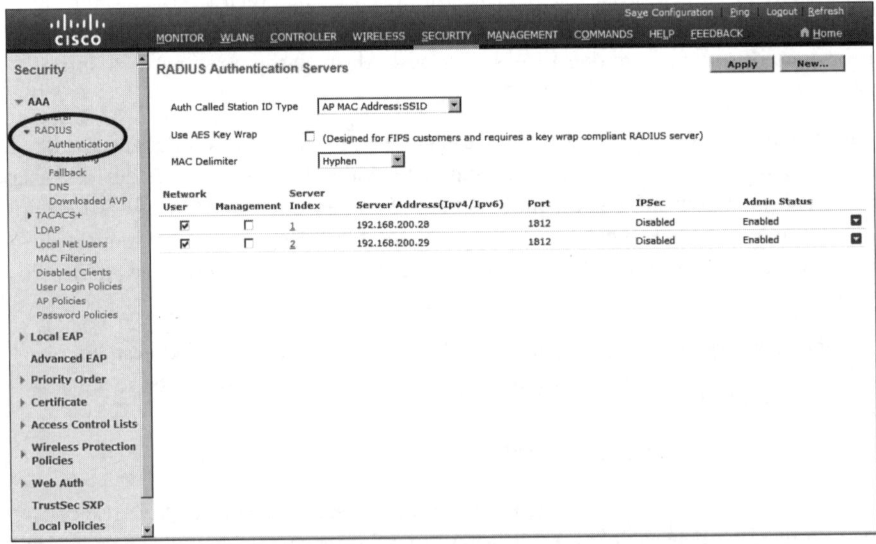

Figure 15-2 *Displaying the List of RADIUS Authentication Servers*

Next, enter the server's IP address, shared secret key, and port number, as shown in Figure 15-3. Because the controller already had two other RADIUS servers configured, the server at 192.168.200.30 will be index number 3. Be sure to set the server status to **Enabled** so that the controller can begin using it. At the bottom of the page, you can select the type of user that will be authenticated with the server. Check **Network User** to authenticate wireless clients or **Management** to authenticate wireless administrators that will access the controller's management functions. Click **Apply** to complete the server configuration.

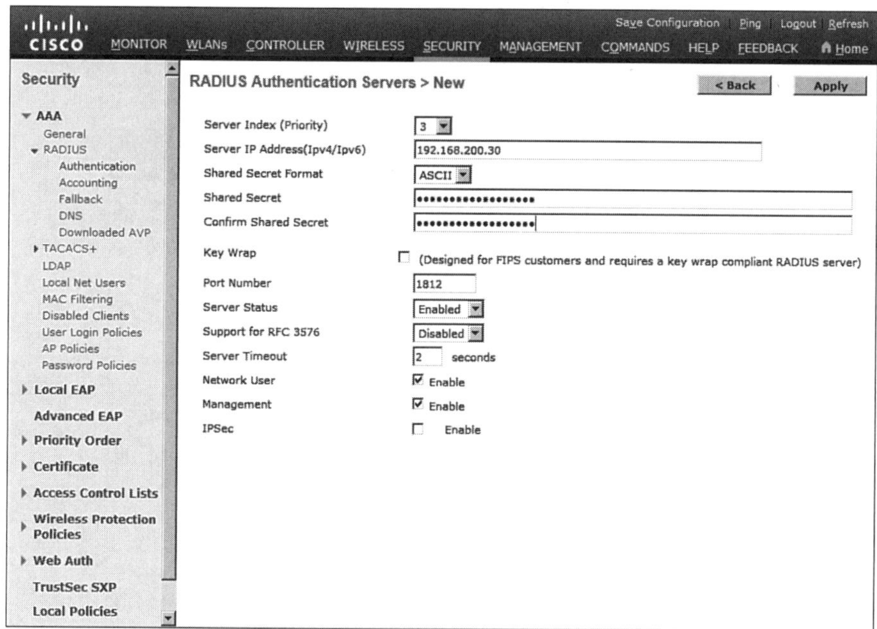

Figure 15-3 *Configuring a New RADIUS Server*

The process on a converged controller is similar, except that RADIUS servers are put into groups, then the group is applied as part of an authentication method list. The method list is used for authentication in any WLANs that are configured. Use the following steps to create a new RADIUS server.

Step 1. Select **Configuration > Security.**

Step 2. Under **Security > AAA > Radius > Servers**, click the **New** button to create a new RADIUS server entry. Enter the server's name, IP address, and shared secret key string. Repeat this step to create any further RADIUS servers.

Step 3. Create a RADIUS server group by selecting Security > AAA > Server Groups > Radius. Move desired servers from the Available Servers list to the Assigned Servers list.

Step 4. Select **Security > AAA > Method Lists > Authentication** and define a new method that uses the RADIUS server. Move desired server groups from the **Available Server Groups** list to the **Assigned Server Groups** list.

Creating a Dynamic Interface

In Chapter 10, "Implementing Controller-based Deployments," you learned about the different types of controller interfaces. A dynamic interface is used to connect the controller to a VLAN on the wired network. When you create a WLAN, you will bind the dynamic interface (and VLAN) to a wireless network.

To create a new dynamic interface on a centralized controller, navigate to **Controller > Interfaces**. You should see a list of all the controller interfaces that are currently configured. Click the **New** button to define a new interface. Enter a name for the interface and the VLAN number it will be bound to. In Figure 15-4, the interface named Engineering is mapped to wired VLAN 100. Click the **Apply** button.

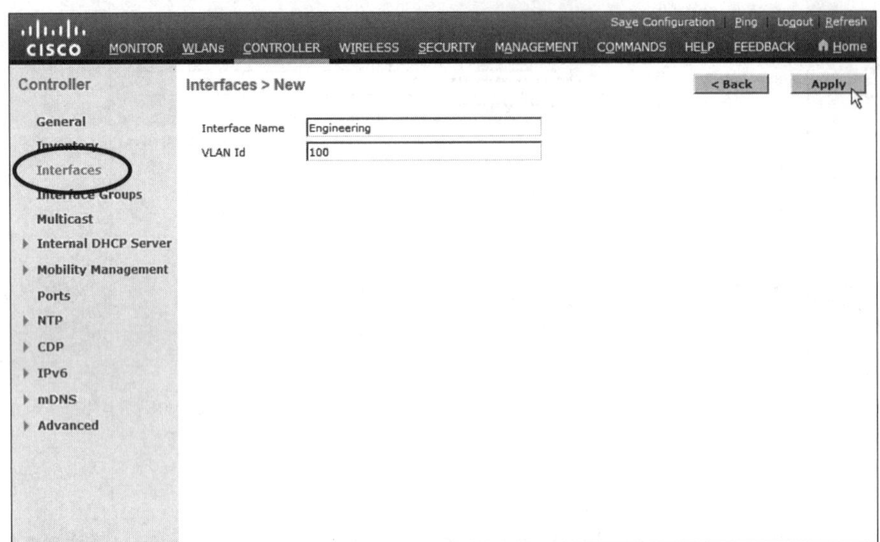

Figure 15-4 *Defining a Dynamic Interface Name and VLAN ID on a Centralized Controller*

Next, enter the IP address, subnet mask, and gateway address for the interface. You should also define primary and secondary DHCP server addresses that the controller will use when it relays DHCP requests from clients that are bound to the interface. Figure 15-5 shows how interface Engineering has been configured with IP address 192.168.100.10. Click the **Apply** button to complete the interface configuration and return to the list of interfaces.

The process is similar on a converged controller. Create the interface by selecting **Configuration > Controller > System > VLAN > Layer2 VLAN** and entering a VLAN number and name as shown in Figure 15-6. In essence, you are creating a VLAN on the switch that is hosting the WLC.

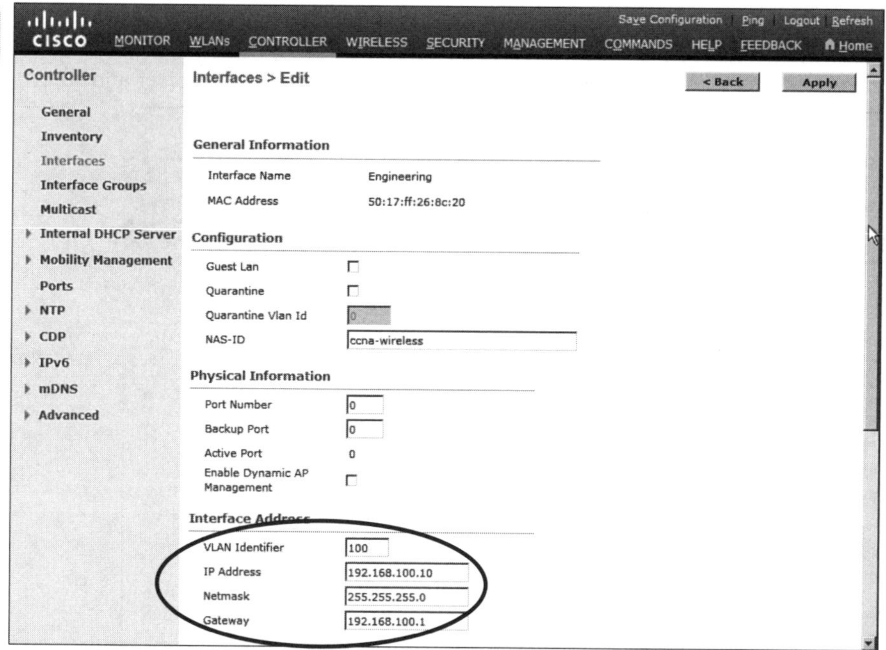

Figure 15-5 *Editing the Dynamic Interface Parameters on a Centralized Controller*

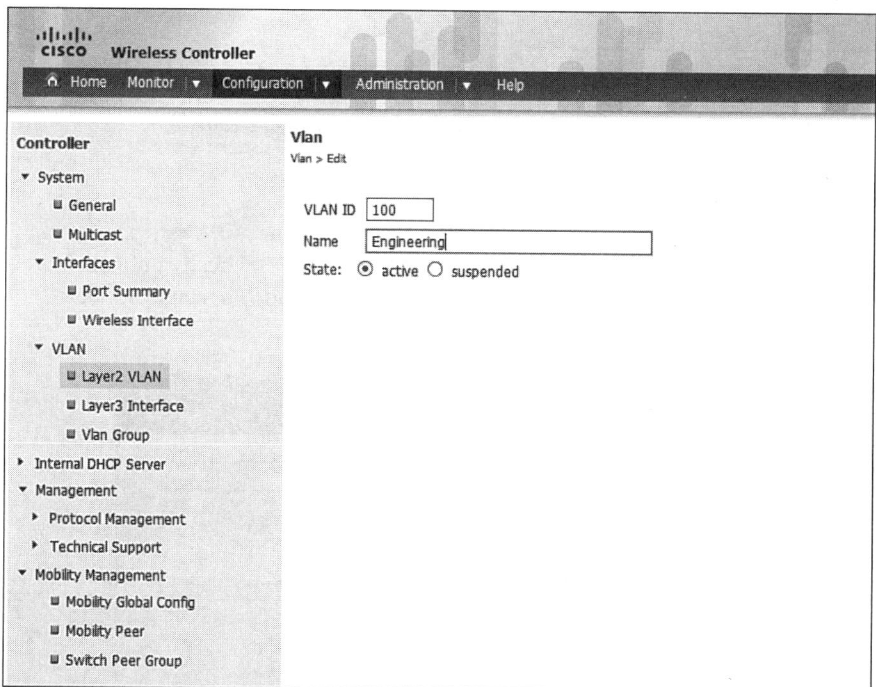

Figure 15-6 *Defining a VLAN on a Converged Controller*

Next, the dynamic interface needs a way to bring Layer 3 connectivity to the Layer 2 VLAN. Select **Configuration > System > VLAN > Layer3 Interface**, then click **New**. Enter the interface description, IP addressing information, and a DHCP server address as shown in Figure 15-7.

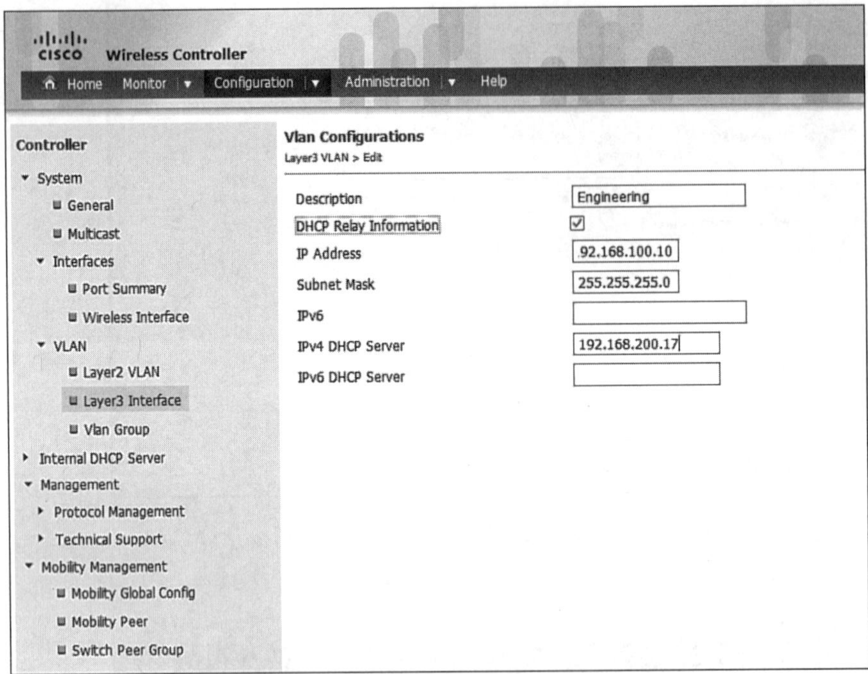

Figure 15-7 *Defining a Dynamic VLAN Interface on a Converged Controller*

Creating a New WLAN

You can display a list of the currently defined WLANs by selecting **WLANs** from the top menu bar. In Figure 15-8, the controller has one WLAN called guest already defined. You can create a new WLAN by selecting **Create New** from the drop-down menu and then clicking the **Go** button.

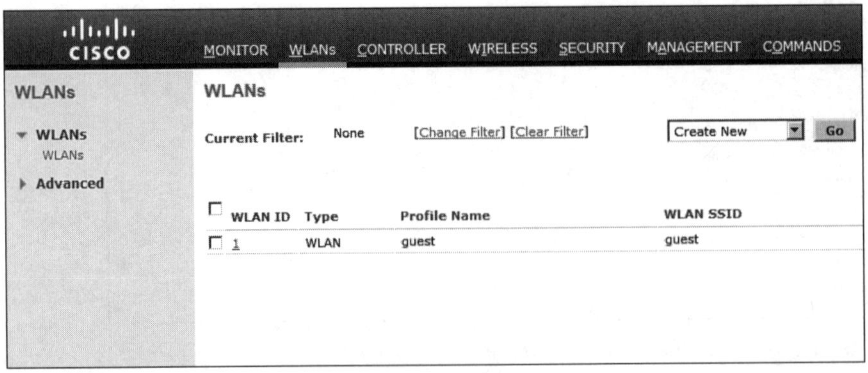

Figure 15-8 *Displaying a List of WLANs*

You can display the same list of WLANs on a converged controller by selecting **Configuration > Wireless > WLAN > WLANs.** Click **New** to create a new WLAN or select an existing WLAN from the list to edit its parameters.

Next, enter a descriptive name as the profile name and the SSID text string. In Figure 15-9, the profile name and SSID are identical, just to keep things straightforward. The ID number is used as an index into the list of WLANs that are defined on the controller. The ID number becomes useful when you use templates in Prime Infrastructure (PI) to configure WLANs on multiple controllers at the same time.

Tip WLAN templates are applied to specific WLAN ID numbers on controllers. The WLAN ID is only locally significant and is not passed between controllers. As a rule, you should keep the sequence of WLAN names and IDs consistent across multiple controllers so that any configuration templates you use in the future will be applied to the correct WLANs.

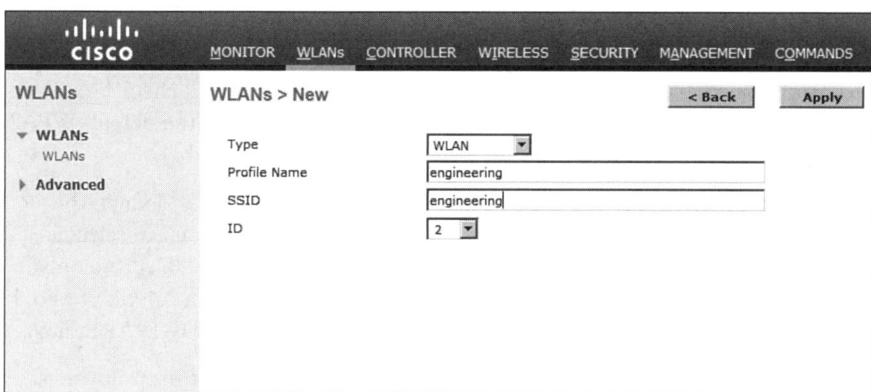

Figure 15-9 *Creating a New WLAN*

Click the **Apply** button to create the new WLAN. The next page will allow you to edit four categories of parameters, corresponding to the tabs across the top as shown in Figure 15-10. On a converged controller, you will have to select the newly created WLAN again from the list of WLANs. By default, the General tab is selected.

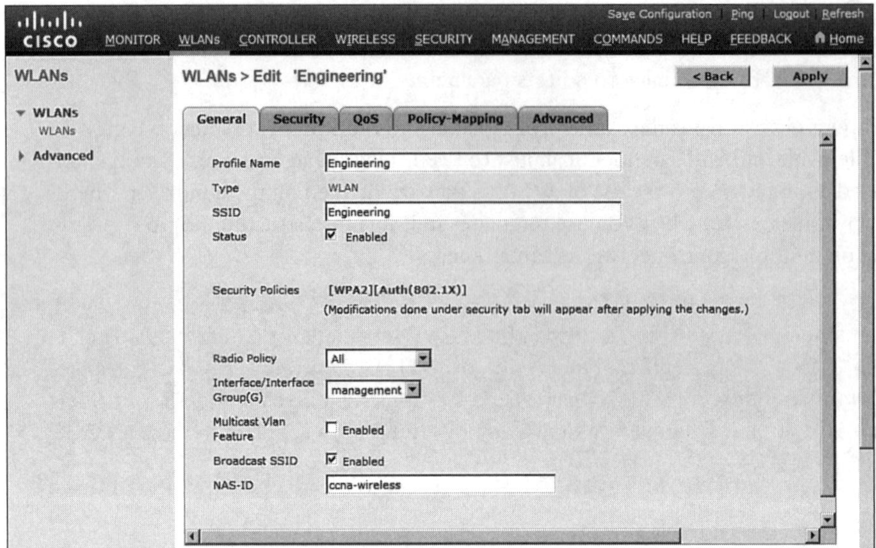

Figure 15-10 *Configuring the General WLAN Parameters*

You can control whether the WLAN is enabled or disabled with the Status check box. Even though the General page shows a specific security policy for the WLAN (the default WPA2 with 802.1x), you can make changes in a later step through the Security tab.

Under Radio Policy, select the type of radios that will offer the WLAN. By default, the WLAN will be offered on all radios that are joined with the controller. You can select a more specific policy with 802.11a only, 802.11a/g only, 802.11g only, or 802.11b/g only. For example, if you are creating a new WLAN for devices that have only a 2.4-GHz radio, it probably does not make sense to advertise the WLAN on both 2.4- and 5-GHz AP radios.

Next, select the controller interface that will be bound to the WLAN. The drop-down list contains all the interface names that are available. In Figure 15-10, the new engineering WLAN will be bound to the Engineering interface.

Finally, use the **Broadcast SSID** check box to select whether the APs should broadcast the SSID name in the beacons. Broadcasting SSIDs is usually more convenient for users, because their devices can learn and display the SSID names automatically. In fact, most devices actually need the SSID in the beacons to understand that the AP is still available for that SSID. Hiding the SSID name, by not broadcasting it, does not really provide any worthwhile security. Instead, it just prevents user devices from discovering an SSID and trying to use it as a default network.

Configuring WLAN Security

Select the **Security** tab to configure the security settings. By default, the Layer 2 security tab is selected. From the Layer 2 Security drop-down menu, select the appropriate security scheme to use. Table 15-2 lists the types that are available. You can also check the **MAC Filtering** check box to use client MAC addresses as authentication credentials.

Table 15-2 Layer 2 WLAN Security Types

Option	Description
None	Open authentication
WPA+WPA2	Wi-Fi protected access WPA or WPA2
802.1x	EAP authentication with dynamic WEP
Static WEP	WEP key security
Static WEP + 802.1x	EAP authentication or static WEP
CKIP	Cisco Key Integrity Protocol
None + EAP Passthrough	Open authentication with remote EAP authentication

In Figure 15-11, WPA+WPA2 security is selected. In the remainder of the page, you can set parameters that are specific to the security scheme. For example, WPA2 with AES is used, but WPA and TKIP are not.

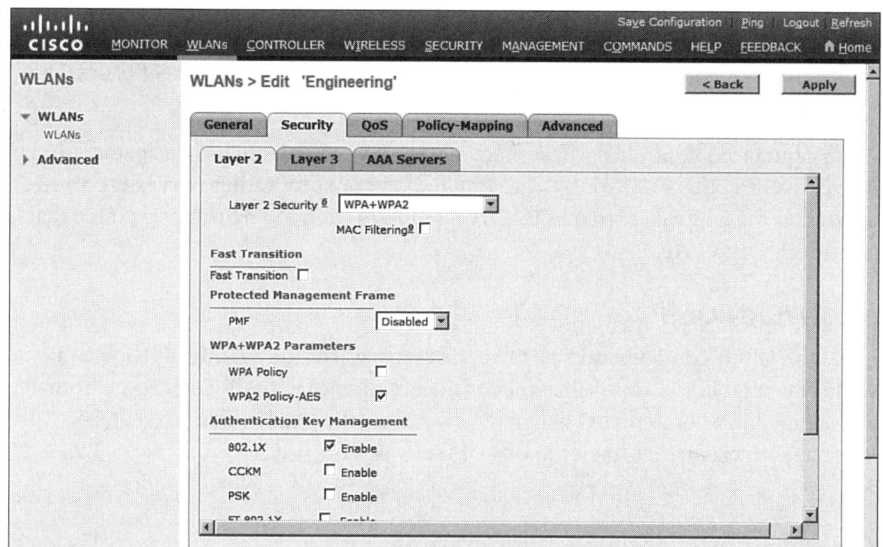

Figure 15-11 *Configuring Layer 2 WLAN Security*

If you choose a Layer 2 security scheme that requires a RADIUS server, the controller will use the global list of servers you have defined under Security > AAA > RADIUS > Authentication. You can override that list by identifying up to three specific RADIUS servers in the WLAN configuration. Display the **AAA Servers** tab, then under each server, you can select a specific server IP address from the drop-down menu of globally defined servers. Servers 1, 2, and 3 are tried in sequential order until one of them responds. In Figure 15-12, Server 1 is being set from a list of servers at 192.168.200.28, 192.168.200.29, and 192.168.200.30.

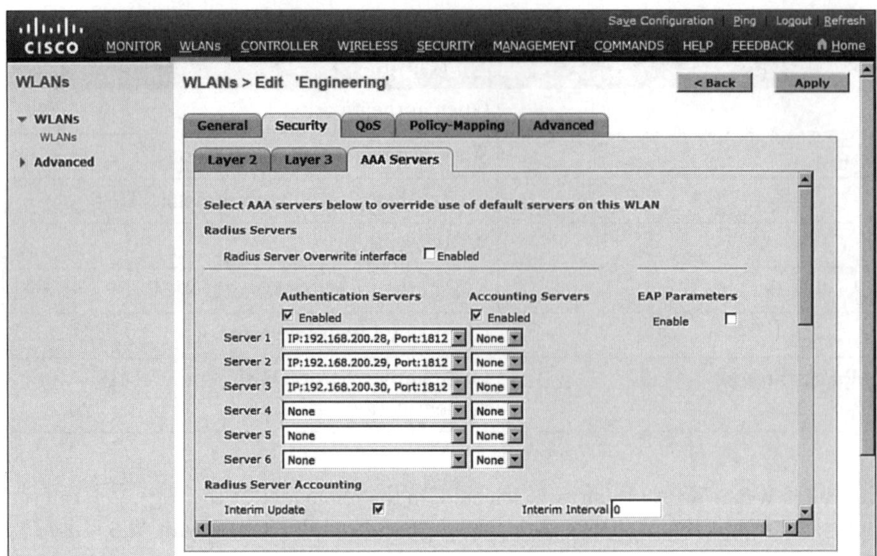

Figure 15-12 *Selecting RADIUS Servers for WLAN Authentication*

A converged controller is configured similarly, except that a method list is used to specify the authentication servers. Method lists are configured under **Configuration > Security > AAA > Method Lists.**

By default, a centralized controller will contact a RADIUS server from its management interface. You can override this behavior by checking the box next to **Radius Server Overwrite Interface**, so that the controller sources RADIUS requests from the dynamic interface that is associated with the WLAN.

Configuring WLAN QoS

Display the **QoS** tab to configure quality of service settings for the WLAN, as shown in Figure 15-13. By default, the controller will consider all frames in the WLAN to be normal data, to be handled in a "best effort" manner. You can set the Quality of Service (QoS) drop-down menu to classify all frames in one of the following ways:

- Platinum (voice)
- Gold (video)
- Silver (best effort)
- Bronze (background)

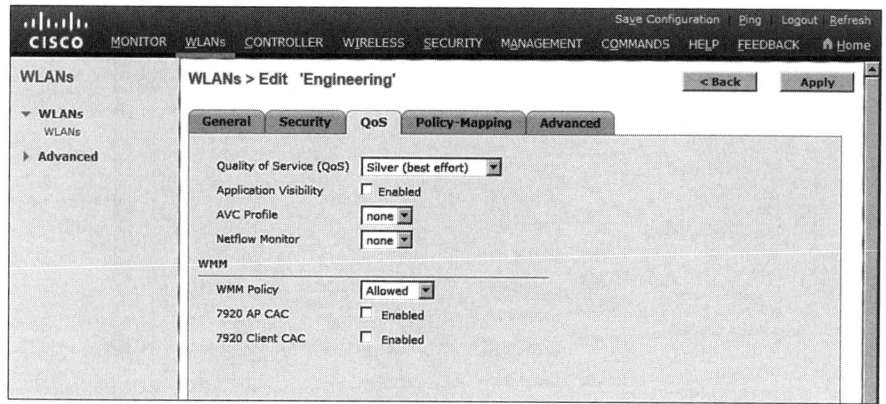

Figure 15-13 *Configuring QoS Settings*

You can also set the Wi-Fi Multimedia (WMM) policy, call admission control (CAC) policies, and bandwidth parameters on the QoS page.

Configuring Advanced WLAN Settings

Finally, display the **Advanced** tab to configure a variety of advanced WLAN settings. From the page shown in Figure 15-14, you can enable functions such as coverage hole detection, peer-to-peer blocking, client exclusion, client load limits, and so on.

Although most of the advanced settings are beyond the scope of the CCNA Wireless level, you should be aware of a few defaults that might affect your wireless clients.

By default, client sessions with the WLAN are limited to 1800 seconds (30 minutes). Once that session time expires, a client will be required to reauthenticate. This setting is controlled by the Enable Session Timeout check box and the Timeout field.

A controller maintains a set of security policies that are used to detect potentially malicious wireless clients. If a client exhibits a certain behavior, the controller can exclude it from the WLAN for a period of time. By default, all clients are subject to the policies configured under **Security > Wireless Protection Policies > Client Exclusion Policies**. These policies include excessive 802.11 association failures, 802.11 authentication failures, 802.1x authentication failures, web authentication failures, and IP address theft or reuse. Offending clients will be automatically excluded or blocked for 60 seconds, as a deterrent to attacks on the wireless network.

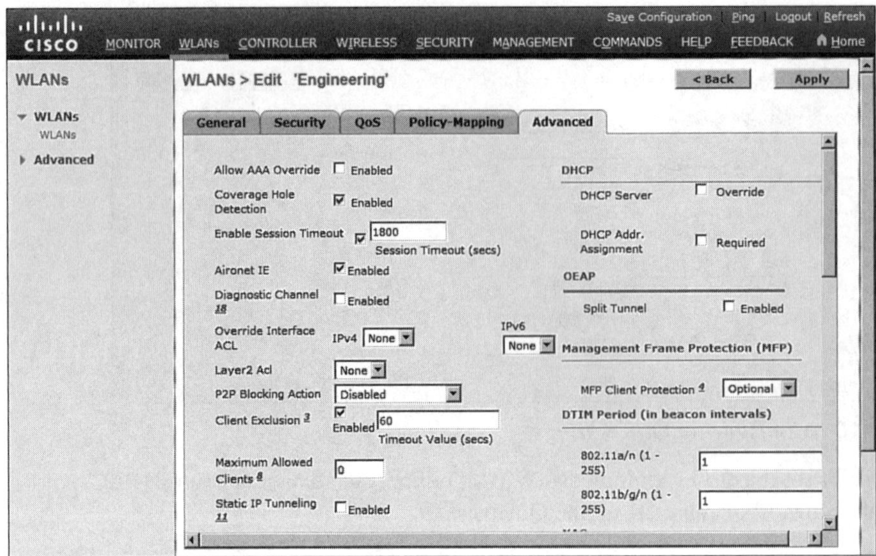

Figure 15-14 *Configuring Advanced WLAN Settings*

> **Tip** Is 60 seconds really enough time to deter an attack coming from a wireless client? In the case of a brute-force attack, where passwords are guessed from a dictionary of possibilities, 60 seconds is enough to disrupt and delay an attacker's progress. What might have taken 2 minutes to find a matching password without an exclusion policy would take 15 years with one.

Finalizing WLAN Configuration

When you are satisfied with the settings in each of the WLAN configuration tabs, click the **Apply** button. The WLAN will be created and added to the controller configuration. In Figure 15-15, the engineering WLAN has been added as WLAN ID 2 and is enabled for use.

Save Configuration Ping Logout Refresh
MONITOR WLANs CONTROLLER WIRELESS SECURITY MANAGEMENT COMMANDS HELP FEEDBACK Home

WLANs | WLANs | Entries 1 - 2 of 2

Current Filter: None [Change Filter] [Clear Filter] Create New Go

WLAN ID	Type	Profile Name	WLAN SSID	Admin Status	Security Policies
1	WLAN	Guest	Guest	Disabled	None
2	WLAN	Engineering	Engineering	Disabled	[WPA2][Auth(802.1X)]

Figure 15-15 *Displaying WLANs Configured on a Controller*

Be aware that by default, a controller will not allow management traffic that is initiated from a WLAN. That means you (or anybody else) cannot access the controller GUI or CLI from a wireless device that is associated to the WLAN. This is considered to be a good security practice because the controller is kept isolated from networks that might be easily accessible or where someone might eavesdrop on the management session traffic. Instead, you can access the controller through its wired interfaces.

You can change the default behavior on a global basis (all WLANs) by selecting **Management > Mgmt Via Wireless**, as shown in Figure 15-16. Check the box to allow management sessions from any WLAN that is configured on the controller.

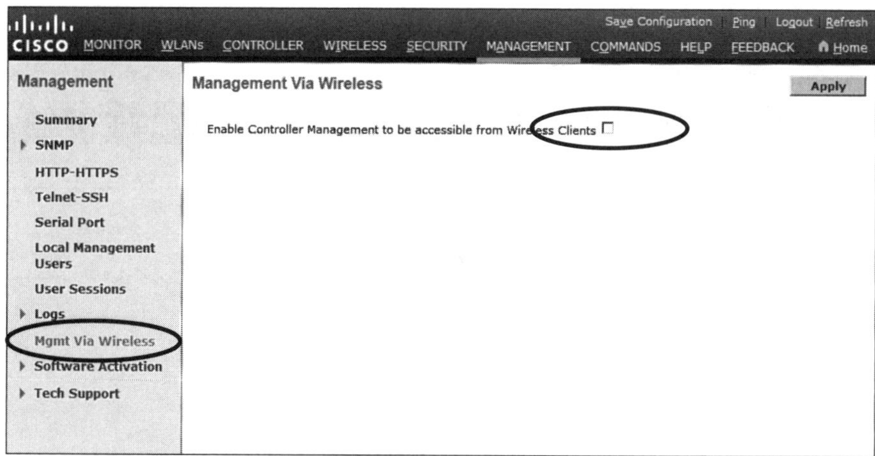

Figure 15-16 *Configuring Management Access from Wireless Networks*

Exam Preparation Tasks

As mentioned in the section, "How to Use This Book," in the Introduction, you have a couple of choices for exam preparation: the exercises here, Chapter 21, "Final Review," and the exam simulation questions on the DVD.

Review All Key Topics

Review the most important topics in this chapter, noted with the Key Topic icon in the outer margin of the page. Table 15-3 lists a reference of these key topics and the page numbers on which each is found.

Table 15-3 Key Topics for Chapter 15

Key Topic Element	Description	Page Number
Figure 15-5	Creating a dynamic interface	359
Figure 15-9	Creating a WLAN	361
Figure 15-11	Configuring WLAN security	363

This chapter covers the following topics:

- **Guest Network Overview**—This section describes a guest wireless network and how it can be used to segregate guests from other users on a network.
- **Configuring a Guest Network**—This section covers the process needed to implement a guest wireless LAN.

This chapter covers the following exam topics:

- 5.0—Configuration of Client Connectivity
- 5.1—Identify authentication mechanisms
  - 5.1a—LDAP, RADIUS, local authentication, WebAuth, 802.1X, PSK
- 5.2—Configuring WLAN authentication mechanisms on the controller
  - 5.2a—WebAuth, 802.1X, PSK
- 5.5—Describe wireless guest networking
  - 5.5a—Anchor controller
  - 5.5b—Foreign controller

Implementing a Wireless Guest Network

In Chapter 15, "Configuring a WLAN," you learned how to define and configure a new wireless LAN to support a community of clients that have something in common. You can even configure multiple WLANs to support multiple user communities. In most cases, the WLAN users are trusted at some level because they are a necessary part of your enterprise.

What about guest users, who might not be trusted or integral to your business? Guest users commonly need to access the wireless network as a convenience. This chapter discusses the steps you can take to configure a guest network as an extension to your wireless infrastructure.

"Do I Know This Already?" Quiz

The "Do I Know This Already?" quiz allows you to assess whether you should read this entire chapter thoroughly or jump to the "Exam Preparation Tasks" section. If you are in doubt about your answers to these questions or your own assessment of your knowledge of the topics, read the entire chapter. Table 16-1 lists the major headings in this chapter and their corresponding "Do I Know This Already?" quiz questions. You can find the answers in Appendix A, "Answers to the 'Do I Know This Already?' Quizzes."

Table 16-1 "Do I Know This Already?" Section-to-Question Mapping

Foundation Topics Section	Questions
Guest Network Overview	1–6
Configuring a Guest Network	7

Caution The goal of self-assessment is to gauge your mastery of the topics in this chapter. If you do not know the answer to a question or are only partially sure of the answer, you should mark that question as wrong for purposes of the self-assessment. Giving yourself credit for an answer you correctly guess skews your self-assessment results and might provide you with a false sense of security.

1. Which one of the following should be used to contain visitors and transient users of a wireless network?
   a. WPA2 enterprise
   b. Guest WLAN
   c. One-time WEP
   d. Broadcast SSID
2. Suppose a data WLAN and a guest WLAN are configured on a controller and mapped to two VLANs. Which one of the following is a true statement?
   a. The controller can route traffic between the two WLANs.
   b. The controller will bridge traffic between the two WLANs.
   c. The controller cannot route packets between the two WLANs.
   d. The controller can route packets between the two WLANs, but not the two VLANs.
3. To create a guest WLAN, which one of the following must be configured on a wireless controller?
   a. A private WLAN
   b. A guest mobility group
   c. A guest BSS
   d. A regular WLAN
4. Which one of the following correctly finishes this sentence? By default, all guest WLANs defined on controllers in an enterprise...
   a. are merged into one VLAN and subnet.
   b. are connected by CAPWAP tunnels.
   c. must be assigned the same WLAN ID number.
   d. are isolated from each other.
5. Which one of the following is necessary to merge guest WLANs from multiple controllers onto a common guest WLAN on a controller?
   a. RF group
   b. Global WLAN
   c. Mobility anchor
   d. Master controller
   e. Prime Infrastructure templates

6. In a wireless guest network, which one of the following statements is correct?
   a. A client associates with a guest mobility anchor controller and is tunneled to a guest foreign controller.
   b. A client associates with a guest foreign controller and is tunneled to a guest mobility anchor controller.
   c. A client associates with a guest mobility anchor and then must reassociate with a guest foreign controller.
   d. A client associates with a guest foreign controller and then must reassociate with a guest mobility anchor controller.

7. Which of the following pairs of phrases makes this sentence correct? You can configure ____________ as a ____________ for a guest WLAN.
   a. only one controller, mobility anchor
   b. multiple controllers, mobility anchor
   c. a mobility anchor, foreign controller
   d. a foreign controller, mobility anchor

Foundation Topics

Guest Network Overview

Wireless LANs are usually configured to support specific groups of clients or client devices. For example, one WLAN might support wireless users in the Engineering department, even if that department is scattered in several buildings or locations. Other WLANs might support a sales staff, teachers, students, and so on. These examples segment wireless users by function or the need to access certain enterprise resources. Each WLAN might have a different set of security policies from the others.

You might also decide to create WLANs to support different types of wireless devices. For example, one WLAN could be configured to support all medical devices in a hospital that can use only Wi-Fi Protected Access Version 2 (WPA2) with a pre-shared key (PSK). A separate WLAN could be created for users with medical devices that support WPA2 Enterprise, with digital certificates. In these cases, WLANs are created according to the wireless device capabilities.

As a wireless network administrator, you might be asked to provide connectivity for users who do not fall into any convenient category. Guest users are normally temporary visitors who need to access a wireless network to make their work and their time onsite more convenient. Because guests are not regular, trusted employees, you should always try to offer some basic network access while containing and isolating them from the trusted portion of your network.

In Figure 16-1, both guests and engineering staff are able to use the same wireless infrastructure, while the two user groups are kept isolated from each other. The engineering users can communicate directly with the company resources. However, the guest users are commonly placed within a demilitarized zone (DMZ) that has limited access and is secured by a firewall.

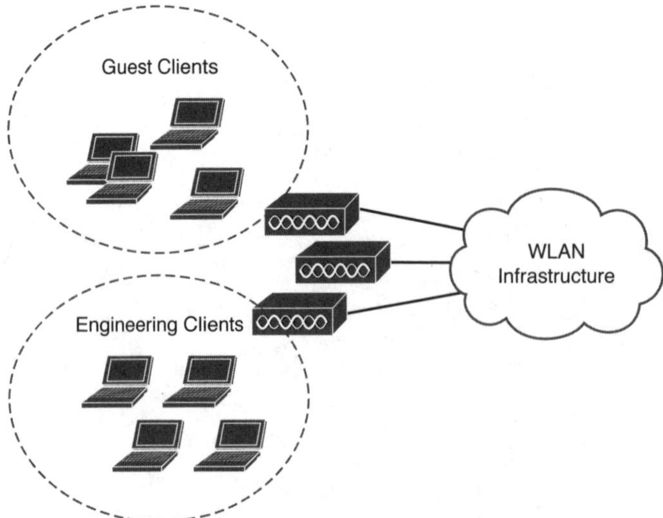

Figure 16-1 *Isolating Guest Wireless Users from Other User Groups*

Building a guest wireless network might seem like a complex task; however, it is really no different from building any other WLAN that is tailored for a user community. The trick is to provide the appropriate degree of isolation from the rest of the enterprise network.

The guest WLAN can be bound to a guest VLAN that is isolated from other VLANs, as shown in Figure 16-2. Before guest users can access the guest WLAN, they should be authenticated somehow. In addition, before they can access resources on any other WLAN or VLAN, a router or firewall should permit and provide the access.

16

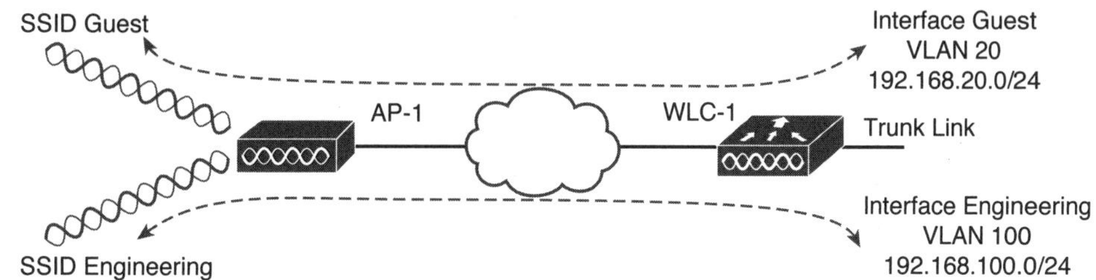

Figure 16-2 *Isolation Between a Guest and Other WLANs*

In Figure 16-2, the Guest WLAN advertises service set identifier (SSID) Guest and is bound to the controller's Guest interface on VLAN 20. The same access point (AP) and controller infrastructure has an Engineering WLAN that is bound to the controller's Engineering interface on VLAN 100.

Because all web browsers on all platforms use HTTP and HTTPS, the web browser is a universal interface for users to be authenticated before granting them wireless access. Cisco wireless LAN controllers (WLCs) support web authentication for this purpose. Users are presented with a web authentication splash page that includes a challenge for credentials.

Web authentication can be handled locally on the WLC for smaller environments through local web authentication (LWA). You can configure LWA in the following modes:

- LWA with an internal database on the WLC
- LWA with an external database on a RADIUS or LDAP server
- LWA with an external redirect after authentication
- LWA with an external splash page redirect, using an internal database on the WLC

When there are many controllers providing web authentication, it makes sense to use LWA with an external database on a RADIUS server, keeping the user database centralized. The next logical progression is to move the web authentication page onto the central server too. This is called central web authentication (CWA).

Scaling the Guest Network

Building a guest WLAN on a single controller is straightforward. The guest WLAN is just like any other WLAN defined on the controller. In larger installations, you might have more than one controller. In that case, each guest WLAN terminates on its own controller, making it difficult to isolate all guest clients in a single DMZ or behind a single firewall.

Recall from Chapter 12, "Understanding Roaming," that Cisco WLCs can support Layer 3 roaming by automatically building a tunnel between the first controller a client associates with and the controller where the client is currently located. In effect, the client is tunneled from a foreign controller back to the original anchor controller. This same tunneling strategy can be leveraged to funnel guest clients from any controller into a mobility anchor controller where guests share a common IP subnet and security policies.

Where Layer 3 roaming builds controller-to-controller tunnels to follow clients as they move, mobility anchors are configured ahead of time so that guest clients will be tunneled to one or more predetermined anchor controllers. Figure 16-3 illustrates the concept with three WLCs. Each WLC is configured with its own guest WLAN, but only WLC-1 is identified as a mobility anchor. The other two, WLC-2 and WLC-3, become foreign controllers that point to WLC-1 as their mobility anchor controller. Regardless of which controller a guest user joins, the user will be tunneled to the anchor and connected into the guest VLAN. You can also identify several mobility anchors so that guest users can be distributed across them to balance the load.

Tip In many implementations, the controller used as a mobility anchor for a guest network does not even have any APs joined to it. Instead, it acts as the final destination for the guest WLANs across an entire enterprise network. Without APs to support, the anchor controller can devote more resources toward handling guest users.

Key Topic

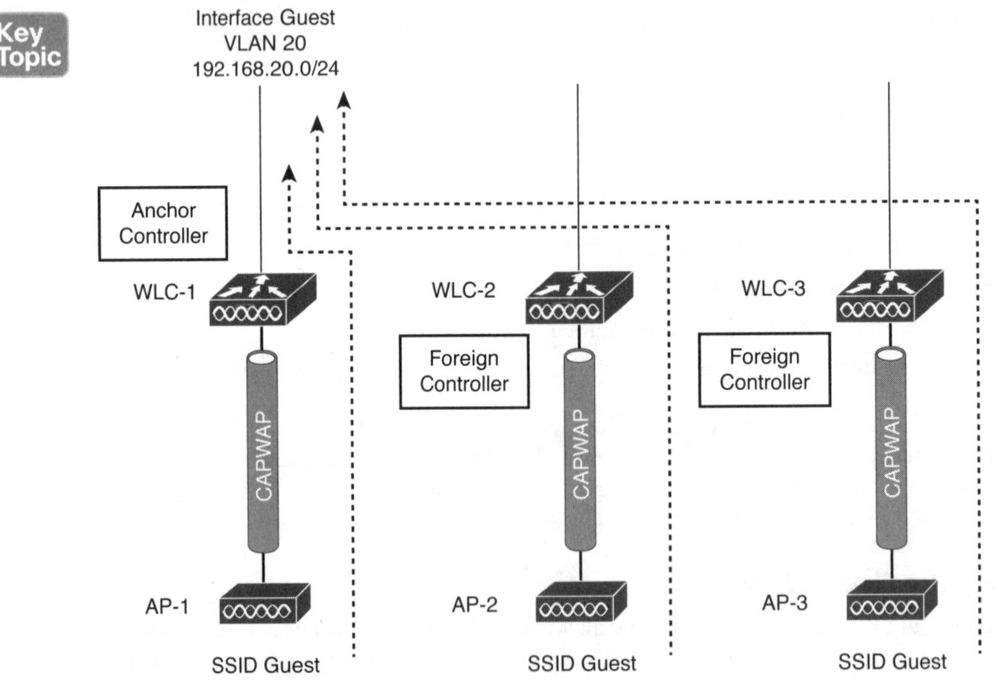

Figure 16-3 *Using Mobility Anchors to Consolidate Guest Wireless Clients*

Configuring a Guest Network

You can use the following steps to configure a guest network. As you work through the steps, notice that the guest network requires a dynamic interface, a WLAN, and an authentication method—much like any other WLAN.

Step 1. Create a dynamic interface for the guest WLAN. Under **Controller > Interfaces > New**, define the dynamic interface, the VLAN ID, and the IP addressing information. Figures 16-4 and 16-5 show an interface named Guest configured for VLAN 20 and the 192.168.20.0/24 subnet.

Figure 16-4 *Creating a Controller Interface for a Guest WLAN*

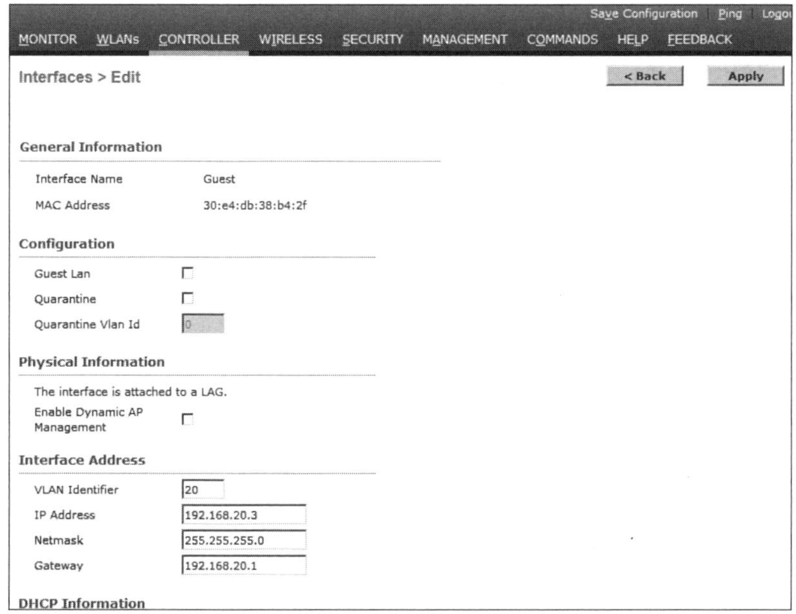

Figure 16-5 *Configuring IP Address Information on the Guest Interface*

Step 2. Create the guest WLAN.

Select **WLAN > New** to define a new WLAN, and then enter the profile name and SSID. In Figure 16-6, the controller has been configured with a second WLAN (ID 2) that uses SSID Guest.

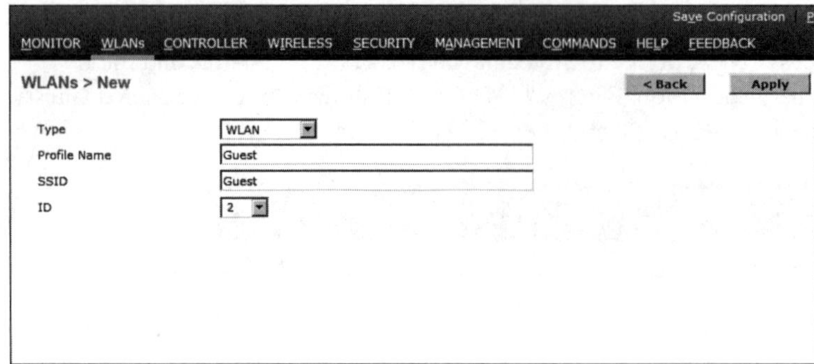

Figure 16-6 *Creating a Guest WLAN*

Step 3. Bind the guest WLAN to the guest WLAN interface.

On the **General** tab of the WLAN, select the guest controller interface to be used. In Figure 16-7, the Guest WLAN is configured to use the Guest dynamic interface. The dynamic interface does not matter on the foreign controller, as traffic is sent to the anchor and its dynamic interface. If PSK authentication is used, only the foreign controller needs the PSK configuration. If external RADIUS authentication is used, only the anchor controller needs the RADIUS configuration. All other WLAN parameters must be identical on the anchor and foreign controllers; otherwise, the two controllers will conclude that their WLANs are different and so no tunneling should occur.

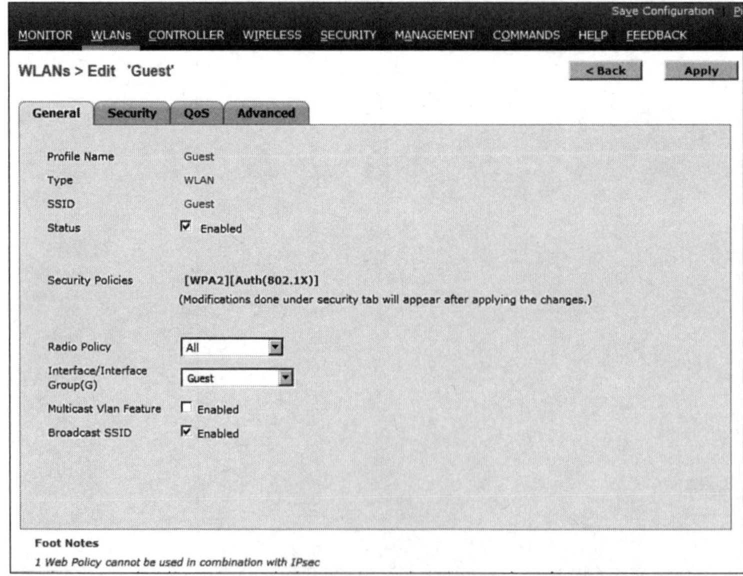

Figure 16-7 *Assigning a Dynamic Interface to the Guest WLAN*

Step 4. Configure the wireless security method.

On the Security tab, you can select the Layer 2 tab to choose a wireless security scheme to be used on the WLAN. In Figure 16-8, open authentication will be used because the None method has been selected.

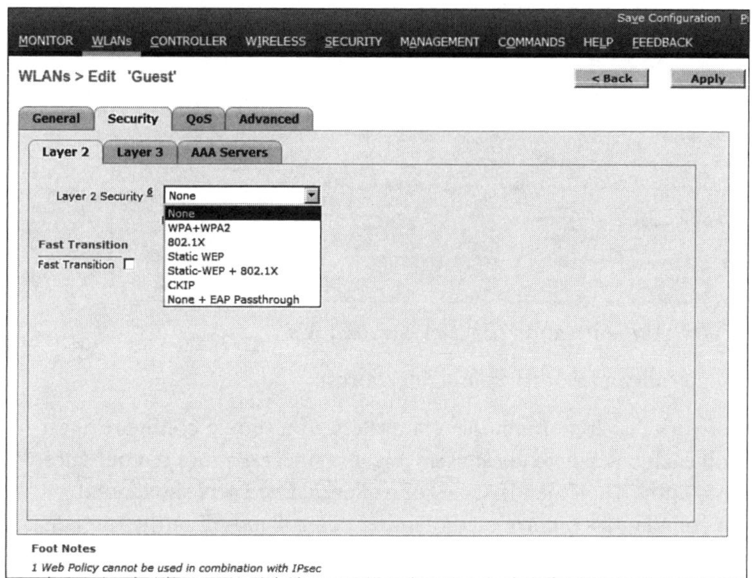

Figure 16-8 *Selecting Open Authentication for the Guest WLAN*

Step 5. Configure web authentication.

Select the **Security > Layer 3** tab, then choose Layer 3 Security type **Web Policy**, as shown in Figure 16-9. When the **Authentication** radio button is selected (the default), web authentication will be performed locally on the WLC. You will also need to define local usernames that will be used when guest users authenticate.

Be sure to visit the **QoS** and **Advanced** tabs to complete the guest WLAN configuration.

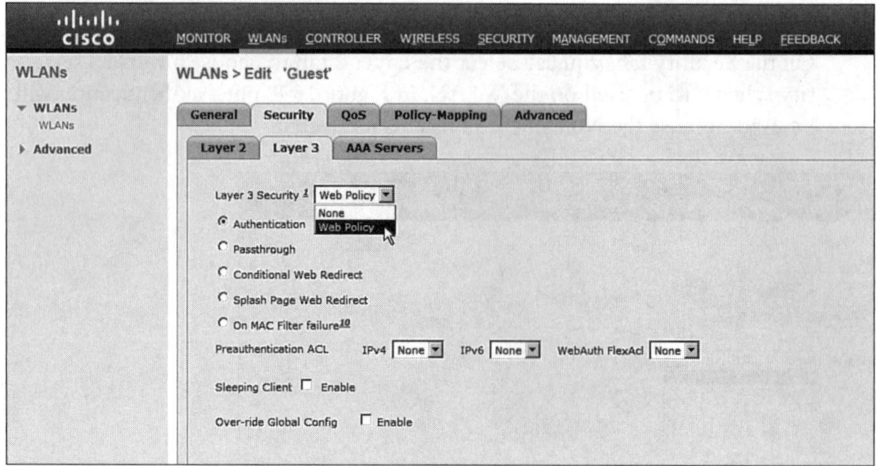

Figure 16-9 *Selecting Web Authentication for the Guest WLAN*

Step 6. Configure mobility anchors (for larger networks).

If your network consists of multiple controllers, you should configure guest WLANs on each one where guest users might connect. Be sure to configure them consistently. Then identify one controller that will serve as a mobility anchor for all guest users hosted by other controllers. All of the foreign controllers (the ones you are configuring) should be configured in the same mobility group to allow roaming, as described in Chapter 12, "Understanding Roaming." The anchor controller does not need to be in the same mobility group because no roaming is expected between APs on the foreign controller and APs on the anchor. In fact, it is common practice to purposely configure the anchor in a different mobility group to prevent any risk of roaming.

Be aware that even the anchor controller must be configured with an anchor controller (itself) so that it will accept guest wireless tunnels from the foreign guest controllers. Select the **WLANs** tab to display the list of WLANs. At the far-right end of the guest WLAN entry, right-click the blue triangle, and then select **Mobility Anchors** from the drop-down menu, as shown in Figure 16-10.

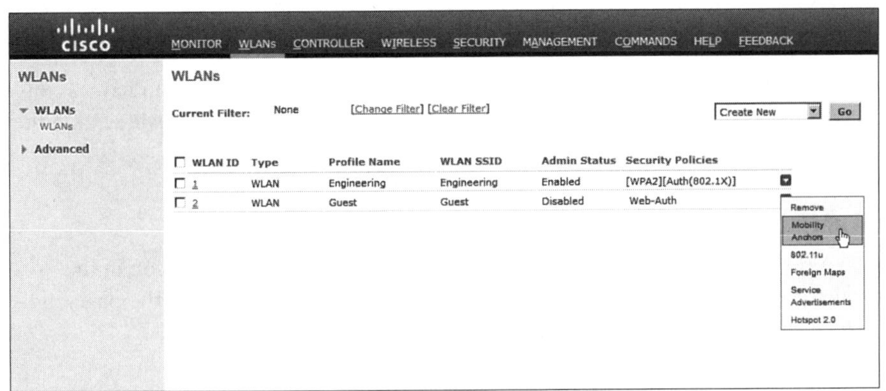

Figure 16-10 *Displaying Mobility Anchors for a Guest WLAN*

From the **Switch IP Address (Anchor)** drop-down menu, select the anchor controller from the list of controllers that are members of the mobility group. The local entry that is displayed in the list of switch IP addresses represents the controller you are configuring. Click the **Mobility Anchor Create** button as shown in Figure 16-11. Once the foreign and anchor controllers know about their new relationship, they will display the status of their mobility tunnel. You should see the control and data paths listed as "**up**."

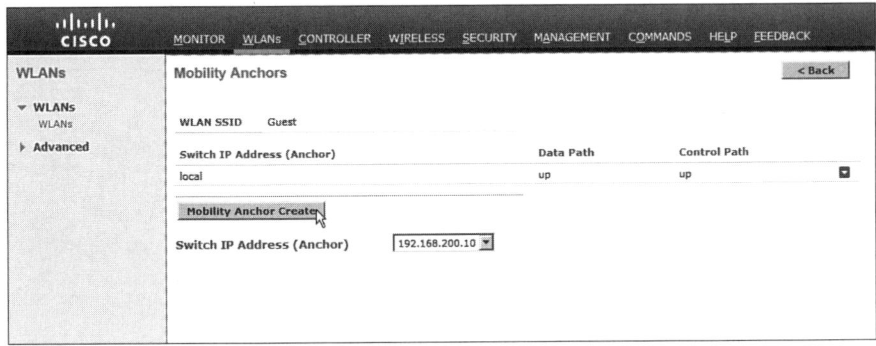

Figure 16-11 *Identifying a Mobility Anchor for a Guest WLAN*

Exam Preparation Tasks

As mentioned in the section, "How to Use This Book," in the Introduction, you have a couple of choices for exam preparation: the exercises here, Chapter 21, "Final Review," and the exam simulation questions on the DVD.

Review All Key Topics

Review the most important topics in this chapter, noted with the Key Topic icon in the outer margin of the page. Table 16-2 lists a reference of these key topics and the page numbers on which each is found.

Table 16-2 Key Topics for Chapter 16

Key Topic Element	Description	Page Number
Figure 16-2	WLAN isolation	375
Figure 16-3	Scaling the guest WLAN	376

Define Key Terms

Define the following key terms from this chapter and check your answers in the glossary:

central web authentication (CWA), guest WLAN, local web authentication (LWA), mobility anchor

This chapter covers the following topics:

- **Configuring Common Wireless Clients**—This section provides an overview of several common client device platforms and how Wi-Fi is configured on them.
- **Cisco Compatible Extensions (CCX)**—This section describes the CCX program and how it is used to certify compatibility with sets of Cisco features and extensions.

This chapter covers the following exam topics:

- 1.2—Interpret RF signal measurements
  - 1.2c—Device capabilities (smartphones, laptops, tablets)
- 5.3—Configure client connectivity in different operating systems
  - 5.3a—Android, MacOS, iOS, Windows
- 6.3—Validate client settings
  - 6.3a—SSID
  - 6.3b—Security
  - 6.3c—Device driver version
- 7.4—Describe the requirements of client real-time and non-real-time applications

CHAPTER 17

Configuring Client Connectivity

A Cisco wireless network consists of wireless LAN controllers (WLCs), lightweight access points (LAPs), and wireless client devices. Even though the majority of this book is devoted to the controllers and access points (APs), the CCNA Wireless exam also includes client configuration. Why? When you build and support a wireless network, you often need to help your users configure and troubleshoot their devices so that they can use your network.

Wireless networks suffer from the bring-your-own-devices (BYOD) syndrome, where users often carry all sorts of wireless devices with them. Each device might use a different operating system, different wireless adapter hardware, and have different capabilities. This chapter covers the most common types of wireless clients.

Tip Exam topic 5.3a lists "MacOS" as a client operating system. In reality, this means Mac OS X.

"Do I Know This Already?" Quiz

The "Do I Know This Already?" quiz allows you to assess whether you should read this entire chapter thoroughly or jump to the "Exam Preparation Tasks" section. If you are in doubt about your answers to these questions or your own assessment of your knowledge of the topics, read the entire chapter. Table 17-1 lists the major headings in this chapter and their corresponding "Do I Know This Already?" quiz questions. You can find the answers in Appendix A, "Answers to the 'Do I Know This Already?' Quizzes."

Table 17-1 "Do I Know This Already?" Section-to-Question Mapping

Foundation Topics Section	Questions
Configuring Common Wireless Clients	1–2
Cisco Compatible Extensions (CCX)	3–9

Caution The goal of self-assessment is to gauge your mastery of the topics in this chapter. If you do not know the answer to a question or are only partially sure of the answer, you should mark that question as wrong for purposes of the self-assessment. Giving yourself credit for an answer you correctly guess skews your self-assessment results and might provide you with a false sense of security.

1. Which one of the following does a Windows 7 machine use to find a wireless network to join?
   a. WLAN Chooser
   b. WLAN AutoConfig Service
   c. WLAN Scanner
   d. ZeroScan Service
2. When a Windows 7 machine scans for available wireless networks, which one of the following does it do first?
   a. Scans by sending ad hoc advertisements
   b. Scans by sending probes for a specific SSID name
   c. Scans by sending probes with a null SSID name
   d. Scans by sending association requests to a list of known BSSIDs
3. CCX is used to certify which one of the following?
   a. Interoperability between wireless hardware manufacturers
   b. Compatibility with Cisco wireless features
   c. RF coverage
   d. Wireless networking professionals
4. To date, how many versions of CCX have been defined?
   a. 1
   b. 4
   c. 5
   d. 10
5. Someone has purchased a new 802.11 wireless device to use in an enterprise that has a Cisco unified wireless network. After reading through the device specifications, you realize that it is not certified for any CCX version at all. Which one of the following most correctly describes the outcome?
   a. The device will not work on the network.
   b. The device will likely work fine.
   c. The device must support at least one CCX version to associate with the network.
   d. The device is compatible with all CCX versions because CCX is part of the 802.11 standard.
6. A wireless device is certified for CCXv1. Which one of the following is a correct statement?
   a. The device is compatible with all Cisco features.
   b. The device is compatible with WPA.
   c. The device can support MFP.
   d. The device is compatible with 802.11.

7. WPA2 with 802.1x and AES was introduced in which one of the following CCX versions?
   a. CCXv1
   b. CCXv2
   c. CCXv3
   d. CCXv4
   e. CCXv5
8. Which one of the following is a CCX Lite module?
   a. CCXv1
   b. Voice
   c. Crypto
   d. Video
9. A device is certified as CCX Lite. Which one of the following modules is mandatory for that certification?
   a. CCXv5
   b. Foundation
   c. Mobility
   d. Survey

Foundation Topics

Configuring Common Wireless Clients

As you work through this chapter, keep in mind that the CCNA Wireless exam blueprint covers configuration of four common wireless client device platforms and validation of their settings. Each of the platforms is described in the sections that follow. You should become familiar with the basic Wi-Fi configuration of each platform, along with simple ways to verify a wireless connection. The device's MAC address is often useful when you need to troubleshoot further from the WLC or a management platform. The Wi-Fi driver software version number can be important too, as newer wireless features and bug fixes might require newer driver releases.

Considering Wireless Client Requirements

You might be familiar with the term bring your own device (BYOD), where any sort of mobile device might be brought into an environment that has a wireless network. The users who bring the devices simply expect them to work and have good connectivity. As a wireless network administrator, would it be easy to satisfy all users? That is a difficult question to answer because you really need to know more about the devices and what they do so that you can design your wireless network to support them properly.

To approach such a problem, you should consider the wireless client requirements. The wireless clients that are covered in this chapter are common mobile devices, such as laptops and smartphones. What sort of requirements do they have? All you really know is the type of device and what operating system it runs. You might also find out some information about the wireless radio inside—perhaps which bands it supports, which wireless security schemes it can use, the receiver sensitivity of the radio, and so on. These specifications are important, but they all revolve around the 802.11 operability and not really around performance or the quality of the user experience.

A better approach is to consider what types of applications are being used on the wireless devices. Think about how an application is using its data and what the end user is expecting from it. If the application must send and receive data in a timely manner, it is known as a *real-time application*. Examples include voice over IP (VoIP), videoconferencing, collaboration, and Citrix remote desktop. Non-real-time applications are not so dependent upon immediate response or timely data exchange. Such applications include email, web browsing, and social media.

You might have noticed a pattern—real-time applications involve voice and video; non-real-time applications include ordinary data. Real-time applications require special consideration as you design, configure, and operate a wireless network. The following effects need to be minimized so that voice and video sessions can be heard and seen consistently, without interruption or corruption.

- **Latency**—The amount of time required to deliver a packet or frame from a transmitter to a receiver

- **Jitter**—The variance of the end-to-end latency experienced as consecutive packets arrive at a receiver
- **Packet loss**—The percentage of packets sent that do not arrive at the receiver

To keep these factors minimized, the adverse conditions in a wireless environment must be controlled. For example, a source of interference can cause packet errors that interrupt a voice or video stream. As packets are lost, they can be retransmitted and delayed, increasing latency and jitter. Other factors like poor radio frequency (RF) coverage, high channel utilization, and excessive collisions can also impede good data throughput and integrity.

As you look closely at client devices and their applications, think about the many wireless features and mechanisms that you can use to make improvements to your network. A good AP layout can address RF coverage, expected client density, efficient roaming, and so on. Disabling lower data rates, enabling transmit beamforming, and load balancing clients across APs are some examples of ways to improve efficiency and throughput. Leveraging CleanAir can detect and help mitigate interfering sources and rogue APs.

The following sections provide an overview of a few client types that you will encounter. You should know how to configure the clients to join a wireless network and how to verify proper operation. There are many other types of client devices too—wireless phones, voice communication badges, asset location tags, tablets, printers, bar code scanners, cameras, and even specialized items such as hospital beds and IV pumps. All of these devices need to coexist and work properly, and you will need to figure out how to best accomplish that.

Understanding Windows Wi-Fi

Microsoft Windows 7, 8.1, and 10 all include a stock wireless client that offers basic connectivity options. The configuration is very similar in each operating system, with only slight differences in the GUI. To access the wireless client, first use the actions in Table 17-2 to look for the wireless icon that indicates the current network status. If the machine is currently connected, the icon shows a sequence of bars or arcs to indicate the received signal strength indicator (RSSI) from the AP. If it is not connected, the icon will show gray bars and a star or asterisk instead.

Table 17-2 How to Find the Wireless Status Icon on Windows Machines

Windows	Action
7	Display the taskbar and look for the wireless icon.
8.1	Move the cursor to the upper-right corner of the screen, select **Settings**, and then look for the wireless icon.
10	Display the taskbar and look for the wireless icon.

You can click the wireless network icon to see a list of service set identifiers (SSIDs) that have been broadcast and discovered, as shown in Figure 17-1. SSIDs that use open authentication and no other security method are marked by a wireless icon with a gold shield with an exclamation mark. SSIDs that use a wireless security method with encryption are marked by a regular wireless icon.

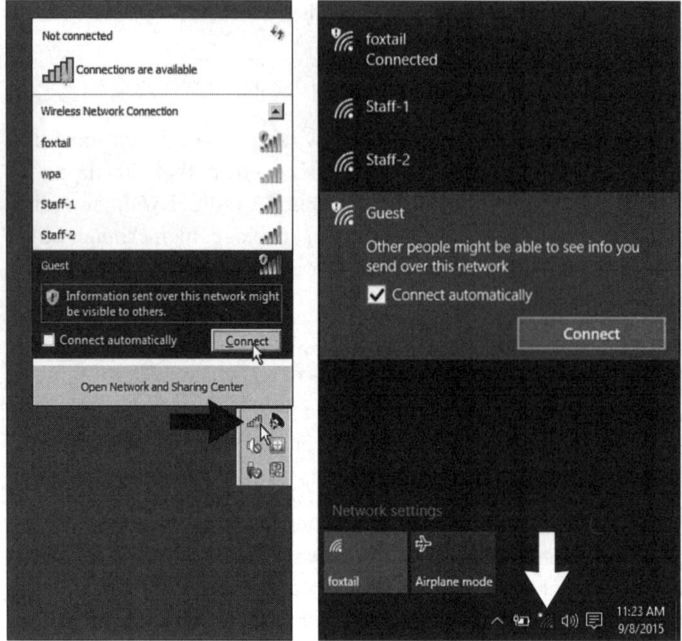

Figure 17-1 *Displaying a List of Available SSIDs*

By default, a Windows PC does not have a prepopulated list of SSIDs to use. Over time, it maintains a list of "preferred" network names from SSIDs that you manually connect to or manually define. Windows 7, 8.1, and 10 machines use a process called WLAN AutoConfig Service to scan for a network, using the following sequence of steps:

1. Scan for available networks by transmitting probe requests with a null or empty SSID name. If a preferred network is found, connect to it.
2. Scan for each preferred network with specific probe requests; if one is found, connect to it.
3. Scan for any preferred network that is an ad hoc (peer-to-peer) network; if one is found, connect to it.
4. No known networks are found; present a list of available networks for manual connection.

To connect to one of the listed networks, click its name and then click the **Connect** button that appears. If the wireless LAN uses a security mechanism, enter the security key or credential when you are prompted to do so. You can configure the machine to automatically connect to the SSID in the future by checking the **Connect Automatically** check box.

You can manually populate a list of preferred wireless networks or edit their properties. You will need to open the Network and Sharing Center, then add or make changes to a network profile. The procedure in each version of Windows is slightly different, so you should perform the appropriate actions listed in Table 17-3.

Table 17-3 How to Open the Network and Sharing Center in Windows

Windows	Action
7	**1.** Click the **Open Network and Sharing Center** link. **2.** Click the **Manage Wireless Networks** link. **3.** Click **Add.** **4.** Click **Manually create a network profile.**
8.1	**1.** Move the cursor to the upper-right corner of the screen. **2.** Select **Settings.** **3.** Select the **Set up a new connection or network** link. **4.** Select **Manually connect to a wireless network**, then click **Next.**
10	**1.** Click the wireless icon in the taskbar. **2.** Select **Network Settings.** **3.** Select **Network and Sharing Center.** **4.** Select **Set up a new connection or network.** **5.** Select **Manually connect to a wireless network**, then click **Next.**

Tip You can follow the same sequence of steps to create an ad hoc wireless network, where client devices can communicate directly with each other in an independent basic service set (IBSS). Rather than selecting Manually Create a Network Profile, select **Create an Ad Hoc Network.** Then you can complete the ad hoc network parameters described in the rest of this section. Be aware that an ad hoc network is not the same as Wi-Fi Direct.

As shown in Figure 17-2, you can enter the network name (SSID) and security and encryption types. You can also specify whether the PC should automatically connect to the network each time the SSID is detected, even if the SSID is not broadcast in any beacon frames.

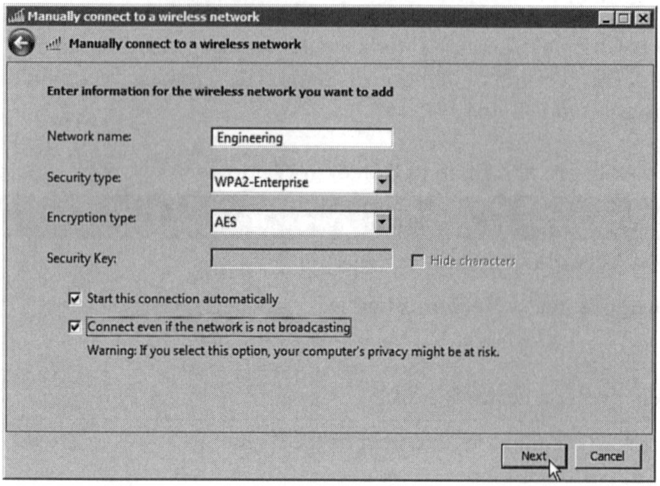

Figure 17-2 *Manually Configuring a New Wireless Network*

The built-in Windows wireless client does not offer many specific configuration options; however, you might find more options by configuring the wireless adapter. From the Network and Sharing Center, select **Change Adapter Settings** to display a list of installed adapters. Right-click a wireless adapter and select **Properties** to display the adapter properties and a list of installed protocols, as shown in Figure 17-3. Click the **Configure** button to bring up a window of adapter driver properties. Finally, display the **Advanced** tab to display a list of parameters and values, as shown in Figure 17-4. The list of parameters varies from one adapter to another, depending on what settings the manufacturer offers.

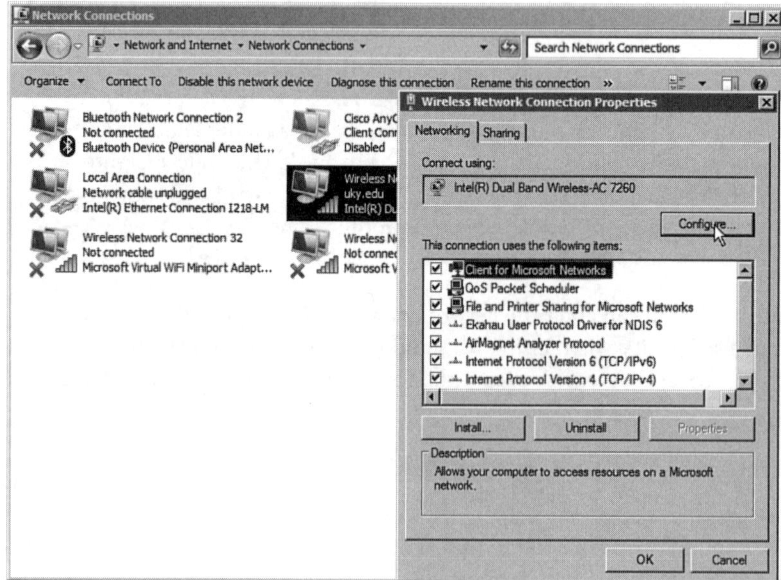

Figure 17-3 *Configuring Wireless Adapter Properties*

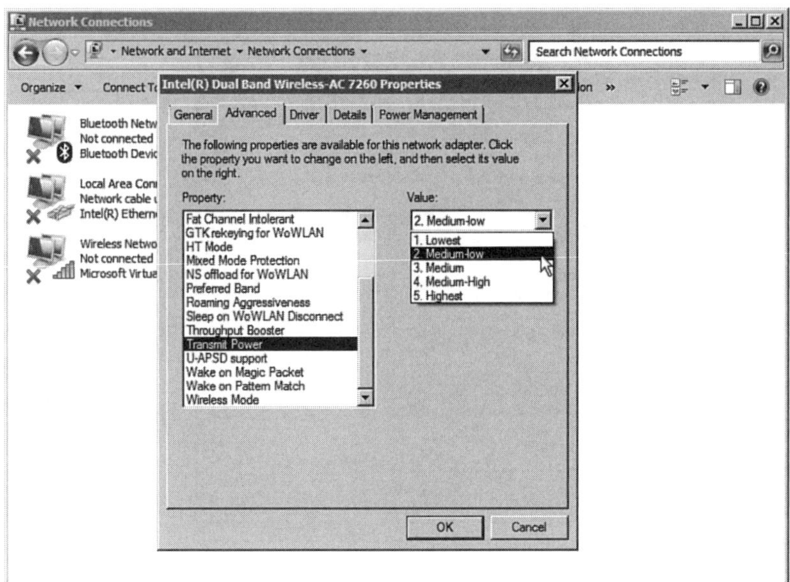

Figure 17-4 *Configuring Advanced Wireless Adapter Settings*

You can verify the status of a wireless connection by right-clicking the wireless icon, then selecting **Open Network and Sharing Center**. If the machine is connected to a wireless network, you can click the Internet connection as shown in Figure 17-5. A new window will display the current network state, including IPv4 and IPv6 connectivity, the SSID, the wireless data rate offered, the signal quality, and a count of bytes sent and received. You can click the Details button to see more detailed information, as shown in Figure 17-6.

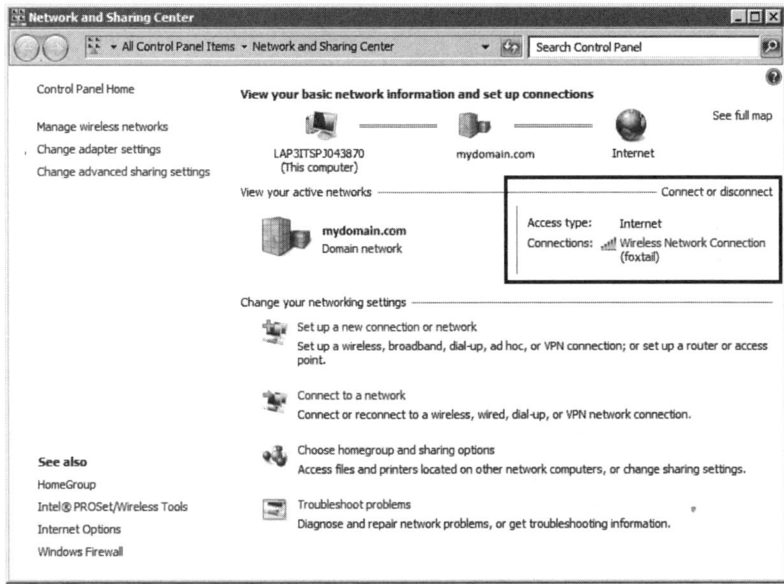

Figure 17-5 *Displaying the Wireless Connection Screen*

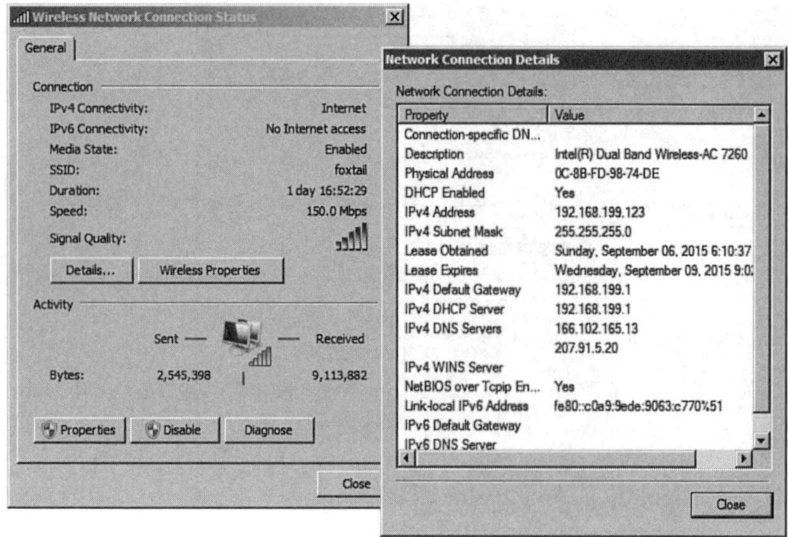

Figure 17-6 *Displaying Detailed Connection Status Information*

From the Wireless Network Connection Status window shown on the left side of Figure 17-6, you can click the **Wireless Properties** button to access configuration information about the wireless network profile that is in use. The **Disable** button can be used to disable the wireless network adapter, while the **Diagnose** button runs a series of tests that can be helpful in troubleshooting connection issues.

Usually it is a good practice to keep the wireless network adapter updated with a current driver version. You can verify the driver version in use by clicking the **Properties** button, then selecting the **Driver** tab as shown in Figure 17-7.

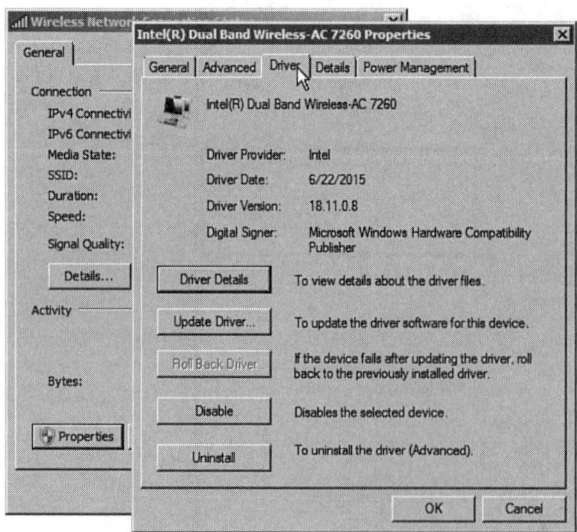

Figure 17-7 *Verifying the Network Adapter Driver Version*

Understanding Android Wi-Fi

Devices based on the Android operating system use a built-in driver and utility to manage connections to wireless networks. Android devices can discover a list of available networks and can manage manually configured networks too.

First, you should enable the wireless adapter by selecting **Settings > Wi-Fi** and then sliding the **Wi-Fi** switch to the on position, as shown in Figure 17-8. You can manage individual wireless connections from the same screen. The list shows the SSIDs of networks that have been discovered, in addition to those that are locally configured. After a network has been learned and connected to at least once, the device will automatically try to use it again in the future.

17

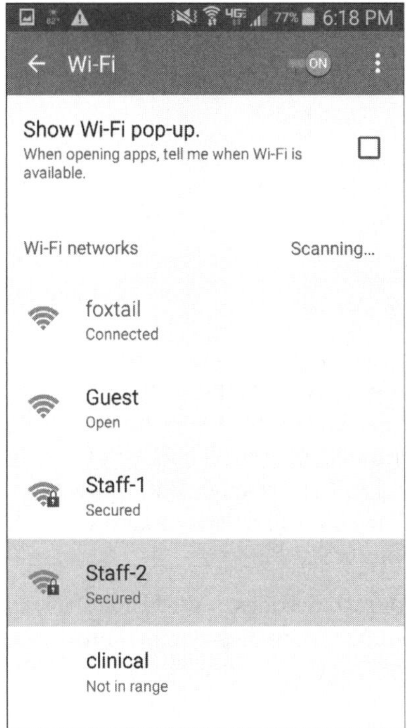

Figure 17-8 *Displaying a List of Wireless Networks on an Android Device*

You can manually add a new network by selecting the **Add Wi-Fi Network** link at the bottom of the network list. Enter the SSID and security parameters as shown in Figure 17-9, and then select the **Save** button. After a network has been learned, you can edit its properties by selecting the network from the list with a long-press and then selecting **Modify Network Config**. You can also delete a network profile by selecting it with a long-press and then selecting **Forget Network**.

Figure 17-9 *Adding a Wireless Network on an Android Device*

Android natively supports both WPA and WPA2 Personal and Enterprise security. Enterprise security commonly includes Transport Layer Security (TLS), Protected Extensible Authentication Protocol (PEAP), and Tunneled TLS (TTLS). Also, Android devices support Wi-Fi Direct, allowing direct communication with a small number of other devices in a peer-to-peer fashion, without requiring an AP. Although Wi-Fi Direct is derived from 802.11 ad hoc networks, it is incompatible with ad hoc networking because it supports additional negotiation and security features.

You can verify the status of a wireless connection by going to **Settings > Wi-Fi**. One of the Wi-Fi network names should be listed as "Connected." You can display more information about it by selecting it, as shown in Figure 17-10.

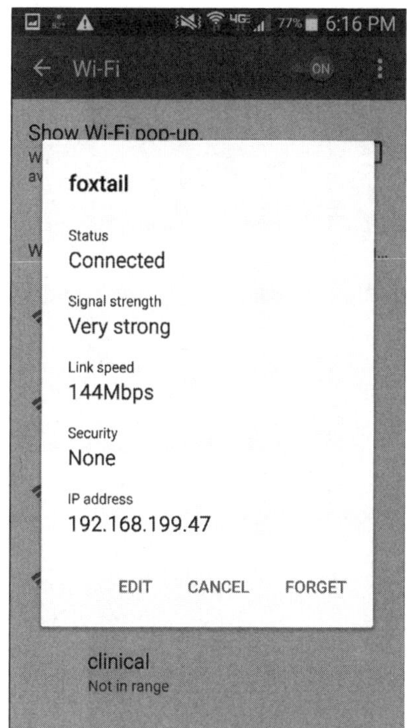

Figure 17-10 *Displaying the Wireless Status on an Android Device*

Understanding MacOS X Wi-Fi

Apple devices use a built-in wireless adapter and a configuration utility to manage networks that are discovered and manually defined. You can view a list of discovered networks by clicking the wireless icon at the top of the screen, as shown in Figure 17-11. To connect to one of the networks, click its name. You can also turn the Wi-Fi adapter off and on from the links at the top of the list.

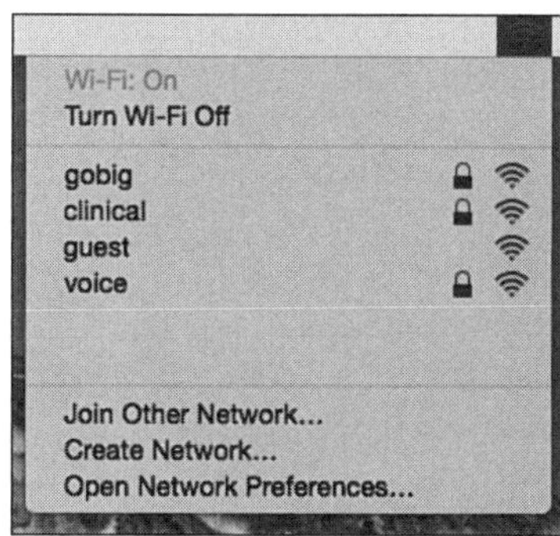

Figure 17-11 *Displaying Discovered Wireless Networks in MacOS X*

To access the wireless configuration utility, select **System Preferences**, and then select **Network**. Figure 17-12 shows an example, with all available network adapters listed down the left side. From this window, you can enable or disable the wireless adapter.

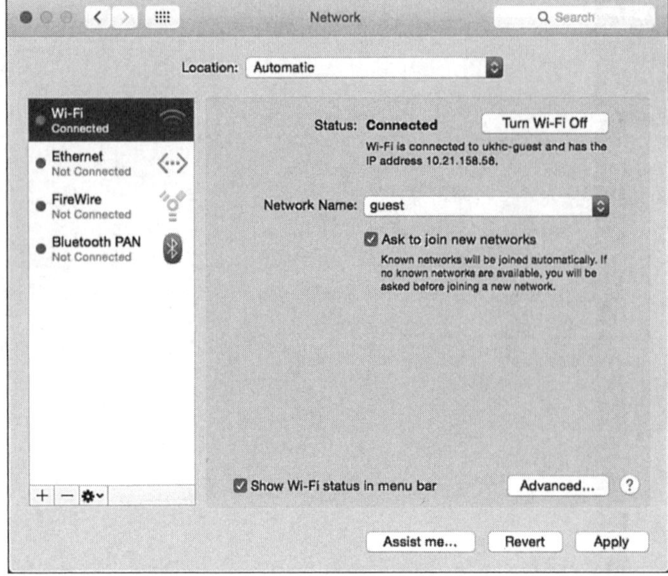

Figure 17-12 *Accessing the MacOS X Network Properties*

You can also select **Wi-Fi** and then click the **Advanced** button to display and edit the network connection configurations. The advanced settings window, as shown in Figure 17-13, has seven tabs across the top. The Wi-Fi tab contains a list of preferred networks—SSIDs that have already been configured. The networks will be tried in sequential order; you can change the order by dragging networks up or down in the list.

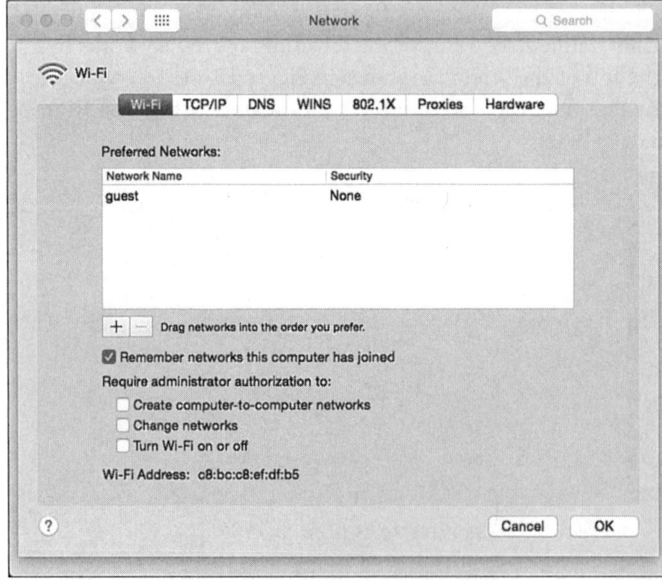

Figure 17-13 *Displaying a List of Preferred Wireless Networks*

You can create a new wireless network by clicking the **+** (plus sign) button. As shown in Figure 17-14, you can enter an SSID and security parameters for the new network profile.

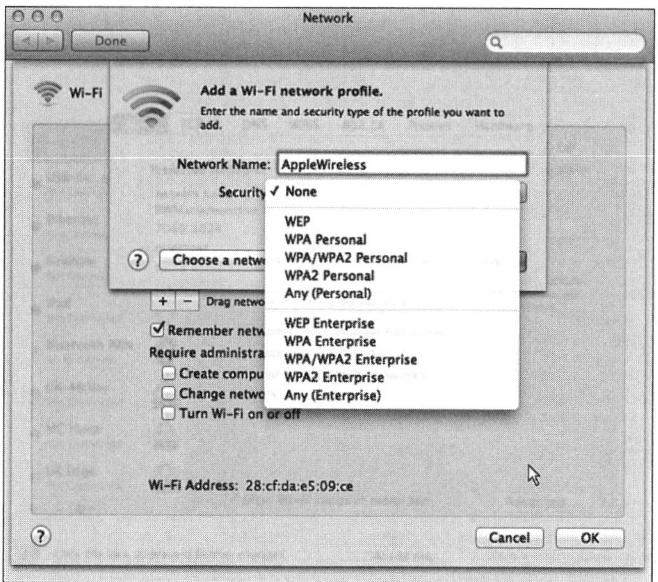

Figure 17-14 *Creating a New Wireless Network Profile*

Sometimes you might need to verify the network adapter software version or wireless capabilities. You can do that by clicking the Apple logo in the upper-left corner of the screen. Next, select **About This Mac** and the **Overview** tab, as shown in Figure 17-15. Detailed wireless information can be displayed by clicking the **System Report** button. In the report output, select **Network > Wi-Fi**, as shown in the example report in Figure 17-16.

Figure 17-15 *Displaying System Information in MacOS X*

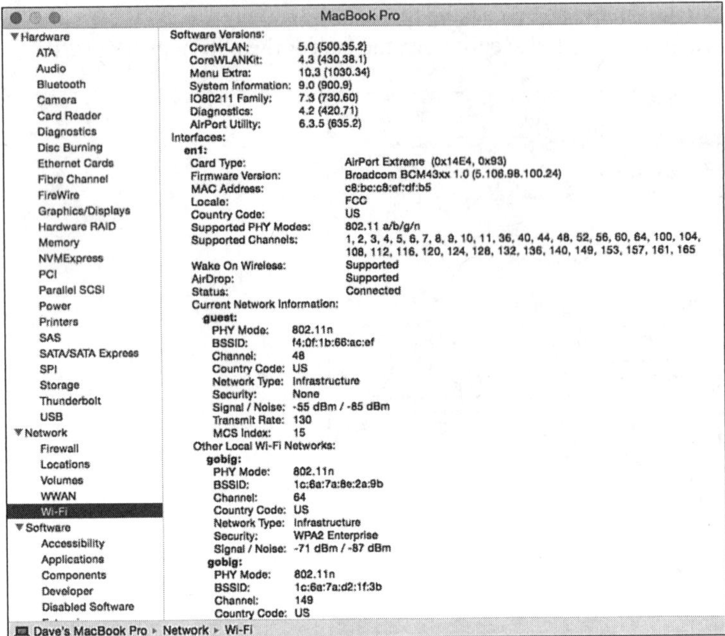

Figure 17-16 *Displaying a Report of Wi-Fi Network Parameters*

Understanding Apple iOS Wi-Fi

Apple iPhones running iOS can connect to Wi-Fi networks using a built-in network adapter and driver. You can view and control the Wi-Fi connectivity by pressing the home button and selecting Settings, as shown in Figure 17-17. Select **Wi-Fi** to manage the connections.

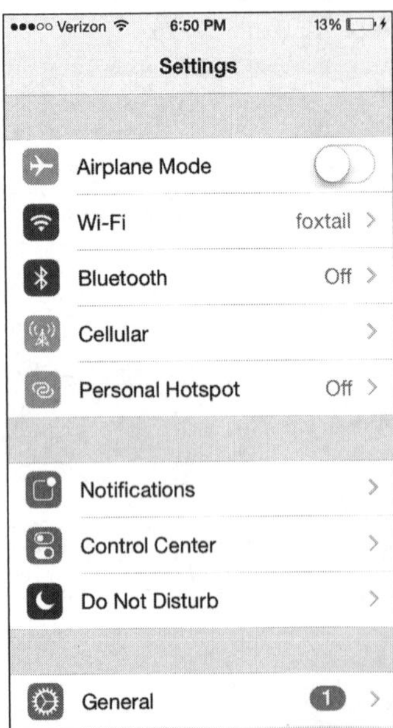

Figure 17-17 *Accessing Wireless Settings on an iOS Device*

Figure 17-18 shows an example list of wireless networks that have been discovered. If the device is connected to a network, a check mark will be shown to the left of the network name. You can select a network name and then select the **Join** or **Forget** link to connect or disconnect from the SSID. You can also manually define a network by selecting **Other** at the bottom of the network list. Enter the network name and security parameters as shown in Figure 17-19, then select **Join** to connect.

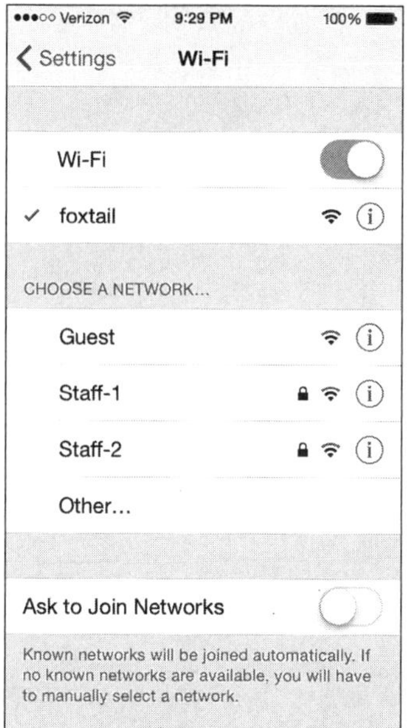

Figure 17-18 *Displaying a List of Wireless Networks on an iOS Device*

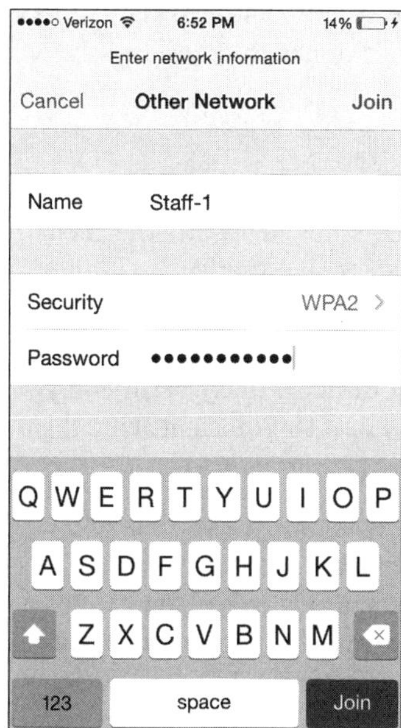

Figure 17-19 *Manually Defining a New Network on an iOS Device*

When the iOS device is connected to a network, you can display basic information about it by selecting the network name in the Wi-Fi settings screen. Figure 17-20 shows the IP addressing parameters for the connection named "foxtail." The device will not display detailed information about the wireless adapter and the current RF parameters natively; you have to install a third-party application to do that.

Figure 17-20 *Displaying Connection Information on an iOS Device*

iOS devices support WPA and WPA2 Personal and Enterprise security and EAP-TLS. Wi-Fi Direct is also supported for impromptu peer-to-peer communication with other devices, without the need for an AP.

Cisco Compatibility Extensions

The wireless clients described in the previous sections are fairly straightforward; the client has a wireless network adapter and controls the SSID and wireless security that are used to associate with an AP. Beyond that, the AP can make a safe assumption that the client complies with the 802.11 standard and supports certain data rates, but it knows little else about the client and its capabilities. Just like the AP, the client device is likely certified by the Wi-Fi Alliance for one of the 802.11 rate protocols (as in 802.11b/a/n/ac), making them compatible.

For example, without thorough testing, how do you know whether a wireless client and its driver software release support Wi-Fi Protected Access Version 2 (WPA2) with EAP Transport Layer Security (EAP-TLS) or some other security scheme? How do you know whether a client can optimally transport audio and video over wireless? Suppose that your enterprise just purchased several hundred wireless communication or medical devices. How can you be certain which wireless functions and security features the devices support?

To remove some of the unknowns, Cisco created the Cisco Compatibility Extensions (CCX) program. Cisco defines a set of features as part of a specific CCX version. Wireless device manufacturers can implement the features in their devices and then submit their devices for testing and validation. If a device passes the interoperability tests, it receives a "Cisco Certified Compatibility" designation.

The CCX program really has two goals:

- Take advantage of Cisco enhancements and innovations above what is defined in the 802.11 standard
- Verify that a client supports each enhancement correctly

Over time, Cisco has developed CCX in phases or versions. To date, there are five versions, each building on its predecessor with an increasing set of features. Table 17-4 lists some of the 70 features, along with the CCX versions that support them. Notice how the more traditional and general features such as 802.11 are supported in all versions, essentially over a long period of time as WLAN technology has evolved. Features available only in v4 and v5 tend to be interactive, where the client works with the wireless infrastructure to report information about itself.

For example, management frame protection (MFP) addresses an inherent weakness in the management frames that an AP transmits. When a client receives a management frame, it implicitly trusts that the frame came from an AP and that the frame contents have not been tampered with. To secure management frames, both the AP and the client must participate to encrypt and authenticate each frame. Only CCXv5 clients are equipped to use frames protected with MFP.

Table 17-4 Feature Support in CCX Versions 1–5

Feature	v1	v2	v3	v4	v5
IEEE 802.11 (general support for the standard as a whole)	X	X	X	X	X
Wi-Fi compliance	X	X	X	X	X
IEEE 802.1s	X	X	X	X	X
Windows Hardware Quality Labs (WHQL)	X	X	X	X	X
WPA		X	X	X	X
AP-assisted client roaming		X	X	X	X
RF scanning and reporting		X	X	X	X
AP-specified client maximum transmit power		X	X	X	X
Wi-Fi Multimedia (WMM)			X	X	X
Call admission control (CAC)				X	X
Client keepalive				X	X
Client link test				X	X
Unscheduled automatic power save delivery (U-APSD)				X	X

Feature	v1	v2	v3	v4	v5
Client location reporting				X	X
Performance reporting					X
Diagnostic channel					X
Roaming and real-time diagnostics					X
Management frame protection (MFP)					X

Tip What if a device is not certified for any CCX version? Chances are that it will work just fine on a Cisco wireless infrastructure. CCX certifies extended features that are specific to Cisco networks—not features that are needed for basic wireless operation.

Each CCX version contains more complex and interactive features than the version before it, but the features are organized more by the version number than by function. Some devices that are designed for a specific application, such as a wireless phone or a locator tag, do not have a need to support the entire list of features in a CCX version. To simplify the compatibility process for these devices, Cisco introduced the CCX Lite designation.

CCX Lite is organized into four basic categories or modules, according to device function:

- **Foundation**—The core set of features that are common to most general-purpose devices
- **Voice**—Features specific to voice communication devices, such as WMM, CAC, expedited bandwidth request, and voice metrics
- **Location**—Features specific to near-real-time location reporting, usually used with RFID tags
- **Management**—Features specific to client management, such as link test, diagnostic channel, client reporting, and roaming and real-time diagnostics

A device must be compliant with the Foundation module to achieve CCX Lite certification. The other modules are optional for application-specific devices.

For the CCNA Wireless exam, be familiar with the CCX basics and know the CCX Lite modules. Understand the general principles without memorizing when specific CCX features were incorporated into which CCX version. As the 802.11 standard has evolved and rolled in various amendments over time, the standard has also solved many of the problems that some CCX features were meant to solve. For your reference, Table 17-5 lists the wireless security and authentication schemes along with the CCX versions.

Table 17-5 Wireless Security Support in CCX Versions 1–5

Feature	v1	v2	v3	v4	v5
IEEE 802.1x	X	X	X	X	X
LEAP	X	X	X	X	X

Feature	v1	v2	v3	v4	v5
PEAP-GTC (PEAP with EAP-GTC)		X	X	X	X
EAP-FAST			X	X	X
PEAP-MSCHAP (PEAP with EAP-MSCHAPv2)				X	X
EAP-TLS				X	X
WPA — 802.1x + WPA TKIP		X	X	X	X
with LEAP		X	X	X	X
with PEAP-GTC		X	X	X	X
with EAP-FAST			X	X	X
with PEAP-MSCHAP				X	X
with EAP-TLS				X	X
WPA2 — 802.1x + AES (802.11i)			X	X	X
with LEAP			X	X	X
with PEAP-GTC			X	X	X
with EAP-FAST			X	X	X
with PEAP-MSCHAP				X	X
with EAP-TLS				X	X
Management frame protection (MFP)					X

Table 17-5 might seem daunting, especially if you have to remember which CCX versions correspond to one of the many security features listed. Notice that the table can be broken down into four main divisions: 802.1x, WPA, WPA2, and MFP. Within each division, the same set of LEAP, PEAP-GTC, EAP-FAST, PEAP-MSCHAP, and EAP-TLS schemes are repeated. Therefore, you might benefit from memorizing the following rules of thumb:

- 802.1x is covered in all versions.
- WPA and its schemes were all introduced in CCXv2.
- WPA2 and its schemes were all introduced in CCXv3.

Except:

- EAP-FAST was introduced in CCXv3.
- PEAP-MSCHAP and EAP-TLS were introduced in CCXv4.
- MFP was introduced in CCXv5.

For example, without looking at the table, which CCX versions support WPA2 with EAP-TLS? From the third rule, you know that WPA2 is supported in Versions 3 and later, except that EAP-TLS is Version 4 and later. Therefore, your answer should be CCXv4 and CCXv5.

Exam Preparation Tasks

As mentioned in the section, "How to Use This Book," in the Introduction, you have a couple of choices for exam preparation: the exercises here, Chapter 21, "Final Review," and the exam simulation questions on the DVD.

Review All Key Topics

Review the most important topics in this chapter, noted with the Key Topic icon in the outer margin of the page. Table 17-6 lists a reference of these key topics and the page numbers on which each is found.

Table 17-6 Key Topics for Chapter 17

Key Topic Element	Description	Page Number
Paragraph	Wireless client requirements	388
Table 17-3	Creating a wireless profile on a Windows device	391
Paragraph	Creating a wireless profile on an Android device	395
Figure 17-12	Creating a wireless profile on a MacOS device	398
Figure 17-18	Creating a wireless profile on an iOS device	401
Table 17-4	CCX versions	403
List	CCX Lite modules	404

Define Key Terms

Define the following key terms from this chapter and check your answers in the glossary:

Cisco Compatibility Extensions (CCX), CCX Lite

This chapter covers the following topics:

- **Cisco Unified Access Overview**—This section provides a summary of the major Cisco network management platforms that can be used to manage and monitor a wireless network.
- **Using Prime Infrastructure**—This section discusses Cisco Prime Infrastructure and its web-based management interface. It also introduces various ways you can monitor a Cisco wireless network and users. In this section, you will learn more about spatial maps that are available in Prime Infrastructure and how they can be used to provide a graphical representation of a wireless network in a physical space.

This chapter covers the following exam topics:

- 4.5—Identify wireless network and client management and configuration platform options
  - 4.5b—Prime infrastructure
  - 4.5d—ISE

CHAPTER 18

Managing Cisco Wireless Networks

A Cisco unified wireless network is based on an architecture of wireless LAN controllers, access points (APs), and, of course, many users. You can configure, monitor, and manage the APs through their controller, and the controller through its own management interface. As a network scales, management tasks can become tedious because you have to visit more than one controller to apply the same configuration changes or to monitor wireless events. Even further, you might have thousands of users to manage with some sort of access policies and monitor in case of problems. This chapter provides an overview of the tools and interfaces that Cisco offers that you can leverage to configure, manage, and monitor network devices and clients.

"Do I Know This Already?" Quiz

The "Do I Know This Already?" quiz allows you to assess whether you should read this entire chapter thoroughly or jump to the "Exam Preparation Tasks" section. If you are in doubt about your answers to these questions or your own assessment of your knowledge of the topics, read the entire chapter. Table 18-1 lists the major headings in this chapter and their corresponding "Do I Know This Already?" quiz questions. You can find the answers in Appendix A, "Answers to the 'Do I Know This Already?' Quizzes."

Table 18-1 "Do I Know This Already?" Section-to-Question Mapping

Foundation Topics Section	Questions
Cisco Unified Access Overview	1–2
Using Prime Infrastructure	3–9

Caution The goal of self-assessment is to gauge your mastery of the topics in this chapter. If you do not know the answer to a question or are only partially sure of the answer, you should mark that question as wrong for purposes of the self-assessment. Giving yourself credit for an answer you correctly guess skews your self-assessment results and might provide you with a false sense of security.

1. Which one of the following is used as the central management platform for Cisco wired and wireless networks?
   a. Master Controller
   b. Cisco MSE
   c. Prime Infrastructure
   d. Cisco ISE
2. Cisco Prime Infrastructure can be integrated with which one of the following platforms to provide location-based services for wireless clients and other devices?
   a. ISE
   b. LSE
   c. MSE
   d. WSE
3. What are three benefits of using Cisco Prime Infrastructure?
   a. Wireless planning
   b. Wireless management
   c. Wireless troubleshooting
   d. Wireless active site surveys
4. In the Alarm Summary bar at the bottom of the PI screen, what is represented by the orange triangle pointing downward?
   a. Helpful cautions about RF parameters
   b. Minor alarms from controllers
   c. Major alarms from controllers
   d. A summary of all alarm types
5. If an alarm goes unacknowledged in PI, what will happen to it?
   a. Nothing; the alarm will be active forever until it is acknowledged.
   b. After 15 days, the alarm will be automatically acknowledged.
   c. After 1 hour, the alarm will be automatically acknowledged.
   d. After 1 day, the AP that is the source of the alarm will be disabled.
6. To see a list of specific alarms and their time stamps in Cisco Prime Infrastructure, you should look in which one of the following areas?
   a. **Reports > Alarms**
   b. **Dashboard > Alarm Viewer**
   c. **Alarm Summary**
   d. **Alarm Browser**

7. The Prime Infrastructure user interface is made up of which one of the following components?
   a. Servlets
   b. Dashlets
   c. Panes
   d. Apps
8. Which one of the following PI menu selections enables you to find a list of maps?
   a. **Maps > Wireless Maps > Site Maps**
   b. **Configure > Maps**
   c. **Dashboard > Wireless > Maps**
   d. **Monitor > Site Maps**
9. PI maps are organized into which one of the following hierarchies?
   a. Campus > building > floor
   b. Enterprise > department > building
   c. Building > floor > room
   d. Domain > building > floor

Foundation Topics

Cisco Unified Access Overview

In the previous chapters of this book, you have learned about autonomous, cloud-based, and lightweight APs, as well as wireless LAN controllers and wireless controller modules. Each of these devices offers some sort of management interface that you can use for configuration, monitoring, and troubleshooting. It would be nice to have a way to manage everything, all in one place.

Now consider that your enterprise network might also be built on Cisco LAN switches, providing network connectivity for APs and wired devices. It would be even nicer to have one place to manage the wired and wireless networks. Don't forget about all the people and devices that connect to those networks—you probably have to enforce some sort of policies on them to allow network access or access to resources on the network.

Cisco has developed a strategy that integrates all of these management functions into an overall network architecture. The Cisco Unified Access architecture consists of three main areas:

- **One Network**—A single network infrastructure that converges both wired and wireless networks together. This includes autonomous (IOS), cloud managed (Meraki), centralized (AireOS), FlexConnect (AireOS), and converged (IOS-XE) wireless designs.
- **One Policy**—All secure access control (wired, wireless, VPN) is created and managed centrally. The same policy management platform provides visibility in all connected users and devices for identity management, posture assessment, and data collection.
- **One Management**—All network devices (wireless controllers, APs, and switches) can be configured, managed, and monitored centrally. Best practices and workflow tasks can be deployed to devices.

Figure 18-1 illustrates how the three "One" areas fit into an overall network infrastructure. All of the networking devices normally found in a network diagram are part of the One Network. To effectively manage the network, the following Cisco platforms in the One Management and One Policy areas must work together:

- **Prime Infrastructure (PI)**—Serves as a "single pane of glass" for all management functions. PI offers configuration and monitoring of all wired and wireless network devices, as well as visibility into all wired and wireless clients. From PI, you can deploy features and best practices to manage devices, manage lifecycle tasks, and generate reports.

  PI also maintains spatial maps that show things like AP heatmaps of buildings and areas, as well as device locations. PI can also integrate with autonomous APs and the Meraki cloud management Dashboard.
- **Mobility Services Engine (MSE)**—A platform that integrates with PI and maintains location data for location-based tracking services and interference source visualization. MSE can also integrate Cisco Connected Mobile Experiences (CMX) to deliver location-based services to customers in retail stores, hospitals, hotels, museums, and so on.

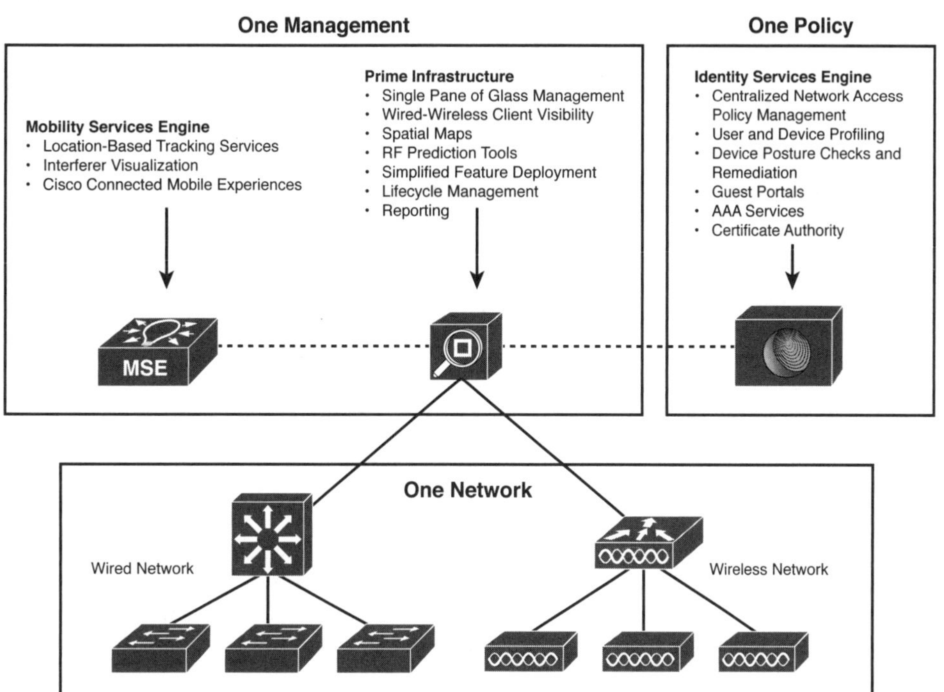

Figure 18-1 *Overview of the Cisco ONE Network for Unified Access*

- **Identity Services Engine (ISE)**—A central platform for managing network access policies that can be applied to wired or wireless networks and VPNs. ISE can profile users and their devices and perform posture checks and remediation according to defined policies. Guest portals can be built and customized through ISE. The same platform also offers a certificate authority and AAA services for controlling network access.

At the CCNA Wireless level, you should have a basic understanding of the components shown in Figure 18-1 and how they interact with each other. For example, you should remember from Chapter 14, "Wireless Security Fundamentals," that some wireless security methods require a RADIUS server. You should also know that Cisco ISE can be used to provide that AAA service, as well as many other robust policies that can control network access to users. ISE plays an important role in assessing user devices to find useful information about the hardware, software, and user identity, as well as their posture in relation to enterprise requirements.

More importantly, you should have a good working knowledge of Prime Infrastructure and how you can use it for basic day-to-day monitoring and customer support. You should understand how to navigate your way through the PI management console screen and how to use PI maps to visualize conditions in the network. These topics are covered in more detail in the following sections. You should also know how to leverage PI to troubleshoot problems that are reported, as covered in Chapter 20, "Troubleshooting WLAN Connectivity."

Using Prime Infrastructure

Cisco Prime Infrastructure is a browser-based software application that offers the capability to manage wired and wireless network deployments through a single interface. Benefits of Prime Infrastructure include the following:

- Using spatial maps to track devices and show their locations
- Wireless planning tools for AP placement and radio frequency (RF) parameters
- Controller and AP deployment through configuration templates
- Monitoring of controllers, APs, and wireless client devices
- Troubleshooting through alerts, events, wireless interference analysis, and a built-in client troubleshooting tool
- Extensive set of reports that can be automated or run on demand
- Integration with ISE for network access policy management

Note Prime Infrastructure has undergone an evolution over time. You might come across the names of its earlier generations as you read and study: Cisco Wireless Control System (WCS) and Cisco Prime Network Control System (NCS). Keep in mind that the CCNA WIFUND 200-355 exam is limited to Prime Infrastructure version 2.2.

Once PI is installed and configured, you can connect to it with a secure web browser session pointed to the IP address of the PI server. Installing and initially configuring PI is beyond the scope of the CCNA Wireless exam. Enter your username and password and click the **Login** button, as shown in Figure 18-2.

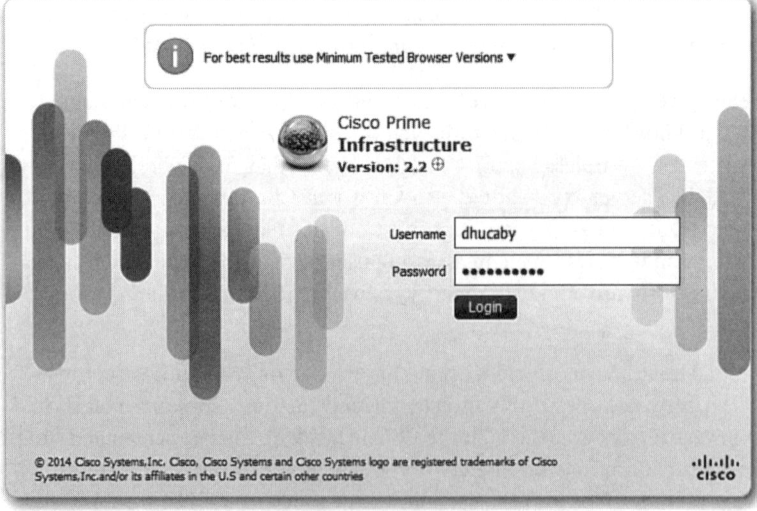

Figure 18-2 *PI Login Screen*

Once you log in to PI, you see a home page like the one shown in Figure 18-3.

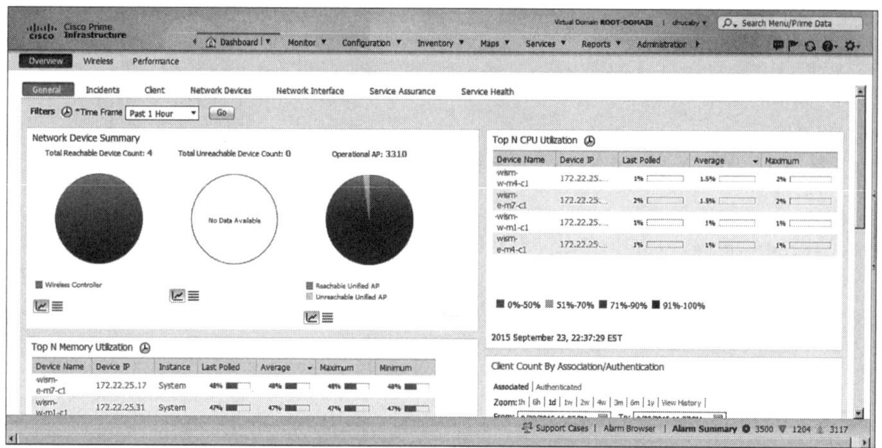

Figure 18-3 *Prime Infrastructure Home Page Layout*

The home page is organized into several sections or areas. The Task Area is a row of drop-down menus organized into lifecycle tasks, as listed in Table 18-2.

Table 18-2 Menus Displayed in the Main PI Task Area

Lifecycle Task	Description
Dashboard	Display concise dashboards of network activity or information
Monitor	Display common day-to-day monitoring, troubleshooting, maintenance, and operations dashboards
Configuration	Manage configuration templates and profiles that can be deployed onto the network infrastructure
Inventory	Manage the inventory of network devices, their software, and configuration archives
Maps	Manage and view network topology maps and spatial maps of wireless information
Services	Access mobility services and Application Visibility and Control (AVC) services
Reports	Create, view, and run a robust set of reports
Administration	Manage the Prime Infrastructure server

When you hover the cursor over one of the task menus, PI displays categories and lists of specific parameters that relate to the task. For example, as Figure 18-4 illustrates, hovering over the **Monitor** task displays a menu of all the resources that you can monitor, organized into three columns.

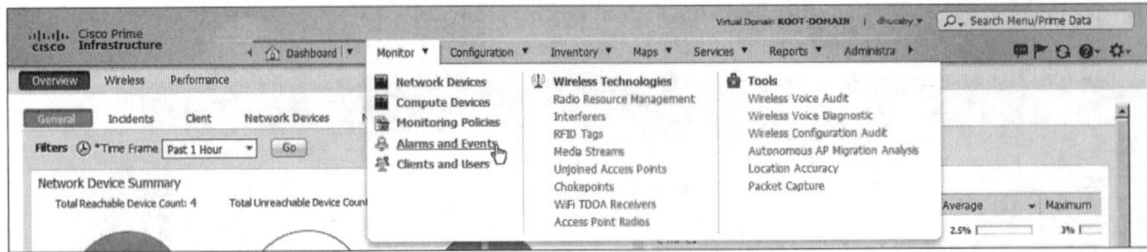

Figure 18-4 *Prime Infrastructure Task Area Menu*

When you select a menu item, the rest of the screen is updated with relevant information. Most screens are made up of individual "dashlets," or small parts of a dashboard display. You can customize how each dashlet is displayed by hovering the cursor over the dashlet's upper-right corner. Figure 18-5 shows the dashlet controls that appear. Selecting the pencil icon lets you change the dashlet title and refresh interval. The question mark displays a brief description of the dashlet. You can also manually refresh the dashlet contents, maximize its size, collapse it out of view, or delete it from the dashboard completely.

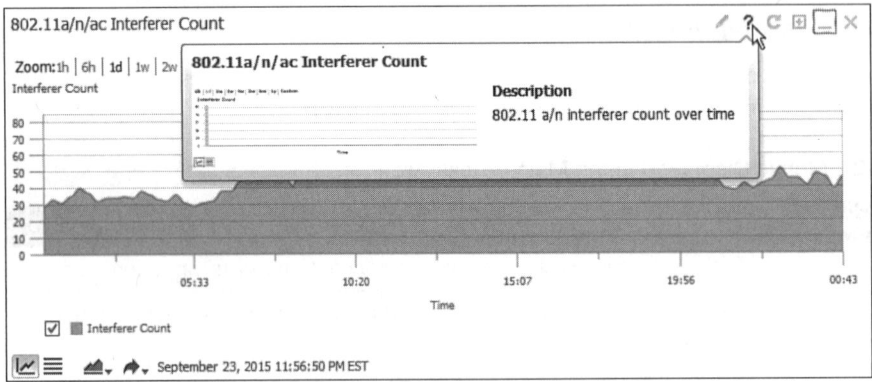

Figure 18-5 *Using the Dashlet Controls*

You can also add new dashlets to the dashboard. Begin by selecting the gear icon in the upper-right corner of the main PI screen, then select **Add Dashlet(s)** as shown in Figure 18-6. Click the **Add** link beside the desired dashlet.

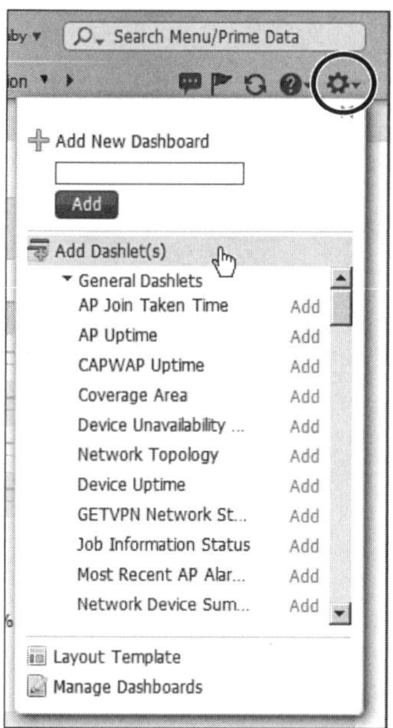

Figure 18-6 *Adding New Dashlets to the PI Dashboard*

> **Tip** You can return to the PI home page at any time by clicking the small house-shaped icon located next to the Dashboard menu in the Task Area.

The main PI screen also provides visibility into alarms that are occurring on the network. As you use PI on a day-to-day basis, you should know how to view alarm information and how to deal with it. These topics are discussed in the following section.

Alarms in the Dashboard

As PI receives alarms from controllers and other wireless management devices, it categorizes them by severity level and displays an Alarm Summary count in a narrow bar across the bottom of the screen. There are three severity levels, as follows:

- **Critical**—Denoted by a red circle containing a ×
- **Major**—Denoted by an orange downward-pointing triangular arrow
- **Minor**—Denoted by a yellow upward-pointing triangular arrow

In Figure 18-7, the alarm bar indicates that there are 3558 critical alarms, 1204 major alarms, and 3311 minor alarms. Hovering the cursor over the Alarm Summary area brings up the Alarm Summary window, which lists a more detailed alarm breakdown by severity.

Category	Critical	Major	Minor
Alarm Summary	3558	1204	3311
Adhoc Rogue	0	0	39
AP	29	0	177
Application Performance	0	0	0
Autonomous AP	0	0	0
Carrier Ethernet	0	0	0
Cisco Interfaces and Mod	0	0	0
Clients	0	0	0
Compute Servers	0	0	0

Figure 18-7 *Displaying the Alarm Summary*

To see a list of the current alarms, you can hover over or click the **Alarm Browser** in the alarm bar. The Alarm Browser will expand to show a list of alarms and their severity, status, source of the failure, time stamp, category, and condition. You can access this same Alarm Browser by selecting **Monitor > Alarms and Events** from the main PI navigation menu (as previously shown in Figure 18-4).

The Alarm Browser allows you to see alarms and their status at a glance, as shown in Figure 18-8. You can click the small right-pointing triangle at the left end of an alarm to view more details about it. PI will remember each alarm it receives for a default period of 15 days or until someone takes some action on it. Notice that each alarm has a check box in the far-left column. You can check the box next to one or more alarms and then use the **Change Status**, **Assign**, or **Annotation** menus, or the **Delete** button to select an action to take. Table 18-3 lists the menus and possible actions you can take on alarms. Figure 18-9 shows an example where Change Status has been selected so that the alarm could be acknowledged.

Severity	Message	Status	Failure Source	Timestamp	Owner	Category	Condition
Critical	Security-risk Interferer 'WiFi I...	Not Acknowle...	AP hazard-a109-ap6, Interfac...	September 23, 2015 11:41:1...		Security	Interferer Security Traps
Critical	IDS 'NULL probe resp 1' Signa...	Not Acknowle...	WLAN Controller pcf-wism-w-...	September 23, 2015 11:38:5...		Security	Signature attack
Critical	CPU Receive Multicast Queue ...	Not Acknowle...	WLAN Controller pcf-wism-w-...	September 23, 2015 11:38:1...		Controller	CPU RX Multicast queu...
Critical	Security-risk Interferer 'WiFi I...	Not Acknowle...	AP mdp-he644c-ap64, Interfa...	September 23, 2015 11:37:2...		Security	Interferer Security Traps
Critical	IDS 'Auth flood' Signature att...	Not Acknowle...	WLAN Controller pcf-wism-w-...	September 23, 2015 11:36:2...		Security	Signature attack
Critical	IDS 'Auth flood' Signature att...	Not Acknowle...	WLAN Controller pcf-wism-e-...	September 23, 2015 11:35:5...		Security	Signature attack
Critical	CPU Receive Multicast Queue ...	Not Acknowle...	WLAN Controller pcf-wism-e-...	September 23, 2015 11:32:3...		Controller	CPU RX Multicast queu...
Critical	Controller '172.22.25.15' de...	Not Acknowle...	WLAN Controller pcf-wism-e-...	September 23, 2015 11:32:1...		Security	Controller Detected Du...
Critical	CPU Receive Multicast Queue ...	Not Acknowle...	WLAN Controller pcf-wism-e-...	September 23, 2015 11:26:3...		Controller	CPU RX Multicast queu...

Figure 18-8 *Managing Alarms in Prime Infrastructure*

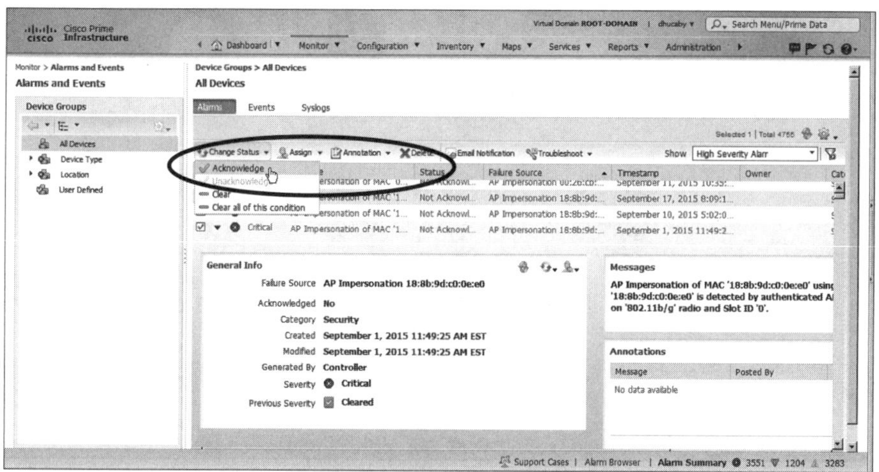

Figure 18-9 *Changing the Alarm State to Acknowledge*

Table 18-3 Alarm Actions

Menu	Action	Description
Change Status	Acknowledge	The alarm has been checked and can be removed from the list.
	Unacknowledge	The alarm should be added back to the list.
	Clear	Remove the alarm from the list, but PI will keep a record of it.
	Clear all of this condition	Remove the alarm and others like it from the list
Assign	Assign to Me	The alarm will remain in your own alarm list.
	Select Owner	Assign the alarm to a different PI user.
	Unassign	Take the alarm out of your alarm list.
Annotation	Note	Leave a text note to annotate the alarm.
Delete		Make PI forget about the alarm.
Email Notification		Select alarm types to be emailed.

Monitoring a Wireless Network with Prime Infrastructure

Aside from dealing with alarms as they arrive, there are many other aspects of a wireless network that you can monitor with Prime Infrastructure. For example, you might need to know the number of APs and wireless clients that are live on the network. The number of APs can be an important factor in a department's budget, plans for future network growth, for sizing wireless controller platforms, and for gauging the AP load across your controllers. You can do that through two dashlets that are displayed on the **Dashboard > Overview > General** menu, as shown in Figure 18-10.

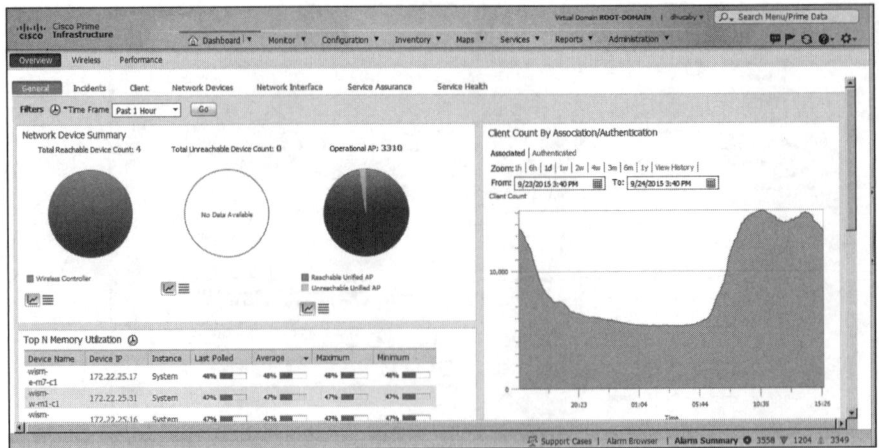

Figure 18-10 *Monitoring Wireless AP and Client Counts*

Table 18-4 lists some other common statistics and alarms that you should watch on a day-to-day basis, along with the menu locations where you can find them.

Table 18-4 Common Monitoring Tasks and the Their PI Menu Locations

Topics to Monitor	Prime Infrastructure Menu
Rogue access points	Alarm Summary (alarm bar across the bottom)
Non–Wi-Fi interference sources	**Dashboard > Wireless > CleanAir**
Interference profile violations	
Air quality index	
Security score and top issues	**Dashboard > Wireless > Security**
Security attacks detected	

Using Prime Infrastructure Maps

As you work with wireless controllers and APs, you might find yourself getting lost in the names and numbers without having a visual concept of things like AP location and RF coverage in an area. Fortunately, PI can help! PI can provide a graphical representation of a wireless network, complete with maps, physical locations, predictive RF coverage, and interactive data displays. In other words, PI will help you see your wireless network as it really is—APs and clients, along with sources of interference and rogue devices, distributed throughout a building or outdoor area.

PI can use an image file (PNG, JPG, or GIF format) as the background behind objects and data that it displays. For example, you can upload the floor plan of a building into PI and have the APs and clients that are located on that floor shown in relation to their actual locations.

PI maps are organized in a tree-like structure. A campus contains one or more buildings or outdoor areas. Each building can contain one or more floor maps. By default, maps are placed into a system campus. You can define your own campuses and your own buildings as you add maps into PI.

Tip The CCNA Wireless exam blueprint focuses on using a PI server that is already configured and ready to use. You should not have to worry about how to create and organize the maps or add APs to them—just have a basic knowledge of how to display various wireless data.

You can access the PI maps by selecting **Maps > Wireless Maps > Site Maps**. The list in the far-left column contains the map tree structure; the rest of the page contains a single flat list of every campus, building, and floor map. If you click a building name in the tree list, then the rest of the page will contain thumbnail maps of each floor along with the number of APs and radios, as shown in Figure 18-11.

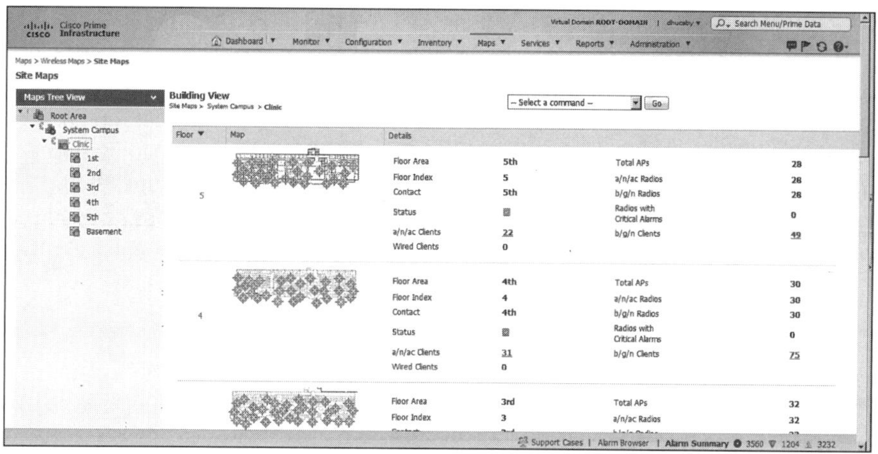

Figure 18-11 *Example of PI Building Maps*

You can click a map name or a thumbnail image in the list to display it, as shown in Figure 18-12. The map consists of the background image, usually a building floor plan or a drawing of an outdoor area, overlaid with AP icons and data. For example, the AP icons in the figure are shown in their current locations with labels that display the AP names.

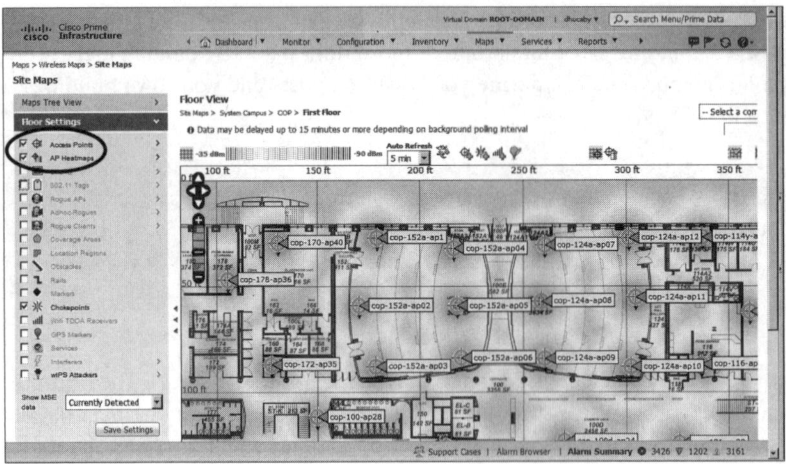

Figure 18-12 *PI Map Showing AP Locations*

A map can display a variety of things, depending on what you have selected in the list of Floor Settings that is displayed on the left side of the map. Figure 18-13 shows the Floor Settings list, along with other settings that are specific to a displayed object type. In this example, access points, AP heatmaps, clients, 802.11 Tags (devices attached to assets for tracking purposes), and chokepoints have been selected for display. When access points are selected, you can choose what information to show in each AP label on the map by selecting a parameter in the **Display** drop-down menu, as shown on the right in Figure 18-13. For instance, AP names are displayed by default, but you can choose things like channel numbers, transmit power levels, AP MAC addresses, controller IP address where the AP is joined, channel utilization, air quality, the number of associated clients, and so on.

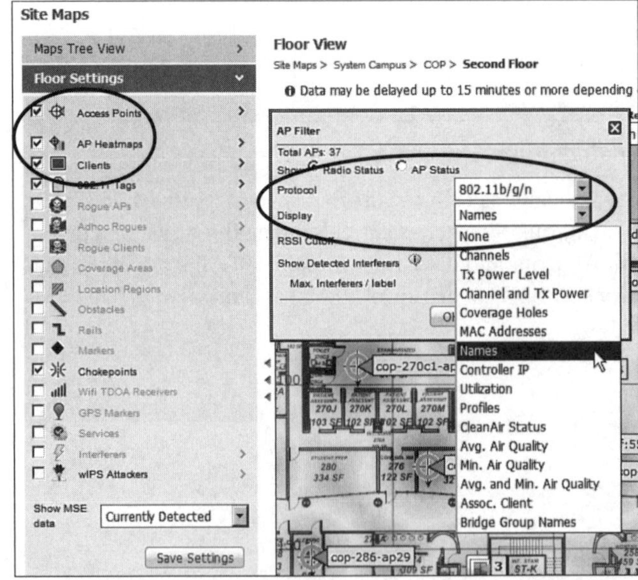

Figure 18-13 *Selecting the Devices and Labels to Display on a Map*

Table 18-5 lists the possible display choices under Floor Settings. A map can get quite busy with icons and labels, so you might want to check the boxes next to only a few things of interest.

Table 18-5 PI Map Display Settings

Displayed Item	Description
Access Points	APs that are known to PI
AP Heatmaps	Colorized representations of the AP signal strengths
Clients	Wireless clients and their MAC addresses
802.11 Tags	RFID tags
Rogue APs	APs that are not part of the enterprise network
Adhoc Rogues	Devices advertising ad hoc networks
Rogue Clients	Clients not known to PI
Coverage Areas	Area expected to be covered by RF signals
Location Regions	Boundaries used to constrain the location of client devices
Obstacles	Preconfigured RF obstacles drawn on the map
Rails	Lines where devices are shown, though they are constantly roaming over a floor or outside the map
Markers	Pointers placed on a map as reference points
Chokepoints	Asset tag chokepoints
Wifi TDOA Receivers	Asset tag receivers
GPS Markers	Wi-Fi devices used to correlate accurate GPS location information onto a map
Services	Locations where location-based services are provided
Interferers	Detected non–Wi-Fi interference sources
wIPS Attackers	Devices that trigger wireless IPS signatures during attacks

18

By default, a map is shown with dynamic information. PI computes the RF signal strength for each AP and displays the results as a colored heatmap. The colors represent the signal strength that might be received in each location on the map. The color scale is shown above the heatmap. Red represents a strong signal (–35 dBm), progressing through orange, yellow, green, and then blues and purples at the weak end of the scale (–90 dBm). The red color does not mean that being close to the AP is bad; it just represents the "heat" of the signal, or how strong it is in relation to orange, yellow, green, blue, and so on.

You can also control which APs contribute to the heatmap computation. For example, you might want to see what would happen if you were to remove an AP or two. Click the right-pointing arrow next to AP Heatmaps to display a list of contributing APs that are located on the map. Then select or deselect specific APs and observe the effect on the heatmap.

The heatmap that PI computes is based on many of the RF principles you learned about in Chapter 3, "RF Signals in the Real World." Based on each map location, PI can compute the free-space loss based on the distance from each of the APs. What about things like absorption, where the walls of a building attenuate or reduce RF signal strength? At a minimum, a PI map contains only the AP icons positioned over a floor plan background image. You might be able to see objects such as walls, doors, and elevators on the map, but PI is not able to interpret the drawing at all. Instead, if you want to know about obstacles and compute their influence, you can edit the map to define the physical objects and their dBm attenuation values. The more information that is put into a map, the more accurate PI can be when it produces the RF heatmap.

PI also updates the AP icons based on current conditions. A green icon represents an AP radio that is working properly, with no faults or alarms. A yellow icon represents an AP radio with a minor alarm, while a red icon indicates an AP radio with a major alarm. By default, PI updates a map every 5 minutes.

While a map is displayed, you can click an icon to display more information about it. For example, Figure 18-14 shows a small window that popped up to display information about the AP named cop-250-ap21. From this window, you can find the AP's MAC address, model number, and the IP address of the controller it has joined. You can select the 802.11a/n/ac or 802.11b/g/n tab to display information about that specific radio, including channel number and transmit power level.

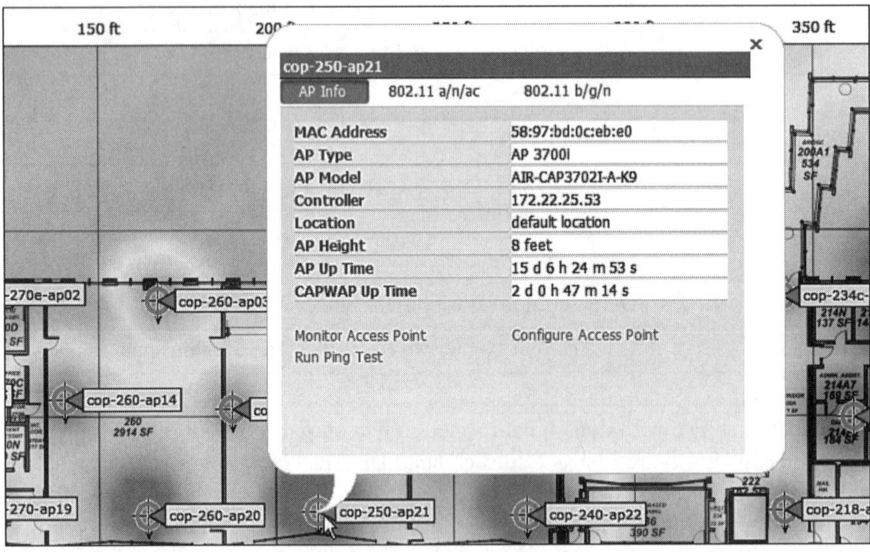

Figure 18-14 *Displaying Information About an AP on a Map*

Likewise, you can check the box next to **Clients** to display any clients that are located within the area of the map. Client locations are determined by triangulating their signals as received from nearby APs. Clients can be shown with a MAC address, IP address, username, or an asset label. Figure 18-15 shows an example floor map with clients and APs displayed. Sometimes more than one client will be located in the same place. Rather than try to display multiple MAC address labels cluttered together, multiple clients are shown with a label that indicates the number of clients there. The client icon also gets larger as the number of clients increases. In Figure 18-15, you can see icons where 3, 4, 5, 6, 11, 24, 26, and even 65 clients are located! You can click any client icon to see more-detailed information.

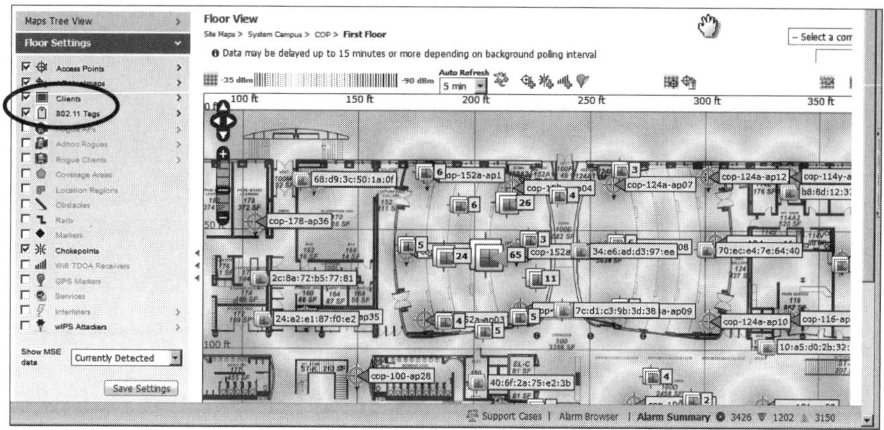

Figure 18-15 *Displaying Wireless Client Locations on a Map*

PI is also quite adept at displaying sources of interference on maps. You can select the **Interferers** check box to show interferers in the locations that PI has determined based on CleanAir information gathered from the controllers in the network. Interferer locations are marked with a yellow lightning-bolt icon, along with a label that identifies the type of interference. You can also view an estimated area that an interferer is impacting by opening the Interferers options and checking the **Show Zone of Impact** check box. In Figure 18-16, several Bluetooth Link interferers are displayed in their locations. The zones of impact are shown as colored circles. Notice how the Bluetooth Link circles are rather small, while the microwave oven in the upper-left corner is affecting quite a large area of the wireless network.

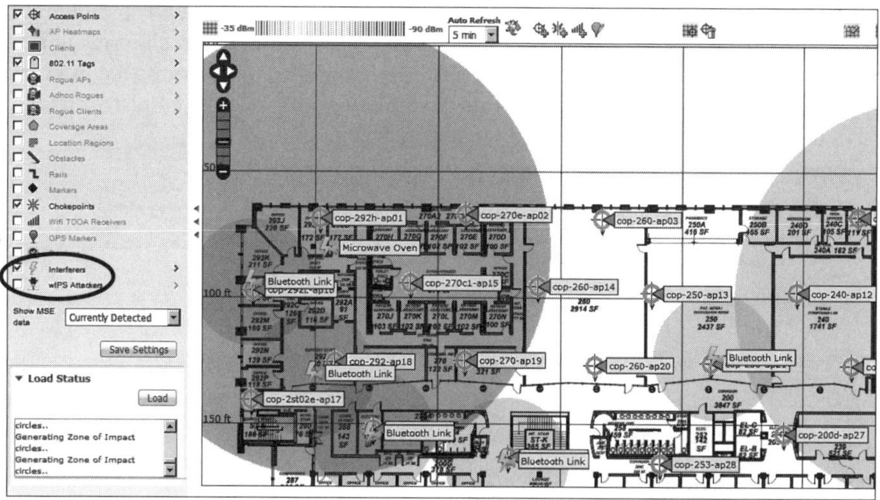

Figure 18-16 *Displaying Sources of Interference on a Map*

Finally, you will likely want to know where rogue APs and rogue clients are located when they come within range of your network. If you select **Rogue APs**, **Rogue Clients**, and **Adhoc Rogues**, those devices will be displayed with icons depicting a red circle with a skull, a gray circle with skull and crossbones, and red squares with skull and crossbones, respectively. In Figure 18-17, you can see several types of devices on the map. The AP locations are not shown, while client locations are. You can see two Bluetooth Link interferers, along with a WiMAX Fixed station that is affecting a large area. There are also several rogue APs located toward the bottom of the map.

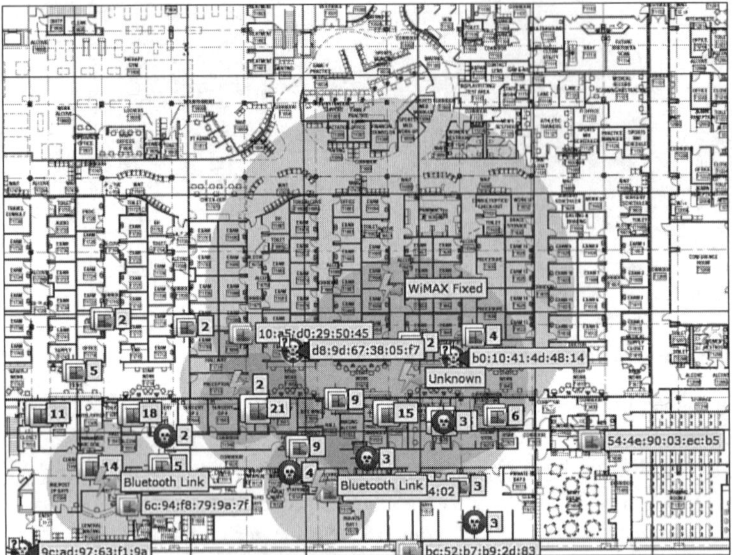

Figure 18-17 *Displaying Wireless Client Locations on a Map to Detect Rogue Devices*

Configuring Devices with PI

Prime Infrastructure can be used for more than monitoring a wireless network. It can also be used to configure controllers, lightweight APs, and autonomous APs through configuration templates. You can select the **Configuration** menu in the navigation bar to choose a template type, as shown in Figure 18-18. Select **Controller Configuration Groups**, **Lightweight Access Points**, or **Autonomous Access Points** to define new templates. Templates can be applied to devices by selecting **Scheduled Configuration Task**.

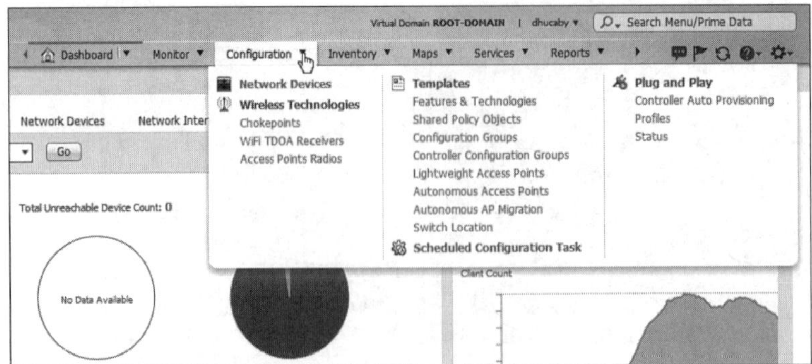

Figure 18-18 *Using PI to Configure Wireless Network Devices*

Exam Preparation Tasks

As mentioned in the section, "How to Use This Book," in the Introduction, you have a couple of choices for exam preparation: the exercises here, Chapter 21, "Final Review," and the exam simulation questions on the DVD.

Review All Key Topics

Review the most important topics in this chapter, noted with the Key Topic icon in the outer margin of the page. Table 18-6 lists a reference of these key topics and the page numbers on which each is found.

Table 18-6 Key Topics for Chapter 18

Key Topic Element	Description	Page Number
Figure 18-1	Cisco ONE Network for Unified Access	413
Figure 18-3	Prime Infrastructure home page organization	415
Table 18-2	Major functions in the PI navigation area	415
Figure 18-7	Alarms at a glance	418
Figure 18-12	Displaying AP information in maps	422
Figure 18-16	Displaying interferers in maps	425

This chapter covers the following topics:

- **Understanding Types of Interference**—This section describes common technologies and devices that can cause wireless interference.
- **Using Tools to Detect and Manage Interference**—This section covers CleanAir operation and explains how you can configure it to deal with interference automatically and efficiently.

This chapter covers the following exam topics:

- 1.2—Interpret RF signal measurements
  - 1.2b—Differentiate interference vs. noise
- 6.4—Employ appropriate controller tools to assist troubleshooting
  - 6.4c—Monitor pages
    - 6.4c(i)—CleanAir (controller GUI)
- 7.3—Identify proper application of site survey tools
  - 7.3a—Spectrum analyzer

CHAPTER 19

Dealing with Wireless Interference

With careful design and planning, 802.11 devices can operate as a fully functional wireless network. However, many readily available products do not use the 802.11 standard. When 802.11 and non-802.11 devices come together, the two can interfere with each other. Wireless interference can make WLAN performance sluggish or completely unusable. This chapter covers some common types of devices that can cause interference and the Cisco CleanAir features that can detect and react to the interference sources.

"Do I Know This Already?" Quiz

The "Do I Know This Already?" quiz allows you to assess whether you should read this entire chapter thoroughly or jump to the "Exam Preparation Tasks" section. If you are in doubt about your answers to these questions or your own assessment of your knowledge of the topics, read the entire chapter. Table 19-1 lists the major headings in this chapter and their corresponding "Do I Know This Already?" quiz questions. You can find the answers in Appendix A, "Answers to the 'Do I Know This Already?' Quizzes."

Table 19-1 "Do I Know This Already?" Section-to-Question Mapping

Foundation Topics Section	Questions
Understanding Types of Interference	1–6
Using Tools to Detect and Manage Interference	7–13

Caution The goal of self-assessment is to gauge your mastery of the topics in this chapter. If you do not know the answer to a question or are only partially sure of the answer, you should mark that question as wrong for purposes of the self-assessment. Giving yourself credit for an answer you correctly guess skews your self-assessment results and might provide you with a false sense of security.

1. DECT cordless phone devices in the United States use which one of the following designations to differentiate from European DECT devices?
   a. DECT 1.0
   b. DECT 2.4
   c. DECT 5.8
   d. DECT 6.0
2. Bluetooth is designed to cover which one of the following areas?
   a. Metropolitan
   b. Personal area
   c. Wide area
   d. Local area
3. Bluetooth operates in which one of the following frequency bands?
   a. 900 MHz
   b. 2.4 GHz
   c. 5 GHz
   d. 11 GHz
4. ZigBee is used for which two of the following common applications?
   a. Building automation
   b. GPS location
   c. Energy management
   d. RFID device location
5. ZigBee belongs to which one of the following families of standards?
   a. IEEE 802.11
   b. IEEE 802.3
   c. IEEE 802.15.4
   d. IEEE 802.16
6. The IEEE 802.16 standard defines which one of the following technologies?
   a. Token Ring
   b. ZigBee
   c. Bluetooth
   d. WiMAX
7. Suppose you decide to perform spectrum analysis in an area of your network where problems have been reported. Which one of the following tools could you use to connect with a Cisco Aironet 3700 AP to collect and display live spectrum data?
   a. Cisco Meraki Dashboard
   b. Cisco Mobility Services Engine

c. MetaGeek Chanalyzer
d. Wireless LAN controller

8. A spectrum analyzer should be used to perform which one of the following tasks?
   a. Investigate wireless interference
   b. Investigate client roaming problems
   c. Measure wireless throughput
   d. Perform a wireless site survey

9. CleanAir adds which one of the following capabilities to a Cisco lightweight AP?
   a. Wireless mesh
   b. Rogue filtration
   c. Spectral multiplexing
   d. Spectrum analysis

10. Cisco CleanAir analyzes which one of the following types of RF signals?
   a. Non-802.11
   b. 802.3
   c. RRM
   d. CAPWAP

11. By default, is Cisco CleanAir enabled or disabled on a controller?
   a. Enabled
   b. Disabled

12. Suppose that an AP has detected an interference source and reported it with RSSI –58, duty cycle 1 percent, and severity 4. Which one of the following statements is most correct?
   a. The interfering source is very severe.
   b. The interfering source is constantly transmitting.
   c. The interfering source is too weak to be detected.
   d. The interfering source is not severe.

13. When an interference source is detected and classified, the controller assigns which one of the following to uniquely identify the same source across several reporting APs?
   a. BSSID
   b. Cluster ID
   c. ISSID
   d. Actual MAC address

Foundation Topics

Understanding Types of Interference

Recall from Chapter 3, "RF Signals in the Real World," that APs can interfere with each other. If two APs are configured to use the same channel and are in close proximity to each other, co-channel interference results. If the APs are set to use adjacent or overlapping channels, adjacent channel interference occurs.

While those types of interference can certainly be destructive, they involve devices that are based on the 802.11 standard. For example, each access point (AP) transmits on a specific channel (possibly the wrong one!), uses a standardized channel width, and always transmits frames in the 802.11 format. As well, each AP should also follow the 802.11 rules for clear channel assessment (CCA) to maintain some etiquette to share the airtime.

Rogue APs can be a significant and pesky source of interference because they usually belong to someone else. In other words, someone outside your organization is free to bring up their own APs on channels of their choosing. As long as signals from their APs can be received within your own AP cells, you might have to deal with the interference. To mitigate the problem, you must do one of the following:

- Find the rogue AP and its owner, and then convince the owner to remove the AP or change its channel.
- Move your own AP to a different channel, which may cause other nearby APs to be moved too.

When 802.11 devices interfere with each other, the result is usually poor performance due to frame retransmissions, errors, and the lack of available airtime. In other words, the 802.11 data can still be detected but not always correctly received. In contrast, non-802.11 devices do not have to obey any of the familiar 802.11 rules. When a non-802.11 device transmits, the result is completely incompatible with 802.11. APs and 802.11 clients will view the signal as unintelligible and regard it as noise.

The following sections provide an overview of some common non-802.11 devices that can interfere with a WLAN. As you work through this chapter, keep the following two terms in mind:

- **Interference**—802.11 signals that come from sources other than expected APs
- **Noise**—Signals or radio frequency (RF) energy that reduces the signal-to-noise ratio (SNR) and disrupts transmission or reception of an 802.11 signal

Bluetooth

Bluetooth is a technology used to form a personal-area network (PAN), in an effort to unify telephony and computing devices. Today, Bluetooth can be found integrated into cell phones, tablets, laptops, desktops, printers, headsets, cameras, and video game consoles. Bluetooth has low power consumption, making it a good choice for mobile, battery-powered devices.

Bluetooth began as Versions 1.0 and 1.0b, developed by the Bluetooth Special Interest Group (SIG). For a time, several Bluetooth versions were incorporated into the IEEE 802.15.1 standard, but that standard is no longer maintained. The Bluetooth SIG continued to develop its own standard, currently published as core Version 4.

Tip You can find the Bluetooth SIG at http://www.bluetooth.org.

Bluetooth devices are grouped into three classes according to their radiated power. Classes 1 and 2 are the most common and use a maximum transmit power level of 1 mW and 2.5 mW, respectively. Because Bluetooth operates as a PAN, class 1 and 2 devices use a relatively low transmit power level and have a range of only 35 feet. Less common, "industrial" Bluetooth class 3 devices can operate at up to 100 mW.

Bluetooth Low Energy (BLE) was designed for the Internet of Things (IoT), allowing small devices such as smartphones and tablets to transmit up to 20 dBm over a range of 100 meters. Apple has implemented BLE as its iBeacon technology, commonly used to interface with shoppers' mobile devices in retail stores. iBeacon can gather location information from devices, detect shoppers' proximity to items, push notifications such as advertisements and coupons to devices, and collect mobile payments.

Up to eight devices can be paired or linked into a PAN, with one device taking a master role and the others operating as slaves. Such tiny network cells are commonly called *piconets*. Devices operate in the 2.4-GHz ISM band, but are not compatible with the 802.11 standard. Bluetooth uses a frequency-hopping spread spectrum (FHSS) technique, with devices typically moving through a predefined sequence of 79 channels with a bandwidth of 1 MHz each. BLE uses 40 channels over the same span of frequencies and is based on Bluetooth specification 4.2.

Bluetooth transmitters could potentially interfere with the majority of the 2.4-GHz band because their channels overlap with the three non-overlapping 802.11 channels. Bluetooth devices can interfere at a close range because of their low transmit power. If there are many Bluetooth devices in an 802.11 cell, they can create a saturation effect that tends to starve wireless LAN devices for airtime.

Be aware that people commonly carry Bluetooth phones, headsets, and computer peripherals right into your WLAN. However, you might have a difficult time finding them and convincing their owners to leave them outside your wireless network. People typically hold Bluetooth devices close to themselves, where their phones are also held. The Bluetooth's short range usually prevents it from impacting APs, but it has the potential to impact client devices close to the users.

ZigBee

ZigBee is wireless LAN technology that is based on relatively low power consumption and low data rates (20 to 250 Kbps). As a result, it offers reliable communication. ZigBee is commonly used for energy management and home and building automation applications.

ZigBee is defined in the IEEE 802.15.4 standard. It allocates the 2.4-GHz ISM band into 16 channels of 5 MHz each. Even though ZigBee uses the same band as 802.11 devices, it has a low duty cycle and does not utilize a channel much of the time. As well, ZigBee devices normally use a low transmit power level, which minimizes interference, but can ramp up to a maximum of 60 mW when necessary.

Tip You can find the ZigBee Alliance at http://www.zigbee.org.

Cordless Phones

Cordless phones use several wireless technologies to connect remote handsets to a central base station. Phones that are advertised to use the 2.4- and 5.8-GHz bands do just that—and can cause significant interference with nearby WLANs. Cordless phones can use one channel at a time, but can also change channels dynamically. As well, transmit power levels can rise up to 250 mW, overpowering an AP at maximum power.

The Digital Enhanced Cordless Telecommunications (DECT) standard was developed by the European Telecommunications Standards Institute (ETSI) and uses the upper portion of the 1.8 GHz band in Europe, Asia, Australia, and South America. In the United States, cordless phones are based on DECT 6.0, which uses the 1.9-GHz band.

Because DECT and DECT 6.0 phones do not use the 2.4-GHz ISM band, they should not interfere with 802.11 WLANs. However, some similar "DECT-like" phones may operate in the 2.4- and 5.8-GHz bands and interfere.

Microwave Ovens

You might not think of a microwave oven as a communication device. After all, microwave ovens are designed to cook food—not to transmit data. To heat food and liquids and make popcorn, a microwave oven transmits RF energy into a sealed cavity. The energy is meant to stay inside the oven where it can penetrate food items.

In practice, the RF shielding around microwave oven doors is not ideal, allowing some amount of energy to leak out into the surrounding area. Like many other consumer devices, microwave ovens are free to use the 2.4-GHz ISM band. In fact, most microwaves produce a signal that spreads over a large portion of the band. The signal is simply crudely transmitted energy that does not need to follow any standard or frame format. Microwaves are commonly rated to generate around 700 W of power inside the oven. Leaked energy often interferes with nearby APs and 802.11 devices.

To mitigate interference coming from microwave ovens, you can move the oven farther away from WLAN coverage areas. Even better, suggest that the oven be swapped out for a commercial model that has higher-quality RF shielding around the oven and its door.

WiMAX

Worldwide Interoperability for Microwave Access (WiMAX) is a wireless technology designed to provide "last mile" broadband access to consumers within a geographic area.

WiMAX does not require line of sight with a base station, so it can offer connectivity to many fixed and mobile users within a 3 to 10-km radius.

WiMAX is defined by the WiMAX Forum and published as the IEEE 802.16 standard. Although WiMAX, with its central base station and a shared wireless medium, sounds similar to 802.11 WLANs, the two are incompatible. WiMAX operates in several bands between 2 and 11 GHz and from 10 to 66 GHz. Depending on the frequency being used, WiMAX can possibly interfere with 802.11 devices, but such interference is highly unlikely. No widely deployed solutions use the ISM bands; the systems that are advertised for ISM are not supported by any major WiMAX players.

Tip You can find the WiMAX Forum at http://www.wimaxforum.org.

Other Devices

You may encounter other types of non-802.11 devices in and around a WLAN. The following devices can cause varying degrees of interference:

- **Canopy**—A fixed wireless broadband technology developed by Motorola for Internet service providers; uses the 900-MHz, 2.4-GHz, 5.2-GHz, 5.4-GHz, and 5.7-GHz bands.
- **Continuous transmitter**—A device that transmits a continuous, generic waveform that causes steady interference.
- **Jammer**—A device that is designed to disrupt radio signals so that channels or bands become completely unusable.
- **SuperAG**—A proprietary set of extensions developed by Atheros to make Wi-Fi transmissions more efficient. SuperG (802.11g) and SuperAG (both 802.11a and 802.11g) define schemes to compress frames, send bursts of frames, and bond channels for improved throughput. However, they are incompatible with the 802.11 standard and can cause interference.
- **Video camera**—Wireless security cameras that transmit on the 900-MHz, 2.4-GHz, and 5.8-GHz bands with analog or non-802.11 signals.
- **Wi-Fi invalid channel**—Wireless devices that use a nonstandard channel or one that is slightly offset from the familiar channel numbers and center frequencies in the 2.4- and 5-GHz bands. These devices are proprietary and can be difficult to detect because they sit on unexpected frequencies. They can overlap normal 802.11 channels and cause interference.
- **Wi-Fi inverted**—Devices that invert the components of an RF signal from what is normally expected. The inverted signals appear as noise to 802.11 devices. However, two inverted devices can correctly receive and use each other's signal and operate as an undetectable wireless bridge.
- **Xbox**—A video game console developed by Microsoft. Its wireless controller uses a frequency-hopping technique that can interfere with 802.11 devices in the 2.4-GHz band.

Tip You might encounter other technologies such as Wi-Fi Direct and Near Field Communication (NFC) in your environment. Neither one is likely to interfere with 802.11. NFC is used for very close range (10 cm) communication between devices. It uses non-802.11 frequencies. Wi-Fi Direct is a means to allow convenient peer-to-peer communication without an AP, while remaining compatible with 802.11 and any nearby APs. Because it is based on 802.11, Wi-Fi Direct does not interfere with Wi-Fi, but it can impact it. Wi-Fi Direct increases the channel utilization; as more devices use it simultaneously, the 802.11 channels may become unusable.

Using Tools to Detect and Manage Interference

As you have learned in this book, WLANs use the same unlicensed bands as many other technologies and devices. If the RF conditions in your environment are superb, such that your 802.11 APs and clients can enjoy clear channels with low noise and no interference, users will be happy and your job will become easier. However, it is all too easy for someone to power up a rogue AP or a non-802.11 device that begins to interfere with your network.

If some portion of your wireless network begins to have degraded performance, wireless interference might be occurring there. How should you approach such a problem? First, you should figure out what type of device is generating the interference. Then you should attempt to locate the device so that you can negotiate with its owner to have it disabled. If that is not possible, you should move your AP onto a different channel that is clear from interference. The following sections discuss two approaches to analyzing the RF spectrum—one manual and one automatic.

Spectrum Analyzers

With no visibility into a Wi-Fi band, it is difficult to know whether anything is interfering with your network. A spectrum analyzer detects and measures the RF energy that is present on a frequency as it sweeps through the band and displays it in a visible format. The display can be quite versatile, showing things like RF signal strength across the band in real time and the RF duty cycle. The information is displayed in color and can be shown by frequency or over time, where snapshots of the frequency graph are cascaded into a moving queue or "waterfall," giving a visual history of the RF energy. All RF data that is collected can also be recorded, saved, and played back at a later time for further analysis.

A spectrum analyzer can also perform complex analysis of the RF data that is collected. APs and service set identifiers (SSIDs) can be identified, as well as co-channel or neighboring channel interference. Many spectrum analyzers can perform signature analysis to identify the type of device that is interfering with Wi-Fi networks. You can also add a directional antenna and manually walk through an area to track down the source of interference.

Normally, spectrum analyzers are manual tools that require human intervention. You must physically visit a location with the spectrum analysis application and hardware to gather the RF activity that is occurring there. The MetaGeek Chanalyzer is a popular third-party spectrum analysis software tool. It runs on a Windows-based machine and can interface with the MetaGeek Wi-Spy 2.4x (2.4 GHz) and Wi-Spy DBx (2.4 and 5 GHz) USB spectrum adapter. The Chanalyzer software can also connect to a Cisco AP configured in Spectrum Expert Connect (SE-Connect) mode to leverage it as a remote sensor.

Figure 19-1 shows an example Chanalyzer session for the 2.4-GHz band. The upper-right graph displays signal amplitude over the frequency range. The graph underneath shows the "waterfall" history over the same range. Because the waterfall slowly scrolls downward, you can see what has happened on any frequency at a glance. The graph to the left shows the same waterfall, only over a longer history. When using the USB receiver, you must do a bit of your own analysis to identify shapes and signatures in the graphs, with the assistance of a set of overlay templates. In Figure 19-1, however, Chanalyzer has been connected to a Cisco 3702 AP in SE-Connect mode. The remote AP supplies the spectrum data, as well as detects and identifies sources of interference, which are listed at the bottom of the screen.

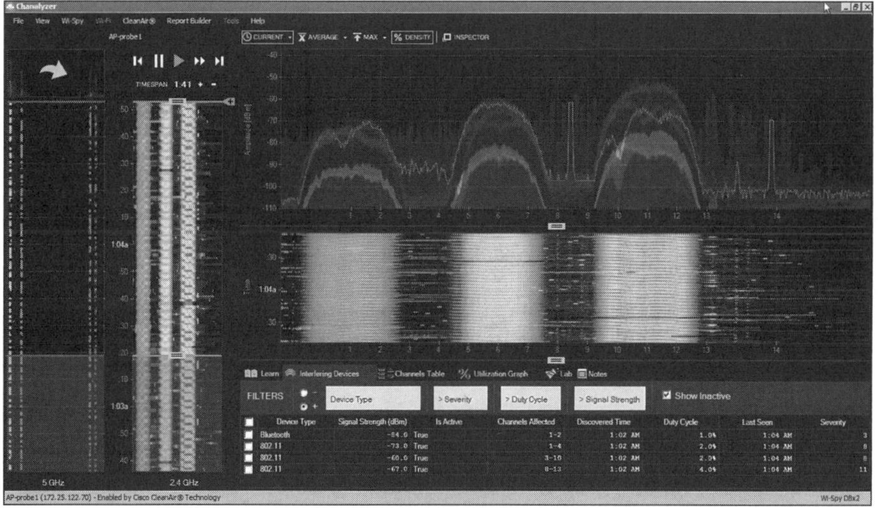

Figure 19-1 *Spectrum Analysis with MetaGeek Chanalyzer and a Cisco AP*

AirMagnet also offers its Spectrum XT spectrum analyzer, which integrates software with a USB-based spectrum receiver for versatile analysis. While Spectrum XT cannot connect to a Cisco AP for remote spectrum data, it can integrate with other AirMagnet tools so that the spectrum information can be collected over an area during a wireless site survey. Spectrum XT can also detect and classify signatures it finds in the data, as shown in Figure 19-2.

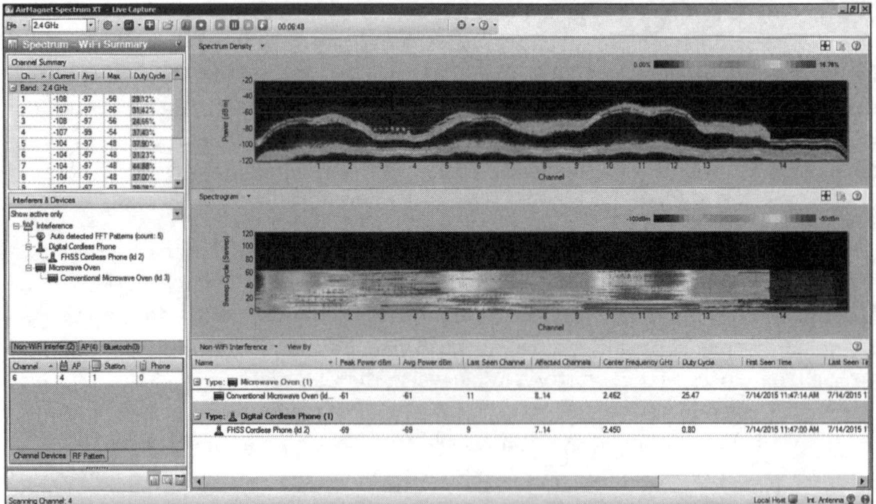

Figure 19-2 *Spectrum Analysis with AirMagnet Spectrum XT*

Cisco cloud-based wireless networks offer spectrum analysis too, through the Cisco Meraki RF Spectrum feature. From the Cisco Meraki Dashboard, select **Wireless > RF Spectrum**, then select an AP from the list. You will be able to see a display of signal strength across the frequency range, a waterfall history display, and channel utilization or a list of interfering APs, as shown in Figure 19-3. The spectrum analysis is performed by hardware integrated in the AP, so it is not necessary to carry a spectrum analyzer onsite to where the AP is located. Cisco Meraki spectrum analysis is still a manual process as you must initiate it from the Dashboard.

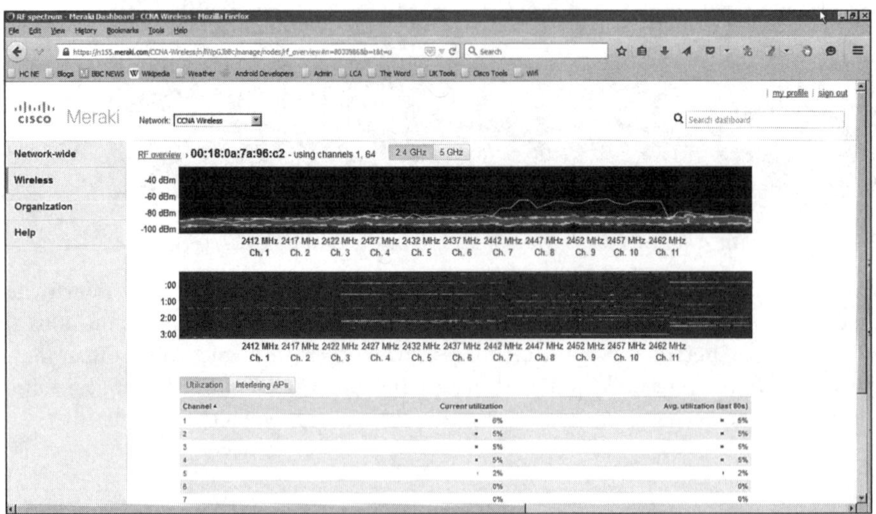

Figure 19-3 *Spectrum Analysis with Cisco Meraki*

Cisco CleanAir

Any Cisco lightweight AP can measure both noise and interference as it scans the channels in a band, as part of the Radio Resource Management (RRM) process. Figure 19-4 shows an example of the information gathered from the 2.4-GHz radio of an AP. The noise level appears to be very low and acceptable on every channel. The Interference by Channel graph displays the received strength of an interference source in dBm on the left vertical axis (dark blue) and the duty cycle of the interference in percent on the right vertical axis (red). Figure 19-4 shows fairly strong interference on channels 4 through 6, but at a very low duty cycle. Although that is good information to have, can you tell what sort of thing is causing the interference?

> **Tip** You can display similar results from a wireless LAN controller GUI by selecting **Monitor > Access Points > Radios > 802.11a/n/ac** or **802.11b/g/n.** Find an AP of interest in the list, and then scroll over to the right side of the page. Click the blue drop-down menu and select **Details.**

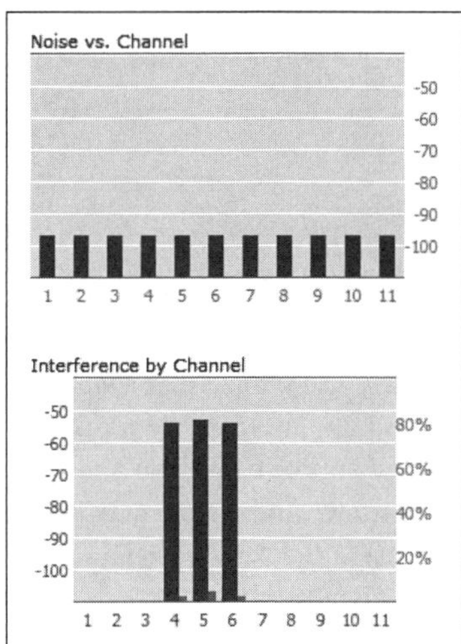

Figure 19-4 *Basic Channel Quality Information Gathered by an AP*

To accurately detect and identify interference, you should use a spectrum analyzer. Rather than rely on your own ability to recognize interference patterns, rely on one of the many spectrum analyzers that offer their own intelligence. They can recognize and identify specific types of devices that are causing interference based on patterns and signatures in the spectrum data.

Now imagine carrying a spectrum analyzer throughout an entire WLAN to look for wireless interference. You never know where interference might crop up or how long it will last. What if you could have a spectrum analyzer permanently located at each AP?

Cisco CleanAir does just that; APs such as the Cisco Aironet 3700, 2700, and 2600 models have spectrum analysis capability built right in to the radio hardware. While a CleanAir

AP is busy operating its normal basic service sets (BSSs) on a channel, it can also monitor RF energy on that channel, analyze the data, and report specific information about any interfering devices—all without interrupting normal WLAN operation. This is all done with the Spectrum Analysis Engine (SAgE) chipset, operating in parallel with the normal 802.11 Wi-Fi chipset in the AP. The SAgE is always on and scans through the frequency range at a high resolution once per second. The high-resolution bandwidth enables the SAgE to identify interference sources with a high degree of accuracy.

Anything that the AP receives and recognizes as an 802.11 frame is processed normally by the split MAC architecture. Other signals that cannot be demodulated according to any known modulation and coding scheme must be coming from a non-802.11 source. That signal information is processed by the spectrum analysis hardware in the AP, as shown in Figure 19-5.

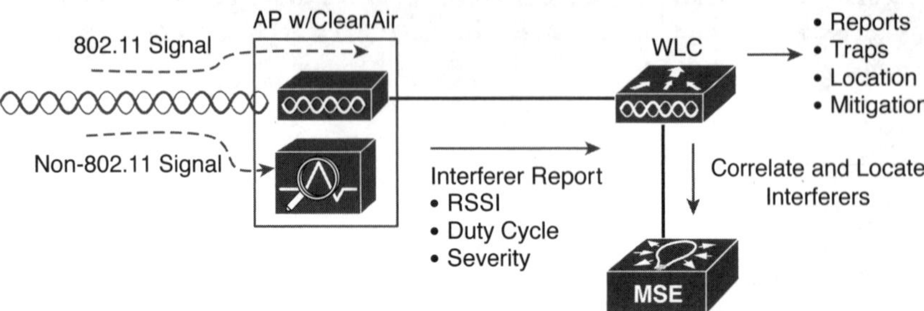

Figure 19-5 *Overview of CleanAir Operation*

The spectrum information from every AP is sent up to the corresponding wireless LAN controller (WLC), where it can be collected and processed. If an interference source is received by more than one AP, the controller can usually correlate the data and realize that a single source is involved and not several different ones. WLCs can also pass interference reports to a Mobility Services Engine (MSE) to determine an interference source's location and display it on a Prime Infrastructure map. With CleanAir, interference can be automatically detected and identified, and its source located—which should make your job easier!

Beyond that, a Cisco unified wireless network can even react to wireless interference automatically. Recall that the RRM process is responsible for working out a channel reuse plan and assigning APs to use specific channels in a band—all on a periodic basis. Event-driven RRM can react to interference immediately, without waiting for the next scheduled RRM iteration, so that an AP can be moved to a different channel to escape the interference.

Enabling CleanAir

CleanAir operates on each band independently. You can enable or disable it globally for all APs on a controller by selecting **Wireless > 802.11a/n** or **802.11b/g/n > CleanAir** and using the **CleanAir** check box, as shown in Figure 19-6. By default, CleanAir is disabled globally on a controller.

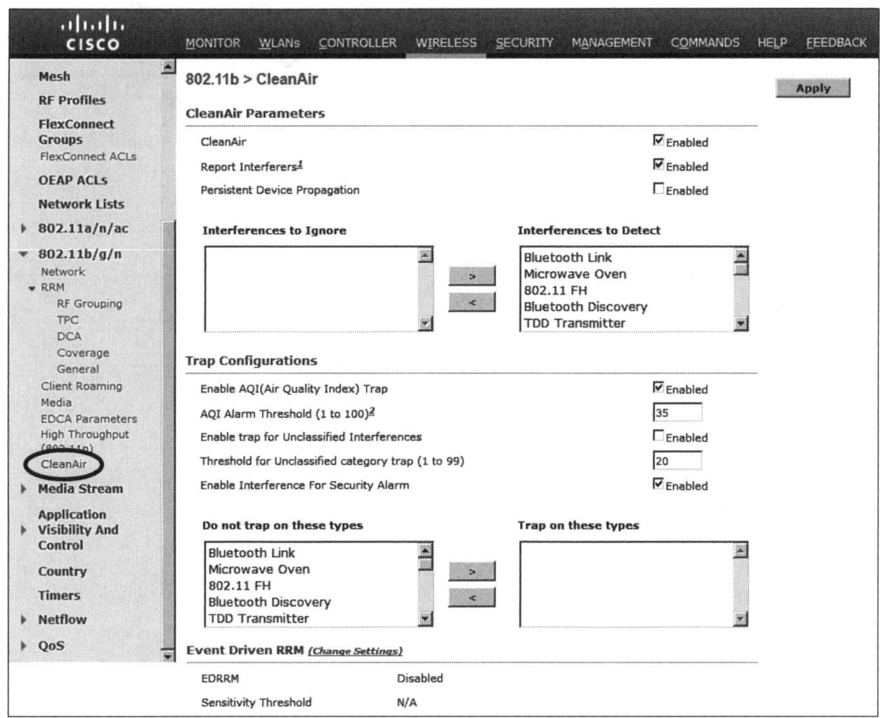

Figure 19-6 *Enabling CleanAir Globally on a Controller*

By default, APs will report the interference types listed in Table 19-2 to their respective controller. You can change this behavior by selecting a type and moving it to the **Interferences to Ignore** or **Interferences to Detect** list. You can also select which types will generate an SNMP trap from the controller when they are detected. Otherwise, any types not selected will not be reported.

Table 19-2 CleanAir Interference Types and Their Default Actions

Interference Type	Report	Trap
802.11 FH (frequency hopping)	X	
802.15.4 (ZigBee)	X	
Bluetooth discovery	X	
Bluetooth link	X	
Canopy	X	
Continuous transmitter	X	X
DECT-like phone	X	
Jammer	X	X
Microwave oven	X	X

Interference Type	Report	Trap
SuperAG	X	
TDD transmitter	X	X
Video camera	X	X
Wi-Fi invalid channel	X	X
Wi-Fi inverted	X	X
WiMAX fixed	X	X
WiMAX mobile	X	X
Xbox	X	

Tip An AP must be configured for either local or monitor mode before it can generate CleanAir interference reports. Reporting is not possible in the Spectrum Expert Connect (SE-Connect) mode.

As interference sources are detected and classified according to interference type, the AP also measures the received signal strength indicator (RSSI) and the duty cycle of the interferer. The duty cycle is the percentage of time the source is transmitting on the channel, which indicates its persistence or how much of the airtime the interferer is consuming. The AP combines the RSSI and duty cycle into a severity index value. Severity ranges from 0 (not severe) to 100 (very severe). Interference with a high severity rating can render a channel unusable.

Interference detection reports sent to a controller include the AP name, interference type, affected channel, time stamp, severity, duty cycle, and RSSI. The controller then tries to determine whether the same interference source is involved in reports coming from multiple APs. If so, the source is uniquely identified by assigning it a cluster ID. A cluster ID is actually a pseudo-MAC address that represents the non-802.11 device with a familiar wireless identifier.

You can display a list of interference detection reports on a controller by selecting **Monitor > CleanAir > 802.11a/n/ac** or **802.11b/g/n > Interference Devices.** Figure 19-7 shows an example list.

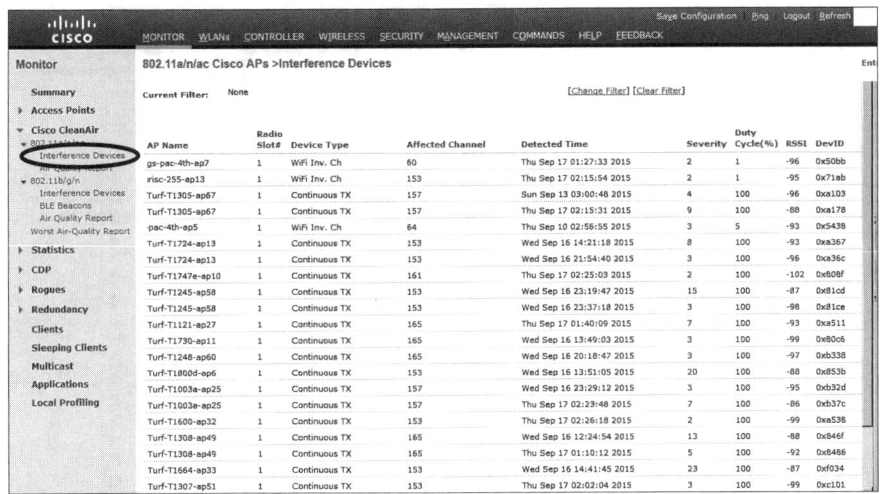

Figure 19-7 *Example List of Interference Device Reports*

Air-Quality Index

As APs and controllers work together to generate a list of interference reports, the list can grow quite long. For example, the controller from Figure 19-7 has a list of 25 reports from the 5-GHz 802.11a/n/ac band. In addition, the same controller has 401 reports on the 2.4-GHz 802.11b/g/n band. To get a feel for the RF conditions on any one channel and AP, you would have to read through the list of reports manually and guess the cumulative effect that various interferers were having.

Cisco WLCs can do a better analysis by calculating an air-quality index (AQI) for each AP and its channels. The AQI indicates Wi-Fi health within an AP's cell, as indicated by a scale from 0 (unusable) to 100 (perfect). You can display the air quality metrics for every AP on a controller by selecting **Monitor > CleanAir > 802.11a/n/ac** or **802.11b/g/n > CleanAir > Air Quality Report**, as shown in Figure 19-8. You can see a summary of the AP with the worst air-quality rating in each band by selecting **Worst Air-Quality Report**.

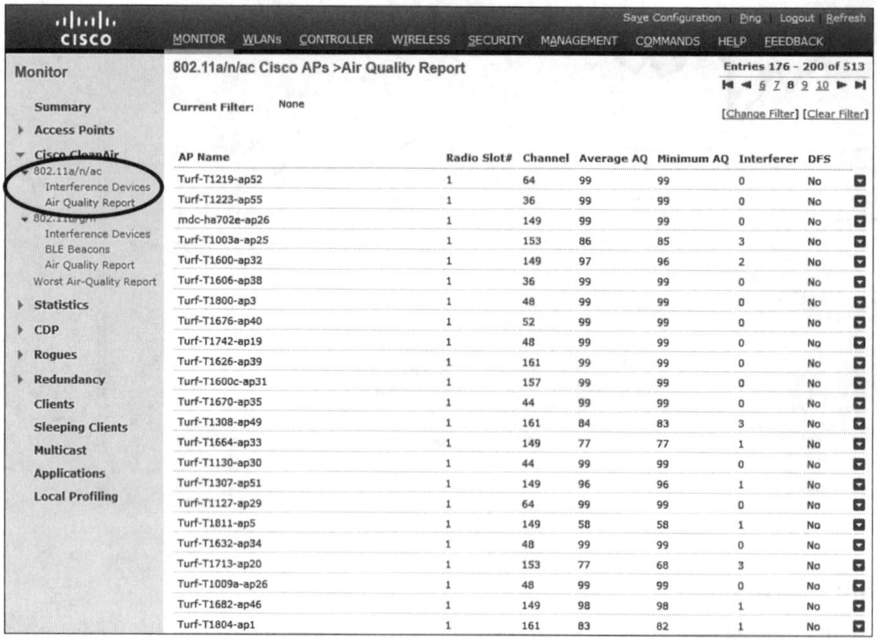

Save Configuration | Ping | Logout | Refresh

MONITOR WLANs CONTROLLER WIRELESS SECURITY MANAGEMENT COMMANDS HELP FEEDBACK

Monitor

- Summary
- Access Points
- Cisco CleanAir
  - 802.11a/n/ac
    - Interference Devices
    - Air Quality Report
  - 802.11b/g/n
    - Interference Devices
    - BLE Beacons
    - Air Quality Report
  - Worst Air-Quality Report
- Statistics
- CDP
- Rogues
- Redundancy
- Clients
- Sleeping Clients
- Multicast
- Applications
- Local Profiling

802.11a/n/ac Cisco APs >Air Quality Report

Entries 176 - 200 of 513

6 7 8 9 10

Current Filter: None

[Change Filter] [Clear Filter]

AP Name	Radio Slot#	Channel	Average AQ	Minimum AQ	Interferer	DFS
Turf-T1219-ap52	1	64	99	99	0	No
Turf-T1223-ap55	1	36	99	99	0	No
mdc-ha702e-ap26	1	149	99	99	0	No
Turf-T1003a-ap25	1	153	86	85	3	No
Turf-T1600-ap32	1	149	97	96	2	No
Turf-T1606-ap38	1	36	99	99	0	No
Turf-T1800-ap3	1	48	99	99	0	No
Turf-T1676-ap40	1	52	99	99	0	No
Turf-T1742-ap19	1	48	99	99	0	No
Turf-T1626-ap39	1	161	99	99	0	No
Turf-T1600c-ap31	1	157	99	99	0	No
Turf-T1670-ap35	1	44	99	99	0	No
Turf-T1308-ap49	1	161	84	83	3	No
Turf-T1664-ap33	1	149	77	77	1	No
Turf-T1130-ap30	1	44	99	99	0	No
Turf-T1307-ap51	1	149	96	96	1	No
Turf-T1127-ap29	1	64	99	99	0	No
Turf-T1811-ap5	1	149	58	58	1	No
Turf-T1632-ap34	1	48	99	99	0	No
Turf-T1713-ap20	1	153	77	68	3	No
Turf-T1009a-ap26	1	48	99	99	0	No
Turf-T1682-ap46	1	149	98	98	1	No
Turf-T1804-ap1	1	161	83	82	1	No

Figure 19-8 *Displaying Air-Quality Indices for all APs on a Controller*

Air-quality ratings are updated dynamically. Each AP measures RF conditions once a second and then calculates an air quality value every 15 seconds and a summary every 30 seconds. By default, these values are reported to the AP's controller every 15 minutes.

You can also view an AP's CleanAir activity more frequently through the rapid update mode. To access this mode, use **Monitor > Access Points > 802.11a/n/ac** or **802.11b/g/n** to display a list of APs. Choose an AP, and then select **CleanAir** from the blue triangular drop-down menu on the right side of the list. In rapid update mode, the controller automatically refreshes the page every 30 seconds with updated CleanAir data.

Rapid update mode also shows more detailed CleanAir information from an AP. In Figure 19-9, the AP has detected interference from a microwave oven. The air quality is shown as a bar graph. Normally only the one channel used by an AP is shown; if the AP is in monitor mode, all channels are shown. The same page also shows channel utilization and interference power measured by the AP.

Controllers display air quality on a per-AP (and channel) basis, and this information is aggregated further by Prime Infrastructure (PI). Air quality is summarized for the entire set of controllers managed in the enterprise.

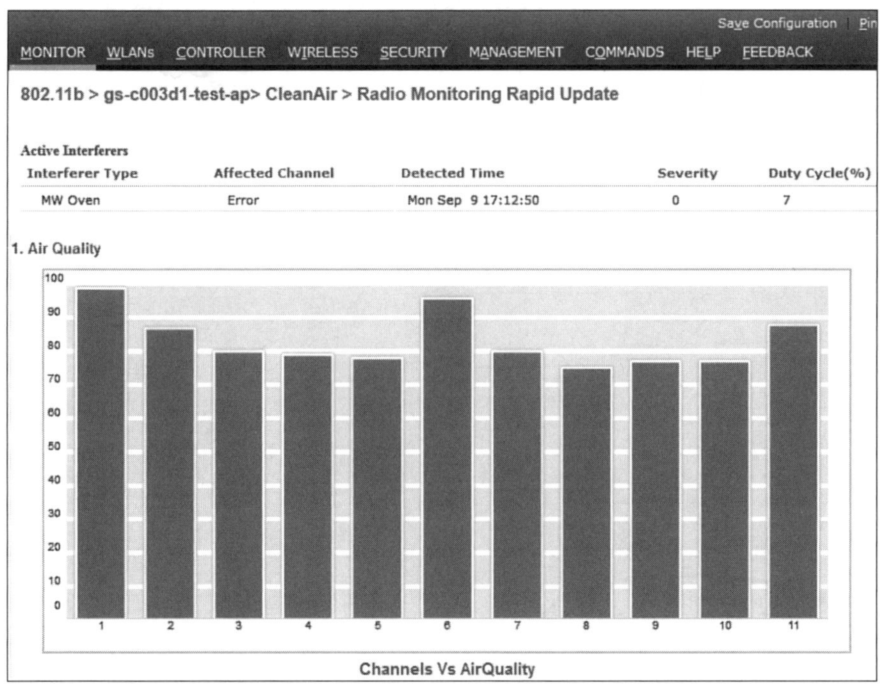

Figure 19-9 *Displaying Detailed CleanAir Data in Rapid Update Mode*

Using Event-Driven RRM

By default, APs and controllers work together to detect, classify, and report wireless interference from non-802.11 devices. CleanAir and RRM can work together so that controllers actually take some action on interference events at the regular RRM intervals. By default, RRM runs the dynamic channel allocation (DCA) algorithm every 10 minutes, but you can increase the interval up to 24 hours. If non-802.11 interference occurs near an AP, the controller must wait until the next DCA interval before it can move the AP away from the unusable channel.

When Event-Driven RRM (ED-RRM) is enabled, the normal periodic RRM DCA process is triggered immediately in response to interference reported by an AP. ED-RRM must be enabled and then triggered based on an AQI threshold. You can set the threshold to Low (AQI 35), Medium (AQI 50), or High (AQI 60).

First, enable ED-RRM globally on a controller. ED-RRM uses the DCA function to change an AP's channel and work out any other channel allocation changes that might be needed. Therefore, navigate to the DCA configuration by selecting **Wireless > 802.11a/n/ac** or **802.11b/g/n > RRM > DCA.** Scroll to the bottom of the page to the Event Driven RRM section, as shown in Figure 19-10. Once you check the **EDRRM** box, you will be able to select a **Sensitivity Threshold** from the drop-down list. By default, the threshold is set to **Medium.** You can select Low, Medium, High, or Custom.

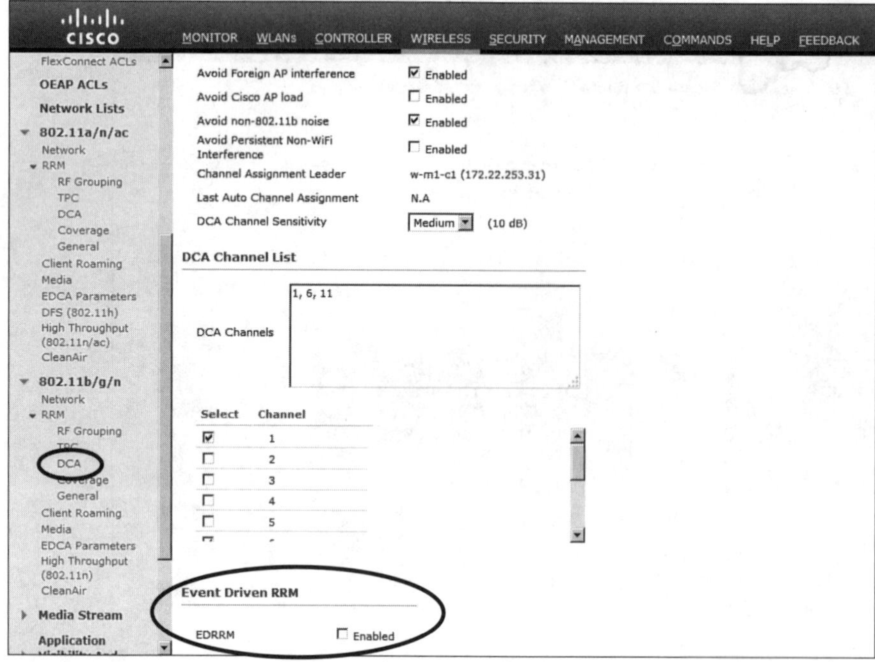

Figure 19-10 *Enabling ED-RRM*

Exam Preparation Tasks

As mentioned in the section "How to Use This Book" in the Introduction, you have a couple of choices for exam preparation: the exercises here, Chapter 21, "Final Review," and the exam simulation questions on the DVD.

Review All Key Topics

Review the most important topics in this chapter, noted with the Key Topic icon in the outer margin of the page. Table 19-3 lists a reference of these key topics and the page numbers on which each is found.

Table 19-3 Key Topics for Chapter 19

Key Topic Element	Description	Page Number
List	Interference and noise	432
Paragraph	CleanAir operation	440
Paragraph	Air-quality index	443

Define Key Terms

Define the following key terms from this chapter and check your answers in the glossary:

air-quality index (AQI), Cisco CleanAir, cluster ID, duty cycle, Event-Driven RRM (ED-RRM), interference, noise, piconet, pseudo-MAC address, rogue AP, spectrum analyzer

This chapter covers the following topics:

- **Troubleshooting Client Connectivity**—This section covers some strategies and methods you can use when faced with wireless clients that report problems connecting to the network.
- **Troubleshooting AP Connectivity**—This section describes some troubleshooting steps you can use to figure out why an access point is not connecting or operating properly.
- **Checking the RF Environment**—This section provides an overview of third-party tools that you can leverage to detect the presence of APs and SSIDs at a location. It also covers tools that scan channels, map 802.11 activity, analyze wireless traffic, and analyze the RF spectrum.

This chapter covers the following exam topics:

- 6.0—Performing Client Connectivity Troubleshooting
- 6.1—Validating WLAN configuration settings at the infrastructure side
  - 6.1a—Security settings
  - 6.1b—SSID settings
- 6.2—Validating AP infrastructure settings
  - 6.2a—Port level configuration
  - 6.2b—Power source
  - 6.2c—AP and antenna orientation and position
- 6.3—Validate client settings
  - 6.3a—SSID
  - 6.3b—Security
- 6.4—Employ appropriate controller tools to assist troubleshooting
  - 6.4a—GUI logs
  - 6.4b—CLI show commands
- 6.5—Identify appropriate third-party tools to assist troubleshooting
  - 6.5a—OS-based Client utilities
  - 6.5b—Wi-Fi scanners
  - 6.5c—RF mapping tool

CHAPTER 20

Troubleshooting WLAN Connectivity

As a CCNA Wireless engineer, you will be expected to perform some basic troubleshooting work when wireless problems arise. The CCNA Wireless exam blueprint focuses on some troubleshooting tools that are available on Cisco Wireless LAN Controllers (WLCs), Wireless Controller Modules (WCMs), and Prime Infrastructure (PI), as well as some third-party tools. This chapter helps you get some perspective on wireless problems, develop a troubleshooting strategy, and become comfortable using the tools at your disposal.

"Do I Know This Already?" Quiz

The "Do I Know This Already?" quiz allows you to assess whether you should read this entire chapter thoroughly or jump to the "Exam Preparation Tasks" section. If you are in doubt about your answers to these questions or your own assessment of your knowledge of the topics, read the entire chapter. Table 20-1 lists the major headings in this chapter and their corresponding "Do I Know This Already?" quiz questions. You can find the answers in Appendix A, "Answers to the 'Do I Know This Already?' Quizzes."

Table 20-1 "Do I Know This Already?" Section-to-Question Mapping

Foundation Topics Section	Questions
Troubleshooting Client Connectivity	1–7
Troubleshooting AP Connectivity	8
Checking the RF Environment	9–10

Caution The goal of self-assessment is to gauge your mastery of the topics in this chapter. If you do not know the answer to a question or are only partially sure of the answer, you should mark that question as wrong for purposes of the self-assessment. Giving yourself credit for an answer you correctly guess skews your self-assessment results and might provide you with a false sense of security.

1. To get PI or a wireless controller to display information about a specific wireless client, you go to the **Monitor > Clients** page. Which one of the following pieces of information should you input to obtain the best troubleshooting data?
   a. WLC IP address
   b. SSID
   c. Client's MAC address
   d. AP name
2. Which one of the following states indicates that a wireless client has met all of the requirements to begin using a wireless network?
   a. 8021X_REQD
   b. START
   c. RUN
   d. L2AUTHCOMPLETE
   e. READY
   f. COMPLETE
3. Suppose that you search for a wireless client on a controller and notice that it is associated. Which one of the following parameters would confirm that the client has completed the association process with the controller and is ready to pass data?
   a. Client's IP address
   b. AP name and IP address
   c. Associated AP status
   d. RUN policy manager state
4. If a client is shown to be in the 8021X_REQD state, even though the end user tried to join the wireless network several minutes ago, which one of the following best describes the client's current condition?
   a. The client does not support any of the 802.11 amendments.
   b. The client failed to authenticate itself properly.
   c. Spanning Tree Protocol is blocking the AP's uplink.
   d. The client failed to receive an IP address.

5. To troubleshoot a client's connection to the wireless network, you decide to use a link test from the controller. The client is a Windows-based machine, uses an adapter that supports 802.11n, is configured to support all possible data rates, and supports CCXv1. Which one of the following link tests will the controller perform with the client?
   a. CCXv1 test frames
   b. ICMP echo packets
   c. Round-trip time (RTT) measurements
   d. RSSI measurements at client and AP

6. Which of the following are required on the client's wireless adapter before a CCX link test can be performed on a controller? (Select all that apply.)
   a. CCXv1
   b. CCXv2
   c. CCXv4
   d. CCXv5
   e. Support for any CCX version

7. Suppose that you have a large wireless network with several controllers, many APs, a RADIUS server, a syslog server, and Prime Infrastructure. A user has reported connectivity problems in a specific building location, but gave no details about the AP or controller he tried to join. Which one of the following represents the most efficient troubleshooting method you can use to find information about the client?
   a. Go to the client's location and use your own computer to associate with the network, then find out which AP and controller you are using
   b. Search for the client's MAC address on each controller
   c. Search for the client's MAC address on Prime Infrastructure
   d. Search for the client's MAC address on the RADIUS server

8. To find a client from a wireless controller GUI, which one of the following should you select?
   a. **Find > Clients**
   b. **Monitor > Clients**
   c. **Management > Clients**
   d. **Monitor > Summary**

9. Suppose that you have just received news that no users can connect with a newly installed lightweight AP. You decide to examine the switch configuration where the AP is connected, knowing that it needs to be bound to VLAN 11. Which one of the following switch interface configurations is correct?

   a. **switchport**
      switchport mode access
      no shutdown

   b. **switchport**
      switchport trunk allowed vlan 1-11
      switchport trunk encapsulation dot1q
      switchport mode trunk

   c. **switchport**
      switchport access vlan 11
      switchport mode access
      spanning-tree portfast
      shutdown

   d. **switchport**
      switchport access vlan 11
      switchport mode access
      no shutdown

10. Suppose you would like to scan the channels in the 5-GHz band to see which SSIDs are available to clients on which channels in a certain area. Which one of the following tools is a Wi-Fi scanner that is suited for this purpose?

   a. Ekahau Site Survey Pro

   b. Savvius OmniPeek

   c. MetaGeek inSSIDer Office

   d. AirMagnet Spectrum XT

11. Ekahau Site Survey Pro is an example of which one of the following third-party wireless tools?

   a. Spectrum analyzer

   b. Packet analyzer

   c. RF mapping tool

   d. Wi-Fi scanner

Foundation Topics

Troubleshooting Client Connectivity

When one or more network users report that they are having problems, your first course of action should be to gather more information. Begin with a broad perspective and then try to ask pointed questions that will narrow the scope of possible causes. You do not want to panic or waste time chasing irrelevant things. Instead, ask questions and try to notice patterns or similarities in the answers you receive.

For example, if you get reports from many people in the same area, perhaps an AP is misconfigured or malfunctioning. Reports from many areas or from a single service set identifier (SSID) may indicate problems with a controller configuration. However, if you receive a report of only one wireless user having problems, it might not make sense to spend time troubleshooting a controller, where many users are supported. Instead, you should focus on that one user's client device and its interaction with an AP.

As you prepare to troubleshoot a single wireless client, think about all of the things a client needs to join and use the network. Figure 20-1 illustrates the following conditions that must be met for a successful association:

- Client is within RF range of an AP, asks to associate
- Client authenticates
- Client requests and receives an IP address

20

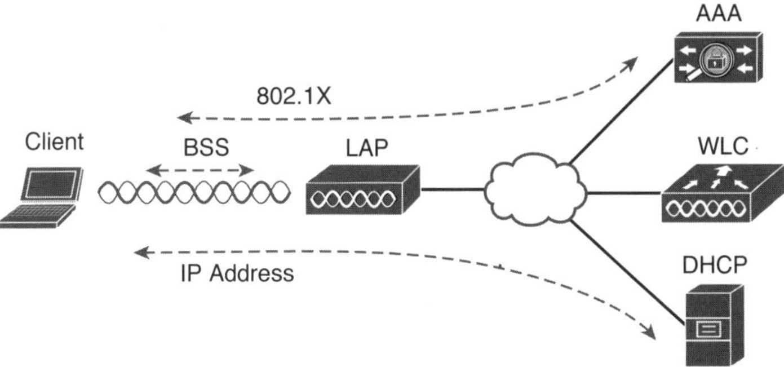

Figure 20-1 *Conditions for a Successful Wireless Association*

Try to gather information from the end user to see what the client is experiencing. "I cannot connect" or "The Wi-Fi is down" might actually mean that the user's device cannot associate, cannot get an IP address, or cannot authenticate. A closer inspection of the device might reveal more clues. Therefore, at a minimum, you will need the wireless adapter MAC address from the client device, as well as its physical location. The end user might try to tell you about a specific AP that is in the room or within view. Record that information too, but remember that the client device selects which AP it wants to use—not the human user. The device may well be using a completely different AP.

The sections in this chapter start by focusing on a single client device and then broaden outward, where multiple clients might be affected.

Troubleshooting Clients from PI

Most of your time managing and monitoring a wireless network will be spent in Prime Infrastructure. PI is also a convenient place to begin troubleshooting client connectivity issues. With a little information about the client, PI can display the client's current state and past history on the wireless network.

You should begin by searching for a client that is having an issue. Enter the client's wireless MAC address into the search box at the upper-right corner of the PI screen, as shown in Figure 20-2. If PI has been integrated with Cisco Identity Services Engine (ISE) in your environment, you might be able to enter a username into the search field instead.

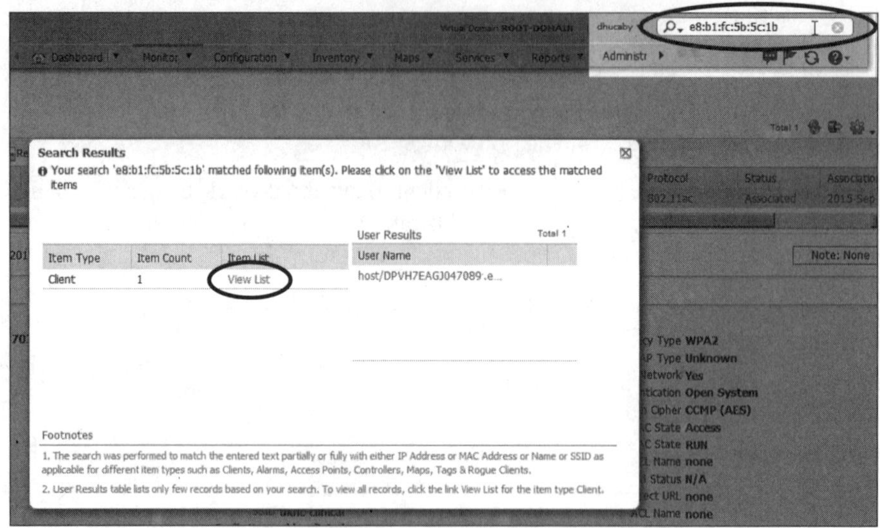

Figure 20-2 *Searching for a Client in PI*

The Search Results window will list any entries that PI can find about the client. In Figure 20-2, PI has found one instance of client MAC address e8:b1:fc:5b:5c:1b. Click the **View List** link to display more information about the client. Figure 20-3 shows an example. At a glance, you can see the client's MAC address, IP address, IP type, username, the wireless network adapter vendor (Intel), location (the name of the PI map, which is obscured in the figure), device name (the WLC or WCM hosting the client), the controller interface (blue), VLAN (36), 802.11 protocol (802.11ac), client status (Associated), and the association time.

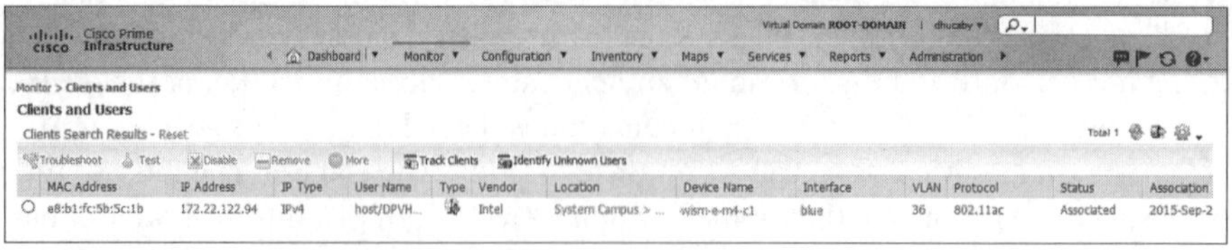

Cisco Prime Infrastructure
Virtual Domain ROOT-DOMAIN | dhucaby
Dashboard Monitor Configuration Inventory Maps Services Reports Administration
Monitor > Clients and Users
Clients and Users
Clients Search Results - Reset
Total 1
Troubleshoot Test Disable Remove More Track Clients Identify Unknown Users

MAC Address	IP Address	IP Type	User Name	Type	Vendor	Location	Device Name	Interface	VLAN	Protocol	Status	Association
e8:b1:fc:5b:5c:1b	172.22.122.94	IPv4	host/DPVH...		Intel	System Campus > ...	wism-e-m4-c1	blue	36	802.11ac	Associated	2015-Sep-2

Figure 20-3 *Displaying a Client in PI*

This is all very helpful information because you may have already learned more about the client. For example, you now know its IP address, a user or host name, which controller it has joined, which controller interface and VLAN it is using, and that it has an active association with an AP.

You can display much more detailed information about the client by clicking the radio button to the left of the client entry. Figure 20-4 continues with the example client, showing details about the client's general configuration, AP/controller session, and security settings. From this information, you can confirm which 802.11 authentication, wireless security policy, encryption, and Extensible Authentication Protocol (EAP) type the client is using.

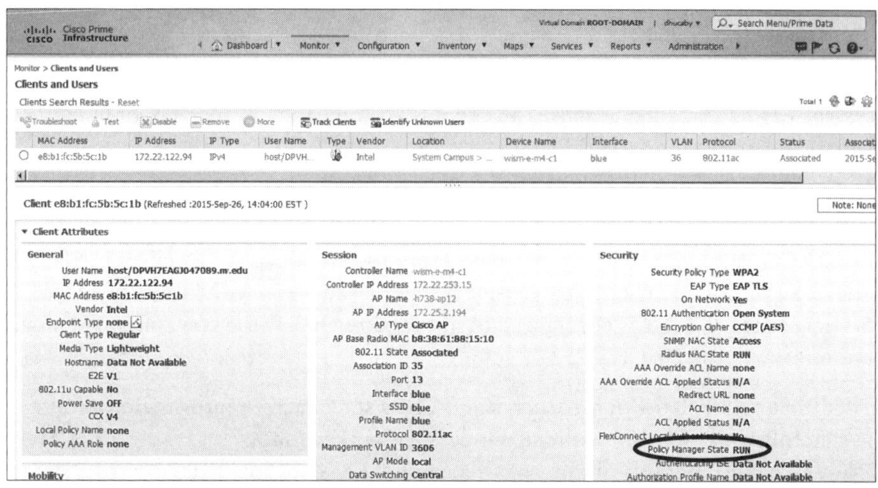

Figure 20-4 *Displaying Client Details in PI*

Perhaps the most important information about the client is listed as the Policy Manager State, which is circled in Figure 20-4. Before a controller will permit a client to fully associate with a basic service set (BSS), the client must progress through a sequence of states. Each state refers to a policy that the client must meet before moving on to the next state. Table 20-2 lists and describes the client policy states. You should understand the states and what they mean, but you should not spend time memorizing the table.

Table 20-2 Possible WLC Client States

State	Description
START	Client activity has just begun.
AUTHCHECK	Client must pass Layer 2 authentication policy.
8021X_REQD	Client must pass 802.1x authentication.
L2AUTHCOMPLETE	Layer 2 policy is complete; Layer 3 policies can begin.
WEP_REQD	Client must authenticate with Wired Equivalent Privacy (WEP).
DHCP_REQD	WLC is waiting to learn the client's IP address.
WEBAUTH_REQD	Client must pass web authentication.
RUN	Client has passed Layer 2 and Layer 3 policies, successfully associated, and can pass traffic.

A probing client always begins in the START state and then moves into Layer 2 policy states and Layer 3 policy states. For example, if the client is attempting to associate with a WLAN that is configured for some form of 802.1x authentication, the client must pass through the 8021X _ REQD state. If it successfully authenticates, it can move further down the list of states.

Ultimately, each client should end up in the RUN state, where it has fully associated with the BSS and is permitted to pass traffic over the WLAN. If you find a client that is consistently shown in a state other than RUN, the client must be having a problem passing the policy of that state.

For example, a client that is stuck in 8021X _ REQD is likely having trouble authenticating successfully. That could be because the client is sending an incorrect key or has an invalid certificate, or because the RADIUS server is down.

A client stuck in DHCP _ REQD is having trouble obtaining an IP address. The controller monitors the Dynamic Host Configuration Protocol (DHCP) request of each client, as well as the DHCP offer returned to each client. If an offer is not seen, the client is stuck waiting. (One exception is a client that is using a static IP address, without the need for DHCP. So long as the WLAN is configured to not require DHCP, the controller will move the client on through the DHCP _ REQD state.)

You can continue to scroll down the Clients and Users screen to see information about the client's mobility relationship with the wireless network, as shown in Figure 20-5. The client is shown to have mobility status Local, meaning it has not roamed away from the initial controller it joined.

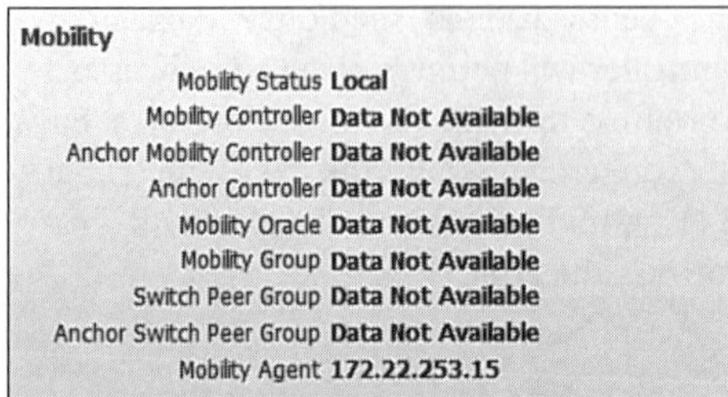

Figure 20-5 *Displaying Client Mobility Details*

Scroll down further to see detailed information about the client's 802.11 link with the AP. For example, Figure 20-6 shows receive and transmit counters for the client, as well as its current received signal strength indicator (RSSI), signal-to-noise ratio (SNR), association uptime, current transmit data rate (Modulation Coding Scheme [MCS] value), and supported data rates. From this information, you can verify that the AP is receiving the client with a good, strong signal (–40 dBm) and a good SNR value (57).

Key Topic

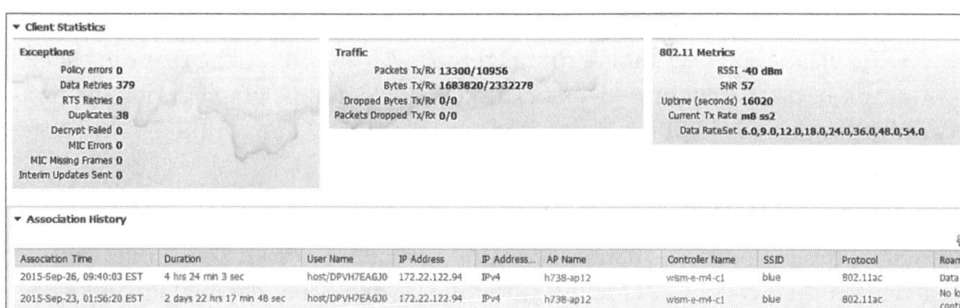

Figure 20-6 *Displaying Client RF Statistics*

Remember that the SNR measures how many dB the signal is above the noise floor. The SNR can be a low value for the 802.11a/g modulation schemes, higher for 802.11n, and even higher for the greater 802.11ac data rates. With the client's strong signal and high SNR, you can see that it is able to use MCS 8 and two spatial streams (m8, ss2) with the AP. The client statistics also show some very important counters that relate to the RF conditions. The client has had only 379 data retries or retransmissions out of 13,300 packets transmitted, or a total of 2.8 percent retries. That indicates that the channel is not overutilized and that the client has been very successful at transmitting frames to the AP without contention from other stations on the same channel.

At the bottom of Figure 20-6, notice that PI provides a history of the client's AP associations over time. Each line represents an association event, with a time stamp and duration, along with the AP and controller names, SSID, 802.11 protocol, and a reason for the event. From the reason listed, you can learn more about why the client changed its association or why the controller updated the entry.

20

Keep scrolling down to find more useful information about the client's history on the wireless network. In Figure 20-7, you can see a small map that indicates the current location of the client as a blue square. The map identifies in which campus, building, and floor the client is located, as well as an approximate location within the floor area. This information can be quite useful if you need to physically go and find the client device. After all, the device is probably mobile and may have moved since the time a problem was reported.

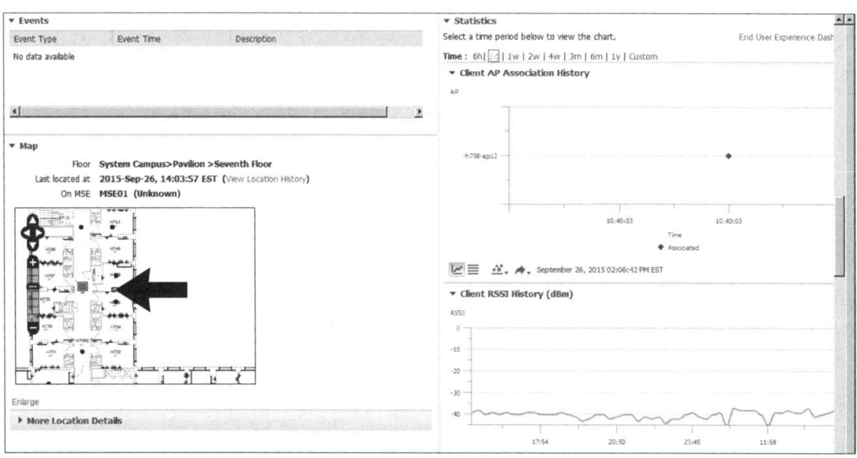

Figure 20-7 *Displaying Client Location and RF History*

There are also graphs that show when the client changed its associations, along with the client RSSI and SNR, all graphed over time. From Figure 20-7, you can assume that the client has been stationary, because only one AP association is shown on the graph during the past day. You can also see that the RSSI has been steady at around –40 dBm. Although it is not shown in the figure, the SNR has also been steady and strong.

So far, this section has presented results and figures from a client that has a successful association. What should you do with a client that is truly having problems? You should still begin by searching for the client in Prime Infrastructure, then use any detailed information to get more clues about the problem.

For example, suppose you searched for a client that reported connectivity problems and found the information shown in Figure 20-8. Notice that the client has no IP address listed, yet it has an Associated status with the AP. Now look at the Policy Manager State, which is DHCP_REQD instead of RUN. The controller is waiting for the client to successfully obtain an IP address from a DHCP server, but that has not yet completed. Most likely, the DHCP address scope is exhausted or the client is trying to use a static IP address on a WLAN that is configured to require DHCP address assignments.

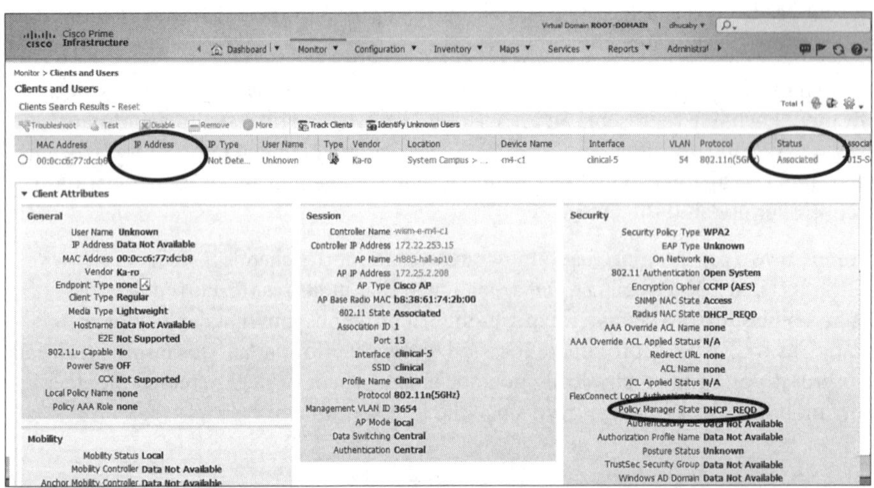

Figure 20-8 *Troubleshooting a Client with IP Addressing Problems*

Suppose a WLAN is configured to use some form of EAP for client authentication. If a client fails to authenticate correctly, PI will indicate that the controller has kept the client in the DOT1X_REQD state. This can happen if the credentials are entered incorrectly or if a RADIUS server has an expired digital certificate.

PI can also provide some clues about RF problems that a client is experiencing before you have to travel onsite to take further measurements. Figure 20-9 shows an example associated client. The Client Statistics section shows that the client is currently being received at RSSI –71 dBm, with an SNR of 27. Because of the low signal strength and low SNR, the performance must be somewhat low. Out of 586,144 packets transmitted, the client has had 115,091 data retries, or 19.6 percent retransmissions. That might explain why the client has a current Tx rate using the M5 MCS with two spatial streams. Figure 20-10 also shows that the client almost always experiences an RSSI of –70 dBm or less, and an SNR that always hovers between 25 and 30.

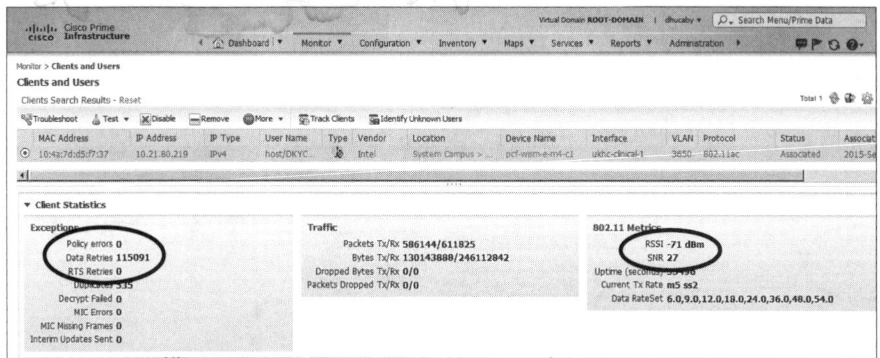

Figure 20-9 *Troubleshooting Client RF Problems with PI*

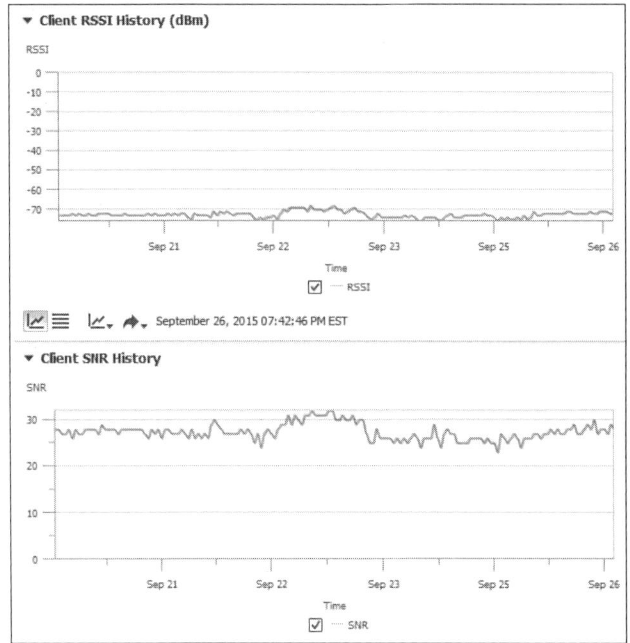

Figure 20-10 *Troubleshooting Poor Client RSSI and SNR with PI*

Testing a Client from PI

Prime Infrastructure offers a quick way to test the link between the controller and the client device. Once you have searched for a client, select its radio button, then select **Test > Link Test** above the client list. A short test to gauge the RF conditions between the controller and the client will run and the results will be displayed.

If the client does not support Cisco Compatible Extensions Version 4 (CCXv4) or CCXv5, the controller will run a ping test consisting of 20 500-byte Internet Control Message

Protocol (ICMP) echo packets sent to the client's IP address. The controller should receive replies to each of the ping packets if the wireless link is good and if the client supports ping traffic. The controller also records the RSSI of the client device and the SNR and reports the test results, as shown in Figure 20-11. In this case, the controller sent 20 test packets, but the client echoed only 4 of them back successfully. This could indicate RF problems between the AP and the client.

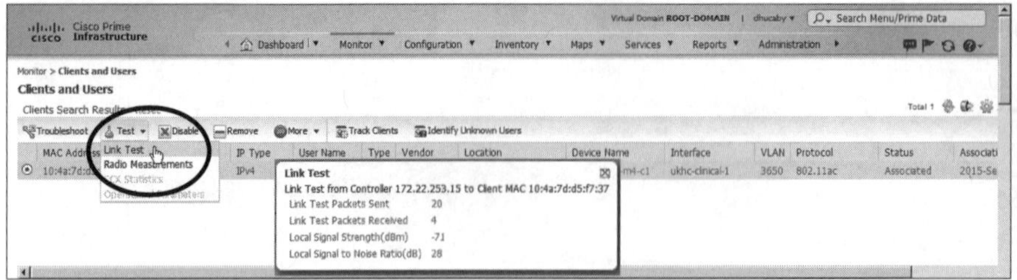

Figure 20-11 *Running a Link Test to a Wireless Client*

Notice that the ping test reports only a single RSSI value. Even though a wireless link is bidirectional and involves two devices, the AP and the client, the controller can report only on the RSSI of the signal it receives from the client. Naturally, the client can (and probably does) measure the RSSI of the AP's signal that it receives, but it cannot share that information with the controller using ping packets.

If you perform a link test on a client that does support CCXv4 or CCXv5, the controller can gather much more information about the conditions at *both* ends of the link. In that case, the link test uses CCX messages rather than pings. The controller can still measure the RSSI of the client's signal, plus the client can return a message that contains the AP's RSSI from the client's perspective. This gives a signal strength reading in *both* directions.

You can also perform an automatic sequence of troubleshooting steps by selecting a client and then clicking the **Troubleshoot** button above the client list. PI will check to see if the client has an 802.11 association, if it can pass 802.1X authentication, and if it has an IP address. The results of the tests are shown, along with a problem description and a list of recommendations to resolve the problem. In Figure 20-12, the client has passed everything except the IP address assignment test, so PI has offered several recommendations.

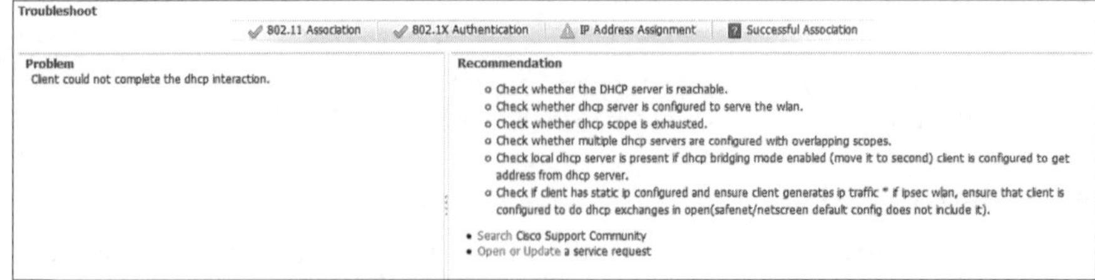

Figure 20-12 *Displaying the Results of Client Troubleshooting Tests*

Troubleshooting Clients from the Controller

Prime Infrastructure offers a "single pane of glass" interface into wireless networks by communicating with and gathering information from the wireless controllers. You can perform quite a bit of troubleshooting directly through the controller GUI and CLI too—much of it the same as from PI. This section presents a summary of the controller-based troubleshooting knowledge required for the CCNA Wireless exam.

As a wireless client probes and attempts to associate with an AP, it is essentially communicating with the controller. You can access a wealth of troubleshooting information from the controller, as long as you know the client's MAC address.

You can view a client's current status by navigating to **Monitor > Clients.** The controller will display every client that is associated to any of its APs. To find a specific client in the long list of clients, click the **Change Filter** link. You can then filter the list based on MAC address, AP name, WLAN profile or SSID, client status, client radio type, and so on. In Figure 20-13, the list will be filtered to display only client MAC address 00:15:70:f2:1c:c1.

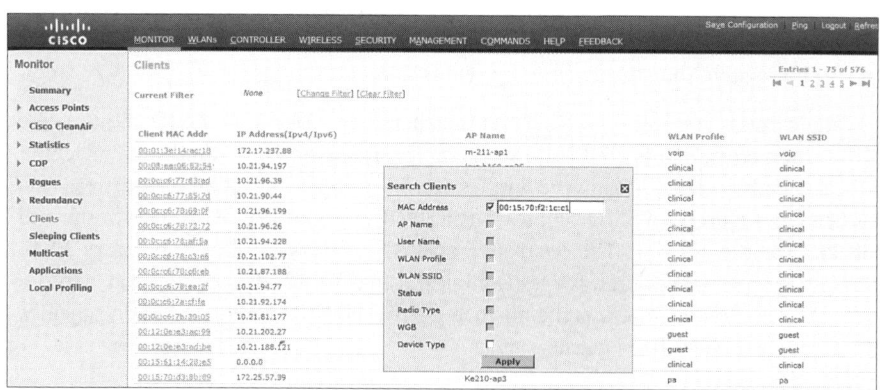

Figure 20-13 *Displaying and Filtering Client Status Information on a Controller*

Click the client MAC address link to display all the detailed information known about the client. The information that is shown is very similar to the client details that Prime Infrastructure shows, including client statistics, the client's policy manager state, security parameters, and RF readings.

You can also select the blue arrow icon at the right end of the client entry to display a drop-down menu to manage the client's association, as shown in Figure 20-14. Selecting **Remove** will deauthenticate the client and force it off the network, so that it will attempt to associate again. Selecting **Disable** will add the client's MAC address to the list of disabled clients and will force the client off the network.

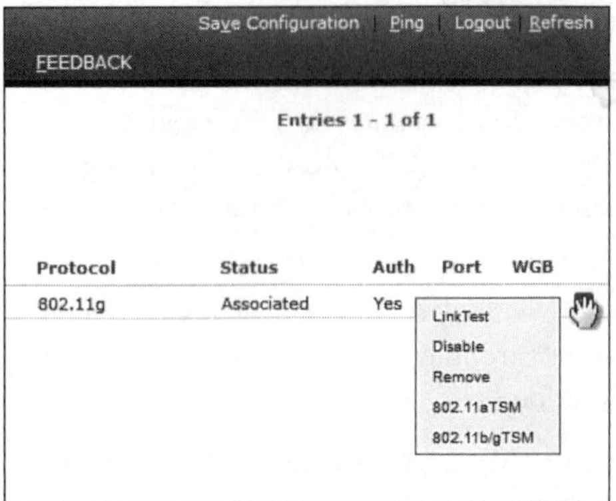

Figure 20-14 *Managing a Client Association*

Verifying Client WLAN Settings

If an end user reports a problem connecting to the wireless network, you should verify that the client device has been configured with wireless settings that match those of the WLAN. If the two do not match, then the association will fail.

First, view the wireless connection settings on the client and look for the SSID and the wireless security parameters. Figure 20-15 shows example parameters on a Windows 7 machine that were displayed by right-clicking the wireless connection and selecting **Properties**. The client has been configured for SSID "clinical" using WPA2 Enterprise, AES encryption, and Microsoft PEAP authentication. The controller's WLAN settings are shown in Figure 20-16. The controller has been configured for SSID clinical using WPA2, AES encryption, and pre-shared key (PSK) authentication. It is the mismatch between WPA2 authentication schemes that is preventing the client from connecting.

Key Topic

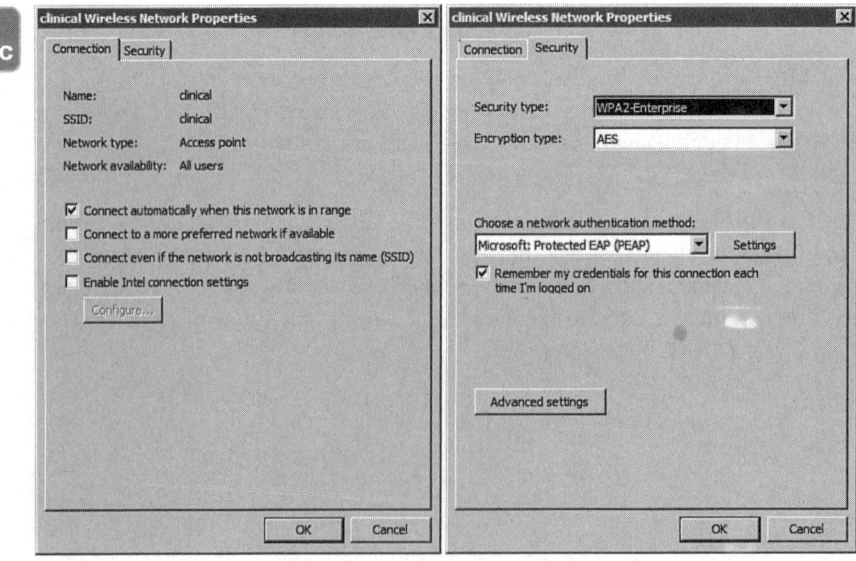

Figure 20-15 *Displaying WLAN Settings on a Windows 7 Client*

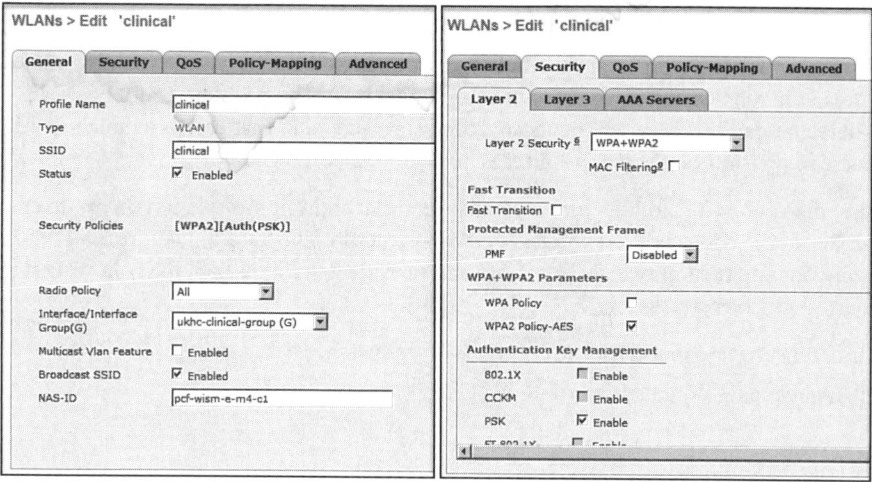

Figure 20-16 *Displaying WLAN Settings on a Controller for Comparison with Client Settings*

Tip If a client cannot associate after you exhaust your attempts at troubleshooting, be aware that the client may be listed in the controller as an excluded or disabled client. A client can be added to the exclusion list automatically, when the client's activity matches one of the controller's wireless protection policy signatures. A client can also be moved to the disabled clients list manually, usually as a result of violating a local security policy. Navigate to **Security > Disabled Clients** and look for the client's MAC address in the list. If the list is long, you can also use the search tool to search for the MAC address on that page.

Viewing Controller Logs

A wireless LAN controller maintains two types of logs that can be useful for troubleshooting:

- A trap log, which records events such as detected rogue devices, AP changes, channel changes, and invalid settings
- A message log, which contains system conditions for the controller as a whole

You can view the logs with the controller GUI and the CLI. Table 20-3 lists the menus and commands needed to display the log contents in either management interface.

Table 20-3 Methods to Display Controller Log Contents

Log Type	GUI Menu	CLI Command
Trap log	**Monitor > Most Recent Traps > View All**	**show traplog**
Message log	**Management > Logs > Message Logs**	**show msglog**

Troubleshooting AP Connectivity

In cases where you get reports from multiple users who are all having problems in the same general area, you might need to focus your efforts on an AP. The problem could be as simple as a defective radio, where no clients are receiving a signal. In that case, you might have to go onsite to confirm that the transmitter is not working correctly.

Otherwise, the split-MAC architecture creates several different points where you can troubleshoot. Recall the Cisco unified wireless network structure illustrated in Figure 20-17. To successfully operate the lightweight AP (LAP) and provide a working BSS, the following two things must work correctly:

- The LAP must have connectivity to its access layer switch.
- The LAP must have connectivity to its WLC.

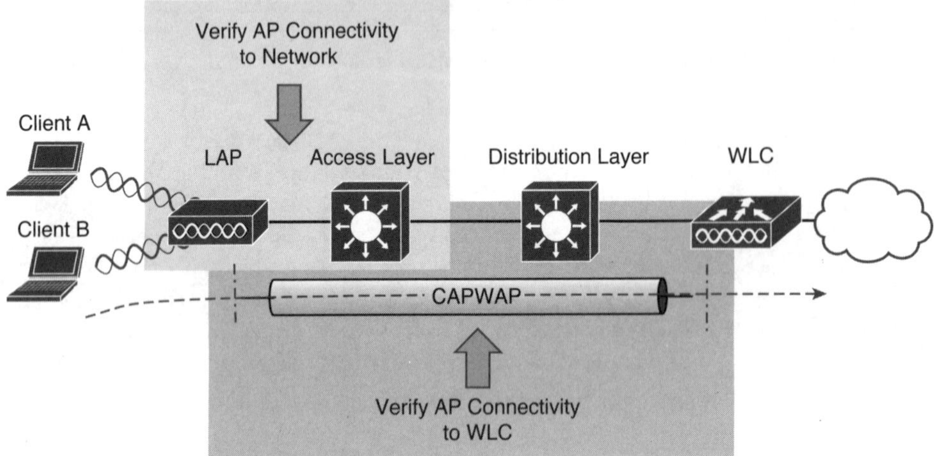

Figure 20-17 *Verifying AP Connectivity in a Cisco Unified Wireless Network*

Verifying AP-to-WLC Connectivity

First, verify the connectivity between an AP and a controller. Usually you will do this when a new AP is installed, to make sure it is able to discover and join a controller before clients arrive and try to use the wireless network. You can also do this at any time as a quick check of the AP's health.

The easiest approach is to simply look for the AP in the list of live APs that have joined the controller. If you know which controller the AP should join, open a management session to it. Navigate to **Wireless > All APs > Change Filter**, and then enter the AP's MAC address or some portion of its name. If the search reveals a live AP that is joined to the controller, verify the IP address that the AP is using and make sure that the AP Uptime shows a valid working duration, as shown in Figure 20-18.

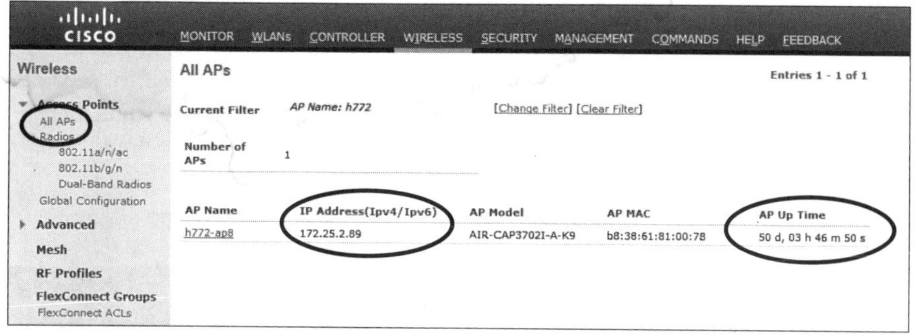

Figure 20-18 *Verifying That an AP Is Alive*

As long as the controller shows the AP with an appropriate IP address, you can assume that there is a working CAPWAP tunnel between the two. If clients are reporting problems with one SSID that they have in common, you should review the WLAN configuration on the controller to make sure it is bound to the correct controller interface and to the correct VLAN.

If your network is large and you have many controllers, you might not know which one the AP has joined. You can look from a more broad perspective by searching for the AP in PI.

Verifying AP-to-Network Connectivity

If you do not find the AP joined to a controller, you will have to move your focus further away from the controller and onto the AP and its wired connection.

Before an AP can boot up and operate correctly, it must have a power source. Most likely, an AP gets its power from the access layer switch as Power over Ethernet (PoE) over the Ethernet cabling. The more radios an AP supports, the more power it can consume. Therefore, different AP models can require different amounts of power. You should verify the minimum PoE requirements of an AP and compare that with the PoE capability of the switch.

The 802.3af standard specifies that a PoE switch can provide up to 15.4 watts to a PoE device. Switch ports using the 802.3at standard can offer up to 30 watts PoE on an interface. When you look for the AP power requirements, be sure that the required power includes all radios in operation.

Once the AP has sufficient power, does it have an IP address? Without the help of a controller, you might have to connect to the AP console and watch the logging information scroll by as the AP tries to boot, get an address, and find a controller to join. You can also query the DHCP server to see whether the AP has an active address lease. If it is not able to get an address from a DHCP server, check the address scope on the server to ensure that the address space is not exhausted.

Tip To connect to the CLI of an AP, you need to enter some credentials. By default, log in with username Cisco and password Cisco. The default enable secret password is also Cisco.

If the AP is having trouble joining a controller, verify that the switch port configuration where the AP is connected. A lightweight AP needs only a single VLAN to support the CAPWAP tunnel. All WLANs are transported over the tunnel without the need for separate VLANs. In contrast, an autonomous AP has no CAPWAP tunnel, so it needs a trunk link that can carry individual WLANs over VLANs. The switch port configuration should look like one of those shown in Table 20-4.

Table 20-4 Switch Port Configuration to Support an AP

Lightweight AP (Access Link)	Autonomous AP (Trunk Link)
interface gigabitethernet1/0/1	interface gigabitethernet1/0/1
switchport	switchport
switchport access vlan 100	switchport trunk allowed vlan 100,101,102,103
switchport mode access	switchport trunk native vlan 100
spanning-tree portfast	switchport trunk encapsulation dot1q
no shutdown	switchport mode trunk
	no shutdown

Finally, recall that a lightweight AP tries a variety of methods to discover viable controllers to join. A common method is to configure a DHCP server to send DHCP option 43 with lease offers to APs. Option 43 is a string of hex digits that contains the IP addresses of one or more controllers. The DHCP server might not have option 43 configured at all, or it could have a typo or error in the hex string.

Sometimes you might connect an AP and wait a very long time for it to join a controller, only to find that it does not. First, check the controller licensing to make sure that there are enough available licenses for the AP. If you still cannot figure out what the AP is doing, you can connect directly to its console port and watch the logging information scroll by as the AP attempts to discover controllers.

The console output listed in Example 20-1 shows that the AP is not able to obtain an IP address so it can join the wired network. In Example 20-2, the AP picked up a list of three candidate controller IP addresses (192.168.90.22, 192.168.90.23, and 192.168.90.16) from the DHCP server. However, the AP then tries to initiate a Datagram Transport Layer Security (DTLS) tunnel (part of CAPWAP) to a controller known as m7-c1 at address 172.22.253.17, and successfully joins it. Perhaps this AP was previously configured with a primary controller address elsewhere before it was installed on the network. Therefore, it used an unexpected controller address.

Example 20-1 *AP Console Output Showing an IP Address Problem*

```
*Mar  1 00:13:33.515: %CDP_PD-4-POWER_OK: Full power - INJECTOR_DETECTED_PD inline
  ccpower source
*Mar  1 00:13:34.537: %LINK-3-UPDOWN: Interface Dot11Radio1, changed state to up
*Mar  1 00:13:35.537: %LINEPROTO-5-UPDOWN: Line protocol on Interface Dot11Radio1,
  changed state to up
*Mar  1 00:13:35.563: %LINK-3-UPDOWN: Interface Dot11Radio0, changed state to up
*Mar  1 00:13:36.563: %LINEPROTO-5-UPDOWN: Line protocol on Interface Dot11Radio0,
  changed state to up
*Mar  1 00:13:57.962: %CAPWAP-3-ERRORLOG: Not sending discovery request AP does not
  have an Ip !!
*Mar  1 00:14:17.962: %CAPWAP-3-ERRORLOG: Not sending discovery request AP does not
  have an Ip !!
```

Example 20-2 *Verifying Candidate Controller Addresses from the AP Console*

```
*Mar  1 00:16:18.971: %CAPWAP-5-DHCP_OPTION_43: Controller address 192.168.90.22
  obtained through DHCP
*Mar  1 00:16:18.971: %CAPWAP-5-DHCP_OPTION_43: Controller address 192.168.90.23
  obtained through DHCP
*Mar  1 00:16:18.971: %CAPWAP-5-DHCP_OPTION_43: Controller address 192.168.90.16
  obtained through DHCP
*Mar  1 00:16:19.012: %CAPWAP-3-ERRORLOG: Could Not resolve CISCO-CAPWAP-CONTROLLER
*Mar  1 00:16:29.020: %CAPWAP-3-ERRORLOG: Selected MWAR m7-c1'(index 0).
*Mar  1 00:16:29.020: %CAPWAP-3-ERRORLOG: Go join a capwap controller
*Sep 12 14:16:04.000: %CAPWAP-5-DTLSREQSEND: DTLS connection request sent peer_ip:
  172.22.253.17 peer_port: 5246
*Sep 12 14:16:04.791: %CAPWAP-5-DTLSREQSUCC: DTLS connection created successfully
  peer_ip: 172.22.253.17 peer_port: 5246
*Sep 12 14:16:04.792: %CAPWAP-5-SENDJOIN: sending Join Request to 172.22.253.17
*Sep 12 14:16:05.069: %LINK-3-UPDOWN: Interface Dot11Radio0, changed state to down
*Sep 12 14:16:05.108: %LINK-5-CHANGED: Interface Dot11Radio0, changed state to reset
*Sep 12 14:16:05.117: %CAPWAP-5-JOINEDCONTROLLER: AP has joined controller m7-c1
```

Verifying the AP and Antenna Orientation

Suppose you have verified that an AP is working properly and has joined a controller, but users near the AP still report connectivity issues. You might consider looking at the AP to make sure it has been mounted properly so that the RF coverage works as designed. If the AP has external antennas, make sure that the antennas are oriented appropriately.

Indoor AP models such as the Cisco Aironet 3702i, 2702i, and 1702i are designed to be mounted flat against a ceiling. The small omnidirectional antennas inside the AP case are oriented such that the RF signal will be dispersed slightly downward and away from the AP in all directions. That simply means the AP can cover the most floor area when it is mounted facedown and flat against the ceiling.

If you find that an AP with internal antennas has been mounted on a wall, the antennas will be oriented perpendicular to the wall. This causes the RF signals to be dispersed along the wall in all directions, effectively ruining the broad floor coverage the AP should have had.

APs with external antennas, such as the Cisco Aironet 3702e and 2702e, have antennas that protrude and can be easily reoriented. Even when an AP is installed with its antennas oriented correctly, someone may come along and knock the antennas if they are within reach. If that happens, you may never know about the reduced coverage until a wireless user calls to complain. To correctly orient the antennas of a wall-mounted AP, turn the top two antennas facing straight up, the bottom two facing straight down, the center left facing left, and the center right facing right—all parallel with the wall.

Checking the RF Environment

To investigate problems that could involve things like 802.11 traffic, client roaming, RF interference, or co-channel or adjacent channel interference, you might need to leverage some third-party tools. The CCNA Wireless exam blueprint lists several topics related to a variety of tools. You should not need to know how to install and use the tools, but you should know which tools are useful for specific scenarios.

The operating systems on common Windows- and Mac OS X–based wireless client devices offer some basic utilities that you can use to display all of the SSIDs that are being broadcast or advertised. As Figure 20-19 shows, the list of SSIDs is handy when you need to select and connect to one, but is of limited value if you need to troubleshoot a problem. The utility does show each SSID and a bar-like indicator of the APs' signal strengths.

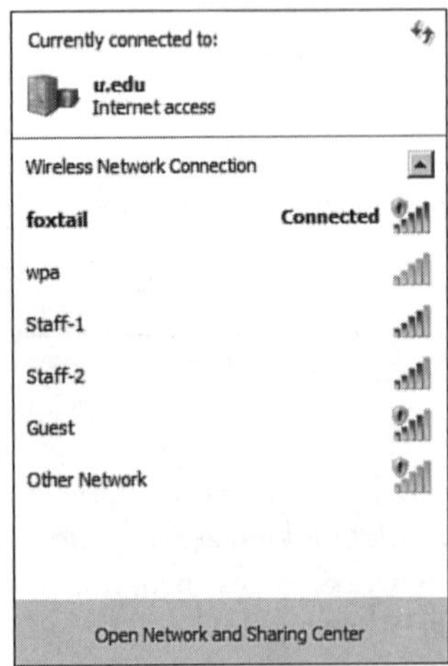

Figure 20-19 *Using a Client OS–based Utility to List Available SSIDs*

Wi-Fi scanning tools are more useful for quick scans and walkthrough surveys of an area, to see all of the active APs and their channel use. Typical examples are MetaGeek inSSIDer Office, Android Wifi Analyzer, and Fluke AirMagnet WiFi Analyzer, shown in Figures 20-20 through 20-22. The MetaGeek inSSIDer Office and Android Wifi Analyzer tools both scan all 2.4- and 5-GHz channels and display any SSIDs overheard on each. You can also see BSSID information that contains the SSID name, AP MAC address, wireless security settings, RSSI, and channel number used. At a glance, you can detect channel overlap and gauge co-channel and adjacent channel interference. For example, if you see two instances of the same SSID on the same channel, it is easy to check the signal strength separation to make sure that the modulation and coding schemes will operate correctly.

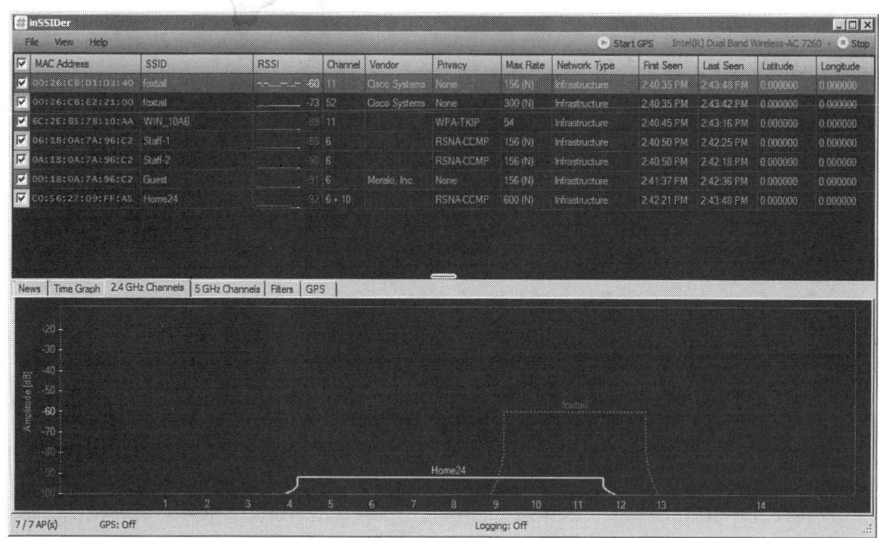

Figure 20-20 *Scanning Channels with MetaGeek inSSIDer Office*

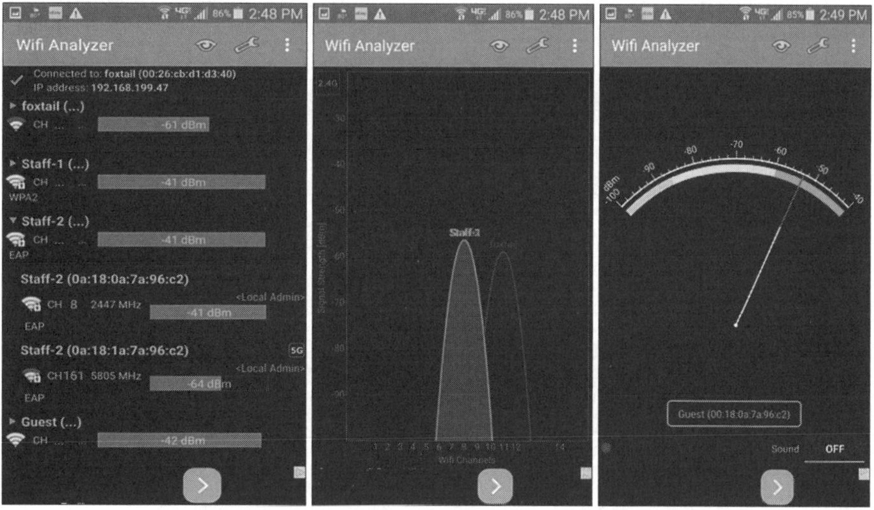

Figure 20-21 *Scanning Channels with Android Wifi Analyzer*

Fluke AirMagnet WiFi Analyzer, shown in Figure 20-22, can also scan channels and display SSIDs and BSSIDs. It can also do much, much more. WiFi Analyzer is a robust tool that scans all channels and performs many types of analysis on the transmissions that are received. It also offers "expert" advice about conditions that are detected.

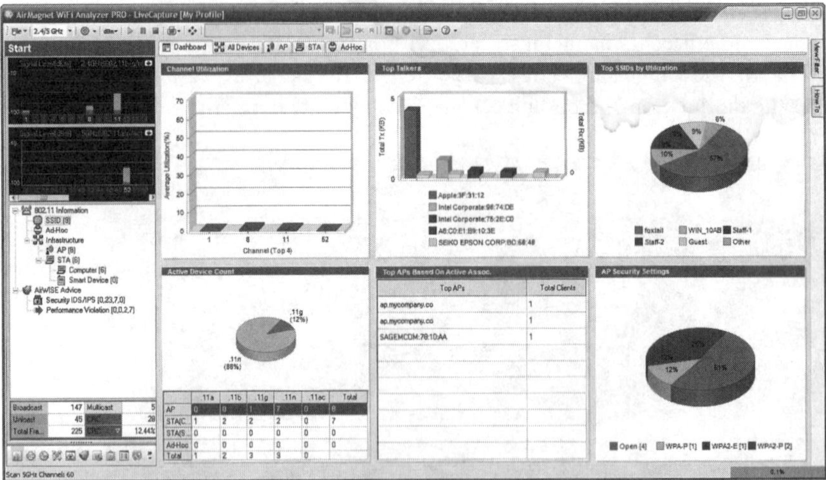

Figure 20-22 *Analyzing Wi-Fi Activity with Fluke AirMagnet WiFi Analyzer*

You can leverage a wireless packet analyzer such as Savvius OmniPeek or Wireshark to capture 802.11 frames and decode the contents for further analysis. Because packet analyzers can interpret the contents of wireless frames and their payloads (assuming the frames do not use a strong encryption), they are most useful when you need to troubleshoot low-level problems between devices. For example, you can capture wireless data to see exactly how a client device is communicating with an AP, how a client handles a roaming condition, how the quality of a voice call is being handled, and so on. Figure 20-23 shows an example of an OmniPeek wireless capture and analysis.

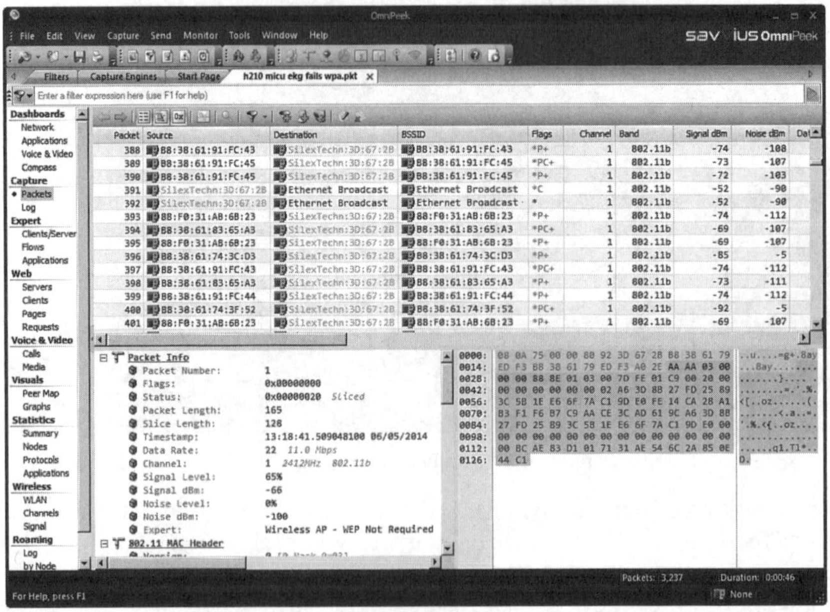

Figure 20-23 *Analyzing Wi-Fi Frames Captured Over the Air with Savvius OmniPeek*

You might also need to leverage third-party RF mapping tools to perform site surveys, where RF signal strength, SNR, and many other parameters are measured over an area and displayed on spatial maps. RF mapping tools are covered in greater detail in Chapter 7, "Planning Coverage with Wireless APs."

Spectrum analyzers are special-purpose tools that you can use to measure RF energy across a range of frequencies, to detect the presence of 802.11 APs and many types of interfering sources. Spectrum analysis is covered in greater detail in Chapter 19, "Dealing with Wireless Interference."

Table 20-5 provides a summary of typical applications of third-party tools, their common uses, and examples of tools and vendors.

Key Topic

Table 20-5 Third-Party Wireless Troubleshooting Tools

Application	Common Uses	Example Tools
OS-based client utilities	Simple scan of SSIDs that are broadcast in a location	Windows Wireless Network Connection Apple Mac OS X AirPort and AirPort Extreme
Wi-Fi scanners	Detailed scan of available SSIDs Display of AP signal strength Survey of channel use and availability	MetaGeek inSSIDer Office Android Wifi Analyzer Fluke AirMagnet WiFi Analyzer
RF mapping tools	Site surveys (active and passive) Spatial mapping of RF signals Verify RF coverage	Fluke AirMagnet Survey Pro Ekahau Site Survey Pro VisiWave Site Survey
Packet analysis	802.11 packet captures Robust analysis	Savvius OmniPeek Wireshark
Spectrum analysis	RF signal and noise analysis across a range of frequencies Identify and locate sources of interference	Fluke AirMagnet Spectrum XT MetaGeek Chanalyzer

20

Exam Preparation Tasks

As mentioned in the section, "How to Use This Book," in the Introduction, you have a couple of choices for exam preparation: the exercises here, Chapter 21, "Final Review," and the exam simulation questions on the DVD.

Review All Key Topics

Review the most important topics in this chapter, noted with the Key Topic icon in the outer margin of the page. Table 20-6 lists a reference of these key topics and the page numbers on which each is found.

Table 20-6 Key Topics for Chapter 20

Key Topic Element	Description	Page Number
Figure 20-1	Anatomy of a client association	453
Table 20-2	Possible WLC client states	455
Figure 20-6	Displaying client RF statistics	457
Figure 20-12	Running a troubleshooting session in PI	460
Figures 20-15 and 20-16	Comparing wireless security settings	462, 463
Table 20-4	Example switch port configurations for APs	466
Table 20-5	Third-party wireless troubleshooting tools	471

This chapter covers the following topics:

- **Advice About the Exam Event**—This section provides an overview of the exam structure and the types of questions you will encounter. It also discusses some strategies for managing your time during the exam, reviewing before the exam, and preparing yourself to sit through the exam.
- **Exam Engine and Questions on the DVD**—This section describes how to install and use the Pearson online exam engine in order to access and take 200-355 WIFUND practice exams to better prepare you for exam day.
- **Final Thoughts**—This brief section provides some concluding bits of encouragement about your exam results.

CHAPTER 21

Final Review

Congratulations! You made it through the book, and now it is time to finish getting ready for the exam. This chapter helps you get ready to take and pass the exam. You should know the content and topics. Now you need to think about what will happen during the exam and what you need to do to prepare your mind for it. At this point, you should be focused on getting yourself ready to pass.

Advice About the Exam Event

Now that you have finished the bulk of this book, you could just register for your Cisco 200-355 WIFUND exam, show up, and take the exam. However, if you spend a little time thinking about the exam event itself and learning more about the user interface of the real Cisco exams and the environment at the Vue testing centers, you will be better prepared—particularly if this is your first Cisco exam.

Learn the Question Types Using the Cisco Certification Exam Tutorial

During the time leading up to your exam, think more about the different types of exam questions and have a plan for how to approach them. One of the best ways to learn about the exam questions is to use the Cisco Certification Exam Tutorial.

To find the Cisco Certification Exam Tutorial, go to Cisco.com and search for "exam tutorial." The tutorial sits inside a web page with a Flash presentation of the exam user interface. Each type of exam question is presented, along with a real-time demonstration of the actions you might take when answering the question. You can also click the **Try Me** button to reset the question and practice interacting and answering the question yourself.

You can expect to find the following types of questions on the exam. (The example questions depicted in Figures 21-1 through 21-7 serve only to demonstrate the exam question formats; they have nothing to do with the actual CCNA Wireless 200-355 WIFUND exam content.)

- **Multiple choice, single answer**—The question has several possible answers, but only one correct one. Figure 21-1 shows an example.

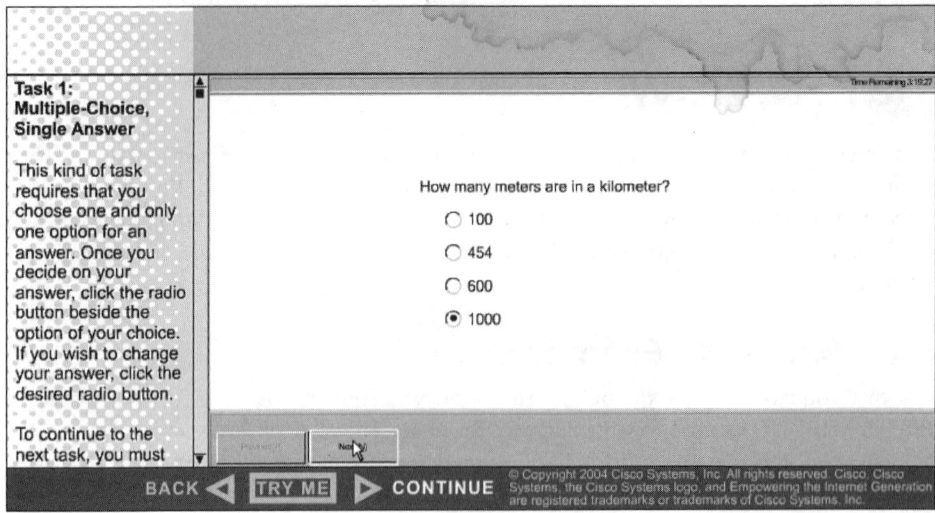

Figure 21-1 *Example Multiple-Choice, Single-Answer Exam Question*

- **Multiple choice, multiple answer**—The question has several possible answers, with a given number of correct ones. Figure 21-2 shows an example.

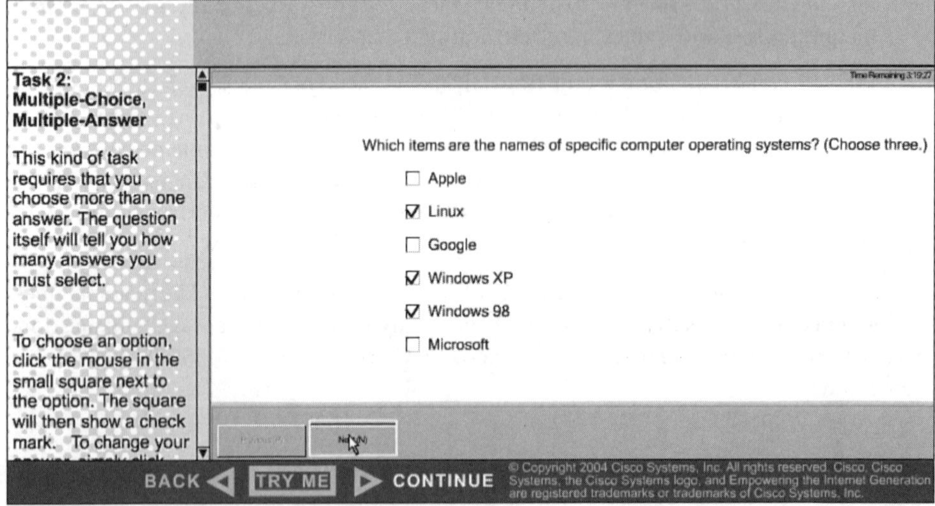

Figure 21-2 *Example Multiple-Choice, Multiple-Answer Exam Question*

- **Drag and drop**—The question has a series of items that you must drag and drop into boxes that represent the correct category, correct sequence, and so on. Figure 21-3 shows an example.

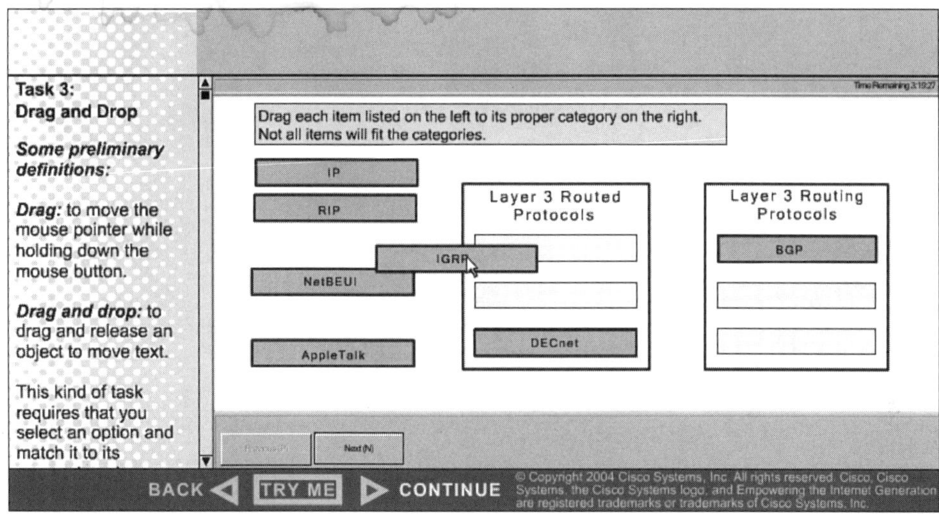

Figure 21-3 *Example Drag-and-Drop Exam Question*

- **Fill in the blank**—The question has one or more blank answers that you must fill in. Figure 21-4 shows an example.

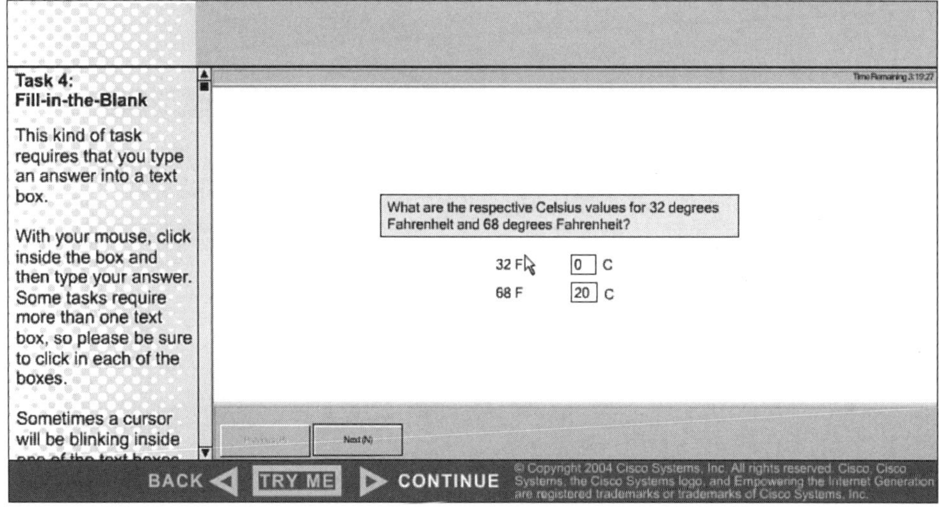

Figure 21-4 *Example Fill-in-the-Blank Exam Question*

- **Simulation**—The question includes a description and a network diagram. You can click a network device and interact with it through a simulated command-line interface (CLI) session. Figure 21-5 shows an example.

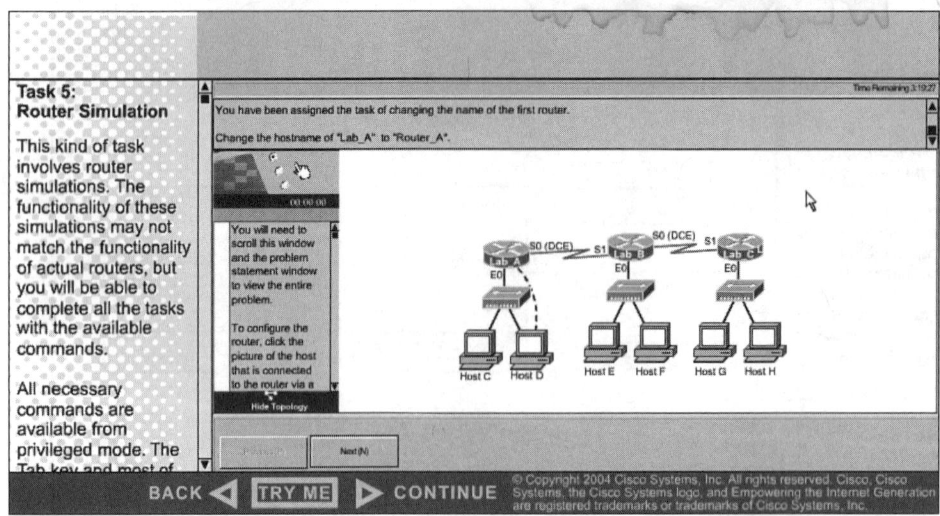

Figure 21-5 *Example Simulation Exam Question*

- **Testlet**—The question includes a detailed scenario and a set of questions that you must select and answer. Figure 21-6 shows an example.

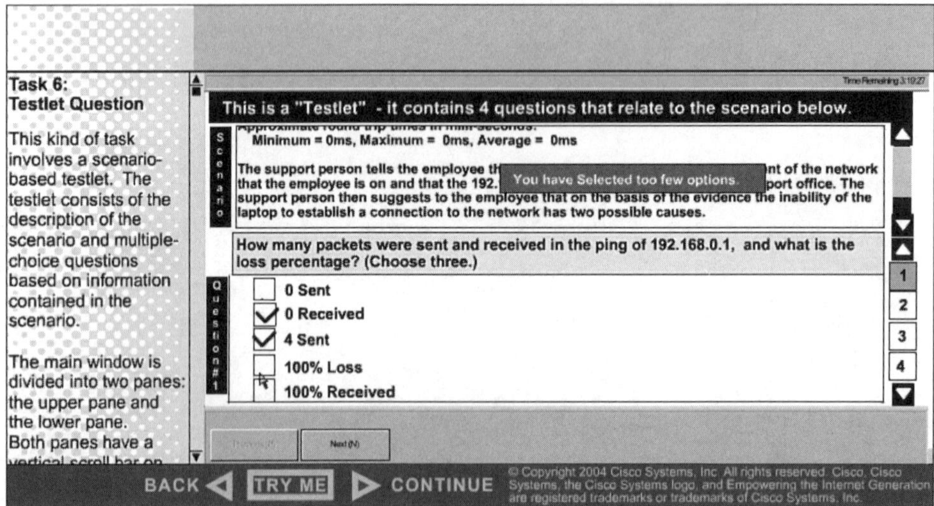

Figure 21-6 *Example Testlet Exam Question*

- **Simlet**—The question includes a scenario and a set of questions that you must answer based on your interaction with a simulated network device. Figure 21-7 shows an example.

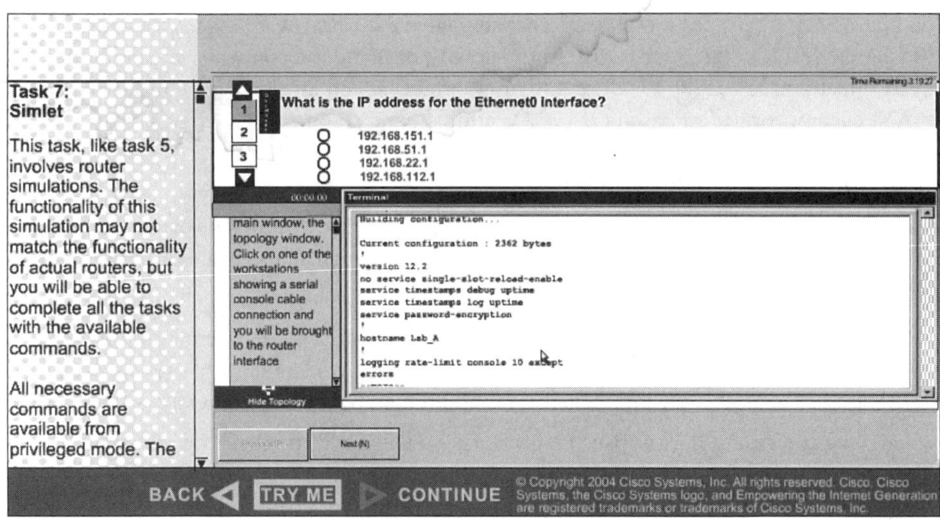

Figure 21-7 *Example Simlet Exam Question*

You should find the multiple-choice questions fairly straightforward because they have only one correct answer. Read through the possible answers carefully so that you can eliminate the obviously incorrect ones. You might find that some answers appear to be similar or are not easy to dismiss. Look for subtle differences and any key words that relate to concepts you have learned.

Multiple-choice questions that require multiple answers sometimes prove more difficult. Fortunately, the questions always state the number of correct answers you should enter. Pay close attention to that number, and then use the answer check boxes to select and narrow down your final answers.

Drag-and-drop questions present you with a list of objects that you must drag and drop into the correct locations in a blank list. Sometimes you will need to sort the objects into two different lists. Sometimes you will need to select only the objects that match a category and then place them in sequential order. Pay close attention to the stated goals and the order that you should put the answers in. If you need to change any of your answers, just drag them back to their starting positions and try again.

The simulation and simlet question formats usually involve network devices such as routers, switches, and firewalls that have a CLI to interact with. Most likely, you will not find such questions on the CCNA Wireless exam. Even though Cisco Wireless LAN controllers and access points (APs) have a CLI that you can access, you are not really expected to until you move to more advanced certifications.

Testlet questions include a short set of questions to answer. The questions are listed on the right side of the exam, usually numbered in sequence. Read through the scenario description, and then select one of the multiple-choice questions to answer. Do not forget to move through the other multiple-choice questions and answer them all before moving on to the next exam question.

You might encounter a testlet question that simulates the Cisco Wireless LAN Controller (WLC) graphical user interface (GUI). Know how to navigate the controller to find important information such as the IP address of an interface, which interface is bound to a WLAN, client information based on a MAC address, and so on.

Think About Your Time Budget

On exam day, keep an eye on your progress as you move through the questions. Budget your time so that you have enough to make your way through all the exam questions. You might find yourself struggling between two feelings:

- **I'm going too slowly!**—If your pace is too slow, you might not have enough time to answer all the questions. You might also find that you are spending what seems like an eternity on one pesky question when you should be moving on to others.
- **I'm going too fast!**—If your pace is too fast, you will get through all the questions, but you might be rushing without being thorough. Remember that you need to read both the questions and the answers completely so that you fully understand them.

During the exam, you need to be able to somehow know whether you are moving quickly enough to answer all the questions, while not rushing. The exam user interface shows some useful information—a countdown timer and a question counter. The question counter shows the question number you are currently answering and the total number of questions on your exam.

Unfortunately, treating each question equally does not give you an accurate time estimate. For example, if your exam allows 90 minutes and your exam has 45 questions, you have an average of 2 minutes per question. Suppose that 40 minutes have elapsed and you have answered 20 questions. At 2 minutes per question, it seems like you would be right on schedule. However, several factors make that kind of estimate difficult to run before the exam.

First, Cisco does not tell us beforehand the exact number of questions for each exam. For example, Cisco.com lists the CCNA Wireless 200-355 WIFUND exam as having from 60 to 70 questions in 90 minutes. You will not know exactly how many questions are on your exam until you go through the initial screens that lead up to the point where you click **Start Exam** and the exam actually begins. As a worst case, 70 questions in 90 minutes works out to an average of slightly over a minute per question.

Next, some questions clearly take a lot more time to answer than others. These are commonly called "time-burner" questions. Consider the following comparison:

- **Normal-time questions**—Multiple-choice and drag-and-drop questions, approximately 1 minute each
- **Time burners**—Simulation, simlet, and testlet questions, approximately 6 to 8 minutes each

Cisco does not tell us why you might get 70 questions and someone else taking the same exam might get 60 questions. It seems reasonable to think that the person with 60 questions might have a few more of the time burners, making the two exams even out.

Even though testlet and simlet questions contain several individual multiple-choice questions (each graded and scored independently), the exam software counts each testlet and simlet question as one question in the question counter. For example, if a testlet question has four embedded multiple-choice questions, the exam software's question counter will show it counting as one exam question.

During the exam, as you encounter each question, resist the temptation to skim through it. Try to deliberately read it from start to finish so that you do not skip over any important words or information. For example, a question might ask "which one is not..." If you skip over the word *not*, you will likely get the answer wrong.

Scenario descriptions can be lengthy, especially when they set the stage for a complex problem. Be aware that the text will be located in a scrolling window that might be hard to read or navigate because of the cramped screen real estate. Network diagrams can be equally cumbersome because they have to show many icons, links, addresses, and other information in a small space.

Other Pre-Exam Suggestions

Here are just a few more suggestions for things to think about before exam day arrives. First, consider the following strategies for reviewing the exam content:

- Go back through the "Do I Know This Already?" quizzes at the beginning of each chapter. You should be able to tell which content areas you might need to review again.
- Open this book to the table of contents page. Read down through the entries until you find a topic that seems foreign or does not come to mind right away. Spend time reviewing the corresponding chapter or section to refresh your memory.
- Use the practice questions on the accompanying DVD. You might not find every type of exam question there, but you should get a thorough sample of the exam content. If you get a practice question in the multiple-choice, single-answer format, think about what might happen if you see that same question on the real exam in another format.
- Keep a running list of topics, acronyms, or concepts that you feel you do not understand completely or are taking too much time remembering. Go back and review the things on your list.
- Join in the discussions on the Cisco Learning Network. Try to answer questions asked by other learners. The process of answering, even if you keep your answer to yourself, makes you think much harder about the topic. When someone posts an answer with which you disagree, think about why and talk about it online. This is a great way to both learn more and build confidence.

Next, think about the things you might need to do right before your exam time:

- Get some earplugs. Testing centers often have some, but if you do not want to chance it, come prepared. The testing center is usually a room inside the space of a company that does something else as well. There could be people talking in nearby rooms, in addition to other office noises. Earplugs can help. Headphones and electronic devices are not permitted.

- The testing center usually provides a white-erase card and a marker, but does not allow you to bring in any notes. Some people like to spend the first minute of the exam writing down some notes on the white-erase card for reference. For example, you might want to write out a table of mW-to-dBm value conversions. If you plan to do that, practice making those notes ahead of time. Before each practice exam, transcribe those lists, just like you expect to do at the real exam.
- Plan your travel to the testing center with enough time so that you will not be rushing to make it there by your scheduled exam time.
- If you tend to be nervous before exams, practice your favorite relaxation techniques for a few minutes before each practice exam, just to be ready to use them.
- Rest the night before the exam, rather than staying up late to study. Clarity of thought is more important than learning one extra fact, especially because the exam requires so much analysis and thinking.
- You can bring personal effects into the building and the testing company's space, but not into the actual room in which you take the exam. So, take as little extra stuff with you as possible. If you have a safe place to leave briefcases, purses, electronics, and so on, leave them there. However, the testing center should have a place to store your things as well. Simply put, the less you bring, the less you have to worry about storing.
- Find a restroom before going into the testing center. If you cannot find one, of course you can use one in the testing center. The testing personnel will direct you and give you time before your exam starts.
- Do not drink a large quantity of liquid before your exam begins. Once the exam has started, the timer will not stop while you go to the restroom.

Exam Engine and Questions on the DVD

The DVD in the back of the book includes the Pearson Cert Practice Test engine. This software presents you with a set of multiple-choice questions, covering the topics you will be likely find on the real exam. The Pearson Cert Practice Test engine lets you study the exam content (using study mode) or take a simulated exam (in practice exam mode).

The DVD in the back of the book contains the exam engine. Once installed, you can then activate and download the current 200-355 WIFUND practice exam from Pearson's website. Installation of the exam engine takes place in two steps:

Step 1. Install the exam engine from the DVD.

Step 2. Activate and download the WIFUND practice exam.

Install the Exam Engine

The following are the steps you should perform to install the software:

Step 1. Insert the DVD into your computer.

Step 2. The software that automatically runs is the Cisco Press software to access and use all DVD-based features, including the exam engine and the DVD-only appendices. From the main menu, click the option to **Install the Exam Engine**.

Step 3. Respond to the prompt windows as you would with any typical software installation process.

The installation process gives you the option to activate your exam with the activation code supplied on the paper in the DVD sleeve. This process requires that you establish a Pearson website login. You will need this login in order to activate the exam. Therefore, please register when prompted. If you already have a Pearson website login, there is no need to register again; just use your existing login.

Activate and Download the Practice Exam

Once the exam engine is installed, you should then activate the exam associated with this book (if you did not do so during the installation process) as follows:

Step 1. Start the Pearson Cert Practice Test (PCPT) software.

Step 2. To activate and download the exam associated with this book, from the **My Products** or **Tools** tab, click the **Activate** button.

Step 3 At the next screen, enter the Activation Key from the paper inside the cardboard DVD holder in the back of the book. Once entered, click the **Activate** button.

Step 4. The activation process will download the practice exam. Click **Next**; then click **Finish**.

Once the activation process is completed, the My Products tab should list your new exam. If you do not see the exam, make sure you selected the **My Products** tab on the menu. At this point, the software and practice exam are ready to use. Simply select the exam, and click the **Use** button.

To update a particular exam you have already activated and downloaded, simply select the **Tools** tab, and select the **Update Products** button. Updating your exams will ensure you have the latest changes and updates to the exam data.

If you wish to check for updates to the Pearson Cert Practice Test exam engine software, simply select the **Tools** tab, and click the **Update Application** button. This will ensure you are running the latest version of the software engine.

Activating Other Exams

The exam software installation process, and the registration process, only has to happen once. Then, for each new exam, only a few steps are required. For instance, if you buy another new Cisco Press Official Cert Guide or Pearson IT Certification Cert Guide, remove the activation code from the DVD sleeve in the back of that book—you don't even need the DVD at this point. From there, all you have to do is start the exam engine (if not still up and running), and perform Steps 2 through 4 from the previous list.

Premium Edition

In addition to the free practice exam provided on the DVD, you can purchase additional exams with expanded functionality directly from Pearson IT Certification. The Premium Edition of this title contains an additional two full practice exams as well as an eBook (in both PDF and ePub format). In addition, the Premium Edition title also has remediation for each question to the specific part of the eBook that relates to that question.

Because you have purchased the print version of this title, you can purchase the Premium Edition at a deep discount. There is a coupon code in the DVD sleeve that contains a one-time-use code, as well as instructions for where you can purchase the Premium Edition.

To view the Premium Edition product page, go to http://www.ciscopress.com/title/9780134307138.

Using the Exam Engine

The Pearson Cert Practice Test engine on the DVD lets you access a database of questions created specifically for this book. The Pearson Cert Practice Test engine can be used either in study mode or practice exam mode, as follows:

- **Study mode**—Study mode is most useful when you want to use the questions for learning and practicing. In study mode, you can select options such as randomizing the order of the questions and answers, automatically viewing answers to the questions as you go, testing on specific topics, and many other options.
- **Practice exam mode**—This mode presents questions in a timed environment, providing you with a more exam-realistic experience. It also restricts your ability to see your score as you progress through the exam and view answers to questions as you are taking the exam. These timed exams not only allow you to study for the actual 200-355 WIFUND exam, but also help you simulate the time pressure that occurs on the actual exam.

When doing your final preparation, you can use study mode, practice exam mode, or both. However, after you have seen each question a couple of times, you will likely start to remember the questions, and the usefulness of the exam database may go down. So, consider the following options when using the exam engine:

- Use the question database for review. Use study mode to study the questions by chapter, just as with the other final review steps listed in this chapter. Consider upgrading to the Premium Edition of this book if you want to take additional simulated exams.
- Save the question database, not using it for review during your review of each book part. Save it until the end, so that you will not have seen the questions before. Then, use practice exam mode to simulate the exam.

To select the exam engine mode, click on the **My Products** tab. Select the exam you wish to use from the list of available exams, then click the **Use** button. The test engine should display a window from which you can choose **Study Mode** or **Practice Exam Mode**. When in study mode, you can further choose the book chapters, limiting the questions to those explained in the specified chapters of the book.

The Cisco Learning Network

Cisco provides a wide variety of CCNA Wireless preparation tools at a Cisco website called the Cisco Learning Network. Resources found there include sample questions, forums on each Cisco exam, video-based learning games, and information about each exam.

To reach the Cisco Learning Network, go to https://learningnetwork.cisco.com, or use a search engine to search for "Cisco Learning Network." To access some of the features/resources, you need to use the login you created at Cisco.com. If you don't have such a login, you can register for free. To register, simply go to Cisco.com, click **Register** at the top of the page, and supply some information.

Final Thoughts

Congratulations for working your way this far through this book. Nothing about Cisco certification exams is easy, but they are well worth your time and hard work. At the end of the exam, you will receive your final score and news of your passing or failing. If you pass, congratulate yourself and breathe a sigh of relief at not having to study more.

If you fail, remind yourself that you are not a failure. It is never a disgraceful thing to fail a Cisco exam, as long as you decide to try it again. Anybody who has ever taken a Cisco exam knows that to be true; just ask the people who have attempted a CCIE lab exam. As soon as you can after learning that you failed, take a few minutes to write down as many exam questions as you can remember. Note which questions left you uneasy. Next, schedule to take the same exam again. Allow a few days so that you can study the topics that gave you trouble. The exam score should also break down the entire exam into major topics, each with its respective score. Do not be discouraged about starting over with your studies; the majority of it is already behind you. Just spend time brushing up on the "low spots" where you lack knowledge or confidence. Go for it and do your best!

APPENDIX A

Answers to the "Do I Know This Already?" Quizzes

Chapter 1

1. C. The IEEE 802.11 standard focuses on wireless LAN definitions, methods, and operation. It is made up of many pieces, as described in Chapter 2, "RF Standards." Sometimes you might see IEEE 802.11x, which refers to the many subparts of 802.11. Be aware of the subtle difference between that and 802.1x, which defines port-based network access control.
2. B, E. Wireless LANs use the 2.4-GHz and 5-GHz bands. Be careful to notice the difference between megahertz (MHz) and gigahertz (GHz). Also remember that 5.5 Mbps and 11 Mbps are some of the common data rates used in wireless LANs, but those are not involved when you need to identify the frequency band.
3. A. When the two power levels are the same, the result is 0 dB. As long as you remember the first handy Law of Zero, you will find exam questions like this easy. If not, you will need to remember that $dB = 10\log_{10} (100\ mW / 100\ mW) = 10\log_{10} (1) = 0\ dB$.
4. C. At first glance, 17 mW and 34 mW might seem like odd numbers to work with. Notice that if you double 17, you get 34. The second handy dB fact says that doubling a power level will increase the dB value by 3.
5. D. Start with transmitter A's level of 1 mW and try to figure out some simple operations that can be used to get to transmitter B's level of 100 mW. Remember the handy Laws of 3s and 10s, which use multiplication by 2 and 10. In this case, 1 mW × 10 = 10 mW × 10 = 100 mW. Each multiplication by 10 adds 10 dB, so the end result is 10 + 10 = 20 dB. Notice that transmitter B is being compared to A (the reference level), which is 1 mW. You could also state the end result in dB-milliwatt (dBm).
6. C. This question involves a *reduction* in the power level, so the dB value must be negative. Try to find a simple way to start with 100 and get to 40 by multiplying or dividing by 2 or 10. In this case, 100 / 10 = 10; 10 × 2 = 20; 20 × 2 = 40. Dividing by 10 reduced the dB value by 10 dB; then multiplying by 2 increased the total by +3 dB; multiplying again by 2 increased the total by +3 more dB. In other words, dB = –10 + 3 + 3 = –4 dB.
7. B. Remember that the EIRP involves radiated power, and that is calculated using only the transmitter components. The EIRP is the sum of the transmitter power level (+20 dBm), the cable loss (–2 dB), and the antenna gain (+5 dBi). Therefore, the EIRP is +23 dBm.

8. D. A high SNR is best, where the received signal strength is more elevated above the noise floor. A 30-dBm SNR separates the signal from the noise more than a 10-dBm SNR does. Likewise, a higher RSSI value means that the signal strength alone is higher. The RSSI scale ranges from 0 (highest) to –100 (lowest).
9. C. DSSS supports 1-, 2-, 5.5-, and 11-Mbps data rates through different combinations of coding and modulation schemes. FHSS is locked to 1 or 2 Mbps. With the exception of 6 and 9 Mbps, only OFDM supports the highest data rates of all the modulation types.
10. C, B, A, D. The correct order is C, B, A, D or DBPSK (2 possible phase changes), DQPSK (4 possible phase changes), 16-QAM (16 possible phase/amplitude changes), 64-QAM (64 possible phase/amplitude changes).
11. B, C. Both 16-QAM and 64-QAM alter the amplitude and phase of a signal.
12. C. OFDM uses 48 subcarriers in a single 20-MHz-wide channel, allowing it to transmit data bits in parallel. DSSS uses a single 22-MHz channel with only one main carrier signal.

Chapter 2

1. C. The ITU-R allocated the ISM bands for global use.
2. B. The U-NII-1 band is the first of four 5-GHz bands set aside for wireless LAN use.
3. D. The EIRP is always limited to +36 dBm in the 2.4-GHz band, except in the case of point-to-point links.
4. D. The IEEE 802.11 standard is the official specification for wireless LAN operation.
5. C. Only channels 1, 6, and 11 are non-overlapping. The 2.4-GHz channels are spaced 5 MHz apart, whereas the DSSS channel width is 22 MHz.
6. D. The first U-NII-1 channel is labeled channel 36.
7. C, D, E, G. IEEE 802.11a is strictly for 5 GHz, 802.11n includes both 2.4- and 5-GHz bands, and 802.11ac is limited to 5 GHz. The IEEE 802.11-2012 standard has all of these amendments rolled up into one document. IEEE 802.11g and 802.11b deal with the 2.4-GHz band.
8. C, D. Both 802.11g and 802.11a define OFDM use, even though the two standards use different bands.
9. A. The maximum theoretical data rate of 802.11b is 11 Mbps, 802.11a is 54 Mbps, and 802.11n is 600 Mbps.
10. B. The device has two transmitters and three receivers. The number of spatial streams supported would be added after the 2×3 designation.
11. C. 802.11n is limited to aggregating two 20-MHz channels for a total width of 40 MHz.
12. A, E. Devices using 802.11n or 802.11ac can use multiple radio chains and multiple spatial streams.
13. B. The 802.11ac amendment supports 256-QAM in both Wave 1 and Wave 2.

14. D. 802.11ac supports a maximum of eight spatial streams, although only three are supported in Wave 1 and four in Wave 2.
15. D. Only the Wi-Fi Alliance tests and certifies wireless products according to industry standards.

Chapter 3

1. C. Because both transmitters are using the same channel, the interference is described as co-channel.
2. E. Cisco recommends a separation of *at least* 19 dB, so +20 dB is the only correct answer.
3. B. The two channels being used are adjacent, so their signals overlap by some degree. The resulting interference is called adjacent channel interference.
4. D. In the 2.4-GHz band, channels 1, 6, and 11 are the only ones that are spaced far enough apart (five channel numbers) that they do not overlap.
5. A. Energy traveling in an electromagnetic wave spreads in three dimensions, weakening the signal strength over a distance.
6. B. The 802.11b and g devices operate at 2.4 GHz, which is less affected by free space loss than the 802.11a device, at 5 GHz.
7. D. By switching to a less-complex modulation scheme, more of the data stream can be repeated to overcome worsening RF conditions. This can be done automatically through DRS.
8. B. As a signal is reflected, a new copy travels in a different direction. Each copy of the signal takes a different path to reach the receiver; thus, the name *multipath*.
9. D. As a signal passes through a wall, the building material absorbs some of the RF energy, reducing the signal strength by some amount.
10. B. The first Fresnel zone is an elliptical area along the length of a signal path that should be kept free of obstructions. When an object extends into a significant portion of the Fresnel zone, the signal can be diffracted and distorted.

Chapter 4

1. B, D. The E and H plane plots are used to show a side view and a top-down view, respectively, with the antenna in the center of the plots.
2. B. The H plane is also known as the azimuth plane because measurements are taken at every azimuth angle around the base of the antenna.
3. D. The beamwidth is the angle measured between the two points on a radiation pattern plot that are 3 dB below the maximum.
4. D. The orientation of the electrical and magnetic components of the electromagnetic wave with respect to the horizon is known as the polarization.
5. B. Cisco antennas are designed to use vertical polarization. Because the dipole antenna is mounted correctly (pointing straight up or down), the wave will be vertically polarized.

6. B. A parabolic dish antenna has the greatest gain because it focuses the RF energy into a tight beam.
7. A, E. An omnidirectional antenna is usually used to cover a large area. Therefore, it has a large beamwidth. Because it covers a large area, its gain is usually low.
8. C. Integrated antennas are omnidirectional.
9. B. Orienting a dipole so that its cylinder points toward a receiver will probably cause the received signal to become weaker. That is because the donut-shaped radiation pattern extends outward in all directions away from the length of the antenna. By pointing the antenna at the receiver, the strongest part of the signal has been rotated away from the receiver. The radiation pattern is weakest along the length of the antenna.
10. C. Lightning arrestors cannot protect against direct lightning strikes on an antenna.

Chapter 5

1. A, B. WPANs and WLANs can both use the unlicensed 2.4-GHz ISM band.
2. B. WLANs require half-duplex operation because all stations must contend for use of a channel to transmit frames.
3. C. An AP offers a basic service set (BSS).
4. B. The AP at the heart of a BSS or cell identifies itself (and the BSS) with a basic service set identifier (BSSID). It also uses an SSID to identify the wireless network, but that is not unique to the AP or BSS. Finally, the radio MAC address is used as the basis for the BSSID value, but the value can be altered to form the BSSID for each SSID that the AP supports.
5. D. In a BSS, the 802.11 standard requires all traffic to pass through an AP. The only exception is the 802.11z amendment, which permits an AP to coordinate direct client-to-client traffic without passing through the AP.
6. A. True: "The DS connects two BSSs to form an ESS"—The distribution system connects two basic service sets (APs) to form an extended service set.

   B. False: "The BSA of a BSS looks like a MAC address"—The basic service area of a BSS is its coverage area or cell, which has nothing to do with a MAC address.

   C. False: "The SSID of a STA must be unique within the ESS"—The service set identifier can be common across one or many BSSs in an ESS.

   D. True: "The BSSID is unique for each SSID in a BSS"—An AP in a BSS uses its radio MAC address as the basis for its BSSIDs, but each SSID has a unique BSSID value.
7. E. Roaming implies that the building has some wireless APs that are interconnected. Therefore, the client must first associate with a BSS. The BSS must connect to a switched infrastructure through a DS. The DS must extend to at least one more AP through an ESS. Finally, the same SSID has to be defined on every AP in the ESS.
8. D. An independent basic service set is also called an ad hoc network.
9. B. A workgroup bridge acts as a wireless client, but bridges traffic to and from a wired device connected to it.

10. B. In a mesh network, each mesh AP builds a standalone BSS. The APs relay client traffic to each other over wireless backhaul links, rather than wired Ethernet. A wireless LAN controller is necessary.

Chapter 6

1. D. An 802.11 frame can contain up to four different address fields.
2. B. Frames are marked as going to the distribution system (DS) or from the DS.
3. D. The Address1 field always contains the RA.
4. A. 802.11 devices can participate in the distributed coordination function (DCF).
5. C. A wireless client uses the network allocation vector (NAV) to predict the number of timeslots required for the channel to become free so that a frame can be transmitted.
6. D. Frames are separated by the distributed interframe space (DIFS).
7. B. A probe request frame is sent to ask any listening APs to identify themselves.
8. B. A wireless device must send an ACK frame, one of the 802.11 control frames, back to the source of each unicast frame that is received.
9. A, B. A client can join a basic service set (BSS) as long as it has at least one mandatory rate in common with the AP and supports all of the AP's mandatory rates.
10. A. In a passive scan, a client simply listens to any beacons that are transmitted by nearby APs. In contrast, probes are sent by the client to discover APs in an active scan.
11. D. A client must first be authenticated to the BSS before it can request to be associated.
12. C. As long as the client can move from one BSS to another without losing a signal or getting disassociated or deauthenticated, it can probe for a new AP and send a reassociation frame to reassociate itself with the existing SSID.

Chapter 7

1. B, C, D. The transmit power directly affects the range of the AP's signal. The supported modulation and coding schemes can affect the range because the simpler schemes can tolerate a lower SNR and a weaker signal, implying a greater range. The more complex schemes offer better data rates, but need a better signal quality within a shorter range. The supported data rates also affect the range because they directly affect the modulation and coding schemes that are used.
2. B, D. If you have already tested the AP's signal and determined that it reaches every location in the lobby area, the problem is not that the AP's transmit power is insufficient. Instead, the problem is occurring because the small client devices must be using a transmit power that is lower than that of the AP. In other words, the client's signals are not strong enough to reach the AP, so the two have asymmetric power levels. One solution is to increase the client's transmit power level (if possible) to be identical to the AP's. Another solution is to lower the data rate on the AP so that its signal will be usable at the client's location. A lower data rate uses less complex modulation and coding schemes, which stay intelligible at farther distances.

3. D. The 1-Mbps data rate is already disabled, which limits the cell size to some extent. You can reduce it further by disabling the 2-Mbps data rate.
4. C. If the problem is occurring some distance away from the replacement AP, the replacement AP must be working correctly within its immediate area. If the replacement had a 1-dBm transmit power, it could not be causing any interference at a great distance away. The problem is likely occurring because the lowest data rates have been enabled on the AP. The lower rates effectively extend the replacement AP's cell size into the cells of other APs farther away. If the channels are identical, the replacement could be causing co-channel interference in other cells, degrading client performance and roaming.
5. C. Roaming is entirely up to the client. The client runs a roaming algorithm that compares current conditions to a threshold. When the signal quality or other factors drop below the threshold, the client tries to roam.
6. D. Whereas an association request is used to join a BSS, a reassociation request is used to move from one BSS to another within the same ESS.
7. B. Roaming algorithms are not standardized at all. Instead, each manufacturer might have its own interpretation of an algorithm. Wireless clients can scan a set of available channels when they anticipate roaming, to look for a new AP. Cisco APs and controllers can also prime a Cisco-compatible client (CCX Versions 3 and later) with a list of viable APs ahead of time, so that the client can save time without having to scan channels.
8. B. To promote clean roaming, neighboring APs should use different, non-overlapping channels. In addition, APs should be located such that their coverage overlaps each other by some amount, usually 15 percent to 20 percent.
9. C. Adjacent APs should always use different, non-overlapping channels.
10. A, C. The fourth-floor APs will not interfere with the main office AP on channel 6. However, the other third-floor APs and the second-floor AP all use channel 6. Those signals could penetrate the floor and interfere with the main office AP, causing roaming issues.
11. A. If the building is under construction, the walls have probably not been built yet. Therefore, it doesn't make sense to try a passive or active site survey because there are no APs to measure and no final building materials to affect the RF signals. Instead, a predictive survey is used to calculate AP locations and RF coverage over a virtual area before APs have been deployed.
12. C. Only the active site survey can use the survey device to associate to the APs as a normal client would.
13. B. A passive site survey would provide all of the information needed. Because the passive survey tool listens to all APs that are in range of a location, you would learn of legitimate and rogue APs as well as the RF conditions.
14. C. AP-on-a-stick refers to a test AP that is mounted on a pole, ladder, tripod, or other stick-like object, at a height at which the AP would be permanently mounted. At that height, realistic measurements can be taken of the AP's cell size in the actual location where it will be used.

15. A. In an active site survey, the survey device associates with only one AP at a time—just as any normal wireless client does.

Chapter 8

1. A. An autonomous AP can operate independently, without the need for a centralized wireless LAN controller.
2. A. Client-to-client traffic typically passes through an autonomous AP, although clients can use Direct Link Setup (DLS) to communicate directly after coordinating with the AP.
3. B. The Cisco Meraki APs are autonomous APs that are managed through a centralized platform in the Meraki cloud.
4. B. A lightweight AP (LAP) transports client traffic through a tunnel back to a wireless LAN controller. Therefore, client-to-client traffic typically passes through the AP, through the controller, and back through the AP. If DLS is used, two wireless clients can communicate directly without passing through the AP and controller, but only after the communication has been coordinated with the AP.
5. C. On a lightweight AP, the MAC function is divided between the AP hardware and the wireless LAN controller (WLC). Therefore, the architecture is known as split-MAC.
6. B. An LAP builds a CAPWAP (Control and Provisioning of Wireless Access Points protocol) tunnel with a WLC.
7. A. Only the CAPWAP control tunnel is secured by default. Client data passes over the CAPWAP data tunnel, but is optionally encrypted. DHCP requests are client data and are not encrypted by default. Finally, 802.11 beacons are sent over the air from an LAP, so they are not encrypted or transported by CAPWAP.
8. A. A trunk link carrying three virtual LANs (VLANs) is not needed at all. A lightweight AP in local mode needs only an access link with a single VLAN; everything else is carried over the CAPWAP tunnel to a WLC. The WLC will need to be connected to three VLANs so that it can work with the LAP to bind them to the three service set identifiers (SSIDs).
9. D. Because the network is built with a WLC and LAPs, CAPWAP tunnels are required. One CAPWAP tunnel connects each LAP to the WLC, for a total of 32 tunnels. CAPWAP encapsulates wireless traffic inside an additional IP header, so the tunnel packets are routable across a Layer 3 network. That means the LAPs and WLC can reside on any IP subnet as long as the subnets are reachable. There are no restrictions for the LAPs and WLC to live on the same Layer 2 VLAN or Layer 3 IP subnet.
10. D. In a converged design, an access layer switch also functions as a WLC so that all user access (wired and wireless) converges in a single layer. Catalyst 3650, 3850, and 4500 offer converged wireless capability.
11. C. A converged wireless design is based on staging a controller in some or all of the access layer switches. Therefore, the number of controllers is usually higher than in the centralized model, which has a small number of larger-capacity controllers. The autonomous and cloud-based models do not use controllers at all.

12. B. FlexConnect is normally used in remote branch sites because it offers local switching so that branch users can access local resources if the WAN link or CAPWAP tunnel is down.
13. A, B. You can have multiple WLCs in a Cisco wireless network, so you could add a second 5520 or replace the existing one with a more robust model. You should not try to expand the coverage of each AP, rather than expand the capacity of the WLC.
14. B, D. The 1850 AP offers 802.11ac Wave 2 right out of the box. You could also leverage the 3700 model because it supports 802.11ac Wave 1 now and will support Wave 2 with the addition of a future expansion module.
15. B. The maximum number of APs is limited by the switch stack as a whole, not by individual member switches in the stack. Therefore, a maximum of 50 lightweight APs can be joined to the stack.

Chapter 9

1. C. A trunk link is needed to carry multiple service set identifier (SSIDs) to multiple virtual LANs (VLANs).
2. C. An autonomous AP is a standalone AP; it offers a basic service set (BSS) and connects to a distribution system (DS), all without the need for a centralized controller.
3. A, C. An autonomous AP has a console port for configuration and management and an Ethernet port to connect to the wired network. Service ports and dynamic interfaces are used on wireless LAN controllers instead.
4. D. The answer is all of the above because the sticker lists the MAC address that is used as the base address for both radios as well as the Ethernet port.
5. A, B. An autonomous AP tries to use Dynamic Host Configuration Protocol (DHCP) by default, but you can configure a static address if necessary.
6. A, B, C. You can use all of the methods except the AP management GUI to find the AP's IP address. Without the IP address, you would not be able to open a browser to the management GUI.
7. B, C. The radios are disabled and no SSIDs are configured. This prevents the AP from becoming active until you have properly configured it.
8. B, E. Each AP radio can host its own unique set of SSIDs. Also, the AP must assign an IP address to its BVI1 interface for management traffic.
9. B, C. A TFTP or FTP server is necessary, along with an appropriate lightweight code image. An autonomous code image is not needed because the AP is already running one.
10. C. You should use the **archive download-sw** command, which also specifies the TFTP server address and filename.
11. D. Cisco Meraki APs are cloud-based, so you must do all management and configuration through the cloud network management interface.
12. C. The AP will connect with the Cisco Meraki cloud network to register itself. At that point, you must browse to the cloud network and claim the AP so that it can be associated with your Meraki Dashboard and account.

Chapter 10

1. B. Controller ports are physical connections to the switched network infrastructure.
2. C. The service port is used for out-of-band management.
3. A. The distribution system ports are usually configured as unconditional 802.1Q trunks.
4. C. Controllers use a link aggregation group (LAG) to bundle the ports together.
5. D. CAPWAP tunnels always terminate on the AP-manager interface. All the APs discover the controller by that interface and its IP address. The management interface can terminate CAPWAP tunnels if no AP-manager interface exists.
6. C. The virtual interface is used to relay DHCP requests from wireless clients.
7. D. A dynamic interface makes a logical connection between a WLAN and a VLAN, all internal to the controller.
8. A. The controller will begin its initial setup to build a bootstrap configuration.
9. A, D. You can either connect to the controller console port or use a web browser to run through the initial setup procedure. The console will use CLI only, while the service port is used for a web interface. A Cisco 2504 Wireless Controller does not have a service port, so a web browser is used from an Ethernet port instead.
10. D. Because the access switch hosts both a switch and a Wireless Controller Module (WCM) function, you should connect to it using the switch management address.
11. B, C. The Apply button made the change active, but didn't save it across the reboot. You would need to click the **Save Configuration** button to save the change permanently.
12. A. To save a copy of the controller's configuration, you can upload the configuration file to a remotely connected TFTP, FTP, or SFTP server
13. B. A WLC can store a primary and a backup code image. One file can be run until the controller is rebooted.
14. A, D. TFTP and FTP are the only two methods supported.
15. A. File transfers are always named from the viewpoint of the controller, as if the controller is a client getting a file from a remote server. In this case, the code image file should be downloaded to the controller.
16. D. Lightweight APs will compare their own code image releases to that of the controller they intend to join. If the controller has a different release, the APs will download the matching release from the controller automatically.

Chapter 11

1. B. An AP will discover all possible WLCs before attempting to build a CAPWAP tunnel or join a controller.
2. C. After an AP boots, it compares its own software image to that of the controller it has joined. If the images differ, the AP downloads a new image from the controller.
3. F. An AP can learn controller addresses from all of the listed methods.

4. C. An AP will try the three primed addresses (primary, secondary, and tertiary) first before any other method.
5. C. If an AP cannot find a viable controller, it reboots and tries the discovery process all over again.
6. B. The AP priority determines which APs can join a controller when the controller fills with APs.
7. D. If the primary controller responds to an AP's discovery methods, the AP will always try to join it first, ahead of any other controller. Configuring an AP with a primary controller is the most specific method because it points the AP to a predetermined controller. Other methods are possible, but they can yield ambiguous results that could send an AP to one of several possible controllers.
8. D. APs use CAPWAP keepalive messages that are sent to the controller every 30 seconds.
9. D. The AP Fallback feature allows APs to fall back or revert to a primary controller at any time.
10. C. N+N redundancy is being used because there are two active controllers and no standby or backup controllers.

Chapter 12

1. B. The client must associate with a basic service set (BSS) offered by an AP.
2. A. The client device is in complete control over the roaming decision, based on its own roaming algorithm. It uses active scanning and probing to discover other candidate APs that it might roam to.
3. C. Because a single controller is involved, the roam occurs in an intracontroller fashion. Even though the client thinks it is associating with APs, the associations actually occur at the controller, thanks to the split-MAC architecture.
4. C. Intracontroller roaming is the most efficient because the reassociation and client authentication occur within a single controller.
5. C. Cisco Centralized Key Management (CCKM) is used to cache key information between a client and an AP. The cached information is then used as a quick check when a client roams to a different AP.
6. C. Intercontroller roaming supports Layer 3 roaming when a client moves from one controller to another and when the client's IP subnet changes between controllers.
7. D. In a Layer 2 roam, the client's IP subnet does not change as it moves between controllers. Therefore, there is no need to tunnel the client data between the controllers; instead, the client simply gets handed off to the new controller.
8. B. A client can always choose to renew or obtain an IP address, but it does not have to. The client can continue to use its same IP address during either Layer 2 or Layer 3 roams.
9. D. The anchor controller, where the client starts, maintains the client's state and builds a tunnel to the foreign controller, where the client has now roamed.

10. C. Controllers A and B are listed in each other's mobility list, so they are known to each other. However, they are configured with different mobility group names. Clients may roam between the two controllers, but CCKM and key caching information will not be exchanged.
11. B. A Mobility Agent (MA) terminates the CAPWAP tunnels from APs that are joined to the controller.
12. A. Each MA must be joined to an Mobility Controller (MC) so that mobility events can be coordinated and managed.
13. A. The Point of Presence (PoP) anchors the client to a wired subnet so that the client's IP address can stay consistent across AP roams.
14. E. The controllers can be designated as a single Switch Peer Group (SPG) to make localized roaming more efficient. Because converged controllers are contained in specific Cisco switch models, SPG derives its name from the LAN switch platforms. Keep in mind that the controllers in an SPG must also be joined to an MC.
15. B. Each converged controller must operate as a Mobility Agent (MA) because it terminates CAPWAP tunnels connecting the lightweight APs.

Chapter 13

1. C. A data rate marked as mandatory by an AP must be supported by any client that intends to associate with the AP.
2. B. You can configure one or more data rates as mandatory. In fact, the 1-, 2-, 5.5-, and 11-Mbps data rates in the 2.4-GHz band are set as mandatory by default.
3. B. Broadcast management frames are sent at the lowest mandatory data rate. Unicast management frames can be sent at any optimal supported or mandatory data rate.
4. B. 802.11n and 802.11ac support is enabled by default. Only 20-MHz channels will be used until 40-MHz or wider channels are enabled.
5. C. RRM monitors and adjusts all APs in a single RF group. The RF group may contain one or more controllers.
6. C. By default, all APs joined to a controller belong to one common RF group. The group can be extended to any other controller that has APs within range by configuring that controller with the same RF group name. To build an RF group, APs send neighbor messages so that they can be discovered. If one controller's APs hear neighbor messages sent from another controller's APs, and the RF group names match, the RF group is extended to include both controllers.
7. D. The transmit power control (TPC) algorithm adjusts the power level used by each AP in an RF group.
8. C. The goal of dynamic channel allocation (DCA) is to maintain an efficient channel layout and avoid interference and noise. Therefore, DCA might choose to move the AP to a different channel.
9. A. TPC and DCA are RRM algorithms that run on a per-RF group basis. Therefore, the RF group leader runs the algorithms.

10. D. A failed radio will probably cause a hole or weakness in the RF coverage around the AP. Coverage hole detection mitigation (CHDM) can detect the failure based on the weak signal clients in that area are experiencing. The algorithm can also boost the transmit power level in neighboring APs to help heal the coverage hole or other coverage gaps that are detected.

Chapter 14

1. D. A secure wireless connection between a client and an access point (AP) should have all of the listed security components.
2. C. The message integrity check (MIC) is used to protect data against tampering.
3. D. Wireless Equivalent Privacy (WEP) is a wireless encryption method that has been found to be vulnerable and is not recommended for use.
4. A. Open authentication is used so that the client can associate with the AP and can then authenticate through 802.1x and Extensible Authentication Protocol (EAP).
5. C. A controller becomes an authenticator in the 802.1x process.
6. B. Protected EAP (PEAP) uses a server certificate, but clients authenticate using more traditional means without a certificate.
7. D. EAP Transport Layer Security (EAP-TLS) requires digital certificates on both the AS and the supplicants.
8. C. Counter/CBC-MAC Protocol (CCMP) is currently the most secure data encryption and integrity method for wireless data.
9. B. Wi-Fi Protected Access Version 2 (WPA2) requires CCMP, whereas WPA does not.
10. A, C. Pre-shared keys (PSKs) can be used in WPA personal and WPA2 personal modes. Enterprise mode requires 802.1x authentication.
11. B, D. Management Frame Protection (MFP) requires a secure connection between an AP and a CCXv5 client. Therefore, WPA2 and Cisco Compatible Extensions Version 5 (CCXv5) are needed.
12. B. WPA2 personal requires a pre-shared key (PSK). The same key must be configured on the WLAN, which gets propagated to all APs that are joined to the controller, in addition to every client that might associate with the WLAN.
13. B, C. Only WEP and Temporal Key Integrity Protocol (TKIP) have been deprecated.

Chapter 15

1. C, D. A wireless LAN (WLAN) binds a service set identifier (SSID) to a controller interface, so that the controller can link the wired and wireless networks. Although the WLAN ultimately reaches a wired virtual LAN (VLAN), it does so only through a controller interface. It is the interface that is configured with a VLAN number.
2. C. You can configure a maximum of 512 WLANs on a controller. However, a maximum of only 16 of them can be configured on an access point (AP).

3. B. Each AP supports a maximum of 16 WLANs. Even so, you should always try to limit the number of WLANs to five or fewer.
4. B. The BSS for each WLAN must be advertised, requiring airtime for beacons. A growing number of WLANs results in a growing number of beacons needed, which results in a diminishing amount of airtime left available for data frames.
5. A, C. The SSID and controller interface are the only parameters from the list that are necessary. The VLAN number is not necessary because it is supplied when a controller interface is configured.
6. B. The WLAN ID is used internally as an index into the list of WLANs on a controller. Therefore, it is not made visible to any clients.

Chapter 16

1. B. A guest WLAN is normally used to provide limited network access to guest clients, while keeping them isolated from the rest of the network.
2. C. By itself, the controller cannot route packets between WLANs; any connectivity must be provided by an external router or firewall.
3. D. A guest WLAN is no different from a data or regular WLAN. The only differences are the type of user authentication and the external means to keep the guest virtual LAN (VLAN) isolated from the other networks.
4. D. A guest WLAN on one controller is completely separate from the guest WLAN defined on another controller. The guest WLANs can be bound to a common VLAN so that they share a common IP subnet, but the WLANs are not merged or joined by default.
5. C. Guest WLANs can be merged toward a common controller if each of the controllers identifies the same controller as a mobility anchor.
6. B. A wireless guest network works like a Layer 3 roaming scenario in reverse—the client associates with a foreign controller. The foreign controller then tunnels the guest traffic to a guest mobility anchor controller.
7. B. You can configure more than one mobility anchor for a guest WLAN. Guest clients will be load balanced across the anchor controllers.

Chapter 17

1. B. Windows 7 uses a process called the WLAN AutoConfig Service to scan for a usable wireless network.
2. C. The machine will transmit probe requests containing a null or empty service set identifier (SSID) name. This is done so that it will learn about all APs and SSIDs that are within range.
3. B. Cisco Compatibility Extensions (CCX) certifies compatibility with a set of Cisco innovations and features.
4. C. CCX has five versions.

5. B. Even though the device has no CCX certification at all, it will most likely work fine on the network. CCX measures compatibility with Cisco features, not with the 802.11 standard.
6. D. CCXv1 is the oldest version and has few compatible features. One of the features is the initial 802.11 standard.
7. C. WPA2 with 802.1x was introduced in CCXv3 and so is supported in it and later versions.
8. B. CCX Lite includes the Foundation, Voice, Location, and Management modules.
9. B. The Foundation module is mandatory because it contains the core set of compatible features.

Chapter 18

1. C. Prime Infrastructure serves as the centralized management platform and can integrate with Cisco Identity Services Engine (ISE) and Cisco Mobility Services Engine (MSE) for additional services.
2. C. Cisco Mobility Services Engine (MSE) is used to provide location-based tracking to Cisco Prime Infrastructure.
3. A, B, C. Prime Infrastructure can be used to plan, manage, and troubleshoot wireless networks. It can also be used to perform predictive or planning surveys, but not active site surveys.
4. C. The downward-pointing orange triangle represents major alarms that have been received from wireless controllers.
5. B. Unacknowledged alarms are automatically acknowledged after 15 days.
6. D. The Alarm Browser, found in the alarm bar across the bottom of the PI screen, displays a list of individual alarms and details. Alarm Summary is a bit different, as it displays a concise breakdown of alarm sources and types.
7. B. The PI Dashboard is made up of a collection of dashlets that you can customize.
8. A. To access the maps, you should select **Maps > Wireless Maps > Site Maps** from the main PI screen.
9. A. PI maps are organized according to campus, building, then floor.

Chapter 19

1. D. DECT 6.0 refers to U.S. devices.
2. B. Bluetooth forms a personal-area network (PAN) and has a short range.
3. B. Bluetooth operates in the 2.4-GHz band and can affect 802.11b/g/n devices.
4. A, C. ZigBee is used for building automation and for energy management.
5. C. ZigBee belongs to the IEEE 802.15.4 family of standards.
6. D. The IEEE 802.16 standard defines WiMAX.

7. C. MetaGeek Chanalyzer is a spectrum analyzer that can collect spectrum data from its own USB receiver or connect to a Cisco AP to collect data remotely.
8. A. A spectrum analyzer is used to look for wireless interference across a spectrum of frequencies.
9. D. CleanAir adds spectrum analysis capabilities to a Cisco lightweight AP.
10. A. CleanAir analyzes non-802.11 signals to detect and classify devices that interfere with 802.11 AP cells.
11. B. By default, Cisco CleanAir is disabled on a controller.
12. D. Because CleanAir has assigned a severity value of 4, the interference is likely not severe. The severity scale runs from 0 (not severe) to 100 (very severe).
13. B. A unique cluster ID is assigned to each uniquely identified interferer. The cluster ID is also known as a pseudo-MAC address. Non-802.11 devices do not use regular MAC addresses, so a virtual MAC address is created and used as a label.

Chapter 20

1. C. By entering the client's MAC address, the controller can display information about it straightaway. The other answers might also lead to useful information, but only after you spend more time sifting through the data.
2. C. The RUN state is the final policy manager state, indicating that the client is a fully functional member of the basic service set (BSS).
3. D. From the controller's perspective, a client must go through a sequence of state changes before it can be fully associated and joined to the network. Only when a client is in the RUN state is it fully operational.
4. B. The client must have failed to authenticate with the 802.1x method that is configured on the WLAN. Perhaps a RADIUS server is down, the client is sending an incorrect username or password, or the client's digital certificate is invalid.
5. B. Because the client supports only Cisco Compatible Extensions Version 1 (CCXv1), the controller uses ping tests with Internet Control Message Protocol (ICMP) packets. The controller can record received signal strength indicator (RSSI) measurements of the client's signal, but the lack of robust CCX support prevents the client from relaying its own RSSI measurements of the AP's signal.
6. C, D. The client must support CCXv4 or CCXv5 before it can accept the CCX link test frames and return information about its own radio to the controller.
7. C. You should leverage Prime Infrastructure and its central location in the wireless network. Assuming that every controller is configured to send Simple Network Management Protocol (SNMP) traps to PI, you should be able to find useful information about the client with just a single search through the PI database.
8. B. Go to Monitor > Clients, from which you can filter the results based on a client's MAC address, AP name, and so on.

9. D. Answer D is correct because it provides VLAN 11 to the AP over an access mode link. Answer A is incorrect because the access VLAN number is left to the default (VLAN 1). Answer B is incorrect, even though a lightweight AP (LAP) can use a trunk link, as long as the trunk is configured with the AP's VLAN number as the 802.1Q native VLAN. The configuration allows VLAN 11 over the trunk, but will use the default native VLAN 1 because it does not define a specific native VLAN number. Answer C is incorrect because the switch interface is left in the shutdown state.
10. C. MetaGeek inSSIDer Office is a Wi-Fi scanner tool that can map service set identifiers (SSIDs) to channels for quick analysis. Other tools such as OmniPeek can achieve the same result, but they are packet analyzers and not strictly Wi-Fi scanners.
11. C. ESS Pro is an example of an RF mapping tool, used to measure 802.11 signals over a map of an area.

APPENDIX B

Modulation and Coding Schemes

Table B-1 lists the possible modulation and coding methods used for direct sequence spread spectrum (DSSS) and orthogonal frequency-division multiplexing (OFDM) for 802.11b/g and 802.11a wireless LANs.

Table B-1 DSSS and OFDM Data Rates Used for 802.11b/g and 802.11a

Modulation and Coding	DSSS Data Rate (Mbps)	OFDM Data Rate (Mbps)
DBPSK	1	
DQPSK	2	
CCK	5.5	
OFDM BPSK 1/2		6
OFDM BPSK 3/4		9
CCK	11	
OFDM QPSK 1/2		12
OFDM QPSK 3/4		18
OFDM 16-QAM 1/2		24
OFDM 16-QAM 3/4		36
OFDM 64-QAM 2/3		48
OFDM 64-QAM 3/4		54

Table B-2 lists the possible modulation coding schemes (MCS) used in 802.11n wireless LANs. The resulting data rates also vary according to the number of spatial streams in use (1 to 4), the guard interval (800 or 400 ns), and the channel width (20 or 40 MHz).

Table B-2 Modulation and Coding Schemes and Data Rates Used for 802.11n

MCS Index	Spatial Streams	Modulation and Coding	Data Rate (Mbps) Guard Interval = 800 ns		Guard Interval = 400 ns	
			20-MHz Channel	40-MHz Channel	20-MHz Channel	40-MHz Channel
0	1	BPSK 1/2	6.5	13.5	7.2	15
1	1	QPSK 1/2	13	27	14.4	30
2	1	QPSK 3/4	19.5	40.5	21.7	45
3	1	16-QAM 1/2	26	54	28.9	60
4	1	16-QAM 3/4	39	81	43.3	90
5	1	64-QAM 2/3	52	108	57.8	120
6	1	64-QAM 3/4	58.5	121.5	65	135
7	1	64-QAM 5/6	65	135	72.2	150
8	1	BPSK 1/2	13	27	14.4	30
9	2	QPSK 1/2	26	54	28.9	60
10	2	QPSK 3/4	39	81	43.3	90
11	2	16-QAM 1/2	52	108	57.8	120
12	2	16-QAM 3/4	78	162	86.7	180
13	2	64-QAM 2/3	104	216	115.6	240
14	2	64-QAM 3/4	117	243	130.3	270
15	2	64-QAM 5/6	130	270	144.4	300
16	3	BPSK 1/2	19.5	40.5	21.7	45
17	3	QPSK 1/2	39	81	43.3	90
18	3	QPSK 3/4	58.5	121.5	65	135
19	3	16-QAM 1/2	78	162	86.7	180
20	3	16-QAM 3/4	117	243	130	270
21	3	64-QAM 2/3	156	324	173.3	360
22	3	64-QAM 3/4	175.5	364.5	195	405
23	3	64-QAM 5/6	195	405	216.7	450
24	4	BPSK 1/2	26	54	28.9	60
25	4	QPSK 1/2	52	108	57.8	120
26	4	QPSK 3/4	78	162	86.7	180

MCS Index	Spatial Streams	Modulation and Coding	Data Rate (Mbps) Guard Interval = 800 ns 20-MHz Channel	40-MHz Channel	Guard Interval = 400 ns 20-MHz Channel	40-MHz Channel
27	4	16-QAM 1/2	104	216	115.6	240
28	4	16-QAM 3/4	156	324	173.3	360
29	4	64-QAM 2/3	208	432	231.1	480
30	4	64-QAM 3/4	234	486	260	540
31	4	64-QAM 5/6	260	540	288.9	600

Table B-3 lists the possible MCS used in 802.11ac wireless LANs. The resulting data rates also vary according to the number of spatial streams in use (1 to 4), the guard interval (800 or 400 ns), and the channel width (20, 40, 80, or 160 MHz).

Table B-3 Modulation and Coding Schemes and Data Rates Used for 802.11ac

MCS Index	Spatial Streams	Modulation and Coding	Data Rate (Mbps) Guard Interval = 800 ns 20-MHz Channel	40-MHz Channel	80-MHz Channel	160-MHz Channel	Guard Interval = 400 ns 20-MHz Channel	40-MHz Channel	80-MHz Channel	160-MHz Channel
0	1	BPSK 1/2	6.5	13.5	29.3	58.5	7.2	15	32.5	65
1	1	QPSK 1/2	13	27	58.5	117	14.4	30	65	130
2	1	QPSK 3/4	19.5	40.5	87.8	175.5	21.7	45	97.5	195
3	1	16-QAM 1/2	26	54	117	234	28.9	60	130	260
4	1	16-QAM 3/4	39	81	175.5	351	43.3	90	195	390
5	1	64-QAM 2/3	52	108	234	468	57.8	120	260	520

MCS Index	Spatial Streams	Modulation and Coding	Data Rate (Mbps) Guard Interval = 800 ns				Guard Interval = 400 ns			
			20-MHz Channel	40-MHz Channel	80-MHz Channel	160-MHz Channel	20-MHz Channel	40-MHz Channel	80-MHz Channel	160-MHz Channel
6	1	64-QAM 3/4	58.5	121.5	263.3	526.5	65	135	292.5	585
7	1	64-QAM 5/6	65	135	292.5	585	72.2	150	325	650
8	1	256-QAM 3/4	78	162	351	702	86.7	180	390	780
9	1	256-QAM 5/6	—	180	390	780	—	200	433.3	866.7
0	2	BPSK 1/2	13	27	58.6	117	14.4	30	65	130
1	2	QPSK 1/2	26	54	117	234	28.8	60	130	260
2	2	QPSK 3/4	39	81	175.6	351	43.4	90	195	390
3	2	16-QAM 1/2	52	108	234	468	57.8	120	260	520
4	2	16-QAM 3/4	78	162	351	702	86.6	180	390	780
5	2	64-QAM 2/3	104	216	468	936	115.6	240	520	1040
6	2	64-QAM 3/4	117	243	526.6	1053	130	270	585	1170
7	2	64-QAM 5/6	130	270	585	1170	144.4	300	650	1300
8	2	256-QAM 3/4	156	324	702	1404	173.4	360	780	1560

MCS Index	Spatial Streams	Modulation and Coding	Data Rate (Mbps) Guard Interval = 800 ns 20-MHz Channel	40-MHz Channel	80-MHz Channel	160-MHz Channel	Guard Interval = 400 ns 20-MHz Channel	40-MHz Channel	80-MHz Channel	160-MHz Channel
9	2	256-QAM 5/6	—	360	780	1560	—	400	866.7	1733.4
0	3	BPSK 1/2	19.5	40.5	87.9	175.5	21.6	45	97.5	195
1	3	QPSK 1/2	39	81	175.5	351	43.2	90	195	390
2	3	QPSK 3/4	58.5	121.5	263.4	526.5	65.1	135	292.5	585
3	3	16-QAM 1/2	78	162	351	702	86.7	180	390	780
4	3	16-QAM 3/4	117	243	526.5	1053	129.9	270	585	1170
5	3	64-QAM 2/3	156	324	702	1404	173.4	360	780	1560
6	3	64-QAM 3/4	175.5	364.5	789.9	1579.5	195	405	877.5	1755
7	3	64-QAM 5/6	195	405	877.5	1755	216.6	450	975	1950
8	3	256-QAM 3/4	234	486	1053	2106	260.1	540	1170	2340
9	3	256-QAM 5/6	—	540	1170	2340	—	600	1299.9	2600.1
0	4	BPSK 1/2	26	54	117.2	234	28.8	60	130	260
1	4	QPSK 1/2	52	108	234	468	57.6	120	260	520

MCS Index	Spatial Streams	Modulation and Coding	Data Rate (Mbps) Guard Interval = 800 ns 20-MHz Channel	40-MHz Channel	80-MHz Channel	160-MHz Channel	Guard Interval = 400 ns 20-MHz Channel	40-MHz Channel	80-MHz Channel	160-MHz Channel
2	4	QPSK 3/4	78	162	351.2	702	86.8	180	390	780
3	4	16-QAM 1/2	104	216	468	936	115.6	240	520	1040
4	4	16-QAM 3/4	156	324	702	1404	173.2	360	780	1560
5	4	64-QAM 2/3	208	432	936	1872	231.2	480	1040	2080
6	4	64-QAM 3/4	234	486	1053.2	2106	260	540	1170	2340
7	4	64-QAM 5/6	260	540	1170	2340	288.8	600	1300	2600
8	4	256-QAM 3/4	312	648	1404	2808	346.8	720	1560	3120
9	4	256-QAM 5/6	—	720	1560	3120	—	800	1733.2	3466.8

CCNA Wireless 200-355 Exam Updates

Over time, reader feedback allows Cisco Press to gauge which topics give our readers the most problems when taking the exams. To assist readers with those topics, the authors create new materials clarifying and expanding upon those troublesome exam topics. As mentioned in the Introduction, the additional content about the exam is contained in a PDF document on this book's companion website, at http://www.ciscopress.com/title/9781587144578.

This appendix is intended to provide you with updated information if Cisco makes minor modifications to the exam upon which this book is based. When Cisco releases an entirely new exam, the changes are usually too extensive to provide in a simple update appendix. In those cases, you might need to consult the new edition of the book for the updated content.

This appendix attempts to fill the void that occurs with any print book. In particular, this appendix does the following:

- Mentions technical items that might not have been mentioned elsewhere in the book
- Covers new topics if Cisco adds new content to the exam over time
- Provides a way to get up-to-the-minute current information about content for the exam

Always Get the Latest at the Companion Website

You are reading the version of this appendix that was available when your book was printed. However, given that the main purpose of this appendix is to be a living, changing document, it is important that you look for the latest version online at the book's companion website. To do so:

Step 1. Browse to http://www.ciscopress.com/title/9781587144578.

Step 2. Select the Appendix option under the More Information box.

Step 3. Download the latest "Appendix C" document.

Note The downloaded document has a version number. Comparing the version of the print Appendix C (Version 1.0) with the latest online version of this appendix, you should do the following:

- **Same version**—Ignore the PDF that you downloaded from the companion website.
- **Website has a later version**—Ignore this Appendix C in your book and read only the latest version that you downloaded from the companion website.

Technical Content

The current version of this appendix does not contain any additional technical coverage.

KEY TERMS GLOSSARY

802.11w An 802.11 amendment that focuses on protecting management frames.

802.1x An IEEE standard that defines port-based access control for wired and wireless networks.

A

absorption The effect of an RF signal meeting a material that absorbs or attenuates the signal strength by some amount.

access point (AP) A device that provides wireless service for clients within its coverage area or cell.

active scanning A method used by wireless clients to actively scan for available APs by sending probe request frames.

active site survey A method used to measure wireless LAN coverage and performance by analyzing the survey device itself as it interacts with the APs as it is moved throughout an area.

ad hoc network *See* independent basic service set (IBSS).

air-quality index (AQI) A scale from 0 to 100 that indicates how usable an 802.11 channel is, based on the number and intensity of interfering sources.

amplifier An active device that adds gain to an RF signal.

amplitude The height from the top peak to the bottom peak of a signal's waveform; also known as the peak-to-peak amplitude.

anchor controller The original controller a client was associated with before a Layer 3 inter-controller roam occurs. An anchor controller can also be used for tunneling clients on a guest WLAN or with a static anchor. Traffic is tunneled from the client's current controller (the foreign controller) back to the anchor.

AP-manager interface A logical link that can be configured to terminate CAPWAP tunnels from lightweight APs.

AP-on-a-stick A site survey method used to measure the coverage area of a single AP that is mounted on a pole, ladder, or "stick." The survey is usually formed before APs are deployed in an area.

association The process by which a wireless device becomes a functioning member of a BSS.

asymmetric power problem The scenario where the AP and a client use differing transmit power levels such that the messages sent by device 1 are received and understood by device 2, but the replies from device 2 are too weak to be understood by device 1.

attenuator A passive device that introduces additional loss to an RF signal.

authentication server (AS) An 802.1x entity that authenticates users or clients based on their credentials, as matched against a user database. In a wireless network, a RADIUS server is an AS.

authenticator An 802.1x entity that exists as a network device that provides access to the network. In a wireless network, a WLC acts as an authenticator.

autonomous AP A wireless AP operating in a standalone mode, such that it can provide a fully functional BSS and connect to the DS.

B

backoff timer The random amount of time a wireless client must wait before attempting to transmit a frame.

band A contiguous range of frequencies.

bandwidth The range of frequencies used by a single channel or a single RF signal.

Barker 11 code An 11-bit sequence of encoded bits that represents a single data bit.

basic service set (BSS) Wireless service provided by an AP to one or more associated clients.

basic service set identifier (BSSID) A unique MAC address that is used to identify the AP that is providing a BSS.

beamwidth A measure of the angle of a radiation pattern in both the E and H planes, where the signal strength is 3 dB below the maximum value.

block acknowledgment A feature used in 802.11n that permits a burst of data frames to be followed by a single acknowledgment message, improving throughput.

BSS basic rate A data rate that is required to be supported between an AP and a wireless client.

BSSID method An active site survey method where the survey client is locked to a specific BSSID so that the cell of a single AP can be measured.

C

CAPWAP Discovery Request A message sent by a lightweight AP to discover one or more wireless LAN controllers. Any controllers that receive the request should return a CAPWAP Discovery Response message to the AP.

CAPWAP Join Request A message sent by a lightweight AP to a specific WLC indicating the AP's desire to join or associate with the controller. If the AP is accepted, the WLC returns a CAPWAP Join Response message.

carrier signal The basic, steady RF signal that is used to carry other useful information.

CCX Lite A CCX certification program that is organized in modules, according to specific applications for wireless devices.

cell The area of wireless coverage provided by an AP; also known as the basic service area.

central web authentication (CWA) A method of wireless user authentication that uses a web authentication page and a user database that are both located centrally on a RADIUS server, rather than locally on the wireless controller.

certificate authority (CA) A trusted entity that generates and signs digital certificates.

channel An arbitrary index that points to a specific frequency within a band.

channel aggregation An 802.11n feature that allows two 20-MHz OFDM channels to be aggregated or bonded into a single 40-MHz channel.

channel reuse The pattern of APs and their channels, arranged such that neighboring APs never use the same channels.

chip A bit produced by a coder.

Cisco CleanAir Wireless technology used to detect, classify, report, and react to non-802.11 interference.

Cisco Compatibility Extensions (CCX) A wireless device certification that verifies compatibility with a set of Cisco-developed features. CCX is defined in five versions.

clear channel assessment (CCA) The process a wireless devices uses to determine whether a channel is clear and available to use.

cloud-based AP A Cisco Meraki autonomous AP that is managed from the Meraki cloud network.

cluster ID A unique identifier that a WLC assigns to a non-802.11 device found to be interfering with an AP. *See also* pseudo-MAC address.

co-channel interference RF signal interference caused by two or more transmitters using the same frequency or channel.

coder A function that converts data bits into multiple encoded bits before transmission, to provide resilience against noise and interference.

collision avoidance The technique used by 802.11 devices to proactively avoid collisions on a channel.

Complementary Code Keying (CCK) An encoding method that takes either 4 or 8 data bits at a time to create a 6-bit or 8-bit symbol, respectively. The symbols are fed into DQPSK to modulate the carrier signal.

contention window The range of values that a wireless station can use to compute a random backoff timer duration.

controller interface A logical connection that a wireless controller uses internally.

controller port A physical connection to an external switched network.

Counter/CBC-MAC Protocol (CCMP) A wireless security scheme based on 802.11i that uses AES counter mode for encryption and CBC-MAC for data integrity.

coverage hole An area that is left without good RF coverage. A coverage hole can be caused by a radio failure or a weak signal in an area.

D

dBd The gain of an antenna, measured in dB, as compared to a simple dipole antenna.

dBi The gain of an antenna, measured in dB, as compared to an isotropic reference antenna.

dBm The power level of a signal measured in dB, as compared to a reference signal power of 1 milliwatt.

DCA *See* dynamic channel allocation (DCA).

decibel (dB) A logarithmic function that compares one absolute measurement to another.

delivery traffic indication message (DTIM) A beacon sent at regular intervals that indicates whether buffered broadcast and multicast frames will be sent for clients that have been in a power save mode.

demodulation The receiver's process of interpreting changes in the carrier signal to recover the original information being sent.

differential binary phase shift keying (DBPSK) A modulation method that takes 1 bit of encoded data and changes the phase of the carrier signal in one of two ways.

differential quadrature phase shift keying (DQPSK) A modulation method that takes 2 bits of encoded data and changes the phase of the carrier signal in one of four ways.

diffraction The effect of an RF signal approaching an opaque object, causing the electromagnetic waves to bend around the object.

dipole An omnidirectional antenna composed of two wire segments.

direct sequence spread spectrum (DSSS) A wireless LAN method where a transmitter uses a single fixed, wide channel to send data.

directional antenna A type of antenna that propagates an RF signal in a narrow range of directions.

distributed coordination function (DCF) The method used by each wireless device to coordinate the use of a wireless channel.

distribution system (DS) The wired Ethernet that connects to an AP and transports traffic between a wired and wireless network.

distribution system port A physical interface that connects a wireless controller to a switched network and carries both AP and management traffic.

duty cycle A measure of the percentage of time a device transmits on a given frequency.

dynamic channel allocation (DCA) An RRM algorithm that monitors APs in an RF group and adjusts their channel assignment based on poor RF conditions.

dynamic interface An internal logical link that connects a VLAN to a WLAN. Traffic passing through a dynamic interface also passes through a VLAN on a distribution system port.

dynamic rate shifting A mechanism used by an 802.11 device to change the Modulation Coding Scheme (MCS) according to dynamic RF signal conditions.

E

EAP Flexible Authentication by Secure Tunneling (EAP-FAST) A Cisco authentication method that is based on EAP and uses a PAC as a credential for outer authentication and a TLS tunnel for inner authentication.

EAP-TLS An authentication method that uses digital certificates on both the server and the supplicant for mutual authentication. A TLS tunnel is used during client authentication and key exchanges.

effective isotropic radiated power (EIRP) The resulting signal power level, measured in dBm, of the combination of a transmitter, cable, and an antenna, as measured at the antenna.

enterprise mode 802.1x EAP-based authentication requirement for WPA or WPA2.

E plane The "elevation" plane passing through an antenna that shows a side view of the radiation pattern.

Event-Driven RRM (ED-RRM) Using Cisco CleanAir to trigger the RRM DCA process automatically, as interference is detected.

extended service set (ESS) Multiple APs that are connected by a common switched infrastructure.

Extensible Authentication Protocol (EAP) A standardized authentication framework that is used by a variety of authentication methods.

F

foreign controller The current controller a client is associated with after a Layer 3 intercontroller roam occurs. Traffic is tunneled from the foreign controller back to an anchor controller so that the client retains connectivity to its original VLAN and subnet.

free-space path loss The degradation of an RF signal's strength as it travels through free space.

frequency The number of times a signal makes one complete up and down cycle in 1 second.

frequency hopping spread spectrum (FHSS) A wireless LAN method where a transmitter "hops" between frequencies all across a band.

Fresnel zone The elliptical shaped space between a transmitter and receiver that must be kept clear of objects, else the RF signal will be degraded.

G–H

gain A measure of how effectively an antenna can focus RF energy in a certain direction.

guard interval (GI) The amount of time required between OFDM symbols to prevent intersymbol interference. In 802.11n, the guard interval can be reduced from 800 ns to 400 ns.

guest WLAN A wireless LAN that is specially created to support guest clients.

hertz (Hz) A unit of frequency equaling one cycle per second.

high throughput (HT) The techniques defined in 802.11n and used to scale performance to a maximum of 600 Mbps.

H plane The "azimuth" plane passing through an antenna that shows a top-down view of the radiation pattern.

I–J–K

in phase The condition when the cycles of two identical signals are in sync with each other.

independent basic service set (IBSS) An impromptu wireless network formed between two or more devices without an AP or a BSS; also known as an ad hoc network.

infrastructure mode The operating mode of an AP that is providing a BSS for wireless clients.

integrated antenna A very small omnidirectional antenna that is set inside a device's outer case.

intercontroller roaming Client roaming that occurs between two APs that are joined to two different controllers.

interference Signals coming from 802.11 devices other than expected or known APs.

interframe space The amount of time the 802.11 standard defines to separate adjacent frames on a channel.

intersymbol interference (ISI) Data corruption caused by OFDM symbols arriving too close together at a receiver, usually caused by signals that take different paths from transmitter to receiver.

intracontroller roaming Client roaming that occurs between two APs joined to the same controller.

isotropic antenna An ideal, theoretical antenna that radiates RF equally in every direction.

L

Layer 2 roam An intercontroller roam where the WLANs of the two controllers are configured for the same Layer 2 VLAN ID; also known as a local-to-local roam.

Layer 3 roam An intercontroller roam where the WLANs of the two controllers are configured for different VLAN IDs; also known as a local-to-foreign roam. To support the roaming client, a tunnel is built between the controllers so that client data can pass between the client's current controller and its original controller.

lightning arrestor A device used to protect a transmitter or receiver from large transient voltages that might be induced by lightning around an antenna.

Lightweight EAP (LEAP) A legacy Cisco proprietary wireless security method.

link aggregation group (LAG) A grouping or bundling of multiple physical links into a single logical link.

link budget The cumulative sum of gains and losses measured in dB over the complete RF signal path; a transmitter's power level must overcome the link budget so that the signal can reach a receiver effectively.

local web authentication (LWA) A method of wireless user authentication that occurs locally on a WLC through the use of local user accounts and a web portal.

M

management frame protection (MFP) A method developed by Cisco to protect wireless clients and APs from attacks involving spoofed management frames.

management interface A logical link that is used for normal management traffic. If an AP-manager interface is not configured, the management interface also terminates CAPWAP tunnels from APs.

mandatory data rate An 802.11 data rate that must be supported by a client before it can associate with an AP.

maximal-ratio combining (MRC) An 802.11n technique that takes multiple copies of a signal, received over multiple antennas, and combines them to reconstruct the original signal.

mesh network A network of APs used to cover a large area without the need for wired Ethernet cabling; client traffic is bridged from AP to AP over a backhaul network.

message integrity check (MIC) A cryptographic value computed from the contents of a data frame and used to detect tampering.

Mobility Agent (MA) A wireless LAN controller function that terminates CAPWAP tunnels from APs, as well as maintains a client database and enforces security and QoS policies.

mobility anchor A wireless LAN controller that acts as the anchor or home base for remote wireless clients that are joined to a different controller.

Mobility Controller (MC) A wireless LAN controller function that manages one or more MAs, handles RRM, performs WIPS, and manages guest access.

mobility domain A logical grouping of all mobility groups within an enterprise.

mobility group A logical grouping of one or more MCs between which efficient roaming is expected.

mobility subdomain A logical grouping of one MC along with the MAs relying on the MC for roaming efficiency.

modulation The transmitter's process of altering the carrier signal according to some other information source.

monopole A very short omnidirectional antenna composed of a single wire segment set over a metal ground plane.

multipath Reflected copies of an RF signal arrive at a receiver after taking different paths through free space.

N

N+1 redundancy High availability offered by N number of active controllers plus one idle standby controller.

N+N redundancy High availability offered by N number of active controllers. The AP load is distributed across the active controllers, so no additional backup controller is used.

N+N+1 redundancy High availability offered by N number of active controllers plus one idle standby controller.

narrowband RF signals that use a very narrow range of frequencies.

neighboring channel interference RF signal interference caused by two or more transmitters using channels that are different, but do not completely overlap.

network allocation vector (NAV) An internal timer maintained by each wireless device that measures the number of timeslots before a transmission may be attempted.

noise Signals or RF energy that do not come from 802.11 sources.

noise floor The average power level of noise measured at a specific frequency.

Null Data Packet (NDP) The explicit method for transmit beamforming specified by the 802.11ac amendment.

O

omnidirectional antenna A type of antenna that propagates an RF signal in a broad range of directions in order to cover a large area.

open authentication An 802.11 authentication method that requires clients to associate with an AP without providing any credentials at all.

open system authentication A simple method used to verify that a wireless device uses 802.11 before it is permitted to join a BSS.

orthogonal frequency-division multiplexing (OFDM) A data transmission method that sends data bits in parallel over multiple frequencies within a single 20-MHz-wide channel. Each frequency represents a single subcarrier.

out of phase The condition when the cycles of one signal are shifted in time in relation to another signal.

P–Q

parabolic dish antenna A highly directional antenna that uses a passive dish shaped like a parabola to focus an RF signal into a tight beam.

passive scanning A method used to scan for available APs by listening to their beacon frames.

passive site survey A method to measure wireless LAN coverage by analyzing information that is overheard by listening to existing APs as you move throughout an area.

patch antenna A directional antenna that has a planar surface and is usually mounted on a wall or column.

personal mode Pre-shared key authentication as applied to WPA or WPA2.

phase A measure of shift in time relative to the start of a cycle; ranges between 0 and 360 degrees.

physical carrier sense To determine whether a channel is available, a device simply listens to any signals that might be present.

piconet A very small network cell used to connect multiple devices. Common examples are personal-area networks using technologies such as Bluetooth or Bluetooth Low Energy.

point-to-point bridge An AP configured to bridge a wired network to a companion bridge at the far end of a line-of-sight path.

Point of Attachment(PoA) The controller that anchors a client's IP address for Layer 3 roaming.

Point of Presence (PoP) The controller where a client is currently associated.

polar plot A round graph that is divided into 360 degrees around an antenna and into concentric circles that represent decreasing dB values. The antenna is always placed at the center of the plot.

polarization The orientation (horizontal, vertical, circular, and so on) of a propagating wave with respect to the ground.

post-deployment site survey A site survey (active or passive) performed after APs have been deployed, in order to validate and verify RF coverage in an area.

predictive survey A method used to predict or calculate RF coverage and an AP layout without collecting any data from live APs.

pre-deployment site survey A predictive or calculated site survey performed before APs are deployed, in order to size and design the wireless coverage for an area.

primed controller address The name or IP address of a controller that is configured in advance on an AP.

protected access credential (PAC) Special-purpose data that is used as an authentication credential in EAP-FAST.

Protected EAP (PEAP) An authentication method that uses a certificate on the AS for outer authentication and a TLS tunnel for inner authentication. Clients can provide their credentials through either MS-CHAPv2 or GTC.

Protected Management Frames (PMF) A service provided by 802.11w that protects a set of 802.11 Robust Management frames and Robust Action frames.

protection mechanism A method of supporting backward compatibility between an advanced and a legacy wireless standard, such as 802.11g and 802.11b, respectively. For example, each 802.11g OFDM transmission is flagged with RTS/CTS messages sent in the lower-rate DSSS format.

pseudo-MAC address A virtual MAC address that a controller assigns to each uniquely identified non-802.11 interferer so that it can be reported and displayed. *See also* cluster ID.

Public Key Infrastructure (PKI) An enterprise-wide system that generates and revokes digital certificates for client authentication.

quadrature amplitude modulation (QAM) A modulation method that combines QPSK phase shifting with multiple amplitude levels to produce a greater number of unique changes to the carrier signal. The number preceding the QAM name designates how many carrier signal changes are possible.

R

radiation pattern A plot that shows the relative signal strength in dBm at every angle around an antenna.

radio frequency (RF) The portion of the frequency spectrum between 3 kHz and 300 GHz.

RADIUS server An authentication server used with 802.1x to authenticate wireless clients.

reassociation The process by which a wireless client changes its association from one BSS to another as it moves.

received signal strength indicator (RSSI) The measure of signal strength (in dBm) as seen by the receiver. RSSI is normally negative (0 to –100) because the received signal is always a degraded form of the original signal that was sent.

reflection The effect of an RF signal meeting a dense, reflective material, such that it is sent in a different direction.

refraction The effect of an RF signal meeting the boundary between two different materials, causing its trajectory to change slightly.

repeater A device that repeats or retransmits signals it receives, effectively expanding the wireless coverage area.

RF group A logical grouping of wireless LAN controllers that operates as a single RF domain. RRM algorithms run on a per-RF group basis.

RF group leader A controller that is elected to handle all of the RRM algorithms for the entire RF group.

roaming The process a wireless client uses to move from one AP to another as it changes location.

rogue AP A wireless AP that operates outside local administrative control.

RRM Radio Resource Management; a set of algorithms that is used to maintain a stable and optimum wireless network even in a changing RF environment.

S

scattering The effect of an RF signal meeting a rough or uneven surface, causing it to be reflected or scattered in many different directions.

sensitivity level The RSSI threshold (in dBm) that divides unintelligible RF signals from useful ones.

service port A physical nontrunking interface that connects a wireless controller to a switched network and carries only out-of-band management traffic.

service set identifier (SSID) A text string that is used to identify a wireless network.

shared key authentication A method used to authenticate a wireless device with a BSS by using a shared WEP key.

signal-to-noise ratio (SNR) A measure of received signal quality, calculated as the difference between the signal's RSSI and the noise floor. A higher SNR is preferred.

spatial multiplexing Distributing streams of data across multiple radio chains with spatial diversity.

spatial stream An independent stream of data that is sent over a radio chain through free space. One spatial stream is separate from others due to the unique path it travels through space.

spectrum analyzer A device that sweeps through a range of frequencies and displays signals that it receives. The signal data can be processed and displayed in a variety of ways to assist in the analysis.

spread spectrum RF signals that spread the information being sent over a wide range of frequencies.

SSID method An active site survey method where the survey client associates to a specific SSID on any AP.

stateful switchover (SSO) High availability offered by controllers configured as a failover pair. One controller is active and supports the AP and client load, while the other controller is a hot standby. Stateful information about APs and clients in the RUN state is synchronized between the active and standby units for an efficient failover.

station (STA) An 802.11 client device that is associated with a BSS.

supplicant An 802.1x entity that exists as software on a client device and serves to request network access.

supported data rate An 802.11 data rate that can be supported by a client when it associates with an AP.

Switch Peer Group (SPG) A logical grouping of MAs between which frequent and efficient roaming is expected.

symbol A complete group of encoded chips that represents a data bit.

T

Temporal Key Integrity Protocol (TKIP) A wireless security scheme developed before 802.11i that provides a MIC for data integrity, a dynamic method for per-frame WEP encryption keys, and a 48-bit initialization vector. The MIC also includes a time stamp and the sender's MAC address.

TPC Transmit power control; an RRM algorithm that adjusts the transmit power level of APs to minimize cell overlap and interference.

traffic indication map (TIM) A list of the association IDs of wireless clients who are in a power save mode but have frames buffered. The TIM is included in beacon frames sent by an AP.

transmit beamforming (TxBF) An 802.11n method to transmit a signal over multiple antennas, each having the signal phase carefully crafted, so that the multiple copies are all in phase at a targeted receiver.

U–V

unscheduled automatic power save deliver (U-APSD) The method defined in 802.11e and WMM that allows a wireless client to enter power save mode and then have buffered frames delivered whenever the client is ready to receive them.

virtual carrier sense The method by which a wireless device calculates that a channel is available, based on frame duration information that is used to set the NAV.

virtual interface A logical link used to support wireless clients with things like DHCP relay and web authentication.

W–X–Y–Z

wavelength The physical distance that a wave travels over one complete cycle.

Wi-Fi Protected Access (WPA) A Wi-Fi Alliance standard that requires pre-shared key or 802.1x authentication, TKIP, and dynamic encryption key management; based on portions of 802.11i before its ratification.

Wireless Control Module (WCM) A wireless controller function that is built into an access layer switch, forming the basis of a converged wireless network.

Wired Equivalent Privacy (WEP) An 802.11 authentication and encryption method that requires clients and APs to use a common WEP key.

wireless intrusion protection system (wIPS) A system that monitors wireless activity to detect malicious behavior according to a set of signatures or patterns.

Wireless Multimedia (WMM) A Wi-Fi Alliance interoperability certification that covers quality of service (QoS) and enhanced power save delivery methods.

workgroup bridge (WGB) An AP that is configured to bridge between a wired device and a wireless network. The WGB acts as a wireless client.

WPA Version 2 (WPA2) A Wi-Fi Alliance standard that requires pre-shared key or 802.1x authentication, TKIP or CCMP, and dynamic encryption key management; based on the complete 802.11i standard after its ratification.

Yagi antenna A directional antenna made up of several parallel wire segments that tend to amplify an RF signal to each other.

Index

Symbols

A

C

D

E

F

G

H

I

J

K

L

M

N

O

P

Q

R

S

T

U

V

W

X – Z